Frommer's®

Los Angeles

18th Edition

by Tara de Lis

WILEY

John Wiley & Sons, Inc.

Published by:

JOHN WILEY & SONS, INC.

111 River St.
Hoboken, NJ 07030-5774

ISBN 978-1-118-02749-3 (paper); 978-1-118-15618-6 (ebk); 978-1-118-15619-3 (ebk); 978-1-118-15620-9 (ebk)

Editor: Stephen Bassman
Production Editor: Jonathan Scott
Cartographer: Nick Trotter
Photo Editor: Richard Fox
Production by Wiley Indianapolis Composition Services
Front cover photo: Mel's Drive-In Diner © Robert Harding/Masterfile
Back cover photo: Marina Del Ray © Damir Frkovic/Masterfile

For information on our other products and services or to obtain technical support, please contact our Customer Care Department within the U.S. at 877/762-2974, outside the U.S. at 317/572-3993 or fax 317/572-4002.

Wiley also publishes its books in a variety of electronic formats. Some content that appears in print may not be available in electronic formats.

Manufactured in the United States of America

5   4   3   2   1

CONTENTS

5 WHERE TO EAT 82

6 WHAT TO SEE & DO IN LOS ANGELES 132

7 THE DISNEYLAND RESORT & KNOTT'S BERRY FARM 195

8 SHOPS & SPAS 217

LIST OF MAPS

ABOUT THE AUTHOR

Tara de Lis, a native Angeleno, has been a professional writer and editor for more than 10 years. She has previously worked for Citysearch.com (as the L.A. City Editor), the Walt Disney Internet Group, and *The Big Issue,* and has been published by *L.A. Times* magazine, Gayot, dineLA, AOL, and CitySpots. She spends her "free time" scoping out new restaurants and hand-crafted cocktails.

ACKNOWLEDGMENTS

I would like to thank everyone who helped me polish off this edition of *Frommer's Los Angeles,* particularly my incredibly supportive editor, Steve Bassman. Others who deserve credit include Matthew Poole and Kristin Luna (authors of the previous edition), Michelle McCue, Danny Guerrero, Juan Flores, Paul Garcia, Brad Thomas, Fred Ascher, Kimberli Partlow, Leslie McLellan, Joan McCraw, Carrie Kommers, Bridgette Casale, Jason Clampet, Lalique Cohen, and Wagstaff Worldwide.

—Tara de Lis

HOW TO CONTACT US

In researching this book, we discovered many wonderful places—hotels, restaurants, shops, and more. We're sure you'll find others. Please tell us about them, so we can share the information with your fellow travelers in upcoming editions. If you were disappointed with a recommendation, we'd love to know that, too. Please write to:

Frommer's Los Angeles, 18th Edition
John Wiley & Sons, Inc. • 111 River St. • Hoboken, NJ 07030-5774
frommersfeedback@wiley.com

ADVISORY & DISCLAIMER

Travel information can change quickly and unexpectedly, and we strongly advise you to confirm important details locally before traveling, including information on visas, health and safety, traffic and transport, accommodations, shopping, and eating out. We also encourage you to stay alert while traveling and to remain aware of your surroundings. Avoid civil disturbances, and keep a close eye on cameras, purses, wallets, and other valuables.

While we have endeavored to ensure that the information contained within this guide is accurate and up-to-date at the time of publication, we make no representations or warranties with respect to the accuracy or completeness of the contents of this work and specifically disclaim all warranties, including without limitation warranties of fitness for a particular purpose. We accept no responsibility or liability for any inaccuracy or errors or omissions, or for any inconvenience, loss, damage, costs, or expenses of any nature whatsoever incurred or suffered by anyone as a result of any advice or information contained in this guide.

The inclusion of a company, organization, or website in this guide as a service provider and/or potential source of further information does not mean that we endorse them or the information they provide. Be aware that information provided through some websites may be unreliable and can change without notice. Neither the publisher nor author shall be liable for any damages arising herefrom.

FROMMER'S STAR RATINGS, ICONS & ABBREVIATIONS

Every hotel, restaurant, and attraction listing in this guide has been ranked for quality, value, service, amenities, and special features using a **star-rating system.** In country, state, and regional guides, we also rate towns and regions to help you narrow down your choices and budget your time accordingly. Hotels and restaurants are rated on a scale of zero (recommended) to three stars (exceptional). Attractions, shopping, nightlife, towns, and regions are rated according to the following scale: zero stars (recommended), one star (highly recommended), two stars (very highly recommended), and three stars (must-see).

In addition to the star-rating system, we also use **seven feature icons** that point you to the great deals, in-the-know advice, and unique experiences that separate travelers from tourists. Throughout the book, look for:

special finds—those places only insiders know about

fun facts—details that make travelers more informed and their trips more fun

kids—best bets for kids and advice for the whole family

special moments—those experiences that memories are made of

overrated—places or experiences not worth your time or money

insider tips—great ways to save time and money

great values—where to get the best deals

The following abbreviations are used for credit cards:

AE	American Express	DISC	Discover	V	Visa
DC	Diners Club	MC	MasterCard		

TRAVEL RESOURCES AT FROMMERS.COM

Frommer's travel resources don't end with this guide. Frommer's website, **www.frommers. com**, has travel information on more than 4,000 destinations. We update features regularly, giving you access to the most current trip-planning information and the best airfare, lodging, and car-rental bargains. You can also listen to podcasts, connect with other Frommers. com members through our active-reader forums, share your travel photos, read blogs from guidebook editors and fellow travelers, and much more.

THE BEST OF LOS ANGELES

The allure of Los Angeles is undeniable. Angelenos know L.A. will never have the sophisticated style of Paris or the historical riches of Rome, but they lay claim to the most entertaining city in the United States, if not the world. It really is warm and sunny most days of the year, movie stars actually do live and dine among regular folk, and you can't throw a Smartphone with hitting an in-line skater at the beach.

Things to Do   If you're going to spend any amount of time in Los Angeles, you'll need a car. How else are you going to squeeze in everything from window shopping on **Rodeo Drive** to cruising **Pacific Coast Highway** to exploring the historic buildings of downtown L.A. to visiting world-class museums like the **Getty Center** and **LACMA?**

Relaxation   L.A. can feel like one big amusement park, as the line between fantasy and reality is often obscured. Get out among the tanned and toned at **Surfrider Beach** in Malibu, check out the **Santa Monica Pier** on a Segway, or melt into the hands—or feet!—of your masseuse at one of the city's top spots for relaxation, such as **Ona Spa.**

Restaurants & Dining   Los Angeles is an international atlas of exotic cuisines: Armenian, Chinese, Japanese, Lebanese, Persian, Peruvian, Thai, Vietnamese, and more. Like everything else in the city, much of L.A.'s dining culture revolves around celebrity-spotting, and places like **The Ivy** at lunch and **Koi** for dinner are usually safe bets. But in SoCal, sometimes it's the chefs themselves that are the real celebrities. Wolfgang Puck makes the rounds at **Spago** and his other fine-dining restaurants when he is in town.

Nightlife & Entertainment   Nightlife in Los Angeles is hopping. Specifically, Hollywood is the happening place to be for drinking and dancing. Storied live music venues like **the Roxy, the Troubadour,** and the **Whisky A Go-Go** continue to build new legacies nightly. Hotel bars across the city, from the **Standard Downtown** to the **Skybar,** still lure locals along with regular guests.

THE most unforgettable
TRAVEL EXPERIENCES

- **Cruising Along the Coast:** Driving along the sunny coastline with the top down and your hair blowing in the warm wind is the quintessential Southern California experience—one that never loses its appeal, even for locals. Stop and visit whatever interests you: a Malibu cantina, the famous Santa Monica Pier, or a South Bay beach—a casual cruise along the shoreline is good for the soul (BYO Mustang convertible). See chapter 10, "Side Trips from Los Angeles," for destination ideas.

- **Visiting Venice Beach's Ocean Front Walk:** You haven't visited L.A. properly until you've rented some skates in Venice and embarrassed yourself in front of thousands while taking in the human carnival around you. Enjoy a front row seat for particularly good people-watching from your table at the Sidewak Café, buy some knockoff sunglasses, and realize how pathetically out of shape you are compared to all the tan and trim locals—all while enjoying the wide beach, blue sea, and assorted performers along the boardwalk. Can't skate? Cowards can rent a bicycle and pedal along the bike path. See p. 138.

- **Basking at the Beach:** This is, after all, L.A.—so get thy buttocks to a beach. Watch a volleyball tournament at Hermosa Beach, take surf lessons at Manhattan Beach, or gawk at the world's vainest weightlifters pumping iron at Venice's Muscle Beach. Surfers are always spotted at the Malibu beaches, and local families prefer to pitch their umbrellas at Zuma Beach. See chapter 6.

- **Visiting the "Happiest Place on Earth," the Disneyland Resort:** The resort's worldwide appeal is evident in the virtual United Nations of revelers traipsing through Adventureland, Fantasyland, Tomorrowland, and Disney's California Adventure park. It won't be long before the song "It's a Small World" seems permanently stuck in your head. See chapter 7.

- **Dining at Spago (or the Ivy or Mastro's):** Dining at one of L.A.'s classic A-list celebrity haunts is an experience to be filed under "Only in L.A." Hear dialogue straight out of *Entourage* while eating fine food prepared for the world's pickiest eaters ("I can't eat *that!* Take it away."). See chapter 5.

- **Cruising Sunset Boulevard:** It's a must for first-time visitors because you'll see a cross section of everything that is L.A.: legendary clubs, studios, and hotels that you'll instantly recognize from the silver screen and TV shows. The journey ends with a trip to Malibu's fabled beaches, where those classy *Baywatch* episodes were filmed (how perfect). See p. 132.

- **Touring the Getty Center:** See the result of unlimited funds and very expensive tastes at this multifaceted cultural center looming large over the city. The ultramodern facility, more airy and inviting than it looks from below, features a museum housing the impressive art collection of deep-pocketed industrialist J. Paul Getty, a postmodern garden, and breathtaking views of L.A. A sleekly high-tech funicular whisks you from freeway level to this virtual city in the clouds. See p. 139.

- **Spending a Day Downtown:** If you're looking for a healthy dose of ethnic culture, you'll find it in Downtown L.A. Take a self-guided tour of the mind-blowing Walt Disney Concert Hall (p. 145) or cutting-edge Museum of Contemporary Art (p. 154), stop in for a snack at the bustling Grand Central Market (p. 227), pick up some inexpensive Mexican handicrafts along colorful and historic Olvera Street, and have dim sum in Chinatown. See chapter 6.

- **Power Shopping:** You'll see "I'd Rather Be Shopping at Nordstrom" license-plate frames on Lexuses all over L.A., evidence that spending money is a major pastime here. Whether it's $5 vintage bowling shirts, $10,000 Beverly Hills baubles, or anything in between, you're sure to find it in L.A.'s cornucopia of consumerism. My favorite shopping zones are the eclectic shops along Abbot Kinney Boulevard, the endless ethnic oddities at the Grand Central Market in Downtown L.A., and the ultratrendy, alternative stores such as GR2 and Giant Robot along Sawtelle Boulevard in Japantown (p. 224). (Also, see "Where to Find Hollywood's Hand-Me-Downs," p. 237.) See chapter 8.

- **Strolling Wilshire Boulevard's Museum Row:** Natural history meets pop culture meets modern art along Museum Row. La Brea Tar Pits, Petersen Automotive Museum, Craft & Folk Art Museum, and Los Angeles County Museum of Art campus are all shoulder-to-shoulder in the heart of L.A. The only problem is that it's too much to see in a single day. See chapter 6.

- **Taking a Gourmet Picnic to the Hollywood Bowl:** What better way to spend a typically warm L.A. evening than under the stars with a picnic basket, a bottle of wine, and some world-class entertainment? In addition to being the summer home of the Los Angeles Philharmonic, the Bowl hosts visiting performers ranging from chamber music quartets to jazz greats to national touring acts like Radiohead and Rod Stewart. The imposing white Frank Lloyd Wright–designed band shell always elicits appreciative gasps from first-time Bowl-goers. See p. 259.

- **Taking a Tour of the Walt Disney Concert Hall:** Built with a lot of Disney money but without a trace of goofiness, this stunning accomplishment of art and architecture is the crown jewel of Downtown. You'd have to fly to Spain to see architect Frank Gehry's similar architectural masterpiece, the Guggenheim Museum. The dramatically curvaceous stainless-steel exterior houses one of the most acoustically perfect concert halls in the world. The self-guided audio walking tour, narrated by actor John Lithgow, is superb. See p. 145.

- **Taking a Studio Tour:** This is why you're vacationing in L.A.—to see where movie magic is being made. Studio tours are an entertaining opportunity to get a peek at the stage sets for sitcom and talk shows (sometimes during filming), and you never know who you're going to see emerging from his or her Star Wagon. See "Studio Tours," on p. 173.

- **Visiting Santa Catalina Island:** Taking a day trip to Catalina makes for a most adventurous day: a scenic boat ride; oodles of shopping, snorkeling, and scuba diving; golf; hiking trails; waffle cones; sunburns; and DUI-free barhopping. *Tip:* The helicopter taxi is a lot cheaper than you'd expect. See chapter 10.

THE best SPLURGE HOTELS

- **The Ambrose** (1255 20th St., Santa Monica; ✆ **877/4-AMBROSE** [2627673]): Take a break from the fast-paced L.A. scene at this stylish 77-room boutique Arts and Crafts hideaway that offers a soothing, peaceful environment—tranquil Japanese garden, koi pond, trickling fountains—and plenty of free perks (including complimentary taxi shuttle service). See p. 50.

- **Beach House Hotel Hermosa Beach** (1300 The Strand, Hermosa Beach; ✆ **888/895-4559**): Romance-seeking couples will never want to leave this beautiful boutique resort offering plush, luxury-laden studio suites. Book one overlooking the sand and sunbathers for the ultimate beach getaway. See p. 47.

o **Beverly Hills Hotel and Bungalows** (9641 Sunset Blvd., Beverly Hills; © 800/283-8885): Spending at least 1 night at this Hollywood icon is well worth the heavy hit to your credit card. Take afternoon tea in the famous Polo Lounge next to Reese Witherspoon, swim laps in the same pool Katharine Hepburn once dove into fully clothed, and eat pancakes in the fabled Fountain Coffee Shop. Ah, yes, the Pink Palace is still the place to relive Hollywood's Golden Age. See p. 55.

o **Casa del Mar** (1910 Ocean Way, Santa Monica; © 800/898-6999): This impeccably restored Renaissance Revival–style hotel is the grande dame of L.A.'s beachfront hotels, ideally situated in the midst of the Santa Monica scene and offering panoramic views of the ocean from every room. See p. 42.

o **Chateau Marmont** (8221 Sunset Blvd., West Hollywood; © 800/242-8328): Modeled after an elegant Loire Valley castle, the 1920s-era Chateau oozes Old Hollywood. Secreted above the Sunset Strip, its ghosts from the past include Greta Garbo, Errol Flynn, Natalie Wood, Marlon Brando, James Dean, Marilyn Monroe, Clark Gable, and Jean Harlow. See p. 56.

o **Millennium Biltmore Hotel Los Angeles** (506 S. Grand Ave., Downtown; © 800/245-8673): Eye-poppingly magnificent, the Biltmore has been hosting royalty, U.S. presidents, and international celebs since 1923. You've seen it in *Chinatown, Ghostbusters, Bugsy,* and *Beverly Hills Cop*—now see it for real. See p. 75.

o **Montage Beverly Hills** (225 N. Canon Dr., Beverly Hills; © 310/860-7800): This ultradeluxe hotel opened in late 2008, but it already feels like it's been here forever. It's equal parts Old Hollywood glamour and Spanish Revival decadence. The rooms are spacious and gorgeous, and the spa will melt away any amount of stress. Shoppers and star-watchers will delight at the Golden Triangle location. See p. 58.

o **The Mosaic Hotel Beverly Hills** (125 S. Spalding Dr., Beverly Hills; © 800/463-4466): You'll want to redecorate your own bedroom by the time you check out of this gorgeous boutique hotel. Huge rainforest shower heads, Frette linens, Bulgari bath products, Wolfgang Puck refreshments, and piles of pillows all add up to hotel heaven. It's the perfect blend of art, luxury, service, prime location, and value. See p. 64.

o **Shutters on the Beach** (1 Pico Blvd., Santa Monica; © 800/334-9000): If a luxurious oceanfront room at Shutters doesn't add romance to your relationship, it's hard to imagine what will. It's like staying at a really rich friend's East Coast beach house. See p. 46.

o **Terranea Resort** (6610 Rancho Palos Verdes Dr. S., Rancho Palos Verdes; © 866/802-8000): This sprawling oceanfront resort reminds me of the higher-end luxury properties in Orange County. Between the seven restaurants and nine-hole golf course, there's little reason to leave paradise. You honestly forget you're still in L.A. County. See p. 47.

THE best MODERATELY PRICED HOTELS

o **Casa Malibu** (22752 Pacific Coast Hwy., Malibu; © 800/831-0858): This well-maintained hotel has a terrific beachfront location. Innkeepers don't come any friendlier, and oceanfront Malibu accommodations don't get more affordable. See p. 52.

- **Carlyle Inn** (1119 S. Robertson Blvd.; ✆ **800/322-7595**): This hidden gem, cleverly tucked away in the heart of West L.A., offers a pleasing courtyard setting, a dash of Deco-inspired style, and a complimentary, generous breakfast spread. It's a real find for those in search of value-priced comforts. See p. 65.

- **Élan Hotel** (8435 Beverly Blvd., Los Angeles; ✆ **866/203-2212**): This former retirement home has been transformed into one of L.A.'s best boutique-style hotels (and one of the city's best values). Its Beverly Boulevard location isn't pretty, but it's within walking distance of dozens of restaurants and Hollywood attractions. See p. 66.

- **Figueroa Hotel** (939 S. Figueroa St., Los Angeles; ✆ **800/421-9092**): My favorite Downtown lodging is this venerable 1925 building re-created as a Spanish Colonial–Gothic palace. Fun and funky, the exotically decorated guest rooms have far more style than your average hotel; what's more, this gentrified corner of Downtown offers easy, car-free Metro Line access to Hollywood and Universal Studios. See p. 74.

- **The Hotel California** (1670 Ocean Ave., Santa Monica; ✆ **866/571-0000**): You'll like livin' it up at this hacienda-style beachfront motel that charges less than half the price of its fancy-pants neighbors. You'll dig the hotel's surfer/sun-worshiper ambience, cheery rooms with California-themed decor, and direct access to the sand via a private path. See p. 51.

- **Inn at Playa del Rey** (435 Culver Blvd., Playa del Rey; ✆ **310/574-1920**): If you crave the slower pace and personal attention that only a bed-and-breakfast can offer, book a room at this inn, which merges easy airport access with a one-of-a-kind natural setting, thoughtful service, and luxury comforts. The spacious View Suites—complete with a two-sided fireplace that casts a romantic glow on the king-size bed and the Jacuzzi for two—are the ideal choice for celebrating couples. See p. 49.

THE most unforgettable
DINING EXPERIENCES

- **The Bazaar by José Andrés** (465 S. La Cienega Blvd., Beverly Hills; ✆ **310/246-5555**): Walking into this SLS Hotel restaurant is total sensory overload: four separate areas all in one open space, with lots of shiny glitz and glam, artwork, and eye candy (it's one of the *most* popular restaurants in town right now). Spanish celebrity chef José Andrés put L.A. on the dining map with his traditional and contemporary take on tapas. The cocktails alone are worth a visit—margarita with salt "air," anyone? For the ultimate splurge, take one of the 30 seats at tasting-menu-only "secret" restaurant-within-a-restaurant SAAM. See p. 98.

- **Cut** (9500 Wilshire Blvd., Beverly Hills; ✆ **310/276-8500**): Tom and Katie may not be regulars anymore (they used to be a fixture here), but A-listers still frequent the place, and because the room is so open, they have nowhere to hide. It's all in the details at Wolfgang Puck's steakhouse, from perfectly cooked steaks to top-notch service to Sherry Yard's amazing desserts. See p. 101.

- **House of Blues Gospel Brunch** (8430 Sunset Blvd., West Hollywood; ✆ **323/848-5100**): For more than a decade, the HOB has hosted a raucous Sunday brunch that's simmering with high-energy gospel music and all-you-can-eat Southern home cookin'. It's a booty-shaking brunch. See p. 117.

o **Koi** (730 N. La Cienega Blvd., West Hollywood; ✆ 310/659-9449): The combination of soothing feng shui ambience and superb Asian fusion cuisine has made Koi one of the hottest restaurants in L.A. Hollywood's biggest celebrities—Colin Farrell, Joe Jonas, Jennifer Hudson, Demi and Ashton—come here often to nosh on addictive dishes such as baked crab rolls with edible rice paper and miso-bronzed black cod. See p. 107.

o **La Cachette Bistro** (1733 Ocean Ave., Santa Monica; ✆ 310/434-9509): Though there are entrée-size portions available, I suggest sticking with the "French tapas." It represents small-plates-style dining at its best, a culinary adventure in different tastes. It's also nice to see a successful chef, Jean François Meteigner, still spending time in his own kitchen. See p 93.

o **The Little Door** (8164 W. 3rd St., Los Angeles; ✆ 323/951-1210): Consistently voted one of L.A.'s most romantic restaurants is this French/Mediterranean charmer hidden behind a little door on 3rd Street. Sit at the shaded patio among the fragrant bougainvillea while sipping champagne and you'd swear you're in Provence. See p. 113.

o **Pizzeria Mozza & Osteria Mozza** (641 N. Highland Ave., Los Angeles; ✆ 323/297-0101; and 6602 Melrose Ave., Los Angeles; ✆ 323/297-0100): Still one of the hottest reservations in town, side-by-side Pizzeria Mozza and Osteria Mozza are a must-stop. Every time I eat at either, I spend the next few days dreamily contemplating how simple yet brilliant my meal was. See p. 116 and p. 113.

o **Ray's and Stark Bar** (5905 Wilshire Blvd., Los Angeles; ✆ 323/857-6180): This is hands down L.A.'s best museum restaurant. While it doesn't have the sweeping vistas of the one at the Getty, the patio is adjacent to the famous lamp-post installation. Both food and drink are topnotch. It's something special.

o **Rivera** (1050 S. Flower St., Los Angeles; ✆ 213/749-1460): It's so exciting to see more and more amazing restaurants popping up Downtown. Out of all of them, I like this newcomer best, not only for the creative pan-Latin and Mexican cuisine, but also for incredible mixology program. See p. 120.

o **Saddle Peak Lodge** (419 Cold Canyon Rd., Calabasas; ✆ 818/222-3888): In L.A., a romantic restaurant is one without cellphone service (that would be in the hills above Malibu). This converted hunting lodge is quite the quixotic setting for a game-centric meal for two. Candlelit tables, a crackling fireplace, and a *Wine Spectator*–endorsed wine list are sure bets for creating *la mood d'amour*. See p. 97.

o **Savory** (29169 Heathercliff Rd., Malibu; ✆ 310/589-8997): This cozy eatery has a casual enough vibe to make it an instant favorite among laid-back Malibu regulars, but the sensational California fare attracts foodies from all over the city. It's high time that Malibu attained a restaurant of this caliber. See p. 94.

THE best THINGS TO DO FOR FREE (OR ALMOST)

o **Cruising Mulholland Drive:** Ride past the homes with million-dollar views, and then stop at the public viewing pullouts to see the splayed-out city in all its smoggy glory. It's even more romantic at night, when the lights of the city and the valley twinkle below. See p. 171.

o **Evening Jazz Performances:** The Los Angeles County Museum of Art offers free jazz concerts every Friday evening April through November. It's the perfect coda to a satisfying day of art appreciation. See p. 248.

- **Free Admission Days to L.A.'s Museums:** If it's free, baby, it's for me. Almost all of L.A.'s art galleries and museums are open free to the public 1 day of the week or month, and several never charge admission. See p. 147.
- **Hollywood Bowl Rehearsals:** Few people know about the Bowl's morning rehearsals with the L.A. Phil, which are generally open to the public on Tuesday and Thursday mornings and absolutely free. Bring coffee and doughnuts and enjoy the best seats in the house. See p. 259.
- **Going to the Getty Center:** I already mentioned it above and I'll mention it again here: One of L.A.'s best attractions is free, though parking has jumped to $15 per car . See p. 139.
- **Paying Your Respects at the Cemeteries of the Stars:** Spend some downtime with Humphrey Bogart, Clark Gable, Karen Carpenter, and all their famous pals at L.A.'s most enduring celebrity hangouts. Six public cemeteries showcase the final performances of Bette Davis, Lucille Ball, Marilyn Monroe, and dozens more famous names. See p. 180.
- **Watching One of Your Favorite TV Sitcoms Being Taped:** Alternately boring and fascinating (the old hurry-up-and-wait syndrome), being an audience member gives you the chance to wander the soundstage, marvel at the cheesy three-wall sets that look so real on TV, and get an inside look at the bloopers that never make it to broadcast—and are often far more entertaining than the scripted dialogue. See p. 117.

THE best OUTDOOR EXPERIENCES

- **Dining by Helicopter:** Impress your sweetie with a helicopter tour of the city that ends with a front-door drop-off at a romantic restaurant. Get that ring ready. See p. 176.
- **Learning How to Surf:** What could be more fun during your L.A. vacation than learning how to surf on the same breaks that the Beach Boys immortalized? Surfing schools such as **Learn to Surf L.A.** in Manhattan Beach will guarantee you'll get up on a longboard and be surfing the easy waves in one short lesson. See p. 191.
- **Taking a Sunset Margarita Horse Ride:** Whoever thought this one up is a genius: Drive to Sunset Ranch Hollywood Stables in Griffith Park, hop on a big ol' horse, and take a scenic ride through the park to a Mexican restaurant in Burbank. Eat, drink, and be merry; then ride back to the ranch under warm, starry skies. See p. 189.
- **Watching a Polo Match:** May through early October, polo matches are held on weekends at the Will Rogers Polo Club. Enjoy a leisurely picnic lunch among the wide green fields, mighty oaks, and whitewashed fences. See p. 194.

THE best OFFBEAT EXPERIENCES

- **Attending Movie Screenings in a Cemetery:** Pack a picnic basket and head to the Hollywood Forever Cemetery for a summer Saturday evening of classic cinema projected onto the mortuary wall. Arrive early, because people are just dying to get here. (6000 Santa Monica Blvd., Hollywood; www.cinespia.org). See p. 264.

- **Auditioning as a Game Show Contestant:** You, too, could be the next contestant on *The Price Is Right* or *Wheel of Fortune*. Fame and fortune are just a phone call away, so set up that audition before you arrive in L.A. See p. 178.

- **Comparing French Dips:** For more than 100 years, a debate has waged in this town—who made the first French dip sandwich? **Philippe the Original** (1001 N. Alameda St.; ✆ 213/628-3781) claims it was a policeman (or was it a fireman?) at the restaurant who asked for the crusty roll to be dipped in pan drippings, and **Cole's** (118 E. 6th St.; ✆ 213/622-4090) credits a customer with sore gums. The historic locations are both Downtown, so it's easy to do a cross-neighborhood taste test. Me? I don't dare take sides. But I will say the lamb is the best bet at both. See p. 126 and 125.

- **Going to ArcLight Cinemas** (6360 W. Sunset Blvd., Hollywood; ✆ 323/464-4226): "The World's Most Private Public Theater" hosts 21-and-over movie screenings, where you can sip cocktails while watching first-run flicks. Seats are reserved in advance, ushers keep it quiet, late arrivals are forbidden, and there's even a lounge serving appetizers. See p. 265.

- **Listening to Jon Brion:** Make reservations far in advance to see producer, songwriter, and multi-instrumentalist legend Jon Brion play at the Largo supper club (366 N. La Cienega Blvd., Los Angeles; ✆ 310/855-0350; www.largo-la.com). His ability to make up songs on the spot from titles shouted from the audience is mind-blowing. See p. 247.

- **Visiting Roscoe's House of Chicken 'n' Waffles** (1514 N. Gower St., Hollywood; ✆ 323/466-7453): You haven't seen everything until you've seen Southern-fried chicken and waffles on the same plate. Roscoe's is a Hollywood institution where a polyglot of L.A.'s population comes for chicken-and-cheese omelets and sweet-potato pie. The friendly atmosphere and creative combinations make for a fun, adventuresome, and inexpensive dining experience. See p. 118.

LOS ANGELES IN DEPTH

Los Angeles ranks as the second-largest city in the nation; its citizens hail from 140 countries and speak 86 different languages. In fact, Los Angeles is one of only two U.S. cities without a majority population.

But unlike many of the world's greatest metropolitan destinations, L.A. is seen more in the context of the present—even the future—than the past. This young city is all the more intriguing because that past is fresh and easily excavated (both figuratively and literally); the sense of simultaneously having one foot in yesterday and one in tomorrow is part of what makes discovering L.A. so rewarding. In this chapter, we give you a little rundown on the history of El Pueblo de Nuestra Señora la Reina de Los Angeles (the Town of Our Lady the Queen of the Angels), along with some other useful background on the local views and customs that give an insight into the city and its inhabitants.

LOS ANGELES TODAY

Having survived a long, leisurely pioneering infancy and a slightly uncouth adolescence, Los Angeles has blossomed into one of the world's major cultural centers. The movies, TV shows, and music produced here are seen and heard throughout the world; the pop products of the city's efforts govern who we are, how we spend our time, and how we think more than we like to admit.

As Los Angeles hurtles through the 21st century, the city is going through some drastic changes. Intense growth and increased ethnic diversity have fueled a climate of political and philosophical change; in many ways, there are two L.A.s, existing in parallel universes. There's the beautiful showbiz town, home of starlets and hunks who cruise palm-tree-lined streets in sleek convertibles on their way to the studio. The other universe is a multiethnic Pacific Rim metropolis, swelling uncomfortably from the influx of new residents, yet enriching the city with cultural diversity. In this other L.A., you'll encounter Vietnamese, Ethiopian, Russian, and Salvadoran enclaves in formerly run-down parts of town. You'll find a city straining to grow technologically into a new century, right next to the town eager to preserve its golden (and sometimes isolationist) roots.

LOOKING BACK AT LOS ANGELES

In the Beginning

Los Angeles was founded by the Spanish on the site of a Native American village in 1781, but it wasn't until after the first film studio was established, in 1911, that Los Angeles really took off. Within 5 years, movies such as D. W. Griffith's *Birth of a Nation* were being produced by the hundreds. By World War I, the Hollywood studio system was firmly entrenched, with the young trio of Charlie Chaplin, Douglas Fairbanks, and "America's Sweetheart," Mary Pickford, at its fore.

As the box office boomed in the 1920s and 1930s, so did the population of Los Angeles. Easterners came to the burgeoning urban paradise in droves to find their fortunes. The world-famous Hollywood sign, erected in 1923, was built as an advertisement for just one of many fledgling real-estate developments that began to crop up on the "outskirts" of the city. Los Angeles was even more alluring during the Great Depression. As Americans ached for an escape from their less-than-inspiring reality, Hollywood's cinematic fantasies were there to oblige. With each glamorous, idyllic portrayal of California, Los Angeles's popularity—and population—grew.

QUEST FOR WATER   As the city expanded, so did the need for water. Most great American cities grew from small settlements on rivers or lakes, freshwater sources vital to everyday life and commerce. Not L.A.—it was founded in the middle of an arid basin. The Los Angeles River has always been too unpredictable to support the city's growth, and today it is merely a series of flood-control channels operated by the Department of Water and Power. The quest for water has provided some of L.A.'s most gripping real-life drama. As early as 1799, Spanish padres at the new Mission San Fernando dammed the river to provide for their water needs, causing an uprising among settlers downstream. Disputes continued up to the incidents that inspired the movie *Chinatown,* about the early battle for the rights to the Owens Valley's abundant

DATELINE

1781 Los Angeles is founded.

1821 Spain grants independence to Mexico and, therefore, to California.

1850 California becomes the 31st state.

1875 The Santa Fe Railroad reaches Los Angeles.

1881 The *Los Angeles Times* begins publication.

1892 Oil is discovered in Downtown Los Angeles.

1900 The population of California approaches 1.5 million; Los Angeles has more than 102,000 residents.

1902 The first movie house, the Electric Theatre, opens.

1909 Santa Monica Pier is erected to accommodate cargo and passenger ships.

1911 Hollywood's first film studio is established.

1912 More than 16 motion-picture companies are operating out of Hollywood.

water, which William Mulholland and Fred Eaton "stole" with their new California aqueduct. Resentment from Northern California continues up to the present time, as L.A. residents continue to reap the agricultural, domestic, and electrical benefits of what many claim was never rightfully theirs.

THE TRIUMPH OF CAR CULTURE   The opening of the Arroyo Seco Parkway in 1940, linking Downtown L.A. and Pasadena with the first of what would be a network of freeways, ushered in a new era for the city. From that time on, car culture flourished in Los Angeles, becoming perhaps the city's most distinctive feature. (For more on this subject, see "From Horseless Carriages to Hot Rods," p. 17.) America's automotive industry successfully conspired to undermine Los Angeles's public transportation system by halting the trolley service that once plied Downtown and advocating the construction of auto-friendly roads. The growth of the freeways led to the development of L.A.'s suburban sprawl, turning Los Angeles into a city without a single geographical focus. The suburbs became firmly entrenched in the L.A. landscape during World War II, when shipyards and munitions factories, as well as aerospace giants McDonnell Douglas, Lockheed, Rockwell, and General Dynamics, opened their doors in Southern California and the workers who flocked here needed affordable housing.

THE POSTWAR ERA   After the war, the threat of television put the movie industry into a tailspin. But instead of being destroyed by the "tube," Hollywood was strengthened when that industry made its home here as well. Soon afterward, in the 1950s and 1960s, the avant-garde discovered Los Angeles, too; the city became popular with artists, beatniks, and hippies, many of whom settled in Venice.

The 1970s gave rise to a number of exotic religions and cults that found eager adherents in Southern California. The spiritual "New Age" born in the "Me" decade found life into the 1980s, in the face of a population growing beyond manageable limits, an increasingly polluted environment, and escalating social ills. At the same time, California became very rich. Real-estate values soared, banks and businesses prospered, and the entertainment industry boomed.

1913 Cecil B. DeMille directs the film industry's first full-length feature, *The Squaw Man.*

1923 The Hollywood sign (which at the time read HOLLYWOODLAND) is erected to advertise a real-estate development.

1927 The first "talkie" is released: *The Jazz Singer,* with Al Jolson.

1929 The Academy of Motion Picture Arts and Sciences bestows its first Oscar.

1940 L.A.'s first freeway, the Arroyo Seco Parkway, connects Hollywood and Pasadena.

1947 The first TV station west of the Mississippi, KTLA, begins broadcasting.

1950 L.A.'s population is nearly two million.

1955 Disneyland opens.

1961 Hollywood's Walk of Fame is started by the Hollywood Chamber of Commerce.

1962 California overtakes New York as the nation's most populous state.

1965 Tension between white LAPD officers and the African-American community fuels riots in Watts.

continues

THE NEW MILLENNIUM   Today, as always, Angelenos are on the leading edge of American pop culture. But they've discovered, as the world wags its finger and shakes its collective head, that success isn't always all it's cracked up to be. The nation's economic, social, and environmental problems have become the city's own, and even become amplified in this larger-than-life arena. The 1991 Rodney King beating and subsequent 1992 rioting, the 1994 Northridge earthquake, the 1996 acquittal of O. J. Simpson, the 1998 *El Niño* floods, the LAPD Rampart scandal in 2000—half the city proclaimed these disasters as signaling the beginning of the end, declaring each time that L.A. would never fully recover. The other half optimistically predicted that adversity would unite the fragmented city and it would emerge, phoenix-like, stronger than ever. Both factions were partially correct—but mostly the city has just gone on with the business of being L.A.

ART & ARCHITECTURE

The movie industry, more than anything else, has defined Los Angeles. The process of moviemaking has never been confined to studio offices and back lots; it spills into the city's streets and other public spaces. The city itself is an extension of the movie set, and Angelenos have always seen it that way. All of Los Angeles has an air of Hollywood surreality (or disposability), even its architecture. The whole city seems a bit larger than life. As a result, L.A. is a veritable Disneyland of architecture and is home to an amalgam of distinctive styles, from Art Deco to Spanish Revival, to coffee-shop kitsch, to suburban ranch, to postmodern—and much more.

Between 1945 and 1966, *Arts & Architecture* magazine focused the design world's attention on L.A. with its series of "Case Study Houses," prototypes for postwar living, which were designed by prominent émigrés like Pierre Koenig, Richard Neutra, and Eero Saarinen. Los Angeles has taken some criticism for not being a "serious" architectural center, but in terms of innovation and style, the city gets high marks.

Although much of it is gone, you can still find some prime examples of the kitschy roadside art that defined L.A. in earlier days. The famous Brown Derby is no more,

1968 Robert F. Kennedy is fatally shot at the Ambassador Hotel after winning California's Democratic Party presidential primary.	**1996** At the conclusion of the "Crime of the Century" trial, O. J. Simpson is found not guilty of the murders of Nicole Brown Simpson and Ron Goldman.
1980 L.A.'s population is nearly three million.	**1997** The J. Paul Getty Center opens on a Brentwood hilltop overlooking L.A.
1984 Los Angeles hosts the Summer Olympic Games.	
1992 More than 40 die and hundreds are injured in the race riots resulting from the acquittal of the police officers involved in the Rodney King beating.	**1998** *El Niño* conditions over the Pacific bring torrential rain, flooding, and landslides to Southern California.
1994 An earthquake measuring 6.8 on the Richter scale shakes the city.	**2000** The country's largest police scandal erupts in L.A., with dozens of Rampart Division officers incriminated in illegal activity.

but you can still find a neon-lit **1950s gas station/spaceship** (at the corner of Little Santa Monica Blvd. and Crescent Dr. in Beverly Hills), in addition to some newer structures carrying on the tradition, such as the former **Chiat/Day offices** in Venice, known affectionately as the "Binoculars Building" (see below).

SANTA MONICA & THE BEACHES When you're strolling the historic canals and streets of Venice, be sure to check out the Binoculars Building at 340 Main St. What would otherwise be an unspectacular contemporary office building is made fantastic by a **three-story pair of binoculars** that frames the entrance. The sculpture is modeled after a design created by Claes Oldenburg and Coosje van Bruggen.

The spacey *Jetsons*-style **Theme Building,** which has always loomed over Los Angeles International Airport, has been joined by a more recent silhouette. The main LAX **control tower,** designed by local architect Kate Diamond to evoke a stylized palm tree, is tailored to present Southern California in its best light. You can go inside to enjoy the view from the Theme Building's observation deck, or have a space-age cocktail at the Technicolor bachelor pad that is the **Encounter at LAX** restaurant.

Constructed on a broad cliff with a steep face, the **Wayfarers Chapel** in Rancho Palos Verdes enjoys a fantastic spot overlooking the waves of the Pacific. It was designed by Lloyd Wright, son of celebrated architect Frank Lloyd Wright. Known locally as the "glass church," Wayfarers is a memorial to Emanuel Swedenborg, an 18th-century Swedish philosopher who claimed to have visions of spirits and heavenly hosts. The church is constructed of glass, redwood, and native stone.

L.A.'S WESTSIDE & BEVERLY HILLS The bold architecture and overwhelming scale of the **Pacific Design Center,** designed by Argentine architect Cesar Pelli, aroused controversy when it was erected in 1975. Sheathed in gently curving cobalt-blue glass, the six-story building houses more than 750,000 square feet of wholesale interior-design showrooms and is known to locals as "the Blue Whale." In 1988 a second boxlike structure, dressed in equally dramatic Kelly green, was added to the design center and surrounded by a protected outdoor plaza. The long-delayed Red Building towers are scheduled to finally open in the summer of 2011.

2005 Antonio Villaraigosa is elected mayor of Los Angeles—he is the first Latino mayor since Cristobal Aguilar in 1872.

2006 The Griffith Observatory reopens in November after a $93-million, 4-year renovation.

2008 A two-train collision kills 25 people and injures 130 others after an engineer fails to heed a traffic signal due to text-messaging.

2009 Economic downturn has Los Angeles in a financial tailspin. Hotel sales plummet while numerous local businesses

shut down. Hopes are pinned on President Barack Obama's economic recovery program.

Michael Jackson dies at age 50 of an administered drug overdose after being rushed to a hospital from his Beverly Hills home.

2011 Hollywood icon and dear friend of Jackson, Elizabeth Taylor passes away at the age of 79 from congestive heart failure.

A protégé of Frank Lloyd Wright and contemporary of Richard Neutra, Austrian architect Rudolph Schindler designed the innovative **Schindler House** for himself in the early 1920s. It's now home to the Los Angeles arm of Austria's Museum of Applied Arts (MAK). The house is noted for its complicated interlocking spaces; the interpenetration of indoors and out; simple, unadorned materials; and technological innovations. Docent-guided tours are conducted at no additional charge on weekends.

HOLLYWOOD   Opened in 1956, the 13-story **Capitol Records Building** tower, just north of the legendary intersection of Hollywood and Vine, is one of the city's most recognizable buildings. The world's first circular office building is often, but incorrectly, said to have been made to resemble a stack of 45s under a turntable stylus.

Conceived by grandiose impresario Sid Grauman, the **Egyptian Theatre** is just down the street from his better-known **Chinese Theatre,** but it remains less altered from its original design, which was based on the then-headline-news discovery of hidden treasures in Pharaohs' tombs—hence the hieroglyphic murals and enormous scarab decoration above the stage. Hollywood's first movie premiere, *Robin Hood,* starring Douglas Fairbanks, was hosted here in 1922. The building has undergone a sensitive restoration by American Cinematheque, which now screens rare, classic, and independent films (see "Movies: Play It Again, Sam," in chapter 9).

Frank Lloyd Wright's **Freeman House,** built in 1924, was designed as an experimental prototype of mass-produced affordable housing. The home's richly patterned "textile-block" exterior is the most famous aspect of the home's design. Situated on a dramatic site overlooking Hollywood, Freeman House is built with the world's first glass-to-glass corner windows. Dancer Martha Graham, bandleader Xavier Cugat, art collector Galka Sheye, photographer Edward Weston, and architects Philip Johnson and Richard Neutra all lived or spent significant time at this house.

DOWNTOWN   For a taste of what Downtown's Bunker Hill was like before the bulldozers, visit the residential neighborhood of **Angelino Heights,** near Echo Park. Entire streets are still filled with stately gingerbread Victorian homes; most still enjoy the beautiful views that led early L.A.'s elite to build here. The 1300 block of Carroll Avenue is the best preserved. Don't be surprised if a film crew is scouting locations while you're there—these blocks often appear on the silver screen.

The **Bradbury Building,** a National Historic Landmark, built in 1893 and designed by George Wyman, is Los Angeles's oldest commercial building and one of the city's most revered architectural achievements. Legend has it that an inexperienced draftsman named George Wyman accepted the $125,000 commission after communicating with his dead brother through a Ouija board. Capped by a magical five-story skylight, Bradbury's courtyard combines glazed brick, ornate Mexican tile floors, rich Belgian marble, Art Nouveau grillwork, handsome oak paneling, and lacelike wrought-iron railings—it's one of the great interior spaces of the 19th century. The glass-topped atrium is often used as a movie and TV set; you've probably seen it before in *Chinatown* and *Blade Runner*.

The **Cathedral of Our Lady of the Angels,** completed in September 2002 at a cost of $163 million and built to last 500 years, is one of L.A.'s newest architectural treasures and the third-largest cathedral in the world. It was designed by award-winning Spanish architect Jose Rafael Moneo and features a 20,000-square-foot plaza with a meditation garden, more than 6,000 crypts and niches (making it the largest crypt mausoleum in the U.S.), mission-style colonnades, biblically inspired gardens, and numerous artworks. The exterior of this austere, sand-colored structure is rather uninspiring and uninviting, but the interior is breathtaking: 12,000 panes of translucent alabaster and larger-than-life tapestries lining the walls create an awe-inspiring sense of magnificence and serenity. The 25,000-pound bronze doors, created by sculptor Robert Graham, pay homage to Ghiberti's bronze baptistery door in Florence. Free self-guided tours are available, and there's a small cafe and gift shop as well.

Built in 1928, the 27-story **Los Angeles City Hall** was the tallest building in the city for more than 30 years. The structure's distinctive ziggurat tower was designed to resemble the Mausoleum at Halicarnassus, one of the seven wonders of the ancient world. The building has been featured in numerous films and television shows, but it is probably best known as the headquarters of the *Daily Planet* in the *Superman* TV series. When it was built, City Hall was the sole exception to an ordinance outlawing buildings taller than 150 feet. Take the elevator to the rarely used 27th-floor Observation Deck—on a clear day you can see to Mount Wilson 15 miles away.

The **L.A. Central Library** is one of L.A.'s early architectural achievements and the third-largest library in the United States. The city rallied to save the library when arson nearly destroyed it in 1986; the triumphant restoration has returned much of its original splendor. Working in the early 1920s, architect Bertram G. Goodhue employed the Egyptian motifs and materials popularized by the discovery of King Tut's tomb, and combined them with a more modern use of concrete block to great effect. Free docent-led art and architecture tours are given daily—call ✆ **213/228-7168.** Walk-in tours last about an hour; they're led Monday through Friday at 12:30pm, and Saturday at 11am and 2pm. **Union Station,** completed in 1939, is one of the finest examples of California mission-style architecture and one of the last of America's great rail stations. With its cathedral-like size and richly paneled ticket lobby and waiting area, it has the attention to detail that characterizes 1930s WPA projects. When you're strolling through these grand historic halls, it's easy to imagine the glamorous movie stars who once boarded *The City of Los Angeles* and *The Super Chief* to journey back East during the glory days of rail travel; it's also easy to picture the many heartfelt reunions between returning soldiers and loved ones following the end of World War II, in the station's heyday. Movies shot here include *Bugsy, The Way We Were,* and *Blade Runner.*

Designed by renowned architect I. M. Pei, **US Bank Tower (also known as Library Tower)** is L.A.'s most distinctive skyscraper (it's the round one) and is the tallest building between Chicago and Singapore. Built in 1989 at a cost of $450 million, the 76-story monolith is both square and rectangular, rising from its 5th Street base in a series of overlapping spirals and cubes. The Bunker Hill Steps wrapping around the west side of the building were inspired by Rome's Spanish Steps. The glass crown at the top—illuminated at night—is the highest building helipad in the world.

WATTS Watts became notorious as the site of riots in the summer of 1965, during which 34 people were killed and more than 1,000 were injured. Today a visit to the **Watts Towers & Art Center** is a lesson in inner-city life. Watts is a high-density land of gray strip malls, well-guarded check-cashing shops, and fast-food restaurants; but it's also a neighborhood of hardworking families struggling to survive in the midst of gangland. Although there's not much for the casual tourist here, the Watts Towers are truly a unique attraction, and the adjoining art gallery illustrates the fierce determination of area residents to maintain cultural integrity.

The Towers—the largest piece of folk art created by a single person—are colorful, 99-foot-tall cement and steel sculptures ornamented with mosaics of bottles, seashells, cups, plates, pottery, and ceramic tiles. They were completed in 1955 by folk artist Simon Rodia, an immigrant Italian tile-setter who worked on them for 33 years in his spare time. Closed in 1994 due to earthquake damage, the towers were reopened in 2001 and now attract more than 20,000 visitors annually. Tours are by request.

PASADENA & ENVIRONS   The two-story **Gamble House,** built in 1908 as a California vacation home for the wealthy family of Procter & Gamble fame, is a sublime example of Arts and Crafts architecture. The interior, designed by the famous Pasadena-based Greene & Greene architectural team, abounds with handcraftsmanship, including intricately carved teak cornices, custom-designed furnishings, elaborate carpets, and a fantastic Tiffany glass door.

Additional elegant Greene & Greene houses (still privately owned) abound 2 blocks away along **Arroyo Terrace,** including nos. **368, 370, 400, 408, 424,** and **440.** The Gamble House bookstore can give you a walking-tour map.

In the late 18th century, Franciscan missionaries established 21 missions up the California coast, from San Diego to Sonoma. Each uniquely beautiful mission was built 1 day's trek from the next, along a path known as El Camino Real ("the Royal Road"), remnants of which still exist. The missions' construction marked the beginning of European settlement of California and the displacement of the Native American population. The two L.A.-area missions are located in the valleys that took their names: the San Fernando Valley and the San Gabriel Valley. A third mission, San Juan Capistrano, is located in Orange County.

Established in 1797, **Mission San Fernando** once controlled more than 1½ million acres, employed 1,500 Native Americans, and boasted more than 22,000 head of cattle and extensive orchards. The fragile adobe mission complex was destroyed several times but was always faithfully rebuilt with low buildings surrounding grassy courtyards. The aging church was replaced in the 1940s and again in the 1970s after an earthquake. The **Convento,** a 250-foot-long colonnaded structure dating from 1810, is the compound's oldest remaining building. Some of the mission's rooms, including the old library and the private salon of the first bishop of California, have been restored to their late-18th-century appearance. A half-dozen padres and many hundreds of Shoshone Indians are buried in the adjacent cemetery.

Founded in 1771, **Mission San Gabriel Arcangel** retains its original facade, notable for its high oblong windows and large capped buttresses said to have been influenced by the cathedral in Cordova, Spain. The mission's self-contained compound encompasses an aqueduct, a cemetery, a tannery, and a winery. Within the church stands a copper font with the distinction of being the first one used to baptize a Native Californian. The most notable contents of the mission's museum are Native American paintings depicting the Stations of the Cross, done on sailcloth, with colors made from crushed desert flower petals.

L.A. IN POPULAR CULTURE: BOOKS & AUTOS

Los Angeles on the Page

NONFICTION   In vivid detail, Edward Jay Epstein's *The Big Picture: The New Logic of Money and Power in Hollywood* (Random House, 2005) delves deep into the modern moviemaking machine with a behind-the-scenes glimpse into the "sexopoly":

the six mega-media companies that control motion picture entertainment (it's a real myth-buster). Love 'em or hate 'em, the saga of the L.A. Lakers makes for good reading in *The Last Season: A Team In Search of Its Soul* by Lakers coach Phil Jackson (Penguin Press, 2004). It's a pro-athlete opera of rape charges, spoiled superstars, team meltdowns, and public feuds. Former Crips gang member Sanyika Shakur documents his life of violence, drugs, and redemption growing up in the streets of South Central L.A. in *Monster: Autobiography of an L.A. Gang Member* (Penguin Books, 1998). *L.A. Exposed: Strange Myths and Curious Legends in the City of Angels* by Paul Young (St. Martin's Press, 2002) is a compelling compendium of dispelled myths, verified rumors, crime lore, conspiracy legends, tall tales, blatant lies, political scandal, and various other fascinating accounts of past and present Los Angeles. Equally titillating is Matt Maranian and Anthony Lovett's *L.A. Bizarro: The Insiders Guide to the Obscure, the Absurd and the Perverse in Los Angeles* (St. Martin's Griffin, 1997), 192 pages of murder sites, sex shops, curiosity shops, dive bars, and various other Southern California scurrility.

FICTION Since the book is almost always better than the movie, try a few of these novels that have been adapted into successful films: James Ellroy's epic crime novel *L.A. Confidential* (Mysterious Press, 1990); Joan Didion's profoundly disturbing *Play It as It Lays* (Farrar, Straus and Giroux, 1990); Joseph Wambaugh's gripping LAPD chronicles, such as *The Onion Field* (Dell, 1974); John Gregory Dunne's cynical and hard-boiled *True Confessions* (Bookthrift Co., 1977); Elmore Leonard's Hollywood-based bestseller *Get Shorty* (HarperTorch, 2002); and Michael Tolkin's absorbing mystery/thriller *The Player* (Grove Press, 1997). And, of course, anything by Raymond Chandler: *Farewell My Lovely, The Big Sleep, The Long Goodbye, The Lady in the Lake,* and *The Postman Always Rings Twice.*

From Horseless Carriages to Hot Rods

The Southern California lifestyle is so closely tied to the automobile that it has given rise to a whole subculture of the car. Since its introduction to the infant city it would grow up with, the automobile has become a pop phenomenon all its own, inextricably intertwined with the personality of L.A.—and the identities of its residents. Although the first "horseless carriages" emerged from the Midwest, it's been Hollywood's influence that has defined the entire nation's passion for the car.

During the early 1920s, movie comedians Laurel and Hardy and the Keystone Cops began to blend their brand of physical humor with the popular Ford Model T. And a visionary coach builder named Harley Earl was busy in his shop on South Main Street, building special vehicles for the movies—the Ben Hur racing chariots—and designing flamboyant custom cars for wealthy movie stars. Earl would later be recruited by General Motors, bringing along with him from Hollywood to Detroit an obsession with style over substance that would culminate in the legendary tail fins of the 1950s.

As movie director Cecil B. DeMille once said, both cars and movies capture Americans' love of motion and speed. Car culture as it was depicted in motion pictures continued to set the pace for the country. In *Rebel Without a Cause,* James Dean's troubled teenager and his hot-rodding buddies assert their independence through their jalopies in scenes filmed on the roads around the Griffith Observatory in the Hollywood Hills. As authorities cracked down on dangerous street racing, locally based *Hot Rod Magazine* helped spawn the movement to create legal drag strips, and the sport of professional drag racing was born. The art of auto-body customizing also came into being here, pioneered by George Barns, the "King of Kustomizers."

The world watched Southern California's physical landscape change to accommodate the four-wheeled resident. In postwar suburban tracts, the garage, which had traditionally been a separate shed, grew attached to the house and became the family's main entrance. The Arroyo Seco Parkway (now the Pasadena Fwy.) opened in 1940; its curvaceous lanes were modeled after the landscaped parkways of the New York City metropolitan area, each turn placed to open up a series of scenic vistas for the driver. (Later L.A. freeways, reflecting a greater concern with speed, were modeled after the straight, efficient autobahns of Europe.)

Meanwhile, businesses in town built signs in an attempt to catch the eye of the driving customer; as the cars got faster, the signs got larger and brighter. A look at the gargantuan billboards on the Sunset Strip shows where that trend ended up. Another scourge of the modern landscape, the minimall, actually started innocently enough in 1927 with the first "supermarket." The term was coined by Hattem's (at the corner of Western Ave. and 43rd St.), where several grocers lined up side by side, set back from the street to provide plentiful parking and one-stop convenience for their customers.

But perhaps the most enduring feature to arise from the phenomenon of the automobile is the drive-up, drive-in, and drive-through business. In the mid-1920s, someone thought to punch through their outer wall to serve the motoring customer. By the next decade, Los Angeles boasted the world's largest collection of establishments that you could patronize from the privacy and comfort of your car. There were drive-up bank-teller windows, drive-through florists and dry cleaners, drive-through dairies (Alta Dena still maintains several in the Southland), and drive-up restaurants. These weren't the impersonal fast-food joints of today, but real restaurants (like the popular Dolores Drive-In chain) with cheerful carhops bringing your freshly made order to you on a window tray.

Perhaps the most popular of these drive-in landmarks are the movie theaters. Los Angeles had the second one built in the country (at the corner of Pico and Westwood boulevards). Long established as a teenage make-out haven, one theater gained popularity in a more spiritual way when Reverend Robert Schuller began to deliver Sunday-morning sermons to a comfortably parked audience at the Orange County Drive-In. His slogan: "Come as you are, in the family car."

The trend to view the car as an extension of the home persists today, with the marketing of mobile phones, scanners, electric shavers, Blu-ray players, and more, all capable of plugging in and functioning inside your car (or even coming as standard equipment). What more could the auto-loving Angeleno ask for?

EATING & DRINKING IN LOS ANGELES

Once upon a time, the culinary culture of Los Angeles was defined by the city's dominant Midwestern heritage. It was mostly a basic meat-and-potatoes fare, or else bad imitations of what passed for good eating in New York or Chicago. Sure, there was always Mexican and Chinese food around, but ethnic cuisine was only acceptable if it was toned down—the spices reduced and the dishes emasculated to fit in with Angelenos' bland-is-best sensibilities. In fact, for far too long the most reliable meal in the city was a burger, a side order of greasy fries, and a drink.

Happily for those seeking more civilized dining, the city's movable feast is now globally varied. As one might expect, the culinary cartography of L.A. parallels the metastasized character of our ethnic communities, with flare-ups of great food emerging in the least-expected places: tucked away in anonymous strip malls and bracketed by a liquor store and a laundry, or hidden in decrepit sections of the inner city. It's no coincidence that the traditional DMZ between the Eastside and the Westside, La Cienega Boulevard, is known as Restaurant Row. It used to be that the wealthy gourmands of Beverly Hills and West L.A. would head east for something a little out of the ordinary, and this was as far as they would drive. Conversely, when the citizens of the Eastside wanted to splurge and step up for the night, they'd head west, winding up in the same place.

The culinary scene remained in this stalemate until the '70s, when California Cuisine first hit the streets, drifting south from Alice Waters's Chez Panisse in Berkeley, daring local chefs to explore the fresh and foreign. Throw in the cacophony of herbs and spices brought to the city by the Pacific Rim immigrants, and you begin to get an idea of what's on the menu at L.A.'s forward-thinking restaurants.

Who are the kitchen gods of L.A.? For starters: Wolfgang Puck, Nobu Matsuhisa, Joaquim Splichal, John Sedlar, Nancy Silverton, Suzanne Goin, Mark Peel, Celestino Drago, and Mary Sue Milliken and Susan Feniger (together known as the "Too Hot Tamales"). What's new? Dining alfresco in mostly smoke-free environments, the evolution of quality fusion fare, upscale Latin-influenced food, more and more chefs featuring "exotic" proteins like pork belly and beef cheeks, and a new wave of destination-dining at boutique and luxury hotels.

And if you're wondering about those A, B, and C ratings you see in the windows of our local eateries, they're the work of the County Public Health Department, which started rating the county's 34,000 food outlets in 1998. Food-selling establishments get inspected several times a year; more than 75% of them get an A, while only 3% get a C. But if you're worried about mouse poop in your pasta, check out www.lapublic health.org/rating so you don't have any reservations about making your reservations.

WHEN TO GO

Many visitors don't realize that Los Angeles—despite its blue ocean, swaying palm trees, green lawns, and forested foothills—is actually the high desert. But with the desert climes tempered by sea breezes and the landscape kept green with water carried by aqueducts from all around the West, L.A. might be the most accommodating desert you've ever visited. No matter how hot it gets, low humidity usually keeps things dry and comfortable.

Tourism peaks during **summer,** when coastal hotels fill to capacity, restaurant reservations can be hard to get, and top attractions are packed with visitors and locals off from work or school. Summer can be miserable in the inland valleys, where daytime temperatures—and that famous L.A. smog—can be stifling, but the beach communities almost always remain comfortable. Moderate temperatures, fewer crowds, and lower hotel rates make travel to L.A. most pleasurable during the **winter.** The city is at its best from early autumn to late spring, when the skies are less smoggy. Rain is rare in Los Angeles—about 34 days a year, on average—but it can cause flooding when it does sneak up on the unsuspecting city; precipitation is most likely from February to April and is virtually unheard of between May and November. Even in January, daytime temperatures reach into the 60s (high teens Celsius) and higher—sometimes up to the 80s (high 20s Celsius).

Los Angeles's Average Temperatures (°F & °C)

	JAN	FEB	MAR	APR	MAY	JUNE	JULY	AUG	SEPT	OCT	NOV	DEC
TEMP (°F)	66/48	68/50	69/51	71/54	73/57	77/60	82/63	84/64	82/63	78/59	73/53	68/50
TEMP (°C])	19/9	20/10	21/11	22/12	23/14	25/16	28/17	29/18	28/17	26/15	23/12	20/10

Pundits claim L.A. has no seasons; it might be more accurate to say the city has its own unique seasons. Two of them are "June Gloom" and "the Santa Anas." The first refers to the ocean fog that keeps the beach cities (and often all of L.A.) overcast into early afternoon; it's most common in June but can occur any time between March and mid-August. The middle of autumn (Oct–Nov) often brings the "Santa Anas," strong, hot winds from across the desert that increase brush-fire danger (surfers love the offshore conditions they usually create).

Winds and coastal fog aside, Los Angeles remains relatively temperate year-round, with an average of 320 sunny days per year and an average mean temperature of 66°F (19°C). It's possible to sunbathe throughout the year, but only die-hard enthusiasts and wet-suited surfers venture into the ocean in winter, when water temps hover around 50° to 55°F (10°–13°C). The water is warmest in summer and fall, usually about 65° to 70°F (18°–21°C), but even then the Pacific can be too chilly for many.

Los Angeles Calendar of Events

For an exhaustive list of events beyond those noted here, check http://events.frommers. com, where you'll find a searchable, up-to-the-minute roster of what's happening in cities all over the world.

JANUARY

Tournament of Roses, Pasadena. A spectacular parade marches down Colorado Boulevard, with lavish floats, music, and extraordinary equestrian entries, followed by the Rose Bowl football game. (It's tradition among parade-goes to camp out along Colorado Boulevard the night before in order to secure a good spot.) Call ℂ **626/449-4100** or see www.tournamentofroses.com for details. January 1.

Martin Luther King, Jr., Parade, Long Beach. This annual parade down Martin Luther King, Jr. Avenue and Anaheim Street ends with a festival in Martin Luther King, Jr., Park. For more information, contact the city manager at ℂ **562/570-6711.** Third Monday in January.

Bob Hope Classic, Palm Springs area. Celebrating its 52nd year in 2011, this PGA golf tournament raises money for charity and includes a celebrity-studded Pro-Am. For spectator information and tickets, call ℂ **760/346-8184.** Mid- to late January.

Santa Barbara International Film Festival, Santa Barbara. For 10 days every year, Santa Barbara does its best impression of Cannes. There's a flurry of foreign and independent film premieres, appearances by actors and directors, and symposia on cinematic topics. For a rundown of events, call ℂ **805/963-0023** or visit www.sbiff.org. Late January to early February.

Chinese New Year & Golden Dragon Parade, Los Angeles. Dragon dancers and martial arts masters parade through the streets of Downtown's Chinatown. Chinese opera and other events are scheduled. For this year's schedule, contact the Chinese Chamber of Commerce at ℂ **213/617-0396** or visit www.lachinesechamber.org. Late January or early February.

FEBRUARY

National Date Festival, Indio (Palm Springs area). Crowds gather for 2 weeks to celebrate the Coachella Valley desert's most beloved cash crop, with events like camel and ostrich races, the Blessing of the Date Garden, and festive Arabian Nights pageants. Plenty of date-sampling booths are set up, along with rides, food vendors, and other county-fair trappings. Call ℂ **800/811-3247** or 760/863-8247, or visit www.datefest.org. Two weeks in February.

Northern Trust Open Golf Tournament, Pacific Palisades. The PGA Tour makes its only Tinseltown appearance at the Riviera Country Club, overlooking the ocean. Expect to see stars in attendance. For information, call the Los Angeles Junior Chamber of Commerce at ☏ **310/454-6591.** Mid-February.

Mardi Gras, West Hollywood. The festivities—including live jazz and lots of food—take place along Santa Monica Boulevard, and in the alley behind Santa Monica Boulevard. Contact the West Hollywood Convention & Visitors Bureau at ☏ **800/368-6020** for details. Late February or early March.

MARCH

Los Angeles Marathon, Downtown. This 26-mile run attracts thousands of participants, from world champions to the guy next door; the big day also features a 5K run/walk and a bike marathon on the same route. The run starts at Dodger Stadium and ends at the Santa Monica Pier. Call ☏ **310/271-7200** or visit www.lamarathon.com for registration or spectator information. Mid March.

California Poppy Blooming Season, Antelope Valley. Less than an hour's drive north of Los Angeles lies the California Poppy Reserve, part of the state park system. In spring, miles of hillside blaze with brilliant hues of red and orange, dazzling the senses of motorists who flock to witness the display. For information and directions, call ☏ **661/723-6077.** Mid-March to mid-May. For information on the annual **California Poppy Festival,** held at full bloom (usually in mid to late Apr), call ☏ **661/723-6077** or visit www.poppyfestival.com.

APRIL

Toyota Grand Prix, Long Beach. An exciting weekend of Indy-class auto racing and entertainment in and around downtown Long Beach draws world-class drivers from the United States and Europe, plus many celebrity contestants and spectators. Contact the Grand Prix Association at ☏ **888/82-SPEED** (827-7333) or www.gplb.com. Mid-April.

Coachella Valley Music & Arts Festival, Indio. Known in colloquial terms as simply "Coachella" this now 3-day extravaganza has become one of the biggest music festivals in the country. People travel from all over the States—and all over the world—for the diverse array of talent. Everyone from Paul McCartney and Madonna to Kraftwerk and Daft Punk have performed on one of the five stages within the Polo Field grounds. For ticket information, log on to the official website, www.coachella.com. Mid-April.

Renaissance Pleasure Faire, Irwindale. This annual event—one of the largest and oldest in the country—takes place at the relatively hidden Santa Fe Dam Recreation Area. It features an Elizabethan marketplace with costumed performers. The fair provides an entire day's activities, including shows, food, and crafts. You're encouraged to come in period costume. For ticket information, call ☏ **626/969-4750,** or log on to the national website, www.renfair.com. Weekends from early April to mid-May.

MAY

Cinco de Mayo, Los Angeles. A weeklong celebration of the Mexican victory over the French Army in 1862 takes place throughout the city. There's a carnival atmosphere with large crowds, live music, dancing, and food. The main festivities are held at El Pueblo de Los Angeles State Historic Park in Downtown; call ☏ **213/628-1274** for information. Other events are held around the city. The week surrounding May 5.

National Orange Show, San Bernardino. An Inland Empire tradition since 1911—when there were more orange groves than houses in Southern California—this weeklong county fair includes stadium events, celebrity entertainment, livestock shows, crafts and food booths, and carnival rides. Call ☏ **909/888-6788.** Second half of May.

Venice Art Walk, Venice Beach. This annual weekend event gives visitors a chance to take docent-guided tours of galleries and studios, plus a Sunday self-guided art walk through the private home studios of more than 50 emerging and well-known artists.

For details, call the Venice Family Clinic, which coordinates the event (📞 **310/392-8630**), or visit its website at www.venice-familyclinic.org. Second half of May.

Long Beach Lesbian & Gay Pride Parade and Festival, Shoreline Park, Long Beach. This event features rock and country music, dancing, food, and more than 100 decorated floats. Call 📞 **562/987-9191** or visit www.longbeachpride.com. Second half of May.

Doheny Blues Festival, Doheny State Beach, Dana Point. This festival features great live music (past acts have included the likes of Little Richard, Los Lobos, and the Black Crowes) on three stages—blues, rock, and soul—at a waterfront grass park. Arts and crafts vendors, memorabilia, and unique displays surround the International Food Court, with restaurants and beverages of all types. Proceeds benefit local charities. Call 📞 **949/362-3366** or log on to www.omegaevents.com. Mid- to late May.

JUNE

Playboy Jazz Festival, Los Angeles. Bill Cosby is the traditional master of ceremonies, presiding over the top jazz musicians at the Hollywood Bowl. Call 📞 **800/745-3000.** Mid-June.

Christopher Street West Festival & Parade, West Hollywood. For more than 40 years, this West Hollywood event has been one of the largest lesbian and gay pride festivals and parades in the world. Outdoor stages, disco- and Western-dance tents, food, and revelry culminate in Sunday's parade down Santa Monica Boulevard. Call 📞 **323/969-8302** or log on to www.lapride.org. Early to mid-June.

Los Angeles Film Festival, Los Angeles. With attendance of more than 60,000, the festival showcases more than 175 American and international indies, short films, and music videos during the 10-day event. Call 📞 **866/345-6337** or log on to www.lafilm-fest.com. Mid to late June.

Mariachi USA Festival, Los Angeles. At this family-oriented celebration of Mexican culture and tradition at the Hollywood Bowl,

festival-goers pack their picnic baskets and enjoy music, folkloric ballet, and related performances by top *grupos*. The all-day, all-night celebration is one of the largest mariachi festivals in the world. For tickets, call 📞 **800/MARIACHI** (627-4224) or 323/850-2000 (the Hollywood Bowl), or log on to www.mariachiusa.com. Mid to late June.

JULY

Lotus Festival, Echo Park. Celebrants gather to witness the spectacular blooms of Echo Lake's floating lotus grove. In keeping with the Asian and South Pacific islands theme, the festivities include tropical music and entertainment, ethnic foods, exotic birds, and plenty of lotus-inspired arts and crafts for sale. Admission is free. Call 📞 **213/413-1622** for information, or log on to www.laparks.org/calendar/lotus/lotus.htm. Second weekend of July.

Beach Festival, Huntington Beach. Two weeks of fun in the sun featuring two surfing competitions—the U.S. Open of Surfing and the world-class Pro of Surfing—plus extreme sports like BMX biking, skateboarding, and more. The festival includes entertainment, food, tons of product booths and giveaways—and plenty of tanned, swimsuit-clad bodies of both sexes. For more information, call 📞 **714/969-3492** or log on to www.surfcityusa.com. End of July.

Festival of Arts & Pageant of the Masters, Laguna Beach. A 70-year tradition in artsy Laguna, this festival centers on a fantastic performance-art production in which actors re-create famous old-masters paintings. Other festivities include live music, crafts sales, art demonstrations and workshops, and the grass-roots Sawdust Festival across the street. Grounds admission is $4 to $7; pageant tickets range from $15 to $150. Call 📞 **800/487-FEST** (487-3378) or 949/494-1145; there's online info at www.foapom.com. July through August.

AUGUST

Nisei Week Japanese Festival, Los Angeles. This weeklong celebration of Japanese culture and heritage—and L.A.'s oldest ethnic festival—is held in the Japanese

American Cultural and Community Center Plaza in Little Tokyo. Festivities include parades, food, Taiko Drum performances, arts, and crafts. Call ✆ **213/687-7193** or log on to www.niseiweek.org. Mid-August.

SEPTEMBER

Los Angeles County Fair, Pomona. Horse racing, arts, agricultural displays, celebrity entertainment, and carnival rides are among the attractions at one of the largest county fairs in the world, held at the Los Angeles County Fair and Exposition Center. Call ✆ **909/623-3111** or visit www.fairplex.com for information. Throughout September.

Long Beach Blues Festival, Long Beach. Great performances by blues legends such as Etta James, Dr. John, and the Allman Brothers make this an event you won't want to miss if you love the blues. The event serves cold beer, wine, and food throughout. Call ✆ **562/985-2999** or log on to www.jazzandblues.org. Labor Day weekend.

Simon Rodia Watts Towers Jazz Festival, Los Angeles. This event pays tribute to the roots of jazz in gospel and blues, as well as celebrating the avant-garde and Latin jazz scene. It's also a great opportunity to visit the Watts Towers. Call ✆ **213/847-4646** or log on to www.wattstowers.us. Late September.

OCTOBER

Catalina Island JazzTrax Festival, Catalina Island. Contemporary jazz greats play at Avalon's legendary Casino Ballroom. This enormously popular festival takes place over 3 consecutive weekends. Call ✆ **866/872-9849** or see www.jazztrax.com for advance ticket sales and a schedule of performers. Three weekends in October.

Hollywood Film Festival, Hollywood. More than 50 films from the U.S. and abroad are screened, with celebrities in abundance. There's also a variety of workshops and marketplaces for aspiring actors and filmmakers. Call ✆ **310/288-1882** or visit www.hollywoodawards.com for info and tickets. Mid-October.

West Hollywood Halloween Costume Carnaval, West Hollywood. This is one of the world's largest Halloween parties. More than 500,000 people, many dressed in outlandish drag couture, party all night along Santa Monica Boulevard. Call ✆ **310/289-2525** or visit www.visitwesthollywood.com for info. October 31.

NOVEMBER

American Indian Arts Marketplace, Autry National Center. For more than 20 years, this showcase of Native American arts and culture, has included traditional dances, music, and arts and crafts, as well as a chance to sample Native American foods. For further details, call ✆ **323/667-2000**. First weekend of November.

American Film Institute's Los Angeles International Film Festival, Los Angeles. Some of the biggest names in the international film community gather to see new movies from around the world. Call ✆ **866/AFI-FEST** (234-3378) or visit www.afi.com for info and tickets. Early November.

Catalina Island Eco Marathon, Catalina Island. Participants run on the island's inner roads, challenging trails, and even attempt to best the "Catalina Crush" hill at mile 19. There's also a 5K and 10K course. Call Spectrum Sports at ✆ **909/399-3553** or visit www.catalinaecomarathon.com. Early November.

Doo Dah Parade, Pasadena. This outrageous spoof of the Rose Parade features such participants as the Briefcase Precision Drill Team and a kazoo-playing marching band. Call ✆ **626/590-1134** or visit www.pasadenadoodahparade.info. Near Thanksgiving.

Hollywood Christmas Parade, Hollywood. This spectacular, star-studded parade marches through the heart of Hollywood. For information, call ✆ **866/727-2331** or visit www.thehollywoodchristmasparade.com. Sunday after Thanksgiving.

DECEMBER

Christmas Boat Parade of Lights. Sailors decorate their crafts with colorful lights. Several Southern California harbors hold nighttime parades; participants range from tiny dinghies with a single strand of lights to showy yachts with Nativity scenes twinkling on deck. Call the following for phone numbers for information and exact times: Ventura, ☎ **805/382-3001;** Marina Del Rey, ☎ **310/670-7130;** Huntington Harbor, ☎ **714/840-7542.**

2 RESPONSIBLE TRAVEL

Responsible tourism is conscientious travel. It means being careful with the environments you explore and respecting the communities you visit. You can find some eco-friendly travel tips and statistics, as well as touring companies and associations— listed by destination under "Your Travel Choice"—at www.ecotourism.org.

Greater Los Angeles is the smoggiest region of the U.S. So if you're concerned about the size of your carbon footprint during your vacation to L.A., the single best effort you can make is to use L.A.'s public transportation system (see "By Public Transportation" in "Getting Around," p. 316). Granted, it's an inferior and often a frustrating experience for anyone who's used to getting around via public transport in NYC, London, or Paris, but it's slowly getting better.

A more realistic alternative is to rent a hybrid car (such as a Toyota Prius). Not only will you save money on gas, but you'll be doing the local air a favor as well. In L.A., a local company called **Simply Hybrid Rental Cars** (☎ **888/359-0055;** www. simplyhybrid.com) rents a wide range of environmentally friendly vehicles ranging from the sensible Toyota Prius to the luxurious Mercedes E320 BlueTEC. As an added bonus, it offers free vehicle delivery and pickup to and from Los Angeles International Airport, Bob Hope Airport (Burbank), Santa Monica, Brentwood, Bel Air, Westwood, Century City, Beverly Hills, West Hollywood, Hollywood, Downtown Los Angeles, Culver City, and Studio City.

Other suggestions for low-impact travel to L.A. include renting a bike to explore the beach communities, staying at eco-friendly inns such as the **Ambrose** hotel in Santa Monica (p. 50), the **Beverly Hilton** (p. 62), or **Hotel Angeleno** (p. 66); and dining at restaurants with an emphasis on organic and sustainability, such as **Rustic Canyon** (p. 93), and **Inn of the Seventh Ray** (p. 97).

LOS ANGELES NEIGHBORHOODS & SUGGESTED ITINERARIES

I f you've left your brain at the office and want someone else to make the tough decisions during your vacation, you'll love this chapter. It's where I tell you what I think you should see and do during your time in L.A. The itineraries are broken down into 1-, 2-, and 3-day sections, depending on how long you're in town. If you've already made your way through "The Best of Los Angeles in 1 Day," the 2-day tour starts where the 1-day schedule left off, and so on.

But if you really want to enjoy even a fraction of what L.A. has to offer, you should plan on staying at least 3 days, preferably a week (besides, it'll increase your chances of getting discovered). And this might seem obvious, but you'll need a car to get around—public transportation in L.A. is improving, but still frustrating.

Before planning your schedule, take a moment to review L.A.'s neighborhoods.

NEIGHBORHOODS IN BRIEF

Los Angeles isn't a single compact city like San Francisco, but a sprawling suburbia comprising dozens of disparate communities located either on the ocean or on the flatlands of a huge desert basin. Ocean breezes push the city's infamous smog inland and through mountain passes into the sprawl of the San Fernando and San Gabriel valleys. Downtown L.A. is in the center of the basin, about 12 miles east of the Pacific Ocean. Most visitors spend the bulk of their time either along the coastline, in Hollywood, or on the city's ever-trendy Westside.

SANTA MONICA & THE BEACHES

These are many people's favorite L.A. communities and get my strong recommendation as one of the premier places to book a hotel for your vacation, especially during summer, when the beaches can be a good 20 degrees cooler than the sweltering parts of the city. Fair warning though: especially in winter, the weather can be downright grey. The 60-mile beachfront stretching from Malibu to the Palos Verdes peninsula has milder weather and less smog than the inland communities, and traffic is lighter, except on summer weekends. The towns along the coast each have a distinct mood and charm, and most are connected via a walk/bike path. They're listed below from north to south.

Malibu   At the northern border of Los Angeles County, 25 miles from Downtown, Malibu was once a privately owned ranch—purchased in 1857 for 10¢ an acre and now the most expensive real estate in L.A. Today its 27 miles of wide beaches, beachfront cliffs, sparsely populated hills, and relative remoteness from the inner city make it popular with rich recluses such as Cher and Mel Gibson. Indeed, the resident lists of Malibu Colony and nearby Broad Beach—oceanfront strips of closely packed mansions—read like a who's who in Hollywood. With plenty of green space and dramatic rocky outcroppings, Malibu's rural beauty is unsurpassed in L.A., and surfers flock to "the 'Bu" for great, if crowded, waves.

Santa Monica   Los Angeles's premier beach community, Santa Monica is known for its festive ocean pier, stylish oceanfront hotels, artsy atmosphere, and large population of homeless residents (I know, that's an oxymoron, but it fits). Shopping is king here, especially along the Third Street Promenade, a pedestrian-only outdoor mall lined with dozens of shops and restaurants.

Venice Beach   Created by tobacco mogul Abbot Kinney (who set out in 1904 to transform a worthless marsh into a resort town modeled after Venice, Italy), Venice Beach has a series of narrow canals connected by one-lane bridges that you'll see as you explore this refreshingly eclectic community. It was once infested with grime and crime, but gentrification has brought scores of great restaurants, boutiques, and rising property values for the canal-side homes and apartment duplexes. Even the movie stars and pop stars are moving in: Kate Beckinsale, Anjelica Huston, and Alanis Morissette reside here. Some of L.A.'s most innovative and interesting architecture lines funky Main Street. But without

question, Venice Beach is best known for its Ocean Front Walk, a nonstop Mardi Gras of thong-wearing skaters, fortunetellers, street musicians, and poseurs of all ages, colors, types, and sizes.

Marina del Rey   Just south of Venice, Marina del Rey is a somewhat quieter, more upscale waterside community best known for its man-made small-craft harbor, the largest of its kind in the world. Fittingly, it offers a wide variety of public boating opportunities, including fishing trips, harbor tours, dinner cruises, and private sailing charters.

Manhattan, Hermosa & Redondo beaches   These are laid-back, mainly residential neighborhoods with modest homes (except for oceanfront real estate), mild weather, and residents happy to have fled the L.A. hubbub. There are excellent beaches for volleyball, surfing, and tanning here, but when it comes to cultural activities, pickings can be slim. The restaurant scene, while limited, has been improving steadily, and some great new bars and clubs have opened near their respective piers.

L.A.'S WESTSIDE & BEVERLY HILLS

The **Westside,** sandwiched between Hollywood and the city's coastal communities, includes some of Los Angeles's most prestigious neighborhoods, virtually all with names you're sure to recognize:

Beverly Hills   Politically distinct from the rest of Los Angeles, Beverly Hills is a famous enclave best known for its palm-tree-lined streets of palatial homes, famous residents (Jack Nicholson, Warren Beatty and Annette Bening), and high-priced shops. But it's not all glitz and glamour; the healthy mix of filthy rich, wannabes, and tourists that comprises downtown Beverly Hills creates a unique—and often snobby-surreal—atmosphere.

West Hollywood   This key-shaped community's epicenter is the intersection of Santa Monica and La Cienega boulevards. Nestled between Beverly Hills and Hollywood, this politically independent—and blissfully fast-food-free—town is home to some of the area's best restaurants, clubs, shops, and art galleries. WeHo, as it's come to be known, is also the center of L.A.'s gay community—you'll know you've arrived when you see the risqué billboards. Encompassing about 2 square miles, it's a pedestrian-friendly place with plenty of metered parking. Highlights include the 1½ miles of Sunset Boulevard known as Sunset Strip, the chic Sunset Plaza retail strip, and the liveliest stretch of Santa Monica Boulevard.

Bel Air & Holmby Hills   In the hills north of Westwood and west of Beverly Hills, these are old-money residential areas that are featured prominently on most maps to the stars' homes.

Brentwood   Brentwood is best known as the famous backdrop to the O. J. Simpson melodrama. The neighborhood itself is generic, a relatively upscale mix of tract homes, restaurants, and strip malls. The Getty Center looms over Brentwood from its hilltop perch next to I-405.

Westwood   An urban village founded in 1929 and home to the University of California at Los Angeles (UCLA), Westwood used to be a hot destination for a night on the town, but it lost much of its appeal in the past decade due to overcrowding and even some minor street violence. Although Westwood is unlikely to regain its old charm, the improved culinary scene has brought new life to the village. The area has been plagued by movie theater closures recently, but the historic Village Theater and the Bruin both survived, so it's still a fun destination for dinner and a flick.

Century City   This is a compact and rather bland area sandwiched between West Los Angeles and Beverly Hills. The primary draws here are the 20th Century Fox studios and the Westfield Century City, a huge open-air shopping mall. Century City's three main thoroughfares are Century Park East, Avenue of the Stars, and Century Park West.

West Los Angeles   West Los Angeles is a label that generally applies to everything that isn't one of the other Westside neighborhoods. It's basically the area south of Santa Monica Boulevard, north of Venice Boulevard, east of Santa Monica and Venice, and west and south of Century City.

HOLLYWOOD   Yes, they still come to the mecca of the film industry—young hopefuls with stars in their eyes gravitate to this historic heart of L.A.'s movie production like moths fluttering to the glare of neon lights. But today's Hollywood is more illusion than industry. Many of the neighborhood's former movie studios have moved to more spacious venues in Burbank, the Westside, and other parts of the city.

Despite the downturn, visitors continue to flock to Hollywood's landmark attractions, such as the star-studded Walk of Fame and Grauman's Chinese Theatre. And now that the city's $1-billion, 30-year revitalization project is in full swing, Hollywood Boulevard is, finally, solidly showing signs that its ascent from a long, seedy slump is permanent. Refurbished movie houses and stylish restaurants and clubs are making a fierce comeback, and two boutique hotels have opened near the Hollywood and Vine Red Line Station: the W and the Redbury. The centerpiece Hollywood & Highland complex anchors the neighborhood, with shopping, entertainment, and a luxury hotel built around the beautiful Kodak Theatre, designed specifically to host the Academy Awards (really, you'll want to poke your head into this gorgeous theater).

Melrose Avenue   Scruffy but fun, Melrose Avenue is the city's funkiest shopping district, catering to often-raucous youth with secondhand and avant-garde clothing shops. There are also a number of good restaurants.

The stretch of Wilshire Boulevard running through the southern part of Hollywood is known as the **Mid-Wilshire** district, or the Miracle Mile. It's lined with tall, contemporary apartment houses and office buildings. The section just east of Fairfax Avenue, known as Museum Row, is home to almost a dozen museums, including the Los Angeles County Museum of Art, the La Brea Tar Pits, and that shrine to L.A. car culture, the Petersen Automotive Museum.

Griffith Park   Up Western Avenue in the northernmost part of Hollywood, this is one of the country's largest urban parks, home

L.A. Neighborhoods in Brief

Map labels:

Thousand Oaks

SAN FERNANDO VALLEY

Tarzana

Woodland Hills

Calabasas

Ventura Fwy.

Mulholland Dr.

Agoura Hills

Westlake Village

TOPANGA STATE PARK

Topanga Canyon Blvd.

MALIBU CREEK STATE PARK

Topanga

Pacific Palisades

Palisades Beach

Trancas

Pacific Coast Hwy.

1

Topanga Beach

Zuma County Beach

Malibu

Santa Monica

Pt. Dume

Santa Monica Bay

0 — 5 mi

0 — 5 km

Legend / Route index:

(1) Lincoln Blvd. / Sepulveda Blvd. / Pacific Coast Hwy.

(2) Santa Monica Blvd. / Glendale Fwy.

(5) Golden State Fwy. / Santa Ana Fwy.

(10) Santa Monica Fwy. / San Bernardino Fwy.

(22) Garden Grove Fwy.

(27) Topanga Canyon Blvd.

(39) Beach Blvd. / San Gabriel Canyon Rd.

(47) Terminal Fwy. / Ocean Blvd.

(55) Newport Fwy. and Blvd.

(57) Orange Fwy.

(60) Pomona Fwy.

(90) Marina Fwy.

(91) Artesia Blvd. & Fwy. / Gardena Fwy. / Riverside Fwy.

(101) Ventura Fwy. / Hollywood Fwy.

(105) Century Fwy.

(110) Pasadena Fwy.

(110) Harbor Fwy.

(134) Ventura Fwy.

(170) Hollywood Fwy.

(210) Foothill Fwy.

(405) San Diego Fwy.

(605) San Gabriel River Fwy.

(710) Long Beach Fwy.

PACIFIC OCEAN

Sacramento

NEVADA

San Francisco

CALIFORNIA

PACIFIC OCEAN

Los Angeles

Legend

(22) State Highway

(101) U.S. Highway

(210) Interstate Highway

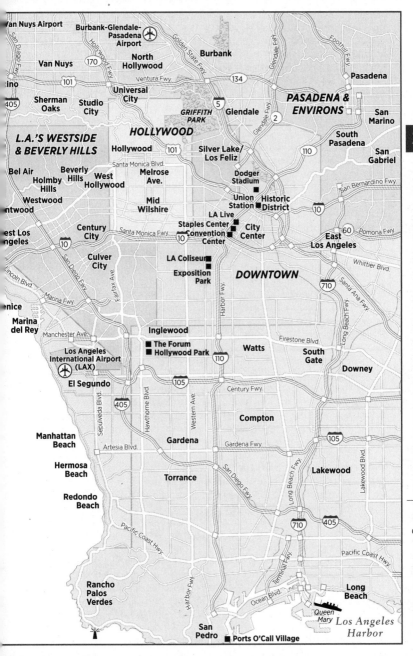

to the Los Angeles Zoo, the famous Griffith Observatory, and the outdoor Greek Theater.

Downtown Despite the relatively recent construction of several major cultural and entertainment centers (such as the Walt Disney Concert Hall, L.A. LIVE, and Cathedral of Our Lady of the Angels) and a handful of trendy restaurants, L.A.'s Downtown isn't the tourist hub it would be in most cities. When it comes to entertaining visitors, the Westside, Hollywood, and beach communities are still far more popular. That said, if you haven't been in years, it's worth another look, particularly for those interested in eclectic restaurants and a bar scene more sophisticated but less pretentious than Hollywood's.

Easily recognized by the tight cluster of high-rise offices—skyscrapers bolstered by earthquake-proof technology—the business center of the city is eerily vacant on weekends and evenings, but the outlying residential communities, such as Koreatown, Little Tokyo, and Chinatown, are enticingly ethnic and vibrant. (See "L.A.'s Ethnic Neighborhoods," in chapter 6, for more information about what to see and do in these and other Downtown ethnic communities.) If you want a tan, head to Santa Monica, but if you want a refreshing dose of non-90210 culture, come here.

El Pueblo de Los Angeles Historic District This is a 44-acre ode to the city's early years and is worth a visit. **Chinatown** is small and touristy but can be plenty of fun for souvenir hunting or traditional dim sum. **Little Tokyo,** on the other hand, is a genuine gathering place for the Southland's Japanese population, with a wide array of shops and restaurants with an authentic flair.

Silver Lake/Los Feliz These residential neighborhoods northwest of Downtown have arty, multicultural areas with unique cafes, theaters, and art galleries—all in equally plentiful proportions, as well as a popular local music scene. It's also worth visiting to admire the old-school architecture styles from early L.A.—Hollywood bungalows and Spanish haciendas, many built to house silent-screen actors.

Exposition Park South and west of Downtown is home to the Los Angeles Memorial Coliseum and the L.A. Sports Arena, as well as the Natural History Museum, the African-American Museum, and the California Science Center. The University of Southern California (USC) is next door.

The San Fernando Valley The San Fernando Valley, known locally as "the Valley," was nationally popularized in the 1980s by the notorious mall-loving "Valley Girl" stereotype. Sandwiched between the Santa Monica and the San Gabriel mountain ranges, most of the Valley is residential and commercial and off the beaten track for tourists. But some of its attractions are bound to draw you over the hill. **Universal City,** located west of Griffith Park between U.S. 101 and California 134, is home to Universal Studios Hollywood and the supersize shopping and entertainment complex City-Walk. About the only reason to go to **Burbank,** west of these other suburbs and north of Universal City, is to see one of your favorite TV shows being filmed at NBC or Warner Brothers Studios. A few good restaurants and shops can be found along Ventura Boulevard, in and around Studio City.

Glendale Glendale is a largely residential community north of Downtown between the Valley and Pasadena. Here you'll find Forest Lawn, the city's best cemetery for very retired movie stars.

Pasadena & Environs Best known as the site of the Tournament of Roses Parade every New Year's Day, **Pasadena** was spared from the tear-down epidemic that swept L.A., so it has a refreshing old-time feel. Once upon a time, Pasadena was every Angeleno's best-kept secret: a quiet community whose slow and careful regentrification meant nonchain restaurants and boutique shopping without the crowds, in a revitalized downtown respectful of its old brick and stone commercial buildings. Although the area's natural and architectural beauty still shines through—so much so that Pasadena remains Hollywood's favorite backyard location for countless movies and TV shows—Old Town has become a pedestrian mall similar to Santa Monica's Third Street Promenade, complete with huge crowds, midrange chain eateries, and standard-issue mall stores. It still gets our vote as a scenic alternative to the congestion of central L.A., but it has lost much of its small-town charm.

Pasadena is also home to the famous California Institute of Technology (CalTech), which boasts 22 Nobel Prize winners among its alumni. The CalTech-operated Jet Propulsion Laboratory was the birthplace of America's space program, and CalTech scientists were the first to report earthquake activity worldwide in the 1930s.

The residential neighborhoods in Pasadena and its adjacent communities—**Arcadia, La Cañada–Flintridge, San Marino,** and **South Pasadena**—are renowned for well-preserved historic homes, from humble bungalows to lavish mansions. These areas feature public gardens, historic neighborhoods, house museums, and quiet bed-and-breakfast inns.

THE BEST OF LOS ANGELES IN 1 DAY

Seeing the top sights of Los Angeles in a single day requires an early start and a bit of stamina, but it's quite doable. This "greatest hits" itinerary begins with L.A.'s sine qua non attraction, Hollywood. After lunch, you'll cruise along Sunset Boulevard to the beach and spend a few hours on foot touring the Santa Monica Pier and Venice Beach. You'll conclude your, like, most excellent day with a live performance under the stars at the legendary Hollywood Bowl. ***Start:*** *Corner of Gower Street and Hollywood Boulevard, and walk west.*

1 Hollywood Walk of Fame ★

Forget the culture/museum stuff—it's time to see for yourself all those famous Hollywood sites you've watched on TV since you were a toddler. Start the day by spending the morning on Hollywood Boulevard, following the path of bronze-and-marble stars along the Walk of Fame. Since 1960 more than 2,400 celebrities have been honored along the world's most famous sidewalk, but you'll need an old-timer to explain who a lot of the now-long-dead entertainers were. For a few bucks, you can buy a map that lists every star; better yet, log on to www.hollywoodchamber.net and "Find Your Favorite Star" (when in doubt, keeping clicking if it doesn't come up right away—the search method isn't always intuitive. Sigh.). See p. 136.

On Hollywood Boulevard, between Highland and La Brea avenues, you'll find:

2 Grauman's Chinese Theatre ★

It's sort of a tourist rite of passage to compare your hands and feet with the famous prints set in cement at the entrance court to Grauman's Chinese Theatre, a tradition started when silent-film star Norma Talmadge "accidentally" stepped in wet cement during the premiere of Cecil B. DeMille's *King of Kings.* Because it's along the Hollywood Walk of Fame, you're already here. Go ahead—compare your shoes to footprints left by Humphrey Bogart or Marilyn Monroe. There are about 160 celebrity squares to scrutinize: See if you can find Whoopi Goldberg's dreadlocks, Bob Hope's nose, Betty Grable's gams, and R2D2's wheels. See p. 133.

L.A. Suggested Itineraries

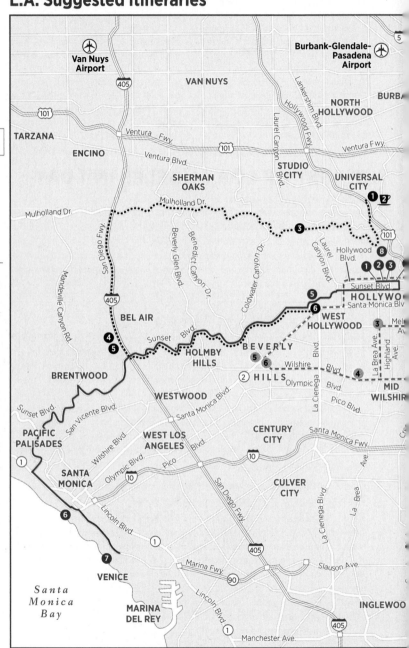

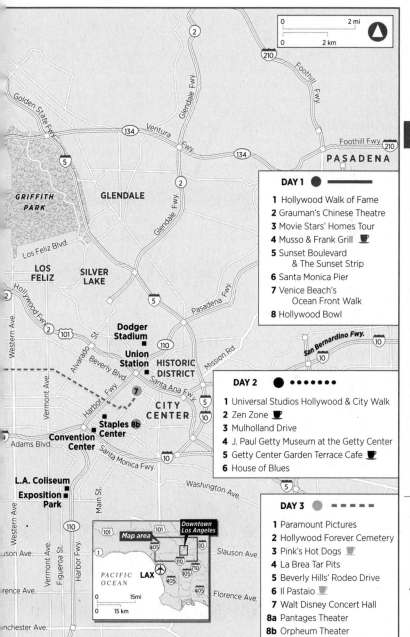

DAY 1

1 Hollywood Walk of Fame
2 Grauman's Chinese Theatre
3 Movie Stars' Homes Tour
4 Musso & Frank Grill ☕
5 Sunset Boulevard
  & The Sunset Strip
6 Santa Monica Pier
7 Venice Beach's
  Ocean Front Walk
8 Hollywood Bowl

DAY 2

1 Universal Studios Hollywood & City Walk
2 Zen Zone ☕
3 Mulholland Drive
4 J. Paul Getty Museum at the Getty Center
5 Getty Center Garden Terrace Cafe ☕
6 House of Blues

DAY 3

1 Paramount Pictures
2 Hollywood Forever Cemetery
3 Pink's Hot Dogs ☕
4 La Brea Tar Pits
5 Beverly Hills' Rodeo Drive
6 Il Pastaio ☕
7 Walt Disney Concert Hall
8a Pantages Theater
8b Orpheum Theater

Stay at Grauman's for the:

3 Movie Stars' Homes Tour ★

Oh, c'mon! You know you want to do it. It's not like you're the only one who feels slightly guilty by paying to peek into the private lives of Tom Cruise, Jennifer Aniston, and Nicolas Cage (hey, nobody forced them to buy a home around Hollywood). Besides, you're already here—the 2-hour tours leave every half-hour between 9:30am and 5:30pm in front of Grauman's Chinese Theatre. Just buy a ticket at the Starline kiosk in front of you, hop into an air-conditioned minibus, and let the voyeurism begin. See p. 175.

4 Musso & Frank Grill ☕ ★

Time for lunch. Walk down the street to Musso & Frank Grill, Hollywood's oldest restaurant (since 1919) and a paragon of Hollywood's halcyon-era grillrooms. Part restaurant, part museum, this is where Faulkner, Hemingway, and Orson Welles derived liquid inspiration during their screenwriting days. Slither into one of the red-leather booths, order one of the legendary martinis or bloody marys from the gruff red-coated waiters, and work on that Atkins diet with a fat rib-eye. 6667 Hollywood Blvd. (at Cherokee Ave.). ℂ 323/467-7788. See p. 115.

After lunch, waddle to your rented convertible red Mustang (you did rent a convertible red Mustang, didn't you?), put in a *Best of the Beach Boys* CD, and slowly cruise the legendary:

5 Sunset Boulevard & The Sunset Strip ★★

This 1-hour -or-so drive takes you from sorta-seedy Hollywood to flamboyant West Hollywood, past the moneyed minimansions of Beverly Hills, through neighborhoods most people can't afford to live in such as Westside and Brentwood, winding your way into the secluded enclave of Pacific Palisades toward Malibu, and finally the Pacific Coast Highway ("PCH," if you're hip). The entire drive takes you through a cross section of nearly everything the western side of Los Angeles has to offer. See p. 132 for an itinerary of the Strip.

Drive south on the PCH into the big-city beach town of Santa Monica, and park at the:

6 Santa Monica Pier ★★

Built in 1908 for passenger and cargo ships, the pier does a pretty good job of recapturing the glory days of Southern California. Buy an ice-cream cone at one of the snack shacks and stroll seaward past the wooden carousel, roller coaster, and arcades, then buy a ticket to ride the Ferris wheel (when's the last time you rode on a Ferris wheel?). See p. 138.

From the pier, walk south to the carnival-like stretch known as:

7 Venice Beach's Ocean Front Walk ★★★

For first-timers, this pseudo-bohemian scene is a bit of a shock to the senses: a surreal assemblage of street performers, musicians, musclemen pumping serious iron, apocalyptic evangelists, break dancers, stoned drummers, and endless schlock shops. By now your feet are probably talking to you, so stop at one of the outdoor cafes and have a beer while taking in the scene. This is also where you can rent a bike and cruise along the 8-mile bike path that runs along the beach.

LOS ANGELES NEIGHBORHOODS & SUGGESTED ITINERARIES | The Best in 1 Day

Pile into the convertible and cruise northeast on Santa Monica Boulevard all the way across town (or take I-10 east to Hwy. 110 north to Hwy. 101 north) to the:

8 Hollywood Bowl ★★★

I've saved the best for last: the Hollywood Bowl. I've yet to meet anyone who wasn't impressed by the Bowl, an elegant, Greek-style natural outdoor amphitheater cradled in a small canyon northeast of Hollywood. Truly, it's one of L.A.'s grandest traditions, watching a live performance under the stars on a warm summer night while noshing on crackers, cheese and wine. It's the summer home of the Los Angeles Philharmonic and Hollywood Bowl orchestras, and often hosts internationally known conductors, soloists, and popular acts ranging from Radiohead to Garrison Keillor. Here's how you do the Bowl the fanciest and easiest way: Reserve a box seat section as far in advance as possible, then pre-order a gourmet picnic basket filled with hot and cold dishes, desserts, and fine wines from the excellent on-site catering department, which will deliver the goodies to your box once you arrive. *Tip*: For those on more of a budget, go for more moderately priced seats (there are two huge monitors, after all), and pick up a simple dinner from a local deli or grocery store, where you can also purchase wine (the Bowl is BYO-friendly for non-lease events). You'll save money and still have a great time. See p. 259.

THE BEST OF LOS ANGELES IN 2 DAYS

On your second day, you'll continue seeing L.A.'s biggest attractions: Universal Studios Hollywood (one of the most popular attractions in L.A.), the massive gazillion-dollar Getty Center, and the rockin' Sunset Strip's House of Blues. It's another full day on your feet, so wear comfortable shoes and make that coffee drink a double. Also, you'll want to make advance reservations: Buy tickets online for Universal Studios, and reserve a table at the House of Blues. *Start: Universal Studios.*

1 Universal Studios Hollywood & CityWalk ★★

A visit to Universal Studios Hollywood will accomplish three classic L.A. experiences in one swoop: taking a studio tour, visiting an amusement park, and strolling through an outdoor megamall. Start with the 1-hour guided tram ride around the studio's 420 acres of actual movie sets, then hit the movie-themed thrill rides and shows, and end with an amble through Universal CityWalk, a 3-block-long, Disney-like promenade crammed with flashy name-brand stores and restaurants (but don't have lunch yet—save that for the Getty Center). Even with an early start, this should take you at least half a day. Also, be sure to splurge on a Front of Line Pass, which could save you hours of standing in lines. See p. 143.

2 Zen Zone 💆

I'm supposed to recommend a dining option here, but I have something you'll like a whole lot better. Along the CityWalk is a place called the Zen Zone, where you can get an inexpensive 20-minute water massage." You lay down fully clothed in what looks like a tanning bed, and strong rotating jets of water massage your backside from neck to toe (a blue rubber sheet keeps you dry). The sensation is a bit weird at first, but after it's over, you'll feel incredibly refreshed. Universal City. ☎ 818/487-7889. See p. 145.

Hop in the convertible, cross over the freeway, turn left on Cahuenga Boulevard, then right onto the famous:

3 Mulholland Drive ★★

This winding, scenic road follows the peaks and canyons of Hollywood Hills (all festooned with seriously huge homes of people who make way too much money). Not only does it offer amazing views of Los Angeles and the San Fernando Valley—you'll find several scenic viewing areas along the drive—it takes you directly to I-405 and our next stop. See p. 171.

Head south on I-405, and just a few miles down the freeway on your right side is the exit for the:

4 J. Paul Getty Museum at the Getty Center ★★

Perched on a hillside in the Santa Monica Mountains and swathed in Italian travertine marble, the Getty Center is stunning in both design and construction cost (roughly $1 billion). Everything about this postmodernist complex elicits oohs and aahs, from Paul Getty's enormous collection of art (including van Gogh's *Irises*) and gorgeous landscaped gardens to the postcard views of Los Angeles and the Pacific Ocean. What's more, entrance to the Getty Center is free, but parking will set you back $15 per car. If you're like me and don't remember a thing from your college art-appreciation class, spend a few bucks for a self-guided audio tour that gives a brief overview of the 250-plus works in the collection. See p. 139.

5 Getty Center Garden Terrace Cafe 🍵 ★

Dining options at the Getty Center range from a self-service cafe to the elegant (though fairly informal) Restaurant, but my favorite place to take a break is the Garden Terrace Cafe, which serves lunch in a beautiful outdoor setting overlooking the Central Garden. You can also pick up a picnic lunch on the Plaza Level and head down to the flower-filled picnic area. 1200 Getty Center Dr. © 310/440-7300. See p. 139 for more about the Getty Center.

Head south again on I-405 (it's rush hour now, so you'll have plenty of time to give your feet and brain a rest), and about a mile down the freeway take the Sunset Boulevard exit. Head east on Sunset until you reach the Sunset Strip and the:

6 House of Blues ★

After sitting in traffic on I-405, it's time for another classic L.A. experience: dinner and a show at the House of Blues. This being L.A., the Sunset Strip HOB consistently books top-tier musicians who live here anyway. If you can make it past the three bars, the upstairs restaurant serves pleasant Southern-style comfort food. Reservations are no longer required, but they are advised for busy nights. Better yet, splurge on the "Dinner Package"—it's $50 extra per person, but includes a full meal upstairs before the concert and reserved seating downstairs during it. Otherwise, the venue is standing room only, which can be frustrating, especially if you are short. By the time the show's over, the action on the Strip will keep you entertained well past midnight. See p. 210.

THE BEST OF LOS ANGELES IN 3 DAYS

On your third day, just lay in bed all day, watch TV, and order room service. Or not. There are plenty of top attractions in L.A. you still haven't seen, and hopefully there's still room on your credit card. Try to make the 10am tour of Paramount Pictures, because you're in for another full day of only-in-L.A. experiences: seeing famous dead people, eating famous chili dogs, staring at a famous pit of tar (heart be still), laughing at price tags along famous Rodeo Drive, and taking a tour of the Frank Gehry-designed Walt Disney Concert Hall. Again, be ready with comfy shoes, strong coffee, and a red convertible. **Start:** *5555 Melrose Ave.*

1 Paramount Pictures ★★

Yes, another studio tour, but this one's my favorite. Paramount is the only major studio still located in Hollywood, so its hallowed grounds are oozing with Hollywood history. The 2-hour cart tour (screw the trams) is both a historical ode to filmmaking and a real-life, behind-the-scenes look at working movie and television facilities in day-to-day operation; ergo, no two tours are alike, and chances of spotting a celebrity are pretty good. What you'll get to see depends on what's being filmed while you're there, but it's cool just to hang out on the other side of that big wall. See p. 173.

Right behind Paramount Pictures on Santa Monica Boulevard is the main entrance to:

2 Hollywood Forever Cemetery ★

This is the "resting place of Hollywood immortals" (whatever). It's 60 minutes well spent walking around the meticulously manicured lawns, searching for familiar names such as Rudolph Valentino, Douglas Fairbanks (Sr. and Jr.), Peter Lorre, and Jayne Mansfield. Fittingly, there's a terrific view of the Hollywood sign from here. You can pick up a map of the stars' burial sites at the flower shop. See p. 180.

For a lunch break, drive about a mile east on Melrose Avenue to La Brea Avenue for:

3 Pink's Hot Dogs 🍴

Why anyone would stand in line for an hour to buy a hot dog is way beyond me, but on weekends the line wraps around the building at Pink's Hot Dogs, an L.A. icon that's been dishing dogs since 1939. About 2,000 of them are served every day in more than 20 varieties, including a heartburn-inducing chili dog made from a secret chili formula that will stick with you for days. If the line's doable, give it a try. 709 N. La Brea Ave. (at Melrose Ave.). ✆ 323/931-4223. See p. 118.

Drive south on La Brea Avenue for about a mile, then turn right (west) onto Wilshire Boulevard. About 10 blocks down on your right side is:

4 La Brea Tar Pits ★★

There's something about this odorous swamp of gooey asphalt oozing to the earth's surface that's fascinating. Perhaps it's the location: smack-dab in the middle of Los Angeles, the last place you'd expect to find this truly bizarre primal pool of hot tar that's been bubbling from the earth for more than 40,000 years. Nearly 400 species of mammals, birds, amphibians, and fish—many of which are now extinct—walked, crawled, landed, swam, or slithered into the sticky sludge, got stuck in the worst way, and stayed forever. It looks like a fake Disney set, complete with cement mastodons in the throes of certain death, wailing from hidden speakers. If you have time, stop in the adjacent Page Museum, which houses the largest and most diverse collection of Ice Age plants and animals in the world. See p. 141.

Head west on Wilshire Boulevard a few miles to Beverly Hills. Just before Santa Monica Boulevard on your right-hand side is:

5 Beverly Hills's Rodeo Drive ★★

Okay, that's enough sightseeing for today—let's go shopping along one of the wealthiest and most famous shopping streets in the world: Rodeo Drive. Within Beverly Hills's Golden Triangle—a 16-square-block area surrounding Rodeo Drive—are the couture shops from high fashion's old guard: Gucci, Dolce & Gabbana, Louis Vuitton, Chanel, Ralph Lauren, Prada, Tiffany, and all the rest. If $15,000 is a bit out of your price range for a suit, the shops off Rodeo are generally not as name-conscious as those on the strip, and you might actually be able to afford something. Surprisingly, parking is a bargain, with nine city-run lots offering 2 hours of free parking.

6 Il Pastaio 🍽 ★

This corner restaurant within the Golden Triangle is *the* place to take a break from shopping and dine on superb Italian food. Ask for a sidewalk table, then order a bottle of chianti, the *arancini* appetizer (trust me), the pumpkin tortelloni in a light sage-and-cream sauce, and for the finale, the silkiest panna cotta you'll ever swoon over. 400 N. Canon Dr. ℭ 310/205-5444. See p. 106.

Head east on Wilshire Boulevard to the Downtown area, turn left on South Figueroa Street, then right on West 1st Street. At South Grand Avenue between 1st and 2nd streets is the:

7 Walt Disney Concert Hall ★★★

The strikingly beautiful Walt Disney Concert Hall is a masterpiece of design by world-renowned architect Frank Gehry. Even if you don't have the slightest interest in architecture, you will experience shock and awe the first time you see the impossibly curvaceous stainless-steel exterior. The 45-minute self-guided audio tour is excellent: Narrated by actor John Lithgow, it takes you all over the building and includes interviews with Gehry. Within is a dazzling 2,265-seat auditorium, but you usually can't see it unless you attend a performance (which I strongly recommend) due to rehearsals. See p. 145.

If you catch a performance at Disney, your tour is done. If you simply toured Disney, you now have two options for a show. To get to the Pantages Theater, head northeast on Grand Ave, turn left onto US-101 N for 9 miles, then take exit 8B for Hollywood Boulevard.

To get to the Orpheum Theatre, head southwest on Grand Street, turn left on 6th Street, right on Broadway, and the theater is on the left side of the street.

8 Pantages & Orpheum Theaters

You really should end your vacation with a grand show at one of L.A.'s major playhouses, preferably the Pantages or Orpheum theater, historical and cultural landmarks that have been meticulously restored. Opened in 1930, the Pantages was the first Art Deco movie palace in the U.S. and site of the Academy Awards from 1949 to 1959. Built in 1926, the Orpheum has hosted performances ranging from Judy Garland's 1933 vaudeville act to Ella Fitzgerald and Duke Ellington. Just being inside either of these historic theaters is a thrill, and seeing a show here is a fitting end to your vacation at the film and entertainment capital of the world. While both are equally majestic, the Pantages has more of a regular schedule, as it's the home of Broadway L.A., which brings major touring productions, such as *Wicked* and *Cats*, to the city. See p. 261 and 260.

3

LOS ANGELES NEIGHBORHOODS & SUGGESTED ITINERARIES | The Best in 3 Days

WHERE TO STAY

4

I n sprawling Los Angeles, location is everything. The neighborhood you choose as a base can make or break your vacation. If you plan to spend your days at the beach but stay Downtown, for example, you're going to lose a lot of valuable relaxation time on the freeway. For business travelers, choosing a location is easy: Pick a hotel near your work event—don't get on the freeways if you don't have to. For vacationers, though, the decision about where to stay is more difficult. Consider where you want to spend most of your time before you commit yourself to a base. But wherever you stay, count on doing a good deal of driving—no hotel in Los Angeles is convenient to everything.

The relatively smog-free beach communities such as **Santa Monica** and **Venice** are understandably popular with visitors—just about everybody loves to stay at the beach. Book ahead because hotels fill up quickly, especially in summer.

If they're not at one of the beach communities, most visitors stay on the city's **Westside,** a short drive from the beach and close to most of L.A.'s colorful sights. The city's most elegant and expensive accommodations are in **Beverly Hills;** a few of the hotels in these neighborhoods, such as the Beverly Hills Hotel, have become visitor attractions unto themselves. As well as being one of the focal points of L.A. nightlife, **West Hollywood** is also home to the greatest range and breadth of hotels, from $300-plus-per-night boutique spots to affordably priced motels.

There are fewer hotels in **Hollywood** than you might expect. Accommodations are generally moderately priced and well maintained but unspectacular. Centrally located between Downtown and Beverly Hills, just a stone's throw from Universal Studios, Hollywood makes a convenient base if you're planning to do a lot of exploring, but it has more tourists and is less visually appealing than some other neighborhoods; the trendier parts; however, are quite congested at night.

With the exception of a couple quirky boutique hotels, **Downtown** lodging options are generally business-oriented, but thanks to direct Metro (L.A.'s subway) connections to Hollywood and Universal Studios, the demographic has begun to shift. The top hotels offer excellent deals on weekend packages. But chances are good that Downtown doesn't embody the picture of L.A. you've been dreaming of; you need a coastal or Westside base for that.

Families might want to head to **Universal City** to be near Universal Studios, or straight to **Anaheim and Disneyland** (see chapter 7). **Pasadena** offers historical charm, small-town ambience, easy access to Downtown L.A., and Stepford-Wives beauty, but driving to the beach can take forever.

Rack Rates   The **rates** quoted in the listings that follow are the rack rates—the maximum rates that a hotel charges for rooms. But rack rates are only guidelines, and there are often many ways around them. *Always* **check each hotel's website for package deals and special Internet rates.**

The hotels listed in this chapter have provided their best estimates for 2012. **Be aware that rates can change at any time** and are subject to availability, seasonal fluctuations, and plain ol' increases.

Pet Policies   I indicate in the listings below those hotels that generally accept pets. However, these policies may have limitations, such as weight and breed restrictions; may require a hefty deposit and/or a signed waiver against damages; and may be revoked at any time. Always inquire when booking if you're bringing Bowser along—*never* just show up with a pet in tow.

BEST HOTEL BETS

Note: In addition to the best hotel bets below, be sure to see "The Best Splurge Hotels" and "The Best Moderately Priced Hotels" in chapter 1. For additional help in choosing a location, see "Neighborhoods in Brief," in chapter 3.

- **Best for Families:** With a great location close to both the beach and boardwalk, a terrific oceanview pool, pet-friendly programs, a new eco-friendly fitness center and spa, and a kids-stay-free policy (plus welcome goodies and special menus for young ones), **Loews Santa Monica Beach Hotel,** 1700 Ocean Ave., Santa Monica (© **866/563-9792** or 310/458-6700), tops my list as L.A.'s best family hotel. See p. 50. Families on a tighter budget might prefer **Hotel Erwin,** 1697 Pacific Ave., Venice (© **800/786-7789** or 310/452-1111), located right next to the carnival-like Venice Beach and boardwalk. The large suites are equipped with full kitchens and a pullout sofa. See p. 53. If you're heading to Universal Studios, stay at the **Sheraton Universal Hotel,** 333 Universal Hollywood Dr., Universal City (© **800/325-3535** or 818/980-1212), which offers free shuttle service to the theme park and adjacent Universal CityWalk, both just a minute away. See p. 78.
- **Best for Business Travelers:** With an oversize work desk, a fax machine, two-line phones, a terrific business/copy center, extensive recreational facilities, plus 24-hour room service and a wet bar for late-night, report-due-in-the-morning munchies, the guest office suites at **Westin Bonaventure Hotel & Suites,** 404 S. Figueroa St. (© **800/WESTIN-1** [937-8461] or 213/624-1000), are Downtown's best accommodations for business travelers. See p. 76. For a more casual California business experience, travelers might enjoy the beachfront **Le Merigot, A JW Marriott Hotel and Spa,** 1740 Ocean Ave., Santa Monica (© **888/539-7899** or 310/395-9700). A short walk from shopping centers, businesses, and major Southern California landmarks, and just steps from the sand, Le Merigot has great meeting spaces, boardrooms, and state-of-the-art amenities and accommodations, including 24-hour clothing mending and pressing, complimentary shoeshine, and more—all perfect for the busy business traveler.

○ **Best Budget Hotel:** The bargain of the beach is the friendly, family-run **Sea Shore Motel,** 2637 Main St., Santa Monica (𝄐 **310/392-2787**), whose motel-basic but beautifully kept rooms couldn't be better located: in the heart of the stylish Main Street shopping and dining district, and just a stone's throw from Santa Monica's pier and sand. See p. 53.

○ **Best for Travelers with Disabilities:** With 25 accessible rooms, the **Sheraton Universal Hotel,** 333 Universal Hollywood Dr., Universal City (𝄐 **800/325-3535** or 818/980-1212), offers the most extensive facilities for wheelchair-using and vision-impaired visitors. Two bathrooms have roll-in showers; the rest have tubs with available benches, lowered closet rods and peepholes, and raised vanities and toilets. There are also strobe kits for door and phone, and Braille symbols on the restaurant menus and on all public facilities. See p. 78. Downtown, the **Westin Bonaventure Hotel & Suites,** 404 S. Figueroa St. (𝄐 **800/WESTIN-1** [937-8461] or 213/624-1000), boasts 39 rooms with similarly extensive auxiliary aids and 15 with roll-in showers. See p. 76. For more information on resources, see "Disabled Travelers" in chapter 11.

○ **Best Hotel Nightlife Scene:** The gorgeous 18th-floor **Penthouse** restaurant, bar, and lounge at the **Huntley Santa Monica Beach,** 1111 2nd St., Santa Monica (𝄐 **310/394-5454**), is my new favorite hotel hangout. It has everything you need for a great night out: a lively bar scene, great food, beautiful 360-degree views of Los Angeles, Santa Monica, and Malibu, and plenty of eye candy. All this and no lines, cover charge, or snobby attitude. See p. 48. For Hollywood eye candy, the **Mondrian,** 8440 Sunset Blvd., West Hollywood (𝄐 **800/697-1791** or 323/650-8999), with its poolside Skybar and a Sunset Strip location, is still a contender for the hottest hotel nightlife scene (p. 58), but for sheer number of rejections at the door, the new king is the rooftop Drai's Lounge at the **W Hollywood,** 6250 Hollywood Blvd. (𝄐 **877/946-8357**). See p. 70.

SANTA MONICA & THE BEACHES

If surf, sand, and sunshine are what you're craving on this vacation, don't consider staying anywhere but here. Not only will you avoid the traffic crush as everyone from the rest of the city flocks to the seaside on clear, sunny days, but you can also soak up the laid-back vibe that only beach communities have.

With its wide beach, iconic Santa Monica Pier, abundant dining and shopping, and easy freeway and airport access, **Santa Monica** is the glittering jewel of the L.A. coast. A **Venice** location puts you at the heart of the wild, colorful human carnival that is Venice Beach, while **Marina del Rey** and Rancho Palos Verdes are ideal destinations for those who want a more sparkling, serene scene. World-famous **Malibu** is the ultimate symbol of the star-studded, sun-soaked coastal L.A. lifestyle, and offers good surf to boot—but be prepared to spend lots of time in the car, as this high-rent enclave is at least a half-hour drive from everything.

LAX is also near the coast, so airport-area accommodations are found in this section as well.

Very Expensive

Casa del Mar ★★★ In a former 1920s Renaissance Revival beach club, this Art Deco stunner is a real dream of a resort hotel, equal in every respect to its sister resort, Shutters, located across the street (see below). Which one you prefer depends on your personal sense of style. While Shutters is outfitted like a chic East Coast beach house, this impeccable, villa-like structure radiates period glamour. The building's U shape awards ocean views to most of the guest rooms, which have summery, European-inspired decor plus abundant luxuries that include sumptuously dressed beds and big, Italian-marble bathrooms. Rooms are laid out for relaxation, not business, so travelers with work on their minds should stay elsewhere. Downstairs is a big, elegant living room with ocean views, a stylish veranda lounge, and the **Catch Restaurant,** which offers a gorgeous oceanfront setting and a varied menu of small plates, salads, sushi and fish-centric entrees.

1910 Ocean Way (next to the Santa Monica Pier), Santa Monica, CA 90405. www.hotelcasadelmar.com. © **800/898-6999** or 310/581-5533. Fax 310/581-5503. 129 units. From $565 double; from $1,275 suite. AE, DC, DISC, MC, V. Valet parking $33. **Amenities:** Oceanfront restaurant; lobby lounge for cocktails and light fare; cafe for daytime dining; concierge; health club w/spa services; heated outdoor pool; room service. *In room:* A/C, TV/DVD, hair dryer, minibar, MP3 docking station, Wi-Fi ($12 per day).

Fairmont Miramar Hotel & Bungalows ★★   The hidden Fairmont Miramar Hotel & Bungalows is for people who prefer their luxury hotels low-key and unobtrusive, yet within walking distance of the area's best attractions. So it's convenient that this gem is only a block from the beach and at the north end of Santa Monica's perpetually crowded Third Street Promenade. The hotel consists of two towers and a bevy of bungalows on 5 acres of grounds. The older, larger rooms in the Pacific Palisades Building are ideal for families; the more modern rooms in the taller Ocean Tower—particularly the corner rooms on the 8th through 10th floors overlooking the Santa Monica Pier or Malibu coastline—are for everyone else. All rooms are well-appointed with goose-down duvets and soundproof windows, and those in the Ocean Tower have balconies. If you're in a splurging mood, get one of the über-romantic garden bungalows. **FIG,** an excellent California-style bistro French brasserie-style restaurant named for the giant tree that fronts the hotel, opened in 2009 (see p. 88). *Tip:* If you have questions, call the hotel directly—the central reservations line often has incorrect information.

101 Wilshire Blvd. (at Ocean Ave.), Santa Monica, CA 90401. www.fairmont.com/santamonica. © **866/540-4470** or 310/576-7777. Fax 310/458-7912. 270 units, 32 bungalows. $349–$469 double; $419–$1,429 bungalow. AE, DC, DISC, MC, V. Valet parking $32. **Amenities:** Restaurant; outdoor lounge; lobby lounge; concierge; health club & spa; heated outdoor pool and whirlpool; room service; Wi-Fi ($13 per day; in lobby). *In room:* A/C, TV/DVD, hair dryer, minibar, Wi-Fi ($13.95 per day).

Malibu Beach Inn ★★   After a $10-million renovation, this beachside hotel is one of the only high-end properties between Santa Monica and Santa Barbara. On the famed "Billionaire's Beach" in the heart of Malibu, the 47-room inn has an understated, contemporary design—I imagine this is what some of the nearby houses feel

More Important Advice on Accommodations

The prices given in this book do not include state and city **hotel taxes,** which run from 12% to 17%, depending upon which municipality the hotel is based in. Most hotels in densely populated parts of the city charge for **parking** (with in-and-out privileges). Also, some provide a **free airport shuttle;** if you're not renting a car, check to see what your hotel offers before you call a cab.

Where to Stay in Santa Monica & the Beaches

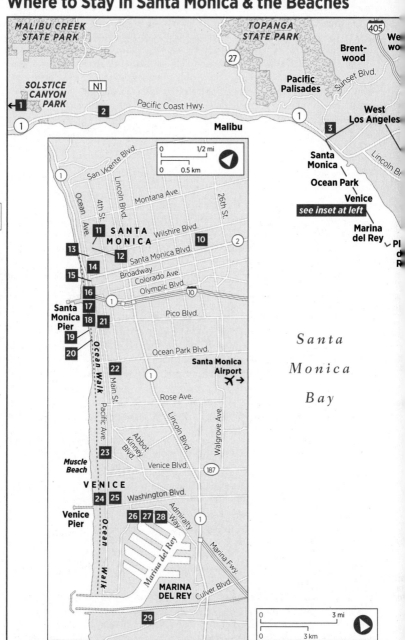

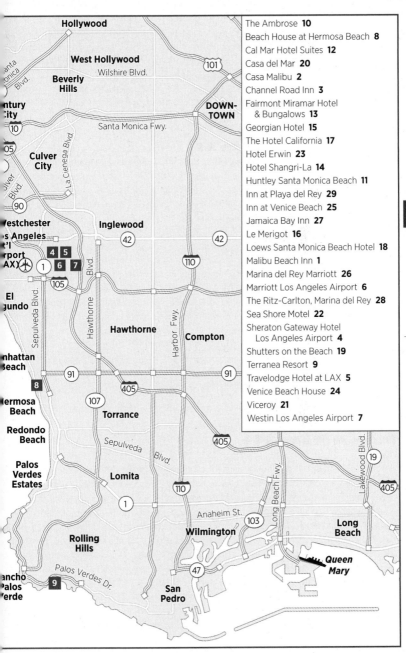

The Ambrose **10**
Beach House at Hermosa Beach **8**
Cal Mar Hotel Suites **12**
Casa del Mar **20**
Casa Malibu **2**
Channel Road Inn **3**
Fairmont Miramar Hotel & Bungalows **13**
Georgian Hotel **15**
The Hotel California **17**
Hotel Erwin **23**
Hotel Shangri-La **14**
Huntley Santa Monica Beach **11**
Inn at Playa del Rey **29**
Inn at Venice Beach **25**
Jamaica Bay Inn **27**
Le Merigot **16**
Loews Santa Monica Beach Hotel **18**
Malibu Beach Inn **1**
Marina del Rey Marriott **26**
Marriott Los Angeles Airport **6**
The Ritz-Carlton, Marina del Rey **28**
Sea Shore Motel **22**
Sheraton Gateway Hotel Los Angeles Airport **4**
Shutters on the Beach **19**
Terranea Resort **9**
Travelodge Hotel at LAX **5**
Venice Beach House **24**
Viceroy **21**
Westin Los Angeles Airport **7**

like. The rooms are tidy with views directly out to the crashing waves and perfect sunsets. Guests can have amenities catered to their wishes—specific wines, CDs, extra towels if you so desire—which definitely ups the luxury factor. The 44-seat Carbon Beach Club dining room is now open to the public (it was formerly guest-only) and has indoor and outdoor seating, just steps from the beach. In the lobby, sit and sip wines around the fireplace. When it's time to go out, the hotel is within walking distance to the Malibu Country Mart and the Malibu Pier.

22878 Pacific Coast Hwy., Malibu. www.malibubeachinn.com. ✆ **800/4-MALIBU** (462-5428) or 310/456-6444. Fax 310/456-1499. 47 units. From $400 double; from $800 suite. AE, DC, DISC, MC, V. Valet parking $23. **Amenities:** Restaurant; lobby lounge; concierge; room service. *In room:* A/C, TV, CD player, hair dryer, minibar, MP3 docking station, free Wi-Fi.

The Ritz-Carlton, Marina del Rey ★★ If you're a watercraft cognoscenti and desire a serene view of more than 5,000 beautiful sailboats and yachts from your private balcony, this is the hotel for you. But it's also business-traveler friendly and not too far from LAX. In typical Ritz-Carlton fashion, the hotel is swathed in soothingly sophisticated decor—French doors leading to small, private balconies, 32-inch plasma-screen televisions, and comfortable goose-down feather beds. The two top floors make up the Ritz-Carlton Club Lounge, with a dedicated concierge, on-the-house cocktails, and complimentary gourmet spreads all day (including breakfast). Thanks to its marina location, the hotel offers yacht and sailing charters and also reserves several slips for boat-bound customers. Venice Beach is about a 15-minute walk, but it's easier to rent a bicycle from the hotel. Unfortunately, the spa was closed at press time, while the hotel looks for a new wellness-company partner. *Tip:* Request one of the "27 series" rooms, which are junior suites that are larger and have the best views. The hotel's restaurant, **jer-ne** (pronounced "journey"), serves California cuisine in a stylishly modern setting.

4375 Admiralty Way, Marina del Rey, CA 90292. www.ritzcarlton.com. ✆ **800/542-8680** or 310/823-1700. Fax 310/823-2403. 304 units. $359–$559 double; from $719 suite. AE, DC, MC, V. Valet parking $35. Pets accepted ($125 cleaning fee). **Amenities:** 2 restaurants (but 1 is seasonal); bar/lounge; bikes; concierge; concierge-level rooms; fitness center; Jacuzzi; heated outdoor pool; room service; spa; 2 tennis courts (lit for night play); basketball court. *In room:* A/C, TV, CD player, hair dryer, minibar, Wi-Fi ($9.95 per day).

Shutters on the Beach ★★★ This Cape Cod–style luxury hotel is directly on the beach, a block from Santa Monica Pier. Only the Shutters' sister property, Casa del Mar (see above), can compete, but Shutters is slightly better because of balconies on every guest room and the more personal boutique-hotel-like ambience. The views and sounds of the ocean are the most outstanding qualities of the spacious, luxuriously outfitted rooms—and pricing is very much based on the scope of said view, some of which have fireplaces and/or whirlpool tubs; all have floor-to-ceiling windows that open. The small swimming pool and the sunny lobby lounge overlooking the sand are two great perches for spotting the celebrities who swear by Shutters as an alternative hangout to smoggy Hollywood. **One Pico,** the hotel's premier restaurant, serves modern American cuisine in a seaside setting. The hotel's **ONE** spa offers guests facials, massages, body scrubs and body treatments, manicures, pedicures, and waxing. *Tip:* The beach-cottage rooms overlooking the sand are more desirable and no more expensive than those in the towers.

1 Pico Blvd., Santa Monica, CA 90405. www.shuttersonthebeach.com. ✆ **800/334-9000** or 310/458-0030. Fax 310/458-4589. 198 units. $575–$995 double; from $1,245 suite. AE, DC, DISC, MC, V. Valet parking $33. **Amenities:** Restaurant; cafe; lobby lounge; babysitting; concierge; health club and spa;

Jacuzzi; outdoor heated pool; room service; sauna; extensive beach-equipment rentals (seasonal). *In room:* TV/DVD, hair dryer, iPod docking station, minibar, Wi-Fi ($13 per day).

Terranea Resort ★★★   This little piece of paradise sprawls across 102 acres of the South Bay coastline. Once the site of Marineland (similar to Sea World), it's sloping green hills, ocean vistas and manicured grounds are among the most luxurious in Southern California. Though the marine mammals of its theme park past are long gone, it's still prime territory for snorkeling, kayaking, and other aquatic activities, not to mention the gorgeous nine-hole golf course on-property. Lodging options include regular guest rooms (even the smallest is at least 450 sq. ft. in size), suites, casitas, bungalows, and villas. Bedding is swoon-worthy, with pillow-top mattresses and fine linen. All rooms include a patio or balcony. There are no less than seven restaurants, though foodies flock to **mar'sel** for Michael Fiorell's seasonal California cuisine. The best view might just be from the patio at the more casual, family-friendly **Nelson's,** though the **Lobby Bar & Lounge** has a great wrap-around balcony to take in the sunsets. Additionally, there's Cal-Med **Catalina Kitchen,** burgers and sandwiches at **Terranea Grill,** healthy fare and protein shakes at the **Spa Café,** and coffee cafe **sea beans.** The indulgent **Spa at Terranea** includes 50,000 sq. ft. of treatment rooms, yoga classes and other wellness pursuits.

6610 Palos Verdes Dr. South, Rancho Palos Verdes, CA 90275. www.terranea.com. © **866/802-8000** or 310/265-2800. Fax 310/265-2700. 582 units. $350–$495 double; from $715 suite. AE,, DISC, MC, V. Valet parking $30; self-parking $20. **Amenities:** 7 restaurants; 3 bars; concierge; business center; 9-hole golf course; health club & spa; Jacuzzi; 3 outdoor heated pools; room service; extensive recreational equipment rentals. *In room:* TV, DVD (upon request), hair dryer, minibar, Wi-Fi (included in the $25 resort fee).

Expensive

Beach House Hotel Hermosa Beach ★★ 📇   Sporting a Cape Cod style that suits the on-the-sand location, this luxurious, romantic inn is composed of beautifully designed and outfitted split-level studio suites. Every bright, sunny unit comes with a plush, furnished living room with a gas fireplace and entertainment center; a microkitchen with china and flatware for four; and an elevated sleeping niche with a down-dressed king-size bed, a second TV, and a generous work area. There are even furnished balconies, many of which overlook the beach. (Believe me—it's worth the extra money to score a beachfront room.) While sofas convert into second beds, the unit configuration is best suited to couples rather than families; more than three is too many. Despite the summertime carnival atmosphere of The Strand, the Beach House keeps serene with double-paned windows and noise-insulated walls. The hotel's small spa offers a wide range of services, including massage treatments (in-room if you prefer) and yoga sessions on the beach in summer. A nice light breakfast is served in the sunny breakfast room overlooking The Strand.

1300 The Strand, Hermosa Beach, CA 90254. www.beach-house.com. © **888/895-4559** or 310/374-3001. Fax 310/372-2115. 96 units. $349–$489 double. Rates include continental breakfast. AE, DC, DISC, MC, V. Valet parking $23. **Amenities:** Room service from two nearby restaurants; spa. *In room:* A/C, TV, CD player, hair dryer, kitchenette, free Wi-Fi.

Channel Road Inn ★★   The innkeeper has used her eye for design to outfit this beautiful 1910 Colonial Revival house in gracious period style. The individually appointed rooms range from "shabby chic" to antique, and all have top-quality textiles and linens, VCRs, and spacious, nicely renovated bathrooms. Some have four-poster beds covered with hand-sewn Amish quilts; others have fireplaces, and still others feature whirlpool tubs. Don't expect much from the promise of an ocean view, however; you'll have to look past a busy street, wires, and rooftops for your sliver of blue. The outdoor areas include a quiet rose garden and private hillside hot tub on the upper lawn. Dominated by an impressive Batchelder tile fireplace, the impeccably decorated living room makes an ideal place to curl up with a book. If you'd rather head outside, the staff will provide bicycles, beach chairs, and towels for your use—the beach is a short walk away. I prefer Channel Road's sister property, the Inn at Playa del Rey (see below); still, this is a beautiful, comfortable, and well-run B&B in a terrific location for beach lovers.

219 W. Channel Rd., Santa Monica, CA 90402. www.channelroadinn.com. ✆ **310/459-1920.** Fax 310/454-9920. 15 units. From $235 double; up to $395 suite. All rates include full breakfast and afternoon tea, wine, and hors d'oeuvres. AE, MC, V. Free parking. **Amenities:** Jacuzzi. *In room:* A/C, TV/VCR (some with DVD), hair dryer, free Wi-Fi.

Georgian Hotel ★ 🛍 This eight-story Art Deco beauty offers luxury comforts, loads of historical charm, and a terrific oceanview location (just across the street from Santa Monica's beach and pier), with prime Ocean Avenue dining just steps away. Established in 1933, the Georgian was popular among Hollywood's Golden Age elite; it even had its own speak-easy, rumored to have been established by Bugsy Siegel. A wonderful veranda with handsome teak furnishings and unobstructed ocean views opens onto a light and airy lobby. Two swift elevators, one very antique, lead to guest rooms that are an ideal blend of nostalgic style and modern-day amenities; you'll find free Wi-Fi and flatscreen TVs. Most rooms have at least a partial or full ocean view, but the best views are above the third floor. Units facing the ocean can be a bit small and noisy, so ask for a Malibu view for the best of both worlds. The back-facing rooms are best for light sleepers—be sure to request one that has a city view, otherwise you'll be looking at the parking lot.

1415 Ocean Ave. (btw. Santa Monica Blvd. and Broadway), Santa Monica, CA 90401. www.georgian hotel.com. ✆ **800/538-8147** or 310/395-9945. Fax 310/451-3374. 84 units. From $255 double; from $355 suite. AE, DC, DISC, MC, V. Valet parking $23 plus tax **Amenities:** Lobby bar; concierge; exercise room; room service. *In room:* TV (DVD in suites only) hair dryer, minibar, free Wi-Fi.

Hotel Shangri-La ★ The iconic Art Deco hotel, originally built in 1939, underwent a $30-million renovation and reopened in 2009, just in time to celebrate its 70th birthday. A hodgepodge of modern fixtures, geometric patterns, and bright accents bring the silver-and-white rooms to life. Other additions include an elevated swimming pool with luxe cabanas, an indoor/outdoor rooftop lounge, and a dining room that sources much of its ingredients from the local farmers' market. Overlooking Ocean Avenue, it's not the quietest building on the block; however, a set of double windows—the outer ones remaining from the original 1930s structure—help to keep some of the noise at bay. All rooms feature kitchenettes with stainless-steel appliances and spacious bathrooms outfitted with both soaking tubs and rainwater showers. The rooftop's panoramic Suite 700 indoor/outdoor lounge, once the private domain of hotel guests, is now open to the public.

1301 Ocean Ave., Santa Monica, 90401. www.shangrila-hotel.com. ✆ **877/999-1301** or 310/394-2791. 71 units. $325–$395 double; from $405 suite. AE, DC, DISC, MC, V. Valet parking $33. **Amenities:** Restaurant; rooftop bar; fitness center; pool; room service. *In room:* A/C, TV/DVD, hair dryer, minibar, MP3 docking station, complimentary Wi-Fi.

Huntley Santa Monica Beach ★★ 🛍 Even though it's in one of Santa Monica's tallest buildings (18 floors), the Huntley is a hidden gem—tucked away behind the Fairmont on the edge of a quiet neighborhood, yet close to Third Street Promenade dining and shopping and just a short walk from the beach. I love this hotel's strikingly stylish lobby, but the coup de grâce is the 18th-floor **Penthouse** restaurant, bar, and lounge. Combine the incredible views of the Santa Monica skyline, a lively bar scene, and good Contemporary American cuisine, and it's no surprise that hotel guests rarely venture elsewhere for drinks and light bites. The Huntley's modern, earth-toned guest rooms offer ocean or mountain views, 42-inch flatscreen TVs, and pillow-top beds with Egyptian cotton linens. Book a room on floors 9 to 17 for ocean views. *Fun tip:* Take a thrilling ride in the street-side glass elevator (acrophobes will prefer the interior lobby elevators).

1111 2nd St. (north of Wilshire Blvd.), Santa Monica, CA 90403. www.thehuntleyhotel.com. ⓒ **310/394-5454.** Fax 310/458-9776. 219 units. $489–$579 double; from $699 suite. AE, DC, DISC, MC, V. Valet parking $30. **Amenities:** Restaurant and bar; lobby cafe; concierge; fitness center; room service. *In room:* A/C, flatscreen TV w/DVD, CD player, hair dryer, Wi-Fi ($9.95 per day), iPod docking station.

Inn at Playa del Rey ★★ 🎁 A half-hour drive from L.A. proper, my favorite L.A. B&B is less than ideal for sightseers with packed itineraries, but great for those looking for romance, a relaxed small-town vibe, or airport convenience. Only 5 minutes from LAX, the pampering inn is as much a sanctuary from the city as it is for the protected wetlands outside the back door. From the street, the contemporary structure looks like a set of condos; inside, it glows with its true character. Fresh, salty breezes and the soft chatter of waterfowl fill a spacious yet cozy fireplace lounge, whose long veranda overlooks peaceful marshland. The impeccably decorated, amenity-laden guest rooms are outfitted in a classy-yet-casual, sophisticated style that evokes the best of Nantucket or Santa Barbara; Marina View rooms have balconies, whirlpool tubs, and fireplaces (worth the splurge, especially if you plan on spending a lot of quality time in your room). The ultimate in romance are the spacious View Suites, whose two-sided fireplaces cast a heavenly glow on both the luxuriously made bed and the inviting double Jacuzzi. A beach suitable for swimming is a short walk away, and bicycles are on hand for cruising the nearby 26-mile coastal path.

435 Culver Blvd., Playa del Rey, CA 90293. www.innatplayadelrey.com. ⓒ **310/574-1920.** Fax 310/574-9920. 21 units. $235–$305 double; from $385 suite. Extra guest $25. Rates include full breakfast and afternoon wine and cheese. AE, MC, V. Free parking. From LAX, take Sepulveda Blvd. north, veering left onto Lincoln Blvd.; turn left at Jefferson Blvd., which turns into Culver Blvd. **Amenities:** Bikes; Jacuzzi. *In room:* A/C, Cable TV/DVD, hair dryer, Wi-Fi (free), iPod docking station.

Le Merigot ★★ If you want something contemporary and spacious, but not too pricey and prestigious, this low-key luxury hotel and spa will fit the bill. Ideally situated on the sandy side of Ocean Avenue in the heart of Santa Monica's beach scene, the 175-room property houses a well-regarded French-California restaurant, **Cézanne,** and the 6,500-square-foot **SPA Le Merigot,** which offers a full range of services along with an outdoor pool and a state-of-the-art fitness center. Some of the contemporary-style guest rooms offer partial ocean views, and all are furnished with plush carpeting, oversize lounge chairs, and pillow-top beds with Italian-cotton linens. Look for clever package deals such as the "California Dreamin'," which includes your choice of a convertible Porsche Boxster or a BMW 3Series rental car; or the "California Surfin' Safari," a deluxe package that offers a 2-hour surf lesson, rejuvenating full-session Swedish massage, and celebratory Blue Crush graduation martinis (how very L.A.).

1740 Ocean Ave., Santa Monica, CA 90401. www.lemerigothotel.com. ⓒ **888/539-7899** or 310/395-9700. Fax 310/395-9200. 175 units. $405–$515 double; from $665 suite. AE, DISC, MC, V. Valet parking $34. **Amenities:** Restaurant; lobby bar; concierge; health club & spa; outdoor pool; room service. *In room:* A/C, TV, minibar, Wi-Fi ($15 per day).

Loews Santa Monica Beach Hotel ★★ ☺   L.A.'s finest family-friendly hotel is also a great choice for anybody looking for comfortable accommodations, an A-1 Santa Monica location, outstanding service, and a wealth of first-rate facilities. Loews isn't exactly beachfront—it's on a hill less than a block away—but the ocean views are fabulous. The dramatic atrium lobby with its playful SoCal style serves as a great backdrop for the spectacular ocean views. Guest rooms have an inviting, contemporary style in light, earthy colors. But the best news is still the top-rated facilities, which include an excellent heated pool, plus the fitness center and spa with a state-of-the-art gym, yoga and Pilates classes, health and fitness counseling, and a full slate of spa and salon services. The **Ocean & Vine** restaurant offers California farm-to-table cuisine and sushi, plus paired wines. The Lobby Bar is a classy spot for a drink.

1700 Ocean Ave. (south of Colorado Blvd.), Santa Monica, CA 90401. www.santamonicaloewshotel. com. ☎ **866/563-9792** or 310/458-6700. Fax 310/458-6761. 342 units. $399–$465 double; from $685 suite. Ask about corporate rates, Internet offers, and other discounts. Children 17 and under stay free in parent's room. AE, DC, DISC, MC, V. Valet parking $34. Pets accepted ($25 cleaning fee). **Amenities:** Restaurant; bar; poolside lunch service; discounted bike rentals; concierge; health club & spa; Jacuzzi; oceanview outdoor heated pool; room service. *In room:* A/C, TV, CD player, hair dryer, minibar, Wi-Fi ($12 per day).

Viceroy ★★   Still on L.A.'s coveted "in" list, is this überchic Santa Monica boutique hotel. It's the startling color scheme that first grabs your attention—parrot green, driftwood gray, and wave-crest white. Then there are the dishes: hundreds of custom-made china plates arranged in symmetrical patterns throughout the hotel and guest rooms, a Kelly Wearstler design. The array of white patent-leather chaises in the lobby seems more for form than function; most guests prefer the more conventional seating in the Cameo Bar or private poolside cabanas. The edgy-English theme is applied to every guest room as well, along with an array of high-tech toys like HD flatscreen TVs and iPod docking stations. Comforts include feather duvets, Egyptian linen, and pillow-top mattresses. The restaurant, **Whist,** serves good Mediterranean-influenced cuisine. You'll also enjoy the location, only a short walk to the beach and in the thick of the shopping, entertainment, and restaurant scene. *Tip:* Splurge for an oceanview room; the only other view is of the hotel parking lot.

1819 Ocean Ave., Santa Monica, CA 90401. www.viceroysantamonica.com. ☎ **800/670-6185** or 310/ 260-7500. Fax 310/260-7515. 162 units. From $380 double; from $580 suite. AE, DC, DISC, MC, V. Valet parking $32. **Amenities:** Restaurant; bar; lounge; concierge; exercise room; 2 heated outdoor pools; room service. *In room:* TV/DVD, hair dryer, minibar, Wi-Fi ($11 per day).

Moderate

The Ambrose ★★   If being within walking distance of the ocean isn't crucial, but a soothing, peaceful environment is, I've found your hotel. In a residential Santa Monica neighborhood, the 77-room Ambrose blends the Arts and Crafts movement with soothing Asian influences—a tranquil Japanese garden, a koi pond, trickling fountains, beautiful artwork, and a profusion of dark woods and mossy palettes. The hotel has been designated a "green" property, meaning that it's committed to conserving the state's natural resources and to low-impact living. Most guest rooms are on the small side but are luxuriously appointed with Matteo Italian bedding, Frette cotton kimonos and bath linens, and surround-sound CD/DVD music systems. Studio rooms come with terraces or balconies. It's the many complimentary amenities that really sold me on the Ambrose: underground parking with direct elevator access, breakfast pastries provided by a local fave Urth Caffe, and even shuttle service around Santa Monica via the hotel's cute-as-all-get-out London taxi (trust me, you'll love this car).

1255 20th St. (at Arizona Ave.), Santa Monica, CA 90404. www.ambrosehotel.com. ✆ **877-AMBROSE** (877/262-7673) or 310/315-1555. Fax 310/315-1556. 77 units. From $235 double. Rates include continental breakfast. AE, DC, DISC, MC, V. Free parking. **Amenities:** Exercise room; room service; complimentary local shuttle. *In room:* TV/VCR/DVD, CD player, hair dryer, minibar, free Wi-Fi.

The Hotel California ★ 👫 On enviable real estate along Ocean Avenue—right next door to the behemoth Loews—this welcoming hacienda-style beachfront motel embodies the surfer/sun-worshiper ambience you'd expect from Santa Monica lodging. The well-tended complex sits above and across an alley from the beach but offers excellent views and direct access to the sand via a private path. The inn offers cheery rooms with California-themed decor, including beds with down comforters, Egyptian-cotton sheets, and surfboard headboards. Five one-bedroom suites also have kitchenettes and trundle beds that make them great for families or longer stays; all rooms have minifridges, 27-inch TVs, and ceiling fans. A handful of rooms only have showers in the bathrooms, so be sure to request a room with a tub from the friendly front-desk staff if it matters to you. (And no, it's not the hotel from the Eagles' hit—that hotel is rumored to be in Mexico, though the album's cover photo is actually of the Beverly Hills Hotel.) *Tip:* Pay a few bucks extra for a courtyard view, as the cheapest rooms face the parking lot and noisy Ocean Avenue. Be sure to check the website for specials.

1670 Ocean Ave. (south of Colorado Ave.), Santa Monica, CA 90401. www.hotelca.com. ✆ **866/571-0000** or 310/393-2363. Fax 310/393-1063. 26 units; 9 monthly rentals. $219–$319 double or suite. AE, DISC, MC, V. Self-parking $25. **Amenities:** Jacuzzi. *In room:* TV/VCR, fridge, hair dryer, free Wi-Fi.

Jamaica Bay Inn ★ Located on prime Mother's Beach adjacent real estate, the Jamaica Bay Inn offers a more affordable alternative to the Ritz, and less of a corporate feel than the Marriott, making it popular with young couples and families when it debuted in late 2010. I remember it's last incarnation as a run-down Best Western, but after the full-scale makeover, it's my choice for a nice stay in the neighborhood. The lobby is welcoming, complete with a simple but stylish lounge area and a fireplace; there are also a few fire pits on the patio. The comfortable rooms, divided between city or marina views (definitely pony up for the latter), reflect a minimalist interpretation of the West Indies theme. Business travelers will appreciate the ergonomic workstations. **Vu Restaurant and Bar** serves a mix of small plates-style molecular gastronomy (one bite of the lobster tail with popcorn Jello and Fritos will change your life), plus larger portions of more familiar American fare like beef tenderloin. *Tip:* Look into the variety of money-saving packages, which may include everything from tasting experiences at the restaurant to complimentary breakfast, and milk and cookies for the kids.

4175 Admiralty Way, Marina Del Rey, CA 90292. www.jamaicabayinn.com. ✆ **888/823-5333** or 310/823-5333. Fax 310/823-1325. 111 units. $209–$254 double; from $259 suite. AE, DISC, MC, V. Valet parking $18; self-parking $14. **Amenities:** Jacuzzi; heated outdoor pool; room service. *In room:* TV, fridge, hair dryer, MP3 docking station, free Wi-Fi ($9.95 per day).

Marina del Rey Marriott ★ 👫 This is not your average Marriott. To attract a more L.A.-hip clientele, this Marina del Rey hotel has made some rather unorthodox modifications to what would typically be a boring business hotel. As soon as you enter the lobby, three of your senses are subliminally put at ease: inhale the Zanzibar Mist, a subtle aromatherapy mixture that circulates throughout the hotel; hear the faint soundtrack of ambient world beats; and gaze into the hypnotic tiers of fire at **Glow,** the hotel's outdoor lounge. Okay, so things get a bit more utilitarian when you enter your guest room, but each is soothingly spacious and comfortably appointed with down comforters and pillows, 32-inch HDTVs, bathrobes, Jacuzzi-style tubs, a work desk, and small balconies with stress-relieving views of the marina or Pacific Ocean. Best of all, this is mainly a business hotel, so the weekend rates are often heavily discounted (check the website for deals).

4100 Admiralty Way (at the north end of the marina), Marina del Rey, CA 90292. www.marriott.com. ⓒ **800/228-9290** or 310/301-3000. Fax 310/448-4870. 370 units. $209–$279 double; from $259 suite. AE, DC, DISC, MC, V. Valet parking $26. **Amenities:** Restaurant; lobby bar; concierge lounge; Glow outdoor lounge; fitness center; pool and whirlpool; room service. *In room:* A/C, HDTV, hair dryer, Wi-Fi ($13 per day).

Venice Beach House ★★ 🎁 Listed on the National Register of Historic Places, this two-story, ivy-covered 1911 Craftsman bungalow is now a homey bed-and-breakfast on one of funky Venice's unique sidewalk streets, just a block from the beach. The interior has a homey lived-in look—shelves of vintage books, antique furnishings, hardwood floors, faded Oriental rugs—that adds charm for romantics but won't live up to the expectations of travelers who like their lodgings to be flawless (or who aren't keen on possibly sharing a bathroom). What's more, the inn hums noisily with activity when there's a full house—seekers of absolute quiet and designer appointments will *not* be comfortable here. Still, the huge repeat clientele base doesn't seem to mind these minor caveats. My favorite room is the upstairs James Peasgood Suite—light and airy, with a double-size Jacuzzi tub, king-size bed, private bathroom, and a small balcony. An expanded continental breakfast with homemade baked goods is served in the sunroom overlooking a splendid garden.

15 30th Ave. (at Speedway, 1 block west of Pacific Ave.), Venice, CA 90291. www.venicebeachhouse. com. ⓒ **310/823-1966.** Fax 310/823-1842. 9 units, 5 with private bathroom. $150 double with shared bathroom; $210–$255 double with private bathroom. Extra person after 2 people $20. Rates include expanded continental breakfast. AE, MC, V. On-site parking $14/day. *In room:* A/C; TV, free Wi-Fi.

Inexpensive

Cal Mar Hotel Suites ★ 🍴 In a residential neighborhood just 2 blocks from the ocean, this garden apartment complex delivers a lot of bang for your vacation buck. Every unit is an apartment-style suite with a living room and pullout sofa, a full-size kitchen with utensils, and a separate bedroom; most are spacious enough to accommodate four in comfort. The building was constructed in the 1950s with an eye for quality (attractive tile work, large closets). While the furnishings aren't luxurious, they're all quite modern and very clean, and everything is well kept. It's easy to be comfortable here for stays of a week or more, especially since it's a mere block from the Third Street Promenade and a short walk to the beach. Rooms are in the process of being updated—for instance, hardwood floors have replaced carpeting in some—but it's not a full-scale renovation, just little touches here and there. The staff is attentive and courteous, which helps account for the high rate of repeat guests. The garden courtyard has an inviting swimming pool and plenty of chaises for lounging. *Tip:* Request a room on the second floor to avoid the sound of stomping feet.

220 California Ave., Santa Monica, CA 90403. www.calmarhotel.com. ⓒ **800/776-6007** or 310/395-5555. Fax 310/451-1111. 36 units. $164–$254 suite. Extra person $10. Children 9 and under stay free in parent's room. AE, DC, DISC, MC, V. Parking $13. **Amenities:** Heated outdoor pool. *In room:* TV, CD player, hair dryer, kitchen, Wi-Fi ($9.95 per day).

Casa Malibu ★★ 🎁 Right on its very own beach, this leftover jewel from Malibu's golden age doesn't try to play the sleek resort game. Instead, the modest, low-rise inn has the cozy and timeless look of a traditional California beach cottage. Wrapped around a palm-studded inner courtyard, the 21 rooms are comfortable and thoughtfully outfitted. Depending on the room, you might find a fireplace, a kitchenette (in a half-dozen or so), a CD player (in suites), a tub (instead of shower only), and/or a private deck over the sand. The upstairs Catalina Suite (Lana Turner's old hide-out) has the best view, while the gorgeous Malibu Suite—the best room in the house and, like the beachfront rooms, located right on the beach—offers state-of-the-art pampering. More than half have ocean views, but even those facing the courtyard are quiet and offer easy beach access. There's also a handsome, wind-shielded brick sun deck that extends directly over the sand. *Tip:* Book well ahead for summer—this one's a favorite of locals and visitors alike.

22752 Pacific Coast Hwy. (about ¼ mile south of Malibu Pier), Malibu, CA 90265. © **800/831-0858** or 310/456-2219. Fax 310/456-5418. 21 units. $169–$259 garden or oceanview double; $249–$299 beachfront double; $499–$529 suite. Rates include continental breakfast. Extra person $15. AE, MC, V. Free parking. **Amenities:** Access to nearby private health club for an additional fee; room service. *In room:* TV/DVD, fridge, hair dryer, free Wi-Fi.

Hotel Erwin ★ ☺

After a year of renovations, this former Best Western was converted to a hip boutique hotel in June 2009. Just off the Venice boardwalk and 200 feet from the beach, the hotel's spacious rooms are brightened with beachy colors and dutifully equipped with new Art Deco–style furnishings, high-definition TVs, and wet bars. The one-bedroom suites are terrific for families, offering master bedrooms with king-size beds, microwaves, dining areas, queen-size sofa sleepers, balconies, and fireplaces. Photos of local scenes and rock-'n'-roll legends along with works by local artists give the public spaces a cool L.A. vibe, and many rooms have at least partial ocean views (the best views are from the top-floor rooms facing the ocean). A restaurant, **Hash,** features various breakfast hash dishes, and the rooftop bar, **High,** has 360-degree views of the beach and surroundings. Stay elsewhere if you don't relish the party-hearty human carnival of Venice Beach.

1697 Pacific Ave. (at 17th Ave.), Venice, CA 90291. www.jdvhotels.com. © **800/786-7789** or 310/452-1111. Fax 310/452-5479. 88 units. $229–$269 double; $259–$369 suite. AE, DC, DISC, MC, V. Valet parking $28. **Amenities:** Restaurant; rooftop lounge; fitness center. *In room:* A/C, flatscreen TV, honor bar, hair dryer, MP3 docking station/iPod-compatible, Wi-Fi ($4.95 per day).

Inn at Venice Beach ☺

This cheery motel at the (relatively) quiet residential south end of Venice is a good choice for travelers who want a near-the-beach, near-the-boardwalk location without being at the center of the fray. Rooms are cheerily colorful (lots of blues and yellows); open-beam ceilings add to the spacious feel. All rooms overlook a cobblestone courtyard, where complimentary continental breakfast is served on warm mornings. It all adds up to a reasonable value for budget-minded travelers (the bi-level loft suites are a great value if there are more than two of you). Because the hotel is just 3 blocks from the ocean on the border between Venice and Marina del Rey, there's an endless parade of people exploring the marina, the beach, or the nearby canals on foot, bike, or in-line skates (rentals are 2 blocks away). About the only thing missing is a pool, but the staff will lend you beach towels for an ocean dip.

327 Washington Blvd., Venice, CA 90291. www.innatvenicebeach.com. © **800/828-0688** or 310/821-2557. Fax 310/827-0289. 43 units. $185–$229 double; $259 suite. Rates include continental breakfast. AE, DC, DISC, MC, V. Parking $8. **Amenities:** Exercise room. *In room:* A/C, TV, fridge, hair dryer, free Wi-Fi.

Sea Shore Motel ⚑

In the heart of Santa Monica's Main Street dining and shopping sector, this small, friendly, family-run motel is one of the best bargains near the beach and the Santa Monica Pier. The Sea Shore is such a well-kept secret that most denizens of stylish Main Street are unaware of the incredible value in their midst. Arranged around a parking courtyard, rooms are small and unremarkable from the outside, but the conscientious management has done a nice job with the interiors, installing 27-inch flatscreen HDTVs, attractive terra-cotta floor tiles, granite countertops, and conveniences like voice mail. *Tip:* Complete with a living room and full kitchen, the 800-square-foot suites that sleep up to six are a phenomenal deal; book them as far in advance as possible (at least a month is recommended).

2637 Main St. (south of Ocean Park Blvd.), Santa Monica, CA 90405. www.seashoremotel.com. ✆ **310/ 392-2787.** Fax 310/392-5167. 24 units. $110–$180 double; $150–$300 suite. Extra person $5. Children 11 and under stay free in parent's room. AE, DISC, MC, V. Free parking. Pets accepted ($10 per night). **Amenities:** Unaffiliated deli in the building. *In room:* Flatscreens, fridge, free Wi-Fi.

ACCOMMODATIONS NEAR LAX
Expensive

Westin Los Angeles Airport ★   This massive 12-story hotel stands a cut above the rest, thanks to an invention that borders on miracle status: Westin's own Heavenly Bed. Touted as "10 layers of heaven"—from the custom pillow-top mattress to the fluffy down comforter and a family of pillows—the Heavenly Bed is the best hotel bed in the business. The like-new rooms are nicely outfitted in chain-standard style, and some have balconies (don't expect anything resembling a view). All of the conveniences are on hand, including a free airport shuttle and a very nice pool and fitness center.

5400 W. Century Blvd., Los Angeles, CA 90045. www.westin.com/losangelesairport. ✆ **800/937-8461** or 310/216-5858. Fax 310/417-4545. 740 units. $209–$269 double; from $349 suite (must be booked over the phone). AE, DC, DISC, MC, V. Valet parking $33; self-parking $22. Pets under 40 lb. allowed. **Amenities:** Restaurant; lobby court for cocktails; free airport transfers; concierge; exercise room; Jacuzzi; heated outdoor pool; room service. *In room:* A/C, TV, hair dryer, minibar, Wi-Fi ($13 per day).

Moderate

Marriott Los Angeles Airport   This huge 18-story Marriott is a good airport choice, designed for travelers on the fly. Rooms are decorated in refreshed chain-hotel style; some have balconies, and now all rooms offer voice mail, two-line phones, high-speed Internet and refrigerators. Future upgrades will include the implementation of HD flatscreen TVs.

5855 W. Century Blvd. (at Airport Blvd.), Los Angeles, CA 90045. www.marriott.com. ✆ **800/228- 9290** or 310/641-5700. Fax 310/337-5358. 1,026 units. $119–$259 double. AE, DC, DISC, MC, V. Valet parking $32; self-parking $26. **Amenities:** 2 restaurants; coffee shop; sports bar; free airport transfers; concierge level; exercise room; Jacuzzi; outdoor heated pool; room service; sauna. *In room:* A/C, TV, hair dryer, minibar, Wi-Fi ($13 per day).

Sheraton Gateway Hotel Los Angeles Airport   This 15-story hotel is so close to the Los Angeles Airport that it literally overlooks the runway. Rooms have a stylish boutique look, Sheraton "Sweet Sleeper" beds, and triple-pane windows that block out even the loudest takeoffs. *Note:* The entire property is smoke-free.

6101 W. Century Blvd. (near Sepulveda Blvd.), Los Angeles, CA 90045. www.sheratonlosangeles.com. ✆ **800/325-3535** or 310/642-1111. Fax 310/645-1414. 802 units. $129–$269 double. AE, DC, DISC, MC, V. Valet parking $24; self-parking $13. **Amenities:** 2 restaurants; cocktail lounge; free airport transfers; concierge; exercise room; Jacuzzi; heated outdoor pool w/cabanas; room service. *In room:* A/C, TV, hair dryer, minibar, Wi-Fi ($11 per day).

Inexpensive

Travelodge Hotel at LAX ✈ The lobby is nondescript and the rooms are standard, but there's a beautiful tropical garden surrounding the pool area, and amenities extend beyond the budget-motel standard, such as courtesy airport/car-rental shuttle service and a free morning paper. Some units have terraces; about two-thirds of the rooms have showers only, so request a tub if you require one. A 24-hour Denny's adjoins the hotel. If you've brought the kids along, request the Sleepy Bear Den, a separate sleeping room designed for children.

5547 W. Century Blvd., Los Angeles, CA 90045. www.travelodgelax.com. ℂ **800/421-3939** or 310/649-4000. Fax 310/649-0311. 147 units. $75–$115 double. Rates include continental breakfast. Extra person $8. Children 17 and under stay free in parent's room. AE, DC, DISC, MC, V. Free parking. Pets accepted ($10 per day, per pet). **Amenities:** 24-hr. restaurant; free airport transfers; exercise room; outdoor heated pool; room service. *In room:* A/C, Cable TV, hair dryer, free Wi-Fi.

L.A.'S WESTSIDE & BEVERLY HILLS

The Westside is home to the city's most centrally located, star-studded, and dining/shopping/spa-centric communities. As such, hotels tend toward the pricey end of the scale—this is where you can find L.A.'s largest concentration of luxury hotels, many of which you've no doubt seen on TV or the big screen. There aren't many bargains to be found, so travelers in search of the best values shouldn't get their hearts set on a Westside location. Even so, I've managed to ferret out a few good mid-priced and budget options.

Very Expensive

Beverly Hills Hotel and Bungalows ★★★ Behind the famous facade (remember the Eagles' *Hotel California* album?) lies this star-studded haven where legends were, and still are, made: The "Pink Palace" was center stage for both deal- and star-making in Hollywood's golden days. Today stars and industry hotshots or, as one member of the staff joked, "all the current rulers of the universe," can still be found lounging around the Olympic-size pool (into which Katharine Hepburn once dove fully clothed) or digging into Dutch apple pancakes in the iconic **Polo Lounge,** where Hunter S. Thompson kicked off his adventure to Las Vegas. It is a truly world-class property.

Following a $250-million restoration about 10 years ago, the hotel's grand lobby and impeccably landscaped grounds retain their over-the-top glory, while the lavish guest rooms—each uniquely decorated in a subdued palette of pinks, greens, apricots, and yellows—boast every state-of-the-art luxury. Many rooms feature private patios, Jacuzzi tubs, kitchens, fireplaces, and/or dining rooms. The 23 bungalows—with two more sizable three-bedroom suites expected to debut in spring 2011 (bye-bye tennis courts)—are more luxurious than ever, and the lush, tropical-like grounds are brimming with exotic trees and flowers that emit divine aromas. Even the outdoor pathways are carpeted, to keep noise to a minimum. Adding one more layer of luxury to the hotel, the **Beverly Hills Hotel Spa by La Prairie** offers European- and Asian-influenced massage and expert facials. Stop by **Bar NINETEEN12** for drinks, which are pricey, or the informal, retro-chic **Fountain Coffee Shop** for lunch or early dinner.

For a truly iconic L.A. dining experience—or just a martini—the old-school vibe at the more upscale **Polo Lounge** can't be beat. *Tip:* Table no. 6, a plush booth, is ideal for its celebrity-spotting vantage point—though the pianist will hear every word you say.

9641 Sunset Blvd. (at Rodeo Dr.), Beverly Hills, CA 90210. www.beverlyhillshotel.com. ✆ **800/283-8885** or 310/276-2251. Fax 310/887-2887. 210 units. $530–$760 double; from $1,150 suite or bungalow. AE, DC, MC, V. Valet parking $34. Pets accepted in bungalows only ($200 non-refundable fee). **Amenities:** 3 restaurants; 2 bars; 2 lounges; free airport transfers; babysitting; concierge; health club; Jacuzzi; Olympic-size outdoor heated pool; room service; spa. *In room:* A/C, TV/VCR, CD player, hair dryer, minibar, Wi-Fi ($10 per day).

Chateau Marmont ★★   Perched secretively in a curve above the Sunset Strip, the Chateau, modeled after an elegant Loire Valley castle, is a landmark from 1920s-era Hollywood; step inside and you'll expect to find John Barrymore or Errol Flynn holding inebriated court in the baronial living room. This historic landmark built its reputation on exclusivity and privacy, which was shattered when John Belushi over-dosed in Bungalow No. 3. The funky luxury oasis revels in its lore-filled past, yet it's hipper and more exclusive than ever. No two of the antiques-filled accommoda-tions—standard rooms, suites, cottages, and bungalows—are alike: The poolside Spanish-style garden cottages are outfitted in Arts and Crafts style, while suites and bungalows may get a 1950s look or a Gothic style. Many units have fireplaces and CD stereos, and all but 11 have kitchenettes or full kitchens. The Chateau Marmont is beautifully kept, eternally chic, and faultlessly service-oriented, but it's not for everybody. This is a place where quirkiness rules, so don't expect traditional luxuries.

8221 Sunset Blvd. (btw. La Cienega and Crescent Heights boulevards), West Hollywood, CA 90046. www.chateaumarmont.com. ✆ **800/242-8328** or 323/656-1010. Fax 323/655-5311. 63 units. From $415 double; from $500 suite; from $545 cottage; from $1,800 bungalow. AE, DC, MC, V. Valet parking $28. Pets accepted ($150 per pet). **Amenities:** Restaurant (serves in lobby, garden, and dining room); bar; con-cierge; exercise room; access to nearby health club; outdoor heated pool w/brick sundeck; room service. *In room:* A/C, TV/DVD, CD player, fridge, hair dryer, minibar, free Wi-Fi, iPod docking station.

Four Seasons Hotel Los Angeles at Beverly Hills ★★★   This intimate-feeling 16-story hotel completed a $33-million renovation in 2010, and attracts a mix of A-list jet-setters loyal to the Four Seasons brand and an L.A. showbiz crowd that cherishes the hotel as an après-event gathering place, especially at Windows Lounge. Like other Four Seasons, the concierge is famously well connected and service staff goes the distance. Guest room luxuries include contemporary furnishings with ele-ments of Old Hollywood, 42-inch LCD flatscreen TVs, custom Stearns & Foster mattresses with heavenly linens and pillows, marble bathrooms with vanity TV, and French doors leading to private balconies. Room rates rise with the elevator, so bar-gain hunters need to sacrifice the view. For not much more money per night, the Premiere King rooms are on the corners of the building, and offer wraparound balco-nies. Along with a full-service spa with several exclusive and organic spa treatments, the view-endowed fourth-floor deck features a saline lap pool with an elevated whirl-pool, Cabana Restaurant, and a glass-walled fitness center. **Culina, Modern Italian** is the new (and quite good) restaurant featuring one of L.A.'s only crudo bars, house-made pasta, brick-oven thin-crust pizza, innovative Italian entrees, and more than 200 wine labels, mostly Italian and available by the carafe. Outside seating is a must on warm days and nights.

300 S. Doheny Dr. (at Burton Way), Los Angeles, CA 90048. www.fourseasons.com/losangeles. ✆ **800/819-5053** or 310/273-2222. Fax 310/859-3824. 285 units. From $525 double; from $745 suite.

Where to Stay in L.A.'s Westside & Beverly Hills

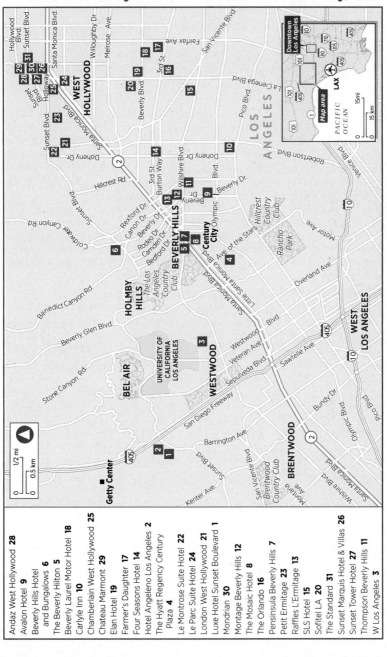

Andaz West Hollywood **28**
Avalon Hotel **9**
Beverly Hills Hotel
  and Bungalows **6**
The Beverly Hilton **5**
Beverly Laurel Motor Hotel **18**
Carlyle Inn **10**
Chamberlain West Hollywood **25**
Chateau Marmont **29**
Elan Hotel **19**
Farmer's Daughter **17**
Four Seasons Hotel **14**
Hotel Angeleno Los Angeles **2**
The Hyatt Regency Century
  Plaza **4**
Le Montrose Suite Hotel **22**
Le Parc Suite Hotel **24**
London West Hollywood **21**
Luxe Hotel Sunset Boulevard **1**
Mondrian **30**
Montage Beverly Hills **12**
The Mosaic Hotel **8**
The Orlando **16**
Pensinsula Beverly Hills **7**
Petit Ermitage **23**
Raffles L'Ermitage **13**
SLS Hotel **15**
Sofitel LA **20**
The Standard **31**
Sunset Marquis Hotel & Villas **26**
Sunset Tower Hotel **27**
Thompson Beverly Hills **11**
W Los Angeles **3**

AE, DC, DISC, MC, V. Valet parking $30. Pets 15 lb. and under welcome. **Amenities:** Restaurant; lounge; poolside grill; concierge; fitness center; Jacuzzi; rooftop heated pool; room service; full-service spa. *In room:* A/C, TV/DVD, CD player, hair dryer, minibar, Wi-Fi ($10 per day).

The Hyatt Regency Century Plaza ★★   Despite the almost foreboding scale, I really like this hotel. The spacious lobby lounge is always my first stop for a cocktail and some great people-watching, followed by a walk around the immense pool and garden area behind the hotel (pack a suit or trunks). The guest rooms are more attractive than you'd expect from a corporate hotel: contemporary furnishings; gorgeous, warm-hued textiles; big closets with terry robes; and almost universally impressive views from the small deck. Hyatt's celestial Grand Bed is a treat, as is the 32-inch LCD flatscreen TV and iPod docking station. **Breeze,** the hotel's beautiful 250-seat restaurant and sushi bar, is popular at lunch, and the **X Bar** is handy for that late-night cocktail-and-appetizers craving. Adjoining the hotel is the tony **Equinox Fitness Club + Spa.** A $20 daily fee allows guests full access to the state-of-the-art fitness center, fitness classes, and locker room. *Tip:* Ask about the hotel's all-new hypo-allergenic rooms, which are recertified every 6 months.

2025 Ave. of the Stars (south of Santa Monica Blvd.), Century City, CA 90067. www.centuryplaza.hyatt. com. ⓒ **800/55-HYATT** (554-9288) or 310/228-1234. Fax 310/551-3355. 726 units. $329–$455 double; from $529 suite. AE, DC, DISC, MC, V. Valet parking $35. Pets under 50 lb. accepted ($30 deposit). **Amenities:** Restaurant; spa cafe; lobby bar; lounge; concierge; access to nearby health club and spa; Jacuzzi; outdoor heated pool; room service; Wi-Fi (free, in lobby). *In room:* A/C, TV, hair dryer, minibar, Wi-Fi ($10 per day).

Mondrian ★★   Theatrical, coveted, sophisticated—this is the kind of place super-hotelier Ian Schrager has created from a once-drab apartment building. Working with designer Philippe Starck, Schrager used the Mondrian's breathtaking views (from every room) as the starting point for his vision of a "hotel in the clouds." Purposely underlit hallways lead to bright, clean rooms done in shades of white, beige, and pale gray and outfitted with simple furniture casually slip-covered in white. Thanks to renovations in 2008, the accommodations themselves—once secondary to the super-hip, star-studded scene, are now much more pleasant. Still, booking a room automatically gets you in to the poolside **Skybar** (soundproof windows on the entire south side of the building have already dealt with a troublesome noise problem in rooms overlooking the raucous late-night scene). In addition to its popular power-dining Asian-Latin fusion restaurant, **Asia de Cuba,** light meals and sushi are served at the **Spin Lounge** in the lobby. Then there's the elegant **Agua Spa,** offering a full range of spa treatments in a Zen-like atmosphere. Thankfully, the beautiful-people staff is getting much better with service than in the old days.

8440 Sunset Blvd., West Hollywood, CA 90069. www.mondrianhotel.com. ⓒ **800/697-1791** or 323/650-8999. Fax 323/650-5215. 237 units. $315–$505 double; from $385 suite. AE, DC, DISC, MC, V. Valet parking $32. **Amenities:** 2 restaurants; bar; concierge; exercise room; outdoor pool; room service; full-service spa. *In room:* A/C, TV/DVD, CD player, hair dryer, minibar, Wi-Fi ($10 per day), iPod docking station.

Montage Beverly Hills ★★★   Smack-dab in the center of the Golden Triangle, a credit card's throw from Rodeo Drive, this resort has it all: beautiful rooms, top-notch service, an excellent spa, and a rooftop restaurant and pool with sweeping views of the city. I like the Spanish Colonial decor—it's warm and inviting, serene and plush, just what you'd expect from the Montage. Because it only opened in late 2008, this definitely feels like a contemporary resort; if you're looking for history, try the Beverly Hills Hotel (see above). All 201 rooms have balconies, extremely comfortable beds, and ample desk space for business travelers. The suites are worth the extra dollars, especially if you like extra living space to spread out; book a Superior Suite and you'll get a complimentary Mercedes-Benz to drive around town during your stay. Private cabanas around the pool are completely decked out with TVs, refrigerators—pretty much anything you could possibly want, they'll get it for you. Get a treatment in the two-story spa; we found that even the facials are relaxing. There's afternoon tea and libations in the lobby, and two restaurants: **Scarpetta** for storied Italian fare from New York–based chef/restaurateur Scott Conant adjacent to the rooftop pool, is the **Conservatory Grill,** a much more casual indoor/outdoor space with lovely views.

225 N. Canon Dr., Beverly Hills, CA 90210. www.montagebeverlyhills.com. © **310/860-7800.** Fax 310/860-7801. 201 units. $475–$775 double; from $925 suite. AE, DC, DISC, MC, V. Parking $30. **Amenities:** 2 restaurants; 1 bar; concierge; state-of-the-art fitness center; rooftop heated pool; room service; full-service spa. *In room:* A/C, TV, hair dryer, minibar, free Wi-Fi.

Peninsula Beverly Hills ★★★   The Peninsula is one of L.A.'s three finest hotels (a group that includes the Beverly Hills Hotel, above, and the Hotel Bel-Air). This stellar brand—like its sister Peninsula properties in exotic locales like Hong Kong, Beijing, and Bangkok—has risen above the rest by making ultraservice its hallmark. Set at Beverly Hills's main crossroads, this gardenlike oasis is impeccable in every respect (although laid-back types will surely consider it too formal). Special features in the large, lavish, European-style guest rooms include controls for everything—lighting, climate, room service (do not disturb sign, of course)—as well as the luxurious Frette-made bed, an extra-large work desk, and round-the-clock personal valets. The 16 private villa suites, ensconced within lush gardens, have gas fireplaces, kitchens, and individual security systems. Sure, rooms are ultraexpensive, but a unique 24-hour check-in/checkout policy—which allows you to keep your room for a full 24 hours, no matter what time you check in—means you get your money's worth. All guests are entitled access to the courtesy Town Car or Rolls-Royce Phantom, within a 3-mile radius. **Belvedere** is one of L.A.'s premier hotel dining room; breakfast is a tradition among CAA agents and their thespian clients (insiders order the nowhere-on-the-menu banana-stuffed brioche French toast), and Sunday brunch is delicious. The mahogany-paneled bar is also popular among the power suits, while the English Garden–style **Living Room** pours L.A.'s best high tea. The Peninsula Spa is worthy of a visit, even if you don't stay at the hotel.

9882 S. Santa Monica Blvd. (at Wilshire Blvd.), Beverly Hills, CA 90212. www.peninsula.com. © **800/462-7899** or 310/551-2888. Fax 310/788-2319. 196 units. $585–$955 double; from $1,550 suite. AE, DC, DISC, MC, V. Parking $28. **Amenities:** Restaurant; bar; concierge; state-of-the-art fitness center; Jacuzzi; rooftop heated lap pool; room service; full-service spa. *In room:* A/C, TV/DVD, hair dryer, minibar, free Wi-Fi.

SLS ★★   After a $230-million renovation, the former staid Le Meridien has been transformed into a whimsical tapestry of living art. Designed by Philippe Starck, the whole place is visually compelling: Life-size photographs of people decorate the elevator walls; mirrors in the rooms are bordered by the outline of human heads; heck, even the TV is projected through a glass wall. Fitness buffs might consider booking an exercise suite that comes outfitted with built-in weighted cables and pulleys (though the hotel gym is so amazing, this is truly for those who don't want to leave their rooms at all). The hotel's restaurant, bar, and retail area, called The Bazaar (which is, fittingly, bizarre), will stimulate all of your senses (see p. 98). The dining rooms (Rojo y Blanca), Bar Centro, and room service are helmed by one of the most inventive chefs in the country right now, José Andrés. For a more exclusive experience, consider

SAAM, the discreet "secret" dining room in the back of the restaurant. For adventurous palates only, dinner here consists of a 22-course, set tasting menu of little bites, with optional wine pairings (for gosh sakes, go for it!). Just be sure to reserve in advance—it can only seat up to 30. Ciel Spa does a fine job living up to its name by creating the illusion that you've arrived at the Pearly Gates through a series of mirrors, bright lighting, and billowy, white drapings. Massages and other treatments are also available in-room. *Tip:* Depending on availability, if you get offered a $20 promotional upgrade to a Terrace Room, take it. The patios aren't spectacular by any means, but they are medium size and semi-private, and it's nice to have a bit of fresh air right off your room.

465 S. La Cienega Blvd., Los Angeles, CA 90048. www.slshotels.com.© **310/247-0400.** Fax 310/247-0315. 297 units. $369–$649 double; from $769 suite. AE, DC, DISC, MC, V. Valet parking $35. **Amenities:** Restaurant; patisserie; lounge; concierge; fitness center; rooftop pool w/private cabanas; room service. *In room:* A/C, TV/DVD, hair dryer, minibar, MP3 docking station, Wi-Fi ($13 per day).

Sofitel LA ★   The Sofitel chain brought its brand of glamour and sophistication to the heart of L.A.'s Westside, adjacent to Beverly Hills and directly across the street from the Beverly Center. With the exception of the Euro beats pumped into the lobby, the Sofitel does everything right. Rooms, though not large, ooze luxury—the thick carpet, high-thread-count linens, and contemporary amenities such as 32-inch plasma TVs, sizable workspaces, and Wi-Fi connections are sure to make anyone comfortable. Suites are lavish, with Bose stereo systems and walk-in closets, as well as flatscreen TVs mounted over soaking tubs in the huge bathrooms. The biggest suite in the house has a full dining space with fireplace, as well as a huge balcony with a full bar. We hear rock stars rent the place after playing shows in town. The dimly lit **Stone Rose** lounge is good spot for late-night cocktails and/or canoodling, and Kerry Simon's **Simon LA** has modern comfort food. The on-site **Le Spa** offers an abundance of indulgent skin treatments, massages, baths, and manicure/pedicures.

8555 Beverly Blvd. (at La Cienega Blvd.), Los Angeles, CA 90048. www.sofitella.com.© **800/SOFITEL** (763-4835) or 310/278-5444. Fax 310/657-2816. 295 units. $280–$400 double; from $475 suite. AE, DC, DISC, MC, V. Valet parking $32. Pets under 30 lb. accepted. **Amenities:** Restaurant; bar; concierge; exercise room; room service; Wi-Fi (free, in lobby). *In room:* A/C, TV/DVD, hair dryer, minibar, Wi-Fi ($9.95 per day).

Sunset Marquis Hotel & Villas ★★ 🛍   This sprawling Mediterranean-style all-suite hotel is the ultimate movie-and-music hostelry, regularly hosting the biggest names in rock and film. (The Rolling Stones, Aerosmith, U2, and even Brad Pitt are all repeat customers.) In fact, the hotel even installed a state-of-the-art recording studio and screening room in the basement for its noteworthy guests. After recording sessions, the musicians can then retire to the dark and sexy **Bar 1200** (a favorite refuge of celebs), where their newly recorded session can be piped in directly. Of course, unless you're staying at the hotel, you'll never get in (which, in itself, is reason enough to stay). The hotel is a short walk from the rowdy Sunset Strip, but it feels a world away, with its 4½ acres of lush gardens, koi ponds, brick paths, and tropical foliage. After completing a $20-million renovation in 2009, the suites have an attractive and comfortable modern style, with streamlined furnishings. The villas take hospitality to a totally new level with private alarm systems and butlers, plus select features like baby grand pianos, flatscreen TVs, and Jacuzzi tubs. Guests who stay in the presidential villa can negotiate the use of an SUV, a Bentley, or a limo during their stay. There are also two separate pool areas, an outdoor bar, a spa, and a restaurant with patio seating. The onsite fine-dining space, known simply as **RESTAURANT,**

does nice renditions of modern American food with fresh ingredients. Off the lobby, **Maximillian Gallery** exhibits contemporary art by emerging and established talent.

1200 Alta Loma Rd. (just south of Sunset Blvd.), West Hollywood, CA 90069. www.sunsetmarquishotel. com. ✆ **800/858-9758** or 310/657-1333. Fax 310/652-5300. 154 units. From $335 double; From $400 junior suite; $550–$1,650 1- or 2-bedroom villa. AE, DC, DISC, MC, V. Valet parking $30. **Amenities:** Restaurant; bar; concierge; free access to Equinox across the street; Jacuzzi; 2 outdoor heated pools; room service; sauna, spa. *In room:* A/C, TV (DVD upon request), fridge, minibar, Wi-Fi ($12 per day); iPod docking station.

Sunset Tower Hotel ★★★

Standing out like an Art Deco pearl among the surrounding architectural swine, the 15-story Sunset Tower was built in 1921 as a luxury apartment for Hollywood's top movie stars—everyone from Jean Harlow and Clark Gable to Marilyn Monroe, Elizabeth Taylor, and Frank Sinatra has lived (or housed lovers) here. The building lost its luster in the '60s and was nearly demolished in the '80s, but when hotelier Jeff Klein bought and renovated the hotel in 2005, it was meticulously restored with fine woods, muted colors, and brass fittings. Guest rooms have floor-to-ceiling windows with wonderful city views, as well as oversize tubs, Egyptian linens, and a soothing aura of Old Hollywood elegance. What better way to spend a day in L.A. than to have a massage and spa treatment at the hotel's **Argyle Spa,** spend the afternoon sunbathing at the pool while noshing on blinis and rosé from the **Terrace** poolside grill, settle into a Plymouth martini and a lobster Cobb at the beautiful **Tower Bar** (a favorite of Jennifer Aniston), then step out the front door and stroll along the famous Sunset Strip?

8358 Sunset Blvd. (on the Sunset Strip), West Hollywood, CA 90069. www.sunsettowerhotel.com. ✆ **800/225-2637** or 323/654-7100. Fax 323/654-9287. 74 units. $295–$325 double; from $345 suite; from $2,500 penthouse. AE, DC, DISC, MC, V. Valet parking $32. Pets accepted ($100 fee). **Amenities:** Restaurant; poolside grill; bar/lounge; concierge; exercise room; heated outdoor pool; room service; full-service spa. *In room:* A/C, TV/DVD, hair dryer, minibar, MP3 docking station, free Wi-Fi.

Thompson Beverly Hills ★★

Beverly Hills got a tad bit cooler with the introduction of the Thompson in 2008, situated along the neighborhood's main drag, Wilshire Boulevard. While all the mirrors almost make you feel like you've stepped into a posh fun house, the rooms are plush and dapper with a nod to California modernism. If you want to spring for an upgrade, you can't go wrong with the signature and sexy Thompson Suite, which has a balcony with sweeping views, a kitchen, two bathrooms (one with a tub, one with a shower, should you feel picky), a sitting area, and a bedroom. The hotel is particularly popular on weekends, when guests have access to the dual-level, mostly members-only rooftop pool and its accompanying bar, **ABH ("Above Beverly Hills"),** offering private cabanas and stunning panoramic views of all of Los Angeles. Though Sundays and Mondays are now locals' nights, it's not as exclusive as it once was. In place of the old Bond Street outpost, the hotel has opened its own French-Italian eatery, which some people refer to as "the Thompson Restaurant." *Tip:* If you want to see the Hollywood sign from your room, ask for something on floors seven through nine.

9360 Wilshire Blvd., Beverly Hills, CA 90212. www.thompsonbeverlyhills.com. ✆ **800/441-5050** or 310/273-1400. Fax 310/859-8551. 107 units. $254–$314 double; from $349 suite. AE, DC, DISC, MC, V. Valet parking $30. **Amenities:** Restaurant; rooftop bar; concierge; fitness center; rooftop pool; room service. *In room:* A/C, TV/DVD, hair dryer, minibar, Wi-Fi ($10 per day), iPod docking station.

Expensive

Andaz West Hollywood ★

For fans of rock-'n'-roll history, please bow your heads in a moment of silence for the former "Riot Hyatt": After a complete overhaul, the hotel reopened as the newly branded Andaz in 2008, wiping clean any remnants of the Sunset Strip glory days. Andaz, a word that means "personal style" in Hindi, is a new brand from Hyatt, and this is the second location. Instead of a front desk, "hosts" holding computer pads in the lounge check you into your room and also act as concierge. In fact, the whole ground floor is one open space with lots of natural light—a striking difference from the dark Hyatt interior. Guest rooms are pretty minimalist in decor, but comfortable; half have views of the Strip (with blackout shades to deal with the flashing lights at night), along with small "sunrooms" where the balconies used to be (no more throwing TVs, you rock stars). The other half face the hillside in the back. *Tip:* On any given day, regardless of the base rate, those facing the Strip are $30 extra, which is definitely worth it for first-time visitors (they are slightly larger, too). If you prefer peace and quiet, save the money and enjoy the more serene view of the hills. Complimentary snacks and nonalcoholic drinks are replenished in your minibar daily, a bonus after a dehydrating night at the clubs. There's a nice pool on the roof with giant round loungers that are first-come, first-served. The restaurant, **RH,** has a stunning open kitchen where chefs prepare Cal-French fare with a seasonal slant.

8401 Sunset Blvd., West Hollywood, CA 90069. http://westhollywood.andaz.hyatt.com. © **323/656-1234.** Fax 323/650-7024. 257 units. $300–$325 double; from $445–$470 suite. AE, DC, MC, V. Valet parking $32. **Amenities:** Restaurant; lounge; concierge; well-equipped exercise room; rooftop pool; room service. *In room:* A/C, TV, hair dryer, minibar, MP3 docking station, free Wi-Fi.

Avalon Hotel ★ 🛏 The first style-conscious boutique hotel on the L.A. scene, this mid-20th-century-inspired gem is located in the heart of Beverly Hills. With a soothing sherbet-hued palette and classic atomic-age furnishings—Eames cabinets, Heywood-Wakefield chairs, Nelson bubble lamps—mixed with smart custom designs, every room looks as if it could star in a *Metropolitan Home* photo spread. But fashion doesn't forsake function at this beautifully designed hotel, which offers enough luxury comforts and amenities to please design-blind travelers, too. The main building is the hub of a chic but low-key scene, but the quieter Canon building features rooms with kitchenettes and/or furnished terraces. No matter where you end up, you'll have easy access to the sunny courtyard, with its retro-hip, amoeba-shaped pool; the fitness room; and **Oliverio,** the groovy, blue-hued Italian restaurant and bar with a contemporary '50s vibe. Service is friendlier than you'll find in other style-minded hotels. *Note:* If you're a light sleeper, request a room away from the pool area, where the occasional nighttime pool party can get loud.

9400 W. Olympic Blvd. (at Beverly Dr.), Beverly Hills, CA 90212. www.avalonbeverlyhills.com. © **800/670-6183** or 310/277-5221. Fax 310/277-4928. 84 units. $248–$400 double; from $400 1-bedroom suite. AE, DC, MC, V. Valet parking $30. **Amenities:** Restaurant; lounge; courtyard pool; room service; Wi-Fi (free, in lobby). *In room:* A/C, TV/DVD, hair dryer, minibar, Wi-Fi ($11 per day).

The Beverly Hilton ★ If you're a fan of awards shows, you'll probably recognize this hotel as the annual home of the star-studded Golden Globe Awards. In the heart of Beverly Hills, this boxlike eight-story hotel has been attracting city business travelers, movie stars, U.S. presidents, royalty, and tourists alike since 1955. It was previously owned by Merv Griffin, who didn't put much into renovations (and it showed), but now the Beverly Hills–based Hilton Corporation has upgraded the entire interior of the hotel as part of an $80-million renovation. All guest rooms have been completely redesigned with a contemporary casual feel and loads of luxury amenities, like 42-inch plasma TVs, Bose Wave Radios, and even 13-inch flatscreen TVs in the bathroom. Many have balconies that offer views of Century City, Beverly Hills, and the Hollywood Hills. During the summer, the ground-level poolside cabana rooms are a good choice—the alluring pool area alone is worth staying here—thanks to sliding doors that open directly onto the sun deck. On the pool level, it's hard to beat the nostalgia of a pupu platter and Scorpion Bowl at the tiki-fied **Trader Vic's Lounge,** and the retro-chic **Circa 55** restaurant is a visual stunner. Other new additions include a huge state-of-the-art fitness room, and the serene **Aqua Star Spa** offering treatments for both men and women.

9876 Wilshire Blvd. (at Santa Monica Blvd.), Beverly Hills, CA 90210. www.beverlyhilton.com. ℂ **800/445-8667** or 310/274-7777. Fax 310/285-1313. 570 units. $265–$395 double; from $425 suite. AE, DC, DISC, MC, V. Valet & self-parking $36. Pets 20 lb. and under accepted ($25 cleaning fee). **Amenities:** 2 restaurants; 3 lounges; concierge; well-equipped exercise room; large heated outdoor pool; room service; full-service spa; Wi-Fi (free, in lobby). *In room:* A/C, TV/VCR, hair dryer, minibar, High-speed internet ($15 per day).

London West Hollywood ★★   This all-suites hotel reopened in 2008 (it used to be the Bel Age) and now combines English charm with California sensibility. The decor is smart and sexy, with lots of marble and glamour in the lobby, clean lines in all 200 suites, and a rooftop pool with sweeping views of Los Angeles. It's fitting for the off-the-Strip location, literally walking distance from famed clubs like the Viper Room and Key Club. Just so you don't forget it's the London, English touches include an English bulldog that sits in the lobby on the weekends and free calls to London, England (with a $1 connection charge). The spacious suites are well designed with sleek furniture (embossed leather upholstery, bleached oak finishes, hand-cut mosaic tiles), and all have some sort of balcony—second-floor suites have full-on patios. The rooftop pool area is reminiscent of an English garden, with topiaries and AstroTurf, plus a lounge area for snacks or lunch; there's also an outdoor seasonal workout and yoga area. The restaurants, from famed London and *Hell's Kitchen* chef Gordon Ramsay, are hit or miss.

1020 N. San Vicente Blvd., West Hollywood, CA 90069. www.thelondonwesthollywood.com. ℂ **866/282-4560** or 310/854-1111. Fax 310/358-7791. 200 units. $309–$609 suites. AE, DC, DISC, MC, V. Valet parking $32. **Amenities:** 2 restaurants; bar; concierge; exercise room; rooftop pool; room service. *In room:* A/C, TV, hair dryer, minibar, free Wi-Fi.

Luxe Hotel Sunset Boulevard ★   Hidden away just a stone's throw from the Getty Center and busy I-405, this low-rise hotel is composed of two levels: The lobby and public areas—plus some rooms—are in the main building, while the most secluded guest rooms (and the Romanesque swimming pool) are uphill on the Garden level. Guest rooms are huge and come with stylish custom furnishings, flatscreen TVs, an iPod base station, and a feather comforter; most have a large balcony or patio. This Luxe appeals equally to business clientele, who appreciate the extensive amenities, and to leisure travelers, who can relax in the open, green setting. A free shuttle lets guests avoid the parking hassles at the Getty Center. The hotel is popular for wedding receptions on weekends, and the spa (sans hair salon) attracts a sizable local clientele, so be prepared for lots of lobby traffic. Still, the overall ambience is very relaxing.

11461 Sunset Blvd. (just east of I-405), Los Angeles, CA 90049. www.luxehotelsunsetblvd.com. ℂ **800/468-3541** or 310/476-6571. Fax 310/471-6310. 161 units. $269–$299 double; $329–$550 suite. Extra person $25. AE, DC, DISC, MC, V. Valet parking $25. **Amenities:** Restaurant; cocktail and piano lounge; concierge; exercise room; outdoor heated pool; spa; tennis court. *In room:* A/C, TV, hair dryer, minibar, MP3 docking station, free Wi-Fi.

The Mosaic Hotel Beverly Hills ★★★ 🏨 The owners pumped in $3 million to overhaul the former Beverly Hills Inn, and the result is spectacular. The lobby is a showcase of functional art, with gleaming tile mosaics; fabrics in deep, rich tones; and a profusion of artfully arranged orchids. Continuing a trend I fully support, a wall has been removed to allow direct access from the check-in desk to the bar and lounge for a Mosaic sake martini. The guest rooms are equally impressive, all done in soothing earth tones with 300-count linens, goose-down comforters and piles of pillows, windows that open onto the quiet neighborhood street or garden courtyard, and minibars stocked with Wolfgang Puck snacks and libations. Other perks include free Wi-Fi, poolside cabanas, and CD players, late room service from the hotel's small restaurant, and a fitness room. *Tip:* If you like to have extra space, the "preferred" corner rooms are worth the extra $50 (you get an extra 50 sq. ft.).

125 Spalding Dr., Beverly Hills, CA 90212. www.mosaichotel.com. © **800/463-4466** or 310/278-0303. Fax 310/278-1728. 49 units. From $350 double; from $700 2-bedroom suite. AE, DC, MC, V. Parking $30. Small pets accepted. **Amenities:** Restaurant; bar; exercise room; heated outdoor pool; room service; sauna. *In room:* A/C, TV, DVD upon request only, CD player, fridge, hair dryer, free Wi-Fi.

Petit Ermitage ★★★ If being surrounded by beautiful young things who may or may not be celebrities while being coddled in a luxurious, relaxed atmosphere is on your agenda, then I've found your new favorite stamping grounds. Nestled on a quiet street in the heart of West Hollywood between Sunset and Santa Monica boulevards, the unassuming, all-suite Petit Ermitage features the owners' impressive personal art collection throughout, hand-painted walls, working fireplaces with handcrafted mantels, 618-thread-count Egyptian-cotton sheets, and globally sourced furnishings. Custom is the name of the game—from the signature soundtrack that plays on the antique gramophone in the lobby and the signature scent wafting throughout the property, to the signature Thermopedic L'Ermitage mattresses in each suite. For an additional $150 to $200, your can opt for a Masters Quarters Suite. Attended by a personal butler, aka "The Liaison to Happiness." *Tip:* This must be booked directly through the hotel, as there's often no availability on the fourth floor, where such rooms are located. Rates are rack only.

The *pièce de résistance* is the hotel's private rooftop club. Fashioned after a private salon, with 360-degree views of the Hollywood Hills, it boasts a heated saltwater pool, Masters Lounge, cabanas, a sunken outdoor living room—complete with cozy couches, fur blankets, and fireplace—and the Butterfly Bar (it's actually a registered hummingbird and butterfly sanctuary). The main dining space in the Hotel and Club features fresh, exotically spiced fare served in a garden setting lush with fragrant blooms and kumquat trees.

8822 Cynthia St., West Hollywood, CA 90069. www.petitermitage.com. © **310/854-1114.** Fax 310/657-2623. 80 suites. $241–$470 suites. AE, DISC, MC, V. Valet parking $30. **Amenities:** Restaurant; private rooftop club w/heated saltwater pool; bar; indoor/outdoor lounge spaces; exercise room; room service. *In room:* TV/ /DVD, hair dryer, minibar, MP3 docking station, free Wi-Fi, custom terry slippers and robes.

W Los Angeles ★★ Design-savvy hipsters looking for cutting-edge style and familiar comforts will enjoy this 15-story, all-suite hotel near UCLA. Hidden behind a severe concrete exterior, this oasis-like property has always had advantages: an all-suite configuration, 2 lush acres of greenery, and eye-catching '60s architectural detailing that's been liberated from its long-standing Sheetrock walls. Rooms range from large two-room suites to two-bed, two-bathroom suites, featuring bold, angular furnishings. The W brand is constantly upgrading its amenities to stay current with new trends and developing technologies. Luxuries include divinely dressed beds, 42-inch plasma screen TVs—and DVD players. The **NineThirty** restaurant serves New American cuisine, while nightlife impresario Rande Gerber's bar, **Whiskey Blue,** still packs locals trendsters in on weekend nights. The well-furnished, garden-like pool area has its own outdoor cafe called the **Backyard,** serving Mediterranean "swimwear fare." The 7,000-square-foot **Bliss Spa** offers hip services like movie-while-you-manicure nail stations and men's and women's lounges that offer snacks to the road-weary.

930 Hilgard Ave., Los Angeles, CA 90024. www.whotels.com. © **877/W-HOTELS** (946-8357) or 310/208-8765. Fax 310/824-0355. 258 units. From $389 1- or 2-bedroom suite. AE, DC, DISC, MC, V. Valet parking $35. Pets under 40 lb. accepted ($25 per night, plus a $100 cleaning fee). **Amenities:** 2 restaurants; lounge; babysitting; concierge; exercise room; outdoor heated pool; room service; spa; Wi-Fi (free, in lobby). *In room:* A/C, TV/DVD, hair dryer, minibar, Wi-Fi ($15 per day), iPod docking stations.

Moderate

Carlyle Inn ★★ 🏆   On an uneventful stretch of Robertson Boulevard just south of Beverly Hills, this four-story inn is one of L.A.'s best midpriced finds. Making the most of a small lot, architects have created an attractive interior courtyard, which almost every room faces, that gives the property a feeling of openness and serenity that most others in this price range lack—not to mention good outdoor space for enjoying the free breakfast at umbrella-covered cafe tables on nice days. The well-planned, contemporary guest rooms are fitted with recessed lighting, quality furnishings, firm bedding, and bathrobes. Suites have pullout sofas but are only slightly larger than standard rooms, so families may be better off in a double/double or connecting rooms. The conscientious manager keeps everything in racing form. The hotel's primary drawback is that it lacks views; curtains must remain drawn at all times to maintain any sense of privacy. Still, it doesn't seem to bother the 90% repeat visitors, who know good value when they find it.

1119 S. Robertson Blvd. (btw. Pico and Olympic boulevards), Los Angeles, CA 90035. www.carlyle-inn. com. © **800/322-7595** or 310/275-4445. Fax 310/859-0496. 32 units. From $199 double; from $229 suite. Rates include buffet breakfast. AE, DC, DISC, MC, V. Parking $11. **Amenities:** Small exercise room; Jacuzzi. *In room:* A/C, TV, hair dryer, minibar, free Wi-Fi).

Chamberlain West Hollywood ★   This four-story boutique hotel in a tree-lined, residential West Hollywood neighborhood looks and feels much like a high-quality Manhattan apartment building (probably because it used to be an apartment building). The location alone is reason enough to stay here, as it's only 2 blocks from the Sunset Strip and Santa Monica Boulevard. If you're young and hip and have plenty of room on your credit card, you won't need your car once it's parked in the underground garage (hell, you won't even need comfortable shoes). If you've been to the Viceroy in Santa Monica, you'll recognize the English Modern decor—dusky grays, greens, and blues among stark white furnishings. Each guest room is a suite with a separate living and sleeping area, and comes pleasantly equipped with a plush king-size bed with Sferra sheets, gas-log fireplace, small balcony, flatscreen TV, DVD/VCR combo, CD player, and large desk. The rooftop pool and cabana are ideal for sunbathing, and the roof has a great view of the city. The small restaurant and bar are good for meeting friends for a drink and appetizers before you hit the town (though I suggest you have dinner elsewhere).

1000 Westmount Dr. (1 block west of La Cienega Blvd.), West Hollywood, CA 90069. www.chamberlain westhollywood.com. © **800/201-9652** or 310/657-7400. Fax 310/854-6744. 114 units. $249–$369 deluxe to 1-bedroom suite. AE, DC, DISC, MC, V. Valet parking $30. **Amenities:** Concierge; newly expanded fitness center; heated rooftop pool; 24-hr. room service; Wi-Fi (free, in lobby). *In room:* A/C, TV/DVD, CD player, hair dryer, Wi-Fi ($11 per day), iHome clock radio/dock station.

Élan Hotel ★ 🏨 The Élan is truly a find: It's not only one of L.A.'s best boutique-style hotels, it's one of the city's best values as well. Rebuilt and freshly renovated from the bones of a 1969 retirement home, the modern structure blends elements from the original facade with a modern, sophisticated decor. Inside, a mod, loungey lobby leads to handsomely appointed guest rooms done in serene earth tones. The design merges form and function beautifully, resulting in amenity-laden and surprisingly luxurious accommodations, considering the price. The standard rooms aren't huge, but high ceilings and thoughtfully designed custom furnishings create the illusion of space, while plush, textured fabrics, beautifully made beds—with cushioned headboards, goose-down comforters, and -high-quality cotton linens—bathrooms with cotton robes, and plush towels elevate comforts well beyond the moderate price point. On the downside, there's no view, no pool, no fitness center (although you can purchase a $14 pass to the nearby health club), no restaurant, and this stretch of Beverly Boulevard isn't exactly the hippest strip in town. But double-pane glass ensures that even boulevard-facing rooms are quiet, and the location in central L.A. is ideal (shoppers will love the walking-distance proximity to the Beverly Center).

8435 Beverly Blvd. (btw. La Cienega Blvd. and Fairfax Ave.), Los Angeles, CA 90048. www.elanhotel. com. ✆ **866/203-2212** or 323/658-6663. Fax 323/658-6640. 49 units. From $189 double. Rates include continental breakfast and evening wine and cheese reception. AE, DC, DISC, MC, V. Valet parking $19 plus tax. **Amenities:** Access to nearby health club ($14). *In room:* A/C, TV, hair dryer, minibar, free Wi-Fi.

Hotel Angeleno Los Angeles ★ This L.A. landmark building is the last of a vanishing breed of circular hotels from the 1960s and 1970s. Formerly a Holiday Inn, it was revamped into a hip, modern destination. The location alone is a good reason to stay here: It's perched beside the city's busiest freeway, a short hop from the popular Getty Center and centrally located in the middle of the beaches, Beverly Hills, and the San Fernando Valley. Each pie-shaped room comes with a private balcony and double-pane glass to keep most of the freeway din at bay—think of it as complimentary white noise—while comfort comes in the form of 300-count Italian linens, feather duvets, and pillow-top mattresses. Little extras like 30-inch plasma TVs, free Wi-Fi, ergonomic workstations, and great views add to the panache. Also a hot spot is the 17-story hotel's penthouse-level **West** supper club and cocktail lounge, is an Italian steakhouse. Additional perks include an outdoor pool with cabanas and a fire pit, a lobby-level cafe, and complimentary pickup and drop-off service to the Getty Center, UCLA, and Westwood. *Tip:* There are only three suites in the hotel, and they must be booked directly; they are not listed on the website.

170 N. Church Lane (at intersection of Sunset Blvd. and I-405), Los Angeles, CA 90049. www.hotel angeleno.com. ✆ **866/ANGELENO** (264-3536) or 310/476-6411. Fax 310/472-1157. 208 units. $179–$209 double; from $249 suite. Rates include evening wine reception. AE, DC, DISC, MC, V. Valet parking free for 1 car; additional vehicles are $20 each. **Amenities:** Rooftop restaurant and lounge; lobby cafe; concierge; exercise room; heated outdoor pool; room service. *In room:* A/C, TV, hair dryer, minibar, free Wi-Fi.

Le Montrose Suite Hotel ★★ 🍴 Nobody pays rack at this terrific all-suite hotel, which offers money-saving specials of every stripe for travelers who want more than a standard room for their accommodations dollars. On a quiet street just 2 blocks from the red-hot Sunset Strip, cozy Le Montrose features large split-level studio and one-bedroom apartments that feel more like comfortable, upscale condos than hotel rooms. Each contemporary-style suite has a sizable living room with gas fireplace, dining area, comfortable sleeping nook (or dedicated bedroom), and very nice bathroom. Executive and one-bedroom suites have kitchenettes (which can be stocked upon request). The two bedrooms are a great deal for families or sharing friends. You have to go up to the roof for anything resembling a view, but once you're up there, you can swim in the saltwater pool, soak in the Jacuzzi, or brush up on your tennis game. There's a fitness center on the fifth floor and the **Privato** restaurant, lounge, and wine bar. This place is a favorite for long-term stays among the music and film crowd, so don't be surprised if you spot a famous face in the hotel's private restaurant during the breakfast hour (open to hotel guests only).

900 Hammond St., West Hollywood, CA 90069. www.lemontrose.com. (© **800/776-0666** or 310/855-1115. Fax 310/657-9192. 133 units. $249–$499 suite. AE, DC, DISC, MC, V. Valet and self-parking $32. Pets accepted ($100 per pet). **Amenities:** Restaurant; 2 bikes; exercise room; Jacuzzi; outdoor heated pool; room service; sauna; tennis court (lit for night play). *In room:* A/C, TV/ /DVD, CD player, hair dryer, minibar, free Wi-Fi, iPod docking station.

Le Parc Suite Hotel ★★   On a quiet, tree-lined residential street, Le Parc is a sophisticated and stylish all-suite hotel that attracts an interesting mix of clientele: Designers stay here because it's a few minutes' walk to the Pacific Design Center; celebrities in the music industry stay because of its low-key neighborhood location; patients and medical consultants check in because it's close to Cedars-Sinai; and tourists enjoy being near the Farmers Market, the Beverly Center, and Museum Row. The renovated apartment-like units are extra large, and they all have a well-outfitted kitchenette, a dining area, a living room with a fireplace, and a balcony. What the hotel lacks in views it makes up for in value and elbowroom, and the rooftop night-lit tennis court is a rare perk in this area. The hotel's intimate bistro-style restaurant, **Knoll** offers contemporary American cuisine and romantic alfresco seating at the rooftop dining area. *Tip:* Ask about tour and bed-and-breakfast packages.

733 N. West Knoll Dr., West Hollywood, CA 90069. www.leparcsuites.com. (© **800/578-4837** or 310/855-8888. Fax 310/659-7812. 154 units. $279–$409 junior or 1-bedroom suite. AE, DC, DISC, MC, V. Parking $30. Pets accepted ($75). **Amenities:** Restaurant w/full bar; concierge; well-equipped exercise room; access to nearby health club; Jacuzzi; outdoor heated pool; room service; sauna; rooftop tennis court (lit for night play). *In room:* A/C, TV/DVD, CD player, hair dryer, kitchenette, minibar, free Wi-Fi.

The Orlando ★   Not only is the Orlando situated between Beverly Hills and West Hollywood, it's also within walking distance of the Grove, the Farmers Market, the Beverly Center, and Restaurant Row (is your credit card sweating yet?). Billed as a European-style boutique hotel, the Orlando has a modern, chic look with custom furnishings and cool color schemes of browns, burnt oranges, and light tans. The large guest rooms are comfortably equipped with 30-inch plasma TVs, iPod docking stations, and beds with 400-thread-count Egyptian-cotton sheets, but you'll probably spend most of your time at the rooftop deck, floating beneath sunny blue skies in the saltwater pool. If you're in a splurging mood, request one of the newly created Hollywood Premium rooms, spacious Executive Garden room with a big ol' king-size bed, personal iPod with surround-sound Bose speakers, and a private patio. There's an onsite Italian restaurant called **Minestraio.**

8384 W. 3rd St. (at Orlando St.), Los Angeles, CA 90048. www.theorlando.com. (© **800/62-HOTEL** (624-6835) or 323/658-6600. Fax 323/653-3464. 98 units. From $189 standard rooms; from $410 executive rooms. AE, DC, DISC, MC, V. Valet parking $29. Pets accepted ($50 per night fee). **Amenities:** Restaurant; bar; exercise room; heated saltwater pool; room service. *In room:* A/C, TV w/On Demand, CD player, hair dryer, minibar, free Wi-Fi, iPod docking station, DVD/iPods available for rental.

The Standard, Hollywood ★ Designed to appeal to the under-35 "it" crowd, André Balazs's swank West Hollywood neo-motel is sometimes absurd, sometimes brilliant, and always provocative (not to mention crowded!). It's a scene worthy of its Sunset Strip location: shag carpeting on the lobby ceiling, blue AstroTurf around the swimming pool, a DJ spinning ambient sounds while a performance artist showing more skin than talent poses in a display case behind the check-in desk—this place is definitely left of center. But look past the retro clutter and often-raucous party scene, and you'll find a level of service more often associated with hotels costing twice as much. Constructed from the bones of a vintage 1964 motel, it boasts comfortably sized rooms outfitted with cobalt blue indoor-outdoor carpeting, silver beanbag chairs, and Warhol's poppy-print curtains, plus private balconies, and minibars whose contents include goodies like sake, condoms, and animal crackers. On the downside, the cheapest rooms face noisy Sunset Boulevard, and the relentless scene can get tiring if you're not into it. *Note:* The 12-story **Downtown Standard,** 550 S. Flower St. (© **213/892-8080**), brings a similar dose of retro-future style and cool attitude to Downtown. It's worth visiting just to check out the retro-glam rooftop bar with its vibrating water-bed pleasure pods, movies projected onto neighboring buildings, and hot waitstaff.

8300 Sunset Blvd. (at Sweetzer Ave.), West Hollywood, CA 90069. www.standardhotel.com. © **323/650-9090.** Fax 323/650-2820. 139 units. $199–$230 double; from $350 suite. AE, DC, DISC, MC, V. Valet parking $29. Pets 20 lb. and under accepted ($100 per pet). **Amenities:** 24-hr. coffee shop; poolside cafe; bar/lounge; concierge; access to nearby health club ($16 per day); outdoor heated pool; room service. *In room:* A/C, TV/DVD, minibar, free Wi-Fi, iPod docking station.

Inexpensive

Beverly Laurel Motor Hotel ⬧ The Beverly Laurel is a great choice for wallet-watching travelers who want a central location and a room with more style than your average motel. Overlooking the parking lot, the budget-basic but well-kept rooms are smartened up with diamond-print spreads and eye-catching artwork; other features include a minifridge, microwave, and ample closet space, and a large kitchenette for an extra 55 bucks. The postage-stamp-size outdoor pool is a little public for carefree sunbathing, but it does the job on hot summer days. Best of all is the motel's own excellent coffee shop, **Swingers** (p. 118)—known for its burgers and malts, and you may even spot your favorite alt-rocker tucking into a 3pm breakfast in the vinyl booth next to yours.

8018 Beverly Blvd. (btw. La Cienega Blvd. and Fairfax Ave.), Los Angeles, CA 90048. © **800/962-3824** (outside CA) or 323/651-2441. Fax 323/651-5225. 52 units. $109–$165 double. AE, DC, MC, V. Free parking. **Amenities:** Outdoor pool. *In room:* A/C, TV, fridge, hair dryer, Wi-Fi ($5.95 per day).

Farmer's Daughter ⬧ Most people end up at the Farmer's Daughter hotel fortuitously because they're waiting to be the next contestants on *The Price Is Right*. The CBS Studios across the street recommends the budget motel to its game show fans, but I recommend it just because I dig this chic little lodge. It's cheery from the moment you walk in the lobby. Bright yellows and cool blues mix well with the country-kitsch theme: rooster wallpaper, faded barn-wood paneling, denim bedspreads, cow-skin rugs, and a parade of inflatable animals that float around the pool. It's obvious that someone with smart fashion sense and a little money turned a dumpy motel into an oasis of stylish affordability. It's also obvious that someone with a good sense of humor was behind the "No Tell" room, which is outfitted with a giant copper-framed mirror above the bed. Money-saving perks include a free DVD library and across-the-street access to an entire farmers' market of inexpensive foodstuffs (p. 137). It is irksome, however, that you have to fork over $20 for a valet to pull your car into a spot that is probably right in front of your room. Since the hotel opened its own comfort food restaurant, **TART,** there's the option of staying in, though in my opinion, it would be a great loss to miss the people-watching and dining experience unique to the iconic Farmers Market. *Tip:* Request a room facing the alley—the view is terrible, but you don't get the 24-hour road noise off Fairfax Avenue.

115 S. Fairfax Ave. (btw. Beverly Dr. and 3rd St.), Los Angeles, CA 90036. www.farmersdaughterhotel. com. © **800/334-1658** or 323/937-3930. Fax 323/932-1608. 66 units. $219 double; from $269 suite. AE, DISC, MC, V. Valet parking $18 plus tax. **Amenities:** Restaurant; bar; morning coffee and tea service; outdoor pool. *In room:* A/C, TV/DVD, movie library, CD player, fridge, free Wi-Fi.

HOLLYWOOD

The geographical area called Hollywood is actually smaller and less glamorous than you might expect. In fact, throughout most of the 1980s and 1990s, Hollywood was pretty much a shambles. But the neighborhood has undergone a major overhaul of late—along the lines of the reinvention of New York City's Times Square—that has turned the seedy area back into tourism central. It's also where many of the hippest clubs in the city are found. The re-gentrification is ongoing, but I still don't recommend heading down dark alleys on moonless nights. That said, Hollywood is definitely cleaner and safer than it has been in decades. What's more, several hotels below are great for travelers looking for good midpriced and budget lodging, and families will like the easy freeway access to Universal Studios. Still, those with an aversion to tourist traps should book elsewhere.

Expensive

The Redbury ★ A smaller sister property to the SLS, the spacious rooms at this stylish Hollywood & Vine boutique hotel feel more like a hipster friend's loft. Owned by lifestyle-curating entertainment company SBE, subtle this is not, from its striking crimson red exterior to its iconic hallway imagery of early Hollywood film vixens like Jean Harlow to the "opa!" Greek-style plate-breaking at Mediterranean eatery **Cleo.** This is not to say its style over substance; in fact, the rooms are quite spacious and feature lots of thoughtful touches like easy-to-operate, single-cup coffeemakers with to-go cups (including lids!); a combo washer/dryer in each unit; and record players with a section of 45s ranging from John Coltrane to Daft Punk. With the smallest "flat" starting at 750 sq. ft., the room is more luxurious than most affordable New York apartments. The only surprise was the lack of a happening nightlife scene; the only bar here is at the restaurant.

1717 Vine St., Hollywood, CA 90028. www.theredbury.com. © **877/962-1717** or 323/962-1717. Fax 323/962-1710. 57 units. From $339–$739. AE, DISC, MC, V. Valet parking $33. **Amenities:** 1 restaurant; 3 bars; free passes to nearby 24[Hr] Fitness; pool privileges at sister property SLS; room service. *In room:* A/C, TV, record player, fridge/minibar, hair dryer, washer/dryer, Wi-Fi ($10 per day).

Renaissance Hollywood Hotel ★ Part of the $615-million Hollywood & Highland project to restore Hollywood to the glory of its heyday, the hotel now serves as Oscar-night headquarters for the frenzy of participants and paparazzi attending the Academy Awards in the Kodak Theatre next door. Despite its high profile, this is principally a convention property and not quite as elite or elegant as the media hype might have you believe. It's also the nicest option in the neighborhood for families, so far as upscale hotels go. Wood-paneled headboards and Technicolor furniture (think *The Jetsons* meets IKEA) paint guest rooms as swinging '50s bachelor pads. Rooms on the seventh floor and up offer truly impressive views: One-third look toward the Pacific Ocean, one-third face the skyline of Downtown L.A., and one-third take in the lush Hollywood Hills (yes, you can see the sign). Sightseeing is virtually unavoidable since the hotel shares the same block as two of the city's most famous landmarks—the Hollywood Walk of Fame and Grauman's Chinese Theatre. The Hollywood Bowl is less than a mile away (check with the concierge about shuttle service), and the subway stops under the hotel complex, offering access to Universal Studios and destinations farther afield.

1755 N. Highland Ave., Hollywood, CA 90028. ℂ **800/769-4774** or 323/856-1200. Fax 323/856-1205. www.renaissancehollywood.com. 637 units. $289 double; $330 executive bedroom; $329 1-bedroom suite. AE, DC, DISC, MC, V. Valet parking $29; self-parking $10. **Amenities:** Restaurant; 2 bars (lobby and poolside); concierge; small exercise room; outdoor pool; room service. *In room:* A/C, TV, hair dryer, minibar, Wi-Fi ($13 per day); iPod docking station.

Roosevelt Hotel, Hollywood ★★ After a $30-million renovation, this venerable, 12-story landmark became *the* place to stay in Hollywood, though lately competition has increased with the openings of the Redbury and the W. But this is the only one of the three with style, exclusivity, models-slash-actresses serving cocktails at the poolside bar, a raucous nightlife scene, *and* history. Host to the first Academy Awards in 1929—not to mention a few famous-name ghosts—this national landmark is Hollywood's only historic hotel still in operation today. Much of the 1927 Spanish-influenced sunken lobby remains the same—the handcrafted columns and dramatic arches are magnificent—but the guest rooms have been completely (and tastefully) renovated with extra-large bathrooms, dark-wood platform beds with luxurious Frette linens, and all the latest high-tech accessories. Rooms on the upper floors have skyline views, while the 60 Rat Pack-style cabana rooms have a balcony or terrace overlooking the Olympic-size pool (whose mural, by the way, was originally painted by David Hockney). The hotel's main restaurant is eclectic **Public Kitchen & Bar** (I loved the diver scallops app, and the steak frites for $19 is a great deal), plus there's also a popular late-night retro-chic burger bar called **25 Degrees.** You'll like the location as well: smack-dab in the touristy section of Hollywood Boulevard, across from Grauman's Chinese Theatre, along the Walk of Fame, and a short cab ride to hot clubs, though there's plenty of nightlife action onsite. The Roosevelt is a playground for the young, hot Hollywood set, with antics from the poolside **Tropicana** bar, **Beacher's Madhouse** theater-like space, and the exclusive **Teddy's** lounge getting as much press as Lindsay Lohan on a bender. **The Spare Room,** playfully named for its two bowling allies, is also popular for board games like Scrabble. For more low-key libations, Library Bar is known for mixology-style cocktails.

7000 Hollywood Blvd., Hollywood, CA 90028. ℂ 800/950-7667 or 323/466-7000. Fax 323/462-8056. www.hollywoodroosevelt.com. 300 units. $231–$339 double; from $299 poolside cabana rooms; from $389 suite. AE, DC, DISC, MC, V. Valet parking $30. Amenities: 2 restaurants; 5 bars; concierge; executive-level rooms; exercise room; Jacuzzi; Olympic-size outdoor pool; 24-hr. room service; spa. In room: A/C, TV/DVD, CD player, hair dryer, minibar, Wi-Fi ($10 per day), iPod docking station.

W Hollywood Hotel ★★ The "It" hotel of 2011 is the W Hollywood, which opened in January 2010 at the corner of Hollywood and Vine and has been the darling of the dig-me crowd ever since. The first and largest LEED-compliant property in L.A., W Hollywood combines eco-conscious construction with stylish design, luxury

Where to Stay in the Hollywood Area

Best Western Hollywood Hills Hotel **5**
Days Inn Hollywood **1**
Magic Castle Hotel **3**
The Redbury **6**
Renaissance Hollywood Hotel **4**
Roosevelt Hotel, Hollywood **2**
W Hollywood Hotel **7**

4

WHERE TO STAY | Hollywood

finishes, dramatic views, and cutting-edge technology (all this for a mere $360 million). All of the W's 305 large studios and one-bedroom suites come with a signature bed with a feather-top mattress, 350-thread-count Egyptian-cotton sheets, and goose down comforter—all the comforts of Caligula—but most of your time will be spent striking a pose at the hotel's signature **Living Room** (essentially a large lobby-cum-lounge); at **Station Hollywood,** an outdoor living room, theater, and lounge (preferred by smokers); at the rooftop pool; at the enormous fitness center; at **Bliss Hollywood,** a 6,075-sq.-ft. full-service spa; or, if you can get in (good luck), at **Drai's Hollywood,** currently the hottest club in Los Angeles. The hotel's signature restaurant is **Delphine,** a 6,000-square-foot indoor/outdoor French bistro and raw bar.

6250 Hollywood Blvd., Hollywood, CA 90028. www.whotels.com/hollywood. ✆ **877/946-8357** or 323/798-1300. 305 units. From $329–$660. AE, DC, DISC, MC, V. Valet parking $35. Pets accepted ($25 per day, with a one-time $100 cleaning fee). **Amenities:** 2 restaurants; 2 lounges; babysitting; concierge; exercise room; outdoor heated pool; room service; spa; Wi-Fi. *In room:* A/C, TV/DVD, CD player, hair dryer, minibar, Wi-Fi ($15 per day).

Inexpensive

Best Western Hollywood Hills Hotel Location is a big selling point for this family-owned (since 1948) member of the reliable Best Western chain: It's just off

U.S. 101 (the Hollywood Fwy.); a Metro Line stop just 3 blocks away means easy, car-free access to Universal Studios; and the famed Hollywood and Vine intersection is just a 5-minute walk away. The entire hotel has been recently renovated in a contemporary style, and all the spiffy guest rooms come with a refrigerator, coffeemaker, microwave, and free Wi-Fi; further renovations to the lobby and exterior began in August 2010 and expect to be completed by January 2011. The rooms in the back building are my favorites, as they sit well back from busy Franklin Avenue, face the gleaming blue-tiled, heated outdoor pool, and have an attractive view of the neighboring hillside. A major convenience is the **101 Hills Coffee Shop,** located off the lower lobby.

6141 Franklin Ave. (btw. Vine and Gower sts.), Hollywood, CA 90028. www.bestwestern.com/hollywood hillshotel. ✆ **800/287-1700** or 323/464-5181. Fax 323/962-0536. 80 units. $169–$199 double. AE, DISC, MC, V. Valet parking $5. Pets accepted ($75 per night). **Amenities:** Coffee shop; heated outdoor pool. *In room:* A/C, cable TV w/HBO, fridge, hair dryer, free Wi-Fi.

Days Inn Hollywood   While it's east of the prime Sunset Strip action, this renovated motel is safe and convenient, and extras like free underground parking and continental breakfast make it an especially good value. Doubles are large enough for families. Some rooms have microwaves, fridges, and coffeemakers; if yours doesn't have a hair dryer or an iron, they're available at the front desk. For maximum bang for your buck, ask for a room overlooking the pool. *Tip:* Ask about AAA, AARP, and other discounted rates (usually they will save you about 10%).

7023 Sunset Blvd. (btw. Highland and La Brea aves.), Hollywood, CA 90028. www.daysinn.com. ✆ **800/329-7466** or 323/464-8344. Fax 323/461-6196. 66 units. $75–$129 double; from $130 for the 1 Jacuzzi suite. Rates include continental breakfast. AE, DC, DISC, MC, V. Free secured parking. **Amenities:** Restaurant; outdoor pool. *In room:* A/C, TV, free Wi-Fi.

Magic Castle Hotel ★ ☺ 🔥   Located a stone's throw from Hollywood Boulevard's attractions, this garden-style hotel/motel at the base of the Hollywood Hills offers L.A.'s best cheap sleeps and is ideal for wallet-watching families or long-term stays. You won't see the Magic Castle Hotel in *Travel + Leisure* anytime soon, but the units are spacious, comfortable, and well kept. Named for the Magic Castle, the illusionist club just uphill, the hotel was once an apartment building; it still feels private and insulated from Franklin Avenue's constant stream of traffic. The units are situated around a central swimming pool. Most are large apartments with fully equipped kitchens complete with a microwave and coffeemaker (grocery shopping service is available as well).

7025 Franklin Ave. (btw. La Brea and Highland aves.), Hollywood, CA 90028. www.magiccastlehotel. com. ✆ **800/741-4915** or 323/851-0800. Fax 323/851-4926. 40 units. $174 double; $214–$314 suite. Rates include continental breakfast. AE, DC, DISC, MC, V. Parking $10. **Amenities:** Outdoor heated pool. *In room:* A/C, cable TV w/HBO, DVD player w/free movie rentals, CD/stereo, hair dryer, free Wi-Fi.

DOWNTOWN

Traditionally the domain of business folk and convention attendees, Downtown L.A. is becoming increasingly attractive to leisure travelers for several reasons: a Rudy Giuliani–style cleanup in the late 1990s; a growing number of cultural attractions, destination dining and great cocktail bars; value weekend packages at hotels that empty out once the workweek ends; and easy, car-free access via the Metro Line to Hollywood and Universal Studios. Every freeway passes through Downtown, so it's a breeze to hop in the car and head off to other neighborhoods (except during weekday

Where to Stay in the Downtown Area

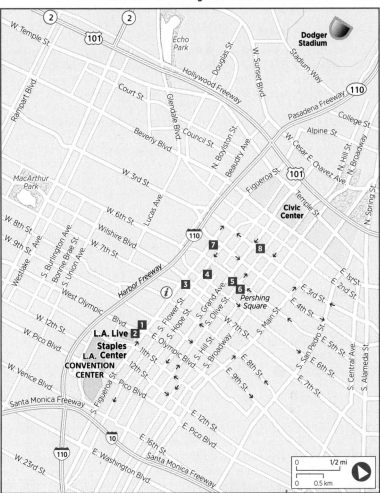

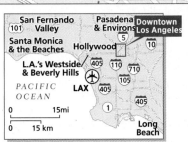

Downtown Standard **4**

Figueroa Hotel **1**

Hilton Checkers Los Angeles **6**

JW Marriott Hotel Los Angeles **2**

Millenium Biltmore Hotel Los Angeles **5**

Omni Los Angeles **8**

The Ritz Carlton, Los Angeles **2**

Westin Bonaventure **7**

Wilshire Grand Los Angeles **3**

rush hour, that is). Consider yourself forewarned, however: Despite the low weekend rates, Downtown L.A. can feel like a ghost town compared to Venice Beach or West Hollywood, particularly after sundown (especially if you're not one for barhopping).

Very Expensive

The Ritz-Carlton Los Angeles ★★★   Opened in February 2010, the Ritz is notable because of its location next to L.A. LIVE, a vast entertainment complex that includes the Staples Center, the Nokia Theatre, and more than a dozen restaurants, in a newly gentrified area of Downtown L.A. The Ritz comprises floors 22 to 26 of a property that it actually shares with the JW Marriott, which represents the high-end branch of the Marriott chain. The hotel is the epitome of luxury, with sleek furnishings, professional service, and lush amenities, like a heated rooftop pool with panoramic views, a sexy Asian-fusion restaurant by Wolfgang Puck, **WP 24;** and an impressive spa and state-of-the-art fitness center. Guest rooms are modern, comfortable and tech-saavy—check out the cool mini TV inside the bathroom mirror! Beds are firm and outfitted with 400-thread count linens. *Note:* Though the two hotels are attached, the entrances and lobbies are separate; for the Ritz, enter on Georgia Street at Olympic Boulevard.

900 W. Olympic Blvd., Los Angeles, CA 90015. www.figueroahotel.com. ℂ **888/275-8063** or 213/743-8800. Fax 213/743-8801. 123 units. From $299 double; from $409 suite. AE, DC, MC, V. Valet parking $40. **Amenities:** 1 restaurant and lounge; concierge and club level; fitness center and spa; heated outdoor pool; room service. *In room:* TV/DVD, small fridge and minibar, Wi-Fi ($13 per day).

Expensive/Moderate

How much you pay at any of the following hotels largely depends on when you come. Some become quite affordable once the business travelers go home; others even offer good-value weekday rates to leisure travelers during periods when rooms would otherwise sit vacant.

Figueroa Hotel ★ 👜   With an artistic eye and a heartfelt commitment to creating exotic, whimsical, and oh-so-anti-corporate-style accommodations, charming owner Uno Thimansson has transformed a 1925-vintage former YWCA residence into one of L.A.'s best moderately priced hotels, and a top pick for affordable Downtown lodging. This venerable 12-story property sits in an increasingly gentrified corner of Downtown, within shouting distance of the L.A. LIVE entertainment complex. The big, airy lobby exudes a romantic Spanish Colonial–Gothic vibe with beamed ceilings and fans, Moroccan chandeliers, soaring columns, tile flooring, and medieval-style furnishings such as big floor pillows made of Kurdish grain sacks, Persian kilims, and exotic fabrics draped from the ceiling. Elevators lead to equally artistic guest rooms that, although poorly lit, are very comfortable. Each comes with a firm, well-made bed with a wrought-iron headboard or canopy and a Georgia O'Keeffe–reminiscent spread, a Mexican-tiled bathroom, and East Asian fabrics that double as blackout drapes. The Casablanca Suite is a Moroccan pleasure den, ideal for romance. Out back you'll find a desert-garden deck with a mosaic-tiled pool and Jacuzzi, and the Verandah Bar, the poolside place to go on warm Southern California nights for a minty mojito and a chat with fellow travelers from around the world.

939 S. Figueroa St. (at Olympic Blvd.), Los Angeles, CA 90015. www.figueroahotel.com. ℂ **800/421-9092** or 213/627-8971. Fax 213/689-0305. 265 units. $164 double; $225–$265 suite. AE, DC, MC, V. Parking $12. **Amenities:** Restaurant; bar; Jacuzzi; outdoor pool. *In room:* A/C, TV, fridge, Wi-Fi ($5 per day).

Hilton Checkers Los Angeles ★ The atmosphere here is as removed from "Hollywood" as an L.A. hotel can get. Built in 1927, the 12-story hotel is a Historic Cultural Monument. Plenty of polished brass complements the neutral sand-colored decor; both accentuate the impressive architectural features that have remained intact during major renovations. Checkers is a European-style hotel, without a lot of flashy amenities and possessing an understated luxury. Rooms are equipped with 42-inch flatscreen TVs, ergonomic workstations, and spacious marble-floored bathrooms. Public areas include a wood-paneled library, a rooftop lap pool, and serene corridors punctuated with Asian antiques. The spa offers everything from aromatherapy body wraps to couples' massage sessions. **Checkers Restaurant** is fine for meals if business keeps you on-property, but otherwise I suggest exploring downtown's impressive array of dining options instead. *Tip:* Be sure to check the website for specials.

535 S. Grand Ave. (btw. 5th and 6th sts.), Los Angeles, CA 90071. www.hiltoncheckers.com. © **800/ HILTONS** (445-8667) or 213/624-0000. Fax 213/626-9906. 188 units. $219–$299 double; from $520 suite. AE, DC, DISC, MC, V. Valet parking $39. **Amenities:** Restaurant; lounge; concierge; exercise room w/men's and women's saunas; Jacuzzi; rooftop heated lap pool; room service; full-service spa. *In room:* A/C, TV, hair dryer, minibar, Wi-Fi ($9.95 per day).

JW Marriott Hotel Los Angeles Opened in February 2010, the JW Marriott is notable because of its location next to L.A. LIVE, a vast entertainment complex that includes the Staples Center, the Nokia Theatre, and more than a dozen restaurants, in a newly gentrified area of Downtown L.A. The JW Marriott represents the high-end branch of the Marriott chain, and the hotel feels luxurious, with sleek furnishings, attentive service, and lush amenities, like an outdoor pool and a spa that it shares with the adjoining Ritz-Carlton hotel. Guest rooms are spacious and modern, and feature color combinations of white, chocolate brown, and orange. Ask for a room on one of the higher floors (the hotel has 21 stories), and you'll be rewarded with excellent views. For a quick bite, **LA Market,** serves three meals per day of American and Americanized favorites. Have a drink at the **Mixing Room,** where mixologists concoct tasty specialty drinks like a cucumber gin martini and a vanilla jasmine cocktail.

900 W. Olympic Blvd. (at Figueroa St.), Los Angeles, CA 90015. www.lalivemarriott.com. © **888/228- 9290** or 213/765-8600. Fax 213/743-3542. 878 units. From $300 double; from $369 suite. AE, DISC, MC, V. Valet parking $40. **Amenities:** 2 restaurants; 2 bars; concierge; fitness center; Jacuzzi; outdoor pool; room service; spa. *In room:* A/C, TV, hair dryer, Wi-Fi ($13 per day).

Millennium Biltmore Hotel Los Angeles ★ The Biltmore is one of those hotels that's worth a visit even if you're not staying here. Built in 1923 and encompassing almost an entire square block, this Italian-Spanish Renaissance landmark is the grande dame of L.A.'s hotels. Chances are you've seen it in many movies, including *The Wedding Crashers, Chinatown, Ghostbusters, Bugsy, Beverly Hills Cop,* and Barbra Streisand's *A Star Is Born.* The hotel lobby—J.F.K.'s campaign headquarters during the 1960 Democratic National Convention—appeared upside-down in *The Poseidon Adventure.* The "wow" factor ends at guest rooms, however, which are a little on the small side (common for older hotels) and aren't quite as eye-popping as the public spaces, but they've recently been redecorated in a style that meshes well with the hotel's vibe. Bathrooms are on the small side as well, but peach-toned marble adds a luxurious edge. A range of dining and cocktail outlets includes **Sai Sai** for modern Asian cuisine and sushi. Pretty, casual **Smeraldi's** serves Continental fare. Off the lobby is the stunning, old-fashioned **Gallery Bar.** Afternoon tea and cocktails are served in the **Rendezvous Court,** which used to be the hotel's original lobby and resembles the interior of a Spanish cathedral, complete with a Moorish ceiling of carved beams and an altarlike baroque doorway. Spend the few bucks to appreciate the Art Deco health club, with its gorgeous Roman-style pool.

506 S. Grand Ave. (btw. 5th and 6th sts.), Los Angeles, CA 90071. www.thebiltmore.com. © **800/245-8673** or 213/624-1011. Fax 213/612-1545. 683 units. $189–$279 double; from $264 suite. Leisure discount packages available. AE, DC, DISC, MC, V. Parking $40. **Amenities:** 3 restaurants; bar; concierge; health club w/original 1923 inlaid pool, Jacuzzi, sauna, and steam room; room service. *In room:* A/C, TV, hair dryer, minibar, Wi-Fi ($9.95 per day per device).

Omni Los Angeles ★   This 17-story tower at the top of Bunker Hill is the best for culture buffs: It's adjacent to the Museum of Contemporary Art and within walking distance of the L.A. Music Center, Walt Disney Concert Hall, and the Cathedral of Our Lady of the Angels. Recognizing the geographical appeal, the hotel caters to theatergoers more than any other demographic, with complimentary car service within a three-mile radius until 11:30pm or midnight most nights (great for dinner/show evenings), late-night dining during performances, and good-value theater packages. An eager-to-please staff runs the property beautifully, and public areas enjoy a graceful air thanks to elegant accents and artworks from the likes of Jim Dine and David Hockney. The spacious, conservatively styled rooms are amenity-packed (including feather and foam pillows, individual climate controls and fluffy robes); business rooms feature extra-large work desks with halogen task lighting and desk-level inputs. Club Level rooms are a great value considering the accompanying free-bies: continental breakfast, all-day beverages and pastries, evening cocktails and appetizers. *Tip:* Request a room overlooking the Walt Disney Concert Hall.

251 S. Olive St., Los Angeles, CA 90012. www.omnihotels.com. © **888/444-6664** or 213/617-3300. Fax 213/617-3399. 453 units. $219–$390 double; from $499 suite. AE, DC, DISC, MC, V. Valet parking $30. **Amenities:** Restaurant; lounge; babysitting; children's programs; concierge; executive-level rooms; exercise room; outdoor heated lap pool; room service. *In room:* A/C, TV, hair dryer, minibar, Wi-Fi ($9.95 per day; free w/Select Guest membership).

Westin Bonaventure Hotel & Suites ★   This 35-story, 1,354-room monolith is the hotel that locals love to hate. The truth is that the Bonaventure is a terrific hotel. It's certainly not for travelers who want intimacy or personality in their accommodations—but with numerous restaurants and bars (the 34th-floor **BonaVista Lounge** slowly rotates 360 degrees), a full-service spa, a monster health club, a business center, and much more on hand, you'll be hard-pressed to want for anything here (except maybe some individualized attention). The hotel's five gleaming glass silos encompass an entire square block and form one of Downtown's most distinctive landmarks. The pie-shaped guest rooms are on the small side, but a wall of windows offering great views and Westin's unparalleled Heavenly Bed—the ultimate in hotel-bed comfort—make for a very comfortable cocoon. With executive workstation, fax, and wet bar, guest office suites are great for business travelers, while tower suites—with living room, extra half-bathroom, minifridge, microwave, and two TVs—are ideal for families. *Tip:* Ask about the "running concierge" program, which offers scenic jogs through historical parts of downtown.

404 S. Figueroa St. (btw. 4th and 5th sts.), Los Angeles, CA 90017. www.westin.com/bonaventure. © **800/WESTIN-1** (937-8461) or 213/624-1000. Fax 213/612-4800. 1,354 units. $169–$289 double; from $249 suite. Ask about specials and packages. AE, DC, DISC, MC, V. Valet parking $40. **Amenities:** 5 restaurants, plus fast-food outlets; 1 bar; concierge; access to 4,500-sq.-ft. health club; outdoor heated lap pool; 24-hr. room service; full-service spa, indoor running track. *In room:* A/C, TV, hair dryer, mini-fridge, Wi-Fi ($13 per day).

😊 family-friendly HOTELS

Beverly Garland's Holiday Inn (p. 78) is a terrific choice for wallet-watching families: Rates are low, the North Hollywood location is close to Universal Studios (a free shuttle ride away), and kids stay and eat free—and even get their own rooms, called KidSuites.

Hotel Erwin (p. 53) gives families a place to stay just off the carnival-like Venice boardwalk. The suites are a terrific choice for the brood, as all feature a full kitchen, a dining area, a pullout sofa, and a connecting door to an adjoining room that lets you form an affordable two-bedroom, two-bathroom suite.

Inn at Venice Beach (p. 53) is ideal for ocean-loving families thanks to its near-the-beach location. The 3-block walk is lined with snack bars, surf shops, and bike and skate rentals. The 12-and-under set is welcomed free of charge, and

everyone starts the day with a complimentary breakfast.

Loews Santa Monica Beach Hotel (p. 50) welcomes kids 10 and under with open arms, activities, and special menus. And with a great location near the beach and Santa Monica amusement pier, the hotel couldn't be better situated for families in search of surf and sun.

Magic Castle Hotel (p. 72) is a good budget choice, with roomy apartment-style suites; it's close to Hollywood Boulevard's family-friendly attractions.

Sheraton Universal Hotel (p. 78) enjoys a terrifically kid-friendly location, adjacent to Universal Studios and the fun CityWalk mall. Plus, they offer family-friendly packages, which include admission to the park.

Wilshire Grand Los Angeles This former Omni hotel is now independently operated and dedicated to business travelers, but weekend rates can be stellar for bargain-hunting vacationers. The taupe-toned rooms are business-hotel average; the best ones have city views or overlook the swimming pool. The executive-level rooms and suites feature extras like plush bathrobes, extra towels, and top-floor views—plus access to the Executive Lounge, which offers free continental breakfast, all-day beverages, and hors d'oeuvres at cocktail hour. The 16-story hotel is centrally located in the heart of Downtown shopping, theater, and dining. The restaurants and bars on-site include an American grill, an upscale Korean barbecue, an Italian trattoria, Japanese cuisine, a tropical lounge in the Trader Vic's vein, and a coffee bar featuring Starbucks brew. I prefer the Omni (see above), but this hotel is a fine choice if you can snag a good rate.

930 Wilshire Blvd. (at Figueroa St.), Los Angeles, CA 90017. www.wilshiregrand.com. © **888/773-2888** or 213/688-7777. Fax 213/612-3989. 900 units. $159–$269 double; from $490 suite. AE, DC, DISC, MC, V. Valet parking $35. **Amenities:** 4 restaurants; bar; concierge; executive-level rooms; exercise room; Jacuzzi; large outdoor heated pool; room service. *In room:* A/C, TV, hair dryer, free Wi-Fi.

UNIVERSAL CITY

If you're planning on visiting the most popular attraction in Los Angeles, Universal Studios Hollywood, you'll save a lot of travel time and hassle by booking a hotel room right next to the park. The hotels listed below are ideally located for quick and easy access to the park; the closest ones are the Hilton Universal City and the Sheraton Universal, which are just a short walk or shuttle ride from the park.

Expensive

Hilton Universal City & Towers   Although this shiny 24-story hotel sits right outside Universal Studios, there's more of a conservative business-traveler feel here than the raucous family-with-young-children vibe you might expect. Still, free adjacent tram service to the theme park and adjacent Universal CityWalk for shopping and dining means that it's hard for families to be better situated. The polished brass and upscale attitude set the businesslike tone, and a light-filled glass lobby leads to a seemingly endless series of conference and banquet rooms, the hotel's bread and butter. The oversize guest rooms are tastefully decorated and constantly refurbished, and have exceptional views (even if the modern, mirror-surfaced windows don't actually open). I prefer the adjacent Sheraton (see below) for leisure stays, but go for the best rate.

555 Universal Hollywood Dr., Universal City, CA 91608. www.universalcity.hilton.com. (C) **800/HILTONS** (445-8667) or 818/506-2500. Fax 818/509-2058. 483 units. $209–$285 double; from $350 suite. AE, DC, DISC, MC, V. Valet parking $23; self-parking $18. **Amenities:** Restaurant; concierge; executive-level rooms; exercise room; Jacuzzi; outdoor heated pool; room service. *In room:* A/C, TV (DVD for rental), hair dryer, minibar, Wi-Fi ($7.95 per day).

Moderate

Beverly Garland's Holiday Inn ☺   The "Beverly Garland" in this 258-room hotel's name is the actress who played Fred MacMurray's wife on *My Three Sons*. Grassy areas and greenery abound at this North Hollywood Holiday Inn, a virtual oasis in the concrete jungle. With upgrades in 2008 and 2009, the hotel has shed dated Southwest-themed fabrics in the spacious (and soundproof) guest rooms; now it's clean lines and neutral colors. Even the pool and lounges got a contemporary overhaul. All of the well-outfitted rooms have balconies overlooking the pleasant grounds, which include a pool and two lighted tennis courts. The staff is very friendly. With Universal Studios just down the street and a free shuttle to the park, the location can't be beat for families. Since proximity to the 101 and 134 freeways also means the constant buzz of traffic, ask for a room facing Vineland Avenue for maximum quiet. *Tip:* If you're bringing the kids along, be sure to inquire about the Kid-Suites, adjoining rooms designed just for kids.

4222 Vineland Ave., North Hollywood, CA 91602. www.beverlygarland.com. (C) **800/238-3759** or 818/980-8000. Fax 818/766-0112. 255 units. $139–$199 double; from $189 suite. Children 12 and under stay free in parent's room and eat free. AE, DC, DISC, MC, V. Self-parking $14. **Amenities:** Restaurant; bar; heated outdoor pool; sauna; 2 tennis courts (lit for night play). *In room:* A/C, TV, hair dryer, Wi-Fi (free).

Sheraton Universal Hotel ★★ ☺   Despite the addition of the sleekly modern Hilton just uphill, the 21-story Sheraton is still considered "the" Universal City hotel of choice for tourists, businesspeople, and industry folks visiting the studios' production offices. Located on the back lot of Universal Studios, it has a spacious 1960s feel, with updated styling and amenities. Although the Sheraton does its share of convention/event business, the hotel feels more leisure-oriented than the Hilton next door (an outdoor elevator connects the two properties). Choose a Lanai room for balconies that overlook the lushly planted pool area, or a Tower room for stunning views and solitude. The hotel is very close to the Hollywood Bowl, and you can practically roll out of bed and into the theme park (via a continuous complimentary shuttle). All suites include Club Level access—worth the money for the extra amenities such as concierge service and free continental breakfast and afternoon hors d'oeuvres. *Tip:* Ask about AAA, AARP, and corporate discounts; also inquire about packages that include theme-park admission.

333 Universal Hollywood Dr., Universal City, CA 91608. www.sheraton.com/universal. ✆ **800/325-3535** or 818/980-1212. Fax 818/985-4980. 451 units. $249–$279 double; from $325 suite. Children stay free in parent's room. AE, DC, DISC, MC, V. Valet parking $23; self-parking $18. **Amenities:** Casual indoor/outdoor restaurant; concierge; executive-level rooms; health club; Jacuzzi; outdoor pool and whirlpool. *In room:* A/C, TV, hair dryer, Wi-Fi (first 45 min. per day free, then $9.95 per day).

Inexpensive

Best Western Mikado Hotel   This Asian-flavored garden hotel has been a Valley fixture for 40-plus years. A 1999 renovation muted but didn't obliterate the kitsch value, which extends from the pagoda-style exterior to the sushi bar (the Valley's oldest) across the driveway. Two-story motel buildings face two well-maintained courtyards, one with a koi pond and wooden footbridge, the other with a shimmering blue-tiled pool and hot tub. The face-lift stripped most of the Asian vibe from guest rooms, which are suitably comfortable and well outfitted. Furnished in 1970s-era chic (leather sofas, earth tones), the one-bedroom apartment is a steal, with enormous rooms and a full-size kitchen. Rates include a full breakfast.

12600 Riverside Dr. (btw. Whitsett and Coldwater Canyon aves.), North Hollywood, CA 91607. www.bestwestern.com/mikadohotel. ✆ **800/780-7234** or 818/763-9141. Fax 818/752-1045. 58 units. $119–$159 double; $250 1-bedroom apartment. Rates include full breakfast. Extra person $10. Children 11 and under stay free in parent's room. AE, DC, DISC, MC, V. Free parking. **Amenities:** Restaurant; cocktail lounge; Jacuzzi; outdoor pool. *In room:* A/C, TV, hair dryer, free Wi-Fi.

PASADENA & ENVIRONS

East of Downtown, Pasadena is serene, well preserved, and architecturally rich. It's close via freeway to both Hollywood and Valley attractions—but forget about basing yourself here if you plan to spend your days at the beach and your nights trolling West Hollywood nightclubs. Those who like a quieter scene will enjoy Pasadena's more bucolic range of accommodations, and the dining and shopping scene stands on its own. Now with the new Metro Gold Line running from Downtown right through Old Town Pasadena and all points east, accessibility to L.A.'s best neighborhoods (without having to deal with traffic) is increasingly easier.

Very Expensive

Langham Huntington Hotel & Spa ★★★   Originally opened in 1907, the opulent Huntington Hotel was one of America's grandest hotels, but not the most earthquake-proof. No matter—the hotel was rebuilt and opened in the same spot in 1991, save its two historic ballrooms, and the astonishing authenticity (including reinstallation of many decorative features) even fools patrons from the hotel's early days. This Spanish-Mediterranean beauty sits on 23 spectacularly landscaped acres that seem a world apart from L.A., though Downtown is only 20 minutes away. Langham Hotels International took over this former Ritz-Carlton in 2008 and has invested significantly in property upgrades. The hotel's dining room, bar, club lounge, and eight cottages have all recently undergone renovations, in addition to its 11,000-square-foot full-service spa, which now offers unique services based upon traditional Chinese medicine. Each oversize guest room is conservatively dressed with Frette linens and has lots of natural light. Spend a few extra dollars on a Club Level room, which features access to the club lounge with dedicated concierge and complimentary gourmet spreads all day (including breakfast). Guests and locals enjoy the Cal-French cuisine of former Patina Group chef David Féau at the **Royce,** where a whimsical menu is now matched by more avant-garde design in the once staid dining room (the sommelier is spot-on in his pairings). The more casual **Terrace** restaurant serves meals at umbrella-covered tables by the pool and hosts an a la carte Sunday brunch. Enjoy craft beer and specialty cocktails drinks in the new **Tap Room.**

1401 S. Oak Knoll Ave., Pasadena, CA 91106. http://pasadena.langhamhotels.com. ℰ **800/591-7481** or 626/568-3900. Fax 626/568-3700. 380 units. $279–$450 double; from $589 suite. AE, DC, MC, V. Valet parking $25. **Amenities:** 2 restaurants; 2 lounges (bar, lobby lounge for high tea); concierge; fitness center; Jacuzzi; heated outdoor pool; room service; full-service spa w/whirlpool, sauna, and steam room; 3 tennis courts (lit for night play). *In room:* A/C, TV, CD player, hair dryer, minibar, Wi-Fi ($9.95 per day).

Moderate

Bissell House Bed & Breakfast ★ If you enjoy the true B&B experience, you'll love the Bissell House. Hidden behind hedges that carefully isolate it from busy Orange Grove Avenue, this antiques-filled 1887 gingerbread Victorian—the former home of the vacuum heiress and now owned by the Hoyman family—offers a unique taste of life on what was once Pasadena's "Millionaire's Row." Outfitted in a traditional chintz-and-cabbage-roses style, all individually decorated rooms have private bathrooms (two with an antique claw-foot tub, one with a whirlpool tub, four with showers only), individual heating and air-conditioning (a B&B rarity), Internet access, and very comfortable beds. If you don't mind stairs, request one of the more spacious top-floor rooms. Most rooms are now equipped with flat screen TVs—all have televisions of some sort—DVDs and premium cable, and the downstairs library features a selection of DVDs for guest use. The beautifully landscaped grounds boast an inviting pool, Jacuzzi, and deck with lounge chairs. Included in the room rate is an elaborately prepared vegetarian breakfast served in the large dining room, as well as an afternoon dessert. *Tip:* A self-serve continental breakfast is also available weekdays for business guests, provided notice is given no later than the night before.

201 Orange Grove Ave. (at Columbia St.), South Pasadena, CA 91030. www.bissellhouse.com. ℰ **800/ 441-3530** or 626/441-3535. Fax 626/441-3671. 7 units. $155–$295 double. Rates include full breakfast. AE, MC, V. Free parking. **Amenities:** Jacuzzi; outdoor pool; DVD library. *In room:* A/C, flatscreen TV (most rooms), hair dryer, free Wi-Fi.

Inexpensive

Saga Motor Hotel 🦋 This 1950s relic of old Route 66 has far more character than most other motels in its price range. The rooms are small, clean, and simply furnished with the basics. The double/doubles are spacious enough for shares, but budget-minded families will prefer the extra-large configuration dedicated to them, with a king-size bed and two doubles. The best rooms are in the front building surrounding the gated swimming pool, shielded from the street and inviting in warm weather. The grounds are attractive and well kept, if you don't count the AstroTurf "lawn" on the pool deck. The location is relatively quiet (considering it's on a busy strip of Colorado Blvd. directly across from Pasadena Community College) and very convenient: just off the Foothill (210) Freeway, about a mile from the Huntington Library, and within 10 minutes of both the Rose Bowl and Old Pasadena. *Note:* The Saga is 100% smoke free; there's no smoking allowed anywhere on its grounds, including the pool and parking lot.

1633 E. Colorado Blvd. (btw. Allen and Sierra Bonita aves.), Pasadena, CA 91106. www.thesagamotor hotel.com. ℰ **800/793-7242** or 626/795-0431. Fax 626/792-0559. 70 units. $92–$94 double; from $135 suite. Rates include continental breakfast. AE, DC, DISC, MC, V. Free parking. Free laundry facilities. Small pets under 15 lb. are allowed ($35 cleaning fee applies). **Amenities:** Outdoor heated pool. *In room:* A/C, cable TV w/HBO, free Wi-Fi.

Where to Stay in the Pasadena Area

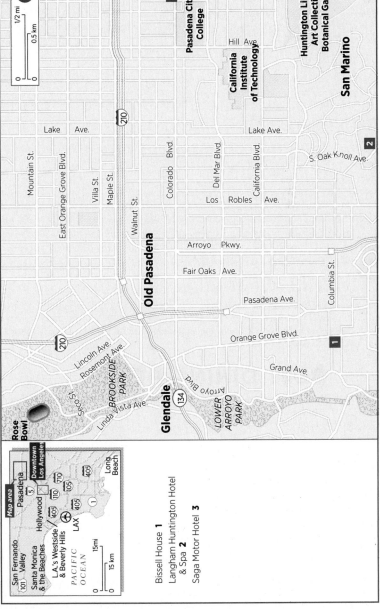

Bissell House **1**

Langham Huntington Hotel & Spa **2**

Saga Motor Hotel **3**

WHERE TO EAT

As one of the world's cultural crossroads, Los Angeles is a veritable international atlas of exotic cuisines: Afghan, Argentine, Armenian, Burmese, Cajun, Cambodian, Caribbean, Cuban, Ethiopian, Indian, Jewish, Korean, Lebanese, Moroccan, Oaxacan, Persian, Peruvian, Spanish, Thai, Vietnamese . . . well, you get the point. Half the fun of visiting Los Angeles is experiencing worldly dishes that only a major metropolis can provide. Whatever you're in the mood for, this town has it covered, and all you need to join the dinner party is an adventurous palate. And since it's L.A., there's always the bonus of spotting celebrities.

Although it's those famous celebrity chef and celebrity-owned restaurants that attract most of the media limelight, the majority of L.A.'s best dining experiences are at its small neighborhood haunts and minimalls, the kind you'll never find unless someone lets you in on the city's dining secrets—and this chapter is full of them.

The restaurants listed below are classified first by area and then by price, using the following categories: Very Expensive, dinner from $75 per person; Expensive, dinner from $50 per person; Moderate, dinner from $35 per person; and Inexpensive, dinner from $20 per person. These categories reflect prices for an appetizer, main course, dessert, and glass of wine.

BEST DINING BETS

Note: In addition to the Best Dining Bets below, see "The Most Unforgettable Dining Experiences," in chapter 1.

- **Best Places for a Power Lunch:** Between 12:30 and 2pm, industry honchos swarm like locusts to a handful of watering holes du jour. Actors, agents, lawyers, and producers flock to perennial favorites the **Ivy** (p. 103), 113 N. Robertson Blvd., West Hollywood (✆ **310/274-8303**), and the L.A. branch of New York's venerable the **Palm** (p. 105), 9001 Santa Monica Blvd., West Hollywood (✆ **310/550-8811**), a steakhouse where the food is impeccable and the conversations read like dialogue from *Entourage.*
- **Best Old-School Diners:** Stand in line for one of the city's best hamburgers at the **Apple Pan,** 10801 Pico Blvd., West L.A. (✆ **310/475-3585**). Choose from the "steakburger" or the saucy "hickory burger"—though regulars know to get extra hickory sauce on the side (for french-fry dipping). The wallpaper at this beloved family-run cottage on the busy Westside looks like it dates from the opening day in 1947. See p. 108. Dating to 1958, **Rae's Restaurant,** 2901 Pico Blvd.,

Santa Monica (© **310/828-7937**), is pretty inconspicuous, but the cash-only, all-American diner is very popular among locals, especially at breakfast time.

o **Best View:** The **Restaurant at the Getty Center,** 1200 Getty Center Dr., West L.A. (© **310/440-6810**), has an in-the-clouds locale that makes for postcard views when the L.A. sky is smog-free. Reservations are recommended, even for lunch and brunch (served Tues–Sun); dinner is served only on Saturday, when the museum is open late. Make reservations online at www.getty.edu. For one of the best views in Los Angeles, the **Penthouse,** 1111 2nd St., Santa Monica (© **310/393-8080**), at the top of the 18-story Huntley Santa Monica Beach, has a 360-degree view of Santa Monica, with Los Angeles to the east, the beach to the west, Malibu to the north, and Venice to the south, not to mention the occasional celeb or two in-house. There is really no bad seat, but the cabanas are definitely prime real estate.

o **Best "Old Hollywood" Restaurant:** Haunted by the ghosts of Faulkner, Fitzgerald, and Hemingway—who drank here during their screenwriting days—**Musso & Frank Grill,** 6667 Hollywood Blvd., Hollywood (© **323/467-7788**), is virtually unchanged since 1919. The atmosphere urges you to order a martini and chicken potpie. Listen to the longtime waitstaff wax nostalgic about the days when Hollywood Boulevard was still fashionable and Orson Welles held court at Musso's. See p. 115.

o **Best Spot for People-Watching:** Nowhere in L.A. is better for people-watching than Venice's Ocean Front Walk, and no restaurant offers a better seat for the action than the **Sidewalk Cafe,** 1401 Ocean Front Walk, Venice (© **310/399-5547**). Unobstructed views of parading skaters, bikers, skateboarders, musclemen, break dancers, street performers, sword swallowers, and other participants in the daily carnival overshadow the food, which is better than it needs to be. See p. 97.

o **Best Spots for Celebrity Sighting:** You'll always find well-known faces frequenting Hollywood hot spots, the most sizzling of which is **Katsuya Hollywood** (p. 113), 6300 Hollywood Blvd. (© **323/871-8777**), the current fave of Jessica Simpson, Janet Jackson, Lauren Conrad, and so on. Other celebrity hangouts include **Koi** (p. 107), 730 N. La Cienega Blvd., West Hollywood (© **310/659-9449**); **Osteria Mozza** (p. 113), 641 N. Highland Ave., Los Angeles (© **323/297-0100**); **Mastro's Steakhouse** (p. 104), 246 N. Canon Dr., Beverly Hills (© **310/888-8782**); **Tower Bar** at the Sunset Tower Hotel, 8358 W. Sunset Blvd., West Hollywood (© **323/848-6677**); the **Ivy** (p. 103), 113 N. Robertson Blvd., West Hollywood (© **310/274-8303**); **Mr. Chow,** 344 N. Camden Dr., Beverly Hills (© **310/278-9911**); and, of course, **Spago Beverly Hills** (p. 105), 176 N. Canon Dr., Beverly Hills (© **310/385-0880**).

o **Best Alfresco Dining:** You'll find that more and more Los Angeles restaurants are eager to create appealing outdoor seating, even if it means placing bistro tables along a busy sidewalk. One of my favorites is the garden patio at the **Little Door,** 8164 W. 3rd St., West Hollywood (© **323/951-1210**), one of the most romantic restaurants in the city. See p. 113. A more affordable way to enjoy a meal outdoors is to stroll **Sunset Boulevard around Sunset Plaza Drive.** At least a half-dozen sidewalk cafes dot this strip—and the people-watching is some of the best in the city. For on-the-beach dining, literally, take a trip to **Back On The Beach Café** at the Annenberg Community Beach House, 445 Palisades Beach Rd., Santa Monica (© **310/393-8282**), where you dine with your feet in the sand.

- **Best Wine List:** Year after year, plenty of other restaurants offer thoughtfully chosen vintages, but no one comes close to toppling **Valentino,** 3115 Pico Blvd., Santa Monica (© **310/829-4313**), which still boasts L.A.'s best cellar and is continually honored with *Wine Spectator's* highest ratings. See p. 91.

- **Best California Cuisine:** Everyone seems to be doing market-to-table cuisine these days, understandable since L.A. is blessed with amazing farmers' markets and produce year-round. At Santa Monica's **Michael's** (p. 90), 1147 3rd St. (© **310/451-0843**), chef/owner Michael McCarty is considered an originator of California cuisine, but others like **Hatfield's,** 6703 Melrose Ave., Los Angeles (© **323/935-2977**); **Josie,** 2424 Pico Blvd., Santa Monica (© **310/581-9888**); and **Forage,** 3823 W. Sunset Blvd., Silver Lake (© **323/663-6885**), always have some of the best season-inspired menus.

- **Best Italian Cuisine:** After more than 40 years in the business, restaurateur Piero Selvaggio is still at the top of his game. Nothing beats the understated elegance of **Valentino,** 3115 Pico Blvd., Santa Monica (© **310/829-4313**), for an authentic Italian dinner. Selvaggio's hospitality is oft imitated (or exaggerated) but never duplicated. Though new-school foodies may chide me for my ode to the old-fashioned, sometimes simple really is best. I dare you to find a better vitello tonnato. See p. 91.

- **Best Mexican Cuisine:** L.A. is teeming with authentic Mexican food—some of the tastiest is even found on mobile taco trucks. For amazing mole, seek out **Guelaguetza,** 3014 W. Olympic Blvd., Los Angeles (© **213/427-0608**), which draws a large Spanish-speaking clientele even thought it's in Koreatown. **La Casita,** 4030 Gage Ave., Bell ([tel **323/773-1898**) is another winner; though it's a more of a trek from the touristy areas.

- **Best Afternoon Tea:** Surrounded by botanical gardens, the tearoom at the **Huntington Library,** 1151 Oxford Rd., San Marino (© **626/683-8131**), is truly an oasis. The Huntington, located in a wealthy residential area near Pasadena, has the added appeal of pre- and post-tea activities, such as strolling the theme gardens, viewing the art gallery or library, and visiting the bookstore/gift shop. Though it's a bit pricey ($28 plus museum admission) the tea is served buffet-style, so you can stuff yourself with fresh-baked scones, finger sandwiches, and strawberries with thick Devonshire cream.

- **Best Value:** Former mayor Richard Riordan's the **Original Pantry,** 877 S. Figueroa St., Downtown (© **213/972-9279**), stays open 24 hours a day, serving up large plates of traditional American comfort food (meatloaf, coleslaw, ham 'n' eggs) that won't win any culinary awards but offers some of the best values in town (you won't leave hungry, that's for sure). See p. 126. Far more upscale but equally value-oriented (particularly, the three-course lunch for $18) is **Joe's Restaurant,** 1023 Abbot Kinney Blvd., Venice (© **310/399-5811**). See p. 92.

- **Best Noshing (While Standing):** Open since 1917, **Grand Central Market,** 317 S. Broadway, Downtown (© **213/624-2378**), is L.A.'s largest and oldest food hall, selling everything from fresh bread, local and exotic produce, and fresh fruit juice to smoked meats, Chinese noodles, and chili.

- **Best for Late-Night Dining:** On the theory that later is better, our vote goes to **Toi on Sunset,** 7505½ Sunset Blvd., West Hollywood (© **323/874-8062**). You'll never feel like the last patron at this place—they're open until 4am—and the terrific Thai food will give your fading brain a spicy kick. See p. 119.

SANTA MONICA & THE BEACHES

Expensive

Boa Steakhouse ★ STEAK   The sophisticated decor eschews the traditional dim steakhouse ambience in favor of a warm, sleek interior highlighted with floor-to-ceiling windows that allow natural light to filter in. Tough decisions abound on the menu: Should you order the bone-in filet mignon, petite filet mignon, Kobe filet mignon, 35-day dry-aged New York strip, bone-in rib-eye, flatiron steak, or porterhouse? Have it prepared with a foie gras butter, tri-peppercorn rub, chef's special J-1 sauce, or creamy horseradish? (Personally, I think it's uncouth to flavor a prime cut of dry-aged beef with anything but salt and pepper.) Sides are purchased separately, the most popular being the homemade crispy fries, macaroni and cheese, and roasted garlic whipped potatoes. As for an appetizer, there's a jumbo lump crab cake with heart of palm salad and Cajun rémoulade. For a pick-me-up dessert, try the refreshing blackberry smash cocktail, a *mojito*-like mixture made with fresh fruit and top-shelf vodka. **Note:** A second Boa Steakhouse is in West Hollywood on the Sunset Strip at 9200 W. Sunset Blvd. (© **310/278-2050**).

101 Santa Monica Blvd. (at Ocean Ave.), Santa Monica. © **310/899-4466.** www.boasteak.com. Reservations recommended. Main courses $28–$44. AE, DC, DISC, MC, V. Lunch Mon–Fri noon–3pm, Sat–Sun noon–5pm; dinner Mon–Wed 5:30–10:30pm, Thurs 5:30–11pm, Fri–Sat 5:30–11:30pm. Valet parking $7 with validation.

Cafe Del Rey ★ CALIFORNIAN   Cafe Del Rey is one of those lively restaurants where everyone seems to be celebrating something on the company's tab. There's a terrific view of the marina's bobbing sailboats, particularly in the summer when the windows facing the harbor are open, creating an indoor-outdoor dining area. The exhibition kitchen focuses on creative preparations of fresh and seasonal foods, but the choices are so varied that it's impossible to accurately categorize the cafe's cuisine. Sure bets are day boat specials like mahi mahi or swordfish, which list both the boats and the captains who brought them in fresh. The *Wine Spectator*–award-winning wine list offers more than 340 selections. **My advice:** Request a table by the window, ask your server what's good today, pair it with a nice bottle of wine, and enjoy a long, leisurely meal.

4451 Admiralty Way (btw. Lincoln and Washington boulevards), Marina del Rey. © **310/823-6395.** www.cafedelreymarina.com. Reservations recommended. Main courses dinner $26–$33, lunch $12–$23. AE, DC, DISC, MC, V. Mon–Fri 11:30am–3pm and 5:30–10pm (until 10:30pm Fri); Sat 11:30am–2:30pm and 5:30–10:30pm; Sun 10:30am–3pm and 5–9:30pm. Valet parking free for lunch, $4 for dinner.

Chez Melange★★ NEW AMERICAN/FUSION Chez Melange turns the big 3-0 in 2012, though it moved from its longtime location in Palos Verdes to the Hollywood Riviera area of Redondo in 2008. Regulars still flock here in droves; it's not unusual to see three generations dining together in the elegant but inviting dining room; couples are a common sight as well. The Chez toast changes weekly; a good rule of thumb is that if it involves truffle oil and eggs, order it. Duck wraps are a tasty DIY appetizer, in which guests assemble their own lettuce cups filled with the rich meat joined by raspberry port sauce and pistachio nuts. Steamed clams also borrow inspiration from Asia, served with sweet Chinese sausage in Thai curry and coconut milk. Hearty twice-cooked pork benefits from braised country greens and cheesy grits

Where to Eat in Santa Monica & the Beaches

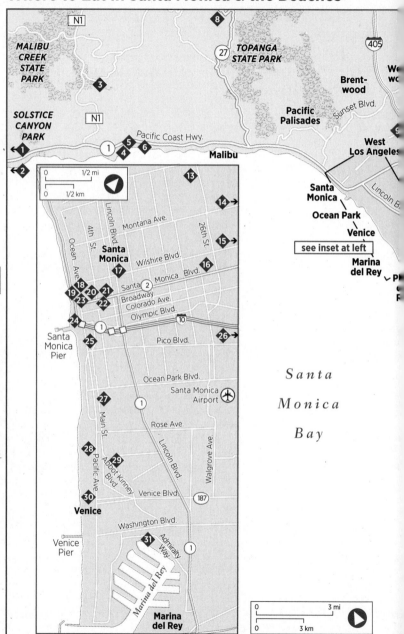

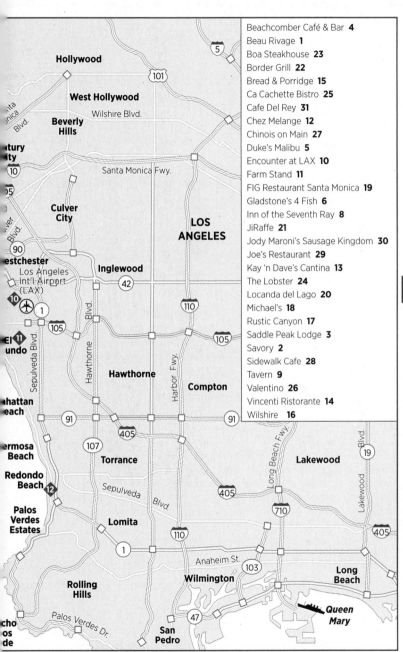

Beachcomber Café & Bar **4**
Beau Rivage **1**
Boa Steakhouse **23**
Border Grill **22**
Bread & Porridge **15**
Ca Cachette Bistro **25**
Cafe Del Rey **31**
Chez Melange **12**
Chinois on Main **27**
Duke's Malibu **5**
Encounter at LAX **10**
Farm Stand **11**
FIG Restaurant Santa Monica **19**
Gladstone's 4 Fish **6**
Inn of the Seventh Ray **8**
JiRaffe **21**
Jody Maroni's Sausage Kingdom **30**
Joe's Restaurant **29**
Kay 'n Dave's Cantina **13**
The Lobster **24**
Locanda del Lago **20**
Michael's **18**
Rustic Canyon **17**
Saddle Peak Lodge **3**
Savory **2**
Sidewalk Cafe **28**
Tavern **9**
Valentino **26**
Vincenti Ristorante **14**
Wilshire **16**

sides. The wine list here is impressive, including the by-the-glass selections. *Tip:* If you're looking for something more casual, the attached Bouzy gastropub shares the same owners and the same kitchen.

1611 S. Catalina Ave. (at Ave. I), Redondo Beach. ✆ **310/540-1222.** www.chezmelange.com. Reservations recommended. Main courses $14–$25. AE, MC, V. Mon–Thurs 5–9:30pm; Fri–Sat 5–10pm; Sun 5–9pm. Valet $4; self-parking in the underground garage free.

Chinois on Main ★★ FUSION   Wolfgang Puck's Franco-Chinese eatery bustles nightly with locals and visitors wowed by the restaurant's reputation and rarely disappointed by the food. The same cannot be said for Puck's latest Asian-inspired eatery, WP24 on the top floor of the Ritz downtown. Go there for the view, come here for the food. Groundbreaking in its time, the restaurant still relies on the quirky East-meets-West mélange of ingredients and technique. The menu is almost equally split between Chinois's signature dishes and seasonal creations. The most famous of the former are Cantonese duck in a sweet-tangy plum sauce, and farm-raised whole catfish that's perfectly deep-fried and dramatically presented. There's also seared Maine sea scallops with pad Thai noodles, and braised Kurobuta pork shoulder served in a hot pot with Chinese eggplant. Try the trio of crème brûlées for dessert. The dining room is as visually colorful as it is acoustically loud. *Tip:* If you like fiery cooking demonstrations, ask for a seat at the kitchen counter.

2709 Main St. (south of Pico Blvd.), Santa Monica. ✆ **310/392-9025.** www.wolfgangpuck.com. Reservations required. Main courses $26–$47. AE, DC, MC, V. Lunch Wed–Fri 11:30am–2pm; dinner Mon–Thurs 6–10pm, Fri–Sat 6–10:30pm, Sun 5:30–10pm. Valet parking $6.

Encounter at LAX CALIFORNIAN   There has always been a restaurant in the spacey Theme Building (since 1961) perched in LAX's midst, though this place has mostly been the domain of fly-by travelers. Angelenos rarely venture up here unless they're waiting for someone on a long-delayed flight and feel like scratching one off the bucket list. The once staid Continental dining room (whose best feature was a panoramic view over the runways) was later transformed into a 1960s *Star Trek* set gone Technicolor. Outer-space lounge music dominates the entire place. The menu features art-food, that L.A. specialty that focuses more on sculptural arrangements than on culinary prowess. That said, the food is of the satisfy-all-tastes variety: roast chicken, grilled salmon, New York steak, and so on. If you're stopping at LAX with kids in tow, not to worry—Encounter's party atmosphere ensures they'll enjoy themselves without disrupting the ambience a bit., and there's even a special "Space Cadet" menu just for them. *A travel advisory:* Fans of tiki bars, Googie architecture and neon "martinis" should at least come up and have a blue cocktail at the lava-lamp-festooned bar, because quirky Encounter is worth an encounter. Purists are advised to join the "Jet Set"—basically a Negroni.

209 World Way (Theme Building, Los Angeles International Airport). ✆ **310/215-5151.** www.encounterrestaurant.com. Reservations recommended for dinner. Main courses dinner $17–$30, lunch $14–$22. AE, DC, DISC, MC, V. Mon–Wed 11am–9pm; Thurs–Sun 11am–9:30pm. Valet parking $6.

FIG Restaurant Santa Monica ★★ CALIFORNIAN   This hidden gem at the Fairmont Miramar Hotel & Bungalows is one of Santa Monica's best—and most consistent—restaurants, FIG's food and drinks feature the freshest local and organically grown ingredients straight from the Santa Monica Farmers Market. The restaurant has a charcuterie and cheese bar, bistro-style tables, and a private dining area that's great for large groups. FIG is definitely casual California style, with its relaxed atmosphere and eco-friendly approach to dining. The menu options are best described as simple

Santa Monica & the Beaches

WHERE TO EAT

Dining in the Dark

Imagine dining at a restaurant where your entire meal—bread, salad, entree, dessert, wine—is served in complete darkness. The pitch-black kind, where you can't see the person you're talking to you or your hand in front of your face. It's called Dining in the Dark, a nouveau European dining trend where specially trained blind or sight-impaired waitstaff serve three-course meals in an opaque dining room. Brought to the States for the first time by German entrepreneur Ben Uphues, this highly entertaining event starts in a lighted lobby at the V-Lounge in Santa Monica, where you select your dinner and drinks from a set menu, then you're introduced to your waiter and escorted to the darkened dining room. It's a bit eerie and awkward at first (good luck if you drop your fork), but my friend and I were surprised at how quickly our other senses kicked into overdrive to make up for our loss of vision (and how loud people felt it necessary to talk to overcompensate). Honestly, I never really got the hang of slicing my steak let alone pouring wine or sharing bites. But from the laughter emanating throughout the darkened dining room, it appeared people were good natured about the awkwardness of their sightless experience. The evening isn't cheap—$99 per person, not including gratuity and drinks—but I guarantee you this will be a dining experience you'll never forget. For more information, log onto www.darkdining.com or call ✆ 800/710-1270.

with a twist, and the presentation is incredible every time. The Sunday brunch is popular with locals; many of whom opt for the "Kegs and Eggs" option, which includes any entrée with endless draft-beer refills. For me, though, it's all about the authentic but gourmet taco bar they set up for the occasion (try the awesome carnitas). *Tip:* For a sweet finale to your dining experience, try the assorted cookie dessert.

101 Wilshire Blvd., Santa Monica. ✆ **310/319-3111.** www.figsantamonica.com. Main courses dinner $18–$38, lunch $13–$24, breakfast/brunch $9–$25. AE, DC, DISC, MC, V. Sun-Mon 7am-2pm; Tues-Sat 7am-2pm and 5-10pm. Valet parking free for up to 3 hr. with validation.

JiRaffe ★★ CALIFORNIAN/FRENCH   The deafening din of conversation at this long-standing restaurant is usually praise for JiRaffe's artistic treatment of the purple Peruvian gnocchi appetizer, with rock shrimp, pearl onions and tomato nage—a signature starter if ever there was one. Also popular are the pepper-crusted ahi tuna, crispy Scottish salmon, the flavorful filet of Prime beef, and caramelized pork chops with smoked bacon, apple chutney, and cider sauce. JiRaffe also wins culinary points for highlighting oft-ignored vegetables such as salsify, Swiss chard, and fennel, as well as complex appetizers that are more like miniature main dishes. I only wish the dishes would change more frequently, but it's been around so long now that there might be revolt. For dessert, say hello to a slice of warm chocolate truffle cake with vanilla bean ice cream and a cup of coffee. *Tip:* The Monday night bistro menu is a terrific bargain, and they don't dumb-down the food either. It offers three courses for $38.

502 Santa Monica Blvd. (corner of 5th St.), Santa Monica. ✆ **310/917-6671.** www.jirafferestaurant.com. Reservations recommended. Main courses $24–$38. AE, MC, V. Mon 6-9pm; Tues-Sat 6-10:30pm. Valet parking $7.

The Lobster ★ SEAFOOD   A seafood shack called the Lobster has been on the Santa Monica Pier since 1923—almost as long as the pier has been standing—but this incarnation is a perpetually lively favorite. The contemporary decor can't compete with the floor-to-ceiling windows offering a million-dollar ocean view, but the space is comfortable. The food is better than it needs to be, given the location, but not quite what it once was. Although the namesake crustacean from Maine is a good choice—get it grilled, steamed, poached—other specialties range from pan-seared crab cakes to wild Columbia River King salmon. Creative appetizers include ahi carpaccio with tangy tobiko wasabi, or steamed mussels and Manila clams with apple-wood bacon. There are a few steaks for landlubbers, and there's a practiced bar dedicated to locals that serves lots of bloody marys garnished with jumbo shrimp. **Tip:** Request a table on the deck and enjoy the 180-degree panoramic view of the Pacific.

1602 Ocean Ave. (at Colorado Blvd.), Santa Monica. © **310/458-9294.** www.thelobster.com. Reservations recommended. Main courses $21–$50. AE, DC, DISC, MC, V. Mon–Thurs 11:30am–10pm; Fri–Sat 11:30am–11pm. Valet parking $8.50 for 1st 3 hr.; $10 maximum.

Michael's ★ CALIFORNIAN   Owner Michael McCarty, L.A.'s answer to Alice Waters, is considered by many to be the father of California cuisine. Since Michael's opened in 1979 (when McCarty was only 25), several top L.A. restaurants have caught up to it, but the market-to-table philosophy remains. Although the furniture and decor are dated, the dining room is filled with contemporary art by Michael's wife, Kim McCarty, and the restaurant's garden is one of the city's most romantic settings. The menu changes seasonally, but you might find things like grilled Mediterranean *loup de mer* with chorizo and mussels, oven-roasted Channel spiny lobster with garlic-fennel potato purée, or grilled pork chop with Calvados apple pan sauce. Don't miss Michael's famous warm mushroom salad, which is prepared in various styles utilizing only market-fresh ingredients. The dry-aged New York strip is also fantastic, as are the steak frites. **Tip:** The cocktail program has now caught up with the times. A new list of "farm to glass" spirits features herbs and fruits grown in the rooftop garden at the restaurant.

1147 3rd St. (north of Wilshire Blvd.), Santa Monica. © **310/451-0843.** www.michaelssantamonica.com. Reservations recommended. Main courses dinner $29–$39, lunch $18–$25. AE, DC, DISC, MC, V. Mon–Fri noon–2:30pm and 6–10pm; Sat 6–10pm. Valet parking $8.

Tavern ★ FRENCH/AMERICAN   Caroline Styne and chef Suzanne Goin already have two successful restaurants in L.A. (including Lucques, p. 104), and this, their third, is the more casual of the bunch. It's a multifaceted concept: A full-service restaurant for breakfast, lunch, and dinner; a bar; and a gourmet grocery and to-go counter called the "larder." The atrium dining room is stunning with butterscotch-colored banquettes, high ceilings, skylights, and real olive trees spaced around the tables. Goin goes out on a limb with some dishes and succeeds—the beautifully cooked orata (sea bream) with snappy English peas, crunchy cashews, soft coconut rice and curry butter was one of the best things I've eaten all year. But the ambitious, Mediterranean-inspired lamb T-bone was, unfortunately, overcooked. The bar is a sexy space with high-backed chairs and seasonal cocktails like the refreshing San Pedro, with Avion silver tequila, Benedictine and muddled strawberries. The larder is bright and sunny, with cases and counters filled with everything from homemade breads and pastries like flaky croissants and rich cupcakes to pre-made salads using farmers' market ingredients like heirloom carrots and beets. Everything is presented personal and homespun, but it's definitely priced for the tony Brentwood neighborhood it inhabits.

11648 San Vicente Blvd. (at Darlington Ave.), Brentwood. © **310/806-6464.** www.tavernla.com. Reservations recommended. Main courses $18–$39. AE, DC, DISC, MC, V. Mon–Fri 8–11am, 11:30am–2:15pm, and 5:30–9:30pm (till 10:30pm Fri); Sat 10am–2:15pm and 5:30–10:30pm; Sun 10am–2:15pm and 5:30–9:30pm. Parking lot behind the restaurant ($4.50 with validation).

The Old Place, Up in Them Thar Hills

In a small town in the Santa Monica Mountains, the **Old Place**, 29983 Mulholland Hwy., Cornell (℗ **818/706-9001;** www.oldplacecornell.com), is reminiscent of another time. It's no wonder, since the rustic wood building served as a post office and general store from 1908 to 1940; although it was transformed into a restaurant in 1970, it still retains an Old Western feel with its dark-wood booths, original wood bar, and dim chandeliers. The menu changes regularly, but it features hearty classic dishes that hearken back to the early 20th century—even the warm, crusty sourdough bread is like edible history. For an appetizer, try the delicious wild mushroom skillet, which is an assortment of fresh local mushrooms served over buttery toast in a cast-iron skillet. For a main, the juicy oak-grilled Black Angus sirloin steak is excellent. The rotating list of specials might include blackened Idaho trout or oak-grilled chicken potpie. Portions are large, so come hungry. *Tip:* The place is tiny, so reservations are a must—they are taken 30 days out and are only available at the following seating times: 5, 6:30, and 8:30pm. Main courses $14–$29. MC, V. Thurs–Fri 4–10pm; Sat–Sun 9am–2pm and 4–10pm. Free parking.

Valentino ★★ NORTHERN ITALIAN Valentino is a good choice if you're splurging on just one special dinner, particularly if you're passionate about wine. For almost 40 years, the ever-so-charming and world-renowned restaurateur, Piero Selvaggio, has greeted guests and helped guide them through the extensive wine list (and taken a lucky few on a tour of his award-winning wine cellar). Dinners here are typically lengthy, multicourse affairs, often involving several bottles of wine to match the cuisine. You might begin with a crisp Verdicchio paired with the seafood spaghetti, which incorporates a fresh medley of baby calamari, clams, prawns and cured fish roe. A rich barolo is the perfect accompaniment to veal osso bucco braised with root vegetables and herbs. If you are looking for a more casual dining experience, Piero's **V-vin wine bar** offers excellent small plates and attractively priced flights of older vintages and rarely seen labels from American and international wineries. Please be aware that jackets are all but required in the elegant dining room.

3115 Pico Blvd. (west of Bundy Dr.), Santa Monica. ℗ **310/829-4313.** www.valentinorestaurant.com. Reservations required. Jackets recommended. Main courses $28–$40. AE, DC, MC, V. Tues–Thurs 5–10pm; Fri 11:30am–2:30pm and 5–10:30pm; Sat 5–10:30pm. Valet parking $5.50.

Vincenti Ristorante ★ NORTHERN ITALIAN Despite newer trends sweeping L.A., finely executed northern Italian cuisine is still going strong, as evidenced by this Westside standout. The menu, praised as "authentically Italian," offers creative fare—house-made gnocchi radicchio sauce with walnuts, spinach pappardelle with wild boar ragu—along with well-prepared classics such as wood oven-roasted fish, game birds, steak and even tripe. Economy-minded diners with upwardly mobile palates can easily stick with hearty appetizers and pastas ($18–$22) and still have some room left for one of Vincenti's tempting *dolci,* particularly the vanilla gelato laced with espresso.

11930 San Vicente Blvd. (west of Montana Ave.), Brentwood. ℗ **310/207-0127.** www.vincentiristorante. com. Reservations recommended. Main courses $25–$44. AE, MC, V. Mon–Sat 6–10pm; Fri noon–2pm. Valet parking $5.

Wilshire ★★ CONTEMPORARY CALIFORNIA   From the moment you walk into the lounge area bathed in soothing hues of burnt orange and amber, you know you're going to enjoy this evening—and it only gets better. Hailed by *Bon Appétit* as one of the top 10 outdoor dining spots in America, the restaurant's split-level garden sanctuary has an almost fairy-tale quality to it, with a centerpiece tree-like sculpture holding dozens of candles in its branches, surrounded by leafy trees, raised fire pits, and soothing sounds of artistic water features. Even if the food were dismal, you'd still enjoy yourself; it's that captivating. Luckily, the cuisine is an ideal match for the setting—a delightfully eclectic menu with a focus on seasonal, organic, and local ingredients: steamed mussels in a red curry coconut broth; English pea soup with olive oil-friend croutons; hedgehog-mushroom risotto; and roasted red pepper and burrata salad. My advice is to order the whole fried Thai snapper with citrus soy dipping sauce and sesame soba as the main dish, surround it with the aforementioned appetizers, and dine family style. There's also a very popular happy hour with special pricing for drinks and light fare such as signature hamburgers, Kobe-style sliders, Kumamoto oyster dynamite, pizzas, skewers, and kabobs, Monday through Saturday (5–7pm). *Tip:* Ask the waitstaff if Andrew has time to visit your table—he's a pleasure to talk with and loves to meet his guests.

2454 Wilshire Blvd., Santa Monica. ℂ **310/586-1707.** www.wilshirerestaurant.com. Reservations recommended. Main courses $17–$45. AE, DC, MC, V. Mon–Fri 11:30am–2:30pm and 6–10pm; Sat 6–10pm. Bar/bar menu Mon–Wed 6–10pm, Thurs–Sat 6pm–midnight. Valet parking $10.

Moderate

Border Grill ★ LATIN AMERICAN   Before Mary Sue Milliken and Susan Feniger spiced up cable TV with *Too Hot Tamales,* they opened this vibrant, cavernous, and *muy* loud space that's packed every night with locals and tourists. This is not your Combo #7 kind of place. You'll get things like freshly made corn masa filled with tender roast duck, *guajillo* chili sauce, and roasted sweet peppers; plantain empanadas with chipotle salsa and Mexican *crema;* or the übertender roasted lamb tacos with strips of poblano chilies and manchego cheese. If it's on special, order the grilled chicken enchiladas verdes simmered in green mole sauce with Oaxacan cheese and hand-rolled corn tortillas. To join in on the nonstop fiesta, start with one of their margaritas or mojitos. *Tip:* The happy hour menu (Mon–Fri 4–7pm, Fri–Sat after 10pm) has tasty $3 treats such as tacos, chile poppers, and ceviche shots; margaritas are only $5.

1445 4th St. (btw. Broadway and Santa Monica Blvd.), Santa Monica. ℂ **310/451-1655.** www.bordergrill.com. Reservations recommended. Main courses $19–$29. AE, DC, DISC, MC, V. Sun–Thurs 11:30am–10pm; Fri–Sat 11:30am–11pm. Meters, parking lots.

Joe's Restaurant ★★ 🔥 CALIFORNIAN   This is one of L.A.'s best dining bargains. Chef/owner Joe Miller gutted and completely remodeled a tiny, quirky storefront, adding a far more spacious dining room and display wine room (though the best tables are still tucked away on the trellised outdoor patio complete with a gurgling waterfall). But don't let the upscale additions dissuade your budgeted appetite—Joe's remains a hidden treasure for those with a champagne palate but a seltzer pocketbook. For lunch, the three-course menu is only $18—things like California sand dabs with cherry tomato, arugula, and Maine sweet shrimp, with a fresh mixed green salad or one of Miller's exquisite soups. Seasonal dinner entrees are equally sophisticated: beet risotto with grilled asparagus, fallow deer wrapped in bacon (served in a black currant sauce with a side of roasted root vegetables), monkfish in

Santa Monica & the Beaches

WHERE TO EAT

a saffron broth, or wild striped bass with curried cauliflower coulis. *Tip:* Brunch is among the best in town.

1023 Abbot Kinney Blvd., Venice. © **310/399-5811.** www.joesrestaurant.com. Reservations recommended. Main courses dinner $19–$31, lunch $13–$18. AE, MC, V. Lunch Tues–Fri noon–2:30pm; dinner Sun and Tues–Thurs 6–10pm, Fri–Sat 6–11pm; brunch Sat–Sun 11am–2:30pm. Free street parking; valet parking $5 weekdays, $6 weekends.

La Cachette Bistro ★★ FRENCH   Widely considered one of the most influential French chefs in America, Jean François Meteigner literally wrote the book on this cuisine—*Cuisine Naturelle*—a revolutionary approach to French cooking that eschews heavy creams, butter, and complex recipes in favor of dishes that are simple, light, full of flavor, and 90% free of cream and butter. His flagship fine-dining restaurant in Century City, La Cachette, set the standard for 10 years, but in 2009, he closed down the upscale, elegant eatery and opened this more casual bistro in Santa Monica. Meteigner is still very much the driving force in the kitchen—and popular dishes like the in-shell "eggs and caviar" from his early days at L.A.'s once beloved L'Orangerie can still be ordered (in advance only), but now he's also serving more affordable "French tapas" (small plates) like the excellent smoked trout with perfectly cooked potatoes and homemade sour cream; fork-tender braised pork cheeks; and seared squid in a mint pesto sauce (even if you don't normally like calamari, order this dish and you'll see a whole new side of squid.) Main courses include coq au vin and New Zealand lamb chops.

1733 Ocean Ave, Santa Monica, CA 90401. © **310/434-9509.** www.lacachettebistro.com. Reservations recommended. Main courses $14–$22 lunch, $19–$27 dinner. AE, DC, MC, V. Lunch Tue–Fri noon–2:30pm; dinner Tue–Sun 6pm–closing. Valet parking $6.50 (dinner-only).

Locanda del Lago ★ NORTHERN ITALIAN   In a sea of mediocre restaurants along Santa Monica's Third Street Promenade this corner trattoria is a breath of fresh air. Locanda del Lago (Inn of the Lake) specializes in cuisine from Northern Italy's Lombardy region. On sunny days, there's no better place in L.A. to people-watch than at the trattoria's outdoor patio, savoring a glass of chianti while tucking into the house specialty—*osso buco alla Milanese,* a veal shank slow-cooked in white wine and vegetables, topped with traditional *gremolata* (a parsley, garlic, and lemon zest mixture) and served with saffron risotto. Better yet, visit during happy hour for deep discounts on drinks and select appetizers, like the farmers market vegetables baked in Fata Paper (which helps them retain their natural flavors) and presented tableside,

231 Arizona Ave. (at 3rd St.), Santa Monica. © **310/451-3525.** www.lagosantamonica.com. Reservations recommended. Main courses $22–$34. AE, DC, DISC, MC, V. Mon–Thurs and Sun 11:30am–10pm; Fri–Sat 11am–11pm. Valet parking $5 with validation; public parking garages nearby.

Rustic Canyon ★★ CALIFORNIAN   Locals flock to this popular restaurant for simply prepared, wine-friendly cuisine. It's a compact but comfortable room with a few tables in the bar area, and it can get deafeningly loud, but that's half the fun. The chef utilizes top seasonal ingredients with an emphasis on organic, sustainable fare: arugula salad with mandarin oranges and pistachios; roasted prawns with beets and spring onions; amazing handmade sweet pea ravioli with bacon confit. There's even one dynamite burger, which is almost big enough for two, and fries. People drive across town for Zoe Nathan's desserts like the hot cinnamon-sugar doughnuts. Rustic Canyon isn't open for lunch, but the owners opened a daytime cafe and bakery called **Huckleberry** just a hop and a skip across the street (1014 Wilshire Blvd., Santa Monica; © **310/451-2311;** www.huckleberrycafe.com). Get fantastic sandwiches

SEA BREEZES & SUNSETS: OCEANVIEW
DINING in malibu

o **Beachcomber Café at Malibu Pier** ★★, 23000 Pacific Coast Hwy. (📞 **310/456-9800;** www.thebeachcombercafe.com). Easily my top pick for beachside Malibu dining is this relative newcomer to the Malibu dining scene, run by Michael Jordon, a Master Sommelier and one of the top wine experts in the country (and a delight to chat with, so be sure to ask him to drop by your table to recommend wines). At the foot of the newly renovated Malibu Pier, the Beachcomber features design and decor that speak to the seaside gems of a bygone era, with lots of dark, polished woods, historic photos of surfing legends, and shiny brass trimmings. On a warm day, beg for a patio table overlooking Surfrider Beach, then immediately order the agave margarita, superb clam chowder, and tiny ahi tacos. For entrees I highly recommend the salmon filet with jasmine rice or the wild-mushroom-and-truffle mac and cheese. After your feast, digest with a leisurely stroll down the pier to watch the surfers and bask in the Malibu sun. The Beachcomber is open daily for lunch and dinner from 11am to 10pm. Validated parking for $6 is available in a lot directly south of the pier, or you can prowl for free street parking along PCH.

o **Beau Rivage,** 26025 Pacific Coast Hwy. (at Corral Canyon; 📞 **310/456-5733;** www.beau-rivagerestaurant.com). Though it's my only pick located on the *other* side of PCH from the beach, this romantic Mediterranean restaurant (whose name means "beautiful shore") has nearly unobstructed ocean views. The baby-pink villa and its flagstone dining patio are overgrown with flowering vines. The place is prettiest at sunset; romantic lighting takes over after dark. The menu is composed of country French and Italian dishes with plenty of moderately priced pastas, many with seafood. Other main courses are more expensive; they include chicken, duck, rabbit, and lamb, all traditionally prepared. An older, nicely dressed crowd tends to dine at this special-occasion place. It's open Wednesday through Friday from 5 to 11pm, and Saturday and Sunday from 11am to 11pm. There's a large lot for free self-parking. *Tip:* The weekend brunch menu, which isn't limited to breakfast dishes, is a less pricey alternative to dinner.

o **Duke's Malibu** ★, 21150 Pacific Coast Hwy. (at Las Flores

on home-baked breads and some of the best pastries in town, including delectable fruit crostadas, éclairs, puddings, and cookies—it's hard to choose a favorite.

1119 Wilshire Blvd. (btw. 11th and 12th sts.), Santa Monica. 📞 **310/393-7050.** www.rusticcanyonwinebar.com. Reservations recommended. Main courses $18–$32. AE, MC, V. Daily 5:30–10:30pm. Valet parking $6.50.

Savory ★★ 🏠 CALIFORNIAN   This is a restaurant I wish were in my neighborhood—or anywhere closer than the northern edge of Malibu, for that matter. Located

Canyon; ☏ **310/317-0777;** www.dukesmalibu.com). Lovers of Hawaii and all things Polynesian will thrive in this outpost of the Hawaiian chain. Imagine a South Pacific T.G.I. Friday's where the food is secondary to the decor, then add a rocky perch atop breaking waves, and you have this surfing-themed crowd-pleaser. It's worth a visit for the memorabilia alone—the place is named for Hawaiian surf legend "Duke" Kahanamoku. Duke's offers up pretty good food at inflated but not outrageous prices. You'll find plenty of fresh fish prepared in the Hawaiian regional style, hearty surf and turf, a smattering of chicken and pasta dishes, and plenty of pupus to accompany Duke's Day-Glo tropical cocktails. As the name Barefoot Bar suggests, in this area, guests can remove their footwear and curl their toes in the sand. The Sunday brunch buffet is a tasty deal at $24 for adults and $12 for kids. It's open Monday through Friday from 3 to 9pm; Tuesday through Thursday for lunch from 11:30am to 3pm, dinner from 5 to 9pm; Friday for lunch from 11:30am to 3pm, dinner from 5 to 9:30pm; Saturday for lunch from 11:30am to 3pm, dinner from 4:30 to 10pm. Sunday brunch takes place from 10am to 3pm, and dinner from 4 to 9pm. Valet parking is $4.

○ **Gladstone's 4 Fish,** 17300 Pacific Coast Hwy. (at Sunset Blvd.; ☏ **310/454-3474;** www.gladstones.com). Gladstone's is totally immersed in the Malibu scene. It shares a parking lot with a public beach, so the restaurant's wooden deck has a constant view of surfers, bikini-clad sunbathers, and other beachgoers. At busy times, Gladstone's even sets up picnic-style tables on the sand. Prices are moderate, and the atmosphere is casual. The menu offers several pages of fresh fish and seafood, augmented by a few salads and other meals for landlubbers—quality has improved somewhat since local hospitality group SBE took over the space, but it's still mostly tourist food, though the large portions get the job done. Gladstone's is popular for afternoon/evening drinking and offers nearly 20 seafood appetizer platters; it's also known for its decadent chocolate dessert, the Mile High Chocolate Cake, large enough for the whole table. It's open Monday through Thursday from 11am to 9:30pm, Friday from 11am to 11pm, Saturday from 9am to 11pm, and Sunday from 9am to 10pm. Parking is $5.50.

in the corner of a shopping center, this isn't the kind of place one accidentally stumbles upon, which is just as well since it's already packed every night of the week. Locals love it because Malibu isn't exactly West Hollywood when it comes to foodie finds; other, like myself are willing to make a pilgrimage to dine on chef/owner Paul Shoemaker's sensibly priced but exquisitely prepared market-fresh fare. Walking in the door, the enticing smell of freshly baked pizza beckons diners further. Made in a stone oven from starter several hundred years old, the crispy crust is spot-on. For starters, I recommend anything with burrata; thanks to the chef's connections, they source only the best. King salmon is sensuously seared, and served with fresh Bloomsdale spinach. Risotto was also impressive in consistency, presentation and wine pairing (I'm not one for buttery Chardonnay, but it worked with this dish). **Note:** Portions are smaller than typical entrees, but I'd hesitate to refer to the them as small plates. Ask your server for ordering advice.

29169 Heathercliff Rd. (off PCH), Malibu **310/589-8997.** www.savorymalibu.com. Reservations recommended. Main courses $12–$16. AE, MC, V. Sun–Thurs 5:30–9pm; Fri–Sat 5:30–10pm. Free lot.

Inexpensive

Bread & Porridge ★ 🖤 AMERICAN   A dozen tables are all that comprise this neighborhood cafe, but steady streams of locals mill outside, reading their newspapers and waiting for a vacant seat. Once inside, surrounded by the vintage fruit-crate labels adorning the walls and tabletops, you can sample the delicious breakfasts, fresh salads and sandwiches, and super-affordable entrees. There's a vaguely international twist to the menu, which leaps from breakfast quesadillas and omelets—all served with black beans and salsa—to the Southern comfort of Cajun crab cakes and coleslaw and typical Italian pastas adorned with Roma tomatoes and plenty of garlic. All menu items are truck-stop cheap, but with an inventive elegance that makes this a best-kept secret. This place thoughtfully serves breakfast all day; get a short stack of one of five varieties of pancakes with any meal.

2315 Wilshire Blvd. (3 blocks west of 26th St.), Santa Monica. **🕾310/453-4941.** www.breadandporridge. com. Main courses $7–$18. AE, MC, V. Mon–Fri 7am–2pm; Sat–Sun 7am–3pm. Metered street parking.

Farm Stand ★★ 🖤 MEDITERRANEAN/TURKISH   Opened in 2006, this critical darling is somehow still one of the best kept secrets in town. It probably has something to do with its location on old-fashioned Main Street in sleepy El Segundo. And a quick scan of the menu doesn't do the food justice; a dish like roasted eggplant dip might not sound inspired, but I've never had better baba ghanoush; the same can be said of the bell pepper stuffed with basmati rice, ground beef, and house-made tomato sauce. The restaurant even infuses its own olive oils, one with cilantro and jalapeno, the other with ancho chile. I'm also impressed with the restaurant's commitment to vegetarian, vegan and gluten-free diners (even most of the pastas can substitute a brown-rice base).

422 Main St. (at Pine Ave.), El Segundo. **🕾310/640-3276.** www.farmstand.us. Main courses $9.50–$18. AE, MC, V. Mon–Fri 11am–10pm; Sat–Sun 4–10pm. Street parking.

Jody Maroni's Sausage Kingdom ★★ 🍴 GRILL   Your cardiologist might not approve, but Jody Maroni's all-natural, preservative-free "haute dogs" are some of the best wieners in town. The grungy walk-up (or in-line skate-up) counter looks fairly foreboding—you wouldn't know there was gourmet fare behind that hot dog stand facade, from which at least 24 different grilled sausage sandwiches are served up. Bypass the traditional hot Italian and try the Toulouse garlic, tequila chicken, all-chicken apple, or the Polish pork (made with dark beer). Each is served on a freshly baked onion roll and smothered with onions and peppers. Burgers, BLTs, and rotisserie chicken are also served, but why bother? **Tip:** The stand closes when it rains. Other locations include the Valley's Universal CityWalk (🕾 **818/622-5639**), and inside LAX Terminals 6, where you can pick up some last-minute vacuum-packed sausages for home.

2011 Ocean Front Walk (north of Venice Blvd.), Venice. **🕾310/822-5639.** www.jodymaroni.com. Sandwiches $5–$8. MC, V. Daily 10am–sunset.

Kay 'n Dave's Cantina ☺ BREAKFAST/MEXICAN   A neighborhood favorite since 1995, Kay 'n Dave's is well known for serving big portions of healthy (cooked lard-free) Mexican food at low prices. Come early—and be prepared to wait—for breakfast, as local devotees line up for fluffy French toast, zesty omelets, or one of the best breakfast burritos in town. Spinach and chicken enchiladas in tomatillo salsa, seafood fajitas tostada, vegetable-filled corn tamales, and other Mexican specialties are served in huge portions, making this mostly locals eatery a great choice to energize for (or reenergize after) an action-packed day of sightseeing. Bring the family—there's a kids' menu and plenty of crayon artwork.

262 26th St. (south of San Vicente Blvd.), Brentwood. © **310/260-1355.** www.kayndaves.com. Main courses $6-$20. AE, MC, V. Mon-Fri 11am-9:30pm; Sat 8:30am-9:30pm; Sun 8:30am-9pm. Metered street parking.

Sidewalk Cafe AMERICAN/BREAKFAST   Nowhere in L.A. is the people-watching better than along Ocean Front Walk. The constantly bustling Sidewalk Cafe is ensconced in one of Venice's few remaining early-20th-century buildings. The best seats, of course, are out front, around overcrowded open-air tables, all with perfect views of the crowd, which provides nonstop entertainment. The menu is extensive, and the food is better than it has to be at a location like this. Choose from the seriously overstuffed sandwiches or other oversized, American, Italian and Mexican favorites.

1401 Ocean Front Walk (btw. Horizon Ave. and Market St.), Venice. © **310/399-5547.** www.thesidewalk cafe.com. No reservations. Main courses $8.95-$20. MC, V. Daily 8am-midnight. Pay lots, street parking.

MALIBU

Inn of the Seventh Ray ★★ ORGANIC/VEGETARIAN   This former church in the beautiful (some say spiritual) Topanga Canyon oozes "aura" and is the perfect setting for a romantic dining experience, far from the bright lights of the city. About half of the seating is outdoors, at tables overlooking a creek and endless tangles of untamed vines and shrubs. Inside, the dining room is rustic, with a sloped roof and a glass wall offering mountain views. Everything is prepared from scratch, and foods are organic and chemical- and preservative-free, with a large vegan menu. The fish are caught in deep water far offshore and served the same day; you can even order unpasteurized wines that are quite good. Even the water is ionized. Ten main dishes from the seasonally changing menu are available daily, but are now served a la carte, a change from the once multi-course meals. There's everything from raw flax crackers with tapenade as a starter and Macadamia nut "cheese" to New York steak cut from naturally fed beef.

128 Old Topanga Canyon Rd. (Calif. 27), Topanga. © **310/455-1311.** www.innoftheseventhray.com. Reservations recommended. Main courses $13-$45. AE, DC, DISC, MC, V. Brunch/lunch Mon-Fri 11:30am-3pm, Sat 10:30am-3pm, Sun 9:30am-3pm; dinner daily 5:30-10pm. Valet parking $4 (during busy periods only; other free street parking).

Saddle Peak Lodge ★★ AMERICAN   When you've had it with the L.A. noise and traffic, it's time to hop in the car for a leisurely drive high in the hills above Malibu to Saddle Peak Lodge, an old hunting lodge that has been converted into a hidden, albeit popular, restaurant. It looks exactly like a hunting lodge should—a rustic, weathered ol' three-story building made of massive timbers and native rock that's been gussied up with Teddy-era antiques, a crackling fireplace, and a heady collection of stuffed game. *Vegetarians beware:* The menu is custom-made for meat lovers. There's grilled lamb loin and braised lamb shank; crispy-skin wild Scottish salmon; and the house specialty—roasted elk tenderloin that's so tender you can cut it with a fork. You'll need a strong selection of rich reds to pair with this genre of cuisine, hence the lengthy *Wine Spectator*–endorsed wine list. The restaurant also hosts a very popular Sunday brunch on the garden terrace, serving equally adventurous dishes such as thick buffalo burgers and the wild game trio. *Tip:* Though the restaurant is blue-jean-friendly, business casual attire is suggested and preferred.

419 Cold Canyon Rd. (call for directions), Calabasas. © **818/222-3888.** www.saddlepeaklodge.com. Main courses $29–$54. AE, DC, MC, V. Wed–Thurs 6–9pm; Fri–Sat 6–10pm; Sun 10:30am–2pm and 5–9pm. Valet parking $4.

L.A.'S WESTSIDE & BEVERLY HILLS

Expensive

The Bazaar by José Andrés ★★★ SPANISH/TAPAS The Bazaar is the Disneyland of culinary adventures, and it's helping to solidify L.A.'s on the dining map. It's a Philippe Starck–designed playground for celebrity chef José Andrés—host of the PBS show *Cooking in Spain*—who serves up avant-garde Spanish cuisine. Located in the splashy new SLS Hotel, it's four separate spaces in one open room, and it's sensory overload, from bullfighter pictures and the open kitchen in Rojo, to the calming relaxed vibe in Blanca, to the pink and glossy Patisserie. You'll get traditional tapas like garlic shrimp, salt cod fritters, and impeccable Spanish *jamon,* but it's the "modern tapas" menu and Andrés' molecular gastronomy techniques that gets us excited. We can't get enough of the "Philly cheesesteak," a hollowed out bread filled with oozy cheese and topped with thinly sliced seared Kobe beef, or anything with the "spherical" olives—juice-filled olive "skin" that dissolves in your mouth like magic. Picking candies like saffron gelee in "edible paper" from jars in the Patisserie makes us giddy with delight. *Tip:* I said it in the hotels chapter and it's worth repeating here that there's nothing like a meal at the restaurant-within-a-restaurant SAAM (kind of like Andrés' minibar at Café Atlantico in Washington, D.C.) Unlike the rest of the bustling space, it's small, intimate, and the ultimate in culinary adventure. Trust the chef to prepare 22 courses of mind-blowing molecular gastronomy at its best. Even cocktails get the José treatment at **Bar Centro:** Margaritas come with salt "air," and caipirinhas are made tableside with liquid nitrogen. It's the best (and most expensive, at $20 a pop) slushy cocktail we ever tasted.

465 S. La Cienega Blvd. (in SLS Hotel), Beverly Hills. © **310/246-5555.** www.thebazaar.com. Reservations required. Tapas $9–$38. SAAM tasting menu (food only) $120 per person. AE, DC, DISC, MC, V. Daily 10am–10pm. Valet parking $12.

BLT Steak ★★ STEAKHOUSE The BLT stands for Bistro Laurent Tourondel, and it's the brand that Laurent Tourondel successfully launched from New York City to Hong Kong. Tourondel's not-so-humble beginnings as Chef to the Admiral in the French Navy marked his early training with French classicism, but make no mistake: This man has taught his legions how to cook a rib-eye. The lively restaurant's prime Sunset Strip location—scion of the legendary old Le Dome space—pulls in a steady dose of the Armani-and-Jimmy-Choo-clad crowd, dutifully attended to by WAMs (waiter/actress/models) waiting for a bigger break than 20% of your $300 tab. Each meal starts with *fromage*-enhanced, softball-size popovers that are astonishingly light

Where to Eat in L.A.'s Westside & Beverly Hills

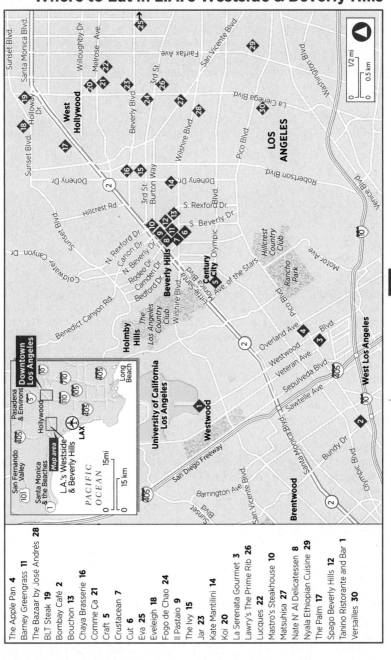

The Apple Pan **4**
Barney Greengrass **11**
The Bazaar by José Andrés **28**
BLT Steak **19**
Bombay Café **2**
Bouchon **13**
Chaya Brasserie **16**
Comme Ça **21**
Craft **5**
Crustacean **7**
Cut **6**
Eva **25**
Eveleigh **18**
Fogo de Chao **24**
Il Pastaio **9**
The Ivy **15**
Jar **23**
Kate Mantilini **14**
Koi **20**
La Serenata Gourmet **3**
Lawry's The Prime Rib **26**
Lucques **22**
Mastro's Steakhouse **10**
Matsuhisa **27**
Nate N' Al Delicatessen **8**
Nyala Ethiopian Cuisine **29**
The Palm **17**
Spago Beverly Hills **12**
Tanino Ristorante and Bar **1**
Versailles **30**

and flavorful, a fitting segue to the 22-ounce bone-in rib-eye, cooked perfectly to your liking and with an octet of sauces to choose from. Our party of four eviscerated a flurry of cocktails, Kumamoto oysters, wonderful side dishes, wines, and desserts, and as we waddled our 7 pounds of leftovers to the parking lot, the vote was unanimous: BLT was one of the most enjoyable steak dining experience we've had in L.A. in years.

8720 W. Sunset Blvd., West Hollywood. ✆ **310/360-1950.** www.bltsteak.com. Reservations recommended. Main courses $27–$55. AE, DC, MC, V. Mon–Thurs 6–10:30pm; Fri–Sat 6–11:30pm; Sun 5:30–10pm. Valet parking $10.

Bouchon ★ FRENCH BISTRO The highly anticipated Bouchon restaurant, the third such French-style bistro created by renowned Chef Thomas Keller (of Napa Valley's the French Laundry fame), made a grand entrance in Beverley Hills in mid-November '09. The name, derived from a specific style of cafe that existed in the French province of Lyon, hints at a classic bistro menu with selections such as steak frites, mussels meunière, *soupe à l'oignon*, quiche Lorraine, foie gras pâté, and other French classics. At the restaurant's Bar Bouchon, diners may choose from small-plate options or oysters from the raw bar, complemented by a glass of Southern California wine or White Apron, a new pilsner-style beer crafted especially for Bouchon. **Tip:** The space is nice and the service stellar, but fans of the original Bouchon in Napa may be disappointed in the inconsistent quality of the food at this outpost.

235 N. Canon Dr. (at Dayton Way), Beverly Hills. ✆ **310/271-9910.** www.bouchonbistro.com. Reservations recommended. Main courses $18–$45. AE, DC, MC, V. Restaurant daily 11:30am–2:30pm and 5:30–10:30pm. Bar daily 11:30am–midnight. Valet parking $8.

Comme Ça ★★ FRENCH BRASSERIE This is a contemporary take on a traditional brasserie: white leather banquettes, mirrors everywhere, chalkboard walls with nightly specials written on them, and knickknack-filled shelves. A bustling bar is the perfect spot for handcrafted fresh-fruit cocktails or a glass of wine and a plate of cheese—the counter has more than 30 varieties and an expert *fromager*. Start with selections from the impressively stocked raw bar. The young and trendy (and, occasionally, the famous) flock here for traditional brasserie dishes like steak frites; delicious escargot doused in parsley butter and miniature croutons; coq au vin; and braised short ribs with potato purée. The rich onion soup is a winner, not overly cheesed-out or gloopy like so many lesser renditions; and the burger is truly one to behold. The only downside is the noise level, which some find abrasive and others think just adds to the bustling atmosphere.

8479 Melrose Ave. (just east of La Cienega Blvd.), West Hollywood. ✆ **323/782-1104.** www.commecarestaurant.com. Reservations recommended. Main courses $17–$29. AE, DISC, MC, V. Daily 10am–10pm. Valet parking $5.50 lunch, $8 dinner.

Craft ★★ NEW AMERICAN The L.A. outpost of the celebrity chef Tom Colicchio's farm-to-table concept, Craft is ironically housed adjacent to the Century City's "Death Star" building. It's fitting, as CAA agents certainly have ample expense accounts to regularly afford the high-quality but pricey proteins. Braised short ribs were some of the best I've had in years. Fermented fruit served with the Liberty Farms duck compensated for a heavy hand with the salt, though I preferred the duck tortellini, with its earthy mushroom consommé. The freshness of the ingredients in the salads remind you that sometimes the best dishes are the most simple. Lightly dressed wild mache with tangerines and hazelnuts bursts with flavor, and pea tendrils with burrata is divine. Finish with a trio of artisan cheeses or the strawberry shortcake with balsamic sorbet.

10100 Constellation Blvd. (btw. Ave. of the Stars and Century Park E), Century City. ☏ **323/782-1104.** www.craftrestaurant.com. Reservations recommended. Main courses $28–$54. AE, DISC, MC, V. Mon-Thurs 6–10pm; Fri-Sat 6–10:30pm. Valet $8; Self-parking free after 5pm (enter the garage on Constellation Blvd.).

Crustacean ★ SEAFOOD/VIETNAMESE   Helene An, matriarch and executive chef of the An family restaurants, is by title a Vietnamese princess, great-granddaughter of the vice king of Vietnam. When she and her family fled from Saigon penniless in 1975, they relocated to San Francisco, purchased a small deli, and introduced the city to their now-legendary recipe: An Family's Famous Roast Crab and Garlic Noodles. These two dishes spawned a Horatio Alger story and a family restaurant dynasty. With the Indochina-themed decor—a curvaceous copper bar, balcony seating, a bamboo garden, a waterfall, and an 80-foot-long "stream" topped with glass and filled with exotic koi—the Beverly Hills location is pure drama from the moment you walk in. What you won't see is the Secret Kitchen (literally, it's off-limits to even most of the staff), where the An family's signature dishes such as tiger prawns with garlic noodles, whole Maine lobster in tamarind sauce, and roast Dungeness crab are prepared.

9646 Little Santa Monica Blvd. (at Bedford St.), Beverly Hills. ☏ **310/205-8990.** www.anfamily.com. Reservations recommended. Main courses $20–$46. AE, DC, DISC, MC, V. Mon-Thurs 11:30am–2:30pm and 5:30–10:30pm; Fri 11:30am–2:30pm and 5:30–11:30pm; Sat 5:30–11:30pm. Valet parking $5.50.

Cut ★★ STEAK   This has been a power dinner spot for entertainment industry heavyweights since it opened at the Beverly Wilshire hotel in 2006. Think of this as special occasion—or, like everyone else, expense account—dining. The decor is chic if not sparse, perfect for seeing any of the myriad celebs walk in and dine (Tom and Katie used to be regulars). It's one open space with few nooks for hiding, and all scene—but there's still substance. Linen-wrapped meat is brought to the table so you can learn the difference between Japanese Kobe beef at $120 for a six-ounce filet (this is the most expensive steak in town), American Wagyu, and Illinois corn-fed USDA prime. The steaks are grilled over hardwood and charcoal and finished under a 1,200°F broiler, ensuring a buttery, juicy cut. Everything is a heightened experience, including side dishes: creamed spinach comes topped with an organic sunny-side-up egg; mac and cheese is made with Quebec cheddar; potatoes aren't simply *au gratin*, they're a beautiful *tarte tatin*. Sherry Yard's desserts are fantastic, and the wine list is exemplary (and pricey). Across the hall is **Sidebar,** a great spot for people-watching while sipping a martini and noshing on Kobe beef sliders.

9500 Wilshire Blvd. (in the Beverly Wilshire Hotel), Beverly Hills. ☏ **310/276-8500.** www.wolfgangpuck.com. Reservations required. Main courses $40–$120. AE, DISC, MC, V. Mon-Thurs 7–10pm; Fri 6–11pm; Sat 5:30–11pm. Valet parking $12.

Eva ★ NEW AMERICAN Chef/owner Mark Gold, an alum of both the Patina Group and Water Grill has created a darling bistro-style restaurant with a small but focused menu. The vibe is down to earth, with friendly staff playing multiple roles as needed. The same person who greeted us as the hostess also ended up being our waitress and mixologist. Parsnip soup is enlivened with prominent bay leaf flavors as well as tangerine foam. The foie gras tourchon was more like a velvety log (one of the best I've had in recent memory). We also enjoyed the texture of the udon noodles in the lobster Bolognese, but we wish the hand-harvested scallops had been a touch or two less cooked through.

7548 Beverly Blvd. (btw. Gardner St. and Vista St.), Los Angeles. ☏ **323/634-0700.** www.evarestaurantla.com. Reservations recommended. Three-course menu starts at $39. AE, MC, V. Tues-Thurs 5:30–10pm; Fri 11:30am–2pm, 5:30–11pm; Sat 5:30–11pm; Sun 3–9:30pm. Valet $3.50.

Eveleigh ★ CALIFORNIAN/MEDITERRANEAN   If we had a food category called Euro-fabulous, I'd easily affix that tag to this hopping new eatery that manages to appeal to both trendsetters and foodies. Hidden behind trellises and shrubbery on the Sunset Strip of all places, the sexy space is strangely one of the few in the neighborhood that takes advantage of the killer view off its back patio, where I highly recommend sitting—not only for the city vistas, but also because the later it gets, the higher the din surrounding the bar in the main dining room. And who can blame them? The bartenders know what they're doing, whether it's stirring a classic Manhattan or crafting the specialty, Mezcal-based Blood and Smoke. Start with shucked oysters in a peppery vinaigrette, or the plump pot-roasted mussels (and get extra bread to sop up the complex broth. Short rib lovers should broaden their horizons with the braised beef cheeks, which are only mildly more gamey. And the roasted barramundi boasts crispy skin and flavorful romesco salsa—I just wish there were more of it on the plate. *Tip:* The name is pronounced "EVER-lee," despite the missing "r."

8752 Sunset Blvd., West Hollywood. ✆ **424/239-1630.** www.theeveleigh.com. Reservations recommended. Main courses $16–$29. AE, DISC, MC, V. Dinner Sun–Wed 5–10pm; Thurs–Sat 5–10:30pm; brunch Sat–Sun 10am–3pm. Valet parking $4.50.

Fogo de Chão ★ BRAZILIAN/STEAK   What was started long ago by four brothers in Brazil, finally made its way to California—Beverly Hills, even—and has become a Restaurant Row staple. Pronounced *fo-go dee SHOWN,* this enormous Southern Brazilian–style steakhouse is packed nightly with fans of the *churrasco* style of cooking *carne*—large cuts of meat slow-roasted over an open wood flame, then deftly sliced and continuously served onto your plate until you give in and flip your disk to red (you'll see). It's a prix-fixe system where everything on the menu except alcohol is available for a flat fee, and the superb waitstaff are always hovering nearby with meat-laden platters in the off-chance that you actually clear your plate. Truly, it's Bacchanalia revisited as you wander wide-eyed around the dazzling salad bar (be careful not to ruin your appetite). The gluttony continues with mountains of freshly roasted meats and endless side dishes, all washed down with rich red wines from among the 10,000 bottles that surround you in two-story, temperature-controlled

The Sturgeon King, Take 2

New Yorkers suffering L.A. culture shock can seek comfort food on the fifth floor of the Barneys New York department store in Beverly Hills. The elevator doors open and *voilà*—a **Barney Greengrass** on the Left Coast. This authentic—and expensive—New York deli not only air-delivers its renowned smoked sturgeon and Nova Scotia salmon direct from the Big Apple, but it has even bejeweled the swanky lunch spot with subway-style tiles. You'll have to move quickly to get a coveted table on the outdoor terrace—all those power lunchers from the entertainment industry won't hesitate. The raison d'être dishes here are the Nova Scotia salmon (or sturgeon) scrambled with eggs and onion, cheese blintzes, and chopped chicken liver sandwiches—all washed down with New York–style seltzer water on tap. It's open Monday, Tuesday, Wednesday, and Friday from 8:30am to 6pm; Thursday and Saturday from 9:30am to 7pm; and Sunday from 9:30am to 6pm. 9570 Wilshire Blvd. (at Camden Dr.), Beverly Hills. ✆ **310/777-5877.**

towers of glass and steel. Dessert? Good luck! *Tip:* The lunch menu is identical to dinner—a savings of more than $20 per person.

133 N. La Cienega Blvd. (btw. W. 3rd St. and Beverly Blvd.), Beverly Hills. © **310/289-7755.** www. fogodechao.com. Reservations recommended. Fixed-price menu $35 lunch; $57 dinner. AE, DC, DISC, MC, V. Lunch Mon–Fri 11:30am–2pm; dinner Mon–Thurs 5–10pm, Fri 5–10:30pm, Sat 4:30–10:30pm, Sun 4–9:30pm. Valet parking $5.50.

The Ivy ★ AMERICAN   If you're willing to endure the cold shoulder to ogle L.A.'s celebrities and pay lots for a perfect meal, the Ivy can be enjoyable. This snobby place attracts one of the most industry-heavy crowds in the city and treats celebrities and nobodies as differently as Brahmans and untouchables. Just past the cool reception lie two disarmingly countrified dining rooms filled with rustic antiques, comfortably worn chintz, and hanging baskets of fragrant flowers. Huge roses bloom everywhere, including out on the charming brick patio (where the highest-profile patrons are seated and dutifully ignore the stares). The Ivy's Caesar salad is nice, as are the plump and crispy crab cakes. Recommended dishes include spinach linguine with a peppery tomato-basil sauce, prime rib dusted with Cajun spices, and tender lime-marinated grilled chicken. There's even a good burger and fried chicken. The wine list is notable, and there's always a terrific variety of desserts (pink boxes are on hand for chocolate-chip cookies to go).

113 N. Robertson Blvd. (btw. 3rd St. and Beverly Blvd.), West Hollywood. © **310/274-8303.** Reservations recommended. Main courses $25–$60. AE, DC, DISC, MC, V. Daily 10am–10pm. Valet parking $5.50.

Jar ★★ MODERN CHOPHOUSE   Jar offers everything you could hope for in a sophisticated American restaurant: a warm and relaxed setting, excellent service, and generous servings of reliably good comfort food. The braised Kurobuta pork shank and a Kobe-style filet of beef—both perfectly cooked, simply seasoned—are divinely flavorful. It was always chef Suzanne Tracht's dream to open a contemporary version of a 1940s-era chophouse, and you can tell that she's putting her best into every plate that leaves the kitchen. Everything she makes is a lesson in quality and simplicity. Among her most popular dishes are the Niman Ranch char sui pork chops and her coup de grâce—a sensational pot roast with caramelized onions and carrots. An extensive wine list and martini menu are two good reasons to arrive early and stay for a nightcap at the beautiful Parisian-style bar. *Tip:* Suzanne's Sunday brunch is one of the best in the city; try the corn pancakes or the lobster Benedict.

8225 Beverly Blvd. (at Harper Ave.), West Hollywood. © **323/655-6566.** www.thejar.com. Reservations recommended. Main courses $21–$42. AE, DC, DISC, MC, V. Mon–Thurs 5:30–10pm; Fri–Sat 5:30–11pm; Sun 10am–2pm and 5:30–10pm. Valet parking $6.

5

WHERE TO EAT

L.A.'s Westside & Beverly Hills

Lawry's The Prime Rib STEAK/SEAFOOD   Most Americans know Lawry's only as a brand of seasoned salt (which was invented here). Going to this family-run institution is an old-world event, where the main menu offerings are four cuts of Prime rib that vary in thickness from two fingers to an entire hand. Every standing rib roast is dry-aged for 2 to 3 weeks, sprinkled with Lawry's famous seasoning, and then roasted on a bed of rock salt. A carver wheels the cooked beef tableside, then slices it properly, rare to well-done. All dinners come with creamy whipped horseradish, Yorkshire pudding, and the Original Spinning Bowl Salad (drenched in Lawry's signature sherry French dressing). Lawry's moved across the street from its original location years ago but retained its throwback-to-the-1930s clubroom atmosphere, complete with Persian-carpeted oak floors, high-backed chairs, and European oil paintings.

100 N. La Cienega Blvd. (north of Wilshire Blvd.), Beverly Hills. © **310/652-2827.** www.lawrysonline. com. Reservations recommended. Main courses $20–$40. AE, DC, DISC, MC, V. Mon–Thurs 5–10pm; Fri 5–11pm; Sat 4:30–11pm; Sun 4–10pm. Valet parking $6.

Lucques ★★ FRENCH/MEDITERRANEAN   Once Los Angeles became accustomed to this restaurant's unusual name—["]Lucques" is a variety of French olive, pronounced "Luke"—local foodies fell hard for this quietly and comfortably sophisticated flagship of former Campanile chef Suzanne Goin. The old brick building, once silent star Harold Lloyd's carriage house, is decorated in muted, clubby colors with subdued lighting that extends to the handsome enclosed patio. Goin cooks with bold flavors, fresh-from-the-farm produce, and an instinctive feel for the food of the Mediterranean. The short and oft-changed menu makes the most of unusual ingredients such as salt cod and oxtails. Standout dishes include Tuscan bean soup with tangy greens and pistou, grilled duck breast served alongside braised red cabbage with chanterelle mushrooms and chestnuts, and a perfect vanilla *pòt de crème* for dessert. Lucques's bar menu, featuring steak frites béarnaise, omelets, and tantalizing hors d'oeuvres (olives, warm almonds, sea salt, chewy bread), is a godsend for late-night diners, and the bartenders make a mean vodka Collins. *Tip:* On Sundays, Lucques offers a bargain $45 prix-fixe three-course dinner from a weekly changing menu.

8474 Melrose Ave. (east of La Cienega Blvd.), West Hollywood. © **323/655-6277.** www.lucques.com. Reservations recommended. Main courses $27–$34. AE, DC, MC, V. Lunch Tues–Sat noon–2:30pm; dinner Mon–Thurs 6–10pm, Fri–Sat 6–10:30pm, Sun 5–10pm. Metered street parking; valet parking $5.50.

Mastro's Steakhouse ★★★ STEAK/SEAFOOD   This is one of the best steakhouses in Southern California. Typical of an upscale steakhouse, the dimly lit dining room on the first floor has a dark, leathery, serious men's club feel to it, so be sure to request a table on the second floor, where the bar, live music, and cool vibe are located. Slide into a plush black leather booth, order a Mastro Dry Ice Martini (which comes with the shaker, so it takes only one to get a groove on), and start off the feast with an Iced Seafood Tower—a massive pyramid of crab legs, lobster, shrimp, clams, and oysters. The Fred Flintstone–size slabs of hand-cut USDA beef are served on sizzling plates heated to 400°F (204°C) so your steak stays warm and juicy throughout the meal. Greens are always a good idea—as is the decadent lobster mashed potatoes. The bad news is that a bone-in rib-eye runs about $50; the good news is that one will feed three normal-size people. *Tip:* Service runs the gamut from fawing to forgetful, often depending on how much you drop. Consider sitting at the downstairs bar for a more casual experience, though you'll miss the priceless people-watching around the piano bar upstairs.

246 N. Canon Dr. (btw. Dayton Way and Wilshire Blvd.), Beverly Hills. © **310/888-8782.** www. mastrossteakhouse.com. Reservations recommended. Main courses $26–$84. AE, DC, MC, V. Restaurant Sun–Thurs 5–11pm, Fri–Sat 5pm–midnight. Lounge daily 4:30pm–1am. Valet parking $7.

Matsuhisa ★ JAPANESE/PERUVIAN Japanese chef/owner Nobuyuki Matsuhisa arrived in Los Angeles via Peru in 1987 and opened what may be the most creative restaurant in the city. A true master of fish cookery, Matsuhisa creates unusual dishes by combining Japanese flavors with South American spices and salsas (he was the first to introduce Americans to yellowtail sashimi with sliced jalapeños). Broiled sea bass with black truffles, miso-flavored black cod, sautéed squid with garlic and soy, tempura sea urchin in a shiso leaf, and Dungeness crab tossed with chilies and cream are just a few examples of the masterfully prepared dishes available, in addition to thickly sliced nigiri and creative sushi rolls. The small, crowded main dining room suffers from poor lighting and precious lack of privacy; many big names are ushered through to private dining rooms. Expect a bit of attitude from the staff as well. In short, this is a landmark eatery, but compared to others at similar price points it's now past its prime. *Note:* Matsuhisa's very local outpost of his successful **Nobu** chain is right up the street (903 N. La Cienega Blvd., © **310/657-5711**). It's more scene-y, so it tends to appeal to a younger demographic.

129 N. La Cienega Blvd. (north of Wilshire Blvd.), Beverly Hills. © **310/659-9639.** www.nobumatsuhisa. com. Reservations required. Main courses $28–$38; sushi $6–$18 per order; full *omakase* dinner from $90. AE, DC, MC, V. Mon–Fri 11:45am–2:15pm and 5:45–10:15pm; Sat–Sun 5:45–10:15pm. Valet parking $5.50.

The Palm ★ STEAK/LOBSTER The child of the famous New York restaurant of the same name, the Palm is one of the top traditional American eateries in the city. In both food and ambience, this West Coast WeHo apple hasn't fallen far from the proverbial tree. The restaurant is brightly lit, bustling with energy, and playfully decorated with dozens of celebrity caricatures on the walls. Live Nova Scotia lobsters are flown in almost daily and then broiled over charcoal and served with big bowls of melted butter. Most are enormous (3–7 lb.) and, although they're obscenely expensive, can be shared. The steaks and swordfish are similarly sized, perfectly grilled to order, and served a la carte by cheeky white-jacketed waiters who have been around since the Nixon administration. For dessert, stick with the Palm's perfect New York cheesecake, flown in straight from the Bronx.

9001 Santa Monica Blvd. (btw. Doheny Dr. and Robertson Blvd.), West Hollywood. © **310/550-8811.** www.thepalm.com. Reservations recommended. Main courses dinner $23–$68, lobsters $28 per pound; lunch $14–$24. AE, DC, MC, V. Mon–Thurs noon–10pm; Fri noon–11pm; Sat 5–11pm; Sun 5–9:30pm. Valet parking $6.

Spago Beverly Hills ★★ CALIFORNIAN Despite all the hoopla—and years of stiff competition—Spago may not be quite the pioneer it once was, but it's still very respectable. Wolfgang Puck's talented henchman Lee Hefter presides over the kitchen, delivering the culinary sophistication demanded by an upscale Beverly Hills crowd. This high-style indoor/outdoor space glows with the aura of big bucks, celebrities, and the well-honed California cuisine that set the standard. Men will feel most comfortable in jacket (suggested, but not required). All eyes may be on the romantically twinkle-lit outdoor patio (the most coveted tables). Menu highlights include the appetizer of foie gras "three ways;" crayfish salad; savory duck either honey-lacquered and topped with foie gras or Cantonese-style with a citrus tang; slow-roasted Sonoma lamb with braised greens; smoked salmon pizza; and rich Austrian dishes from "Wolfie's" childhood, such as spicy beef goulash and perfect veal schnitzel.

176 N. Canon Dr. (north of Wilshire Blvd.), Beverly Hills. © 310/385-0880. www.wolfgangpuck.com. Reservations required. Jacket advised for men. Main courses $32–$45, tasting menu $140. AE, DC, DISC, MC, V. Lunch Mon–Sat noon–2:30pm; dinner daily 6–10pm. Valet parking $8.

Moderate

Bombay Café ★ INDIAN   This friendly sleeper is one of L.A.'s most popular Indian spots, serving quite good curries and kormas typical of South Indian street food. Once seated, immediately order *sev puri* for the table; these crispy little crackers topped with chopped potatoes, onions, and chutneys are the perfect accompaniment to what's sure to be an extended menu-reading session. Also recommended are the burrito-like "frankies," juicy little bread rolls stuffed with lamb, chicken, or cauliflower. The best dishes come from the tandoor and include chicken marinated overnight in yogurt and spice masala and skewered. While some dishes are authentically spicy, plenty of others have a mellow flavor for less incendiary palates. The main gripe among locals, though, are the prices; it's more spendy than most Indian food.

12021 W. Pico Blvd. (at Bundy Dr.), Los Angeles. © 310/473-3388. www.bombaycafe-la.com. Reservations recommended for dinner. Main courses $11–$19. MC, V. Mon–Fri 11:30am–3pm and 5–10pm (Fri till 11pm); Sat noon–3pm and 5–11pm; Sun noon–3pm and 5–10pm. Metered street parking (lunch); valet parking $4.75 (dinner).

Chaya Brasserie ★ FRENCH/JAPANESE   Open for more than 25 years, Chaya is still one of Los Angeles's most reliable restaurants. This Continental bistro with Asian overtones is popular with film agents during lunch and a particularly beautiful assembly of stars at night. The place is loved for its high-concept East/West dishes, unpretentious atmosphere, and attractive waitstaff. Despite a high noise level and odd Motown/rock soundtrack, the stage-lit dining room feels sensuous and swoony. On warm afternoons and evenings, the best tables are on the outside terrace, overlooking the busy street, but I prefer the interior. The best way to order is off the three- or five-course tasting menu, though there are gems in the a la carte section, such as smoky yellowtail mole. Porcini risotto utilizes organic farro to get earthy effect. Black Angus beef filet is nicely salted and served with a subtle bone marrow jus and wasabi potato puree. *Note:* There's also a Chaya near the beach, **Chaya Venice** (110 Navy St., Venice; © 310/396-1179), and the splashy newest location at the City National Plaza (525 S. Flower St., Downtown; © 213/236-9577).

8741 Alden Dr. (east of Robertson Blvd.), Los Angeles. © 310/859-8833. www.thechaya.com. Reservations recommended. Main courses dinner $15–$27, lunch $10–$16. AE, MC, V. Mon–Thurs 11am–2:30pm and 6–10:30pm; Fri–Sat 11am–2:30pm and 6–11pm; Sun 11am–3pm and 6–10pm. Valet parking $7.

Il Pastaio ★ NORTHERN ITALIAN   Sicilian-born chef/owner Giacomino Drago (scion of L.A.'s well-known Drago restaurateur family) hit the jackpot with this hugely successful, value-priced trattoria located on a busy corner in the shopping district of Beverly Hills. All day long, Giacomino's fans take a break from work or shopping and converse over glasses of chianti and plates of oh-so-authentic pasta. You'll swoon over the *arancini,* breaded rice cones filled with mozzarella cheese and peas, then fried crispy brown (highly addictive); the pumpkin tortelloni in a light sage-and-cream sauce; the *arrabbiata,* a simple penne pasta dish in a fantastic spicy tomato-and-garlic sauce; and for dessert, the silky panna cotta. There's almost always a wait—and not much room to wait in—but by meal's end it always seems worth it.

400 N. Canon Dr. (at Brighton Way), Beverly Hills. © **310/205-5444.** www.giacominodrago.com. Main courses $12–$30 lunch, $13–$30 dinner. AE, DC, MC, V. Mon–Wed 11:30am–11pm; Thu–Sat 11:30am–midnight; Sun 11:30am–10pm. Valet parking $7.

Koi ★ ASIAN FUSION   Even after almost 10 years, this place still attracts Hollywood's A-list crowd. Incorporating feng shui elements, the minimalist, earthen-hued interior has a calming ambience that is a welcome relief from the hectic La Cienega scene just outside the ornately carved gates. The chef's fusions of Japanese and Californian cuisine account for the repeat clientele. As is the case for trendy restaurants like this, the food is overpriced, but good—if you're not a purist and you like big, bold flavors. Start with the refreshing cucumber *sunomono* tower flavored with sweet vinegar and edible flowers, followed by a baked crab roll with edible rice paper, the tuna tartare and avocado on crispy won tons, the yellowtail carpaccio delicately flavored with grape-seed oil, and black cod bronzed with miso that's warm-butter soft and exploding with sweet flavor. *Tip:* Request one of the horseshoe booths on the back patio amid Buddha statues and candlelight.

730 N. La Cienega Blvd. (btw. Melrose Ave. and Santa Monica Blvd.), West Hollywood. © **310/659-9449.** www.koirestaurant.com. Reservations recommended. Main courses $14–$50. AE, DC, DISC, MC, V. Sun–Wed 6–11pm; Thurs 6–11:30pm; Fri–Sat 6pm–midnight. Valet parking $8.

Tanino Ristorante and Bar ★★ REGIONAL ITALIAN   It's worth visiting Tanino just to marvel at the 1929 Italianate Renaissance–style building, one of only 12 remaining since Westwood's founding days. The magnificent original ceiling frescoes, carvings, murals, and artisan plaster blend well with the checkerboard terrazzo marble flooring, sumptuous booths, wrought-iron chandeliers, and candlelit tables—an ideal setting for a romantic evening. Chef/owner Tanino Drago (of L.A.'s well-known Drago restaurateur family) has created a menu based on regional dishes, many of which are from his native home of Sicily. Wild mushroom soup, with just a small touch of truffle oil, makes a great start to the meal. For pastas, the pumpkin tortelloni in a flavorful sage-and-cream sauce is delicious, but I actually preferred the baked spaghetti with eggplant served in a light tomato basil sauce—think of it as eggplant Parmesan meets spaghetti. Spigola, similar to striped bass, isn't always on the menu—it depends if they get a batch that day from the Motherland—but if it, it's a must. The whole, delicate fish is baked in salt and deboned tableside. *Tip:* Linger a bit after your meal to enjoy a glass of grappa by the fireplace.

1043 Westwood Blvd. (btw. Kinross and Weyburn sts.), Westwood. © **310/208-0444.** www.tanino. com. Reservations recommended. Main courses $13–$40. AE, DC, MC, V. Mon–Fri 11am–2:30pm and 5–10:30 pm; Sat 5–10:30pm; Sun 4:30–10pm. Valet parking $6.

Waterloo & City ★ BRITISH GASTROPUB   Gastropubs have come and gone in one form or another in waves since the trend first hit back in the mid-2000s, but none have had as distinctly a British take as this one. On the outskirts of Culver City near the Marina del Rey border—it's kind of in the middle of nowhere, really, sits this former coffee shop, which has been transformed into a casually chic neighborhood favorite and destination dining institution. There's a whole section of charcuterie—and not just the usual suspects. If you're adventurous enough to try a smoked tongue and carrot terrine, I highly recommend it. The Caesar salad is also far from passé; it's wrapped in a giant "crouton," beautifully dressed and topped with white anchovies. Missteps are small: the short rib is beautifully cooked, but benefits from a pinch of salt. For dessert, you may discover a new favorite triple cream cheese or try the seasonal "limey" pie with ginger sorbet and Key lime confit.

12517 Washington Blvd., Culver City. © **310/391-4222.** www.waterlooandcity.com. Main courses $19–$26. AE, MC, V. Mon–Sat 6–10pm; Sun 5–9pm. Free street parking.

I'LL TAKE THE FIFTH...TASTE

Since opening its original location on La Brea in 2009, **Umami Burger,** 850 S. La Brea Ave. (℃ **323/931-3000;** www.umamiburger.com)—named after the fifth taste profile, savory or "umami"—has become something of a cult classic, spawning sister restaurants all over the city. While the signature burger remains the most popular, I'm partial to the smoky triple pork burger (ground pork, chorizo, and applewood-smoked bacon) topped with manchego cheese and pimento aioli. The menu varies slightly at each location, as does the availability of beer and wine verses a full bar (the tiny original will remain alcohol-free). Be sure to try the sweet potato fries, too. Also at 1520 N. Cahuenga Blvd., Hollywood (℃ **323/469-3100**); 4655 Hollywood Blvd., Los Feliz (℃ **323/669-3922**); 500 Broadway, Santa Monica (℃ **310/451-1300**); and 12159 Ventura Blvd., Studio City (℃ **818/286-9004**).

Inexpensive

The Apple Pan ★ DINER   There are no tables—just a U-shaped counter—at this classic American burger shack and hugely popular L.A. landmark. Open since 1947, the Apple Pan is a diner that looks—and acts—the part. It's famous for juicy burgers, grumpy service, and an authentic, frills-free atmosphere. The hickory burger is best, though the tuna sandwich also has its share of fans. Ham, egg salad, and Swiss-cheese sandwiches round out the menu. Definitely order fries and, if you're in the mood, the house-baked apple pie. Expect to wait a bit during the lunch rush (don't worry, the honor-system line moves pretty fast).

10801 Pico Blvd. (east of Westwood Blvd.), Los Angeles. ℃ **310/475-3585.** www.applepan.com. Most menu items under $6. No credit cards. Tues–Thurs and Sun 11am–midnight; Fri–Sat 11am–1am. Free parking.

Kate Mantilini ★★ TRADITIONAL AMERICAN/BREAKFAST   It's rare to find a restaurant that feels comfortably familiar yet cutting-edge trendy at the same time—and also happens to be one of L.A.'s few late-night eateries. Kate Mantilini fits the bill perfectly. One of the first to bring meatloaf back into fashion, Kate's offers a huge menu of upscale truck-stop favorites such as "white" chili (made with chicken, white beans, and jack cheese); grilled steaks, chicken, and fish; a few token pastas; and just about anything you might crave. At 2am, nothing quite beats a steaming bowl of lentil-vegetable soup and some garlic-cheese toast, unless your taste runs to fresh oysters, a candy-bar-ice-cream pie, and a dry martini—yep, Kate has it all.

9101 Wilshire Blvd. (at Doheny Dr.), Beverly Hills. ℃ **310/278-3699.** www.katemantilinirestaurant.com. Reservations accepted only for parties of 6 or more. Main courses $13–$25. AE, MC, V. Mon 11:30am–10pm; Tues–Thurs 11:30am–midnight; Fri 11:30am–1am; Sat 11am–1am; Sun 10am–10pm. Valet parking $5.

La Serenata Gourmet ★★ MEXICAN   Westsiders rejoiced when this branch of Boyle Heights's award-winning La Serenata de Girabaldi began serving its authentic, innovative Mexican cuisine just a block away from the Westside Pavilion shopping center. This place is casual, fun, and intensely delicious. Local favorites are the Mexican shrimp in rich *mojo de ajo* sauce, fish tacos, shrimp enchiladas, pork *gorditas,* and tender beef tongue in tomatillo sauce. All dishes are accented with hand-patted corn tortillas, and fresh chips served with flavorful, fresh salsas. It's always packed to capacity, so try to avoid the prime lunch and dinner hours.

10924 W. Pico Blvd. (at Westwood Blvd.), West L.A. ☎**310/441-9667.** www.laserenataonline.com. Main courses $9.95–$24. DISC, MC, V. Mon–Fri 11:30am–10pm; Fri 11am–3pm ;Sat–Sun 9am–10:30pm. Metered street parking.

Nate 'n Al Delicatessen ★ DELI/BREAKFAST   If you want to know where old-money, rich-and-famous types go for comfort food, look no further. Despite its location in the center of Beverly Hills's "Golden Triangle," Nate 'n Al has remained unchanged since 1945, from the Naugahyde booths to the motherly waitresses, who treat you the same whether you're a house-account celebrity regular or just a visitor stopping in for an overstuffed pastrami on rye, beef brisket, or short ribs. The too-salty chicken soup keeps Nate 'n Al from being the best L.A. deli (actually, I'd be hard-pressed to choose any one deli as the city's best), but staples such as chopped liver, dense potato pancakes, blintzes, borscht, and well-dilled pickles more than make up for it. *Tip:* This is a little-known and low-rent hot spot for celebrity spying.

414 N. Beverly Dr. (at Brighton Way), Beverly Hills. ☎**310/274-0101.** www.natenal.com. Main courses $9.50–$16. AE, DISC, MC, V. Daily 7am–9pm. Public parking lot next door; 2 hr. free; after 6pm, it's a flat-rate of $5.

Nyala Ethiopian Cuisine ★ 🍴 ETHIOPIAN   There are no fewer than four or five (who can keep track?) Ethiopian eateries along two compact blocks of Fairfax, but Nyala is one of the largest and still the most popular. In a mellow setting, an ethnically mixed crowd finds common ground in the expertly spiced (smoldering rather than fiery) cuisine. For the uninitiated, Ethiopian food is a mosaic of chopped salads, chunky stews, and saucy vegetables, all served on a colorful enamel platter for communal enjoyment. There are no utensils, merely a basket of *injera,* the thick, sour, plate-size pancake that triples as utensil, plate, and bread. Choices range from hearty chicken or lamb chunks stewed with tomatoes and onions to a parade of vegetarian choices (lentils, split peas, collard greens), each with a distinctive marinade. African beers and honey wine are perfect accompaniments. *Tip:* The weekday lunch buffet is a great deal.

1076 S. Fairfax Ave. (south of Olympic Blvd.), Los Angeles. ☎**323/936-5918.** www.nyala-la.com. Reservations recommended. Main courses $7–$12. AE, DC, MC, V. Mon–Sat 11:30am–10:30pm; Sun noon–10pm. Metered street parking.

Versailles ★ CARIBBEAN/CUBAN   Outfitted with Formica tabletops and looking something like an ethnic IHOP, Versailles feels much like any number of restaurants in Miami that cater to the Cuban community. The menu reads like a veritable survey of Havana-style cookery and includes specialties such as "Moros y Cristianos" (flavorful black beans with white rice), *ropa vieja* (a stringy beef stew), and fried whole fish (usually sea bass). Anybody who's eaten here will tell you the same thing: "Order the shredded roast pork." Tossed with the restaurant's trademark garlic-citrus sauce, it's highly addictive. Equally fetching is the garlic chicken—succulent, slow roasted, and smothered in onions and garlic-citrus sauce. Almost everything is served with black beans and rice; wine and beer are available. Because meals are good, bountiful, and cheap, there's often a wait.

1415 S. La Cienega Blvd. (south of Pico Blvd.), Los Angeles. ☎**310/289-0392.** www.versaillescuban. com. Main courses $11–$22. AE, MC, V. Sun–Thurs 11am–10pm; Fri–Sat 11am–11pm. Free parking.

HOLLYWOOD & WEST HOLLYWOOD

Expensive

Ammo ★ CONTEMPORARY AMERICAN Ammo has been around since 1996—not an easy feat for an L.A. restaurant. Thanks to chef/couple team Daniel Mattern (chef) and Roxana Jullapat (pastry chef) it's better than ever. For a restaurant that's not at all fussy, the attention to detail is refreshing. The ambiance is airy, with lots of light wood and soft lighting at night. Even the cool indie soundtrack is curated by GM Benny Bohm, himself a musician. The menu changes all the time, but anything wood-roasted is a good bet. We loved the thick asparagus with burrata, lemon, and hazelnuts. Pacific clams rested in a complex broth of white wine and pickled chili with sweet fennel sausage. Sand dabs are an old favorite, but here they are given contemporary treatment thanks to a crunchy celery root slaw side. Don't leave without trying Jullapat's desserts such as sticky toffee pudding with dates, tangerines and brown-butter ice cream.

1155 N. Highland Ave. (at Lexington Ave.), Los Angeles. ✆ **323/871-2666.** www.ammocafe.com. Main courses $15–$29. AE, MC, V. Lunch Mon–Fri 11:30am–2:30pm; dinner Mon–Thu 6–10pm, Fri–Sat 5:30–11pm, Sun 5–9pm; brunch Sun 10am–2:30pm. Valet $6.

Animal ♨[CONTEMPORARY AMERICAN If you're a vegetarian, just move on. Then again, even as a meat lover, I'm moving on. A stone's throw from the 24-hour Canter's Delicatessen in the heart of the Fairfax District, chefs Jon Shook and Vinny Dotolo turned a former teahouse into one of the most talked-about restaurants in L.A. (and the country: In 2009, they were named two of *Food & Wine* magazine's Best New Chefs). Clearly, all the attention has gone to their heads. A recent visit was one of my most disappointing meals of the year. A friend summed it up best, "communist food at capitalist prices." Yes, pig's tail is mostly fat, but $11 seems a bit steep for a "Buffalo-style" appetizer lacking in crispiness. Rabbit loin actually tasted better without the bacon wrapped around it (how is that even possible?), and the rock cod, while nicely cooked, was drowning in brown butter. The best on the menu were the balsamic pork ribs, which were a textural success, but a touch too sweet. It's a shame because the chefs started out so strong and have a passion for artisanal and seasonal ingredients. I miss the days when Animal could be counted on for its sensational pork belly with kimchi and peanuts.

435 N. Fairfax Ave. (btw. Oakwood and Rosewood aves.), Los Angeles. ✆ **323/782-9225.** www.animal-restaurant.com. Main courses $27–$35. AE, MC, V. Sun–Thurs 6–11pm; Fri–Sat 6pm–1am. Valet parking $5.

Campanile ★★ CALIFORNIAN/MEDITERRANEAN Built as Charlie Chaplin's private offices in 1928, this Tuscan-style building has a multilevel layout with flower-bedecked interior balconies, a bubbling fountain, and a skylight through which diners can see the campanile (bell tower). Often ranked as one of L.A.'s finest restaurants, a meal here might begin with fried zucchini flowers drizzled with melted mozzarella, or lamb carpaccio surrounded by artichoke leaves—a dish that arrives looking like one of van Gogh's sunflowers. Chef/owner and Spago alumnus Mark Peel

Grilled Cheese Night

Every Thursday evening, Campanile (see above) hosts a hugely popular Grilled Cheese Night. The menu offers 12 different gourmet sandwiches along with appetizers.

Where to Eat in the Hollywood Area

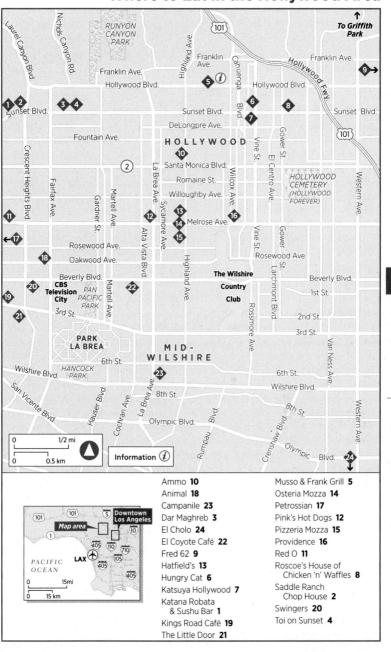

Ammo **10**
Animal **18**
Campanile **23**
Dar Maghreb **3**
El Cholo **24**
El Coyote Café **22**
Fred 62 **9**
Hatfield's **13**
Hungry Cat **6**
Katsuya Hollywood **7**
Katana Robata
  & Sushu Bar **1**
Kings Road Café **19**
The Little Door **21**

Musso & Frank Grill **5**
Osteria Mozza **14**
Petrossian **17**
Pink's Hot Dogs **12**
Pizzeria Mozza **15**
Providence **16**
Red O **11**
Roscoe's House of
  Chicken 'n' Waffles **8**
Saddle Ranch
  Chop House **2**
Swingers **20**
Toi on Sunset **4**

heads up the kitchen and is particularly known for his grills and roasts. Try the wood-grilled prime rib smeared with black-olive tapenade; pappardelle with braised rabbit, roasted tomato, and collard greens; or the rosemary-charred lamb with artichokes and fava beans. **Tip:** On Monday nights, chef Peel offers a $38 three-course family-style themed menu that's been voted Best Monday Night Dinner by *Los Angeles* magazine.

624 S. La Brea Ave. (north of Wilshire Blvd.), Los Angeles. (Ⓒ **323/938-1447.** www.campanile restaurant.com. Reservations recommended. Main courses $26-$38. AE, DC, DISC, MC, V. Mon-Wed noon-2:30pm and 6-10pm; Thurs-Fri noon-2:30pm and 5:30-11pm; Sat 9:30am-1:30pm and 5:30-11pm; Sun 9:30am-1:30pm. Valet parking $6.50.

Dar Maghreb ★★ MOROCCAN   If you're a lone diner in search of a quick bite, this isn't the place for you. Dinner at Dar Maghreb is an entertaining dining experience that improves exponentially the larger your party and the longer you linger. Enter an exotic Arab world of genie waitresses who wash your hands with warm water, and belly dancers who shimmy around an exquisite fountain in the center of a patio. You'll feel like a guest in an ornately tiled palace as you dine at traditional tables on either low sofas or goatskin cushions. Nothing is available a la carte here. The fixed-price meal is a multicourse feast, starting with bread and traditional Moroccan salads, followed by *b'stilla*, an appetizer of shredded chicken, eggs, almonds, and spices wrapped in a flaky pastry shell and topped with powdered sugar and cinnamon. All is eaten with your hands—a sensual experience that grows on you as the night progresses.

7651 Sunset Blvd. (at Stanley Ave.), Hollywood. (Ⓒ **323/876-7651.** www.darmaghrebrestaurant.com. Reservations recommended. Fixed-price dinner $37 (half-price for children 5-11). DC, MC, V. Mon-Fri 6-11pm; Sat 5:30-11pm; Sun 5:30-10:30pm. Valet parking $4.50.

Hatfield's ★★★ NEW AMERICAN   After a move to this larger Melrose location in 2010, savory/sweet chef couple Quinn and Karen Hatfield have achieved a new level of sophistication without pretension, from food and beverage to service and décor. Request one of the twin booths against the south wall in the sparsely stylish main dining room for maximum comfort and the best view of the exhibition kitchen. Quinn's signature starter, a variation on the *croque madame*, sandwiches yellowtail sashimi and prosciutto between brioche. Mains follow suit: supple slow-baked salmon almost melts in your mouth, and oven-roasted veal loin is reminiscent of the best bockwurst. Beverage director Peter Birmingham elevates wine pairings to poetry. **Tip:** Karen's specialty dessert, a chocolate and peanut butter truffle cake—think molten meets soufflé—is an off-menu secret.

6703 Melrose Ave. (at Citrus Ave.), Los Angeles. (Ⓒ **323/935-2977.** www.hatfieldsrestaurant.com. Reservations recommended. Main courses $28-$36. AE, MC, V. Mon-Thurs 11:45am-2:15pm and 6-10pm; Fri 11:45am-2:15pm and 6-10:30pm; Sat 6-10:30pm; Sun 6-10pm. Valet parking $7.

Katana Robata & Sushi Bar ★ JAPANESE/ROBATA   In the City of Sushi, you need to stand out from the crowd if you want to run a successful Japanese restaurant. And that's just what they did at Katana. The restaurant has sex appeal, with steel beams, metallic screens, exotic woods, and worn brick, and a fantastic patio overlooking the Sunset Strip. Katana is known for its *robata-yaki*, a traditional Japanese style of cooking where meats, fish, and vegetables are cooked on small bamboo skewers over imported *bincho tan* coal that imparts a unique smoky essence to the food. The sushi is very good, but it's the incredibly flavorful skewers that you'll want to sample: foie gras and asparagus wrapped with filet mignon, fresh lobster with a peppercorn-miso glaze, giant seared scallops with shiitake mushrooms, and Kurobuta pork and pineapple drizzled with plum sauce. Be sure to start the adventure with a $18 Sake Sampler.

5

Hollywood & West Hollywood

WHERE TO EAT

8439 W. Sunset Blvd. (near La Cienega Blvd.), West Hollywood. ✆ **323/650-8585.** www.katanarobata. com. Reservations recommended. Main courses $12–$35. AE, DC, DISC, MC, V. Dinner Sun–Mon 6–11pm; Tues–Wed 6–11:30pm; Thurs–Sat 6pm–12:30am. Valet parking $9 for the first 3 hr. with validation; $20 max.

Katsuya Hollywood ★★ JAPANESE   Anchoring the corner of Hollywood and Vine, this überhip restaurant has all the L.A. tourists and snooties agog. Capitalizing on their raging success of the original Katsuya by Starck in Brentwood, the SBE group once again partnered with designer Philippe Starck and master sushi chef Katsuya Uechi to create this shrine to sushi and high-design. The decor is an intriguing mix of gleaming white leather and chrome furniture, overblown images of a geisha's facial parts, and a sinister black banner bearing the *kanji* symbol for Katsuya. Katsuya's must-try signature dishes include the crispy rice with spicy tuna, the Kobe filet with foie gras and plum soy sauce, and the baked whitefish with truffle in a shell of salt. Reservations may be difficult to get, particularly on a weekend night, so be sure to call as far in advance as possible, and then strut past the paparazzi staked outside on your way in.

6300 Hollywood Blvd. (at Vine St.), Hollywood. ✆ **323/871-8777.** www.sbe.com/katsuya. Reservations recommended. Main courses $22–$55. AE, DC, DISC, MC, V. Mon 11am–2:30pm and 5:30–11pm; Tues–Thurs 11:30am–2:30pm and 5:30pm–midnight; Fri 11am–2:30pm and 5:30pm–12:30am; Sun 4:30–11pm. Valet parking $10.

The Little Door ★★ FRENCH/MEDITERRANEAN   For more than a decade, this provincial hideaway off 3rd Street has been voted one of L.A.'s most romantic restaurants. There are four dining areas situated throughout a converted cottage-style house, the most popular being the lush "Patio" with its tile fountain and koi pond. If you can't get a table here, ask for one in the back room by the fireplace, which is both quieter and roomier. Fittingly, the cuisine is French/Mediterranean, ranging from a terrine of duck foie gras with strawberries to pistachio-encrusted scallops with Moroccan greens to rosemary-encrusted rack of lamb in a parsnip purée. It's pricey ($28 for couscous?), the tables are a tad too close together, and the attitude from the servers can be a bit . . . er . . . French. But when it all comes together perfectly—the candlelit table, an attentive waiter, a warm summer night, a nice glass of wine, a soupçon of foie gras melting on your tongue—it's easy to see why the Little Door is where the locals go when they're in the mood for romance.

8164 W. 3rd St. (btw. Crescent Heights and La Jolla sts.), Los Angeles. ✆ **323/951-1210.** www.thelittle-door.com. Reservations recommended. Main courses $28–$44. AE, MC, V. Sun–Thurs 6–10pm; Fri–Sat 6–11pm. Valet parking $6.75.

Osteria Mozza ★★ ITALIAN   This is the kind of place that can be so wonderful, you keep thinking about it for days afterward. The partner restaurant to the bustling Pizzeria Mozza (see below) is an airy, lively, Italianesque space with a central free-standing mozzarella bar, a full bar along the south wall, and an indoor/outdoor dining area that opens onto Melrose Avenue. Dishes are composed of only the finest and freshest ingredients. The result: small-dish heaven for the adventurous epicurean, with standouts like fresh ricotta and egg ravioli with browned butter, grilled whole orata, the buffalo mozzarella with caperberry relish, and for dessert, the *bombolini,* a huckleberry compote with vanilla gelato. The only downside is that service doesn't always mirror the skill of the kitchen. Reservations are taken one month in advance, though walk-ins can be accommodated at the mozzarella and regular bars, which I'd say are the best seats in the house.

6602 Melrose Ave. (at N. Highland Ave.), West Hollywood. ✆ **323/297-0100.** www.mozza-la.com. Reservations recommended. Main courses $17–$29. AE, MC, V. Mon–Fri 5:30–11pm; Sat 5–11pm; Sun 5–10pm. Valet parking $8.

Truck It: The Food Truck Revolution

Over the past few years, a food truck trend has swept L.A. Once known as "roach coaches" (no explanation necessary), this latest wave is actually quite upscale. It totally makes sense for a city with great weather year-round, a dedicated car culture, and a longstanding love for authentic taco trucks. The only downside is that most don't answer their phones (or even have land lines), so the only way to find out where they'll be at any given time is via the Internet or Twitter. The brand credited with founding the phenomenon is **Kogi** (www.kogibbq.com), which specializes in Korean fusion food. Think Korean short rib tacos and kimchi quesadillas. One surefire way to sample a number of outlets at once is via the monthly first-Sundays **Truckit Fest** at Union Station (www.truckitfest.com). My picks include **Gourmet Genie** (www.gourmetgenietogo.com) for nicely spiced lamb sliders; **Global Soul** (www.globalsoultruck.com) for the savory "shrimp toasties"; and **India Jones** (www.indiajoneschowtruck.com) for flavorful chicken tikka masala.

Providence ★★ MODERN AMERICAN/SEAFOOD   Chef Michael Cimarusti and his quadrilingual Italian compatriot, Donato Poto, set out to create the city's preeminent seafood experience. It's a pleasure to just relax at this sleek, modern space, though be advised that during service rushes, the downtime can turn into 20-minute gaps between courses. Cimarusti visits the fish market daily for the choicest seafood available, and the philosophy here is to let the flavors of wild fish prevail. Sauces are intended as a complement—such as striped sea bass in a pea tendril broth or kanpachi in finger-lime crème fraiche. Sadly, there are occasional missteps, including inconsistent scallops—some buttery soft, some more akin to rubber. The two best dishes I've tried were the salt-crusted Santa Barbara prawns and the Wagyu beef—if you get the chance to order either, do so. Lastly, be sure to order anything Cimarusti makes with sea urchin, especially if you don't like uni. Trust me, he might just convert you.

5955 Melrose Ave. (at N. Cahuenga Blvd.), Los Angeles. © **323/460-4170.** www.providencela.com. Reservations recommended. Main courses $45–$49. AE, MC, V. Mon–Thurs 6–10pm; Fri noon–2:30pm and 6–10pm; Sat 5:30–10pm; Sun 5:30–9pm. Valet parking $6.

Moderate

El Coyote Cafe ★ 🍴 MEXICAN   Everyone from 20-something hipsters to slick showbiz player-types, rockers, movie stars, and even regular folk like you and me can be found at this family-owned cantina that has been around since 1931. The rowdy bar scene alone is a great reason to hang out at this highly popular (yet eminently affordable) Mexican restaurant. During prime dining hours, the restaurant's bustling atmosphere spills over into the bar, which is frequently crowded to capacity. Settle in by sampling from the *grande*-size menu of appetizers such as taquitos, quesadillas, and nachos, and be sure to wash them down with a couple of World Famous House Margaritas (a bargain at $7.25, though I prefer the made-from-scratch version for only 50¢ more). The fare is Americanized Mexican, so don't expect much; recommended plates include the "chunky" guacamole, green corn tamales, ostrich tacos (yes, ostrich), and the enchilada Howard smothered with chili *con carne*, named after the restaurant's first regular customer.

7312 Beverly Blvd. (at N. Poinsettia Place), Los Angeles. © **323/939-2255.** www.elcoyotecafe.com. Main courses $8–$15. AE, MC, V. Mon–Thurs and Sun 11am–10pm; Fri–Sat 11am–11pm. Valet parking $3.50.

Hungry Cat ★★ SEAFOOD   Tucked away near the back entrance of Borders at the odd Sunset + Vine complex is this modern, casual, bustling place for local and regional seafood that is simple and seasonal. The raw bar has some of the freshest chilled oysters, crab legs, and Santa Barbara sea urchin (served in the spiny shell); the market lettuces with pecorino cheese, egg, and avocado are a refreshing take on chopped salad; and mussels or clams simmered in chorizo-laden broth are hearty and flavorful. And for you landlubbers, there is exactly one all-meat dish: The pug burger, a towering beef patty (more like a ball) charred to perfection and served with thin, crispy fries. The annual Maryland-style crab feast (one of Lentz's childhood favorites) is one of the most anticipated events for locals. The bar puts out fresh-fruit cocktails; get the "kumquatini" if it's in season. There's a great patio for lunch, brunch, and warm summer nights.

1535 N. Vine St. (near back entrance of Sunset + Vine complex), Hollywood. © **323/462-2155.** www. thehungrycat.com. Main courses $16–$25. AE, MC, V. Mon–Wed noon–11pm; Thurs–Sat noon–midnight; Sun 11am–11pm. Parking garage at Sunset + Vine complex (entrance on Morningstar Court).

Kings Road Cafe ★ AMERICAN   This is the cafe you wish were down the street from your place instead of that Starbucks. The Kings Road Cafe has the perfect combo of everything you'd want in a neighborhood eatery—sunny sidewalk seating, excellent coffee served in big bowl-like cups, great people-watching, attitude-free service, the occasional celebrity sighting, a huge magazine stand right next door, and fresh, healthy, inexpensive food served in large portions. It's open from morning until night, so you can drop by anytime for such local favorites as banana-pecan buttermilk pancakes, fluffy French toast, spinach and shiitake mushroom omelet, blackened ahi with mashed sweet potatoes, and signature panini-style sandwiches. You can pretty much count on waiting for an outside table on weekends, but it gives you time to do a bit of inconspicuous star searching, pick up a few magazines, and check out the Kings Road Cafe Bakery next door (the black currant scones are wonderful).

8361 Beverly Blvd. (at Kings Rd.), Los Angeles. © **323/655-9044.** www.kingsroadcafe.com. Reservations not accepted. Main courses $7.50–$13 breakfast, $8.95–$18 lunch and dinner. AE, MC, V. Mon–Fri 6:30am–8pm; Sat–Sun 6:30am–6:30pm. Metered street parking.

Musso & Frank Grill ★ AMERICAN/CONTINENTAL   A survey of Hollywood restaurants that leaves out Musso & Frank is like a study of Las Vegas singers that fails to mention Wayne Newton. As Hollywood's oldest eatery (since 1919), Musso & Frank is the paragon of Old Hollywood grillrooms. This is where Faulkner and Hemingway drank during their screenwriting days and where Orson Welles used to hold court. The restaurant is still known for its bone-dry martinis and perfectly seasoned bloody marys. The setting is what you'd expect: oak-beamed ceilings, gruff red-coated waiters, red-leather booths and banquettes, and mahogany room dividers. The extensive old-school menu is a veritable survey of American/Continental cookery. Hearty dinners include veal scaloppini Marsala, roast spring lamb with mint jelly, and broiled lobster. Grilled meats are a specialty, as is the Thursday-only chicken potpie. **Tip:** For the full M&F effect, sit at either the counter or request table no. 1 in the west room, which was Charlie Chaplin's regular table.

6667 Hollywood Blvd. (at Cherokee Ave.), Hollywood. © **323/467-7788.** Reservations recommended. Main courses $14–$45. AE, DC, MC, V. Tues–Sat 11am–11pm. Self-parking behind the restaurant $2.25 for 2 hr. with validation.

Petrossian ★★ FRENCH   Petrossian is the best known caviar store in Los Angeles, if not the country (New York is the original and still flagship). This has long been the go-to spot for gourmet goodies. In 2008, it debuted an adjoining restaurant, which in short time has become a dining destination unto itself—and not just for the rich and famous. Prices, while certainly not cheap, are also surprisingly not nearly as cost-prohibitive as one would expect. The signature vodka martini with its trademark caviar cube will get you in the mood for the rest to come. Many of the best dishes are the ones that feature the famous fish roe, such as the bold sturgeon risotto with crème fraiche, and the hearty cauliflower soup with crisp beet chips. Tender striped bass comes not only with caviar, but also playful potato "noodles." Flat iron steak is thinly sliced and expertly prepared (no caviar in this one, but it's plenty good on its own), The dreamy vanilla panna cotta is studded with espresso "roe" and served with cardamom shortbread cookies.

321 N. Robertson Blvd. (at Rosewood Ave.), West Hollywood. ✆ 310/271-6300. www.petrossian.com. Reservations recommended. Main courses $15–$32. AE, DISC, MC, V. Mon-Fri 11am-10pm; Sat 10am-10pm; Sun 10am-4pm. Metered street parking meters (free after 6pm).

Pizzeria Mozza ★★ ITALIAN   Open since 2006, this is still one of the hardest reservations to get in town. Locals call up to a month in advance for an opportunity to experience celeb chef Nancy Silverton's—she founded the famed La Brea Bakery—artisanal pies. When she partnered with Mario Batali, L.A.'s foodies swooned and surged. In contrast to the restaurant's celebrity status (everyone from Scarlett Johansen to Jake Gyllenhaal to Mario Batali himself are often here), the ambience and decor are entirely unpretentious. There are about a dozen tables and two first-come, first-served bars (one is situated in front of the pizza ovens) that are always packed. The pizzas are small and inexpensive enough for everyone to order their own. Favorites are the house-made fennel sausage with *panna* (cream) and red onion; stinging nettles and salami with *cacio di Roma* cheese; and the squash blossoms, tomato and burrata. But the toppings are secondary to Nancy's complex crust—in true Italian style, each is wafer-thin in the middle, yet impossibly puffy, crunchy, and flavorful on the edges. For dessert, the butterscotch *budino* with Maldon sea salt is a must-try; even stubborn non-sweet tooths worship it. Fittingly, the wines are all Italian, and moderately priced between $33 and $50. *Tip:* There are seats at the bar for walk-ins, but be prepared for a lengthy wait during peak hours.

641 N. Highland Ave. (at Melrose Ave.), West Hollywood/Los Angeles. ✆ 323/297-0101. www.mozza-la.com. Reservations required. Main courses $10–$23. AE, MC, V. Daily noon-midnight. Valet parking $8.50 at lunch; $10 at dinner.

Red O ★ MEXICAN   This packed concept restaurant by Chicago chef and TV personality Rick Bayless is his first in Los Angeles, and if nothing else, it's worth a visit for the great people-watching (it's a cougar den), tart margaritas, and a few stand-out dishes. It was a bold move for a Midwesterner to bring Mexican to Los Angeles, a city certainly not lacking in the cuisine, and while results are mixed, when he's on, he's good. Guacamole is made-to-order, a chunky and a satisfying start. For appetizers, the Dungeness crab satisfies but is overpowered by its too-sweet grilled pineapple accompaniment. Sea scallops are nicely textured but get a little lost in the bigger flavors of citrus, herbs and nuts. On the other hand, the souped-up lamb tacos succeed on many levels. *Sopes* are solid, and marinated rib-eye is cooked over coals to great effect. Mexican hot fudge closes the meal on a sweet note.

8155 Melrose Ave. (at Kilkea Dr.), West Hollywood/Los Angeles. ✆ 323/655-5009. www.redorestaurant.com. Reservations recommended. Main courses $14–$29. AE, MC, V. Sun-Thurs 6-11pm; Fri-Sat 5:30pm-midnight. Valet parking $8.

Saddle Ranch Chop House AMERICAN   Let's say you wake up one morning in L.A. and you say to yourself, "Hey, I'm really in a mood to ride a mechanical bull today." Well, pardner, you're in luck. Smack-dab on the Sunset Strip is this sort of wild-west Hard Rock Cafe where everything is done Texas-style—the drinks are tall and stiff, the platters of fried chicken and ribs are ginormous, and when a buxom cowgirl is riding the bull like a rodeo pro, the fellers tend to get a bit *loco*. The huge pine-wood building—fashioned after an Old Western saloon—is impossible to miss. Yes, they lay on the cheesy Western theme a bit thick, and no local over the age of 24 would ever admit going to such a blatant tourist trap, but after a couple of Sweet Tea vodka cocktails, you can't help but loosen up and get into the hoedown spirit. **Note:** There's a second Saddle Ranch location at Universal Studios' CityWalk (℃ 818/760-9680), near the entrance to the park.

8371 Sunset Blvd. (at La Cienega Blvd.), West Hollywood. ℃ 323/656-2007. www.srrestaurants.com. Reservations recommended for dinner. Main courses $12–$23, breakfast $9–$16. AE, DC, DISC, MC, V. Mon–Fri 11am–2am; Sat–Sat 8am–2am. Valet parking $2 before 4pm, $8 with validation after 4pm.

Inexpensive

El Cholo ★★ MEXICAN   L.A.'s oldest Mexican restaurant (Gary Cooper and Bing Crosby were regulars, and Jack Nicholson and Warren Beatty still are), El Cholo has been serving up authentic Mexican cuisine in this pink adobe hacienda since 1925, even though the once-outlying mid-Wilshire neighborhood around it has since turned into Koreatown. El Cholo's *muy* strong margaritas, invitingly messy nachos—the first served in the U.S.—and classic combination dinners don't break new culinary ground, but the kitchen has perfected these standards over 80 years. Other specialties include seasonally available green-corn tamales and creative, sizzling vegetarian fajitas that go way beyond just eliminating the meat. The atmosphere is festive, as people from all parts of town dine happily in the many rambling rooms that compose the restaurant. Westsiders head to El Cholo's Santa Monica branch at 1025 Wilshire Blvd. (at 11th St.; ℃ 310/899-1106). **Note:** Be prepared for a long wait on weekends.

1121 S. Western Ave. (south of Olympic Blvd.), Los Angeles. ℃ 323/734-2773. www.elcholo.com. Reservations suggested. Main courses $9.95–$16. AE, DC, DISC, MC, V. Mon–Thurs 11am–10pm; Fri–Sat 11am–11pm; Sun 11am–9pm. Valet parking $5.

Fred 62 AMERICAN/BREAKFAST   Opened in the heart of trendy Los Feliz by chef Fred Eric, this slightly skewed 24-hour coffee shop comes by its retro kitsch honestly. Eric remodeled the tiny corner diner with spiffy 1950s car-culture icons, including hood-ornament sconces and blue service-station smocks for the waitstaff. He then named it after himself (and his birth year, 1962) and peppered the menu with cutesy-sounding dishes. There's the "hotter than hell" penne pasta, a "white trash" tuna and "poorest boy" fried chicken sandwiches, burgers, salads, tofu scrambles, and a handful of Asian noodle bowls, including " NOO*DEL–I Noodle," a cryptic name for vermicelli noodles and Thai vegetables in lemongrass broth. You might feel like you've stepped into a Route 66 beatnik diner in TV land, but the clientele is very real and the food is comforting (slow service, though). Don't miss the old-fashioned shakes or malts, or the red velvet cake. *Tip:* Arrive early on weekends; after 10am (okay, 11am for the truly decadent), this is hungover-hipster central.

1850 N. Vermont Ave. (at Russell Ave.), Los Feliz. ✆ **323/667-0062.** www.fred62.com. Main courses $7–$15. MC, V. Open 24 hr. Metered street parking.

Pink's Hot Dogs ☺ HOT DOGS   Pink's isn't your usual guidebook recommendation, but then again, this corner stand isn't your typical hot dog shack. This L.A. icon grew around the late Paul and Betty Pink, who opened for business in 1939 selling 10¢ wieners from a used hot dog cart. Now this place serves 2,000 dogs every day on Pink's soft steamed rolls. There are 24 varieties of dogs available, many coined by the celebrities who order them. Martha Stewart once stopped her caravan to order a 10-incher with mustard, relish, onions, chopped tomatoes, sauerkraut, bacon, and sour cream, and now you, too, can order a "Martha Stewart" dog. The heartburn-inducing chili dogs (made from Betty's chili formula that's still a secret) are craved by even the most upstanding, health-conscious Angelenos. Lots of folklore emanates from this wiener shack: Bruce Willis reportedly proposed to Demi Moore in the parking lot, and Orson Welles holds the record for the most hot dogs consumed in one sitting (18). Even though the dogs are churned out every 30 seconds, expect to wait in line even at midnight—you'll invariably meet a true crossroads of Los Angeles cultures.

709 N. La Brea Ave. (at Melrose Ave.), West Hollywood. ✆ **323/931-4223.** www.pinkshollywood.com. Chili dog $3.30. No credit cards. Sun–Thurs 9:30am–2am; Fri–Sat 9:30am–3am. Free lot; metered street parking.

Roscoe's House of Chicken 'n' Waffles BREAKFAST/SOUTHERN   It sounds like a bad joke—fried chicken and waffles on the same plate. But Roscoe's is one of those places that you have to visit at least once to see how it works (and judging by the wait, it definitely works). A chicken-and-cheese omelet isn't everyone's ideal way to begin the day, but it's de rigueur at Roscoe's. At lunch, few calorie-unconscious diners can resist the juicy fried chicken smothered in gravy and onions, a house specialty that's served with waffles or grits and biscuits. Large chicken-salad bowls and chicken sandwiches also provide plenty of cluck for the buck. Homemade corn bread, sweet-potato pie, homemade potato salad, and corn on the cob are available as side orders. Granted, the waffles are of Eggo quality and come with enough whipped butter to stop your heart, but the Southern fried chicken is addictive. *Tip:* The waffles tend to come a bit undercooked, so ask for them crispy.

1514 N. Gower St. (at Sunset Blvd.), Los Angeles. ✆ **323/466-7453.** www.roscoeschickenandwaffles. com. Main courses $6.40–$16. AE, DISC, MC, V. Sun–Thurs 8:30am–midnight; Fri–Sat 8:30am–4am. Metered street parking, pay lots, valet parking Fri–Sat only $10.

Swingers AMERICAN/DINER/BREAKFAST   Resurrected from a motel coffee shop, Swingers was transformed by a couple of L.A. hipster nightclub owners into a 1990s version of comfy Americana. The interior seems like a slice of the 1950s until you notice the plaid upholstery and Warhol-esque graphics, which contrast nicely with the retro red-white-and-blue Swingers logo adorning *everything*. Guests at the attached Beverly Laurel Motor Hotel chow down alongside body-pierced industry hounds from nearby record companies, while a soundtrack that runs the gamut from punk rock to *Schoolhouse Rock* plays in the background. It's not all attitude, though—you'll enjoy a menu of high-quality diner favorites with trendy crowd-pleasers: Steel-cut Irish oatmeal, blue corn nachos, grilled Jamaican jerk chicken, and a selection of tofu-enhanced vegetarian dishes are just a few of the eclectic offerings. *Note:* There's a second location in Santa Monica at 802 Broadway (at Lincoln Ave.; ℂ **310/393-9793**).

8020 Beverly Blvd. (west of Fairfax Ave.), Los Angeles. ℂ **323/653-5858.** www.swingersdiner.com. Most items less than $9. AE, DISC, MC, V. Daily 6am–4am. Metered street parking.

Toi on Sunset ★★ 🔪 THAI   Because it's open *really* late, Toi has been a fave of two generations of Hollywood hipsters, who have been making postclubbing excursions to this rock-'n'-roll eatery a few blocks from the Sunset Strip since 1986. After all the hype, it's surprising to say that this is still one of L.A.'s best bargains for Thai food (hands down *the* best for one with such a cool vibe). Everything is nicely prepared and served in portions so generous the word *enormous* seems inadequate. Menu highlights include tangy seafood soup in a hot and sour lime broth, and the house specialty: chicken curry *somen,* a spicy dish with green curry and mint sauce spooned over thin Japanese rice noodles. Personally, I like anything spicy here that I can sop up with the special brown rice. Vegetarians will be pleased with the vast selection of meat-free items. Pad Thai is always a reliable choice. The interior is a noisy amalgam of cultish movie posters, rock-'n'-roll memorabilia, and haphazardly placed industrial-issue dinette sets, and the plates, flatware, and drinking glasses are cheap coffee-shop issue. In other words, it's all about the food and the scene—neither will disappoint. *Note:* Beer, wine and sake are only served until midnight.

7505½ Sunset Blvd. (at Gardner St.), West Hollywood. ℂ **323/874-8062.** www.toirockinthaifood.com. Reservations accepted only for parties of 6 or more. Main courses $6–$17. MC, V. Daily 11am–4am.

DOWNTOWN
Expensive

Drago Centro ★ ITALIAN   Celestino Drago, chef/owner of Santa Monica's Drago has created one of the splashiest new-ish, restaurants Downtown. On the ground floor of the City National Bank building, the room is filled with creamy leather banquettes, stunning Murano chandeliers, and a custom-designed glass wine room that showcases bottles from the extensive collection. Expense-account office workers and Drago fans enjoy the refined Italian cuisine, which is inspired by different regions of Italy: perfectly cooked *branzino,* a flaky whitefish in seafood broth, tender veal chop with sweetbreads; and we could eat the pappardelle ribbons with pheasant and morel mushrooms every day. Service is exemplary, a ballet of precision. *Tip:* The bar and outdoor lounge is a great spot for thin-crust pizzas (oh, the pizza bianca is good) and fresh-fruit cocktails, and don't forget to check out the exhibition kitchen set up in the former bank vault, which is used for private parties.

525 S. Flower St. (at 5th St.), Downtown. ℂ **213/228-8998.** www.dragocentro.com. Reservations recommended. Main courses dinner $18–$35, lunch $17–$25. AE, DC, MC, V. Mon–Fri 11:30am–2:30pm and 5–10pm; Sat 5–10pm. Sun 5–9. Valet parking $5 for up to 2 hr. before 5pm; 3 hrs free after 5pm, $7 flat-rate after 3 hrs.

L.A. live

We'd be remiss not to mention all the new eateries at L.A. LIVE, the high-voltage (literally; there are giant LED screens lighting up the courtyard), massive complex that opened near Staples Center and the Los Angeles Convention Center at the end of 2008. Sure, most of the restaurants are chains, but at least most are local chains, and, really, we're just glad to have so many options for lunch and dinner in the area now. The famed Latin music mecca, the Conga Room, relocated here, and with it came **Boca** (© 213/745-0162; www.conga room.com), a pan-Latin dining room that looks into the nightclub and is a great option for dinner and a show. **Rock'N Fish** (© 213/748-4020; www. rocknfishlalive.com) is a popular steak and seafood restaurant from Manhattan Beach; don't miss the Navy Grog, a potent rum drink. **The Farm of Beverly Hills** (© 213/747-4555; www.thefarmof beverlyhills.com) has comfort food and lighter fare like salads and sandwiches, all made with seasonal ingredients. The largest **Katsuya** (© 213/747-9797; www.

sbe.com/katsuya) in L.A. opened in spring 2009 and is a stylish spot for sushi (the baked-crab hand roll is dynamite) and well-crafted, fresh-fruit cocktails. A **Trader Vic's** (© 213/785-3330; www.tradervicsla.com) opened in 2009, and while it isn't as tiki-rific as the original, it's great to have a second location for Scorpion Bowls and pupu platters. **Wolfgang Puck Bar & Grill** (© 213/748-9700; www.wolfgangpuck.com) showcases the celebrity chef's simpler side. **Rosa Mexicano** (© 213/746-0001; www. rosamexicano.com) brings surprisingly excellent Mexican cuisine from New York. There's also a **Lawry's Carvery** (© 213/222-2212; www.lawrysonline. com), **New Zealand Natural** (© 213/ 748-4696; www.nznusa.com) ice cream, a huge **ESPN Zone** (© 213/765-7070; www.espnzone.com), **Fleming's Steakhouse and Wine Bar** (© 213/745-9911; www.flemingssteakhouse.com), a **Yard House** (© 213/745-9273; www.yard house.com) for beer and bar food lovers, and of course a **Starbucks.**

Patina ★★ FRENCH   When celebrity L.A. restaurateur Joachim Splichal moved his flagship Patina restaurant from Melrose Avenue to the new Walt Disney Concert Hall, it raised one pertinent question: "Is it as good as the old Patina?" If you arrived after a performance ended, you wouldn't hear the answer anyway. Billowing walls of laser-cut walnut and floor-to-ceiling glass panels only augment the hubbub as droves of smartly clad fans of the performing arts dine on Splichal's signature dishes of wild game and the de rigueur ahi tuna appetizer. The après-show performances continue with a trio of carts—mounds of caviar, giant rib-eye steaks for two, and expensive cheeses—crisscrossing the dining room. Vegetarian dishes and wine pairings are also available, as are prix-fixe theater menus. Jackets are suggested but not required for dinner. *Tip:* If you want a quiet, romantic dinner, ask the hostess to schedule it at the *start* of a performance.

141 S. Grand Ave. (near 1st St.), Los Angeles. © **213/972-3331.** www.patinagroup.com. Reservations recommended. Main courses $38–$48 dinner. AE, DC, MC, V. Tues–Sat 5–9:30pm; Sun 4–9:30pm (on L.A. Philharmonic performance evenings, the last seating takes place 30 min. after the concert ends). Closed Mon. Valet parking $8 with validation.

Rivera ★★ LATIN   Chef John Sedlar was so instrumental to the L.A. dining scene in the '80s and '90s that the food world was turned on its head when he reemerged

Where to Eat in the Downtown Area

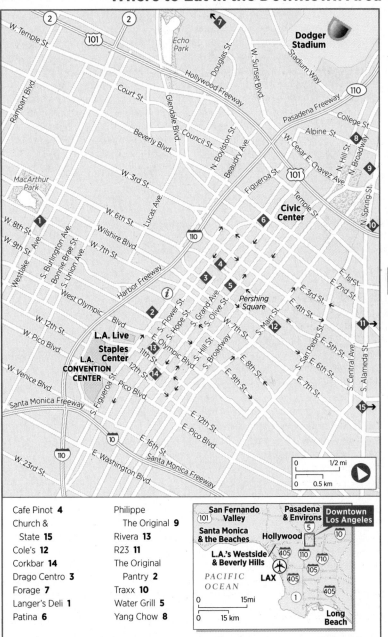

Cafe Pinot **4**

Church &
  State **15**

Cole's **12**

Corkbar **14**

Drago Centro **3**

Forage **7**

Langer's Deli **1**

Patina **6**

Philippe
  The Original **9**

Rivera **13**

R23 **11**

The Original
  Pantry **2**

Traxx **10**

Water Grill **5**

Yang Chow **8**

at this stunning new pan-Latin restaurant. Sedlar literally wrote the book on modern Southwest cuisine, bringing into play flavors like chipotle, which is almost as ubiquitous as basil these days. The menu explores flavors from Mexico, Spain, and South and Central America, and each of three dining areas is themed accordingly; though the menus are interchangeable, so you order off of either regardless of where you are seated. Dishes include pasilla chiles with braised goat, cinnamon and pine nuts; snails in vinho verde sauce with garlic peppers and Spanish ham; and coffee-braised Kurobuta pork tenderloin in a sugar cane sauce. The cocktail program is impressive, with a wide range of premium spirits available, though the ones with mezcal or tequila are not surprisingly the bar's strong suit. Since day one, the Donaji has been a favorite, and is rimmed with cricket salt. The restaurant is just a hop, skip, and a jump away from Staples Center, by the way. *Tip:* For a more affordable taste of the chef's culinary process (and equally great cocktails), try **Playa,** 7360 Beverly Blvd., Los Angeles (© **323/933-5300**). I highly recommend the maize cakes (basically tacos—just don't call them that), particularly the warm version with pork belly confit, chile-lime jicama, and masala; and the cool one with mojito-poached shrimp, braised cabbage and mustard ice cream.

1050 S. Flower St. (at 11th St.), Downtown. © **213/749-1460.** www.riverarestaurant.com. Reservations recommended. Main courses dinner $23–$29, lunch $12–$17. AE, DC, DISC, MC, V. Mon–Fri 11:30am–2pm and 5:30–10:30pm; Sat 5:30–10:30pm; Sun 5:30–10pm. Valet parking $5 with validation.

Water Grill ★★ SEAFOOD Widely considered to be one of the best seafood houses in the city, Water Grill is popular with the suit-and-tie crowd at lunch, and with concertgoers en route to the Music Center at night. The dining room is a stylish and sophisticated fusion of wood, leather, and brass, but it gets a lighthearted lift from cavorting papier-mâché fish that play against an aquamarine ceiling. The restaurant is known for its shellfish; among the appetizers are a dozen different oysters, Nantucket Bay scallops, and Alaskan king crab "nuggets." Main courses are imaginative dishes influenced by coastal cuisines of Hawaii, the Pacific Northwest, New Orleans, and New England, among others. Selections from the menu may range from sautéed Columbia River sturgeon with roasted beet risotto to line-caught Pacific swordfish with peppadew hummus and pomegranate couscous. For dessert, try the Meyer lemon tart, or the chocolate cherry devil's food cake.

544 S. Grand Ave. (btw. 5th and 6th sts.), Downtown. © **213/891-0900.** www.watergrill.com. Reservations recommended. Main courses $21–$46. AE, DC, DISC, MC, V. Mon–Tues 11:30am–9:30pm; Wed–Fri 11:30am–10pm; Sat 5–10pm; Sun 4:30–9pm. Valet parking 3 hr. with validation $8.

Moderate

Café Pinot ★★ ☺ CALIFORNIAN/FRENCH A member of superstar-chef Joachim Splichal's L.A. restaurant empire, Café Pinot is less formal and lighter on the palate—and the pocketbook—than his Patina restaurant at the Walt Disney Concert Hall. The restaurant's location, in the front garden of the L.A. Public Library, makes it a natural for Downtown business folk; at night there's a free shuttle to the Music Center. Be sure to request a table on the shaded patio. Splichal has installed a giant rotisserie in the kitchen, and this is where the best meals come from. The moist, tender mustard-crusted roast chicken is your best bet. *Tip:* There's an unofficial kids' menu with items like chicken fingers and burgers and fries, depending on availability, but the restaurant is well adept at catering to young palates.

family-friendly RESTAURANTS

Café Pinot (p. 122) and **Pinot Bistro** (p. 126) are upscale offshoots of chic Patina that don't often come to mind when you're searching for family eats, and many kids are certainly too antsy to behave during an entire bistro meal. But the Pinot dynasty welcomes little ones with a special child-friendly menu, and kids 10 and under can order anything from the menu free of charge. It's a great way to enjoy L.A.'s finest and stay close to your budget, too.

On the other end of the scale is **Pink's Hot Dogs** (p. 118) in Hollywood, an institution that has been serving politically incorrect franks for what seems like forever. Everyone loves Pink's chili dogs, but you may never get the orange grease stains out of your kids' clothes.

The Mexican minichain **Kay 'n Dave's Cantina** (p. 97) is a great spot to fuel up with the kids at the start of a long day. They serve five kinds of fluffy pancakes, a killer breakfast burrito, enchiladas, fajitas, and more—all cooked lard-free—plus there's a kids' menu and crayons at every table.

Miceli's (p. 127), in Universal City, is a cavernous Italian restaurant that the whole family is sure to love. The gimmick? The waitstaff sings show tunes or opera favorites while (and sometimes instead of) serving. Kids will love the boisterous atmosphere, which might even drown them out.

Jerry's Famous Deli (p. 127), in Studio City, is frequented mostly by industry types who populate this Valley community; their kids often sport baseball caps or production T-shirts from Mom's or Dad's latest project. Jerry's has the most extensive deli menu in town and a casual, coffee-shop atmosphere. Families flock here for lunch, early dinner, and (crowded) weekend breakfast.

700 W. 5th St. (btw. Grand and Flower sts., next to the L.A. Public Library), Downtown. © **213/239-6500.** www.patinagroup.com. Reservations recommended. Main courses $18–$34. AE, DC, DISC, MC, V. Lunch Mon–Fri 11:30am–2:30pm; dinner Mon–Tues 5–9pm, Wed–Thurs 5–9:30pm, Fri–Sat 5–10pm, Sun 4:30–9pm. Lunch parking is available at the adjacent library $6 for 2hr. with validation; dinner valet at the restaurant $7.

Church & State ★ FRENCH BRASSERIE   This is one of the city's hippest French restaurants, found in the most unlikely of places. Hidden in an industrial neighborhood Downtown, on the ground floor of the Biscuit Lofts, this hip French bistro creates classic dishes like garlicky escargot topped with buttery puff pastry, steak frites with béarnaise sauce, and house-made charcuterie like potted duck and veal terrine. Crisp, thin-crust tartes are ideal to share. Adventurous eaters will flock to the crispy pig's ears, braised octopus, and roasted bone marrow. The room is exactly what you'd imagine finding in an urban setting: high ceilings, brick walls, mirrored columns, and an open kitchen bustling with chefs. The wine list is just as exemplary as the menu—mostly French varietals priced right for the neighborhood. During the day, the place is crawling with artists and loft dwellers from the building; at night it might seem a bit out of the way and uninhabited, until you see all the expensive sedans lining the street.

1850 Industrial St. (at Matteo St.), Downtown. © **213/405-1434.** www.churchandstatebistro.com. Reservations recommended. Main courses $11–$27. AE, DC, DISC, MC, V. Lunch Mon–Fri 11:30am–2:30pm. Dinner Mon–Thurs 6–10pm; Fri 6–11pm; Sat 5:30–11pm. Sun 5:30–9pm. Metered street parking (free after 6pm) and nearby lots.

Corkbar ★ WINE BAR   Set in the ground floor of the new EVO lofts in the South Park neighborhood of Downtown, this sleek, stylish spot is great for tasting the best of California wine country without ever having to hit the 101. The entire wine list is comprised of big and small labels from Napa and Sonoma to the Central Coast. The menu offers wine-friendly dishes like puffy cheddar *gougères,* a burger with Asiago cheese and herbs, and a tasty Brussels sprout salad with shredded duck confit and hazelnuts. With a huge patio and ample parking, this is a good stop before or after a night at Staples Center or the Nokia Theatre, which are just a few blocks away, and the huge patio is the perfect spot for happy hour sips (and discounted menu items). *Tip:* Visit on "Test Kitchen Tuesdays," when the chef tries out small portions of a new dish he's considering adding to the menu. There's one item featured per week for only $2.

403 W. 12th St. (at Grand Ave.), Downtown. ✆ **213/746-0050.** www.corkbar.com. Main courses $10–$20. AE, DC, DISC, MC, V. Tues–Fri 11am–close; Sat–Mon 3pm–close. Metered street parking (free after 6pm) and nearby lots.

Forage ★★ CALIFORNIAN   The brainchild of chef/owner Jason Kim, Forage follows the philosophy that top quality farmers' market fare shouldn't be the exclusive domaine of fine-dining restaurants. The starving Silver Lake artist has as much right to healthy, locavore food as famous actors who share the same zip code. He built it, and boy did they come. It's the perfect restaurant for this gentrified but still bohemian neighborhood. The menu changes daily, but certain dishes are fixtures. My favorite is the luscious pork belly sandwich, which packs in the fresh vegetables along with decadent, creamy aioli. Healthier options may include Jidori chicken from the in-house rotisserie, Blue Lake beans, and a beluga lentil and barley salad.

3823 W. Sunset Blvd., (btw. Hyperion Ave. and Lucille Ave.), Los Angeles/Silver Lake. ✆ **323/663-6885.** www.foragela.com. Main courses $11–$20. MC, V. Tues–Sat 11:30am–3pm and 5:30–9:30pm. Metered street parking.

R23 ★★ 🍴 JAPANESE/SUSHI   This gallery-like space in Downtown's out-of-the-way warehouse/artist-loft district has been the secret of sushi connoisseurs since 1991. At the back of R23's single, large exposed-brick dining room, the 12-seat sushi bar shines like a beacon; what appear at first to be ceramic wall ornaments are really stylish sushi platters hanging in wait for large orders. Salmon, yellowtail, shrimp, tuna, and scallops are among the always-fresh selections; an excellent offering if available is seared *toro,* in which the rich belly tuna absorbs a delectable, smoky flavor from the grill. Though R23's sublimely perfect sushi is the star, the short but inventive menu includes pungent miso-based soup with mixed seafood, sautéed scallops with shiitake mushrooms, deep-fried sawa crab, fresh Dungeness crab salad, and roasted Hama Hama oysters with sea urchin on top. Browse a wide selection of premium wines and sakes, which were chosen specifically to pair with the food.

923 E. 2nd St. (btw. Alameda St. and Santa Fe Ave.), Downtown. ✆ **213/687-7178.** www.r23.com. Reservations recommended. Main courses $12–$20; sushi $6–$14. AE, DC, DISC, MC, V. Mon–Fri 11:30am–2pm and 5:30–10:30pm; Sat 5:30–10:30pm. Sun 5:30–9pm. Free parking.

Traxx ★ 🍴 CALIFORNIAN   There's always been a restaurant—of some sort—inside the Union Station passenger concourse, but Traxx is the first to do justice to its grand, historic setting. Showcasing a stylish mix of retro-evocative Art Deco character with sleek contemporary touches, the interior blends seamlessly with the station's architecture. Elegant enough for a romantic dinner, yet welcoming to the casual commuter in search of a stylish lunch or sit-down snack, Traxx features a menu with the same cosmopolitan flavor as the station itself. Samples range from "small plates" of grilled asparagus with CaraCara orange mayo and P.E.I. mussels in a spicy tomato-saffron broth, to main dishes such as house-cured pork loin with mission fig polenta and chicken and green chile posole.

800 N. Alameda St. (at Cesar E. Chavez Ave., in Union Station), Chinatown. © **213/625-1999.** www.traxxrestaurant.com. Reservations recommended for dinner. Main courses $14–$26. AE, DC, MC, V. Lunch Mon–Fri 11:30am–2:30pm; Dinner Mon–Thurs 5:30–9pm, Fri 5:30–9:30pm, Sat 5–9:30pm. Free valet parking with validation.

Yang Chow Restaurant CHINESE   Open for more than 30 years, family-operated Yang Chow is one of Downtown's most popular Chinese restaurants. It's not the dining room's bland and functional decor that accrues accolades; what makes Yang Chow so popular is an interesting menu of seafood specialties complementing well-done Chinese standards. After covering the Mandarin and Szechuan basics—sweet-and-sour pork, shrimp with broccoli, moo shu chicken—the kitchen leaps into high gear, concocting zesty dishes such as sautéed pork shreds with spicy garlic sauce, hot and spicy whole fish, and spicy Hunan beef. The key to having a terrific meal is to first order the house specialties—Slippery Shrimp and plump steamed pork dumplings—and then ask for recommendations from your server.

819 N. Broadway (at Alpine St.), Chinatown. © **213/625-0811.** www.yangchow.com. Reservations recommended on weekends. Main courses $10–$20. AE, DC, MC, V. Sun–Thurs 11:30am–9:45pm; Fri–Sat 11:30am–10:45pm. Validated 2-hr. parking lot behind the building for 75¢.

Inexpensive

Cole's, Originators of the French Dip ★ 🏛TAVERN   There are two schools
of thought about where the French dip originated: One is that it was at **Philippe the Original** (p. 126); the other is here at what used to be called Cole's P.E. Buffet. To add flame to the debate, Cedd Moses, the nightlife impresario who spent $2 million to renovate the restaurant and bar, added "originators of the French dip" to the name when he reopened it in 2008. Once touted as being the oldest operating restaurant in Los Angeles, Cole's is an institution dating back to 1908, when it served as a stopover for travelers going through the Pacific Electric building. Today it looks as old as it ever did, except now the bartenders are handsome young sorts who throw together classic cocktails like Sazeracs and Rickey's. Chef Neal Fraser helped revamp the menu, making the lamb and beef sandwiches more palatable than ever, but here you dip the bread yourself (at Philippe, the counter maidens do it for you). Make sure you save room for the fantastic apple or pecan pie. *Tip:* Look for the door with a picture of a cocktail on it, walk in, and you'll find Varnish, a speak-easy-type bar with its own drink menu.

118 E. 6th St. (at Main St.), Downtown. © **213/622-4090.** www.colesfrenchdip.com. French dips $6.40. MC, V. Sun–Wed 11:30am–10pm; Thurs 11:30am–11pm; Fri–Sat 11:30am–1am. Metered street parking; pay lots.

Langer's Deli BREAKFAST/DELI   A leader in L.A.'s long-running deli war—Al
Langer and his son Norm have been serving the business community and displaced New Yorkers since 1947—this deli/institution makes some of the best kishka and matzo-ball soup this side of the Hudson. For many, however, it's the fresh chopped liver, lean and spicy hot pastrami sandwiches on crispy rye, and melt-in-your-mouth corned beef that make Langer's L.A.'s best deli. *Tip:* The most sought after sandwich among locals, by far, is the famous No. 19, with pastrami, Swiss cheese, coleslaw, and Russian-style dressing. After the riots, when things got dicey around this MacArthur Park neighborhood, the restaurant began a curbside pickup service: Phone in your order with an ETA, and they'll wait for you at the curb—with change.

704 S. Alvarado St. (at 7th St.), Los Angeles. ℰ **213/483-8050.** www.langersdeli.com. Main courses $11–$23. MC, V. Mon–Sat 8am–4pm. Free 1-hr. parking with validation (at 7th and Westlake).

The Original Pantry AMERICAN/BREAKFAST   This bastion of blue-collar cooking has been serving huge portions of comfort food round-the-clock since 1924. The cash-only Pantry is popular with politicos, who come here for weekday lunches, and with conferencegoers en route to the nearby L.A. Convention Center. The well-worn restaurant is also a welcoming beacon to hungry clubbers after hours. A bowl of celery stalks, carrot sticks, and whole radishes greets you at your Formica table, and creamy coleslaw and sourdough bread come free with every meal. The menu? It's a chalkboard hanging on the wall. Famous for quantity rather than quality, the Pantry serves huge T-bone steaks, densely packed hamburger loaf, macaroni and cheese, and other American favorites. A typical breakfast—served all day—consists of a huge stack of hot cakes, a big slab of sweet cured ham, home fries, and coffee.

877 S. Figueroa St. (at 9th St.), Downtown. ℰ **213/972-9279.** www.pantrycafe.com. Main courses $6–$14. No credit cards. Daily 24 hr. Free parking across the street with validation.

Philippe The Original 🎯 BREAKFAST/SANDWICHES   Good old-fashioned value is what this legendary landmark cafeteria is all about. Popular with both South Central project residents and Beverly Hills elite—along with lawyers, jurors, and tourists—Philippe's unspectacular dining room with sawdust floors is one of the few places in L.A. where everyone can get along. Philippe's claims to have invented the French dip sandwich at this location in 1908; it remains the most popular menu item. Patrons line up and then watch while their choice of beef, pork, ham, turkey, or lamb is sliced and layered onto crusty French bread that's been dipped (or double-dipped) in meat juices. A hearty breakfast, served daily from 6 to 10:30am, is worthwhile if only for Philippe's uncommonly good cinnamon-dipped French toast. Beer and wine are available. For added entertainment, snag a booth in the Train Room, which houses the nifty Model Train Museum. *Tip:* After all these years, a regular coffee at Philippe the Original is still one of the best deals in town: 9¢.

1001 N. Alameda St. (at Ord St.), Chinatown. ℰ **213/628-3781.** www.philippes.com. Most items under $8. No credit cards. Daily 6am–10pm. Free parking.

UNIVERSAL CITY

You can choose from among more than three dozen dining options at Universal Studios, including chains like Bubba Gump Shrimp Co., Bucca di Beppo, and Saddle Ranch in Universal CityWalk. But just in case you need a respite from the frenzied theme-park atmosphere, we've also included some of our favorite San Fernando Valley restaurants, which are within easy driving distance of Universal Studios.

Expensive

Pinot Bistro ★ ☺ CALIFORNIAN/FRENCH   When the Valley crowd doesn't want to make the drive to Patina, they pack into Pinot Bistro, one of Joachim Splichal's cadre of successful restaurants. The Valley's only great bistro is designed with dark woods, etched glass, and cream-colored walls that scream "trendy French" almost as loudly as the rich, straightforward cooking. The menu, a symphony of California and Continental elements, includes a beautiful hand-chopped organic beef tartar with quail egg and herb salads, and sea scallops in a spinach pesto coulis with lemon essence—both studies in culinary perfection. The generously portioned main dishes continue the gourmet theme: crispy whitefish with potato brandade, wild risotto with a Parmesan crisp, grilled lamb with wilted greens ragout, and duck confit. The service is good, attentive, and unobtrusive. Many regulars prefer Pinot Bistro at lunch, when a slightly less expensive menu is served to a more easygoing crowd. *Tip:* You might not normally bring your kids to a bistro—but this one offers a special menu for its junior diners, which includes an entree, such as mac and cheese, fish and chips, or chicken fingers—plus dessert—for about $8.

12969 Ventura Blvd. (west of Coldwater Canyon Ave.), Studio City. ✆ **818/990-0500.** www.patina-group.com. Reservations recommended. Main courses $18–$37. AE, DC, DISC, MC, V. Lunch Mon–Fri noon–2pm; dinner Sun–Mon 5:30–9pm; Tues–Thurs 5:30–9:30pm, Fri–Sat 5:30–10pm. Valet parking $3.50.

Moderate

Casa Vega ★ 🍷 MEXICAN   Every neighborhood needs a friendly dive that's open until 2am, and Casa Vega has been the local favorite for nearly half a century. A faux-weathered adobe exterior conceals red Naugahyde booths lurking among fake potted plants and 1960s amateur oil paintings of dark-eyed Mexican children and cape-waving bullfighters. (The decor achieves critical mass at Christmas, when everything drips with tinsel.) Locals and celebs love this family-owned and -operated place for its strong, cheap margaritas; bottomless baskets of hot and salty chips; and traditional combination dinners, which all come with Casa Vega's patented tostada-style dinner salad. On warm days, ask for a table on the patio, and be prepared to wait for a table on weekends. **Tip:** There's an awesome, very modern bowling alley next door, Pinz, beloved by local families and Valley hipsters (if such a thing truly exists).

13301 Ventura Blvd. (at Fulton Ave.), Sherman Oaks. ✆ **818/788-4868.** www.casavega.com. Reservations not accepted. Main courses $12–$20. AE, DC, DISC, MC, V. Daily 11:30am–2am. Metered street parking; valet parking $3.50

Jerry's Famous Deli ★ ☺ BREAKFAST/DELI   Here's a simple yet sizable deli where all the Valley's hipsters go to relieve their late-night munchies. This place probably has one of the largest menus in America—a tome that spans cultures and continents, from Central America to China to New York. From salads and sandwiches to steak-and-seafood platters, everything—including breakfast—is served all day. Jerry's is consistently good at lox and eggs, pastrami sandwiches, potato pancakes, and all the deli staples. It's also an integral part of L.A.'s cultural landscape and a favorite of the show-business types—and their kids. Jerry's is a popular spot for families who populate the adjacent foothill neighborhoods. It even has a full bar.

12711 Ventura Blvd. (just east of Coldwater Canyon Ave.), Studio City. ✆ **818/980-4245.** www.jerrysfamousdeli.com. Main courses dinner $9–$28; sandwiches and salads $7–$17; breakfast $5–$15. AE, MC, V. Daily 24 hr. Free parking.

Miceli's ☺ TRADITIONAL ITALIAN   Mostaccioli marinara, lasagna, thin-crust pizza, and eggplant parmigiana are indicative of the Sicilian-style fare at this cavernous, stained-glass-windowed Italian restaurant adjacent to Universal City. The waitstaff sings show tunes or opera favorites in between (and sometimes instead of) serving dinner; make sure you have enough chianti to get into the spirit of it all. This is a great place for kids but is too rollicking for romance.

3655 Cahuenga Blvd. (east of Lankershim Blvd.), Universal City. ✆ **323/851-3344.** www.micelisrestaurant.com. Main courses $12–$19; pizza $13–$23. AE, DC, MC, V. Sun–Thurs 11:30am–10pm; Fri–Sat 11:30am–11pm. Complimentary valet.

Inexpensive

Du-par's Restaurant & Bakery ★ TRADITIONAL AMERICAN/BREAK-FAST   It's been called a "culinary wax museum," the last of a dying breed, the kind of coffee shop Donna Reed took the family to for blue-plate specials. This isn't a trendy new theme place, it's the real deal—and that motherly waitress who calls everyone under 60 "hon" has probably been slinging hash here for 20 or 30 years. Du-par's is popular among old-timers who made it part of their daily routine decades ago, show-business denizens who eschew the industry watering holes, a new generation that appreciates a tasty, cheap meal . . . well, everyone, really. It's common knowledge that Du-par's makes the best buttermilk pancakes in town, though some prefer the eggy, perfect French toast (extra crispy around the edges, please). Mouthwatering pies (blueberry cream cheese, coconut cream, and more) line the front display case and can be had for a song. *Tip*: Du-par's serves early morning "beat the clock" specials from 4 to 6am, and blue-plate specials from 6 to 11am.

12036 Ventura Blvd. (1 block east of Laurel Canyon Blvd.), Studio City. © **818/766-4437.** www.du-pars. com. All items under $11. AE, DC, DISC, MC, V. Daily 24 hr. Free parking. Pasadena & Environs

Expensive

Bistro 45 ★★ CALIFORNIAN/FRENCH   All class, yet never stuffy, Bistro 45 is a favorite among Pasadena's old guard and nouvelle riche. The restaurant's warm, light ambience and gallery-like decor are an unexpected surprise after the ornately historic Art Deco exterior, and provide a romantic backdrop for owner Robert Simon's award-winning cuisine. The seasonally inspired menu changes frequently; dishes might include braised veal short ribs with Asian five spice, rock shrimp risotto with saffron, pan-roasted monkfish with garlic polenta, roasted veal loin filled with Roquefort, Fanny Bay oyster salad, and Nebraska pork with figs. For dessert, try the "chocolate soup," a creamy soufflé served with warm chocolate sauce and vanilla ice cream. The knowledgeable waitstaff can answer questions about the excellent wine list; Bistro 45 appears regularly on *Wine Spectator*'s Best Of lists and hosts special-event wine dinners.

45 S. Mentor Ave. (btw. Colorado Blvd. and Green St.), Pasadena. © **626/795-2478.** www.bistro45. com. Reservations recommended. Main courses $16–$34 lunch, $19–$35 dinner. AE, DC, MC, V. Tues-Thurs 11:30am–2:30pm and 5–9pm; Fri 11:30am–2:30pm and 5–10pm; Sat 5–10pm; Sun 5–8:30pm. Valet parking $4.50.

The Raymond ★ NEW AMERICAN   With its easy-to-miss setting in a sleepy part of Pasadena, the Raymond is a jewel even few locals know about. This Craftsman cottage was once the caretaker's house for a grand Victorian hotel called the Raymond. Though the city has grown to surround it, the place maintains an enchanting air of seclusion, romance, and serenity. In 2005 the classic restaurant got a face-lift, as did the haute American- and European-inspired menu, which changes seasonally. A typical dinner may start with locally grown organic lettuces simply dressed in artisan olive oil, lemon, and smoked salt or pork belly in a bourbon barrel-aged maple. Popular entrees can be straightforward American, like 48-hour braised short ribs and Prime New York steak, or more avant garde—for instance a duck in potato-butter emulsion or Moroccan-style braised lamb shank. Tables are scattered throughout the house and in the lush English garden, and there's plenty of free parking (you won't find *that* on the Westside). *Note:* **Bar 1886,** named after the year the Raymond hotel opened, is an experience in and of itself—right down to its secret entrance off

Where to Eat in the Pasadena Area

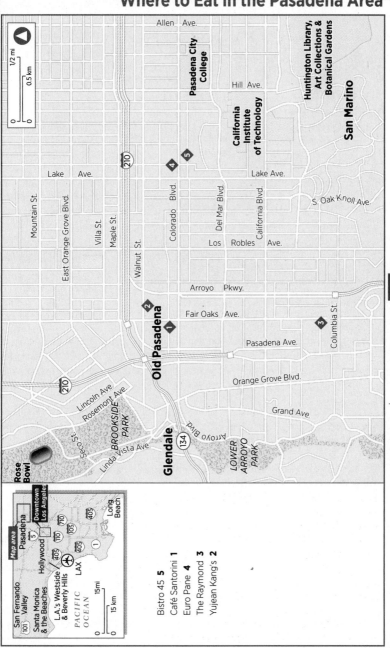

Bistro 45 **5**
Café Santorini **1**
Euro Pane **4**
The Raymond **3**
Yujean Kang's **2**

the parking lot. There are unique handcrafted cocktails, such as the Rose Parade punch and a horseradish egg sour, along with small plates like Kentucky fried quail and grilled octopus.

1250 S. Fair Oaks Ave. (at Columbia St.), Pasadena.© 626/441-3136. www.theraymond.com. Reservations recommended. Main courses $12–$20 lunch, $24–$39 dinner. AE, DC, DISC, MC, V. Tues–Thurs 5:30–9:30pm; Fri 11:30am–2:30pm and 5:30–9:30pm; Sat 9am–2:30pm and 5:30–9:30pm; Sun 9am–2:30pm and 5–9pm. Free parking lot; free valet Fri–Sun.

Moderate

Café Santorini ★ GREEK   Located at ground zero of Pasadena's crowded Old Town shopping mecca, this second-story gem has a secluded Mediterranean ambience, due in part to its historic brick building with patio tables overlooking, but insulated from, the plaza below. In the evening, lighting is subdued and romantic, but ambience is casual; many diners are coming from or going to an adjacent movie-theater complex. The food is terrific and affordable, featuring grilled meats and kabobs, pizzas, fresh and tangy hummus, plenty of warm pita, and other staples of Greek cuisine. The menu includes regional flavors such as lamb, feta cheese, spinach, and Armenian sausage; the vegetarian baked butternut squash is filled with fluffy rice and smoky roasted vegetables.

64 W. Union St. (main entrance at the shopping plaza at the corner of Fair Oaks Ave. and Colorado Blvd.), Pasadena. © 626/564-4200. www.cafesantorini.com. Reservations recommended on weekends. Main courses $10–$31. AE, DC, DISC, MC, V. Mon–Thurs 11am–10pm; Fri–Sat 11am–midnight; Sun 11am–10pm. Valet parking $7 with validation; self-parking across the street $7.

Yujean Kang's Gourmet Chinese Cuisine ★ CHINESE   Many Chinese restaurants put the word *gourmet* in their name, but few really mean it—or deserve it. Not so at Yujean Kang's, where Chinese cuisine is taken to an entirely new level. A master of fusion cuisine, the eponymous chef/owner snatches bits of techniques and flavors from both China and the West, merging them in an entirely fresh way. Can you resist such provocative dishes as "Ants on Tree" (beef sautéed with glass noodles in chili and black sesame seeds), Chinese polenta with shrimp and mushrooms, or sautéed pork chop with fresh leeks? Kang is also a wine aficionado and has assembled a magnificent cellar of California, French, and German wines. Try pairing a German Spätlese with tea-smoked duck salad. The red-wrapped dining room is less subtle than the food, but just as elegant.

67 N. Raymond Ave. (btw. Walnut St. and Colorado Blvd.), Pasadena. © 626/585-0855. www.yujeankangs.com. Reservations recommended. Main courses $8–$10. AE, MC, V. Sun–Thurs 11:30am–2pm and 5–9pm; Fri–Sat 11:30am–2pm and 5–10pm. Valet parking $6 with validation.

Inexpensive

Euro Pane ★ 🍴 BAKERY/CAFE   This tiny little bakery and cafe is off the Old Town beaten path but close to the burgeoning Lake Avenue shopping district. Any day of the week, you'll see locals, office workers, and Cal Tech students and professors all vying for Sumi Chang's fresh-baked pastries, cookies, and sandwiches. Chang has a way with croissants—hers are some of the butteriest, flakiest in town—and breads. A small menu of sandwiches is available, including the yogurt chicken salad laced with dill and lemon (get it on rosemary-currant bread), roasted vegetables and goat cheese (excellent on olive bread), and the dynamite egg salad. People come from all over town for the warm, chopped, slightly runny open-faced sandwich, and the salted caramel macaroons will make you swoon. There isn't much to the decor, but at certain times of day, it's quiet enough to snag a seat, catch your breath, and read one of the free papers laying about.

950 E. Colorado Blvd., Pasadena. ℂ **626/577-1828.** Main courses $7.50–$9. MC, V. Mon–Sat 7am–5:30pm; Sun 7am–3pm. Free street parking.

6

WHAT TO SEE & DO IN LOS ANGELES

You'll need to make a lot of tough decisions if you're touring L.A. for the first time: surfing lessons or a jogging tour? Join the live studio audience at the Tonight Show or Jeopardy!? Go to Disneyland or Universal Studios Hollywood? You get the point; it would take you months to do all the things listed in this chapter. For some help in narrowing down the options, read chapter 1, "The Best of Los Angeles," and chapter 3, "Suggested Los Angeles Itineraries."

To find out what's going on while you're in town, pick up a copy of the free *L.A. Weekly,* the monthly magazine *Los Angeles,* or the Sunday *Los Angeles Times* "The Guide" section; each has detailed listings covering events and entertainment around town, often accompanied by helpful commentary on which activities might be worth your while.

Also, note that you usually have to drive everywhere in L.A. Be sure you have a map handy (or better yet, a GPS) and try to plan your itinerary with as little time on the freeways as possible, *especially* during rush hour.

L.A.'S TOP ATTRACTIONS
Sunset Boulevard & The Sunset Strip ★★

Unless you were raised in a cave, you've undoubtedly heard of L.A.'s Sunset Boulevard. The most famous of the city's many legendary boulevards, it winds dozens of miles over prime real estate as it travels from Downtown (where it briefly turns into Cesar Chavez Avenue between Spring and Figueroa Streets) to the beach, taking its travelers on both a historical and microcosmic journey that defines Los Angeles as a whole—from tacky strip malls and historic movie studios to infamous strip clubs and some of the most coveted zip codes on earth. In fact, driving the stretch from Hollywood to the Pacific should be required for all first-time visitors because it is such a good example of what L.A. is all about: instant gratification.

Bam! From the start, you'll see the **Saharan Motor Hotel,** of many a movie shoot; the Guitar Center's **Hollywood RockWalk,** where superstars like Chuck Berry, Little Richard, Santana, and the Van Halen brothers left handprints or signatures; the **"Riot Hyatt,"** (now the Andaz) where The Doors, Led Zeppelin, and Guns N' Roses crashed and smashed from the '60s through the '80s; and **Chateau Marmont,** where Greta Garbo lived and John Belushi died.

Phew! And you've barely even started. Once you pass the Chateau Marmont, you're officially cruising the **Sunset Strip**—a 1¾-mile stretch of Sunset Boulevard from Crescent Heights Boulevard to Doheny Drive. The tour continues with the **Comedy Store,** where Roseanne Barr, Robin Williams, and David Letterman rose to stardom; Dan Aykroyd's ramshackle **House of Blues,** where the rock stars still show up for an impromptu show; the **Sunset Tower Hotel,** where Clark Gable, Marilyn Monroe, and John Wayne once lived; the ultraexclusive **Skybar** within the Mondrian hotel; the **Viper Room,** once owned by Johnny Depp, and the site of River Phoenix's overdose in 1993; **Whisky A Go-Go,** where the Doors were once a house band; and the **Rainbow Bar & Grill,** where Jimi Hendrix, Bruce Springsteen, and Bob Marley became legends.

Once you emerge from the Strip, things calm down considerably as you drive through the tony neighborhoods of **Beverly Hills, Bel Air, Brentwood,** and **Pacific Palisades.** By the time you've reached **Malibu** and the beach where *Baywatch* was filmed, you'll have seen a vivid cross section of the city and have a pretty good idea of what L.A. is all about.

Iconic Hollywood

Probably the first misconception about Hollywood—at least the areas described here—is that it is crawling with celebrities. You may find one or two at some of the hot spot restaurants and bars, but when we say "iconic" Hollywood, we mean Old Hollywood, or at least the remnants of it. We're talking stars in the sidewalks, the sign, glorious old theaters, the places where the movie industry grew up. A good place to start is near one of the major intersections, like Hollywood and Highland or Sunset and Vine, and walk through the streets from there. You'll find paid parking garages at the shopping and entertainment complexes, lots on many of the side streets, and plenty of metered street parking. Prices get steep on weekend nights (up to $20 or more).

Visitors by the millions flock to **Grauman's Chinese Theatre ★** for its famous entry court, where stars like Elizabeth Taylor, Paul Newman, Ginger Rogers, Humphrey Bogart, Frank Sinatra, Marilyn Monroe, and about 160 others set their signatures and hand-/footprints in concrete (a tradition started when actress Norma Talmadge "accidentally" stepped in wet cement during the premiere of Cecil B. DeMille's *King of Kings*). It's not always hands and feet: Betty Grable's shapely leg; the hoofprints of Gene Autry's horse, Champion; Jimmy Durante's and Bob Hope's trademark noses; Whoopi Goldberg's dreadlocks; George Burns's cigar; and even R2D2's wheels are all captured in cement.

Grauman's is one of the world's great movie palaces and one of Hollywood's finest landmarks. The theater was opened in 1927 by impresario Sid Grauman, a brilliant promoter who's credited with originating the idea of the paparazzi-packed movie "premiere." Outrageously conceived, with both authentic and simulated Chinese embellishments, Grauman's theater was designed to impress. Original Chinese heavenly doves top the facade, and two of the theater's columns once propped up a Ming dynasty temple. The theater is located at 6925 Hollywood Blvd. (btw. Highland and La Brea aves.), Hollywood. Ticket prices vary, but are usually around $15. Call ✆ **323/464-8111** or go to www.manntheaters.com/chinese for showtimes.

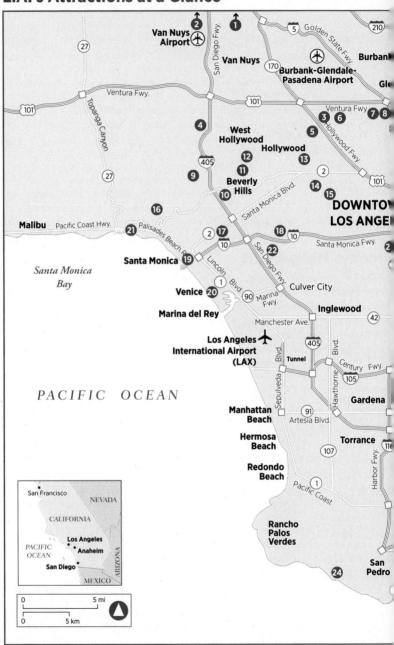

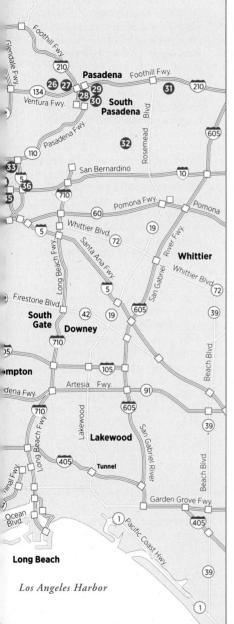

Los Angeles Harbor

Los Angeles Harbor

Money-Saving Tourist Passes

If you're the type who loves to cram as many tourist attractions as possible in one trip, then you might want to consider purchasing a **Hollywood CityPass** or **GO Los Angeles Card.** The CityPass (✆ 888/330-5008; www.citypass.com) booklet includes tickets to four attractions, all within 2 blocks of each other: **Madam Tussauds Hollywood, Starline Tour of Hollywood, Red Line Tours,** and the **Kodak Theatre Guided Tour** *or* the **Hollywood Museum.** Purchase the pass at any of the above attractions, or visit the CityPass website to buy advance passes online. The pass costs $59 for adults ($39 for kids 3–11) and expires 9 days from the first use. Is it a good deal? If you use all the tickets, you end up saving about 45% over individual, full-price admission.

I think the better deal, however, is the **GO Los Angeles Card** (✆ 866/652-3053; www.smartdestinations.com). It offers free or discounted admission to more than 40 of L.A.'s most popular attractions, activities, and tours; has far more flexibility (available in 1-, 2-, 3-, 5, and 7-day increments over a 14-day period); and comes with a nifty little full-color guidebook that fits in your back pocket. The 2-day card costs $100 for adults ($70 for kids 3–12) and doesn't need to be used on consecutive days. The 3-, 5-, and 7-day cards include admission to Universal Studios Hollywood (a great bargain). You can purchase the GO Cards via their website or at the Hollywood Visitor Information Center (6801 Hollywood Blvd. at Highland Ave.; ✆ 323/467-6412).

When the Hollywood honchos realized how limited the footprint space was at Grauman's Chinese Theatre, they came up with another way to pay tribute to the stars: the **Hollywood Walk of Fame ★**, on Hollywood Boulevard between Gower Street and La Brea Avenue, and Vine Street between Yucca Street and Sunset Boulevard. Since 1960 more than 2,400 celebrities have been honored along the world's most famous sidewalk. Each bronze medallion, set into the center of a terrazzo star, pays homage to a famous television, film, radio, theater, or recording personality. Although about a third of them are now obscure—their fame simply hasn't withstood the test of time—millions of visitors are thrilled by the sight of famous names like **James Dean** (1719 Vine St.), **John Lennon** (1750 Vine St.), **Marlon Brando** (1765 Vine St.), **Rudolph Valentino** (6164 Hollywood Blvd.), **Marilyn Monroe** (6744 Hollywood Blvd.), **Elvis Presley** (7080 Hollywood Blvd.)—the only star that has ever been moved—**Greta Garbo** (6901 Hollywood Blvd.), **Louis Armstrong** (7000 Hollywood Blvd.), **Barbra Streisand** (6925 Hollywood Blvd.), and **Eddie Murphy** (7000 Hollywood Blvd.). **Gene Autry** is all over the place: The singing cowboy earned five different stars (a sidewalk record), one in each category.

The sight of bikers, metalheads, homeless wanderers, and hordes of disoriented tourists all treading on memorials to Hollywood's greats makes for a bizarre and somewhat tacky tribute. But the Hollywood Chamber of Commerce has been doing a terrific job sprucing up the pedestrian experience with filmstrip crosswalks, swaying palms, and more. And at least 1 weekend a month, a group of fans calling themselves Star Polishers busy themselves scrubbing tarnished medallions.

The legendary sidewalk is continually adding new names, such as Muhammad Ali in front of the Kodak Theatre. The public is invited to attend dedication ceremonies; the honoree—who pays a whopping $25,000 for the eternal upkeep—is usually in attendance. Contact the **Hollywood Chamber of Commerce,** 7018 Hollywood Blvd., Hollywood, CA 90028 (© 323/469-8311; www.hollywoodchamber.net), for information on who's being honored this week.

Yet another Hollywood icon, the famous 50-foot-high white sheet-metal letters of the HOLLYWOOD **sign** ★ have come to symbolize the movie industry and the city itself. The sign was erected on Mount Lee in 1923 as an advertisement for a real-estate development. The full text originally read HOLLYWOODLAND and was lined with thousands of 20-watt bulbs around the letters (changed periodically by a caretaker who lived in a small house behind the sign). The sign gained notoriety when actress Peg Entwistle leapt to her death from the "H" in 1932. The LAND section was damaged by a landslide, and the entire sign fell into major disrepair until the Hollywood Chamber of Commerce spearheaded a campaign to repair it (Hugh Hefner, Alice Cooper, Gene Autry, and Andy Williams were all major contributors). Officially completed in 1978, the 450-foot-long installation is now protected by a fence and motion detectors. The best view is from down below, at the corner of Sunset Boulevard and Bronson Avenue. *Tip:* It may look like it on a map, but Beachwood Drive does not lead to the sign. If you want to reach the sign on foot (you still won't be able to touch it), it requires a somewhat strenuous (depending on your level of physical fitness) 5-mile round-trip hike on the Brush Canyon Trail in Griffith Park—the trail head is at the end of Canyon Drive. You can also choose to park at the Observatory (it's the same distance either way) and combine two activities in one. For more information, call the Griffith Park headquarters at © **323/913-4688.**

When it opened in 1934, the original **Farmers Market** ★★ at the intersection of 3rd Street and Fairfax Boulevard was little more than an empty lot with wooden stands set up by farmers during the Depression so they could sell directly to city dwellers. Eventually, permanent buildings grew up, including the trademark shingled 10-story clock tower. Today the place has evolved into a sprawling marketplace with a carnival atmosphere, a kind of "turf" version of San Francisco's Fisherman's Wharf. About 70 restaurants, shops, and grocers cater to a mix of workers from the CBS Television City complex, locals, and tourists brought here by the busload. Retailers sell greeting cards, kitchen implements, candles, and souvenirs, but everyone comes for the food stands, which offer oysters, hot doughnuts, Cajun gumbo, fresh-squeezed orange juice, corned beef sandwiches, fresh-pressed peanut butter, and all kinds of international fast foods. You can still buy produce here—it's no longer a farm-fresh bargain, but the selection's better than at the grocery store. Don't miss **Loteria Grill,** 6627 Hollywood Blvd. (© 323/930-2211; www.loteriagrill.com) for *shredded beef* tacos on handmade tortillas (trust me, they aren't your average asada) and cool *aguas frescas,* or **Du-par's** (© 323/933-8446) for a slice of pie. The seafood gumbo and gumbo ya ya at the **Gumbo Pot** (© 323/933-0358) are also very popular.

At the eastern end of the Farmers Market is the **Grove,** a massive 575,000-sq.-ft. Vegas-style retail complex composed of various architectural styles ranging from Art Deco to Italian Renaissance. Miniature streets link the Grove to the Market via a double-deck electric trolley. Granted, it's all a bit Disney-gaudy, but we locals love it. Where else can you power-shop until noon, check all your bags at a drop-off station, see a movie at the 14-screen **Grove Theatre** (© 323/692-0829; www.thegrovela. com), have a concierge secure you an early dinner reservation at **Morels French Steakhouse & Bistro** (© 323/965-9595), and be home by 7pm? The Grove is located at 6333 W. 3rd St. (at Fairfax Ave.), Los Angeles (© **888/315-8883** or 323/900-8080; www.thegrovela.com). It is open Monday through Thursday from

10am to 9pm, Friday and Saturday from 10am to 10pm, and Sunday from 10am to 8pm. Park in either the Grove parking structure (entry on The Grove Dr. or off of Fairfax Blvd.) or the Farmers Market parking lot, which is free for 2 hours with validation from one of the market vendors.

OceanSide Delights

Venice Beach's Ocean Front Walk ★★★ has long been one of L.A.'s most colorful areas and a must-see for any first-time visitor. Founded at the turn of the last century, Venice was a development inspired by its Italian namesake. Authentic gondolas plied miles of inland waterways lined with rococo palaces. In the 1950s, Venice became the stamping grounds of Jack Kerouac, Allen Ginsberg, William S. Burroughs, and other Beats. In the 1960s, this was the epicenter of L.A.'s hippie scene.

Today Venice is still one of the world's most engaging bohemian locales. It's not an exaggeration to say that no visit to L.A. would be complete without a stroll along the famous paved beach path, an almost surreal assemblage of every L.A. stereotype—and then some. Among stalls and stands selling cheap sunglasses, Mexican blankets, and medical marijuana swirls a carnival of humanity that includes bikini-clad in-line skaters, tattooed bikers, tan hunks pumping iron at Muscle Beach, panhandling vets, beautiful wannabes, and plenty of tourists and gawkers. On any given day, you're bound to come across all kinds of performers: mimes, break dancers, stoned drummers, chain-saw jugglers, talking parrots, and the occasional apocalyptic evangelist. The walk is located along the beach in Venice between Venice Boulevard and Rose Avenue.

Parking: Better Secure than Sorry

If you're driving to Venice Beach, pay the $5 to $10 fee for a secured lot, hide your valuables, and walk to the beach—car break-ins aren't uncommon.

About a mile up the Ocean Front Walk from Venice, and making for a great round-trip stroll, is the world-famous **Santa Monica Pier** ★★. Piers have been a tradition in Southern California since the area's 19th-century seaside resort days. Many have long since disappeared (like Pacific Ocean Park, an entire amusement park perched on offshore pilings), and others have been shortened by battering storms and are now mere shadows (or stumps) of their former selves, but you can still experience those halcyon days of yesteryear at the Santa Monica Pier.

Built in 1908 for passenger and cargo ships, the Santa Monica Pier does a pretty good job of recapturing the glory days of Southern California. The wooden wharf is now home to seafood restaurants and snack shacks, a touristy Mexican cantina, a gaily-colored 1920's indoor wooden **carousel** (which Paul Newman operated in *The Sting*), an **aquarium** filled with sharks, rays, octopus, eels, and other local sea life, and a **trapeze school** that offers lessons. The original **Muscle Beach** is also just south of the Pier. Summer evening concerts called **Twilight Dance Series,** which are free and range from big band to Miami-style Latin, draw crowds, as does the small amusement area perched halfway down. Its name, **Pacific Park** (✆ **310/260-8744;** www.pacpark.com), hearkens back to the granddaddy pier amusement park in California, Pacific Ocean Park; this updated version has a **solar-powered Ferris wheel,** a vintage **roller coaster,** and 10 other rides, plus a high-tech **arcade** shootout. But anglers still head to the end to fish, and nostalgia buffs to view the photographic display of the pier's history. This is the last of the great pleasure piers, offering rides, romance, and perfect panoramic views of the bay and mountains.

The Santa Monica Pier is also now home to the official West Coast end of **Route 66.** The end has been long debated, but in November 2009, the sign was planted on the Pier, which now attracts many tourists.

Parking is available for $6 to $8 on both the pier deck and the beachfront nearby. Limited short-term parking is also available. For information on twilight concerts (generally held Thurs mid-June through the end of Aug), call ☎ **310/458-8900** or visit www.santamonicapier.org.

Other Top Attractions

The Getty Center Los Angeles ★★ ☺ Since opening in 1997, the Richard Meier–designed Getty Center has quickly assumed its place in the L.A. landscape (literally and figuratively) as the city's cultural acropolis and international mecca. Headquarters for the Getty Trust's research, educational, philanthropic, and conservational concerns, the postmodernist complex—perched on a hillside in the Santa Monica Mountains and swathed in Italian travertine marble—is most frequently visited for the museum galleries displaying the Getty's enormous collection of Impressionist paintings, truckloads of glimmering French furniture and decorative arts, fine illuminated manuscripts, contemporary photography, and European drawings. I personally think there's nothing more relaxing than spending part of a pretty day just strolling through the Central Garden, which itself is actually a copyrighted work of art by Robert Irwin. The area that's open to the public consists of five two-story pavilions set around an open courtyard, and each gallery within is specially designed to complement the works on display. A sophisticated system of programmable window louvers allows many works (particularly paintings) to be displayed in the natural light in which they were created for the first time in the modern era. One of these is van Gogh's *Irises,* one of the museum's finest and most popular holdings. Trivia buffs will enjoy knowing that the museum spent $53.9 million to acquire this painting; it's displayed in a complex that cost roughly $1 *billion* to construct.

One of the more recent additions to the Getty Center is the Fran and Ray Stark Sculpture Garden. This collection of 28 modern and contemporary outdoor sculptures from the collection of the late legendary film producer Ray Stark and his wife, Fran, was donated to the Getty Museum and features many of the 20th century's greatest sculptors, including works by **Elisabeth Frink**, Joan Miró, and Isamu Noguchi.

Visitors to the center park at the base of the hill and ascend via a cable-driven electric tram. On clear days, the sensation is of being in the clouds, gazing across Los Angeles and the Pacific Ocean (and into a few chic Brentwood backyards). If you're

 Marina Oasis

One of my favorite places in L.A. to get away from it all is a tiny, quiet, little-known park in Marina del Rey that overlooks the mouth of the harbor. All day long you can sit on a bench and enjoy the cool breeze as a never-ending parade of beautiful yachts and sailboats slowly works its way to the ocean or back to the marina. To reach this relaxing oasis, from Venice Beach drive to the south end of Pacific Avenue, turn left on Via Marina, and park in one of the metered spaces (bring quarters and binoculars).

Avoid the masses at the Getty Center by visiting in the late afternoon or evening; the center is open until 9pm Saturdays. The nighttime view is breathtaking, and you can finish with a late dinner on the Westside.

like me and don't remember a thing from your college art-appreciation class, get one of the new GettyGuide Audio Guides at the information desk. The nifty device allows visitors to take their own guided tour through the Getty Museum. The 45-minute human-led architectural tours, offered throughout the day, are also worth looking into. Dining options include several espresso/snack carts, a cafeteria, a self-service cafe, and the elegant (though informal) "Restaurant" offering table service for lunch (Tues–Sat) and dinner (Sat) and Sunday brunch, with breathtaking views overlooking the ocean and mountains (restaurant reservations are recommended, though walk-ins are accepted; call ✆ **310/440-6810** or make reservations online at www.getty.edu).

Realizing that fine-art museums can be boring for kids, the center provides several clever children's programs, including a family room filled with hands-on activities for families; weekend family workshops; Art Detective cards to help parents and kids explore the grounds and galleries; and some tours are geared specifically for families.

Entrance to the Getty Center is free and no reservations are required. Cameras and video cams are permitted, but only if you use existing light (flash units are *verboten*) and limit photos to the permanent collection and outdoor areas.

1200 Getty Center Dr., Los Angeles. ✆ **310/440-7300.** www.getty.edu. Free admission. Tues–Fri 10am–5:30pm; Sat 10am–9pm; Sun 10am–5:30pm. Closed major holidays. Parking $15 (free after 5pm for special evening events and Sat).

The Getty Villa Malibu ★★ ☺   After 8 years and $275 million in renovations, the magnificent Getty Villa is receiving guests again. As the Getty Center was the cultural coup of 1997, a ticket to the renovated Villa was once one of the most sought-after items in the city. Fortunately, it's more accessible now; while you still need to secure advance tickets, for all but busy holiday periods, it can usually be done the day before. And thankfully, the museum has upgraded to the PDF system (versus snail mail). This former residence of oil tycoon J. Paul Getty, built in 1974 on the edge of a Malibu bluff with dazzling views of the ocean, was modeled after a first-century Roman country house buried by the eruption of Mount Vesuvius in A.D. 79—the Villa dei Papiri in Herculaneum, Italy. In fact, as you enter the sun-filled inner courtyard, it's not hard to imagine toga-clad senators wandering the gardens where fountains and bronze busts occupy the same spots as the original villa.

The museum's permanent collection of Greek, Roman, and Etruscan artifacts—dating from 6500 B.C. to A.D. 400—consists of more than 1,200 works in 23 galleries arranged by theme, and five additional galleries for changing exhibitions. Exhibits on display range from everyday items such as coins, jewelry, and sculpture to modern interactive exhibits that illustrate key moments in the history of the ancient Mediterranean. Highlights include *Statue of a Victorious Youth,* a large-scale bronze discovered in an Adriatic shipwreck that is kept in a special climate-controlled room to preserve the metal (it's one of the few life-size Greek bronzes to have survived to modern times), as well as a beautiful 450-seat open-air theater where visitors are encouraged to take a break. Performances of either a Greek comedy or tragedy take place here every September (a commanding rendition of *Elektra* featured Olympia Dukakis). For keeping the kids entertained, the Villa's education team created a hands-on space called the Family Forum where children can partake in art-related activities.

For a more enlightening museum experience, I strongly suggest you rent a $5 Getty-Guide Audio Player, which features commentary from curators and conservators on more than 150 works (it's available at the Pick-Up Desk on Floor 1). Admission to the Getty Villa is free but, unlike the Getty Center, advance tickets are required and can be obtained online or by phone.

17985 Pacific Coast Hwy. (1 mile north of Sunset Blvd.), Pacific Palisades. *C* **310/440-7300.** www. getty.edu. Free admission, but tickets required. Wed–Mon 10am–5pm. Closed major holidays. Parking $15 (free for evening programs).

Griffith Observatory ★★

Made world-famous in the film *Rebel Without a Cause,* Griffith Observatory's bronze domes have been Hollywood Hills landmarks since 1935. Closed for renovation for what seemed like forever, it finally reopened in November 2006 after a $93-million overhaul. The central dome houses the 300-seat **Samuel Oschin Planetarium,** where hourly screenings of a narrated 30-minute projection show called "Centered in the Universe" reveal the stars and planets that are hidden from the naked eye by the city's ubiquitous lights and smog.

The observatory also features 60 space-related exhibits designed to "sparkle your imagination," the highlight being the largest astronomically accurate image ever produced—a 20×152-foot porcelain enamel dazzler that's cleverly called "The Big Picture." It supposedly encompasses a million galaxies, but I lost count after 11. There's also the 200-seat Leonard Nimoy Event Horizon Theater (go Spock!), a Wolfgang Puck "Café at the End of the Universe," and several Zeiss and solar telescopes for public use both day and night.

Truth be told, most locals never actually go inside the observatory; they come to this spot on the south slope of Mount Hollywood for the unparalleled city views. On warm nights, with the lights twinkling below, this is one of the most romantic places in L.A.

2800 E. Observatory Rd. (in Griffith Park, at the end of Vermont Ave.), Los Angeles. *C* **213/473-0800.** www.griffithobservatory.org. Planetarium tickets $7 adults, $5 seniors 60 or older and students with ID, $3 children 5-12. Wed–Fri noon–10pm; Sat–Sun 10am–10pm. Call or check website for planetarium showtimes.

La Brea Tar Pits & Page Museum ★★ ☺

An odorous swamp of gooey asphalt oozes to the earth's surface in the middle of Los Angeles. No, it's not a low-budget horror-movie set—it's La Brea Tar Pits, a truly bizarre primal pool on Museum Row where hot tar has been bubbling from the earth for more than 40,000 years. The bubbling pools may look like a fake Disney set, but they're the real thing and have enticed thirsty animals throughout history. Nearly 400 species of mammals, birds, amphibians, and fish—many of which are now extinct—walked, crawled, landed, swam, or slithered into the sticky sludge, got stuck in the worst way, and stayed forever. In 1906 scientists began a systematic removal and classification of entombed specimens, including ground sloths, giant vultures, mastodons, camels, bears, lizards, and even prehistoric relatives of today's super-rats. Today it's one of the world's richest excavation sites for Ice Age fossils. The best finds are on display in the adjacent **Page Museum at the La Brea Tar Pits,** which houses the largest and most diverse collection of Ice Age plants and tar-stained skeletons in the world. Archaeological work is ongoing; you can watch as scientists clean, identify, and catalog new finds in the Paleontology Laboratory. An entertaining 15-minute film documenting the recoveries is also shown.

5801 Wilshire Blvd. (east of Fairfax Ave.), Los Angeles. © **323/934-7243.** www.tarpits.org. Museum admission $7 adults; $4.50 seniors 62 and older, students with ID, and teens 13-17; $2 children 5-12; free for kids 4 and under; free for everyone the 1st Tues of every month. Daily 9:30am–5pm. Parking $7 with validation, $9 without validation.

L.A. LIVE The new L.A. LIVE "entertainment campus" is the keystone of L.A.'s Downtown gentrification project. This being Los Angeles, the envy-me capital of the world, L.A. LIVE is one of the largest and flashiest mixed-use entertainment complexes in the world, costing $2.5 billion to build and covering more than 6 city blocks (hence its nickname—Times Square West). It's anchored by the **Nokia Theatre,** the **Staples Center** (where the Lakers and Clippers play their home games), and the **Los Angeles Convention Center,** and is crammed with a dozen chain restaurants and cafes, two huge nightclubs, a 14-screen Regal Cinema, the highly interactive **Grammy Museum,** a bowling center, **ESPN's West Coast broadcast headquarters,** and JW Marriott and Ritz-Carlton hotels (both within a 54-story tower). Whether it's worth the trip from Hollywood or the beaches depends on your interest in mega-size sports and entertainment complexes, but I do recommend logging on to the L.A. LIVE website to see who's playing or performing while you're in town. And if you're going to eat when you visit, I suggest Rosa Mexicano or Fleming's Steakhouse.

> ## The Tar-Nished Prince
>
> One of the L.A. sights Prince Charles asked to visit during his trip to Los Angeles was La Brea Tar Pits.

Figueroa St. (btw. Venice and Olympic boulevards), Los Angeles. © **866/548-3452** or 213/763-5483. www.lalive.com.

Madame Tussauds Hollywood In the heart of Hollywood, adjacent to Grauman's Chinese Theatre, the new Madame Tussauds Hollywood is the first-ever to be built from the ground up. This 44,000-square-foot, $55 million, three-story building is home to more than 100 celebrity wax figures that cost up to $300,000 each to create. Lifelike wax figures on display include famous icons: Vivien Leigh, President Barack Obama, Marilyn Monroe, Marlon Brando, Johnny Depp, Justin Timberlake, Lady Gaga, Kobe Bryant, Zac Efron, and many more. Guests can interact with their favorite celebrities without velvet ropes or barriers. The wax figures are artfully displayed in 14 themed areas including the Red Carpet, A-List Party, Spirit of Hollywood, Westerns, Crime, Modern Classics, Making Movies, American Idol, Sport, Action Heroes, Behind the Scenes, and Awards Ceremony.

6933 Hollywood Blvd., Hollywood. © **323/798-1670.** www.madametussauds.com/hollywood. Admission $25 adults, $20 seniors 60 and older and students with ID, $18 children 4-12, free for kids 3 and under.

Six Flags California (Magic Mountain and Hurricane Harbor) ★ ☺ What started as a countrified little amusement park with a couple of relatively tame roller coasters in 1971 has been transformed by Six Flags into a thrill-a-minute daredevil's paradise. The 18 world-class roller coasters (more than any other place in the world) make it enormously popular with teenagers and young adults, and the children's playland—Bugs Bunny World—creates excitement for the pint-size set (kids under 48 in. tall.) Bring an iron constitution; rides with names like Goliath, Déjà Vu, Ninja, Viper, Colossus, and Apocalypse will leave you exiting with queasy expressions. Some rides are themed to action-film characters (such as Superman: Escape From Krypton and the Riddler's Revenge); others are loosely tied to their surroundings, such as the Log Jammer and Swashbuckler. One of the newer thrill rides is **Tatsu,** a "flying beast" that debuted as the tallest, fastest, and longest flying coaster in the world; **Scream!,** where riders are strapped into a "flying chair" and raced upside down seven times at 65 mph; and the redesigned **X2,** where riders rotate 360 degrees forward and backward. Arcade games and summer-only entertainment (stunt shows, animal shows, and parades) round out the park's attractions.

Hurricane Harbor is Six Flags's tropical paradise. It's located right next door to Magic Mountain and is open mid-June through September. You really can't see both in 1 day—so plan accordingly. Bring your own swimsuit; the park has changing rooms with showers and lockers. Like Magic Mountain, areas have themes like a tropical lagoon or an African river (complete with ancient temple ruins). The primary activities are swimming, going down the 20-plus water slides, rafting, playing volleyball, and lounging; many areas are designed especially for the little "buccaneer."

Note: Be sure to check their website for money-saving discounts on admission tickets—you could save up to $25 per ticket by buying online. The amusement park is located about 20 to 30 minutes north of Universal Studios.

Magic Mountain Pkwy. (off Golden State Fwy. [I-5 N.]), Valencia. ☎ **661/255-4100** or 818/367-5965. www.sixflags.com. Magic Mountain $60 adults, $35 children under 48 in. tall, free for kids 2 and under, Harbor $33 adults, $25 children under 48 in. tall, free for kids 2 and under; Magic Mountain daily March to Labor Day and weekends and holidays the rest of the year; Hurricane Harbor daily mid-June to Labor Day and weekends May and Sept. Both parks open at 10:30am, and closing hours vary btw. 6pm and midnight. Hurricane Harbor closed Oct–Apr. Prices and hours are subject to change without notice, so call before you arrive. Parking $15.

Universal Studios Hollywood & CityWalk ★★ ☺ Believing that filmmaking itself is a bona fide attraction, Universal Studios began offering tours to the public in 1964. The concept worked: Today Universal is more than just one of the largest movie studios in the world—it's one of the largest theme parks as well. By integrating shows and rides with behind-the-scenes presentations on moviemaking, Universal created a new genre of theme park, stimulating a number of clone and competitor parks.

 Body Double

Here's a really cheap and easy way to get a great seat at a fancy Hollywood award ceremony: Log on to Seatfiller. com and sign up to be one of those people who makes sure all the front seats are occupied.

The main attraction continues to be the **Studio Tour,** a nearly 1-hour guided tram ride around the company's 420 acres that's "hosted" (via video screen) by Jimmy Fallon. En route you pass production offices before visiting the most extensive backlot reconstruction in Universal's history, including the new New York Street, plus classic stops from *War of the Worlds* and *How the Grinch Stole Christmas.* A new feature of the tour is director Peter Jackson's **King Kong 360 3D,** the largest experience of its kind in the world.

Along the way, the tram encounters several staged "disasters," which I won't divulge here, lest I ruin the surprise (they're all very tame), and a staged street race special effects sequence echoing the action in Universal's *Fast and Furious* movie series. Though the wait to board might appear long, don't be discouraged—each tram carries several hundred people and departures are frequent, so the line moves quickly. The "Front of the Line" ticket option renders it moot.

Other attractions are more typical of high-tech theme-park fare, but all have a film- or TV-oriented slant. The newest of which will be Transformers 3D: The Ride, which opens in the spring of 2012. **The Simpsons Ride** allows guests to join Homer, Marge, Bart, Lisa, and Maggie as they soar high above the fictional "Krustyland" theme park in a "virtual roller coaster," creating the sensation of thrilling drops and turns and a full 360-degree loop. **Revenge of the Mummy** is a high-tech indoor roller coaster that whips you backward and forward through a dark Egyptian tomb filled with creepy Warrior Mummies (and ends a bit too soon). **Jurassic Park—The Ride** is short in duration as well but long on dinosaur animatronics; riders in jungle boats float through a world of five-story-tall T-rexes and airborne raptors that culminates in a pitch-dark vertical drop with a splash ending. **Terminator 2: 3D** is a high-tech cyberwar show that combines live action along with triple-screen 3-D technology, explosions, spraying mists, and laser fire (Arnold prevails, of course). **Shrek 4D** is one of the park's best attractions, a multisensory animated show that combines 3-D effects, a humorous storyline, and "surprise" special effects—the flying dragon chase is wild.

Waterworld is a fast-paced outdoor theater presentation (and far better than the film that inspired it) featuring stunts and special effects performed on and around a small man-made lagoon (arrive at the theater at least 15 min. before the show time listed in the handout park map to ensure seating). Straight ahead of the park's main entrance on Main Street is the **Hollywood Ticket Office,** where you can obtain free tickets (subject to availability) for any TV shows that are taping during your visit—including *The Tonight Show with Jay Leno*—as well as tickets and passes to other local museums, sporting events, and entertainment attractions.

Universal Studios is an exciting place for kids and teens, but just as in any theme park, lines can be brutally long; the wait for a 5-minute ride can sometimes last more than an hour. In summer, the stifling Valley heat can dog you all day. To avoid the crowds, try not to visit on weekends or during school vacations. If you're willing to pay extra money to skip the hassle of standing in line, the park offers a **"Front of Line" pass** with—obviously—front-of-the-line privileges, as well as VIP passes (essentially private tours). You can also save time standing in line by purchasing and printing your tickets online. Log on to **www.universalstudioshollywood.com** for more information. Another ticket option is the **"All You Can Eat"** pass, which allows guests to dine all day at selected in-park restaurants for one price.

The **Southern California CityPass** (② 888/330-5008; www.citypass.com) offers admission to five So Cal attractions including Universal Studios Hollywood and the Disneyland Resort.

Located just outside the gate of Universal Studios Hollywood is **Universal City-Walk** (② 818/622-4455; www.citywalkhollywood.com). If you have any money left from the amusement park, you can spend it at this 3-block-long pedestrian promenade crammed thick with flashy name-brand stores (Billabong, Fossil, Skechers, Abercrombie and Fitch), nightclubs (the Jon Lovitz Comedy Club, Howl at the Moon dueling piano bar, Rumba Room Latin dance club, and the newest outpost of San Francisco's sexy Infusion Lounge), restaurants (Hard Rock Cafe, Daily Grill, Bubba Gumps, Pink's Hot Dogs, Samba Brazilian Steakhouse & Lounge, Saddle Ranch

Glaring Mistake

The only people who weren't applauding the new Walt Disney Concert Hall were the condominium owners across the street. To them the stainless-steel building was a giant Easy-Bake oven—every time the sunlight reflected off the Concert Hall and into the condos, it increased daytime room temperatures up to 15%. The final solution was to dull the finish on certain sections of the Concert Hall.

Chop House—ride the mechanical bull—we dare you!), a six-story 3-D IMAX theater, the 18-screen **CityWalk Cinemas,** a 6,200-seat amphitheater, an indoor skydiving wind tunnel, and even a bowling alley (Take *that,* Disney!). Be sure to stop into the **Zen Zone** (© **818/487-7889**), where you can get an inexpensive 20-minute "aqua massage." You lay down fully clothed in what looks like a tanning bed, and strong rotating jets of water massage your backside from neck-to-toe (a blue rubber sheet keeps you dry). Entrance to CityWalk is free; it's open until 9pm on weekdays and until midnight Friday and Saturday. *Tip:* The sushi at the Wasabi at CityWalk restaurant (© **818/763-8813**) was surprisingly good and very reasonably priced.

Hollywood Fwy. (Universal Center Dr. or Lankershim Blvd. exits), Universal City. © **800-UNIVERSAL** (864-8377) or 818/622-3801. www.universalstudioshollywood.com. Admission $74 adults, $66 children under 48 in. tall, free for kids 2 and under. Winter 10am–6pm; summer 9am–7pm. Hours are subject to change. Parking $12.

Walt Disney Concert Hall ★★★   The strikingly beautiful Walt Disney Concert Hall isn't just the new home of the Los Angeles Philharmonic; it's a key element in an urban revitalization effort now underway Downtown. The Walt Disney family insisted on the best and, with an initial gift of $50 million to build a world-class performance venue, that's what they got: A masterpiece of design by world-renowned architect Frank Gehry, and an acoustical quality that equals or surpasses those of the best concert halls in the world. Similar to Gehry's most famous architectural masterpiece, the Guggenheim Museum in Bilbao, the concert hall's dramatic stainless-steel exterior consists of a series of undulating curved surfaces that partially envelop the entire building, presenting multiple glimmering facades to the surrounding neighborhood. Within is a dazzling 2,265-seat auditorium replete with curved woods and a dazzling array of organ pipes (also designed by Gehry), as well as Joachim Splichal's Patina restaurant, the hip Concert Hall Cafe, a bookstore, and a gift shop.

The 3½-acre Concert Hall is open to the public for viewing, but to witness it in its full glory, do whatever it takes to attend a concert by the world-class **Los Angeles Philharmonic** (p. 258) and the sensational new music director Gustavo Dudamel. Also highly recommended are free audio tours, which lead visitors through the Concert Hall's history from conception to creation. The 45-minute self-guided tour is narrated by actor John Lithgow and includes interviews with Frank Gehry, and former Los Angeles Philharmonic music director Esa-Pekka Salonen, and acoustician Yasuhisa Toyota, among others. One big caveat is that you see just about everything except the auditorium: There's almost always a rehearsal in progress, and the acoustics are so good that there's no discreet way to sneak a peek. The audio tours are available on most nonmatinee days from 10am to 2pm (be sure to check the website for the monthly tour schedule).

111 S. Grand Ave. (at 1st St.). ℂ **323/850-2000** or 213/972-7211. www.disneyhall.com, www.laphil.com, or www.musiccenter.org.

MUSEUMS & GALLERIES

See p. 140 for the **J. Paul Getty collection** at the Getty Center Los Angeles and the Getty Villa Malibu.

L.A.'s Westside & Beverly Hills

Annenberg Space for Photography ★★   If you're a fan of photography, you'll want to schedule time to visit the free Annenberg Space for Photography. The first solely photographic cultural destination in the Los Angeles area, the design for the new 10,000-square-foot facility was modeled on the mechanics of a camera and lens. A circular digital gallery is contained within the square building, while the ceiling features an iris-like design that creates an architectural metaphor for a convex lens. The intimate environment features state-of-the-art, high-definition digital technology as well as traditional prints by some of the world's most renowned and emerging photographers. Previous exhibits ranged from sports photography and international Pictures of the Year to environmental issues such as "Water: Our Thirsty World," featuring the work of award-winning photographers looking at water from environmental, social, political, and cultural perspectives. ***Note:*** Self-parking in the underground garage at Century Park is $3.50 for 3 hours with validation Monday through Friday 8:30am to 4:30pm. Weekdays after 4:30pm and on Saturday and Sunday, parking is a flat rate of $1 with validation.

Tune Time

The organ in the Walt Disney Concert Hall is so complex that it took a full year to tune.

2000 Ave. of the Stars, Century City. ℂ **213/403-3000.** www.annenbergspaceforphotography.com. Free admission. Wed, Fri–Sun 11am–6pm (digital programming ends at 5pm on Thursdays).

Hammer Museum ★   Created by the former chairman and CEO of Occidental Petroleum, the Hammer Museum is ensconced in a two-story Carrara marble building attached to the oil company's offices. It's better known for its high-profile and often provocative visiting exhibits. With a reputation for championing contemporary political and experimental art, the Hammer continues to present often daring and usually popular special exhibits, and it's definitely worth calling ahead to find out what will be there during your visit to L.A. The permanent collection (Armand Hammer's personal collection) consists mostly of traditional western European and Anglo-American art, and contains noteworthy paintings by Toulouse-Lautrec, Rembrandt, Degas, and van Gogh.

10899 Wilshire Blvd. (at Westwood Blvd.), Westwood. ℂ **310/443-7000.** www.hammer.ucla.edu. Admission $7 adults, $5 seniors 65 and over, free for children 17 and under; free for everyone Thurs. Tues–Wed and Fri–Sat 11am–7pm; Thurs 11am–9pm; Sun 11am–5pm. Closed Jan 1, July 4, Thanksgiving, and Christmas. Parking $3 for 1st 3 hr. with validation.

Museum of Tolerance ★   The Museum of Tolerance is designed to expose prejudices, bigotry, and inhumanity while teaching racial and cultural tolerance. Since its opening in 1993, it has hosted four million visitors from around the world, including King Hussein of Jordan and the Dalai Lama. It's located in the Simon Wiesenthal Center, an institute founded by the legendary Nazi hunter. While the Holocaust

free CULTURE

To beef up attendance and give indigent folk like us travel writers a break, almost all of L.A.'s art galleries and museums are open free to the public 1 day of the week or month (or both), and several charge no admission at any time. Use the following list to plan your week around the museums' free-day schedules; refer to the individual attractions listings in this chapter for more information on each museum.

Free Every Day
- J. Paul Getty Museum at the Getty Center
- The Getty Villa Malibu (advance tickets required)
- Paley Center for Media (donation suggested)
- Los Angeles County Museum of Art (*after* 5pm)
- Bergamot Arts Station & Santa Monica Museum of Art
- California African American Museum
- California Science Center
- Annenberg Space for Photography

Free Every Thursday
- Museum of Contemporary Art (MOCA), from 5 to 8pm
- Hammer Museum, from 11am to 9pm
- Japanese American National Museum, from 5 to 8pm
- Skirball Cultural Center, from noon to 9pm

- Geffen Contemporary at MOCA, from 5 to 8pm

Free Every Friday
- Schindler House, from 4 to 6pm

Free Every First Tuesday
- Natural History Museum of Los Angeles County, from 9:30am to 5pm
- Page Museum at La Brea Tar Pits, from 9:30am to 5pm

Free Every First Wednesday
- Craft and Folk Art Museum, from 11am to 5pm

Free Every First Thursday
- Huntington Library, Art Collections & Botanical Gardens, from noon to 4:30pm

Free Every First Friday
- Norton Simon Museum of Art, from 6 to 9pm

Free Every Second Tuesday
- Autry National Center of the American West, from 10am to 5pm
- Los Angeles County Museum of Art, from noon to 8pm

Free Every Third Tuesday
- Los Angeles County Arboretum and Botanic Garden, from 9am to 4:30pm
- Japanese American National Museum, from 10am to 8pm

Free Every Fourth Friday
- Pacific Asia Museum, from 10am to 8pm

figures prominently here, this is not a Jewish museum—it's an academy that broadly campaigns for a live-and-let-live world. Tolerance is an abstract idea that's hard to display, so most of this $50-million museum's exhibits are high-tech and conceptual in nature. Fast-paced interactive displays are designed to touch the heart as well as the mind, and engage everyone from heads of state to Gen Y.

9786 W. Pico Blvd. (at Roxbury Dr.), Los Angeles. ☎ **310/553-8403.** www.museumoftolerance.com. Admission $15 adults, $12 seniors 62 and over, $11 students with ID and children 5–18, free for kids 4 and under. Advance purchase recommended; photo ID required for admission. Mon–Thurs 10am–5pm; Fri 10am–3:15pm.; Sun 11am–5pm. Closed Sat and many Jewish and secular holidays; call for schedule. Free underground parking.

If you've seen *The Witches of Eastwick* or *War and Remembrance,* then you already know how beautiful and opulent the Greystone Mansion and surrounding gardens are. On a gentle slope overlooking Beverly Hills, the 19-acre park is a prime filming location where dozens of TV episodes, movies *(Spiderman, X-Men, Batman, Ghostbusters, The Bodyguard),* commercials, and music videos are filmed annually. It's worth a visit just to admire the matriarch of Beverly Hills mansions and the meticulously groomed gardens. A self-guided tour takes you through the Formal Gardens, Mansion Gardens, and Lower Ground Estate. Picnics are welcome in designated areas. The park is at 905 Loma Vista Dr., just off Doheny Road, and is open daily from 10am to 6pm (to 5pm in the winter). (C) 310/285-6830. Admission is free. For more information, log on to www.greystonemansion.org.

The Paley Center for Media ★ Want to see the Beatles on *The Ed Sullivan Show* (1964), or Edward R. Murrow's examination of Joseph McCarthy (1954), or Arnold Palmer's victory in the 1958 Masters Tournament; or want to listen to radio excerpts like FDR's first "Fireside Chat" (1933) and Orson Welles's famous *War of the Worlds* UFO hoax (1938)? All these, plus a gazillion episodes of *The Twilight Zone, I Love Lucy,* and other beloved series (including numerous pilots never aired on national television), can be viewed within the starkly white walls of architect Richard Meier's neutral, contemporary building. Once you gawk at the celebrity and industry-honcho names adorning every hall, room, and miscellaneous area, it becomes quickly apparent that "library" would be a more fitting name for this collection, since the main attractions—120,000 television and radio programs and commercials—are requested via sophisticated computer catalogs and viewed in private consoles. Although no one sets out to spend a vacation watching TV, it can be tempting once you start browsing the archives. This West Coast branch of the venerable New York facility succeeds in treating our culture's favorite pastime as a legitimate art form of historical significance.

465 N. Beverly Dr. (at Santa Monica Blvd.), Beverly Hills. (C) **310/786-1091.** www.paleycenter.org. Suggested contribution $10 adults, $8 students and seniors, $5 children 13 and under. Wed–Sun noon–5pm. Closed Jan 1, July 4, Thanksgiving, and Christmas. Parking free.

Skirball Cultural Center ★ This strikingly modern museum/cultural center is quick to remind us that Jewish history is about more than the Holocaust. Nestled in the Sepulveda Pass uphill from the Getty Center, the Skirball explores American Jewish life, American democratic values, and the pursuit of the American dream—a theme shared by many immigrant groups. The Skirball's core exhibit, "Visions and Values: Jewish Life from Antiquity to America," chronicles the experiences and accomplishments of the Jewish people over 4,000 years. Related events are held here throughout the year; such as a rollicking festival of klezmer music (a traditional Jewish folk-music style). Call for free docent-led tour times.

2701 N. Sepulveda Blvd. (at Mulholland Dr.), Los Angeles. (C) **310/440-4500.** www.skirball.org. Admission $10 adults, $7 students and seniors 65 and over, $5 children 2–12, free for kids 1 and under; free for everyone Thurs. Tues–Fri noon–5pm; Sat–Sun 10am–5pm. Closed many Jewish and secular holidays; call for schedule. Free parking (except during Sunset Concerts). From I-405, exit at Skirball Center Dr./ Mulholland Dr.

Hollywood

Craft and Folk Art Museum ★   The Craft and Folk Art Museum (CAFAM) has been a catalyst for cultural exploration for more than 40 years. Formerly The Egg and The Eye, an innovative cafe and artist hangout, CAFAM now provides the culturally curious a chance to explore the world through the universal lens of art. Breaking from the traditional, the museum offers a fresh and modern take on "craft and folk art" by featuring thought-provoking exhibitions, ranging from the history of the Tarot to a photojournalist's observations of contemporary Iranian society. Be sure to check out the museum's weekly public programs where you can get your hands dirty and actively participate in interpreting and creating art.

Another great reason to visit is to experience the museum's award-winning shop, which features a curated selection of exquisite handmade goods that represent the best of contemporary craft and traditional folk art from around the world. Plus, these handpicked objects come from fair-trade collectives, women's empowerment projects, and local artisans, so your buying power has a positive social impact.

5814 Wilshire Blvd. (btw. Fairfax and La Brea aves.), Los Angeles. *C* **323/937-4230.** www.cafam.org. Admission $7 adults, $5 seniors and students, free for children 9 and under; free for everyone 1st Wed each month. Tues–Fri 11am–5pm; Sat–Sun noon–6pm. Metered street parking or nearby public lots.

The Hollywood Museum   The historic Max Factor Building—Max Factor was the patriarch of the Hollywood makeup industry—has finally been restored to its original 1935 Art Deco splendor and is now the home of the Hollywood Museum, which features four floors of famous and rare props (including Hannibal Lecter's cell), costumes (Nicole Kidman's from *Moulin Rouge*), scripts, cameras, awards, and numerous vintage photos and posters from the television, stage, and recording industries. Exhibits are arranged for the visitor to experience Hollywood chronologically—from the Silent Era and Golden Era to current production technology and a glimpse into the future of the industry. The museum, located across from the Hollywood & Highland entertainment complex, also houses a library, a screening room, an education center, and a museum-studio gift shop. Private guided tours are available upon request.

L.A.-Style XXX-ercise

Actress Sheila Kelley has taken the L.A. exercise craze in an X-citing new direction with "the S Factor," a workout regimen inspired by striptease and pole dancing. A 1- to 2-hour (depending on class size) intro course is only $40, but be sure to sign up early as they fill up fast (sorry, guys, it's for women only). Check it out at www.sfactor.com.

1660 N. Highland Ave. (at Hollywood Blvd.), Hollywood. *C* **323/464-7776.** www.thehollywood museum.com. Admission and tour $15 adults, $12 seniors and children 11 and under. Wed–Sun 10am–5pm.

Los Angeles County Museum of Art (LACMA) ★★★   For more than 50 years, LACMA has been one of the finest art museums in the nation, housing a 100,000-piece permanent collection that includes works by Degas, Rembrandt, Hockney, and Monet. The huge 20-acre complex—it's the largest visual-arts museum west of Chicago—has been expanded even more with the 2008 opening of the $56-million, three-story **Broad Contemporary Art Museum** (also known as BCAM). Boasting 60,000 sq. ft. of exhibition space, it's the first new art museum built in L.A. since the Getty Center opened in 1997. Opening installations include works by such contemporary artists as Richard Serra, Jeff Koons, Jasper Johns, Andy Warhol, and Roy Lichtenstein.

More recently, the Lynda and Stewart Resnick Exhibition Pavilion was added in 2010. The single-story structure is 45,000 square feet in size, and is now the world's largest custom-built, open-plan museum with natural lighting. Three diverse exhibits inaugurated its debut—one focused on decorative arts, another on ancient Mexican masterworks and the third on European fashion from 1700 to 1915.

Other highlights include LACMA's **Pavilion for Japanese Art,** which has exterior walls made of Kalwall, a translucent material that, like shoji screens, permits the entry of soft natural light. Inside is a collection of Japanese Edo paintings that's rivaled only by the holdings of the emperor of Japan. The **Ahmanson Building** houses the majority of the museum's permanent collections—everything from 2,000-year-old pre-Columbian Mexican ceramics to 19th-century portraiture, to a unique glass collection spanning the centuries. Other displays include one of the nation's largest holdings of costumes and textiles, and an important Indian and Southeast Asian art collection. Free 50-minute guided tours of many of LACMA's special exhibitions are offered weekly—check the museum's online calendar for times and locations.

Ray & Stark's Bar is a new restaurant and outdoor lounge that is one more coup for the LACMA campus. A destination in itself, there's no better (or closer) spot in the neighborhood for enjoying a specialty cocktail, a flatbread pizza from the bar bites menu, or even a full Mediterranean-inspired dinner experience. A must try: the rich, wood-roasted Anaheim chile starter with chorizo, dates, and local goat cheese. While everything is topnotch, the dress code is surprisingly relaxed.

5905 Wilshire Blvd. (btw. Curson and Fairfax aves.), Los Angeles. ✆ **323/857-6000.** www.lacma.org. Admission $15 adults, $10 students and seniors 62 and over, free for children 17 and under; regular exhibitions free for everyone after 5pm, all day the 2nd Tues of every month, and all holidays that fall on Mondays. Mon–Tues and Thurs noon–8pm; Fri noon–9pm; Sat–Sun 11am–8pm. Closed Thanksgiving and Christmas. Parking $7.

Autry National Center of the American West ★★

North of Downtown in Griffith Park, this is one of the country's finest and most comprehensive museums of the American West. More than 100,000 pieces of art and artifacts showcasing the history of the region west of the Mississippi River are intelligently displayed. Evocative exhibits illustrate the everyday lives of early pioneers, not only with antique firearms, tools, saddles, and the like, but also with many hands-on displays that successfully stir the imagination and the heart. Displays include the Southwest Museum of the American Indian Collection and the works of western artists, as well as film clips from the silent days of early Westerns and contemporary movies. Provocative visiting exhibits usually focus on cultural or domestic regional history. Docent-led tours are generally scheduled on Saturdays at 11:30am, 1, and 3pm.

4700 Western Heritage Way, Griffith Park. ✆ **323/667-2000.** www.autrynationalcenter.org. Admission $10 adults, $6 seniors 60 and over and students 13–18, $4 children 3–12, free for kids 2 and under; free for everyone the 2nd Tues of every month. Tues–Fri 10am–4pm (until 8pm Thurs in July & Aug.); Sat–Sun 11am–5pm. Closed Jan 1, July 4, Labor Day, Thanksgiving and the day after Thanksgiving, and Dec 24–25. Free parking.

Petersen Automotive Museum ★★ ☺

When the Petersen opened in 1994, many locals were surprised that it had taken this long for the city of freeways to salute its most important shaper. Indeed, this museum says more about the city than probably any other in L.A. Named for Robert Petersen, the publisher responsible for *Hot Rod* and *Motor Trend* magazines, the four-story, 300,000-square-foot museum displays more than 200 cars and motorcycles, from the historic to the futuristic. Cars on

the first floor are exhibited chronologically in period settings. Other floors are devoted to frequently changing shows of race cars, early motorcycles, famous movie and TV vehicles like the Batmobile, and celebrity wheels. On the third floor is the Discovery Center, a "hands-on" learning center that teaches adults and kids the basic scientific principles of how a car works. Past shows have included a comprehensive exhibit of "woodies" and surf culture, Hollywood "star cars," and the world's fastest and most valuable cars.

6060 Wilshire Blvd. (at Fairfax Ave.), Los Angeles. ✆ **323/930-CARS** (930-2277). www.petersen.org. Admission $10 adults, $5 seniors and students, $3 children 5–12, free for kids 4 and under. Tues–Sun 10am–6pm; Labor Day and Memorial Day 10am–6pm. Closed Jan 1, Thanksgiving, and Christmas. Parking $8.

Downtown

California African American Museum   This small museum is both a celebration of individual African Americans and a living showplace of contemporary culture. The best exhibits are temporary and touch on themes as varied as the human experience. Previous shows have included a sculpture exhibit examining interpretations of home, a survey of African puppetry, and a look at black music in Los Angeles in the 1960s. In the gift shop you'll find sub-Saharan wooden masks and woven baskets, as well as hand-embroidered Ethiopian pillows. There are also posters, children's books, and calendars. The museum offers a full calendar of lectures, concerts, and special events; call for the latest.

600 State Dr., Exposition Park. ✆ **213/744-7432.** www.caamuseum.org. Free admission; donation requested. Tues–Sat 10am–5pm; Sun 11am–5pm. Closed Jan 1, Thanksgiving, and Christmas. Parking $8.

California Science Center ★★ ☺   A $130-million renovation—reinvention, actually—has turned the former Museum of Science and Industry into Exposition Park's most popular attraction. Using high-tech sleight of hand, the center stimulates kids of all ages with questions, answers, and lessons about the world. The museum is organized into themed worlds, and one of the museum's highlights is Tess, a 50-foot animatronic woman whose muscles, bones, organs, and blood vessels are revealed, demonstrating how the body reacts to a variety of external conditions and activities. (Appropriate for children of all ages; Tess doesn't possess reproductive organs.) Another highlight is the **Air and Space Gallery,** a seven-story space where real air- and spacecraft are suspended overhead. Ecosystems is the newest permanent exhibition wing; in it the Earth's various environments can be explored through live habitats and hands-on technology.

Visitors must pay nominal fees, ranging from $2 to $5, to enjoy the science center's more thrilling attractions. You can pedal a bicycle across a high-wire suspended 43 feet above the ground (demonstrating the principle of gravity and counterweights) or get strapped into the **Space Docking Simulator** for a virtual-reality taste of zero gravity. The IMAX theater screen is seven stories high and 90 feet wide, with state-of-the-art surround-sound and 3-D technology. Films are screened throughout the day and are nearly always breathtaking, even the two-dimensional ones.

700 Exposition Park Dr., Exposition Park. ✆ **323/724-3623** or 213/744-7400 (IMAX theater). www.californiasciencecenter.org. Free admission to museum; IMAX theater $8.25 adults; $6 seniors 60 and over, students 13–17, and college students with valid ID; $5 children 3–12. Multishow and group discounts available. Daily 10am–5pm. Closed Jan 1, Thanksgiving, and Christmas. Parking $8.

Grammy Museum ★★ ☺   Open since December 2008 and an anchor to the L.A. LIVE entertainment complex, this $30-million, 30,000-square-foot, four-story

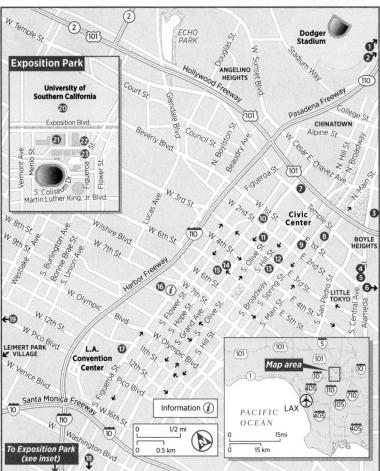

Bradbury Building **12**
California African American Museum **23**
California Science Center **22**
Cathedral of Our Lady of the Angels **7**
Central Library **15**
Charles F. Lummis House (El Alisal) and Garden **1**
City Hall **8**
Geffen Contemporary at MOCA **4**
Grammy Museum **17**
Grand Central Market **13**
Japanese American National Museum **5**
The Los Angeles Times Building **9**

Mariachi Plaza **6**
Museum of Contemporary Art **11**
Museum of Tolerance **19**
Natural History Museum of Los Angeles County **21**
The Southwest Museum **2**
STAPLES Center / L.A. Live **17**
Union Station **3**
University of Southern California **20**
US Bank Tower **14**
Visitors Information Center **16**
Walt Disney Concert Hall **10**
Watts Towers **18**

museum has interactive exhibits that take you from the creative process to the production of 150 different kinds of music: pop, jazz, rock, gospel, country, world, polka, Native American, Hawaiian, blues, hip-hop, opera, classical, and many more. Displays include artifacts like Jennifer Lopez's infamous green Grammy dress, Billie Holiday's costume jewelry, and Leadbelly's prison pardon. There are pods with performance footage and interviews, eight interactive studios where you can mix tracks with some of today's biggest recording producers (kids love this feature), a rooftop terrace, and a 200-seat theater that shows short films. You can't possibly see it all in one visit—except for maybe the die-hard music buffs who will probably never want to leave. *Tip:* The intimate theater is a great place to catch a stripped-down set by legendary performers as varied as the Preservation Hall Jazz Band to Kenny Chesney.

800 W. Olympic Blvd. (at Figueroa St., on the L.A. LIVE campus), Downtown. ℂ **213/765-6800.** www. grammymuseum.org. Admission $13 adults, $12 seniors and students, $11 children 6–17, free for kids 5 and under; $8 after 6pm when there's an evening program. Mon–Fri 11:30am–7:30pm; Sat–Sun 10am–7:30pm. Parking $5 and up.

Japanese American National Museum ★★ 📱 In an architecturally acclaimed modern building in Little Tokyo, this soaring pavilion—designed by renowned architect Gyo Obata—is a private nonprofit institute created to document and celebrate the history of the Japanese in America. The permanent and rotating exhibits chronicle Japanese life in the United States, highlighting distinctive aspects of Japanese-American culture ranging from the internment-camp experience during the early years of World War II to the lives of Japanese Americans in Hawaii. The experience is made even more poignant by the personal accounts of the docents, some of whom are elderly Japanese-American citizens who were interred in these camps during the war. It's a very popular museum, attracting more than 150,000 annual visitors. *Tip:* Don't miss the museum store, which carries excellent gift items ranging from teapots to cool origami sets.

369 E. 1st St. (at Central Ave.), Downtown. ℂ **213/625-0414.** www.janm.org. Admission $9 adults; $5 seniors, students and children 6–17; free for kids 5 and under; free for everyone the 3rd Thurs of every month and every Thurs after 5pm. Wed, Fri–Sat 11am–5pm; Thurs noon–8pm. Closed Jan 1, July 4, Thanksgiving, and Christmas.

The Museum of Contemporary Art, Los Angeles (MOCA) ★ A vital arbiter of new art, architecture, and design with a history of presenting groundbreaking exhibitions, the Museum of Contemporary Art, Los Angeles (MOCA), showcases the most ambitious and challenging art of our time by emerging and mid-career artists, as well as iconic works from its world-renowned permanent collection in three distinct buildings. As Los Angeles's only institution devoted to art created from 1940 to the present, MOCA holds one of the country's finest collections of American and European art with roughly 6,000 objects of various visual mediums—ranging from masterpieces of abstract expressionism and pop art to recent works by young and emerging artists.

MOCA Grand Avenue (250 S. Grand Ave.), which has received numerous design accolades, is a contemporary red sandstone structure by renowned Japanese architect Arata Isozaki. Also at the Grand Avenue location is the museum's popular restaurant, **Lemonade** (Mon and Fri 11am–5pm, Thurs 11am–8pm, Sat–Sun 11am–6pm; ℂ **213/628-0200**).

The museum's second space, on Central Avenue in Little Tokyo (152 N. Central Ave.), was the "Temporary Contemporary" while the Grand structure was being built

A great day IN DOWNTOWN L.A.

If you haven't heard the news, it's hip to hang out in Downtown L.A. these days. What used to be a ghost town after 5pm is speedily becoming a trendy destination as chic hotels (the Standard), bars (Edison), and venues (Walt Disney Concert Hall) sprout up like weeds between all those tall buildings. Start the day early with a 9¢ cup of coffee and cinnamon-dipped French toast at **Philippe the Original** (p. 126). Then make your way to Seventh Street for a self-guided walking tour of a glimpse into the financial, jewelry, theater and fashion districts. (Be sure to print out a map in advance at www.laconservancy.org/tours/Strolling_on_Seventh.pdf). Next up is an audio tour of the spectacular **Walt Disney Concert Hall** (bring a camera).

Time for lunch, so spend a few hours noshing your way through the dozens of ethnic food stalls at the **Grand Central**

Market (p. 227). After lunch, the options abound: tour the poignant **Japanese American National Museum** (p. 154) or **Museum of Contemporary Art** (p. 154). If you did your homework, you already made reservations for a play or performance at the **Dorothy Chandler Pavilion** or **Walt Disney Concert Hall** (see chapter 9). After the show, it's time for a late-night bite at the adjacent fine-dining **Patina** restaurant (p. 120), which seats up to 30 minutes after performance end-time (if you're not hungry for a full meal, consider the impressive cheese cart). Cap off this grand day with a martini at the subterranean **Edison,** quite possibly the most beautiful bar I've ever had the pleasure of drinking in. *Tip:* Be sure to get a DASH shuttle map (p. 319) so you can get around Downtown quickly and easily; rides are only 35¢.

and now presents rotating exhibits in a warehouse-type space that's been renamed the **Geffen Contemporary at MOCA,** for entertainment mogul and art collector David Geffen. Unless there's a visiting exhibit of great interest at the main museum, I recommend that you start at the Geffen building, where it's also easier to park.

The museum's third venue is **MOCA Pacific Design Center** (8687 Melrose Ave., West Hollywood)—it's the compact building next to the Pacific Design Center. Unlike the other two, admission to this gallery is free, and emphasis is on contemporary architecture and design, as well as new work by emerging and established artists.

© **213/626-6222.** www.moca.org. MOCA Grand Avenue and the Geffen Contemporary at MOCA: Admission $10 adults, $5 seniors 65 and over and students, free for children 12 and under; free for everyone Thurs 5-8pm. Mon and Fri 11am-5pm; Thurs 11am-8pm; Sat-Sun 11am-6pm. MOCA Pacific Design Center: Free admission. Tues-Fri 11am-5pm; Sat-Sun 11am-6pm. All MOCA spaces closed Jan 1, July 4, Thanksgiving, and Christmas. Metered street parking or use the Walt Disney Concert Hall garage (enter from Lower Grand Ave. or 2nd St.; $9 flat rate with MOCA validation); $20 deposit required upon entry; $11 refund.

Natural History Museum of Los Angeles County ★★ ☺ The "Dueling Dinosaurs" are not a high school football team, but the trademark symbol of this massive museum: the *Tyrannosaurus rex* and *Triceratops* skeletons are poised in a stance so realistic that every kid feels inspired to imitate their *Jurassic Park* bellows (think *Calvin & Hobbes*). Opened in 1913 in a beautiful domed Beaux-Arts building, the museum tells the story of the planet with 35 million specimens and artifacts, including meteorites dating back 4.5 billion years. It's the largest natural-history museum in the western United States, stocked with a mind-boggling array of wildlife dioramas, ancient Latin American and California history treasures, and prehistoric fossils—including a new exhibit, **Age of Mammals,** that tells the story of the past 65 million years of mammal evolution. The **Dino Lab** is a specially designed room where visitors can watch the work of paleontologists—live and in person—as they prepare the fossils for the **Dinosaur Hall** exhibition, opening in July of 2011. Of particular interest will be the 30-ft. tall "Thomas" the T.rex, whose bones had previously been assembled in the Dino Lab.

The best permanent displays include a walk-through vault of priceless gems and an eyebrow-raising **Insect Zoo.** Kids can dig for fossils, make fossil rubbings, and view live animals such as snakes and lizards in the family-friendly **Discovery Center.** During the summer, from April through Labor Day, the **Butterfly Pavilion** lets visitors walk through an outdoor butterfly conservatory as 40 species flutter through the air and occasionally land on their shirts. For 6 weeks in the fall, timed around Halloween, this enclosed conservatory is transformed into the **Spider Pavilion,** where the beauty of the orb weavers' webs convinces guests to conquer their fears of arachnids.

The museum is adding another outdoor component in July 2011, when 3½ acres of green space open with live, year-round habitats of butterflies, birds, bugs, and pollinating plants as well as nature experiences, including an urban teaching garden and a "Get Dirty Zone." Fall of 2012 will bear witness to the opening of **Under the Sun,** an exhibition focusing on the environmental and cultural history of Southern California. Also, a new rail line connecting Downtown with west Los Angeles will open, and the Expo Line will have a dedicated stop in front of the museum. The museum's renovated store carries everything from butterfly houses and dinosaur toys to ethnic jewelry and guides to the birds of Los Angeles written by museum curators.

900 Exposition Blvd. (btw. Vermont Ave. and Figueroa St.), Exposition Park. ℂ **213/763-DINO** (763-3466). www.nhm.org. Admission $9 adults; $6.50 children 13–17, seniors, and students with ID; $2 children 5–12; free for kids 4 and under; free for everyone 1st Tues of month. Daily 9:30am–5pm. Closed Jan 1, July 4, Thanksgiving, and Christmas. Parking $8 and up.

Santa Monica

Annenberg Community Beach House ★   The reopened Annenberg Community Beach House is a great place for families to relax and play. Originally built in the '20s for Marion Davies, actress and mistress of William Hearst, this mansion was a hot spot for A-list celebs until its recent renovation into a public beach house. This attraction, which opened in 2009, offers a pool (open 10am–6pm in summer), guesthouse facilities, recreation and family fitness classes, a gym, docent tours, volleyball and tennis courts (available upon reservation), beach rentals (chairs, balls, boogie boards, and so on), a nice cafe, and access to the wide beaches of Santa Monica.

415 Pacific Coast Hwy., Santa Monica. ℂ **310/458-4904.** http://beachhouse.smgov.net. Free admission. Daily 8:30am–5:30pm. Parking prices vary seasonally and by the day of the week.

Santa Monica Museum of Art at Bergamot Station ★★   One of Santa Monica's primary cultural destinations is this campuslike art complex just off I-10. The location dates from 1875, when it was a stop for the Red Line trolley, and it retains a quasi-industrial look. Filled with more than 20 galleries, the unique installations on display here range from photography and sculpture to interactive pieces

secrets OF SANTA MONICA

If you're the type of traveler who eschews crowded tourist attractions, here are a few of my favorite places in Santa Monica that only the locals know about:

Camera Obscura It's well named, because even most Santa Monicans don't know about this truly obscure attraction though they've passed right by it countless times. In the Senior Recreation Center in Palisades Park, the Camera Obscura (which is Latin for "dark room") is, well, a dark room that's round and has a white circular table in the middle. Turn the old boat steering wheel, which turns the overhead periscope thingy, and a reverse projection of the park, ocean, and avenue is reflected onto the table (that's your car getting a parking ticket). It's an ancient invention that offers a few minutes of mindless voyeuristic amusement in a modern world. To see it, you have to go into the Senior Center (*mmmm,* smell that Salisbury steak!), give the person at the desk your driver's license, and get the key to the Camera Obscura door located up the stairs to your right. The whole experience is a bit surreal, but fun (and free). It's open Monday to Friday 9am to 2pm and Saturday 11am to 4pm. 1450 Ocean Ave., between Broadway and Santa Monica Boulevard, Santa Monica (☎ **310/458-8644**).

Father's Office If you just want to tuck into a great burger and a beer without having to endure the Santa Monica tourist scene, join the young and beautiful at Father's Office, a small, unpretentious bar and grill that offers 40 beers on tap and one of the best burgers in L.A.—dry-aged sirloin with a composite of apple-wood-smoked bacon, caramelized onion, arugula, Gruyère, and Maytag blue cheese on a French roll. Addictive sweet potato fries are piled into toy shopping carts (you'll see). It's usually standing room only on most evenings, so come early if you want a table. 1018 Montana Ave., at 10th Street, Santa Monica (☎ **310/736-2224;** www.fathersoffice.com).

Chez Jay's It may look like a dumpy bar (okay, it is a dumpy bar), but it's *my* kind of dumpy bar. Located on a multi-million-dollar plot of land near the Santa Monica Pier, this creaky classic was opened by a man named Jay "Peanuts" Fiondella, a gray-bearded old-timer who wouldn't sell out to developers at any price; now that he's gone (may he rest in peace), hopefully it will stay that way. Marlon Brando, Frank Sinatra, Peter Sellers, Kevin Spacey, Madonna, George Clooney—they've all been regulars at one time or another over the years. Rumor has it astronaut Alan Shepard took a peanut from Jay's to the moon and back (and Steve McQueen tried to eat it). Naturally, there's a jukebox in the corner, a marlin mounted on the wall, peanut shells on the floor, and well-worn red vinyl booths. I hear they serve a great steak, but I've never seen the menu. The place is a bit hard to find—look for the little neon sign on the east side of Ocean Avenue, ½ block south of the pier. 1657 Ocean Ave., between Pico Boulevard and Colorado Avenue, Santa Monica (☎ **310/395-1741;** www.chezjays.com).

that are both eclectic and cutting edge. Because of the layout, visitors can park in the free lot and spend the day gallery hopping from one central location rather than driving around town from one gallery to the next. Most pieces are available for purchase. 2525 Michigan Ave. (off Cloverfield Blvd.), Santa Monica. ☎ **310/586-6488.** www.smmoa.org. Pool passes $10 adults; $5 seniors; $4 youth 17 and under. Tues–Sat 11am–6pm. Free parking.

Pasadena

Norton Simon Museum of Art ★★★ 🎁   Named for a food-packing king and financier who reorganized the failing Pasadena Museum of Modern Art, the Norton Simon displays one of the finest private collections of European, American, and Asian art in the world (and yet another feather in the cap of architect Frank Gehry, who redesigned the interior space). Comprehensive collections of masterpieces by Degas, Picasso, Rembrandt, and Goya are augmented by sculpture by Henry Moore and Auguste Rodin, including *The Burghers of Calais,* which greets you at the entrance. The "Blue Four" collection of works by Kandinsky, Jawlensky, Klee, and Feininger is impressive, as is a superb collection of Southeast Asian sculpture. Perhaps the most popular piece is *The Flower Vendor/Girl with Lilies,* by Diego Rivera, followed by *Mulberry Tree,* by Vincent van Gogh. The collection of paintings, sculptures, pastels, and prints by French Impressionist Edgar Degas is among the best in the world. *Tip:* Unless you're an art expert, you'll probably want to take the "Acoustiguide" audio tour—it's $3 well spent.

411 W. Colorado Blvd. (corner of Orange Grove and Colorado Blvd. at the intersection of the Foothill [I-210] and Ventura [Calif. 134] freeways), Pasadena. ⓒ **626/449-6840.** www.nortonsimon.org. Admission $10 adults, $5 seniors 62 and up, free for students and children 17 and under; free for everyone 6–9pm the 1st Fri of every month. Wed–Mon noon–6pm (until 9pm Fri). Free parking.

Pacific Asia Museum   The most striking aspect of this museum is the building itself. Designed in the 1920s in Chinese Imperial Palace style, it's rivaled in flamboyance only by Grauman's Chinese Theatre in Hollywood (see "L.A.'s Top Attractions," earlier in this chapter). Rotating exhibits of 15,000 rare Asian and Pacific Islands art and artifacts span the centuries, from 100 B.C. to the current day. This manageable-size museum is worth a visit, particularly if you're an adherent of Buddhism.

46 N. Los Robles Ave., Pasadena. ⓒ **626/449-2742.** www.pacificasiamuseum.org. Admission $9 adults, $7 students and seniors, free for children 11 and under; free for everyone the 4th Fri of every month. Wed–Sun 10am–6pm. Free parking.

L.A.'S ETHNIC NEIGHBORHOODS

Los Angeles has the highest concentration of Mexicans outside Mexico, Koreans outside Korea, and even Samoans outside Samoa. Tiny Russian, Ethiopian, Armenian, and even British enclaves also coexist throughout L.A. But to call the city a "melting pot" wouldn't be quite accurate; to paraphrase Alex Haley, it's really more of a tossed salad, composed of distinct, albeit overlapping, cultures.

The following neighborhoods all fall under the "Downtown" label, as we've defined it in "Neighborhoods in Brief," in chapter 3.

Boyle Heights

East of Downtown; bounded by U.S. 101, I-10, Calif. 60, and Indiana St.

In the first decades of the 20th century, Boyle Heights was inhabited by Jewish immigrants, who have since migrated west to the Fairfax district and beyond. They left behind the oldest orthodox synagogue in Los Angeles, and Brooklyn Avenue, which has since been renamed Cesar E. Chavez Avenue. Boyle Heights is now the heart of the Latino barrio.

kid-cool ATTRACTIONS IN L.A.

Much of larger-than-life L.A. is as appealing to kids as it is to adults. Many of the city's best attractions, like Venice Beach's **Ocean Front Walk** (p. 138), Hollywood's **Farmers Market** (p. 231), and Downtown's **Olvera Street** (part of El Pueblo de Los Angeles Historic Monument; p. 160) have a kid-friendly, carnival-like atmosphere. The novelty of sights such as the **Walk of Fame** (p. 136) and **Grauman's Chinese Theatre** (p. 133) appeals to kids as well. Older kids in particular love to go on **studio tours** (p. 173) and to **TV tapings** (p. 177).

Then there's the kid-centric museums. Kids who are into dinosaurs will dig the **La Brea Tar Pits** (p. 141) and the cool prehistoric creatures on display at the adjoining **Page Museum** (really, you have to drag your kids *out* of here; p. 141). The **California Science Center** (p. 152) will entertain, stimulate, and even teach (sshhhh) kids about science, technology, biology, and the world around them. The **Natural History Museum** (p. 155), the Science Center's neighbor in Exposition Park, has giant dinosaur skeletons, an insect zoo, and a museum shop packed with terrifically fun model kits and other irresistible toys. The **Petersen Automotive Museum** (p. 150) is packed with cool-looking cars and motorcycles, as well as a science-themed Discovery Center designed just for kids.

Thanks to the **Winnick Family Children's Zoo** (p. 173), the Los Angeles Zoo is an all-day adventure for the kids. This excellent children's zoo has a top-notch petting zoo, exhibition animal-care center, Adventure Theater, and other kid-cool attractions. Or how about an afternoon of **horseback riding** (p. 187) on the trails through the Hollywood hills? Here's one you haven't thought of: the **J. Paul Getty Museum** at the Getty Center (p. 139). Deceptively educational programs for kids include exploratory games such as "The Getty Art Detective" and "Perplexing Paintings." There's also a family room filled with picture books and games, storytelling sessions, weekend family workshops, and self-guided audio tours made specifically for families.

But wait, there's more. Young tourists will also like the surreal **Universal CityWalk** shopping mall (p. 143), the carousel and arcade at **Santa Monica Pier** (p. 138), and the miniature train ride at the **Travel Town Transportation Museum** in Griffith Park (p. 169). If they're sports fans, there's sure to be a few tickets available for a pro **baseball, basketball,** or **soccer** game in town (p. 192). And if all this isn't enough, there's always **Universal Studios Hollywood** (p. 143), **Disneyland** (p. 199), **Knott's Berry Farm** (p. 211), and **Six Flags California** (p. 142) amusement parks. Or heck, just get the kids a toy bucket and shovel and spend the day at **Santa Monica State Beach** (p. 184).

Westsiders come here for cheap Mexican food, but many miss my favorite Boyle Heights sight: Near the corner of Boyle Avenue and 1st Street is **Mariachi Plaza,** a colorful street corner where three-, four-, and five-man mariachi bands stand ready to entertain every afternoon and evening. Resplendent in matching ruffled shirts and tailored bolero jackets with a rainbow of embroidery, the mariachis loiter beneath three-story murals of their forebears with guitars at the ready. It's not unusual to see someone drive up in a minivan, offer a price for a night's entertainment, and carry off an ensemble to play a private party or other gathering. *Tip:* For a truly authentic meal

6

WHAT TO SEE & DO IN LOS ANGELES | L.A.'s Ethnic Neighborhoods in the neighborhood, try either **Birrieria Jalisco,** 1845 E. 1st St. (℃ **323/262-4552**; www.birrieriajalisco.com) for Jalisco-style goat (it's the only thing on the menu), or **La Serenata de Garibaldi,** 1842 E. 1st St. (℃ **323/265-2887;** www.laserenataonline.com) for seafood-centric dishes with many traditional salsas.

Chinatown

Downtown; bounded by N. Broadway, N. Hill St., Bernard St., and Sunset Blvd.

Many Chinese settled in this once-rural area during the second half of the 19th century. Today most Angelenos of Chinese descent are well integrated into the city's suburbs; few can be found living in this rough pocket of Downtown. But though the neighborhood hardly compares in quality or size to the Chinese quarters of London, San Francisco, or New York, Chinatown's bustling little mom-and-pop shops and profusion of ethnic restaurants provide an interesting Downtown diversion.

Chinatown centers on a mall, **Mandarin Plaza,** 970 N. Broadway, reconstructed in 1938 a few blocks from its original site just south of Dodger Stadium. Go on a Sunday morning for dim sum at **Empress Pavilion,** 988 N. Hill St. (℃ **213/617-9898;** www.empresspavilion.com), and then browse through the collection of shops jammed with Chinese slippers, cheap jewelry, and china. You'll also find some upscale stores specializing in inlaid furniture, Asian art, fine silks, and other imports.

Chinatown is especially worth going out of your way for during **Chinese New Year,** a month-long celebration that usually begins in late January. The neighborhood explodes into a colorful fantasy of sights and sounds with the Golden Dragon Parade, a beauty pageant, and a 5K/10K run. There are plenty of firecrackers and all the Lin Go New Year's cakes you can eat. For more information about Chinatown, log on to www.chinatownla.com.

El Pueblo de Los Angeles Historic Monument ★

Enter El Pueblo Historic Monument via Alameda St. across from Union Station.

This historic district was built in the 1930s on the site where the city was founded as an alternative to the razing of a particularly unsightly slum. The result is a contrived nostalgic fantasy of the city's beginnings, a kitschy theme park portraying Latino culture in a Disney-esque fashion. Nevertheless, El Pueblo has proven wildly successful, as L.A.'s Latinos have adopted it as an important cultural monument.

El Pueblo is not without authenticity. Some of L.A.'s oldest buildings are here, and the area really does exude the ambience of Old Mexico. At its core is a Mexican-style marketplace on old brick-paved **Olvera Street,** the district's primary pedestrian street. On weekends the carnival of sights and sounds is heightened by mariachis, piñatas, and more-than-occasional folkloric dancing. Olvera Street and adjacent Main Street are home to about two dozen 19th-century buildings. Free 50-minute walking tours are given Tuesday through Saturday mornings; for tour times, contact **El Pueblo Visitor Center** (622 N. Main St.; ℃ **213/628-1274;** www.lasangelitas.org). Also, don't miss the **Avila Adobe,** at E-10 Olvera St. (Tues–Fri 10am–3pm; Sat–Sun 10am–4:30pm. free admission); built in 1818, it's the oldest building in the city.

Koreatown

West of Downtown; bounded by Wilshire Ave., Crenshaw Blvd., Olympic Blvd., and Vermont Ave.

Here's something you probably didn't know: There are more Koreans in Los Angeles than anywhere else in the world outside of Korea—some 100,000. If you drive down

Western Avenue between Olympic and Wilshire boulevards, it won't take much imagination to believe that you're suddenly in a section of Seoul. Hundreds of signs in Korean script are bolted onto dozens of minimalls and office buildings within this vibrant commercial district. Park the car and spend a few hours browsing the elixir shops, bargain stores, malls, and authentic Korean barbecue joints. You might also want to visit the museum within the **Korean Cultural Center,** 5505 Wilshire Blvd. (Mon–Fri 9am–5pm, Sat 10am–1pm; ✆ **323/936-7141;** www.kccla.org), which houses historical photographs, Korean antiques, and rotating exhibits.

Leimert Park Village

Southwest of Downtown; bounded by Crenshaw Blvd., Vernon Ave., Leimert Blvd., and 43rd Place.

The neighborhood around tiny Leimert Park is becoming a center of African-American artistic life and culture. It features galleries, restaurants, and shops filled with local crafts and African imports. Folks flock here to jazz clubs that evoke the heyday of L.A.'s Central Avenue jazz scene, when greats like Ella Fitzgerald mesmerized audiences. In December, **Kwanzaa** celebrations further enliven Leimert Park.

Little Tokyo

Downtown, southeast of the Civic Center; bounded by 1st, 2nd, San Pedro, and Los Angeles sts.

Like nearby Chinatown, this redeveloped ethnic neighborhood isn't home to the majority of Angelenos of Japanese ancestry; suburban Gardena has that distinction. But Little Tokyo functions as the community's cultural focal point and is home to several malls filled with bakeries, bookshops, restaurants, and boutiques, as well as the occasional Buddhist temple. The **Japanese American National Museum** (p. 154) is here, as is the **Japanese American Cultural and Community Center,** 244 S. San Pedro St. (✆ **213/628-2725;** www.jaccc.org), which regularly offers traditional Kabuki dramas and modern music concerts.

Unfortunately, Little Tokyo is shabbier than almost any district in the Japanese capital, and it has difficulty holding a visitor's attention for much longer than the time it takes to eat lunch. Exceptions to this rule come twice yearly, during the **Cherry Blossom Festival** in spring and **Nisei Week** in late summer. Both heritage festivals celebrate Japanese culture with parades, traditional Ondo street dancing, a carnival, and an arts fair. The Japanese American Network provides a community calendar, a map of Little Tokyo points of interest, and useful Web links online at www.janet.org/janet_little_tokyo/ja_little_tokyo.html.

ARCHITECTURAL HIGHLIGHTS

Because it's more receptive to experimentation than some other American cities, Los Angeles is a veritable Disneyland of architecture. The city is home to an amalgam of distinctive styles: Art Deco, Spanish Revival, coffee-shop kitsch, suburban ranch, postmodern—and much more.

The movie industry, more than anything else, has defined Los Angeles. The process of moviemaking has never been confined to studio offices and back lots; it spills into the city's streets and other public spaces. The city itself is an extension of the movie set, and Angelenos have always seen it that way. All of Los Angeles has an air of Hollywood surreality, even in its architecture. The whole city seems a bit larger than life. Cutting-edge, over-the-top styles that would be out of place in other cities are perfectly at home in L.A. The world's top architects, from Frank Lloyd Wright to Frank

L.A.'S TOP architectural TOURS

The **L.A. Conservancy** (☎ 213/623-2489; www.laconservancy.org) conducts a dozen information-packed walking tours of historic **Downtown L.A.,** seed of today's sprawling metropolis. The most popular is Broadway Historic Theatre & Commercial District, a look at movie palaces, among other area attractions. Other intriguing tours include Angelino Heights, Art Deco, Downtown's Modern Skyline, and tours of the Biltmore Hotel and Union Station. Most tours take place on Saturday mornings at 10am and last about 2½ hours. Call Monday through Friday between 9am and 5pm for information,

or, better yet, click on the "Walking Tours" link on the website.

In **Pasadena,** various tours spotlighting Old Pasadena or the surrounding neighborhoods are intriguing, given this area's history of wealthy estates and ardent preservation. Call **Pasadena Heritage** (☎ 626/441-6333; www.pasadena heritage.org) for a schedule of guided tours, or pick up one of the self-guided walking or driving maps available at the **Pasadena Convention and Visitors Bureau,** 300 E. Green St. (☎ 626/795-9311; www.visitpasadena.com).

Gehry, have flocked to L.A., reveling in the artistic freedom here. Between 1945 and 1966, *Arts & Architecture* magazine focused the design world's attention on L.A. with its series of "Case Study Houses," prototypes for postwar living, many of which were designed by prominent émigrés like Pierre Koenig, Richard Neutra, and Eero Saarinen. Los Angeles has taken some criticism for not being a "serious" architectural center, but in terms of innovation and style, the city gets high marks.

Although much of it is gone, you can still find some prime examples of the kitschy roadside art that defined L.A. in earlier days. The famous Brown Derby is no more, but you can still find a neon-lit **1950s gas station/spaceship** (at the corner of Little Santa Monica Blvd. and Crescent Dr. in Beverly Hills), in addition to some newer structures carrying on the tradition, such as the **"Binocular Building" offices** in Venice (see below).

Santa Monica & the Beaches

When you're strolling the historic canals and streets of Venice, be sure to check out the old **Chiat/Day** offices at 340 Main St. What would otherwise be an unspectacular contemporary office building is made fantastic by a **three-story pair of binoculars** that frames the entrance. The sculpture is modeled after a design created by Claes Oldenburg and Coosje van Bruggen.

When you're on your way in or out of LAX, be sure to stop for a moment to admire the **Control Tower** and **Theme Building.** The spacey *Jetsons*-style Theme Building, which has always loomed over LAX, has been joined by a more recent silhouette. The main control tower, designed by local architect Kate Diamond to evoke a stylized palm tree, is tailored to present Southern California in its best light. You can go inside to enjoy the view from the Theme Building's observation deck, or have a space-age cocktail at the Technicolor bachelor pad that is the **Encounter at LAX** restaurant (p. 88).

Constructed on a broad cliff with a steep face, the **Wayfarers Chapel** in Rancho Palos Verdes enjoys a fantastic spot overlooking the waves of the Pacific. It was designed by Lloyd Wright, son of celebrated architect Frank Lloyd Wright. Known locally as the "glass church," Wayfarers is a memorial to Emanuel Swedenborg, an

18th-century Swedish philosopher who claimed to have visions of spirits and heavenly hosts. The church is constructed of glass, redwood, and native stone. Rare plants, some of which are native to Israel, surround the building. The church is open daily from 8am to 5pm and is located at 5755 Palos Verdes Dr. S. Call ✆ 310/377-1650 or visit www.wayfarerschapel.org in advance to arrange a free escorted tour.

L.A.'s Westside & Beverly Hills

In addition to the sights below, don't miss the **Beverly Hills Hotel** (p. 55), and be sure to wind your way through the wide rural streets of Beverly Hills between Sunset and Santa Monica boulevards.

Church of the Good Shepherd   Built in 1924, this is Beverly Hills's oldest house of worship. The relatively small church (seats only 600) is in the Spanish Colonial Revival style, and its two striking steeples and lovely exterior are noticeable from any direction. In 1950 Elizabeth Taylor and her first husband, Nicky Hilton, were married here. The funerals of Alfred Hitchcock, Gary Cooper, Eva Gabor, and Frank Sinatra were all held here as well.

505 N. Bedford Dr. (at Park Way), Beverly Hills. ✆ **310/285-5425.** www.goodshepherdbeverlyhills.org.

Pacific Design Center   The bold architecture and overwhelming scale of the Pacific Design Center, created by Argentine architect Cesar Pelli, aroused controversy when it was erected in 1975. Sheathed in gently curving cobalt-blue glass, the six-story building houses more than 750,000 square feet of wholesale interior-design showrooms and is known to locals as "the Blue Whale." In 1988 a second boxlike structure, dressed in equally dramatic Kelly green, was added to the design center and surrounded by a protected outdoor plaza. The long-delayed Red Building towers are scheduled to finally open in the summer of 2011. Visitors are welcome during regular business hours and one designated Saturday each month (except June-August). There are two casual Wolfgang Puck restaurants, Red 7 and Spectra.

8687 Melrose Ave. (at San Vicente Blvd.), West Hollywood. ✆ **310/657-0800.** www.pacificdesign center.com. Mon-Fri 9am-5pm; select Saturdays 10am-4pm. Parking varies; daily max typically $14

Schindler House ★   A protégé of Frank Lloyd Wright and contemporary of Richard Neutra, Austrian architect Rudolph Schindler designed this innovative modern house for himself in 1921 and 1922. It's now home to the Los Angeles arm of Austria's Museum of Applied Arts (MAK). The house is noted for its complicated interlocking spaces; the interpenetration of indoors and out; simple, unadorned materials; and technological innovations. Docent-guided tours are conducted at no additional charge on weekends only.

The MAK Center offers guides to L.A.-area buildings by Schindler and other architects, and presents related original exhibitions and creative arts programming. Call for schedules.

835 N. Kings Rd. (north of Melrose Ave.), West Hollywood. ✆ **323/651-1510.** www.makcenter.org. Admission $7 adults, $6 students and seniors, free to children 12 and under; free to everyone Fri after 4pm, Sept 10 (Schindler's birthday), and May 24 (International Museum Day). Wed-Sun 11am-6pm. Closed Jan 1, Thanksgiving, and Christmas. Street parking.

Hollywood

In addition to the buildings listed below, don't miss the **Griffith Observatory** and **Grauman's Chinese Theatre** (see "L.A.'s Top Attractions," earlier in this chapter), and the **Roosevelt Hotel, Hollywood** (p. 70).

Capitol Records Building Opened in 1956, this 13-story tower, just north of the legendary intersection of Hollywood and Vine, is one of the city's most recognizable buildings. The world's first circular office building is often—albeit incorrectly—said to have been made to resemble a stack of 45s under a turntable stylus (it kinda does, though). Nat "King" Cole, Ella Fitzgerald, and Billie Holliday are among the artists featured in the giant exterior mural known as *Hollywood Jazz.* Look down and you'll see the sidewalk stars of Capitol's recording artists (including John Lennon). In the lobby, numerous gold albums are on display.

1750 Vine St. (just north of Hollywood Blvd.). **323/462-6252.**

The Egyptian Theatre Conceived by grandiose impresario Sid Grauman, the Egyptian Theatre is just down the street from his better-known Chinese Theatre, but it remains less altered from its original design, which was based on the then-headline-news discovery of hidden treasures in Pharaohs' tombs—hence the hieroglyphic murals and enormous scarab decoration above the stage. Hollywood's first movie première, *Robin Hood,* starring Douglas Fairbanks, was shown here in 1922, followed by the première of *The Ten Commandments* in 1923. The building has undergone a sensitive restoration by American Cinematheque, which now screens rare, classic, and independent films (see chapter 9 for details). *Tip:* Check the website schedule for screenings hosted by celebrity guest speakers, directors, and actors such as Ron Howard and George Clooney.

> ## Not Quite SOS, but . . .
>
> **The light on the rooftop spire of the Capitol Records building flashes "H-O-L-L-Y-W-O-O-D" in Morse code. Really, it does.**

6712 Hollywood Blvd. (btw. N. Las Palmas Ave. and N. McCadden Place), Hollywood. **323/466-FILM** (466-3456). www.egyptiantheatre.com.

Freeman House Frank Lloyd Wright's Freeman House, built in 1924, was designed as an experimental prototype of mass-produced affordable housing. The home's richly patterned "textile-block" exterior was Wright's invention and is the most famous aspect of the home's design. Situated on a dramatic site overlooking Hollywood, Freeman House is built with the world's first glass-to-glass corner windows. Dancer Martha Graham, bandleader Xavier Cugat, art collector Galka Sheye, photographer Edward Weston, and architects Philip Johnson and Richard Neutra all lived or spent significant time at this house, which became known as an avant-garde salon. The house is currently closed for restoration; call ahead to see if it's open.

1962 Glencoe Way (off Hillcrest Rd., near Highland and Franklin aves.), Hollywood. **323/851-0671.**

Downtown

For a taste of what Downtown's Bunker Hill was like before the bulldozers, visit the residential neighborhood of **Angelino Heights,** near Echo Park. Entire streets are still filled with stately gingerbread Victorian homes; most still enjoy the beautiful views that led early L.A.'s elite to build here. The 1300 block of Carroll Avenue is the best preserved. Don't be surprised if a film crew is scouting locations while you're there—these blocks appear often on the silver screen.

In addition to the buildings listed below, a definite must-see for architecture buffs is the **Walt Disney Concert Hall ★★★** (p. 145).

The Bradbury Building ★ This National Historic Landmark, built in 1893 and designed by George Wyman, is Los Angeles's oldest commercial building and one of the city's most revered architectural achievements. Legend has it that an inexperienced draftsman named George Wyman accepted the $125,000 commission after communicating with his dead brother through a Ouija board. Capped by a magical five-story skylight, Bradbury's courtyard combines glazed brick, ornate Mexican tile floors, rich Belgian marble, Art Nouveau grillwork, handsome oak paneling, and lacelike wrought-iron railings—it's one of the great interior spaces of the 19th century. The glass-topped atrium is often used as a movie and TV set; you've probably seen it before in *Chinatown* and *Blade Runner*.

304 S. Broadway (at 3rd St.), Downtown. ℂ **213/626-1893.** Mon–Fri 9am–6pm; Sat–Sun 9am–5pm.

Cathedral of Our Lady of the Angels ★ Completed in September 2002 at a cost of $163 million and built to last 500 years, this ultracontemporary cathedral is one of L.A.'s newest architectural treasures and the third-largest cathedral in the world. It was designed by award-winning Spanish architect Jose Rafael Moneo and features a 20,000-square-foot plaza with a meditation garden, more than 6,000 crypts and niches (making it the largest crypt mausoleum in the U.S.), mission-style colonnades, biblically inspired gardens, and numerous artworks created by world-acclaimed artists. While most Angelenos admit that the exterior of this austere, sand-colored structure is rather uninspiring and uninviting (the church doors don't face the street, but rather a private plaza in back surrounded by fortresslike walls), the inside is breathtaking: Soaring heights, 12,000 panes of translucent alabaster, and larger-than-life tapestries lining the walls create an awe-inspiring sense of magnificence and serenity. The 25,000-pound bronze doors, created by sculptor Robert Graham, pay homage to Ghiberti's bronze baptistery door in Florence. Free self-guided tours are available, and there's a small cafe and gift shop as well.

555 W. Temple St. (at Grand Ave.), Downtown. ℂ **213/680-5200.** www.olacathedral.org. Mon–Fri 6am–6pm; Sat 9am–6pm; Sun 7am–6pm.

Charles F. Lummis House (El Alisal) and Garden ★ El Alisal is a small, rugged, two-story "castle," built between 1889 and 1910 from large rocks and telephone poles purchased from the Santa Fe Railroad. The architect and creator was Charles F. Lummis, a Harvard graduate, archaeologist, and writer, who walked from Ohio to California and coined the slogan "See America First." A fan of Native American culture, Lummis is credited with popularizing the concept of the "Southwest," referring to New Mexico and Arizona. He often lived the lifestyle of the Indians, and he founded the Southwest Museum (234 Museum Dr.; ℂ **323/667-2000**), a repository of Indian artifacts. Lummis held fabulous parties for the theatrical, political, and artistic elite; his guest list often included Will Rogers and Theodore Roosevelt. The outstanding feature of his house is the fireplace, which was carved by Mount Rushmore creator Gutzon Borglum. The lawn has been turned into an experimental garden of water-conserving plants.

200 E. Ave. 43, Highland Park. ℂ **323/460-5632.** www.socalhistory.org. Free admission. Fri–Sun noon–4pm.

City Hall Built in 1928, the 27-story Los Angeles City Hall was the tallest building in the city for more than 30 years. The structure's distinctive ziggurat tower was designed to resemble the Mausoleum at Halicarnassus, one of the seven wonders of the ancient world. The building has been featured in numerous films and television

Divine Vibrations

Every Wednesday from 12:45 to 1:15pm, the Cathedral of Our Lady of the Angels—the city's $163-million architectural jewel—hosts an **organ recital** that is open to the public and free of charge. The power of the 42-ton organ's 6,019 pipes makes the cathedral vibrate, enabling you to not only hear the music, but also feel it, making the experience physically poignant as well as emotionally moving. Be sure to call ✆ 213/680-5200 to confirm the Wednesday recital.

shows, but it is probably best known as the headquarters of the *Daily Planet* in the *Superman* TV series (or from *Beverly Hills Cop,* depending on your birth date). When it was built, City Hall was the sole exception to an ordinance outlawing buildings taller than 150 feet. While you're here, be sure to take the elevator to the rarely used 27th-floor Observation Deck—on a clear day (yeah, right), you can see to Mount Wilson 15 miles away. Free docent-led tours are available at 10am to noon Monday through Thursday, and self-guided tours are available at other times. Call ✆ **213/978-1995** for tour information.

200 N. Spring St. (btw. 1st and Temple sts.), Downtown. ✆ **213/485-2121.** www.lacity.org/lacity. Mon–Fri 8am–5pm.

L.A. Central Library ★★   This is one of L.A.'s early architectural achievements and the third-largest library in the United States. The city rallied to save the library when arson nearly destroyed it in 1986; the triumphant restoration has returned much of its original splendor. Working in the early 1920s, architect Bertram G. Goodhue employed the Egyptian motifs and materials popularized by the discovery of King Tut's tomb and combined them with a more modern use of concrete block to great effect. Free docent-led art and architecture tours are given daily and last about an hour—call ✆ **213/228-7168.** *Warning:* Parking in this area can involve a heroic effort. Try visiting on the weekend and using the Flower Street parking entrance; the daily max is $8, a relative bargain for downtown.

630 W. 5th St. (btw. Flower St. and Grand Ave.), Downtown. ✆ **213/228-7000.** www.lapl.org/central.

Union Station ★   Union Station, completed in 1939, is one of the finest examples of California mission-style architecture and one of the last of America's great rail stations. It was built with the opulence and attention to detail that characterized 1930s WPA projects, such as its cathedral-like size and richly paneled ticket lobby and waiting area. When you're strolling through these grand historic halls, it's easy to imagine the glamorous movie stars who once boarded *The City of Los Angeles* and *The Super Chief* to journey back East during the glory days of rail travel; it's also easy to picture the many heartfelt reunions between returning soldiers and loved ones following the victorious end to World War II, in the station's heyday. Movies shot here include *Bugsy, The Way We Were,* and *Blade Runner.* There's always been a restaurant in the station; the latest to occupy this unusually beautiful setting is **Traxx** (p. 124).

800 N. Alameda St. (at Cesar E. Chavez Ave.), Downtown.

US Bank Tower (also known as Library Tower)   Designed by renowned architect I. M. Pei, L.A.'s most distinctive skyscraper (it's the round one) is the tallest building between Chicago and Singapore. Built in 1989 at a cost of $450 million, the

76-story monolith is both square and rectangular, rising from its 5th Street base in a series of overlapping spirals and cubes. The Bunker Hill Steps wrapping around the west side of the building were inspired by Rome's Spanish Steps. *"Gee whiz" fact:* The glass crown at the top—illuminated at night—is the highest building helipad in the world.

633 W. 5th St. (at S. Grand Ave.), Downtown.

Watts Towers & Art Center Watts became notorious as the site of riots in the summer of 1965, during which 34 people were killed and more than 1,000 were injured. Today a visit to Watts is a lesson in inner-city life. It's a high-density land of gray strip malls, well-guarded check-cashing shops, and fast-food restaurants; but it's also a neighborhood of hardworking families struggling to survive in the midst of gangland. Although there's not much for the casual tourist here, the Watts Towers are truly a unique attraction, and the adjoining art gallery illustrates the fierce determination of area residents to maintain cultural integrity.

The Towers—the largest piece of folk art created by a single person—are colorful, 99-foot-tall cement and steel sculptures ornamented with mosaics of bottles, seashells, cups, plates, pottery, and ceramic tiles. They were completed in 1955 by folk artist Simon Rodia, an immigrant Italian tile-setter who worked on them for 33 years in his spare time. True fans of decorative ceramics will enjoy the fact that Rodia's day job was at the legendary Malibu Potteries (are those fragments of valuable Malibu tile encrusting the Towers?). Closed in 1994 due to earthquake damage, the towers were triumphantly reopened in 2001 and now attract more than 20,000 visitors annually. Tours are by request.

Note: Next to these designated Cultural Landmarks is the Art Center, which has an interesting collection of ethnic musical instruments as well as several visiting art exhibits throughout the year.

1727 E. 107th St., Watts. © **213/847-4646.** www.wattstowers.us. Art Center: Free admission. Wed–Sat 10am–4pm; Sun noon–4pm. Towers: Admission $7 adults, $3 seniors 55 and over and children 13–17, free for children 12 and under. Thurs–Sat 10:30am–3:30pm; Sun 12:30–3:30pm.

Pasadena & Environs

See "L.A.'s Top Architectural Tours" box (p. 162) and "Sightseeing Tours" (p. 173) for more information on touring the many well-preserved historic neighborhoods in Pasadena. For a quick but profound architectural fix, stroll past Pasadena's grandiose and baroque **City Hall,** 100 N. Garfield Ave., 2 blocks north of Colorado Boulevard; closer inspection will reveal its classical colonnaded courtyard, formal gardens, and spectacular tiled dome.

The Gamble House ★★ The huge two-story Gamble House, built in 1908 as a California vacation home for the wealthy family of Procter & Gamble fame, is a sublime example of Arts and Crafts architecture. The interior, designed by the famous Pasadena-based Greene & Greene architectural team, abounds with handcraftsmanship, including intricately carved teak cornices, custom-designed furnishings, elaborate carpets, and a fantastic Tiffany glass door. No detail was overlooked: Every oak wedge, downspout, air vent, and switch plate contributes to the unified design. Admission is by 1-hour guided tour only, which departs every 15 to 20 minutes. Tickets go on sale on tour days in the bookstore at 10am Thursday through Saturday, and at 11:30am on Sunday. No reservations are necessary, but tours are often sold out, especially on weekends, by 2pm. And don't wear high heels or they'll make you put on slippers. No interior photography is allowed either.

If you can't fit the tour into your schedule but have an affection for Craftsman design, visit the well-stocked bookstore and museum shop, located in the former garage (you can also see the exterior and grounds of the house this way). The bookstore is open Tuesday through Saturday 10am to 5pm, and Sunday 11:30am to 5pm.

Additional elegant Greene & Greene creations (still privately owned) abound 2 blocks away along **Arroyo Terrace,** including nos. **368, 370, 400, 408, 424,** and **440.** The Gamble House bookstore can give you a walking-tour map ($1.50). For occasional opportunities to actually go inside the homes, there's the annual Craftsman Weekend in October, and Bungalow Heaven in April.

4 Westmoreland Place (in the 300 block of N. Orange Grove Blvd.), Pasadena. ℭ **626/793-3334.** www.gamblehouse.org. Most tours $10 adults, $7 students and seniors 65 and over, free for children 11 and under. 2pm tours are $13 per person and must be made at least 1 week in advance. Tours Thurs–Sun noon–3pm. Closed holidays.

Mission San Fernando In the late 18th century, Franciscan missionaries established 21 missions along the California coast from San Diego to Sonoma. Each uniquely beautiful mission was built 1 day's trek from the next, along a path known as El Camino Real ("the Royal Road"), remnants of which still exist. The missions' construction marked the beginning of European settlement of California and the displacement of the Native American population. The two L.A.-area missions are located in the valleys that took their names: the San Fernando Valley and the San Gabriel Valley (see below). A third mission, San Juan Capistrano, is located in Orange County (p. 276).

Established in 1797, Mission San Fernando once controlled more than 1½ million acres, employed 1,500 Native Americans, and boasted more than 22,000 head of cattle and extensive orchards. The fragile adobe mission complex was destroyed several times but was always faithfully rebuilt with low buildings surrounding grassy courtyards. The aging church was replaced in the 1940s and again in the 1970s after an earthquake. The **Convento,** a 250-foot-long colonnaded structure dating from 1810, is the compound's oldest remaining building. Some of the mission's rooms, including the old library and the private salon of the first bishop of California, have been restored to their late-18th-century appearance. A half-dozen padres and many hundreds of Shoshone Indians are buried in the adjacent cemetery.

House Hygiene

The restoration of the Gamble House was so meticulous that workers used dental picks to scrape gunk from the home's 262 rafters.

15151 San Fernando Mission Blvd., Mission Hills. ℭ **818/361-0186.** www.missionscalifornia.com. Admission $4 adults, $3 seniors 65 and over and children 7–15, free for kids 6 and under. Daily 9am–4:30pm. From I-5, exit at San Fernando Mission Blvd. E. and drive 5 blocks to the mission.

Mission San Gabriel Arcangel Founded in 1771, Mission San Gabriel Arcangel retains its original facade, notable for its high oblong windows and large capped buttresses, said to have been influenced by the cathedral in Cordova, Spain. The mission's self-contained compound encompasses an aqueduct, a cemetery, a tannery, and a working winery. Within the church stands a copper font with the distinction of being the first one used to baptize a native Californian. The most notable contents of the mission's museum are Native American paintings depicting the Stations of the Cross, done on sailcloth, with colors made from crushed desert flower petals.

428 S. Mission Dr., San Gabriel (15 min. south of Pasadena). ℂ **626/457-3035.** www.sangabrielmission. org. Admission $5 adults, $4 seniors 62 and over and students, $3 children 6–17, free for kids 5 and under. Daily 9am–4:30pm. Closed holidays.

L.A. PARKS, GARDENS, VIEWS & ZOOS

Parks

In addition to the two excellent examples of urban parkland below, check out **Pan Pacific Park,** a hilly retreat near the Farmers Market and CBS Studios, named for the Art Deco auditorium that, unfortunately, no longer stands at its edge.

GRIFFITH PARK ★★

Mining tycoon Col. Griffith J. Griffith donated these 4,107 acres to the city in 1896 as a Christmas gift. Today Griffith Park (ℂ **323/913-4688**) is one of the largest urban parks in America. There's a lot to do here, including 53 miles of hiking trails (the prettiest is the **Fern Dell trail ★** near the Western Ave. entrance, a shady hideaway cooled by waterfalls and ferns), horseback riding, golfing, swimming, biking, and picnicking (see "Golf, Hiking & Other Fun in the California Sun," later in this chapter). For a general overview of the park, drive the mountainous loop road that winds from the top of Western Avenue, past Griffith Observatory, and down to Vermont Avenue. For a more extensive foray, turn north at the loop road's midsection, onto Mount Hollywood Drive. To reach the golf courses, the **Autry National Center of the American West** (p. 150), or **Los Angeles Zoo** (p. 172), take Los Feliz Boulevard to Riverside Drive, which runs along the park's western edge.

Near the zoo, in a particularly dusty corner of the park, you can find the **Travel Town Transportation Museum,** 5200 Zoo Dr. (ℂ **323/662-5874;** www.travel town.org), a little-known outdoor museum with a small collection of vintage locomotives and old airplanes. Kids love the miniature train ride that circles the perimeter of the museum. The museum is open Monday through Friday from 10am to 4pm, and Saturday and Sunday from 10am to 6pm; admission is free.

WILL ROGERS STATE HISTORIC PARK

Will Rogers willed his private ranch and grounds to the state of California in 1944, and the 168-acre estate is now both a park and a historic site. Visitors may explore the grounds, the former stables, and the 31-room house filled with the original furnishings, including a porch swing in the living room and many Native American rugs and baskets. Charles Lindbergh and his wife, Anne Morrow Lindbergh, hid out here in the 1930s during part of the craze that followed the kidnapping and murder of their first son. There are picnic tables, but no food is sold.

Who's Will Rogers, you ask? He was born in Oklahoma in 1879 and became a cowboy in the Texas Panhandle before drifting into a Wild West show as a folksy, speechifying roper. The "cracker-barrel philosopher" performed lariat tricks while carrying on a humorous deadpan monologue on current events. The showman moved to Los Angeles in 1919, where he become a movie actor as well as the author of numerous books detailing his down-home "cowboy philosophy."

The park (℅ **310/454-8212**) entrance is at 1501 Will Rogers State Park Rd., in Pacific Palisades, between Santa Monica and Malibu. From Santa Monica, take the Pacific Coast Hwy. (Calif. 1) north, turn right onto Sunset Boulevard, and continue to the park entrance. Admission is $12 per vehicle. The park is open daily from 8am to sunset; the house, Thurs–Fri 11am–3pm, Sat–Sun 10am–4pm; and guided Ranch House tours are offered every hour, on the hour, up until one hour before closing

Botanical Gardens

Descanso Gardens ★ Camellias—evergreen flowering shrubs from China and Japan—were the passion of amateur gardener E. Manchester Boddy, who began planting them here in 1941. Today his 150-acre Descanso Gardens contain more than 100,000 camellias in more than 600 varieties, blooming under a canopy of California oak trees. The shrubs now share the limelight with a 5-acre International Rosarium, home to hundreds of varieties. This is a very relaxing place, with paths and streams that wind through the towering forest; it borders a lake, bird sanctuary, Japanese Garden & Tea House, and Boddy House museum. Each season features different plants: daffodils, azaleas, tulips, and lilacs in the spring; chrysanthemums in the fall; and so on. Monthly art exhibits are held in the hospitality house, and the Descanso Café offers light meals daily from 9am to 4:30pm. Guided tram tours, which cost $4, run Tuesday through Friday at 1, 2, and 3pm, and Saturday and Sunday at 11am and 1, 2, and 3pm. Picnicking is allowed in specified areas. *Tip:* Kids dig the mini Enchanted Railroad, which travels around a small area of the park, (adults are allowed onboard, too, though one trip is usually plenty for them). Rides are $3.

1418 Descanso Dr., La Cañada Flintridge (near the intersection of the 2 and 210 freeways). ℅ **818/949-4200.** www.descansogardens.org. Admission $8 adults, $6 students and seniors 62 and over, $3 children 5–12, free for kids 4 and under. Daily 9am–5pm. Closed Christmas. Free parking.

Huntington Library, Art Collections & Botanical Gardens ★★ ☺ The Huntington Library is the jewel in Pasadena's crown. The 207-acre hilltop estate was once home to industrialist and railroad magnate Henry E. Huntington (1850–1927), who bought books on the same massive scale on which he acquired land. The continually expanding collection includes dozens of Shakespeare's first editions, Benjamin Franklin's handwritten autobiography, a Gutenberg Bible from the 1450s, and the earliest known manuscript of Chaucer's *Canterbury Tales*. Although some rare works are available only to visiting scholars, the library has a regularly changing (and always excellent) exhibit showcasing hundreds of different items in the collection.

If you prefer canvas to parchment, Huntington also put together a terrific 18th-century and 19-century British and French art collection. The most celebrated paintings are Gainsborough's *The Blue Boy* and Sir Thomas Lawrence's *Pinkie,* depicting the youthful aunt of Elizabeth Barrett Browning. These and other works of Renaissance paintings and bronzes are displayed in the stately Italianate mansion on the crest of this hillside estate, so you can also get a glimpse of its splendid furnishings. American art is exhibited in additional galleries and includes work ranging from Edward Hopper to Andy Warhol.

But it's the vast **botanical gardens** featuring more than 14,000 different species of plants that draw most locals to the Huntington. The **Japanese Garden** comes complete with a traditional open-air Japanese house, koi-filled stream, and serene Zen garden. There's also an exotic **Desert Garden,** intriguing **Jungle Garden, Bing Children's Garden** (designed specifically for kids 2–7), and the glass-and-steel

Conservatory for Botanical Science, where visitors learn some of the fundamentals of botany via state-of-the-art science stations. The latest addition is a new 4.5-acre **Chinese Garden,** one of the largest of the Huntington's 14 specialized gardens. Highlights include a lake, teahouse, pavilions, and bridges within a landscape of plants native to China.

Because the Huntington surprises many with its size and wealth of activities to choose from, first-timers might want to start with a tour. One-hour garden tours are offered daily, subject to volunteer availability; no reservations or additional fees are required. Times vary, so check at the information desk upon arrival. I also recommend that you tailor your visit to include the popular **English tea,** served Monday, Wednesday, Thursday, and Friday from noon to 4:30pm, and Saturday and Sunday from 10:45am to 4:30pm (last seating at 3:30pm). The tearoom overlooks the Rose Garden (home to 1,000 varieties displayed in chronological order of their breeding), and since the finger sandwiches and desserts are served buffet-style, it's a genteel bargain, even for hearty appetites, at $28 per person (please note that museum admission is a separate required cost). Call ✆ **626/683-8131** for tearoom reservations, which are required and should be made at least 2 weeks in advance.

1151 Oxford Rd., San Marino (near Pasadena, with easy access from Calif. 110 or I-210). ✆ 626/405-2100. www.huntington.org. Weekday admission $15 adults, $12 seniors 65 and over, $10 students and children 12–18, $6 children 5–11, free for kids 4 and under; free for everyone the 1st Thurs of every month. Weekend admission $20 adults, $15 seniors 65 and over, $10 students and children ages 12–18, $6 children ages 5–11, free to children 4 and under. Sept–May Mon and Wed–Fri noon–4:30pm, Sat–Sun 10:30am–4:30pm; June–Aug Wed–Mon 10:30am–4:30pm. Closed major holidays. Free parking.

The Los Angeles County Arboretum and Botanic Garden ★ Tucked into the hillsides of the San Gabriel Mountains, this sprawling horticultural and botanical center was formerly the estate of silver magnate "Lucky" Baldwin—the man responsible for bringing horse racing to Southern California—who lived until 1909 on these lushly planted 127 acres overlooking the Santa Anita racetrack. You might recognize Baldwin's red-and-white Queen Anne cottage from the opening sequence of *Fantasy Island* ("de plane, de plane"); the gardens are also a favorite location for movie filming and local weddings. In addition to spectacular flora (every continent is represented here), the Arboretum boasts a bevy of resident peafowl who seem unafraid of humans—one of the best treats here is being up close when the peacocks, attempting to impress passing hens, unfold their brilliant rainbow plumage. Avid gardeners will want to visit the nursery-like gift shop on the way out. Admission is free every third Tuesday, but note that there is no tram on these days.

301 N. Baldwin Ave., Arcadia. ✆ **626/821-3222.** www.arboretum.org. Admission $8 adults, $6 students and seniors 62 and over, $3 children 5–12, free for kids 4 and under. Daily 9am–5pm (last admission 4:30pm). Closed Christmas. Free parking. From the 210 freeway, take the Baldwin Ave. exit and follow the signs.

Views

It's not always easy to get a good city view in Los Angeles. Even if you find the right vantage, the smog may keep you from having any kind of panorama. But, as they say, on a clear day, you can see forever. One of the best views of the city can be had from **Griffith Observatory** ★★ (p. 141). The view of Santa Monica Bay from the end of **Santa Monica Pier** is also impressive.

Los Angeles is the only major city in the world divided by a mountain range, and the road on top of this range is the famous **Mulholland Drive** ★. It travels 21 miles along the peaks and canyons of Hollywood Hills and the Santa Monica Mountains, separating the Los Angeles basin from the San Fernando Valley. The winding road provides amazing views of the city (particularly at night) and offers many opportunities to pull over and enjoy the view 1,400 feet above sea level.

Completed in 1924, it's named after William Mulholland, the engineer of the aqueduct connecting L.A. and the Valley. Yes, there are celebrities up in them thar hills—Leonardo DiCaprio, Paris Hilton—but you'll never find them, as most of the mansions are well hidden. You don't need to drive the whole road to get the full effect. From Cahuenga Boulevard (near the Hollywood Bowl), take the Mulholland Drive turnoff heading west. After about a mile, you'll see the scenic view area on your left (look for the black iron fence). Park at the small paved parking lot (which closes at sunset), ooh and aah over the view of the L.A. basin, and then drive a few miles farther west until you spot the other scenic view area on your right (dirt this time) overlooking the San Fernando Valley. The whole trip should take you less than an hour. *Tip:* Don't drive here after 3pm on the weekdays—the rush-hour traffic in this area is horrible. Also, no matter what your map says, there is no Mulholland Drive exit off U.S. 101; you have to get on at Cahuenga Boulevard.

ZOOS

Los Angeles Zoo ★ ☺   The L.A. Zoo has been welcoming visitors and busloads of school kids since 1966. In 1982 the zoo inaugurated a display of cuddly koalas, still one of its biggest attractions among 1,100 animals from around the world. Although it's smaller than the world-famous San Diego Zoo, the L.A. Zoo is far easier to fully explore. As much an arboretum as a zoo, the grounds are thick with mature shade trees from around the world that help cool the once-barren grounds, and new habitats are light-years ahead of the cruel concrete roundhouses originally used to exhibit animals (though you can't help feeling that, despite the fancy digs, all the creatures would rather be in their natural habitat).

The zoo's latest attraction is the **Elephants of Asia,** which tracks the history and culture of the animal through Cambodia, China, India, and Thailand. There are bathing pools, sand pits, and no less than five viewing areas for the public.

In 2007 the zoo debuted the $19-million **Campo Gorilla Reserve,** a habitat for seven African lowland gorillas that closely resembles their native West African homeland. Visitors partake in a pseudo-African-jungle experience as they journey along a misty, forested pathway with glassed viewing areas for close-ups of the gorillas living in two separate habitats: one for a family troop of gorillas. There's also the **Sea Lion Cliffs** habitat, where visitors can view the saltwater habitat from an underwater glass viewing area; the Jane Goodall-approved **Chimpanzees of the Mahale Mountains** habitat, where visitors can see plenty of primate activity; the **Red Ape Rainforest,** a natural orangutan habitat; the entertaining **World of Birds** show; and **Dragons of Komodo,** featuring a pair of the world's largest lizard species. The gargantuan Andean condor had me enthralled as well (the facility is renowned in zoological circles for the successful breeding and releasing of California condors, and occasionally some of these majestic and endangered birds are on exhibit).

The zoo offers an audio tour, aptly named Weird and Wonderful, highlighting more than a dozen of the most intriguing residents, including the red-knobbed hornbill, Komodo dragon, double-wattled cassowary, rock hyrax, African wild dog, Chacoan peccary, white-crested turaco, Coquerel's sifaka, fossa, Sichuan takin, mountain tapir, and the Cape griffon vulture. The tour guests hear fascinating facts about the animals, as well as information on the zoo's curators and animal keepers. The tour, which also explains conservation efforts, is also available for downloading in English and Spanish from the zoo's website, under the "Fun Zone" tab.

Kids will also enjoy the **Winnick Family Children's Zoo,** which contains a petting area, exhibition animal-care center, Adventure Theater storytelling and puppet show, and other kid-hip exhibits and activities. *Tip:* To avoid the busloads of rambunctious school kids, arrive after noon.

The Moss Family Conservation Carousel is expected to open in late spring 2011, followed by the Living Amphibians, Insects and Reptiles (LAIR) center in the fall of 2011.

5333 Zoo Dr., Griffith Park. ✆ **323/644-4200.** www.lazoo.org. Admission $14 adults, $11 seniors 62 and over, $9 children 2–12, free for kids 1 and under. Daily 10am–5pm (until 6pm July 1 to Labor Day). Closed Christmas. Free parking.

STUDIO & SIGHTSEEING TOURS

Studio Tours

In addition to the studios list below, **Universal Studios** ★ offers daily 1-hour tram tours of its studio lot as part of the general admission price to the amusement park, which is open from 9am to 7pm in the summer and from 10am to 6pm in the winter. See p. 143 for more information.

NBC Studios ☺ According to a security guard, John Wayne and Redd Foxx once got into a fight here after Wayne refused to ride in the same limo as Foxx, who called the movie star a "redneck." Well, your NBC tour will probably be a bit more docile than that. The guided indoor and outdoor walking tour includes a brief walk-in, unstaged look at *The Tonight Show with Jay Leno* set (see p. 179 for how to get free Leno tickets), and wardrobe, makeup, and prop-building departments. In fact, NBC is the only TV studio that offers the public a behind-the-scenes look at the inner workings of its television operation, and it's a lot less expensive than the competition's studio tours. Granted, it doesn't have the cachet of a major motion picture studio tour, but it's entertaining nonetheless.

Tours depart at the top of the hour Monday through Friday from 9am to 1pm, and tickets are sold at the Guest Relations Department (bring cash—they don't take credit cards). Also, this is one of the few studio tours that doesn't have a minimum age requirement. *Note:* Before you make the drive to Burbank, be sure to call the studio and make sure tours are being offered that day and aren't already sold out.

3000 W. Alameda Ave. (off California St.), Burbank. ✆ **818/840-3537.** Tours $8.50 adults, $7.50 seniors 60 and over, $5 children 5–12, free for kids 4 and under. Mon–Fri 9am–1pm. Parking lots and metered street parking.

Paramount Pictures ★★ Paramount is the only major studio still located in Hollywood, which makes the 2-hour "cart tour" around its Hollywood headquarters far more historically enriching than the modern studios in Burbank (even the wrought-iron gates Gloria Swanson motored through in *Sunset Boulevard* are still there). The tour is both a historical ode to filmmaking and a real-life, behind-the-scenes look at working movie and television facilities in day-to-day operation; ergo, no two tours are alike, and chances of spotting a celebrity are pretty good. Visits typically include a walk-through of the soundstages of TV shows or feature films, though you can't enter while taping is taking place. The $40 tours depart Monday through Friday *by advance reservations* up to one month out, though you can occasionally get lucky with same-day tickets if you are in the neighborhood. You need to be 12 or older to take the tour, and recording equipment is *verboten* (still cameras are ok in certain areas). *Tip:* Unfortunately, tour guests are no longer permitted to have lunch at the commissary.

5555 Melrose Ave. (btw. Gower St. and Van Ness Ave.), Hollywood. © **323/956-1777.** www.paramount studios.com. Tours $40 per person by advance reservation only. Mon–Fri 10am–2pm. Follow signs to parking garages.

Sony Pictures Studio Tour   Although it doesn't have quite the same historical cachet as Warner Brothers or Paramount, a lot of movie history was made at this Culver City lot. Four scenes from the *Wizard of Oz* were filmed here when it was MGM Studios, and although the Yellow Brick Road once ran through the lot, it's no longer there. What you will see on the 2-hour walking tour: sets currently in production, and an opportunity to drop in on the new *Jeopardy!* set (updated in 2009 for its 25th anniversary) or *Wheel of Fortune* when they aren't filming or on hiatus. But the main reason for the tour is the chance to catch a glimpse at the stars who work here (it's one of the busiest studio lots in the world). Tours depart from the Sony Pictures Plaza; be sure to call ahead and make a reservation. *Note:* Photo ID is required of all guests.

10000 W. Washington Blvd., Culver City. © **310/244-8687.** www.sonypicturesstudios.com. Reservations highly recommended; children under 12 not admitted. Tours $33 per person. Tours Mon–Fri at 9:30, 10:30am, 1:30, and 2:30pm, but are subject to change. Free parking.

Warner Bros. Studios ★   The Warner Brothers' "VIP Tour" takes visitors on a 2¼-hour jaunt around the world's busiest movie and TV studio. After a brief introductory film about the history of WB, groups of 12 pile into stretch golf carts for an intimate view of the inner workings of a motion picture and television studio: back-lot streets, soundstages, sets, and craft shops. Because nothing is staged, there's no telling what or who you might encounter, and no two tours are the same. The tour also includes a visit to the Warner Bros. Museum, which contains original costumes, props, sets, scripts, and correspondence from classic WB films and television shows. Advance tickets are recommended and available online via their website, or by calling © **818/972-8687;** otherwise, tickets are sold the day of the tour on a first-come, first-served basis. *Note:* Children 7 and under are not admitted, you must bring a valid photo ID, and they recommend you show up about 30 minutes before the tour starts.

3400 Riverside Dr., Burbank. © **818/972-8687.** www.wbstudiotour.com. Tours $48 per person. Tours Mon–Fri every 20 min. 8:20am–4pm (extended hours during spring and summer). Parking $7 (follow signs to VIP tour parking).

Sightseeing Tours
BUS/VAN TOURS

L.A. Tours (© 323/460-6490; www.latours.net) operates regularly scheduled tours of the city. Plush shuttle buses pick up riders from major hotels for morning or afternoon tours of Sunset Strip, the movie studios, the Farmers Market, Hollywood, homes of the stars, and other attractions. Different itineraries are available, from Downtown and the Music Center to Disneyland or Universal Studios. Tours vary in length from a half-day Beaches & Shopping tour to a full-day Grand City tour. Advance reservations are required.

stargazing IN L.A.: TOP SPOTS FOR SIGHTING CELEBRITIES

Celebrities pop up everywhere in L.A. If you spend enough time here, you'll surely bump into a few of them. If you're in the city for only a short time, however, it's best to go on the offensive.

Restaurants are your surest bet. Dining out is such a popular recreation among Hollywood's elite that you sometimes wonder whether frequently sighted folks like Nicole, Kobe, and Harrison ever actually eat at home. Places like **Dan Tana's, Mr. Chow, Nobu,** the **Ivy, Il Sole, Koi, Osteria Mozza, Cut, the Polo Lounge, the Grill on the Alley** and **Spago Beverly Hills** can almost guarantee sightings most nights of the week. The city's stylish hotels can also be good spots—the poolside cabanas at the **Viceroy** in Santa Monica are a good bet; the **Sunset Tower Hotel** draws stars like Jennifer Aniston to its **Tower Bar** dining room. **Shutters'** lobby lounge is the rendezvous of choice for famous faces heading to dinner at the hotel's **One Pico** restaurant; and spotting stars at the **Beverly Hills Hotel** is almost too easy. The trendiest clubs and bars—**Teddy's, Voyeur, Skybar**—are good for star sighting, but cover charges can be astronomical and the velvet-rope gauntlet oppressive. And A-list sightings aren't a guarantee: Expect a lot of reality show stars from *The Hills* and any one of the Kardashian sisters.

Often the best places to see members of the A-list aren't as obvious as a back-alley stage door or the front room of **Spago.** Shops along Sunset Boulevard are often star-heavy, as are chichi shops within the **Beverly Center** mall. **Book Soup,** that browser's paradise on the Sunset Strip, is usually good for a star or two. A midafternoon stroll along **Melrose Avenue** might also produce a familiar face (particularly at **Fred Segal**), likewise for the chic European-style shops of **Sunset Plaza** or the **Beverly Center.**

Or you can seek out the celebrities on the job. It's not uncommon for star-studded movie productions to use L.A.'s diverse cultural landscape for **location shots;** in fact, it's such a regular occurrence that locals are usually less impressed with an A-list presence than perturbed about the precious parking spaces lost to all those equipment trucks and dressing-room trailers. On-the-street movie shoots are part of what makes L.A. unique, and onlookers gather wherever hastily scrawled production signs point to a hot site.

If you're really intent on seeing as many stars as possible, log on to **www. seeing-stars.com,** a website that keeps tabs on where all the stars shop, eat, stay, and play in L.A.

The other major tour company in L.A. is **Starline Tours ★★** (*©* **800/959-3131;** www.starlinetours.com)—you'll see their air-conditioned minibuses, double-decker Big Red buses, and open-air trolleys all over the city—from Santa Monica into Downtown L.A. Since 1935 Starline has been offering a wide selection of L.A. tours, including the first-ever Movie Stars' Homes tour. Its most popular tour, the 2-hour neighborhood jaunt, departs every half-hour from the front of Grauman's Chinese Theatre between 9:30am and 4pm (you'll see the Starline kiosk to the right of the theater entrance at 6925 Hollywood Blvd.). If you really like driving tours, sign up for the *pièce de résistance:* the 5½-hour Grand Tour of L.A. Check out the website for more tour information.

Plane Spotting at LAX

You've undoubtedly heard of train spotters—those supergeeks sporting a pair of binoculars in one hand and a journal in the other—but what about plane spotters? The hobby of maintaining meticulous records of every type of commercial aircraft spotted has become so popular that the city of El Segundo invested $150,000 into a "hilltop aircraft observation area" near LAX, complete with benches, tables, and telescopes. It's located at the end of the southern runways on West Imperial Avenue between Sepulveda Boulevard and Main Street. For more information, log on to www.planespotting.com.

WALKING TOURS

If you want the classic Hollywood walking tour, **Red Line Tours** (© 323/402-1074; www.redlinetours.com) offers daily sightseeing expeditions to all the famous (and infamous) landmarks in Hollywood. Its unique "live-audio" system allows customers to hear the tour guide even over the city noise; customers wear an audio headset receiver while the tour guide wears a headset microphone transmitter (pretty clever, actually). Trips depart from the Egyptian Theatre (6708 Hollywood Blvd.) at 10am, noon, 2, and 4pm, 7 days a week. Rates are $25 for adults, $18 for students and seniors, and $15 for children ages 9 to 15. Log on to the Red Line Tours website for more information.

The **L.A. Conservancy** (© 213/623-2489; www.laconservancy.org) conducts about a dozen entertaining walking tours of historic Downtown L.A. In Pasadena, **Pasadena Heritage** (© 626/441-6333; www.pasadenaheritage.org) offers a walking tour of Old Pasadena. (For both tours, see the box "L.A.'s Top Architectural Tours," earlier in this chapter.)

Santa Monica Conservancy Walking Tours (© 310/496-3146; www.smconservancy.org) explore the history, architecture, and culture that give Santa Monica its distinctive quality. Choose from docent-guided tours, self-guided tours, and group tours.

BICYCLE TOURS

Perry's Beach Café & Rentals in Santa Monica offers 1½-hour bicycle tours of the Santa Monica and Venice beach communities. It's a great way to explore the area while learning about its history and landmark architecture. The package costs $35 per person and includes a tour guide, an additional 1½-hour bike rental with protective gear, water, and a bike lock. *Note:* A minimum of three people is required for the tour. For more information or to make a reservation, call © 310/939-0000.

HELICOPTER TOURS

Touring L.A. from above is certainly a unique perspective. Just the thrill of riding in a helicopter is worth the price. **Celebrity Helicopters** (© 877/999-2099; www.celebheli.com) offers a wide array of themed trips, ranging from a 35-minute Celebrity Home Tour ($189) to a 25-minute fly-by of the L.A. coastline ($149). Other tour packages are available as well; check the website for more information.

JOGGING TOURS

Off 'N Running Tours (© 310/246-1418; www.offnrunningtours.com) combines sporting with sightseeing, taking joggers on guided runs through Los Angeles. The themed tours, such as "Running from the Paparazzi," are customized to take in the most entertaining areas around the city and can accommodate any skill level for 4 miles. Another popular option is the Mansion Tour, which starts at Santa Monica Boulevard and Rodeo Drive, with a midpoint break at Greystone Mansion, where runners can stroll the grounds while winding down, before taking a route through different neighborhoods on the way back. It's a fun way to get the most out of your morning jog. Tours cost about $60 and include a technical T-shirt, bottle of water, and a cupcake at the end.

BEVERLY HILLS TROLLEY TOURS

The city of Beverly Hills offers inexpensive trolley tours that detail the city's history as well as little-known facts and celebrity tidbits. The tour takes visitors on a 40-minute docent-led tour through the tony avenues of Beverly Hills, including Rodeo Avenue and the Golden Triangle. It runs every Saturday and Sunday on the hour from 11am to 4pm. The fare is a mere $10 for adults and $5 for children 12 and under. The trolley departs at the "Trolley Stop" at the intersection of Rodeo Drive and Dayton Way. For more information, call ✆ **310/285-2442** or log on to www.beverlyhills.org.

LIVE-AUDIENCE TV TAPINGS

Being part of the audience for the taping of a television show might be the quintessential L.A. experience. This is a great way to see Hollywood at work, to find out how your favorite sitcom or talk show is made, and to catch a glimpse of your favorite TV personalities. Timing is important—remember that most series go on hiatus between March and July. And tickets to the top shows are in greater demand than others, so getting your hands on them takes advance planning—and possibly some waiting in line.

Request tickets as far in advance as possible. Several episodes may be shot on a single day, so you may be required to remain in the theater for up to 4 hours (in addition to the recommended 1-hr. early check-in). If you phone at the last moment, you may luck into tickets for your top choice. More likely, however, you'll be given a list of shows that are currently filming, and you won't recognize many of the titles; studios are always taping pilots, few of which end up on the air. But you never know who may be starring in them—look at all the famous faces that have launched new sitcoms in the past couple of years. Tickets are always free, are usually limited to two per person, and are distributed on a first-come, first-served basis. Many shows don't admit children under the age of 10; in some cases, no one under the age of 18 is admitted.

The Cold Truth About Talk Shows

The sets of most talk shows are kept at a cool temperature (the hot lights raise the temperature on stage), so be sure to bring a sweater or jacket. And if you dress well—no T-shirts or shorts—your chances of getting a front-row seat increase dramatically.

Tickets are sometimes given away to the public outside popular tourist sites like Grauman's Chinese Theatre in Hollywood and Universal Studios in the Valley; L.A.'s visitor information centers in Downtown and Hollywood often have tickets as well (see "Visitor Information" in chapter 11). But if you're determined to see a particular show, contact the following suppliers:

HOW TO BE A game show CONTESTANT

So you've been thinking of taking a chance on fame and fortune the next time you're in L.A., eh? Well, both are more attainable than you might think—actress Markie Post's career began with her audition for a game show; and as far as fortune goes, *somebody* has to win the big money.

If you're serious about trying to get on a show, be sure you have some flexibility in your schedule; although most production companies go out of their way to give priority to out-of-town contestants, you should be prepared to return to Los Angeles one or more times for a final audition and/or taping. Here are some tips that might help you prepare:

The Bubblier, the Better: Be friendly, cheerful, and bright at your audition and during taping. Be good-natured when you lose or make mistakes, and above all, be exuberant if you win the "big money." When you're onstage, nothing feels quite real.

Dress for Success: Contestant coordinators look for players who won't alienate viewers. It's awfully hard for a granny in the heartland to relate to a trendy big-city type. So dress as conservatively as possible for your auditions, and avoid the fashion no-nos—white, black, stripes, metallics—that would require lighting and camera adjustments.

Most Unglamorous Advice: Remember income taxes. Should you be lucky enough to win big, bear in mind that all cash winnings, as well as the retail value of all your prizes, will be reported to the IRS as earnings.

Some Game Shows Currently in Production:

Jeopardy! Trivia quiz not for the faint-hearted (the contestant, that is; watching isn't nearly as difficult!). Call ☎ **310/244-5367** or log on to www.sonypictures.com/tv/shows/jeopardy.

Wheel of Fortune Less about your skill with the "hangman"-style puzzles than your luck spinning the carnival wheel. Call ☎ **213/520-5555** or log on to www.wheeloffortune.com.

The Price Is Right Contestants are chosen from the studio audience to test their shopping expertise. Call ☎ **323/575-2448** or log on to www.cbs.com/daytime/price/tickets.

Audiences Unlimited, Inc. (www.tvtickets.com) is a good place to start. It distributes tickets for most of the top sitcoms, including, *America's Funniest Videos, Hot in Cleveland,* and *$#*! My Dad Says.* This service is organized and informative (as is its website), and fully sanctioned by production companies and networks. ABC, for example, no longer handles ticket distribution directly, but refers all inquiries to Audiences Unlimited, Inc. **TVTix** (☎ **323/653-4105;** www.tvtix.com) also distributes tickets for numerous talk and game shows, including *The Tonight Show with Jay Leno* and *Jeopardy!*

You also may want to contact the networks for information on a specific show, including some whose tickets are not available at the above agencies. At **ABC**, all ticket inquiries are referred to Audiences Unlimited (see above), but you may want to check out ABC's website at **www.abc.com** for a colorful look at their lineup and links to specific show sites.

For **CBS Television City,** 7800 Beverly Blvd., Los Angeles, CA 90036, call ☎ **323/575-2458** between Monday and Friday from 9am to 5pm to see what's being filmed while you're in town. Tickets for CBS tapings are distributed on a first-come, first-served basis; you can write in advance to reserve them or pick them up at the studio up to an hour before taping. Tickets for many CBS sitcoms are also available from Audiences Unlimited (see above). For tickets to *The Price Is Right,* call the 24-hour ticket hot line at ✆ **323/575-2448** or log on to www.cbs.com/daytime/price/tickets.

For **NBC,** 3000 W. Alameda Ave., Burbank, CA 91523 (✆ **818/840-3537;** www.nbc.com), call to see what's on while you're in L.A. Tickets for some NBC tapings are available online through www.tvtickets.com. For tickets to *The Tonight Show with Jay Leno* (minimum age to attend this show is 16), visit www.nbc.com/the-tonight-show/tickets 4 to 6 weeks before your visit. Be sure to include four dates you'd like to attend in order of preference, the full name of the person attending, your e-mail address, mailing address, and phone number. NBC hands out a limited number of standby tickets for every *Leno* taping at 8am the morning of every show (lineups start early). For standby tickets, go to the NBC Ticket Box at 3000 W. Alameda Ave.

Paramount Studios also offers free tickets to its live audience shows. All you need to do is call one of the friendly employees at Paramount Guest Relations (✆ **323/956-1777**) between 9am and 5pm on weekdays and make a reservation. For seating reservations for *Dr. Phil,* call ✆ **323/461-7445. Universal Studios** (✆ **800/UNIVERSAL** [864-8377]; www.universalstudios.com) also offers free tickets to its live audience shows. At the amusement park's **Audiences Unlimited ticket booth,** you can obtain free tickets to join the audience for any TV shows that are taping during your visit (subject to availability).

BEACHES

Los Angeles County's 72-mile coastline sports more than 30 miles of beaches, most of which are operated by the **Department of Beaches & Harbors,** 13837 Fiji Way, Marina del Rey (✆ **310/305-9503;** www.beaches.lacounty.gov). County-run beaches usually charge for parking ($3–$12). Alcohol, bonfires, and pets are prohibited. For recorded **surf conditions** (and coastal weather forecast), call ✆ **310/457-9701.** The following are the county's best beaches, listed from north to south.

EL PESCADOR, L.A. PIEDRA & EL MATADOR BEACHES   These rugged and isolated beaches (real finds) front a 2-mile stretch of the Pacific Coast Highway (Calif. 1) between Broad Beach and Decker Canyon roads, a 10-minute drive from the Malibu Pier. Picturesque coves with unusual rock formations are great for sunbathing and picnicking, but swim with caution, as there are no lifeguards. The beaches can be difficult to find; only small signs on the highway mark them. There are a limited number of parking spots atop the bluffs. Descend to the beach via stairs that cling to the cliffs.

ZUMA BEACH COUNTY PARK ★   Jampacked on warm weekends, L.A. County's largest beach park is located off the Pacific Coast Highway (Calif. 1), a mile past Kanan Dume Road. While it can't claim to be the most scenic beach in the Southland, Zuma has the most comprehensive facilities: plenty of restrooms, lifeguards, playgrounds, volleyball courts, and snack bars. The southern stretch, toward Point Dume, is Westward Beach, separated from the noisy highway by sandstone cliffs. A trail leads over the point's headlands to Pirate's Cove, once a popular nude beach.

PARADISE COVE   This private beach in the 28000 block of the Pacific Coast Highway (Calif. 1) charges $25 to park and $5 per person if you walk in—or you can

stargazing IN L.A., PART II: THE LESS-THAN-LIVELY

Almost everybody who visits L.A. hopes to see a celebrity—they are, after all, the city's most common export. But celebrities usually don't cooperate, failing to gather in readily viewable herds. There is, however, an absolutely guaranteed method to approach within 6 feet of many famous stars. Cemeteries are *the* place for stargazing (or at least headstone gazing): The star is always available, and you're going to get a lot more up close and personal than you probably would to anyone who's actually alive. Here is a guide to the most fruitful cemeteries, listed in order of their friendliness to stargazers. If you're looking for someone in particular, log on to www.findagrave.com. (There's a website for *everything*.)

Weathered Victorian and Art Deco memorials add to the decaying charm of **Hollywood Forever** ★★ (formerly Hollywood Memorial Park), 6000 Santa Monica Blvd., Hollywood (© **323/469-1181;** www.hollywoodforever.com). Fittingly, there's a terrific view of the HOLLYWOOD sign over the graves, as many of the founders of the community rest here. The most notable tenant is Rudolph Valentino, who rests in an interior crypt. Outside are Tyrone Power, Jr.; Douglas Fairbanks, Sr.; Cecil B. DeMille (facing Paramount, his old studio); Carl "Alfalfa" Spritzer from *The Little Rascals* (the dog on his grave is not Petey);

Hearst mistress Marion Davies; John Huston; and a headstone for Jayne Mansfield (she's really buried in Pennsylvania with her family). In 2000 Douglas Fairbanks, Jr., joined his dad at Hollywood Forever. The best epitaph is Mel Blanc's "That's all, Folks." Grab a map at the entrance for a self-guided tour.

The Catholic **Holy Cross Cemetery,** 5835 W. Slauson Ave., Culver City (© **310/836-5500;** www.holycross mortuary.com), founded in 1939, hands out maps to the stars' graves. In one area, within mere feet of each other, lie Bing Crosby, Bela Lugosi (buried in his Dracula cape), and Sharon Tate; not far away are Rita Hayworth and Jimmy Durante. Also here are "Tin Man" Jack Haley and "Scarecrow" Ray Bolger, Mary Astor, John Ford, and Gloria Morgan Vanderbilt. More recent arrivals include John Candy and Audrey Meadows.

The front office at **Hillside Memorial Park,** 6001 W. Centinela Ave., Baldwin Hills (© **800/576-1994;** www.hillside memorial.org), can provide a guide to this Jewish cemetery, which has an L.A. landmark: the behemoth tomb of Al Jolson. His rotunda, complete with a bronze reproduction of Jolson and a cascading fountain, is visible from I-405. Also on hand are Jack Benny, Eddie Cantor, Vic Morrow, and Michael Landon.

You just know developers get stomachaches looking at **Westwood Village**

dine at Paradise Cove Restaurant and get validated for 4 hours, making the per-car charge only $3. Changing rooms and showers are included in the price. The beach is often full by noon on weekends.

MALIBU LAGOON STATE BEACH ★★ Not just a pretty white-sand beach, but an estuary and wetlands area as well, Malibu Lagoon is the historic home of the Chumash Indians. The entrance is on the Pacific Coast Highway (Calif. 1) south of Cross Creek Road, and there's a small admission charge. Marine life and shorebirds teem where the creek empties into the sea, and the waves are always mild. The historic **Adamson House** is here, a showplace of Malibu tile now operating as a museum.

Memorial Park, 1218 Glendon Ave., Westwood (☎ **310/474-1579;** www. pbwvmortuary.com), smack-dab in the middle of some of L.A.'s priciest real estate (behind the AVCO office building south of Wilshire Blvd.). But it's not going anywhere, especially when you consider its most famous resident: Marilyn Monroe (entombed in a simple wall crypt, number 24). It's also got Truman Capote, Roy Orbison, John Cassavetes, Armand Hammer, Donna Reed, and Natalie Wood. Walter Matthau and Jack Lemmon are buried here as well, a fitting ending for the Odd Couple.

Forest Lawn Glendale, 1712 S. Glendale Ave. (☎ **800/204-3131;** www.forest lawn.com), likes to pretend it has no celebrities. The most prominent of L.A. cemeteries, it's also the most humorless. The place is full of bad art, all part of the continuing vision of founder Huburt Eaton, who thought cemeteries should be happy places. So he banished those gloomy upright tombstones and monuments in favor of flat, pleasant, character-free, flush-to-the-ground slabs. Contrary to urban legend, Walt Disney was *not* frozen and placed under Cinderella's castle at Disneyland. His cremated remains are in a little garden to the left of the Freedom Mausoleum. Turn around, and just behind you are Errol Flynn and Spencer Tracy. In the Freedom Mausoleum itself are Nat

"King" Cole, Chico Marx, Gummo Marx, and Gracie Allen—finally joined by George Burns. In a columbarium near the Mystery of Life is Humphrey Bogart. Unfortunately, some of the best celebs—such as Clark Gable, Carole Lombard, and Jean Harlow—are in the Great Mausoleum, which you often can't get into unless you're visiting a relative.

You'd think a place that encourages people to visit for fun would understand what the attraction is. But no—Forest Lawn Glendale won't tell you where any of their illustrious guests are, so don't ask. This place is immense—and, frankly, dull in comparison to the previously listed cemeteries, unless you appreciate the kitsch value of the Forest Lawn approach to art.

Forest Lawn Hollywood Hills, 6300 Forest Lawn Dr. (☎ **800/204-3131;** www.forestlawn.com), is slightly less anal than the Glendale branch, but the same basic attitude prevails. On the right lawn, near the statue of George Washington, is Buster Keaton. In the Courts of Remembrance are Lucille Ball, Charles Laughton, and the not-quite-gaudy-enough tomb of Liberace. Outside, in a vault on the Ascension Road side, is Andy Gibb. Bette Davis's sarcophagus is in front of the wall, to the left of the entrance to the Courts. Gene Autry is also buried here, almost within earshot of the museum that bears his name.

SURFRIDER BEACH Without a doubt, L.A.'s best waves roll ashore here. One of the city's most popular surfing spots, this beach is located between the Malibu Pier and the lagoon. In surf lingo, few "locals-only" wave wars are ever fought here—surfing is not as territorial as it can be in other areas, where out-of-towners can be made to feel unwelcome. Surfrider is surrounded by all of Malibu's hustle and bustle; don't come here for peace and quiet, as the surf is always crowded.

TOPANGA STATE BEACH Highway noise prevents solitude at this short, narrow strip of sand located where Topanga Canyon Boulevard emerges from the mountains. Why go? Ask the surfers who wait in line to catch Topanga's excellent right point breaks. There are restrooms and lifeguard services here, and across the street

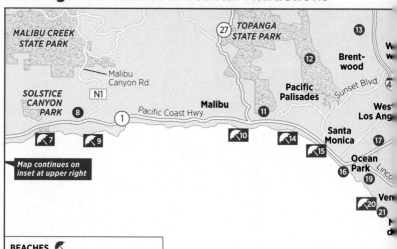

MALIBU CREEK
STATE PARK

Malibu
Canyon Rd.

SOLSTICE
CANYON
PARK **8**

N1

Pacific Coast Hwy.

1

TOPANGA
STATE PARK **27**

12

Brent-
wood

Pacific
Palisades

Sunset Blvd.

Malibu

11

13

W
w

4

West
Los Ang

Santa
Monica

17

7   **9**

10   **14**

15

Map continues on
inset at upper right

Ocean
Park

16   **19**

Linco

20   **21**

Ven

N
d

de

BEACHES 🏖

El Pescador, La Piedra,
  & El Matador Beaches **3**
Hermosa City Beach **23**
Leo Carrillo Beach **2**
Malibu Lagoon State Beach **7**
Manhattan State Beach **22**
North County Line Beach **1**
Paradise Cove **6**
Point Dume Beach **5**
Redondo State Beach **24**
Santa Monica State Beach **15**
Surfrider Beach **9**
Topanga State Beach **10**
Venice Beach **20**
Will Rogers State Beach **14**
Zuma Beach County Park **4**

SIGHTS & ATTRACTIONS ●

Aquarium of the Pacific **25**
Binoculars Building **19**
Getty Center **13**
Getty Villa **11**
Pepperdine University **8**
Queen Mary **26**
Santa Monica Museum
  of Art & Bergamot Station **17**
Santa Monica Pier **16**
Venice Beach's Ocean Front Walk **21**
Will Rogers State Historic Park **12**

Santa

Monica

Bay

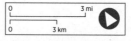

0   3 mi

0   3 km

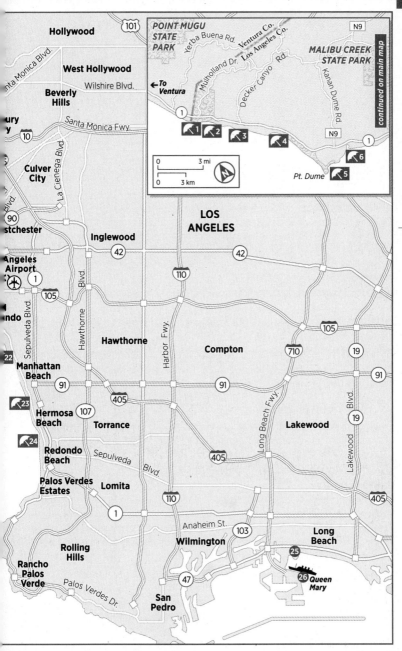

continued on main map

Hollywood

West Hollywood

Beverly Hills

Wilshire Blvd.

Santa Monica Fwy.

Culver City

Inglewood

LOS ANGELES

Hawthorne

Compton

Manhattan Beach

Hermosa Beach

Torrance

Redondo Beach

Sepulveda Blvd.

Palos Verdes Estates

Lomita

Lakewood

Rolling Hills

Rancho Palos Verde

Wilmington

San Pedro

Long Beach

Queen Mary

POINT MUGU STATE PARK

MALIBU CREEK STATE PARK

Yerba Buena Rd.

Mulholland Dr.

Decker Canyon Rd.

Kanan Dume Rd.

Ventura Co.
Los Angeles Co.

To Ventura

Pt. Dume

0   3 mi
0   3 km

6 GOOD DAY, marina del rey

The coastal playground of Marina del Rey offers several fun reasons to spend a day taking advantage of its harborside location. For instance, check out the **Bird-Watching Experience** starting within Burton Chace Park. The 2-hour walks explore the Ballona Wetlands fresh- and saltwater marshes, nesting sites of the great blue- and black-crowned night herons (for reservations for kayaking and bird-watching, call the park at ✆ **310/305-9595**). Kayaks, powerboats, jet skis, and sailboats are also available at **Marina Boat Rentals** (✆ **310/574-2822**).

After an alfresco lunch on the elevated deck overlooking the harbor at **Cafe Del Rey** (p. 85), head over to the **Fisherman's Village,** rent a bicycle at **Daniel's Bikes** (✆ **310/980-4045;**

www.danielsbikesales.com), and spend the afternoon cruising alongside the docks on the South Bay Bicycle Trail (you can even keep the bikes after hours by special request; be sure and get a lock, and you can arrange to leave it at the ice cream shop next door). If it's a Thursday or Saturday during the summer, arrive early for a good seat at the **free classical, jazz, and pop concerts** held at 7pm at Burton Chace Park. After the show, end your fun-filled day with a romantic dinner overlooking the harbor at the **Vu restaurant** within the Jamaica Bay Inn, Marina del Rey (p. 51). For more information about Marina del Rey activities, call the **Marina del Rey Convention & Visitors Bureau** at ✆ **310/305-9545** or log on to www.visitmarinadelrey.com.

you'll find one of the best fresh fish restaurants around, the **Reel Inn,** 18661 Pacific Coast Hwy., Malibu (✆ **310/456-8221**).

WILL ROGERS STATE BEACH Three miles along the Pacific Coast Highway (Calif. 1), between Sunset Boulevard and the Santa Monica border, are named for the American humorist whose ranch-turned-state-historic-park (see "L.A. Parks, Gardens, Views & Zoos," earlier in this chapter) is nestled above the palisades that provide the backdrop for this popular beach. A pay parking lot extends the entire length of the beach, and facilities include restrooms, lifeguards, and a snack hut in season. While the surfing is not the best, the waves are friendly for swimmers, and there are always competitive volleyball games to be found.

SANTA MONICA STATE BEACH The family-friendly beaches on either side of the Santa Monica Pier (see "Oceanside Delights," p. 138) are popular for their white sands and accessibility. There are big parking lots, cafes, and well-maintained restrooms. A paved path runs along the beach, allowing you to walk, bike, or skate to Venice and points south. Colorado Boulevard leads to the pier; turn north on the Pacific Coast Highway (Calif. 1) below the coastline's bluffs, or south along Ocean Avenue—you can find parking in both directions.

VENICE BEACH ★★ Moving south from the city of Santa Monica, the paved pedestrian Promenade becomes Ocean Front Walk and gets progressively weirder until it reaches an apex at Washington Boulevard and the Venice fishing pier. Although there are people who swim and sunbathe, Venice Beach's character is defined by the sea of humanity on the Ocean Front Walk, plus the bevy of boardwalk vendors and old-fashioned pedestrian streets a block away (see "Oceanside Delights," p. 138). Park on the side streets or in the plentiful lots west of Pacific Avenue.

MANHATTAN STATE BEACH   The Beach Boys used to hang out at this wide, friendly beach backed by beautiful oceanview homes. Plenty of parking on 36 blocks of side streets (btw. Rosecrans Ave. and the Hermosa Beach border) draws weekend crowds from the L.A. area. Manhattan has some of the best surfing around as well as restrooms, lifeguards, and volleyball courts. Manhattan Beach Boulevard leads west to the fishing pier and adjacent seafood restaurants.

HERMOSA CITY BEACH ★★   This very wide white-sand beach is one of the best in Southern California and my favorite. Hermosa extends to either side of the pier and includes The Strand, a wide, smooth pedestrian lane that runs its entire length. Main access is at the foot of Pier Avenue, which is lined with interesting shops and cafes with outdoor seating. There's plenty of street parking, as well as restrooms, lifeguards, volleyball courts, a fishing pier, playgrounds, and good surfing.

REDONDO STATE BEACH   Popular with surfers, bicyclists, and joggers, Redondo's white sand and ice-plant-carpeted dunes are just south of tiny King Harbor, along the Esplanade (S. Esplanade Dr.). Get there via the Pacific Coast Highway (Calif. 1) or Torrance Boulevard. Facilities include restrooms, lifeguards, and volleyball courts.

GOLF, HIKING & OTHER FUN IN THE CALIFORNIA SUN

Bisected by the Santa Monica Mountains and fronted by long stretches of beach, Los Angeles is one of the best cities in the world for nature and sports lovers. Where else can you hike in the mountains, in-line skate along the beach, swim in the ocean, enjoy a gourmet meal, and then take in a pro basketball, soccer, hockey, or baseball game—all in the same day?

BICYCLING   Los Angeles, being mostly flat, is great for biking. If you're into distance pedaling, you can do no better than the flat, paved bicycle trail that follows about 22 miles of state beaches, harbors, LAX, and laid-back beach towns such as Venice, Manhattan Beach, Hermosa Beach, and Redondo Beach. The first stretch starts at Will Rogers State Beach in Pacific Palisades and runs south through Santa Monica and Venice to Marina del Rey—about 8 miles. The second stretch—called the **South Bay Bike Trail**—starts at the south end of Marina del Rey and takes you all the way to Torrance Beach. If you want to ride the entire path, you'll have to detour around Marina del Rey, which takes only about 15 minutes. The bike path attracts all levels of riders and gets pretty busy on weekends, so ixnay the time trials. Don't worry about packing food and water—there are plenty of fountains, snack stands, and public restrooms along the trail. For information on this and other city bike routes, log on to www.labikepaths.com. For **guided bicycle tours** of the Santa Monica and Venice beach communities, see "Bicycle Tours," on p. 176.

   The best place to mountain bike in the L.A. region is along the trails of **Malibu Creek State Park** (© **818/880-0367**), in the Santa Monica Mountains between Malibu and the San Fernando Valley in Calabasas. Fifteen miles of trails rise to a maximum of 3,000 feet and are appropriate for intermediate to advanced bikers. Pick up a trail map at the park entrance, 4 miles south of U.S. 101 off Las Virgenes Road, just north of Mulholland Highway. Park admission is $12 per car. For more information on mountain-bike trails in the L.A. region, log on to **www.latrails.com**.

Spokes 'N Stuff has four locations, one of which is 4175 Admiralty Way, Marina del Rey (© 310/306-3332; www.spokes-n-stuff.com), which is open only on weekends; and another at 1715 Ocean Front Walk, behind Loews Hotel, Santa Monica (© **310/395-4748**), which is open every day. They rent 10-speed cruisers and 15-speed mountain bikes for about $7.50 per hour and $22 per day. Another good Santa Monica rental shop is **Blazing Saddles Bike Rentals** (Santa Monica Pier; © **310/393-9778**). The rates are about the same as those at Spokes 'N Stuff. Be sure to ask for a free **self-guided tour map** (it's really handy).

In the Santa Monica Mountains, **Topanga Creek Bicycles,** 1273 N. Topanga Canyon Blvd., Topanga (© **310/455-2111;** www.topangacreekbicycles.com), rents mountain bikes at $75 for a 24-hour period and $50 for each additional day. Every rental comes with a free tour map, a safety helmet, and a flat-tire kit. Water and snacks are available for purchase.

In the South Bay, bike rentals—including tandem bikes—are available 1 block from The Strand at **Hermosa Cyclery,** 20 13th St., Hermosa Beach (© 310/374-7816; www.hermosacyclery.com). Cruisers are $7 per hour; tandems are $13 per hour. FYI, The Strand is an excellent car-free path that's tailor-made for a leisurely bike ride.

FISHING Del Rey Sport Fishing, 13552 Fiji Way, Marina del Rey (© 800/822-3625 or 310/822-3635; www.marinadelreysportfishing.com), has two deep-sea boats departing daily on half- and full-day ocean fishing trips. Of course, it depends on what's running when you're out, but bass, barracuda, halibut, and yellowtail are the most common catches on these party boats. Excursions start at $35 ($25 for kids under 12) for half-day trips; tackle rental is available for $10 as well. Phone for reservations. Note: Anyone 16 years and up needs a fishing license, which can be obtained at just about any sporting goods store.

No permit is required to cast from shore or drop a line from more public piers. Local anglers will hate me for giving away their secret spot, but the **best saltwater fishing spot** in all of L.A. is at the foot of Torrance Boulevard in Redondo Beach.

GOLF The greater Los Angeles area has more than 100 golf courses, which vary in quality from abysmal to superb. Most of the city's public courses are administered by the Department of Recreation and Parks. A new online reservation system allows any player to book a tee time up to 8 days in advance. The non-refundable, non-transferable cost is $5 per person (https://golfreservation.lacity.org/golferla72). You're also still welcome to play any of the courses by showing up and getting on the call sheet (much easier for nine-hole courses versus full ones). Expect to wait for the most popular tee times, but try to use your flexible vacationer status to your advantage by avoiding the early morning rush.

Of the city's seven 18-hole and three 9-hole courses, you can't get more central than the **Rancho Park Golf Course,** 10460 W. Pico Blvd. (© **310/838-7373;** www.rancho.lagolfclubs.com), located smack-dab in the middle of L.A.'s Westside. The par-71 course has lots of tall trees, but not enough to blot out the towering Century City buildings next door. For the money, it's a real bargain (heck, even Bill Clinton golfed here). Rancho also has a 9-hole, par-3 course, as well as a driving range.

For a genuinely woodsy experience, try one of the three courses inside Griffith Park, northeast of Hollywood (see "L.A. Parks, Gardens, Views & Zoos," earlier in this chapter). The courses are extremely well maintained, challenging without being frustrating, and (despite some holes alongside I-5) a great way to leave the city behind.

topanga canyon: NATURE'S SOLUTION TO L.A.'S NOISE POLLUTION

When you've had enough of cellphones, cement, and Mercedes, then it's time to take the short drive from L.A. to Topanga Canyon to bargain shop, drink margaritas, and play cowgirl for a day. Here's the game plan: Call **Los Angeles Horseback Riding** (𝒞 **818/591-2032;** www.losangeleshorsebackriding.com) and make a reservation for a guided horseback ride in the late afternoon. Next, take the winding drive up Topanga Canyon Boulevard to tiny **Topanga,** one of the last art communities left in Southern California—it was the former haunt of Fleetwood Mac, Neil Young, and other music legends of the '60s and '70s—and the perfect antidote to the dig-me L.A. scene. Spend an hour or so picking through the treasure-trove of vintage clothes, accessories, and antiques at **Hidden Treasures** (154 S. Topanga Canyon Blvd.; 𝒞 **310/455-2998**), one of the funkiest little shops I've ever seen (the custom-made sea-theme toilet seat lids are mesmerizing). After the scenic horseback ride through the boulder-strewn Topanga canyons lined with oaks, sycamores, chaparral, and sage, finish off your relaxing day with a leisurely dinner in Topanga at **Abuelitas** (137 S. Topanga Canyon Blvd.; 𝒞 **310/455-8688;** www.abuelitastopanga.com), a popular Mexican restaurant; or try the romantic **Inn of the Seventh Ray** (p. 97).

Bucolic pleasures abound, particularly on the 9-hole **Roosevelt,** on Vermont Avenue across from the Greek Theatre; early morning wildlife often includes deer, rabbits, raccoons, and skunks (fore!). **Wilson** and **Harding** are each 18 holes and start from the main clubhouse off Riverside Drive, the park's main entrance.

Greens fees on all city courses range from $16 to $48 for non-residents; 9-hole courses start at $16 on weekdays and $19 on weekends and holidays. For details on other city courses, or to contact the starter directly by phone, call the Department of Recreation and Parks at 𝒞 **213/625-1040** or log on to the city's parks website at www.laparks.org.

If you're not a fan of crowded city courses, it's well worth the 20-minute drive north to play **Robinson Ranch,** 27734 Sand Canyon Rd., Santa Clarita (𝒞 **661/252-8484;** www.robinsonranchgolf.com), one of the best and least-crowded public courses in the L.A. region (my golfing buddy loves this place). Golfers can choose between two courses, Mountain or Valley, both of which offer challenging, hilly terrain—bring extra balls—and great views of the Santa Clarita Valley. The striking 25,000-square-foot clubhouse makes a nice view as well, and houses a well-stocked pro shop and full-service restaurant. Greens fees for both courses are $87 Monday through Thursday, $117 Friday through Sunday. Carts and practice balls are included.

The **Trump National Golf Club,** 1 Ocean Trails Dr. (𝒞 **310/265-5000;** www.trumpnationallosangeles.com), recently opened in Rancho Palos Verdes. Perched on a bluff overlooking the Pacific Ocean, the course provides a spectacular view from every hole. Originally designed by Pete Dye as the Ocean Trails Golf Course, the property was purchased by developer Donald Trump, who spent more than $250 million to redesign it with elements such as lakes and waterfalls. Located on the Palos Verdes Peninsula, 30 minutes south of Downtown Los Angeles, the course also offers a 45,000-square-foot clubhouse with locker rooms, a pro shop, three dining options, conference rooms, and a grand ballroom. Greens fees at the public course are $275 at peak times, $215 midday, $160 for the afternoon, and $80 after 2:30pm.

Industry Hills Golf Club, 1 Industry Hills Pkwy., Industry Hills (© **626/810-4653;** www.ihgolfclub.com), has two 18-hole courses designed by William Bell. Together they encompass eight lakes, 160 bunkers, and many long fairways. The Eisenhower Course, consistently ranked among *Golf Digest's* top 25 public courses, has extra-large undulating greens and the challenge of thick *Kikuyu* grass. (*Kikuyu,* even coarser than Bermuda's broad-leaf terrain, is often called "Bermuda on steroids.") An adjacent driving range is lit for night use. Greens fees are $70 to $80 Monday through Friday and $100 to $105 Saturday and Sunday, including a cart; call in advance for tee times.

For more information on regional golf courses, log on to www.golfcalifornia.com.

HANG GLIDING Up and down the California coast, it's not uncommon to see people poised on the crests of hills, hanging from enormous colorful kites. You can, too. **Windsports Soaring Center,** 12623 Gridley St., Sylmar (© **818/367-2430;** www.windsports.com), offers instruction and rentals for both novices and experts. A 1-day lesson in a solo hang glider on a bunny hill costs $120 (Wednesday to Sunday, by advance reservation only). If it's more of a thrill you're looking for, choose the 3,000-foot-high tandem flight for $199, which is offered 7 days a week. Beginner lessons are waterside at Dockweiler State Beach Training Flight Park (near LAX), while tandem flights take off from a San Fernando Valley hilltop. Phone for reservations.

HIKING The **Santa Monica Mountains,** a small range that runs only 50 miles from Griffith Park to Point Mugu, on the coast north of Malibu, makes Los Angeles a great place for hiking. The mountains, which peak at 3,111 feet, are part of the Santa Monica Mountains National Recreation Area, a contiguous conglomeration of 350 public parks and 65,000 acres. Many animals live in this area, including deer, coyote, rabbit, skunk, rattlesnake, fox, hawk, and quail. The hills are also home to almost 1,000 drought-resistant plant species, including live oak and coastal sage.

Hiking is best after spring rains, when the hills are green, flowers are in bloom, and the air is clear. Summers can be very hot; hikers should always carry fresh water. Beware of poison oak, a hearty shrub that's common on the West Coast. Usually found among oak trees, poison oak has leaves in groups of three, with waxy surfaces and prominent veins. If you come into contact with this itch-producing plant, you'll end up with a California souvenir that you'll soon regret.

 The Big Sprawl

How crowded is L.A.? If the five-county area was a state, it would surpass all states in total population size, with the exception of California, New York, and Texas.

Santa Ynez Canyon, in Pacific Palisades, is a long and difficult climb that rises steadily for about 3 miles. At the top, hikers are rewarded with fantastic views over the Pacific. At the top is **Trippet Ranch,** a public facility providing water, restrooms, and picnic tables. From Santa Monica, take Pacific Coast Highway (Calif. 1) north; turn right onto Sunset Boulevard and then left onto Palisades Drive. Continue for 2½ miles, turn left onto Verenda de la Montura, and park at the cul-de-sac at the end of the street, where you can find the trail head.

The California coastline north of Santa Monica has more than great beaches and surfing. A new wine country is emerging right here in Los Angeles County, and nothing is quite as exciting to a Master Sommelier as an internationally recognized wine region right in his own backyard.

Within the Malibu region are two officially recognized wine-producing appellations (called American Viticultural Areas, or "AVAs"): Saddle Rock–Malibu AVA and Malibu–Newton Canyon AVA. In fact, there are now more than 50 wineries in these Santa Monica Mountains and at several tasting rooms to visit along the Malibu Wine Country

"Wine Trail," where warm days and cool nights create ideal conditions for growing grapes.

Our Malibu wine country beckons you to come discover and enjoy. So venture off into the Malibu canyons for a relaxing day of wine tasting, then enjoy a great sunset dining experience at one of the scenic Malibu waterfront restaurants, such as the Beachcomber Café at Malibu Pier (p. 94). For a free Wine Trail map, contact the Malibu Chamber of Commerce (② 310/456-9025; www.malibu.org). Cheers!
—Michael "Malibu Mike" Jordan, Master Sommelier

Temescal Canyon, in Pacific Palisades, is far easier than the Santa Ynez trail and far more popular, especially among locals. This is one of the quickest routes into the wilderness. Hikes here are anywhere from 1 to 5 miles. From Santa Monica, take Pacific Coast Highway (Calif. 1) north; turn right onto Temescal Canyon Road, and follow it to the end. Sign in with the gatekeeper, who can also answer your questions.

Will Rogers State Historic Park ★, in Pacific Palisades, is also a terrific place for hiking. An intermediate-level hike from the park's entrance ends at Inspiration Point, a plateau from which you can see a good portion of L.A.'s Westside. See "L.A. Parks, Gardens, Views & Zoos," earlier in this chapter, for complete information.

For more information on hiking in the L.A. region, log on to **www.latrails.com**.

HORSEBACK RIDING   Griffith Park Horse Rental, 480 Riverside Dr. (in the Los Angeles Equestrian Center), Burbank (② 818/840-8401), rents horses by the hour for guided rides through Griffith Park's hills; no experience is necessary. Horse rental start at $25 for 1 hour (it's more for riders over 200 pounds), cash only. The stables are open daily from 8am to 5pm ('til 6pm in the summer), and you must be at least 6 years old to ride. If you have a rider 5 or younger, you can either opt for the pony rides in Griffith Park (p. 169) or an on-site hand-led ride for kids ages 2 to 5. For private lessons, call ② 818/569-3666.

Another popular horseback riding outfit is **Sunset Ranch,** located at 3400 Beachwood Dr. off of Franklin Avenue, just under the HOLLYWOOD sign. Horse rentals are offered daily from 9am to closing (generally, 5pm) for all levels of riders. The ranch is on the edge of Griffith Park with access to 52 miles of trails. Also available are private night rides (very romantic), dinner rides (see "Sunset Margarita Horse Rides," below), and riding lessons. Rates are $25 for a 1-hour ride and $40 for 2 hours, not including tip. No reservations are required. For more information, call ② 323/469-5450 or log on to www.sunsetranchhollywood.com.

This is so cool. Every night except the Saturday of each month (when they host barbecue nights), the Sunset Ranch Hollywood Stables company hosts the **Dinner Ride.** They saddle you up on a big ol' horse, and then y'all take a scenic 1½-hour ride through Griffith Park—with the city lights shining far below—to the Viva Fresh Mexican restaurant in Burbank (dinner and drinks are not included in the price—plan to eat light since the food is very average). After dinner and a margarita, you ride back to the ranch in the dark. Consider yourself warned, however: Many a sore derriere has wished it hadn't been subjected to 180 minutes in the saddle. $115 for the first person; $85 each additional rider. The ranch is located at the very end of Beachwood Drive off Franklin Avenue, just under the HOLLYWOOD sign. For more information, call ✆ 323/469-5450 or log on to www.sunsetranchhollywood.com.

Closer to the ocean in Topanga Canyon is **Los Angeles Horseback Riding** (2623 Old Topanga Canyon Rd., Topanga; ✆ 818/591-2032; www.lahorseback riding.com), a small, friendly outfit that offers guided Western-style trail rides for beginners to advanced riders. It's situated at the top of a 1,800-foot ridgeline—about a 25-minute drive from Santa Monica—with panoramic views of the ocean and San Fernando Valley (best seen on one of the sunset or full-moon rides). What I like about this outfit is that, if the guide feels that the group is experienced enough, she'll pick up the pace to a canter. Although same-day reservations are sometimes possible, try to book at least 3 days in advance. Kids 6 and older are welcome, and kids 17 and under must wear helmets (bring a bike helmet, if possible). Prices start at about $60 for a 1-hour, guided ride, plus tip; 2-hour canyon rides and full-moon trips are available as well.

SAILING   Marina del Rey, the largest man made marina in the world, is the launching point for **Paradise Bound Yacht Charters** (✆ 800/655-0850; www. aaparadiseboundyacht.com). Book Captain Alex's 42-foot sailing vessel for a minimum of 2 hours for $340 an hour for up to six people. The cost covers the services of captain, crew, a hostess, and soft drinks. Food can be catered, or you can bring your own. Touring options include harbor cruises, coastal and sea-life exploration and more. Captain Alex is a retired Navy vet who commanded 4 warships; in the sailing business since 1990, he enjoys "taking care of and pampering his guests."

SEA KAYAKING   Sea kayaking is all the rage in Southern California, a simple and serene way to explore the southern coastline. **Southwind Kayak Center** (17855 Skypark Circle, Irvine; ✆ 800/768-8494 or 949/261-0200; www.southwindkayaks. com) rents a variety of kayaks, including sit-on-top, sit-inside, foot-peddled, hand-peddled and doubles, for use in the bay or open ocean at its Newport Beach rental base. Rates start at $50 per day; instructional classes are available as scheduled on the website, and pre-registration is required. The center also conducts several easygoing guided outings, including a $55 Back to Nature trip that highlights the marine life around Newport. Visit the website for more details.

SKATING   The 22-mile-long South Beach Trail that runs from Pacific Palisades to Torrance is one of the premier skating spots in the country. In-line skating is especially popular, but conventional skates are often seen here, too. Skating is allowed just about everywhere bicycling is, but be advised that cyclists have the right of way. **JS Rentals,** 1501 Ocean Front Walk, Venice (🕾 310/392-7306), is just one of many places to rent wheels in Venice. In the South Bay, in-line skate rentals are available 1 block from The Strand at **Hermosa Cyclery,** 20 13th St., Hermosa Beach (🕾 310/374-7816; www.hermosacyclery.com). Skates cost $6 per hour ($18 for the day); kneepads and wrist guards come with every rental.

SURFING George Freeth (1883–1918), who first surfed Redondo Beach in 1907, is widely credited with introducing the sport to California. But surfing didn't catch on until the 1950s, when CalTech graduate Bob Simmons invented a more maneuverable lightweight fiberglass board. The Beach Boys and other surf-music groups popularized Southern California in the minds of beach-babes and -dudes everywhere, and the rest, as they say, is history.

If you're a first-timer eager to learn the sport, contact **Learn to Surf L.A.** (🕾 310/663-2479; www.learntosurfla.com). This highly respected school features a team of experienced instructors that will supply all necessary equipment and get you up and riding a foam board on your first day (trust me, it's a blast). Private lessons are $120, and group lessons are $75. Another great source for learning to surf is **Malibu Longboards** (🕾 310/467-6898 or 818/990-7633; www.malibulongboards.com), the official surf instruction for Santa Monica College (don't you wish you'd spent a semester here?). The company offers private lessons for $99 for a single person, about $150 for double, as well as group lessons and 5-day surf camps.

If you want to try it on your own, surfboards are available for rent at shops near all top surfing beaches in the L.A. area. **Zuma Jay Surfboards,** 22775 Pacific Coast Hwy., Malibu (🕾 310/456-8044; www.zumajays.com), Malibu's oldest surf shop, is about a half-mile south of Malibu Pier. Rentals are about $20 per day, plus $10 for wet suits in winter. For more information about surfing in Southern California, log on to www.surfline.com.

TENNIS While soft-surface courts are more popular on the East Coast, hard surfaces are most common in California. If your hotel doesn't have a court and can't suggest any courts nearby, try the well-maintained, well-lit **Griffith Park Tennis Courts,** on Commonwealth Road, just east of Vermont Avenue (🕾 323/662-7772). Call or log on to the website of the **City of Los Angeles Department of Recreation and Parks** (🕾 323/644-3536; www.laparks.org/dos/sports/tennis.htm) to

---

 Segway Rentals in Santa Monica

Those weird-looking upright electronic scooters zipping around the Santa Monica beach scene are coming from the **Segway Los Angeles** rental shop near the Santa Monica Pier at 1660 Ocean Ave., 1 block south of the pier (🕾 310/395-1395; www.segway.la). Riding these personal transporters is a hoot: lean forward, go forward; lean back, go back; stand straight up, stop. Simple. After the free 25-minute lesson it becomes intuitive, and then you're on your own to scoot about the paved shoreline path around Venice Beach and the Santa Monica Pier. It's the closest you'll come to being a celebrity (*everyone* checks you out). A 2-hour rental with lesson is $79 plus tax. Guided tours are available for groups of four or more. *Note:* You have to be at least 18 to rent one solo; the minimum age for kids accompanied by a parent is 12. *Note:* There's a 24-hour cancelation policy.

Spectator Sports

This is *so* only-in-L.A.: Surfing instructor and orthodox rabbi Nachum Shifren hosts "Surf and Soul" sermons on the sand in Santa Monica. Not only will the rabbi teach you how to surf, his wise words will empower you to succeed in this competitive world we live in. Yes, even gentiles are welcome (☏ **310/ 877-1482**; www.surfingrabbi.com).

WHAT TO SEE & DO IN LOS ANGELES

see a long list of free tennis courts or make a reservation at a municipal court near you. *Tip:* Spectators can watch free collegiate matches at the UCLA campus's L.A. Tennis Center from October through May. For a schedule of tournaments, call ☏ **310/206-6831.**

WINDSURFING Invented and patented by Hoyle Schweitzer of Torrance in 1968, windsurfing, or sailboarding, is a fun sport that's much more difficult than it looks. **Long Beach Windsurf & Kayak Center,** 3850 E. Ocean Blvd., Long Beach (☏ **562/433-1014;** www.windsurfcenter.com), offers lessons and rentals in Alamitos Bay. A $199 learner's package includes instruction from 8am to noon and use of board and wet suit.

SPECTATOR SPORTS

BASEBALL The **Los Angeles Dodgers** (☏ **866/DODGERS** [363-4377]; www.dodgers.com), winner of nine National League championships and five World Series titles, play at Dodger Stadium, located at 1000 Elysian Park, near Sunset Boulevard. Watching a game at this old-school ballpark is a great way to spend the day, chomping on Dodger Dogs and basking in the sunshine. Tickets are reasonably priced, too. And even if you can't score tickets, you can still take a 90-minute **"Championship Tour" of Dodger Stadium,** including access to the field, the Dodger Dugout, the Dugout Club, the press box, and the Tommy Lasorda Training Center. Tours are offered Tuesday, Thursday, Saturday, and Sunday at 10 and 11:30am through October. The cost is $15 for adults, $10 for seniors (55 and over) and children 14 and under. You can reserve and purchase tour tickets online at www.dodgers.com (click on "Dodger Stadium," then scroll down to "Stadium Tours").

The **Los Angeles Angels of Anaheim** (☏ **888/796-HALO** [796-4256]; www.laangels.com) play American League ball at Anaheim Stadium, at 2000 Gene Autry Way, about 30 minutes from Downtown L.A. The regular Major League baseball season runs from April to October. Log on to either team's website for ticket information.

BASKETBALL Los Angeles has two NBA franchises: the **L.A. Lakers** (www.lakers.com), who have won 11 NBA titles for the city, and the **L.A. Clippers** (www.clippers.com), who haven't won any. Both teams play in the **Staples Center** in Downtown L.A., 1111 S. Figueroa St. Celebrity fans like Jack Nicholson, Leonardo DiCaprio, Ice Cube, and Dyan Cannon have the best tickets, but this 20,000-seater should have room for you—that is, if you have the big bucks for a Lakers ticket or the interest in watching a Clippers game. The season runs from October to April, with 2 months of playoffs following. For tickets to see either team, call ☏ **213/742-7340** or log on to www.staplescenter.com.

FOOTBALL   Los Angeles suffers from an absence of major-league football, but it gets by just fine with two popular college teams (one of whom many locals refer to either proudly or snidely as our professional team, USC). The college season runs September through November; if you're interested in checking out a game, contact **UCLA Bruins Football** (✆ 310/825-2101; www.uclabruins.com) or **USC Trojans Football** (✆ 213/740-2311; www.usctrojans.com).

HORSE RACING   One of the most beautiful tracks in the country, **Santa Anita Racetrack,** 285 W. Huntington Dr., Arcadia (✆ 626/574-7223; www.santaanita.com), offers racing from late December through mid-April. Set against the majestic San Gabriel Mountains, the track was featured in the Marx Brothers' film *A Day at the Races* and in the 1954 version of *A Star Is Born*. On weekdays during the season, the public is invited to watch morning workouts from 5:30 to 10am at Clockers' Corner. Admission is free; be sure to call or check the website for exact post times. *Tip:* The infield is ideal for picnics (no glass or alcohol), as well as getting an up-close look at the horses and jockeys in action—it even has a children's playground.

Just down the road from LAX, the scenic **Hollywood Park Racetrack,** 1050 S. Prairie Ave., Inglewood (✆ 310/419-1500; www.hollywoodpark.com), with its lakes and flowers, features thoroughbred racing from mid-April to July, as well as from mid-November through mid-December. Opened in 1938, it had shareholders that included movie mogul Harry Warner, Walt Disney, and Bing Crosby. Well-placed monitors project views of the backstretch as well as stop-action replays of photo finishes. Races are usually held Thursday through Sunday. Post times are 1pm in summer (7pm on Fri) and 12:30pm on weekends and holidays. General admission is $8; admission to the clubhouse is $10.

ICE HOCKEY   The **L.A. Kings** (✆ 888/546-4752; www.lakings.com) hold court at their Staples Center home (see above); and down the road in Orange County, the **Anaheim Ducks** (✆ 714/704-2400; www.anaheimducks.com) play at the Honda Center (formerly Arrowhead Pond) in Anaheim. The hockey season typically runs from October through mid-April, with playoffs following. Tickets are available at either arena or through Ticketmaster.

SOCCER   Since its inaugural season in 1996, the **Los Angeles Galaxy** (✆ 877/3-GALAXY [877/342-5299]; www.lagalaxy.com) has already won the Major

---

   Getting Dolled Up

If you thought Roller Derby fanned out in the '70s, you've clearly never heard of the L.A. Derby Dolls (1910 W. Temple Ave.; ✆ 310/285-3766; http://derbydolls.com/la). The all-female league was reconceived in 2003; it's actually become a campy, cult-favorite activity among young hipsters, nostalgia-loving oldsters, and a whole lotta lesbians. More than just a match, it's an experience, complete with food trucks, funky merchandise vendors, raffles, live music, and an official after-party at downtown dive bar La Cita. The event is 21+ only. *Tip:* If you want a more mellow after-party, check out under-the-radar 1642 Beer and Wine bar (1642 Temple St.; ✆ 213/989-6836); it's walking distance from the venue and often where losing team members and locals show up.

polo, ANYONE?

Way back in 1930, cowboy humorist Will Rogers got a hankerin' to play some polo, so he cleared the field in front of his Pacific Palisades home for a friendly match with his ponies and celebrity pals. Shortly after, he started his famed **Will Rogers Polo Club,** and of the 25 polo organizations that existed at the time, his polo field is the only one that remains. Matches are still held on weekends from May through early October, and the bucolic setting of wide green fields, whitewashed fences, and majestic oaks is ideal for a leisurely picnic lunch and a bit of respite from the city. The polo field is located at 501 Will Rogers State Park Rd. in Pacific Palisades, off West Sunset Boulevard. For more information, call the club at © **818/509-9965** or log on to its website at www.willrogerspolo.org (there's a great feature on "How to Watch a Polo Game").

League Soccer Cup and earned a reputation as a major force in MLS. But the big draw these days is soccer superstar David Beckham, who joined the roster in 2007. He and his pop-star wife, Victoria Beckham, made international headlines by making Los Angeles their home. In fact, within the first hour following the announcement, the L.A. Galaxy sold more than 500 home-game tickets. Visitors can catch a regular-season game from March through November at the Home Depot Center, 18400 Avalon Blvd. in Carson. Tickets for individual games are available through the Galaxy box office and Ticketmaster.

THE DISNEYLAND RESORT & KNOTT'S BERRY FARM

Get your theme park vacation on. The Disneyland Resort is the undisputed front-runner in family-friendly vacation destinations in Southern California. A short drive away is another appealing amusement park: Knott's Berry Farm. Hosting a far better selection of high-speed roller coasters, it's hugely popular with teens who crave thrill rides.

THE DISNEYLAND RESORT

33 miles S of Los Angeles

There are newer and sometimes larger Disney parks in Florida, Tokyo, France and Hong Kong, but Disneyland—the original and the inspiration for them all—still opens its gates in Anaheim every day, proudly proclaiming itself "The Happiest Place on Earth." In 2001, Disney unveiled a new sister theme park, Disney's California Adventure, along with the shopping/dining/entertainment district called Downtown Disney.

Attractions & Rides Savvy visitors know to use the FASTPASS system for the park's most popular rides—basically an appointment time so you can skip the lines. For little ones, **It's A Small World** is still timeless. Slightly older kids will love the Jack Sparrow scene in another classic, **Pirates of the Caribbean.** Thrill-seekers can count on Space Mountain, Indiana Jones Adventure, the Matterhorn Bobsleds, Big Thunder Mountain Railroad, plus the California Screamin' rollercoaster at California Adventure, for a good time.

Restaurants & Dining Kids will eat up character-dining opportunities, from Chip and Dale at the **Grand Californian's Storytellers Café** to **Lilo & Stitch's Aloha Breakfast** at the Paradise Pier Hotel, plus **Goofy's Kitchen** at Downtown Disney. For a one-of-a-kind experience, make a reservation at the dimly lit **Blue Bayou,** which is located inside the Pirates attraction. For a more upscale, adult-oriented experience, the

Napa Rose competes with Orange County's best fine-dining establishments; **Catal Restaurant** is quite good as well, and more moderately priced.

Nightlife & Entertainment　Downtown Disney isn't just for kids. In fact, even though most shows at the **House of Blues** are all ages, unaccompanied minors aren't even allowed. The impressive live music venue regularly hosts local heroes like Social Distortion to singer/songwriters, tribute bands and club nights. **ESPN Zone** is technically a restaurant, but really a world-class sports bar with more than 175 TV screens.

Characters & Parades　Disneyland and California Adventure are also known for sensational productions such as the seasonal **FANTASMIC!,** which takes its inspiration from *The Sorcerer's Apprentice,* and mixes magic, music, live performance, floats and special effects. California Adventure's electrifying **World of Color** is a lighting and water-feature feat, showcasing beloved Disney film characters and scenes, and takes place nightly in the Paradise Park lagoon.

Essentials

GETTING THERE　To reach the Disneyland Resort by car from LAX, take I-105 east to I-605 north, then I-5 south. From Downtown Los Angeles, take I-5 south until you see signs for Disneyland. The drive from both Downtown L.A. and LAX takes approximately 40 minutes with no traffic. (Right!)

　If Anaheim is your first—or only—destination and you want to avoid L.A. altogether, consider flying directly into **John Wayne Airport** in Santa Ana (✆ 949/252-5200; www.ocair.com), Orange County's largest airport. It's about 15 miles from Disneyland at the intersection of I-405 and California 55. Check to see if your hotel has a free shuttle to and from either airport (some will pick you up at LAX), or call a shuttle service: **Disneyland Resort Express** (✆ 714/978-8855; www.coach america.com); **Xpress** (✆ 800/427-7483; www.execucarexpress.com); **Prime Time** (✆ 800/733-8267; www.primetimeshuttle.com); or **SuperShuttle** (✆ 800/258-3826; www.supershuttle.com). Car-rental agencies at the John Wayne Airport include **Budget** (✆ 800/527-0700; www.budget.com) and **Hertz** (✆ 800/654-3131; www.hertz.com). To reach Anaheim from John Wayne Airport, take California 55 north to I-5 north, and then take the Harbor Boulevard exit and follow signs to THEME PARKS. You can also catch a ride with **Yellow Cab Co.** (✆ 877/733-3305), whose cabs queue up at the Ground Transportation Center on the airport's lower level (reservations not necessary). Expect the fare to Disneyland to cost about $45.

VISITOR INFORMATION　For information on the **Disneyland Resort,** including show schedules and ride closures that apply to the specific day(s) of your visit, call ✆ 714/781-4565 for automated information or ✆ 714/781-7290 to speak to Guest Relations (but expect a long wait). Better yet, log on to the Disneyland Resort's official website at **www.disneyland.com**.

　For information on the Anaheim region, contact the **Anaheim/Orange County Visitor and Convention Bureau,** 800 W. Katella Ave., inside the Anaheim Convention Center (✆ 714/765-8888; www.anaheimoc.org). It's open Monday to Friday from 8am to 5:30pm. Staffers can fill you in on area activities and shopping, as well as send you their *Official Visitors Guide* and information on the AdventureCard, which offers discounts at dozens of local attractions, hotels, restaurants, and shops.

　You can find out everything you need to know about the Disneyland Resort online, beginning with the official site, **www.disneyland.com**, which contains an interactive

CityPass Savings

If your vacation includes a visit to San Diego, look into purchasing a **Southern California CityPass** (www.citypass.com). It includes a 3-Day Park Hopper ticket to Disneyland and Disney's California Adventure, plus a 1-day admission to Universal Studios Hollywood, Sea-World Adventure Park, and the San Diego Zoo or Wild Animal Park. It costs $276 for adults and $229 for children, and if you visit all these attractions, you'll save more than $90.

trip planner, plus special offers (sometimes on airfare or reduced admission). You can also contact a Walt Disney Travel Company specialist at ☏ **866/60-DISNEY** (603-4763) and ask about money-saving package deals.

Numerous unofficial Disney websites provide very detailed—and often judgmental—information about the Disneyland Resort. The best I've found are **Disneyland: Inside & Out** (www.intercotwest.com), an active and friendly website filled with detailed information on every corner of the Disneyland Resort; **LaughingPlace.com** and **MouseInfo.com**, which both feature daily updated headlines and columns on all things Disney; **Mouseplanet.com**, a comprehensive Disneyland information resource that offers features and reviews by guest writers; and **MouseSavers.com**, which helps users save money on lodging and admissions.

ADMISSION, HOURS & INFORMATION   As of press time, admission to *either* Disneyland or Disney's California Adventure, including unlimited rides and all festivities and entertainment, is $76 for adults and children 10 and over, $68 for children 3 to 9, and free for children 2 and under. Parking is $14. A **1-Day Park Hopper ticket,** which allows you to go back and forth as much as you'd like, is $101 for adults and $91 for children. A **2-day Park Hopper ticket** is $161 for adults and children 10 and over, and $146 for children 3 to 9. Other multiday, multipark combination passes are available as well. In addition, many area accommodations offer lodging packages that include admission for 1 or more days. Be sure to check the Disney website, www.disneyland.com, for seasonal ticket specials.

If you plan on arriving during a busy time (when the gates open in the morning, or 11am–2pm), purchase your tickets in advance and get a jump on the crowds at the ticket counters. Advance tickets may be purchased through Disneyland's website (www.disneyland.com), at Disney stores in the United States, by calling the ticket mail-order line (☏ **714/781-4043**), at any nearby Disneyland Resort Good Neighbor Hotel, or as part of your travel package.

Disneyland and Disney's California Adventure are open every day of the year, but operating hours vary, so be sure to call ☏ **714/781-7290** before your visit. The same information, including ride closures and show schedules, can also be found at **www.disneyland.com**. Generally speaking, the parks are open from 9 or 10am to 6 or 7pm on weekdays, fall to spring; and from 8 or 9am to midnight or 1am on weekends, holidays, and during winter, spring, or summer vacation periods. *Tip:* The park's operating hours can give you some idea of what kinds of crowds Disney planners are expecting: The later the parks close, the more people will be there.

WHEN TO GO   The Disneyland Resort is busiest in summer (btw. Memorial Day and Labor Day), on holidays (Thanksgiving week, Christmas week, Presidents' Day weekend, and Easter week), plus weekends year-round. All other periods are

THE art OF THE (PACKAGE) DEAL

If you intend to spend 2 or more nights in Disney territory, it pays to investigate the bevy of packaged vacation options. Start by logging on to www.disneyland.com to peruse the standard package offers, take a virtual tour of Disney hotel properties, and get online price quotes for customized, date-specific packages—including airline tickets. The packages are value-packed timesavers with abundant flexibility. Rates are highly competitive, considering that each package includes multiday and multi-park admission, plus keepsake souvenirs, preferred seating at Disney shows,

Disney pocket guides, and coupon books. If you're staying in a non-Disney hotel (even those in Los Angeles or San Diego), ask whether they sell Disneyland admission packages; many hotels offer inclusive vacation packages that include Disneyland and Disney's California Adventure (and other attractions). To make sure you're getting the absolute best deal, call the official Disney travel planners at **Walt Disney Travel Co.** (**☏ 866/60-DISNEY** [603-4763] or 714/520-5050) and compare their package deals with the ones you've already been quoted.

considered off season. Peak hours are from noon to 5pm; visit the most popular rides before and after these hours, and you'll cut your waiting times substantially. If you plan to arrive during a busy time, buy your tickets in advance and get a jump on the crowds at the ticket booths. For information on purchasing advance tickets, see "Admission, Hours & Information," above.

Attendance falls dramatically during the winter, so the park offers discounted or two-for-one admission to Southern California residents, who may buy up to five tickets per zip code verification. If you'll be visiting the park with someone who lives here, be sure to take advantage of this promotion.

Another secret timesaving tip is to enter Disneyland from the turnstile at the Monorail Station in Downtown Disney. The line is usually shorter and the Monorail will take you straight into Tomorrowland (but it doesn't stop in Disney's California Adventure). Another timesaver is booking your vacation through the Walt Disney Travel Company—those package guests can enter Mickey's Toontown and Fantasyland 1 hour before the general public.

Many visitors tackle Disneyland (or Disney's California Adventure) systematically, beginning at the entrance and working their way clockwise around the park. My advice: Arrive early and run to the most popular rides—the Indiana Jones Adventure, Star Tours, Big Thunder Mountain Railroad, Splash Mountain, the Haunted Mansion, and Pirates of the Caribbean, all in Disneyland; and Twilight Zone Tower of Terror, Soarin' Over California, California Screamin', Grizzly River Run, and It's Tough to Be a Bug rides in Disney's California Adventure. Waits for these rides can last an hour or more in the middle of the day.

This time-honored plan of attack may eventually become obsolete, thanks to Disney's complimentary **FASTPASS** system. Here's how it works: Say you want to ride Space Mountain, but the line is long—*so* long the current wait sign indicates a 75-minute standby. Instead, you can head to the automated FASTPASS ticket dispenser, where you pop in your park ticket to receive a free voucher listing a computer-assigned boarding time later that day. When you return at the assigned time, you enter through the FASTPASS gate and only have to wait about 10 minutes (to the envy of everyone in the slowpoke line). For a complete list for each park, check your official map/guide when you enter and look for the red FP symbol. **Note:** You can obtain a FASTPASS for only one attraction at a time. Also, the FASTPASS system doesn't eliminate the need to arrive at the theme park early, because there's only a limited supply of FASTPASSes available for each attraction on a given day. So if you don't show up until the middle of the afternoon, you might find that all the FAST-PASSes have been distributed to other guests.

Disneyland ★★★

Disneyland is divided into eight sub-areas or "lands" arranged around a central hub, each of which has a number of rides and attractions that are, more or less, related to that land's theme. Be sure to pick up a free park map on the way in, or you'll probably get lost almost immediately.

MAIN STREET U.S.A.   At the park's entrance, Main Street U.S.A. is an idealized version of a turn-of-the-20th-century American small-town street inspired by Marceline, Missouri (Walt Disney's childhood home), and built on a ⅞ scale. Attention to detail here is exceptional—interiors, furnishings, and fixtures conform to the period. As with any real Main Street, the Disney version is essentially a collection of shops and eating places, with a city hall, a fire station, and an old-time silent cinema. Live performances include piano playing at the Carnation ice-cream parlor and Dapper Dan's barbershop quartet along the street. A mixed-media attraction combines a presentation on the life of Walt Disney (The Walt Disney Story) with a patriotic remembrance of Abraham Lincoln. Horse-drawn trolleys, fire engines, and horseless carriages give rides along Main Street and transport visitors to the central hub (properly known as the Central Plaza).

Because there are no major rides, it's best to tour Main Street during the middle of the afternoon, when lines for rides are longest, and in the evening, when walkways can be packed with visitors viewing Disneyland's parades and shows. Stop in at the information booth to the left of the Main Entrance for a schedule of the day's events.

ADVENTURELAND ★★   Inspired by the most exotic regions of Asia, Africa, India, and the South Pacific, Adventureland is home to several popular rides. Here's where you can cavort inside **Tarzan's Treehouse,** a climb-around attraction based on the animated film. Its neighbor is the **Jungle Cruise,** where passengers board a large, authentic-looking Mississippi River paddleboat and float along an Amazon-like river; a spear's throw away is the **Enchanted Tiki Room,** one of the most sedate attractions in Adventureland. Inside, you can sit down and watch a 20-minute musical comedy featuring electronically animated tropical birds, flowers, and "Tiki gods."

The **Indiana Jones Adventure ★★** is Adventureland's star ride. Based on the Steven Spielberg films, this ride takes adventurers into the Temple of the Forbidden Eye in joltingly realistic all-terrain vehicles. Riders follow Indy and experience the perils of bubbling lava pits, whizzing arrows, fire-breathing serpents, collapsing bridges, and the familiar tumbling boulder (an effect that's very realistic to riders in the front seats).

NEW ORLEANS SQUARE   A large, grassy green dotted with gas lamps, New Orleans Square evokes the French Quarter's timeless charm from antebellum mansions to sidewalk cafes and lakefront terraces. Jazz music wafts through the air, and portrait artists line a cobblestone alley of shops. One of Disneyland's most popular rides, **Pirates of the Caribbean,** is located here; visitors still float on boats through

relax . . . THINK FUN, NOT FRANTIC

It's finally here, the dream vacation to the "Happiest Place on Earth!" Whether you're 6 or 60, it's hard to keep from getting caught up in the excitement, even when you're the one responsible for the (seemingly) endless planning stage.

Once you arrive and enter the theme park(s), kids—and plenty of adults—seem to kick into warp speed. But sensory overload doesn't mean you should abandon common sense. Here are just a few suggestions to avoid common pitfalls:

- **Write Down Your Car's Location:** When you're rushing to jump the tram for the park, it's easy to forget that your section/row/floor looks exactly like dozens of others in the parking lot or structure. Take a second to write down your parking location or snap a photo with your phone.

- **Don't Overplan:** Only the most stubbornly energetic parkgoers (and if you have small children in tow, this is definitely not you) can manage to see everything at Disneyland in 1 day. California Adventure is more manageable, but can also be time-consuming at peak capacity. Agree as a group to several "must-do" rides and activities each day, so no one is disappointed by missing their favorite ride or attraction.

- **Pace Yourself:** Why are those folks running to catch the parking lot tram? Relax, the theme parks aren't going anywhere, and trams run constantly during peak arrival and departure hours. While inside the park, stagger long waits in line with easy-entry shows and rides, and remember to sit with a refreshing drink every now and then. It may seem like a good idea to head right for another "must-do," but even the best ride is less fun if you've been cranky for 45 minutes in line.

- **Set a Spending Limit:** Kids should know they have a certain amount to spend on between-meal snacks and Disney souvenirs, so they'll look around and carefully decide which trinket is the one they can't live without.

- **Dress Comfortably:** We mean *really* comfortably, so you can stay that way throughout a long, hot day with lots of walking and lots of standing. Reliable walking shoes (sneakers or walking sandals are best), layered clothing (a sweat shirt or sweater for evening can be welcome, even in summer), sunblock (yes, even in winter) and a hat and/or sunglasses are all must-haves. And be advised, there are lockers inside the park near the entrance to Main Street, so you needn't weigh yourself down by trying to carry everything you brought—and everything you bought—with you at all times.

mock underground caves, but now one of the major scenes is Captain Jack Sparrow and his cohorts from the hit film franchise doing battle with Davy Jones. The venerable **Haunted Mansion** looms here as well, where the dated effects are more funny than scary. Even in the middle of a sweltering summer day, you can dine by the cool moonlight to the sound of crickets in the **Blue Bayou** restaurant, the only eatery inside Disneyland that requires reservations (stop by early in the day to make yours).

CRITTER COUNTRY   An ode to the backwoods, Critter Country is a sort of Frontierland without those pesky settlers. Older kids and grown-ups head straight for **Splash Mountain ★★**, one of the largest water flume rides in the world. Loosely based on the Disney movie *Song of the South,* the ride is lined with about 100 characters that won't stop singing "Zip-A-Dee-Doo-Dah." Be prepared to get wet, especially if someone sizable is in the front seat of your log-shaped boat. The **Many Adventures of Winnie the Pooh** is a spellbinding children's attraction based on Winnie the Pooh and his friends from the Hundred-Acre Wood—Tigger, Eeyore, Piglet, and the gang. The attraction is of the kindler, gentler sort, where you board "hunny bee-hives" and take a slow-moving journey through the Hundred-Acre Wood in endless pursuit of "hunny." (*Tip:* It's a very popular attraction, so be sure to arrive early or make use of FASTPASS.) While it may not be the fastest ride in the park, **Davy Crockett's Explorer Canoes** allow folks to row around Tom Sawyer Island. It's the only ride where you actively control your boat (no underwater rails!). Hop into replica canoes, grab a paddle, and away you go.

FRONTIERLAND   Inspired by 19th-century America, Frontierland features a raft to **Pirate's Lair at Tom Sawyer's Island,** a do-it-yourself play area with live pirates, island caverns, and rope bridges leading to buried treasure. You'll also find the **Big Thunder Mountain Railroad ★**, a runaway roller coaster that races through a deserted 1870s gold mine. Children will dig the petting zoo, and there's an Abe Lincoln–style log cabin; both are great for exploring with the little ones. This is also where you board one of two riverboats—*Mark Twain* and the *Sailing Ship Columbia*—that navigate the waters around Tom Sawyer Island and Fort Wilderness. Beautiful crafts, the riverboats provide lofty perches from which to see Frontierland and New Orleans Square. The *Sailing Ship Columbia,* however, has far more historic and aesthetic appeal. As with the other river craft, the riverboats suspend operations at dusk.

When it's showing (it's a seasonal presentation), head to Frontierland's **Rivers of America** after dark to see the *FANTASMIC!* show. It mixes magic, music, 50 live performers, floats, and sensational special effects. Just as he did in *The Sorcerer's Apprentice,* Mickey Mouse battles evil and conjures good, using his magical powers to create giant water fountains, enormous flowers, and fantasy creatures. There are plenty of pyrotechnics, lasers, and fog, as well as a brand-new, 45-foot-tall Audio-Animatronic dragon that breathes fire and sets the water of the Rivers of America aflame. New enhancements include a new projection system using HD format.

MICKEY'S TOONTOWN ★   This is a colorful, whimsical world inspired by the film *Who Framed Roger Rabbit?*—a wacky, gag-filled land populated by 'toons. It even looks like a cartoon come to life, a trippy, smile-inducing world without a straight line or right angle in sight. In addition to serving as a place where guests can be certain of finding Disney characters at any time during the day, Mickey's Toontown also serves as an elaborate interactive playground where it's okay for the kids to run, climb, and let off steam. There are several rides and play areas, including **Roger Rabbit's Car-ToonSpin, Donald's Boat, Chip 'n' Dale's Treehouse, Gadget's Go Coaster,** and **Mickey's House & Minnie's House.** *Tip:* Because of its popularity with families, Toontown is most crowded during the day but often deserted after dinnertime.

FANTASYLAND   With a storybook theme, this is the catchall "land" for stuff that doesn't quite fit anywhere else. Most of the rides are geared to the under-6 set, including the **King Arthur Carousel, Mad Tea Party, Dumbo the Flying Elephant ride,** and **Casey Jr. Circus Train.** Some, like **Mr. Toad's Wild Ride** and **Peter Pan's Flight,** appeal to grown-ups as well, and are original attractions from opening day in 1955. You'll also find **Alice in Wonderland, Snow White's Scary Adventures, Pinocchio's Daring Journey,** and more.

The most lauded attraction is **it's a small world,** a slow-moving indoor river ride through a saccharine scenario of all the world's children singing the song everybody loves to hate. (Perhaps the ride would be more entertaining if each person got four softballs on the way in?) For a different kind of thrill, try the **Matterhorn Bobsleds,** a zippy roller coaster through chilled caverns and drifting fog banks. It's one of the park's most popular rides and the world's first steel tubular track roller coaster.

TOMORROWLAND ★   Conceived as an optimistic look at the future, Tomorrowland employs an angular, metallic look popularized by futurists like Jules Verne. Longtime favorites include the revamped **Space Mountain ★** (a pitch-black indoor roller coaster that assaults your equilibrium and ears with its near constant side-to-side motions) and **Star Tours,** the original Disney–George Lucas joint venture, with a 3D update due in the summer of 2011. Those with queasy tendencies should sit out this ride: It's a 40-passenger StarSpeeder that encounters a spaceload of misadventures—achieved with wired seats and video effects—on the way to the Moon of Endor. In the **Finding Nemo Submarine Voyage,** the famous Tomorrowland submarines have resurfaced after a hiatus and now dive the Tomorrowland Lagoon with Marlin and Dory in search of Nemo from the Disney film *Finding Nemo.*

Other Tomorrowland attractions include: **Buzz Lightyear Astro Blasters,** where guests pilot their own Star Cruiser through a comical interactive space mission to conquer the Evil Emperor Zurg; the return of *Captain EO,* the 17-minute interactive film that stars Michael Jackson as Captain EO on his quest to change the world; the **Disneyland Monorail,** a "futuristic" elevated monorail that takes you to Downtown Disney and back again (and offers the only practical opportunity for escaping the park during the crowded lunch period and early afternoon); and **Innoventions,** a huge, busy collection of industry-sponsored hands-on exhibits such as the **Dream Home,** a 5,000-plus-square-foot home belonging to the fictional Elias family that provides a glimpse of the emerging digital advances for future high-tech homes. Exhibits, many of which change each year, demonstrate such products as virtual-reality games, voice-activated appliances, and various digital applications.

Disney's California Adventure ★★

In late 2007, Disney executives announced a multiyear expansion plan for the Disneyland Resort, largely focused on creating some new shows and attractions for Disney's California Adventure. The goal, they said, will be to bring more of Walt Disney into Disney's California Adventure, and to celebrate the hope and optimism of California that attracted Walt to the Golden State in the 1920s.

That said, guests to Disney's California Adventure will notice changes taking place around them through 2012, when the park caps its expansion with the opening of a new Car's Land. Until then, all of Disney's California Adventure's popular attractions will generally continue to operate, but expect a few construction fences guiding guests around development sites.

From the entrance, visitors head into four themed "districts," each with rides, interactive attractions, live-action shows, and plenty of dining, snacking, and shopping.

THE GOLDEN STATE ★★   This multidimensional area represents California's history, heritage, and physical attributes. Sound boring? Actually, the park's splashiest attractions are here. **Condor Flats** is a tribute to daring aviators; inside a weathered corrugated test-pilots' hangar is **Soarin' Over California** ★★★, the simulated hang-glider ride that immediately rose to the top on everyone's "ride first" list (I highly recommend FASTPASSing it). It uses cutting-edge technology to combine elevated seats with a spectacular IMAX-style surround-movie—riders literally "soar" over California's scenic lands, feeling the Malibu ocean breeze and smelling the Central Valley orange groves and Yosemite pines.

Nearby, California Adventure's iconic Grizzly Peak towers over the **Grizzly River Run** ★, a splashy gold-country ride through caverns, mine shafts, and water slides; it culminates with a wet plunge into a spouting geyser. Kids can cavort nearby on the **Redwood Creek Challenge Trail,** a forest playground with smoke-jumper cable slides, net climbing, and swaying bridges.

Pacific Wharf was inspired by Monterey's Cannery Row and features mouthwatering demonstration attractions by **Boudin Sourdough Bakery** and **Mission Tortillas.** If you get hungry, each has a food counter where you can enjoy either soup in a sourdough bowl or tacos, burritos, and enchiladas.

PARADISE PIER ★★   Journey back to the glory days of California's beachfront amusement piers—remember Santa Monica, Santa Cruz, and Belmont Park?—on this fantasy boardwalk. Highlights include **California Screamin'** ★★, a classic roller coaster that replicates the whitewashed wooden white-knucklers of the past—but with state-of-the-art steel construction and a smooth, computerized ride that catapults you from zero to 55 mph in less than 5 seconds, then takes a loop-de-loop over the boardwalk. There's also the **Silly Symphony Swings,** a wave swinger themed to Disney's Band Concert; **Mulholland Madness,** a wacky, wild trip along L.A.'s precarious hilltop street that is way scarier than it looks; and **Mickey's Fun Wheel,** featuring unique zigzagging cars that bring a new twist to the familiar ride. Guests can don 3-D glasses as they "shrink" to the size of a toy and hop into fanciful vehicles that travel and twist along a midway-themed route in **Toy Story Mania.** Upon arriving at each game booth, you aim for animated targets using your onboard "toy cannon." The newest addition to the area is a nighttime water spectacular: **World of Color.** Disney animation comes to life in a combination of hundreds of fountains, dazzling LED-produced colors, and a kaleidoscope of audio and visual effects—all projected onto a large water screen.

Paradise Pier also has all the familiar boardwalk games (complete with stuffed prizes); guilty-pleasure fast foods like pizza, corn dogs, and burritos; plus a full-service ocean-themed restaurant called **Ariel's Grotto.**

HOLLYWOOD PICTURES BACKLOT ★★   If you've visited Disney in Florida, you might recognize many elements of this *trompe l'oeil* re-creation of a Hollywood movie studio lot. One of the resort's most anticipated attractions since expanding is the **Twilight Zone Tower of Terror** ★★★. This truly scary ride has been a huge hit since its debut at Walt Disney World. Legend has it that during a violent storm on Halloween night 1939, lightning struck the Hollywood Tower Hotel, causing an entire wing and an elevator full of people to disappear, and you're about to retrace their steps from that fateful night as you become the star in a special Disney episode of . . . *The Twilight Zone.* In this eerily vacant hotel, you tour the lobby, library, and boiler room, and ultimately board the elevator to plunge 13 stories to the fifth dimension and beyond.

The Backlot's other main attraction is *Disney Channel Rocks!,* featuring songs from *Hannah Montana, High School Musical,* and more. Other popular shows include **Monsters, Inc. Mike & Sully to the Rescue!,** where guests ride taxis through Monstropolis on a mission to safely return "Boo" to her bedroom; and **Jim Henson's MuppetVision 3D ★,** an on-screen comedy romp featuring Kermit, Miss Piggy, Gonzo, and Fozzie Bear. Although it's not nearly as entertaining as **It's Tough to Be a Bug** (see below), it has its moments and won't scare the bejesus out of little kids.

At the end of the street, the replica movie palace **Hyperion Theater** presents Broadway-caliber live-action shows of classic Disney films. In the **Disney Animation** building, visitors can participate in different interactive galleries and learn how stories become animated features as told by Disney artists in the Drawn to Animation studio.

A Bug's Land ★ This bug-themed land encompasses **It's Tough to Be a Bug ★★,** **Flik's Fun Fair,** and **Bountiful Valley Farm.** Inspired by the movie *A Bug's Life, It's Tough to Be a Bug* uses 3-D technology to lead the audience on an underground romp in the insect kingdom with bees, termites, grasshoppers, stink bugs, spiders, and a few surprises that keep everyone hopping, ducking, and laughing along. (I could see how little kids might find the show terrifying, however.) The **Flik's Fun Fair** area features bug-themed rides and a water playground designed especially for little ones ages 4 to 7—but sized so their parents can ride along, too. **Bountiful Farm** pays tribute to California's agriculture.

Downtown Disney District ★

Borrowing a page from central Florida's successful Disney compound, the **Downtown Disney District** is a colorful (and very sanitized) "street scene" filled with restaurants, shops, and entertainment for all ages. Options abound: Window-shop with kids in tow, have an upscale dinner for two, or party into the night. The promenade begins at the amusement park gates and stretches toward the Disneyland Hotel; there are nearly 20 shops and boutiques, and a dozen-plus restaurants, live music venues, and entertainment options.

Highlights include **House of Blues,** the blues-jazz restaurant/club that features Delta-inspired cuisine, big-name musicians, and the hand-clapping Sunday Gospel Brunch; **Ralph Brennan's Jazz Kitchen,** a spicy mix of New Orleans traditional foods and live jazz; **ESPN Zone,** the ultimate sports, dining, and entertainment experience, including an interactive game room with a rock-climbing wall; and **World of Disney,** one of the biggest Disney shopping experiences anywhere, with a vast and diverse range of toys, souvenirs, and collectibles. There is also an AMC Theatres 12-screen multiplex, the LEGO Imagination Center, a Sephora cosmetics store, and more.

Where to Stay

For vacation packages at any of the Disneyland Resort hotels, call the Walt Disney Travel Company at **866/60-DISNEY** (603-4763).

VERY EXPENSIVE

The Disneyland Hotel ★★ ☺ The Holy Grail of Disney-goers has always been this, the "Official Hotel of the Magic Kingdom." A monorail connection via Downtown Disney means you'll be able to return to your room anytime, whether to take a

Sneak Preview

Stop by the "Blue Sky Cellar," a converted "aging room" in the Golden
Wine Vinery that now hosts a terrific
preview of all the changes coming to
Disney's California Adventures. It's
updated frequently by Disney's Imagi-
neers and provides a behind-the-scenes
look at the future development projects.

much-needed nap or to change your soaked shorts after riding Splash Mountain. The
theme hotel is an attraction unto itself and is the best choice for families with small
children. The rooms in the midst of a full-scale "reimagination," which will be completed in early 2012; each of the three towers will reflect a distinct "land" within the
park (Adventureland, Fantasyland, and Frontierland). The look will be stylish, but
still family-friendly—down to headboards featuring Sleeping Beauty's Castle with
illuminated fireworks. In-room amenities include movie channels (with free Disney
Channel, naturally) and even Disneyland-themed toiletries and accessories such as
Sneezy on the tissue box. The resort has several restaurants (see below for a review
of **Goofy's Kitchen**), snack bars, and cocktail lounges; every kind of service desk
imaginable; a video-game center; and the Never Land Pool Complex with a white-
sand beach and separate adult pool nearby.

1150 Magic Way, Anaheim, CA 92802. www.disneyland.com. *℘* **714/956-MICKEY** (956-6425) or 778-
6600. Fax 714/956-6582. 990 units. $255–$345 double; from $750 suite. 2-night minimum stay. AE, MC,
V. Valet parking $22; self-parking for up to 2 cars $15. **Amenities:** 2 restaurants; 1 lounge; children's
programs; concierge; small fitness center; Jacuzzi; 3 outdoor pools (including adults-only pool); room
service. *In room:* A/C, TV, fridge, hair dryer, free Wi-Fi.

Disney's Grand Californian Hotel & Spa ★★ ☺ Disney didn't miss the
details when constructing this enormous version of an Arts and Crafts–era lodge
(think Yosemite's Ahwahnee and Pasadena's Gamble House), hiring craftspeople
throughout the state to contribute one-of-a-kind tiles, furniture, sculpture, and artwork. Taking inspiration from California's redwood forests, mission pioneers, and
plein-air painters, designers created a nostalgic yet state-of-the-art high-rise hotel that
has its own private entrance into Disney's California Adventure park and Downtown
Disney District.

Guest rooms are spacious and smartly designed, carrying through the Arts and
Crafts theme surprisingly well considering the hotel's grand scale. The best ones
overlook the park, but you'll pay for that view. Despite the sophisticated air of the
Grand Californian, this is a hotel that truly caters to families, with a bevy of room
configurations including one with a double bed plus bunk beds with a trundle. Since
the hotel provides sleeping bags (rather than rollaways) for kids, this standard-size
room will sleep a family of five—but you have to share the bathroom. *Tip:* Ask for a
free upgrade to a room with a view of the park when you check in—they're pretty
generous about this, space-permitting.

The hotel's two main restaurants are the upscale **Napa Rose** and the **Storytellers
Cafe,** a "character dining" restaurant that's always bustling with excited kids who pay
more attention to Chip and Dale than their eggs and bacon (be sure to make a breakfast reservation). Also on the property is **Mandara Spa,** offering a complete array of
spa services for men and women.

1600 S. Disneyland Dr., Anaheim, CA 92802. www.disneyland.com. *℘* **714/956-MICKEY** (956-6425) or
635-2300. Fax 714/956-6099. 948 units. $300–$500 double; from $600 suite. AE, DC, DISC, MC, V.

Valet parking $22; self-parking $15. **Amenities:** 2 restaurants; lounge; children's center; concierge; concierge-level rooms; Jacuzzi; 2 outdoor pools; room service; spa. *In room:* A/C, TV, fridge, hair dryer, free Wi-Fi.

EXPENSIVE

Disney's Paradise Pier Hotel ★ ☺

The whimsical beach boardwalk theme of this 15-story hotel ties in with the Paradise Pier section of Disney's California Adventure park across the street. The surfer theme salutes the heyday of seaside amusement parks with nautical and beach decor in the guest rooms, nostalgic California artwork, and a water slide modeled after the wooden roller coasters of yesteryear. Book a room at this smallest Disney property only if the other two are full—it's not as "magical" as the original Disneyland Hotel and is soundly trounced by the superlative Grand Californian. It's also not as centrally located as the other two hotels, which could be a problem if you're not fond of walking. It does, however, offer "family suites" that comfortably accommodate families of six or more, as well as Lilo & Stitch's Aloha Breakfast featuring island songs and tableside visits at the hotel's **PCH Grill.** Kids even get to make their own pizzas (pseudo–breakfast pizzas with peanut butter and gummy bears and such, or, for lunch/dinner, traditional pizzas baked in the kitchen oven). *Tip:* Request a room that either overlooks the Paradise Pier section of California Adventure or has direct access to the poolside cabanas.

1717 S. Disneyland Dr., Anaheim, CA 92802. www.disneyland.com. ⓒ **714/956-MICKEY** (956-6425) or 999-0990. Fax 714/956-6582. 489 units. $250–$350 double; from $400 suite. AE, MC, V. Valet parking $22; Self-parking $15. **Amenities:** 2 restaurants; lounge; children's programs; fitness center; Jacuzzi; outdoor pool; room service.*In room:* A/C, TV, fridge, hair dryer, Wi-Fi.

Sheraton Anaheim Hotel ★

This hotel rises to the festive theme-park occasion with its fanciful English Tudor architecture; it's a castle that lures business conventions, Disney-bound families, and local high school proms. The public areas are quiet and elegant—intimate gardens with fountains and koi ponds, and a plush lobby and lounges—which can be a pleasing touch after a frantic day at the amusement park. The rooms are modern and unusually spacious, but otherwise not distinctive. A large swimming pool sits in the center of the complex, surrounded by attractive landscaping. Book suites well in advance; they are often the first room types to go due to the busy conference schedule during the week and families coming in on weekends.

900 S. Disneyland Dr. (at I-5), Anaheim, CA 92802. ⓒ **800/325-3535** or 714/778-1700. Fax 714/535-3889. www.sheraton.com. 489 units. $149–$225 double; $300 suite. AE, DC, MC, V. Parking $10; free Disneyland shuttle. **Amenities:** 1 restaurant; lounge; concierge; fitness center; Jacuzzi; outdoor pool; room service; Wi-Fi (free, in lobby). *In room:* A/C, TV, hair dryer, minibar, Wi-Fi ($9.95 per day).

MODERATE

The Anabella Hotel ★

Uniting several formerly independent low-rise hotels across the street from Disney's California Adventure, the developers behind the Anabella started from scratch, gutting each building to create carefully planned rooms for park-bound families and business travelers alike. The complex features a vaguely mission-style facade of whitewashed walls and red-tiled roofs, though guest room interiors are strictly contemporary in style and modern in appointments. Bathrooms are generously sized and outfitted in honey-toned granite; most have a tub/shower combo—just a few are shower-only. Though parking areas dot the grounds, you'll also find a pleasant garden around the central swimming pool and whirlpool; a separate adult pool hides out next to the street-side fitness room. Business travelers will appreciate the in-room executive desks with high-speed Internet access, while families can take advantage of "kids' suites" complete with bunk beds and separate bedrooms. There's a pleasant indoor-outdoor all-day restaurant, and the hotel is a stop on both the Disney and Convention Center shuttle routes. *Note:* Rooms and rates vary wildly in terms of room size, layout, and occupancy limits; extra time spent at the hotel's website and with the reservationist will pay off in meeting your needs.

1030 W. Katella Ave. (at S. West St.), Anaheim, CA 92802. www.anabellahotel.com. © **800/863-4888** or 714/905-1050. Fax 714/905-1055. 360 units. $99–$209 double. AE, DC, DISC, MC, V. Parking $12. **Amenities:** Restaurant; lounge; concierge; exercise room; Jacuzzi; 2 outdoor heated pools (including adults-only pool); room service. *In room:* A/C, TV, fridge, hair dryer, Wi-Fi ($9.95 per day).

Anaheim Plaza Hotel & Suites ★ 🍴

Although it's located across the street from the Disneyland Resort's main gate, you'll appreciate the way this hotel's clever design shuts out the noisy world. In fact, the seven two-story garden buildings remind me more of 1960s Waikiki than busy Anaheim (maybe it's the palm trees). A key feature is the Olympic-size heated outdoor pool and adjacent whirlpool. The furnishings are motel-bland, but you won't spend much time here anyway. On the plus side, little has changed about the friendly rates, which often drop as low as $69.

1700 S. Harbor Blvd. (at Katella Ave.), Anaheim, CA 92802. www.anaheimplazahotel.com. © **800/631-4144** or 714/772-5900. Fax 714/772-8386. 300 units. $89–$129 double; from $178 suite. AE, DC, DISC, MC, V. Parking $4.60. **Amenities:** Restaurant; lounge; Jacuzzi; large outdoor heated pool; room service (only at breakfast). *In room:* A/C, TV, hair dryer, Wi-Fi ($9.95 per day).

Portofino Inn & Suites ★★ ☺

This complex of low- and high-rise all-suite buildings sports a cheery yellow exterior and family-friendly interior. The location couldn't be better—directly across the street from California Adventure's back side. You can either walk or take the ART (Anaheim Resort Transit) to the front gate. Designed to work as well for business travelers from the nearby Convention Center as for Disney-bound families, the Portofino offers contemporary, stylish furnishings as well as vacation-friendly rates and suites for any family configuration. Families will want a Kids' Suite, which features bunk beds and a sleeper sofa, plus a TV, fridge, and microwave—and that's just in the kids' room. Mom and Dad have a separate bedroom with grown-up comforts like a double vanity, shower massage, and their own TV. Parking and complimentary Internet access are included in the daily resort fee of $9.50.

1831 S. Harbor Blvd. (at Katella Ave.), Anaheim, CA 92802. www.portofinoinnanaheim.com. © **800/398-3963** or 714/782-7600. Fax 714/782-7619. 190 units. $109–$169 double; $132–$259 suite. AE, DC, DISC, MC, V. **Amenities:** Exercise room; Jacuzzi; outdoor heated pool; arcade. *In room:* A/C, TV, hair dryer.

INEXPENSIVE

Candy Cane Inn ★★ 🍴

Take your standard U-shaped motel court with outdoor corridors, spruce it up with cobblestone drives and walkways along with old-time streetlamps, add flowering vines engulfing room balconies, and you have the Candy Cane. The face-lift worked, making this gem near Disneyland's main gate a treat for the stylish bargain hunter. The rooms are decorated in bright floral motifs with comfortable furnishings, including queen-size beds and a separate dressing and vanity area. Breakfast is served in the courtyard, where you can also splash around in a heated pool, whirlpool, or kids' wading pool. If you feel like splurging, request one of the Premium Rooms with extended checkout and nightly turndown service.

1747 S. Harbor Blvd., Anaheim, CA 92802. www.candycaneinn.net. © **800/345-7057** or 714/774-5284. Fax 714/772-1305. 171 units. $95–$179 double. Rates include expanded continental breakfast. AE, DC,

Healthy Snack Options

As a welcome relief to those ubiquitous salty, sugary junk-food stands, both the Disneyland and California Adventure parks offer several bastions of healthful snacking: rustic wooden **fruit stands** teeming with a variety of quality seasonal fresh fruit and juices that sell for a fraction of the price you'd pay for a hot dog, fries, and a Coke. Ask a Disney "Cast Member" (any employee) for the location of the nearest stand.

DISC, MC, V. Free parking and Disneyland shuttle. **Amenities:** Exercise room; Jacuzzi; outdoor heated pool and wading pool. *In room:* A/C, TV, fridge, hair dryer, Wi-Fi (free).

Travelodge Anaheim   Located on the backside of Disneyland, this modest hotel appeals to the budget-conscious traveler who's looking for plenty of free perks such as Wi-Fi and continental breakfast. All rooms have a refrigerator and microwave, and you can relax by the large outdoor heated pool and Jacuzzi while using the laundry room. The extra-large family rooms accommodate virtually any brood, and the public ART shuttles run regularly to the park. *Tip:* Request a Star Light room, in which "stars" appear when you turn off the lights at night (it's free!).

1057 W. Ball Rd., Anaheim, CA 92802. www.travelodge.com. © **800/578-7878** or 714/774-7600. Fax 714/535-6953. 95 units. $90–$110 double; $115 family room with 3 queen-size beds. Rates include full breakfast. AE, DC, DISC, MC, V. Free parking. **Amenities:** Jacuzzi; outdoor heated pool. *In room:* A/C, TV, fridge, hair dryer, free Wi-Fi.

Where to Eat

There's nothing quite like an energetic family vacation to build an appetite, and sooner or later, you'll have to make the inevitable Disney dining decisions: where, when, and for how much? The expanded Disneyland Resort has something for everyone, a respectable lineup that can easily meet your needs for the duration of the typical visit. Until recently, dining options were pretty sparse, limited to those inside Disneyland and some old standbys at the Disneyland Hotel. But Disney's big expansion upped the ante with national theme/concept restaurants along Downtown Disney and competitive dining options at the resort hotels. The best of the bunch are reviewed below. For dining reservations at any place throughout the Disneyland Resort, call © **714/781-DINE** (781-3463).

EXPENSIVE

Napa Rose ★★★ CALIFORNIAN   In the upscale Grand Californian Hotel, Napa Rose is the first really serious (read: on "foodie" radar) restaurant at the resort. Its warm and light dining room mirrors the Arts and Crafts style of the hotel, down to Frank Lloyd Wright stained-glass windows and Craftsman-inspired seating. Executive chef Andrew Sutton was lured away from Napa's chic Auberge du Soleil, bringing with him a wine-country sensibility and passion for fresh California ingredients and inventive preparations. You can see him busy in the impressive open exhibition kitchen, showcasing specialty items like Sierra golden trout, artisan cheeses from Humboldt County and the Gold Country, and the Sonoma rabbit in Sutton's signature braised mushroom-rabbit tart. The tantalizing Seven Sparkling Sins starter platter (for two) features jewel-like portions of foie gras, caviar, oysters, lobster, and other exotic delicacies; the same attention to detail is evident in seasonally composed main-course standouts like grilled yellowtail with tangerine-basil fruit salsa atop savory couscous, or free-range veal osso buco in rich bacon-and-forest-mushroom ragout. Leave room for dessert, to at least share one of pastry chef Jorge Sotelo's creative treats. Napa Rose boasts an impressive and balanced wine list, with 60 by-the-glass choices (and 40-plus sommeliers, the most of any restaurant in the world). Outdoor seating is arranged around a rustic fire pit, facing a landscaped arroyo and California Adventure's distinctive Grizzly Peak. *Tip:* My favorite place to sit is at the counter facing the exhibition kitchen. Also, you can skip all the pomp and circumstance of a full sit-down meal by dining at the restaurant's lounge, which offers full menu service.

1600 S. Disneyland Dr. (in Disney's Grand Californian Hotel). ☏ **714/300-7170.** www.disneyland.com. Reservations strongly recommended. Main courses $26–$40. AE, DC, DISC, MC, V. Daily 11:30am–2pm and 5:30–10pm.

MODERATE

Catal Restaurant/Uva Bar ★★ MEDITERRANEAN/TAPAS

Branching out from the acclaimed Patina restaurant in Los Angeles, high-priest-of-cuisine Joachim Splichal brings us this Spanish-inspired Mediterranean concept duo at the heart of Downtown Disney. The main restaurant, Catal, features a series of intimate second-floor rooms that combine rustic Mediterranean charm with fine dining. Complemented by an international wine list, the menu is a collage of flavors that borrow from France, Spain, Italy, Greece, Morocco, and the Middle East—all united in selections that manage to be intriguing but not overwhelming. Though the menu will vary seasonally, expect to find selections like braised lamb shoulder with spicy red lentil curry, chorizo-spiked Spanish paella, or roasted half chicken with savoy cabbage and Dijon mustard jus. The Uva Bar (*uva* means "grape" in Spanish) is a casual tapas bar at an outdoor courtyard in the middle of the Downtown Disney walkway. Martinis are a standout, and there are 40 different wines by the glass. The affordable menu echoes the pan-Mediterranean influence, even offering many items from the Catal menu; standouts include cabernet-braised short ribs atop horseradish mashed potatoes, marinated olives, and cured Spanish ham; and Andalusian gazpacho with rock shrimp.

Note: For an even more casual Italian experience—and one that's considerably more kid-friendly—try **Naples Ristorante e Pizzeria** (1550 Downtown Disney Dr., [**714/776-6200**]), also a Patina Group restaurant. There are 2-dozen thin crust pizzas, plus sandwiches and salads. 1580 Disneyland Dr. (at Downtown Disney). ☏ **714/774-4442.** www.disneyland.com. Reservations recommended Sun–Thurs, not accepted Fri–Sat for Catal; not accepted for Uva Bar. Main courses $23–$34; tapas $8–$12. AE, DC, DISC, MC, V. Daily 8am–10pm.

Goofy's Kitchen ☺ AMERICAN

Your younger kids will never forgive you if they miss an opportunity to dine with their favorite Disney characters at this colorful, lively restaurant inside the Disneyland Hotel. Known for its entertainment and wacky and off-center Toontown-esque decor, Goofy's Kitchen features tableside visits by a rotating selection of Disney characters (always Goofy, but also may include Jasmine, Pinocchio, or Cinderella), who thrill the youngsters with dancing, autograph signing, and up-close-and-personal encounters. Meals are buffet-style and offer an adequate selection of crowd pleasers and reliable standbys, from made-to-order omeletes at brunch to Prime rib, salmon, Caesar salad, and pastas at dinner. The most popular kid food is the peanut butter pizza (even for breakfast), the buffet of desserts, Mickey Mouse–shaped waffles, and Mickey ear-shaped chicken nuggets. This place isn't really about the food, though, and is definitely *not* for kidless grown-ups (unless you're trying to make up for a deprived childhood). Bring a camera and Disney autograph book for capturing the family's "candid" encounters. *Tip:* Make reservations for an early or late breakfast or dinner to avoid the mayhem.

1150 Magic Way (inside the Disneyland Hotel). ☎ **714/956-6755** or 781-DINE (781-3463). www.disneyland.com. Reservations recommended. Buffet dinner $32 adult, $14 children 3–9; buffet brunch $26 adults, $14 children 3–9. AE, DC, DISC, MC, V. Daily 7am–1pm and 5–9pm.

House of Blues AMERICAN/SOUTHERN   For years, fans have been comparing the House of Blues locations in Las Vegas, L.A., Orlando, and so forth to Disneyland, so this celeb-backed restaurant/nightclub fits right in. The Anaheim HOB follows the calculated backwoods-bayou-meets-Country-Bear-Jamboree formula, and features Delta-inspired stick-to-your-ribs cuisine like gumbo, pan-seared voodoo shrimp, Creole seafood jambalaya, cornmeal-crusted catfish, baby back ribs glazed with Jack Daniel's sauce, and spicy Cajun meatloaf—plus some out-of-place Cal-lite stragglers like fresh catch of the day and wild mushroom penne pasta Sunday's Gospel Brunch is an advance-ticket event of hand-clapping, foot-stomping proportions. HOB's state-of-the-art Music Hall is a welcome addition to the local music scene (advance tickets are highly recommended for big-name bookings).

1530 S. Disneyland Dr. (at Downtown Disney). ☎ **714/778-2583.** www.hob.com. Reservations not accepted for restaurant (tickets required for performances). Main courses $18–$29. AE, DC, DISC, MC, V. Daily 11am–1:30am.

Rainforest Cafe ☺ INTERNATIONAL   Designed to suggest ancient temple ruins in an overgrown Central American jungle, this national chain favorite successfully combines entertainment, retail, and family-friendly dining in one fantasy setting. There are cascading waterfalls inside and out, a canopy of lush vegetation, simulated tropical mists, and even a troupe of colorful parrots beckoning shoppers into the Retail Village. Once seated, diners choose from an amalgam of wildly flavored dishes inspired by Caribbean, Polynesian, Latin, Asian, and Mediterranean cuisines. Masquerading under exotic-sounding names like Shrimpkins (a kids' menu staple of popcorn shrimp and "Jurassic" chicken tidbits) and Mojo Bones (barbecued pork ribs), the food is really fairly familiar: A translated sampling includes Cobb salad, pita sandwiches, pot stickers, shrimp-studded pasta, and charbroiled chicken. Fresh-fruit smoothies and tropical specialty cocktails are offered, as is a best-shared dessert called the Giant Chocolate Volcano. There's a children's menu, and the Rainforest Cafe is one of the few Downtown Disney eateries to have full breakfast service.

1515 S. Disneyland Dr. (at Downtown Disney). ☎ **714/772-0413.** www.rainforestcafe.com. Reservations recommended for peak mealtimes. Main courses $13–$20. AE, DC, DISC, MC, V. Sun–Thurs 8am–11pm; Fri–Sat 8am–midnight.

Ralph Brennan's Jazz Kitchen ★★ CAJUN/CREOLE   If you always thought Disneyland's New Orleans Square was just like the real thing, wait until you see this fun Southern concept restaurant at Downtown Disney. Ralph Brennan, of the New Orleans food dynasty responsible for NOLA landmarks like Commander's Palace and a trio of Big Easy hot spots, commissioned a handful of New Orleans artists to create the handcrafted furnishings that give the Jazz Kitchen its believable French Quarter ambience. Lacy wrought-iron grillwork, cascading ferns, and trickling stone fountains enhance three separate dining choices: The upstairs Carnival Club is an elegant dining salon with silk-draped chandeliers and terrace dining that overlooks the "street scene" below; casual Flambeaux is downstairs, where a bead-encrusted grand piano hints at the nightly live jazz that sizzles in this room; and the Creole Cafe is a quick stop for necessities like muffulettas or beignets. Expect traditional Cajun-Creole fare with heavy-handed seasonings and rich, heart-stopping sauces.

1590 S. Disneyland Dr. (at Downtown Disney). ✆ **714/776-5200.** www.rbjazzkitchen.com. Reservations strongly recommended. Main courses $19–$33; cafe items $6.99–$9.99. AE, DC, DISC, MC, V. Mon–Thurs 11am–10pm; Fri–Sat 11am–11pm; Sun 10am–10pm.

INEXPENSIVE

Tortilla Jo's ☺ MEXICAN   The offerings at this indoor/outdoor eatery are diverse enough to appeal to kids—they get their menu of mini soft tacos and quesadillas—and upscale enough to attract hungry adults (did I mention there are also more than 100 tequilas to choose from?). Guacamole is prepared fresh to-order; if you like it spicy, ask the kitchen to add jalapeños. As the name might suggest, the tortillas are handmade here. Fajitas are a favorite, as are citrus-braised pork carnitas.

1510 Disneyland Dr., (at Downtown Disney). ✆ **714/535-5000.** www.patinagroup.com. Main courses $12–$19. AE, DISC, MC, V. Sun–Thurs 11am–9pm; Fri–Sat 11am–10pm.

KNOTT'S BERRY FARM

30 miles SE of Downtown Los Angeles

Although destined to forever be in the shadow of Mickey's megaresort, the reality is that Knott's doesn't even attempt to compete with the Disney empire; instead, it targets Southern California thrill-seekers (droves of them) by offering a far better selection of scream-inducing thrill rides.

Like Disneyland, Knott's Berry Farm is not without historical background. In 1920 Walter Knott began farming 20 acres of leased land on Hwy. 39 (now Beach Blvd.). When things got tough during the Depression, Mrs. Knott began selling pies, preserves, and home-cooked chicken dinners. Within a year, she was selling 90 meals a day. Lines became so long that Walter decided to create an Old West Ghost Town—America's first theme park—in 1940 as a diversion for waiting customers.

Today Knott's amusement park offers a whopping 165 shows, attractions, and state-of-the-art rides that are far more intense than most of the rides at the Disneyland Resort. Granted, it's less than half the size of the Disney Resort, but if you're more into fast-paced amusement rides than swirling teacups, it offers twice the thrill.

Essentials

GETTING THERE   Knott's Berry Farm is at 8039 Beach Blvd. in Buena Park. It's about a 10-minute ride north on I-5 from Disneyland. From I-5 or California 91, exit south onto Beach Boulevard. The park is about a half-mile south of California 91.

The **Buena Park Convention and Visitors Office,** 6601 Beach Blvd., Ste. 200, Buena Park (© **714/562-3560;** www.buenapark.com), provides specialized information on the area, including Knott's Berry Farm. To learn more about the amusement park before you arrive, call © **714/220-5200** or log on to **www.knotts.com**.

ADMISSION PRICES & OPERATING HOURS Admission to the park, including unlimited access to all rides, shows, and attractions, is $57 for "Regular" (ages 12 and up), $25 for Junior (ages 3–11) and seniors 62 and older, and free for children 2 and under. Admission after 4pm (on any day the park is open past 6pm) is $29 for Regular and $25 for Junior. Parking is $12. Tickets can also be purchased at many Southern California hotels, where discount coupons are sometimes available.

Like Disneyland, Knott's offers discounted admission—$47—for Southern California residents with zip codes 90000 through 93599, so if you're bringing local friends or family members along, try to take advantage of the bargain. Always check the website for deals and discounts, too. Also like Disneyland, Knott's Berry Farm's hours vary from week to week, so call ahead. The park generally opens daily at 10am and closes at 6 or 7pm, except Saturdays, when it stays open until 10pm. Operating hours and prices often change with seasonal promotions, so it's always a good idea to call Knott's Info at © **714/220-5200** for specific hours on the day you plan to visit. Stage shows and special activities are scheduled throughout the day; pick up a schedule at the ticket booth.

Touring the Park

Despite all the high-tech multimillion-dollar rides, Knott's Berry Farm maintains much of its original Old West motif and also features the Peanuts gang: Snoopy, Charlie Brown, Woodstock, and pals are the official costumed characters of Knott's. The park is divided into five themed areas, each one of which features at least one of the thrill roller coasters that are the Knott's claim to fame. The MarketPlace is located adjacent to, but outside of, the theme park, and features 14 unique shops and restaurants, including the original favorite, Mrs. Knott's Chicken Dinner Restaurant, and a T.G.I. Friday's. They've also added a Pink's (© 714/220-5084; www.pinkshollywood.com); the Hollywood hot dog legend, for which people stand in lines wrapped around Melrose, now has a home in the OC. Serving the same great hot dogs and extras, Pink's 72-year tradition is the perfect addition to Knott's casual MarketPlace.

GHOST TOWN

The park's original attraction is a collection of authentic 19th-century buildings relocated from deserted Old West towns in Arizona and California. You can pan for gold, ride an authentic stagecoach, take rickety train cars through the Calico Mine, and get held up aboard the Calico Railroad. If you love wooden roller coasters, don't miss the clackity GhostRider.

Bigfoot Rapids ★★   The longest of its kind in the world, this $10-million, 3½-acre ride is styled like a turn-of-the-20th-century California wilderness park with a raging white-water river, cascading waterfalls, soaring geysers, and old-style ranger stations. Climb aboard a six-seat circular raft and prepare to be bounced, buffeted, tossed, spun, and splashed along fast-moving currents. Let there be no doubt: You will get *extremely* wet on this one.

Calico Railroad   Board this 1881 narrow-gauge steam-engine train—once part of the Denver and Rio Grande Southern Line—for a round-trip tour of half the theme park, interrupted by "bandit" holdups.

Ghost Town Artisans ★★ 🎁   An entertaining holdover from the earliest days of the park, these living-history booths showcase old-time crafts and tall tales presented by costumed blacksmiths, woodcarvers, a spinner, and storytellers who help bring Ghost Town to life for curious kids and history buffs.

GhostRider ★★★   Looming 118 feet high, this coaster is the park's single largest attraction and one of the longest and tallest wooden roller coasters in the world. Riders enter through a replica mine and are strapped into gold, silver, or copper mining cars for an adventure that twists and careens through sudden dips, banked turns, and cheek-flattening G-forces. The ride isn't nearly as smooth and quiet as the steel roller coasters, and that's part of the thrill. Coaster enthusiasts worldwide worship this classic.

Mystery Lodge ★★   This amazing high-tech, trick-of-the-eye tribute to the magic of Native American storytelling is a theater attraction for the whole family. The Old Storyteller takes the audience on a mystical, multisensory journey into the culture of local tribes by employing centuries-old legends passed down through oral history.

Pony Express ★★   The west was never so much fun. This coaster invites you to saddle up on your own pony and then delivers speed and thrills never seen in the Old West before. *Warning:* This ride will leave you wanting more. It's that much fun!

Silver Bullet ★★   This inverted coaster dangles riders from the steel track that weaves its way through the center of the park. Flying over Reflection Lake from the edge of the stagecoach stop to the top of the Log Ride mountain at a height of 146 feet, this high-speed thriller sends riders head over heels six times with cobra rolls, spirals, corkscrews, and other whacked-out whirls.

Timber Mountain Log Ride ★   Riders emerge from a dark and twisting "saw-mill" waterway and plummet down a 42-foot flume for the grand splash. Compared to the other water rides in the park, this one leaves you only slightly sprinkled.

Wild West Stunt Show   This wild and woolly stunt spectacular is a raucous salute to the Old West presented throughout the day in the open-air Wagon Camp Theater.

FIESTA VILLAGE

Here you'll find a south-of-the-border theme—festive markets and an ambience that suggests old Spanish California. A cluster of carnival-style rides (in addition to the roller coasters listed below) includes a 100-year-old merry-go-round, plus Knott's version of Disneyland's Tea Cups, where you can sit-and-spin in your own sombrero. You can stroll the paths of Fiesta Village, which are lined with old-time carnival games and state-of-the-art electronic arcades.

Jaguar! ★★   Loosely themed around a tropical jungle setting, this wild roller coaster includes two heart-in-the-mouth drops and a view of Fiesta Village from high above. It's a good family roller coaster for first-timers or the easily frightened.

La Revolución ★   A real stomach-churner, this ride spins you in circles while swinging back and forth more than 65 feet in the air. It's like being in the rinse cycle of a washing machine that's swinging from a rope.

Montezooma's Revenge ★   Blasting from 0 to 60 mph in 5 seconds, this not-for-the-fainthearted thriller then propels riders through a giant 360-degree loop both forward and backward.

THE BOARDWALK

The park's Boardwalk area is a salute to Southern California's beach culture, where colorful architecture and palm trees are the backdrop for a trio of thrill rides. Other amusements include arcade and boardwalk games, and the **Charles M. Schulz Theatre,** where seasonal productions include a *Snoopy* ice show or holiday pageant (check the marquee or park entertainment schedule for showtimes).

Boomerang ★   This corkscrew scream machine sends you twisting through three head-over-heels loops in less than a minute—but it doesn't end there, since you're sent through the track again . . . backward.

Lazer Invaders ☺   In this adaptation of the classic Lazer Runner, participants equipped with lasers and fiber-optic vests battle for supremacy in a richly evocative atmosphere. Each combatant must make use of protective walls and laser power to vanquish opponents.

Perilous Plunge ★★   Just 34 feet shorter than Niagara Falls, this wet adventure sends riders to a height of 127 feet and then drops them down a 115-foot water chute at a 75-degree angle—15 degrees from a sheer vertical. Prepare for a thorough soaking (a boon on hot days, but best experienced before nightfall, when it can get chilly).

Sky Cabin ★   Just when you were thinking all the rides were for hard-core adrenaline-seekers (most are, actually), this quiet ride offers the same spectacular views at a calmer pace. The slowly rotating "cabin" ascends Knott's vertical tower, providing panoramic views of the park and surrounding area.

Supreme Scream ★★   They could've called this one the Evil Elevator: Seated and fully exposed riders are hoisted straight up a 30-story tower with their feet dangling in the air, then held at the top just long enough to rattle the nerves before plunging downward faster than gravity at more than 60 mph. The whole descent takes only a bowel-shaking 3 seconds. It's one of the tallest (and most unnerving) thrill rides in the world.

Xcelerator ★★★   It's scary just looking at this super-high-tech 1950s-themed roller coaster, which launches you from 0 to 82 mph in $2\frac{1}{3}$ seconds, then whips you straight up 20 stories (with a half-twist thrown in for added addling) and almost straight back down again. It's like riding on the outer edge of a gigantic paper clip.

CAMP SNOOPY

This will probably be the youngsters' favorite area. The first-ever theme-park area dedicated solely to kids, it's meant to re-create a wilderness camp in the High Sierras. Six rustic acres are the playgrounds of Charles Schulz's beagle and his pals, Charlie Brown and Lucy, who greet guests and pose for pictures. There are more than a dozen rides in the camp; several kid-size rides are made especially for the younger set, while the entire family can enjoy others. Scaled-down stock cars, locomotives, 18-wheeler semis, hot-air balloons, and even the Peanuts gang's school bus give kids a playland of their own. There's also a child-size version of Supreme Scream called Woodstock's Airmail, and Joe Cool's GR8 SK8, a miniature thrill ride for the whole family. The biggest thrill ride in the area is Sierra Sidewinder, a traditional roller coaster with the exception that your car spins in circles while you're zooming along the track. It's mild

Getting Soaked at Knott's

Surf's up at **Knott's Soak City Water Park,** a 13-acre water park next door to Knott's Berry Farm, with a theme of surf woodies and longboards of the 1950s Southern California coast. The fun includes the **Pacific Spin,** a multi-person raft ride that drops riders 75 feet into a six-story funnel tube, as well as body slides, speed slides, an artificial wave lagoon, and an area for youngsters with their own pool and beach-shack fun house. The park is at 8039 Beach Blvd. (© 714/220-5200; www.knotts.com). Admission prices are $32 for "Regular" (ages 12 and up), $22 for Junior (ages 3–11), and free for children 2 and under; parking is $12. After 3pm, tickets for all ages are $20. Ask about special promotions and discount coupons (or check the website). The park is open mid-May through early September. Soak City Water Park opens at 10am and closes between 5 and 7pm, based on the season.

enough for the whole family, yet quite thrilling. Interactive attractions include the **Camp Snoopy Theatre,** starring the Peanuts gang (little kids are transfixed by this show).

INDIAN TRAILS

Explore the ride-free Indian Trails cultural area, which offers demonstrations of Native dance and music by authentically costumed Native American and Aztec dancers, singers, and musicians performing in the round on the Indian Trails stage. In addition, the compound showcases a variety of traditional Native American structures from the Pacific Northwest, Great Plains, and Southwest. The area includes four towering totem poles, standing from 15 to 27 feet high; three authentic tepees, representing the Arapaho, Blackfoot, and Nez Percé tribes; and more. The arts and crafts of Native American tribes from the western part of North America are also demonstrated and displayed. While exploring Indian Trails, visitors can enjoy a sampling of Native American foods, including Navajo tacos, Indian fry bread, and fresh-roasted ears of corn.

Where to Stay

Knott's Berry Farm Resort Hotel ★ ☺ Within easy walking distance of Knott's Berry Farm, this nine-story hotel offers the only accommodations near the amusement park. Despite the hotel's lengthy moniker, the exterior and lobby have the look of a business hotel. My two favorite things about this hotel are the Peanuts-themed rooms, complete with Snoopy tuck-in service and Camp Kids bedtime stories (told via the in-room phone by the bed), and free shuttle service to Disneyland, 7 miles away. There's also a large family pool with a children's water play structure, and an arcade. Be sure to inquire about special rates and Knott's multiday vacation package deals.

7675 Crescent Ave. (at Grand Ave.), Buena Park, CA 90620. © **866/752-2444** or 714/995-1111. Fax 714/828-8590. www.knottshotel.com. 320 units. $179 standard room; $224 Snoopy room. Prices vary depending on date of visit and room availability. AE, DC, DISC, MC, V. Parking $12 per night; free Disneyland shuttle. **Amenities:** Restaurant; lounge; concierge; fitness center; Jacuzzi; large outdoor pool; room service; 2 outdoor tennis and basketball courts (lit for night play). *In room:* A/C, TV, hair dryer, Wi-Fi ($10 per day).

Where to Eat

Mrs. Knott's Chicken Dinner Restaurant ☺AMERICAN   Knott's Berry Farm got its start as a roadside diner in 1934, and you can still get a filling—albeit unhealthful—all-American meal without even entering the theme park. Cordelia Knott's down-home cooking was so popular that her husband created a few humble attractions to amuse patrons as they waited to be served. Today more than 1.5 million annual patrons line up around the building to experience Cordelia's original recipe (very similar to the Colonel's, I must admit). Looking just as you'd expect—country cute, with window shutters, old black-and-white photos of the original diner, and calico prints aplenty—the restaurant serves up its featured attraction, the original fried-chicken dinner, complete with soup, salad, warm buttermilk biscuits, mashed potatoes and chicken gravy, and a slice of famous pie (the boysenberry pie is fantastic). Country-fried steak, pot roast, roast turkey, and pork ribs are options, as are sandwiches, salads, and a terrific chicken potpie. Boysenberries abound, from breakfast jam to traditional double-crust pies, and there's even an adjacent takeout shop that's always crowded. If you're not visiting the amusement park, park in the lot that offers 3 free hours.

8039 Beach Blvd. (near La Palma Ave.), Buena Park. ✆ **714/220-5080.** Reservations not accepted. Complete dinners $16. DC, DISC, MC, V. Open daily at 7am; closing times vary.

SHOPS & SPAS

W hether you're looking for trendsetting fashions or just some tourist schlock mementos, Los Angeles has your shopping needs covered like no other place in the world. Heck, Los Angeles practically invented the shopping mall.

But to really shop L.A.-style, you need to combine your outing with a trip to a day spa and make it an all-day event. For example, if you're planning an outing to the Grove, an outdoor mall (highly recommended), you should first make a lunch reservation at **Morels French Steakhouse & Bistro** (© 323/965-9595), and then go online to buy movie tickets to the **Grove Theatres** (© 323/692-0829; www.thegrovela.com). When the big day arrives, you meet your friends for coffee in the morning, hit the shops, check your packages with the Grove concierge, have lunch, see a matinee, pick up your purchases, and call it a day. Nicely done.

A note on shopping hours: Street shops are generally open Monday through Saturday from 10 or 11am to 5 or 6pm. Many are open Sunday, particularly those near the beaches, movie theaters, or clusters of other stores. In addition, quite a few offer extended evening hours 1 night a week, often Wednesday or Thursday. Mall shops take their cue from the anchor department stores and generally open from 10am to 8 or 9pm. On Sunday, shave an hour or two off each side, while holiday periods increase mall hours substantially.

Sales tax in Los Angeles is 9.75%; savvy out-of-state shoppers know to have larger items shipped directly home to save the tax.

SHOPS & SPAS BY 'HOOD

If addresses and phone numbers are not given here, refer to the store's expanded listing by category in "Shopping A to Z," later in this chapter.

L.A.'s Westside & Beverly Hills

Beverly Boulevard (from Robertson Blvd. to La Brea Ave.) ★ Beverly is L.A.'s premier boulevard for mid-20th-century furnishings. Expensive showrooms line the street, but the shop that started it all is **Modernica,** 7366 Beverly Blvd. (© 323/933-0383; www.modernica.net). You can still find vintage Stickley and Noguchi pieces, but Modernica has become best known for the authentic—and more affordable—replicas they offer (Eames storage units are one popular item). **Scent Bar,** 8327 Beverly Blvd. (© 323/782-8300), the sleek retail shop from the wildly popular fragrance website www.luckyscent.com, is the place to go for exclusive fragrances from Monyette Paris and Parfums de Nicolai.

URBAN shopping ADVENTURES

Shopping may be a casual pastime in other cities, but in the urban jungle of Los Angeles, it's a competitive sport. If you're a shopping rookie, you might consider an outing with **Urban Shopping Adventures,** which offers custom guided shopping tours of the L.A. Fashion District—more than 100 sprawling blocks loaded with wholesale and retail venues—and celebrity-frequented boutiques in Westside neighborhoods along Rodeo Drive, Robertson Boulevard, West Third Street, and Melrose Heights. Hosted by shopping expert Christine Silvestri, the 3-hour walking tours start at just $36 per person, and merchants are sometimes willing to provide deep discounts to her tour guests. All shopping excursions include a shopping bag, district map, bottled water, snack bar, and plenty of time to browse at your own pace. She also offers round-trip transportation options such as shuttle, bus, or limousine service from your hotel or your chosen location for an additional cost. Advance reservations are required for all tours, and additional shopping districts are also available upon request. Call (✆ **213/683-9715** or log on to www. urbanshoppingadventures.com.

British designer and rock royalty **Stella McCartney,** 8823 Beverly Blvd. (✆ **310/273-7051;** www.stellamccartney.com), opened her eponymous digs in an ivy-covered 1920s cottage. Here you'll find the entire collection, from ready-to-wear and fragrance to footwear and handbags. At nearby **Erica Courtney,** 7465 Beverly Blvd. (✆ **323/938-2373;** www.ericacourtney.com), celebs like Julia Roberts, Sandra Bullock, and Eva Longoria Parker are all fans of Courtney's drop-dead gorgeous diamonds. If you complain that they just don't make 'em like they used to . . . well, they do at **Re-Mix,** 7605½ Beverly Blvd. (btw. Fairfax and La Brea aves.; ✆ **323/936-6210;** www.remixvintageshoes.com). This shop sells vintage (1920s–1950s)—as well as brand-new reproductions (as in unworn)—shoes for women and men (though the selection is smaller for men), such as wingtips, Joan Crawford pumps, and wedgestyles. It's more like a shoe-store museum. A rack of unworn vintage socks all display their original tags and stickers, and the prices are downright reasonable. Celebrity hipsters and hepcats are often spotted here.

Other vintage wares are found at **Second Time Around Watch Co.,** 8763 Rosewood Ave., West Hollywood (✆ **310/271-6615;** www.secondtimearoundwatchco. com). The city's best selection of collectible timepieces includes dozens of classic Tiffanys, Cartiers, Piagets, and Rolexes, plus rare pocket watches. Priced for collectors, but a fascinating browse for the Swatch crowd, too.

When it's time to unwind and beautify, hit **Ona Spa,** 7373 Beverly Blvd. (just east of Martel Ave.); ✆ **323/931-4442** (p. 239) for a tension-relieving massage; the attached **Privé Salon** is one of the city's trendiest salons where celebrity-sightings are common.

La Brea Avenue (north of Wilshire Blvd.) ★ This is L.A.'s artiest shopping strip. La Brea is anchored by the giant **American Rag,** Maison Midialterna-complex and is also home to lots of great urban antiques stores dealing in Art Deco, Arts and Crafts, 1950s modern, and the like. You'll also find vintage clothiers, furniture galleries, and other warehouse-size stores, as well as some of the city's top restaurants, such as **Campanile** (p. 110).

Upscale seekers of home decor head to **Mortise & Tenon,** 446 S. La Brea Ave. (☎ **323/937-7654;** www.mortisetenon.com), where handcrafted heavy wood pieces sit next to overstuffed, velvet-upholstered sofas and even vintage steel desks. The best place for a snack is the **La Brea Bakery,** 624 S. La Brea Ave. (☎ **323/939-6813;** www.labreabakery.com), which epicureans know from gourmet markets and the attached Campanile restaurant.

Stuffed to the rafters with hardware and fixtures of the past 100 years, **Liz's Antique Hardware,** 453 S. La Brea Ave. (☎ **323/939-4403;** www.lahardware. com), thoughtfully keeps a canister of wet wipes at the register—believe us, you'll need one after sifting through bags and crates of doorknobs, latches, finials, and any other home hardware you can imagine. Perfect sets of Bakelite drawer pulls and antique ceramic bathroom fixtures are some of the more intriguing items. Be prepared to browse for hours, whether you're redecorating or not. There's a respectable collection of coordinating trendy clothing for men and women, too.

Robertson Boulevard (btw. Wilshire and Beverly boulevards) ★   If you're a fan of celeb magazines like *US Weekly,* you simply must pay a visit to one of L.A.'s most popular shopping streets. It's common to see the likes of Jessica Simpson, Lindsay Lohan, and Paris Hilton shopping at trend-obsessed boutiques like **Kitson,** 115 S. Robertson Blvd. (☎ **310/859-2652;** www.shopkitson.com), and **Lisa Kline,** 143 S. Robertson Blvd. (☎ **310/246-0907**). A splashy **Dolce & Gabbana** flagship boutique at 147 N. Robertson Blvd. (☎ **310/247-1571;** www.dolcegabbana.com) has the full spectrum of men's and women's clothing and must-have accessories like sunglasses and jewelry. After shopping like a celebrity, dine among them at the **Ivy** (p. 103).

Just up the street, one of L.A.'s most unique day spas beckon the tired, the stressed, and the famous. **In fact,** skin-care specialist **Kinara Spa,** 656 N. Robertson Blvd. (☎ **310/657-9188;** www.kinaraspa.com), lists among its faithful fans Halle Berry, Naomi Watts, and Jennifer Garner.

Rodeo Drive & Beverly Hills's Golden Triangle (btw. Santa Monica Blvd., Wilshire Blvd., and Crescent Dr., Beverly Hills) ★★   Everyone knows about Rodeo Drive, the city's most famous shopping street. Couture shops from high fashion's old guard are located along these 3 hallowed blocks, along with plenty of newer high-end labels. And there are two examples of the Beverly Hills version of minimalls, albeit more insular and attractive: the **Rodeo Collection,** 421 N. Rodeo Dr. (www.rodeo collection.net), a contemporary center with towering palms; and **2 Rodeo** (www. tworodeo.com), a cobblestoned Italianate piazza at Wilshire Boulevard. The 16-square-block area surrounding Rodeo Drive is known as the Golden Triangle. Shops off Rodeo are generally not as name-conscious as those on the strip (and you might actually be able to afford something), but they're nevertheless plenty upscale. Little Santa Monica Boulevard has a particularly colorful line of specialty stores, and Brighton Way is as young and hip as relatively staid Beverly Hills gets. Parking is a bargain, with seven city-run lots offering 2 hours of free parking.

Window-Shopping—L.A. Style

The gorgeous Bulgari jewelry store at the corner of Rodeo Drive and Wilshire Boulevard—former home of the Brown Derby restaurant—displays many of the priceless (literally) jewels worn by the stars at the big awards ceremonies. Look wealthy and they might even invite you upstairs for an espresso.

The big names to look for here are **Missoni,** 469 N. Rodeo Dr. (☎ **310/246-3060**); **Prada,** 343 N. Rodeo Dr. (☎ **310/278-8661**); **Chanel,** 400 N. Rodeo Dr. (☎ **310/278-5500**); **Bulgari,** 201 N. Rodeo Dr. (☎ **310/858-9216**); **Gucci,** 347 N. Rodeo Dr. (☎ **310/278-3451**); **Hermès,** 434 N. Rodeo Dr. (☎ **310/278-6440**); **Louis Vuitton,** 295 N. Rodeo Dr. (☎ **310/859-0457**); **Polo/Ralph Lauren,** 444 N. Rodeo Dr. (☎ **310/281-7200**); and a three-story **Tiffany & Co.** that's one of the largest Tiffany stores in the world, 210 N. Rodeo Dr. (☎ **310/273-8880**). There's also the ultrachic clothiers **Dolce & Gabbana,** 312 N. Rodeo Dr. (☎ **310/888-8701**); British plaid palace **Burberry,** 9560 Wilshire Blvd. (☎ **310/550-4500**); and **NikeTown,** on the corner of Wilshire Boulevard and Rodeo Drive (☎ **310/275-9998**), a behemoth shrine to the reigning athletic-gear king.

Wilshire Boulevard is also home to New York–style department stores (each in spectacular landmark buildings), like **Saks Fifth Avenue,** 9600 Wilshire Blvd. (☎ **310/275-4211**); **Barneys New York,** 9570 Wilshire Blvd. (☎ **310/276-4400**); and **Neiman Marcus,** 9700 Wilshire Blvd. (☎ **310/550-5900**).

When all that walking and gawking tires you out, do what all the Beverly Hills beauties do: Hit a spa. **Thibiant Beverly Hills Day Spa,** 449 N. Canon Dr. (☎ **310/278-7565;** www.thibiantspa.com), has been offering classic treatments since the 1970s. Guys have a place of their own at the high-end barbershop the **Shave,** 230 S. Beverly Dr. (☎ **310/888-2898;** www.theshavebeverlyhills.com). Those looking for eco-friendly pampering can visit **Chi Nail Bar and Organic Spa,** 9390 Little Santa Monica Blvd. (☎ **310/858-8803;** www.chi-nailbar.com), for treatments and facials. You don't need to stay in one of the fabulously luxurious Beverly Hills hotels to get all the pampering services. At the **Spa at the Four Seasons** (p. 56), California-flavored treatments use everything from pumpkin to caviar in decadent massages and facials. The **Spa at the Peninsula Beverly Hills** (p. 59) uses diamonds, emeralds, rubies, and sapphires in some of their signature treatments. At the **Beverly Hills Hotel Spa by La Prairie** (p. 55), the facials and massages are some of the most expensive in town, but it's a great reason to spend a decadent day at the "Pink Palace" without having to drop $1,000 a night on a suite.

The Sunset Strip (btw. La Cienega Blvd. and Doheny Dr., West Hollywood)   The monster-size billboards advertising the latest rock god make it clear this is rock-'n'-roll territory. The Strip is lined with trendy restaurants, industry-oriented hotels, and dozens of shops offering outrageous fashions and stage accessories. One anomaly is Sunset Plaza, an upscale cluster of Georgian-style shops resembling Beverly Hills at

A Little Bit o' Country

With its red barn facade and easygoing neighborhood vibe, the **Brentwood Country Mart,** which was built in 1948, has recovered rather nicely from a major face-lift in 2006. It's one of the easiest places to shop in L.A. because so many chic stores are in one spot, and parking is free. Be sure to visit the menswear outpost Apartment Number 9, the upscale beauty shop Marie Mason Apothecary, and Farm Shop (great for bakery items, cured meats and other gourmet goodies). The Mart is located at 225 26th St., just off San Vicente Boulevard in Brentwood (☎ **310/451-9877;** www.brentwood countrymart.com).

A Very Beverly Hills Bookstore

If you're a connoisseur of small bookstores, you'll definitely want to pay a visit to the **Taschen** bookstore at 354 N. Beverly Dr., in Beverly Hills (© **310/274-4300**; www.taschen.com). It's the German-based publishing house's first American store and a fitting monument to the company's beautiful, high-quality books. French designer *célèbre* Philippe Starck was commissioned to create the long, narrow store's dramatic interiors—glossy walnut woods, shimmering bronze bookshelves, purple mirrors, and handmade glass walls. Befitting the world's leading art publisher, the artwork alone is worth the trip: Artist Albert Oehlen created 20 computer-generated collages for the walls and ceiling, inspired by the wide selection of Taschen's art, design, and erotic books. Prices range from a few dollars to several thousand for Helmut Newton's *SUMO,* the biggest and most expensive book produced in the 20th century. Truly, Taschen is unlike any other bookstore you've browsed. Open Monday through Saturday 10am to 7pm, Sunday noon to 5pm. A second, smaller location has opened at the Grove, 6333 W. Third St. (© **323/931-1168**).

its snootiest. You'll find **Billy Martin's,** 8605 Sunset Blvd. (© **310/289-5000;** www.billymartin.com), founded by the legendary Yankees manager in 1978. This chic men's Western shop—complete with fireplace and leather sofa—stocks hand-forged silver and gold belt buckles, Lucchese and Liberty boots, and stable staples like flannel shirts. **Book Soup,** 8818 W. Sunset Blvd. (© **310/659-3110;** www.booksoup. com), has long been one of L.A.'s most celebrated bookshops, selling mainstream and small-press books and hosting book signings and readings.

The Sunset Strip's trendiest hotels have in-house spas and spa services—like **Agua at the Mondrian,** 8440 W. Sunset Blvd. (© **323/203-1138;** www.mondrianhotel. com)—which offer great added amenities for hotel guests. But to feel like a real superstar on the Strip, go to the "facialist of the stars": **Ole Henriksen Face/Body,** 8622 W. Sunset Blvd. (© **310/854-7700;** www.olehenriksen.com/spa), is where stunners like Ashley Judd and Charlize Theron go for glowing skin.

West 3rd Street (btw. Fairfax and Robertson boulevards) ★ You can shop until you drop on this trendy strip, anchored on the east end by the **Farmers Market and The Grove** (p. 229). Many of Melrose Avenue's shops have relocated here, along with terrific up-and-comers, several cafes, and restaurants. *Fun* is more the catchword here than *funky,* and the shops (including the vintage-clothing stores) are a bit more refined than those along Melrose. **Traveler's Bookcase,** 8375 W. 3rd St. (© **323/655-0575;** www.travelbooks.com), is one of the best travel bookshops in the West, stocking a huge selection of guidebooks and travel literature, as well as maps and travel accessories.

There's lots more to see along this always-growing street. Refuel at **Chado Tea Room,** 8422½ W. 3rd St. (© **323/655-2056;** www.chadotea.com), a temple for tea lovers. Chado is designed with a nod to Paris's renowned Mariage Frères tea purveyor; one wall is lined with nooks whose recognizable brown tins are filled with more than 250 different varieties of tea from around the world. Among the choices are 15 kinds of Darjeeling, Indian teas blended with rose petals, and ceremonial Chinese and

Japanese blends. You can also get tea meals here, featuring delightful sandwiches and individual pots of any loose tea in the store.

Hollywood

Hollywood Boulevard (btw. Gower St. and La Brea Ave.)   One of Los Angeles's most famous streets is, for the most part, a cheesy tourist strip. But along the Walk of Fame, between the T-shirt shops and greasy pizza parlors, you'll find some excellent poster shops, souvenir stores, and Hollywood-memorabilia dealers worth getting out of your car for—especially if there's a chance of getting your hands on that long-sought-after Ethel Merman autograph or *200 Motels* poster.

Some long-standing purveyors of memorabilia include **Hollywood Book and Poster Company,** 6562 Hollywood Blvd. (✆ **323/465-8764;** www.hollywoodbook andposter.com), which has an excellent collection of posters (from about $20 each), strong in horror and exploitation flicks. Photocopies of around 5,000 movie and television scripts are sold for $15 each—*Pulp Fiction* is just as good in print, by the way—and the store carries music posters and photos.

The legendary **Fredericks of Hollywood,** 6751 Hollywood Blvd. (✆ **323/957-5953;** www.fredericks.com), located just a block east of Hollywood & Highland, is worth a stop if you're looking for devilish dainties. The flagship store features lingerie worn by celebrities like Sharon Stone, Julianne Moore, and Halle Berry.

Larchmont Boulevard (btw. Melrose Ave. and 3rd St.)   Neighbors congregate on this old-fashioned street just east of busy Vine Avenue. As the surrounding Hancock Park homes become increasingly popular with artists and young industry types, the shops and cafes lining Larchmont get more stylish. Sure, chains like Jamba Juice and the Coffee Bean have infiltrated this formerly mom-and-pop terrain, but plenty of unique shopping awaits amid charming elements like diagonal parking, shady trees, and sidewalk bistro tables.

One of L.A.'s landmark independent bookstores is **Chevalier's Books,** 126 N. Larchmont Blvd. (✆ **323/465-1334**), a 60-year Larchmont tradition. If your walking shoes are letting you down, stop into **Village Footwear,** 248 N. Larchmont Blvd. (✆ **323/461-3619**), which specializes in comfort lines like Josef Siebel. Or even better, stop in for a foot—or full-body—massage at **Healing Hands Wellness Center,** 414 N. Larchmont Blvd. (✆ **323/461-7876;** www.healinghandswc.com), which has affordable 1-hour massages starting at $55. An entire afternoon of pampering can be had at **Le Petite Retreat Day Spa,** 331 N. Larchmont Blvd. (✆ **323/466-1028;** www.lprdayspa.com), which offers great packages for couples or a girls' day out.

Melrose Avenue (btw. Fairfax and La Brea aves.) ★★   It's showing some wear—some stretches have become downright ugly—but this is still one of the most exciting shopping streets in the country for cutting-edge fashions (and some eye-popping people-watching, to boot). Melrose is always an entertaining stroll, dotted with plenty of hip restaurants and funky shops selling the latest in clothes, gifts, jewelry, and accessories that are sure to shock. Where else could you find green patent-leather cowboy boots, a 19th-century pocket watch, an inflatable girlfriend, and glow-in-the-dark condoms on the same block? Here are some highlights:

l.a. Eyeworks, 7407 Melrose Ave. (✆ **323/653-8255;** www.laeyeworks.com), revolutionized eyeglass designs from medical supply to stylish accessory, and now their brand is nationwide. **Off the Wall Antiques,** 7325 Melrose Ave. (✆ **323/930-1185;** www.offthewallantiques.com), is filled with neon-flashing, bells-and-whistles kitsch collectibles, from vintage Wurlitzer jukeboxes to life-size fiberglass cows. The L.A. branch of a Bay Area hipster hangout, **Wasteland,** 7248 Melrose Ave. (② **323/653-3028;** www.wastelandclothing.com), has an enormous steel-sculpted facade. There's a lot of leather and denim, and some classic vintage—but mostly funky 1970s-style garb, both vintage and contemporary. An outpost of the edgy **Floyd's Barbershops,** 7300 Melrose Ave. (② **323/965-7600;** www.floydsbarbershops.com), keeps the street's style-for-less theme by charging around $21 for men's and $24 for women's cuts. It's like a salon, music store, and Internet cafe rolled into one.

Melrose Heights (btw. La Cienega Blvd. and Fairfax Ave.) ★★ This posh section of Melrose, anchored by the venerable favorite **Fred Segal,** 8100 Melrose Ave. (② **323/655-3734;** www.fredsegal.com), houses designer boutiques such as **Diane Von Furstenberg,** 8407 Melrose Ave. (② **323/951-1947**), and **Paul Smith,** 8221 Melrose Ave. (② **323/951-4800**). L.A. jewelry designer **Suzanne Felsen,** 8332 Melrose Ave. (② **323/653-5400**), is a celebrity favorite—she transformed a 1920s Spanish home to house her gold and platinum baubles lined with Peruvian opals and Mandarin garnets. Perennial fashion favorite **Marc Jacobs** has three stores at 8400, 8409, and 8410 Melrose Ave., featuring ready-to-wear, accessories, menswear, and the less expensive Marc by Marc Jacobs collection.

Santa Monica & the Beaches

Main Street (btw. Pacific St. and Rose Ave., and Santa Monica and Venice boulevards) ★ An excellent street for strolling, Main Street is crammed with a combination of mall standards and upscale, left-of-center individual boutiques. You can also find plenty of casually hip cafes and restaurants. The primary strip connecting Santa Monica and Venice, Main Street has a relaxed, beach-community vibe that sets it apart from similar strips. The stores here straddle the fashion fence between upscale trendy and beach-bum edgy. Highlights include **Obsolete,** 222 Main St. (near Rose Ave.; ② **310/399-0024**), the most hip antiques store I've ever seen. Collectibles range from antique carnival curios to 19th-century anatomical charts from Belgium (you'd be amazed at how much some of that junk in your attic is worth). **CP Shades,** 2937 Main St. (btw. Ashland and Pier sts.; ② **310/392-0949;** www.cpshades.com), is a San Francisco–based ladies' clothier whose loose and comfy cotton and linen line is carried by many department stores and boutiques. If you're looking for some truly sophisticated, finely crafted eyewear, the friendly **Optical Shop of Aspen,** 2904 Main St. (btw. Ashland and Pier sts.; ② **310/392-0633;** www.opticalshopofaspen. com), is for you. Ask for frames by cutting-edge L.A. designers Bada and Koh Sakai. For aromatherapy nirvana, it's **Cloud's,** 2719 Main St. (② **310/399-2059**), where Jill Cloud (happily assisted by her lovely mom) carries the most heavenly scented candles. Then there's **Arts & Letters,** 2665 Main St. (② **310/392-9076**), a stationery haven that includes invitations by the owner herself, Marilyn Golin. Outdoors types will get lost in 5,600-square-foot **Patagonia,** 2936 Main St. (② **310/314-1776;** www.patagonia.com), where climbers, surfers, skiers, and hikers can gear up in the functional, colorful duds that put this environmentally friendly firm on the map.

Montana Avenue (btw. 17th and 7th sts., Santa Monica; www.montanaave. com) This breezy stretch of slow-traffic Montana has gotten a lot more pricey than in the late 1970s, when tailors and laundromats ruled the roost, but the specialty shops still outnumber the chains. Look around and you can see upscale moms with strollers and cellphones shopping for designer fashions, country home decor, and gourmet takeout.

GR8 FINDS IN WEST L.A.'S j-town

What started off as a magazine has spawned two of L.A.'s most talked-about stores—**Giant Robot,** 2015 Sawtelle Blvd. (☎ **310/478-1819**), and **GR2,** 2062 Sawtelle Blvd. (☎ **310/445-9276**)—and **gr/eats** restaurant, 2050 Sawtelle Blvd. (☎ **310/478-3242;** www.gr-eats.com). Located across the street from each other in West L.A.'s Japantown (at Sawtelle and Olympic boulevards), both shops specialize in a wide range of Asian-American pop-culture items, including T-shirts, books, music, stationery, toys, art, and accessories (check out the Takashi Murakami pins). Several other cool shops and restaurants occupy this 1½-block stretch as well. One of my favorite stores is **Happy Six,** 2115 Sawtelle Blvd. (☎ **310/479-5363**), which sells playful apparel and accessories for men and women that are reminiscent of Hello Kitty on acid. If you're hungry, my favorites along Sawtelle are **Manpuku,** 2125 Sawtelle Blvd. (☎ **310/473-0580;** www.manpuku.us); **Sawtelle Kitchen,** 2024 Sawtelle Blvd. (☎ **310/473-2222;** www.sawtellekitchen.com); and **Hurry Curry of Tokyo,** 2131 Sawtelle Blvd. (☎ **310/473-1640;** www.hurrycurryoftokyo.com). Or you can pop into **Nijiya Market,** 2130 Sawtelle Blvd. (☎ **310/575-3300;** www.nijiya.com), and grab a *bento* (Japanese boxed lunch) to go.

Montana is still original enough for residents from across town to make a special trip here, seeking out distinctive shops like **Shabby Chic,** 1013 Montana Ave. (☎ **310/394-1975;** www.shabbychic.com), a much-copied purveyor of slipcovered sofas and flea-market furnishings, while clotheshorses shop for designer wear at minimalist **Savannah,** 706 Montana Ave. (☎ **310/458-2095**); ultrahip **Jill Roberts,** 920 Montana Ave. (☎ **310/260-1966;** www.jillroberts.com); and sleekly professional **Weathervane,** 1209 Montana Ave. (☎ **310/393-5344**). **Leona Edmiston,** 1007 Montana Ave. (☎ **310/587-1100;** www.leonaedmiston.com), houses the Aussie designer's famed frocks. For more grown-up style, head to **Ponte Vecchio,** 702 Montana Ave. (☎ **310/394-0989;** www.pontev.com), which sells Italian hand-painted dishes and urns. If Valentine's Day is approaching, duck into **Only Hearts,** 1407 Montana Ave. (☎ **310/393-3088;** www.onlyhearts.com), for heart-themed gifts and seductively comfortable intimate apparel. And don't forget the one-of-a-kind shops such as **Sun Precautions,** 1601 Montana Ave. (☎ **310/451-5858;** www.sunprecautions.com), specializing in 100% UV protection apparel, and the second-largest **Kiehl's** store outside of New York City, 1516 Montana Ave. (☎ **310/255-0055;** www.kiehls.com). Skin is taken incredibly seriously at the flagship store and spa **Dermalogica on Montana,** 1022 Montana Ave. (☎ **310/260-8682;** www.dermalogicaonmontana.com), where "touch therapies" and "skin mapping" are just the beginning of the dynamite facials. Enjoy a meal at the local favorite, **Café Montana,** 1534 Montana Ave. (☎ **310/829-3990**), for great people-watching through its floor-to-ceiling glass windows; the original **Father's Office,** 1018 Montana Ave. (☎ **310/736-2224;** www.fathersoffice.com), for microbrews and one of the city's best burgers; or **R+D Kitchen,** 1323 Montana Ave. (☎ **310/395-3314**), for classic California cuisine and cocktails.

Third Street Promenade (3rd St. btw. Wilshire Blvd. and Broadway Ave.; www.downtownsm.com) ★ Packed with those ubiquitous corporate chain stores, restaurants, and cafes (gee, another Starbucks), Santa Monica's pedestrians-only section of

3rd Street is one of the most popular shopping areas in the city. The Promenade bustles all day and well into the evening with a seemingly endless assortment of street performers among the shoppers, bored teens, and home-challenged. There are, however, a few shopping gems squeezed between Gap, Abercrombie & Fitch, and Old Navy. You can easily browse for hours at **Hennessey & Ingalls,** 214 Wilshire Blvd. (*©* **310/458-9074**), a bookstore devoted to art and architecture. **Restoration Hardware,** 1221 Third Street Promenade (*©* **310/458-7992**), is still the retro-current leader for reproduction home furnishings and accessories. **Puzzle Zoo,** 1413 Third Street Promenade (*©* **310/393-9201**), was the original location of this now regional chain and you'll find an array of toys and puzzles, as well as many brain-teasing challenges.

Exhale is perfect for those seeking quiet time and relief from the crowds. There's yoga and Core Fusion classes, the Healing Waters sanctuary with eucalyptus steam rooms, relaxing spa services, and the simply titled "Quiet Room" for rejuvenation. Stores stay open late (often until 1 or 2am on the weekends) for the moviegoing crowds, and there's plenty of public parking in six structures along 2nd and 4th streets between Broadway and Wilshire Boulevard.

Santa Monica Place Mall ★   This spanking-new outdoor shopping mall (300 block of Colorado Ave., between Third Street Promenade and the Santa Monica Pier; www.santamonicaplace.com) opened on August 6, 2010, in Downtown Santa Monica, offering high-end shopping options in true California form (just 2 blocks away from the beach). The mall is anchored by **Bloomingdale's** and **Nordstrom,** and features shops such as **Hugo Boss, Burberry, Kitson,** and more. Distinguishing attributes of the outdoor shopping haven include its pretty view overlooking Santa Monica Beach, unique event space, fine rooftop dining and bar scene, and modern outdoor fireplace.

Silver Lake & Los Feliz

Located at the eastern end of Hollywood and technically part of Los Angeles, these two communities have been rising steadily on the hipness meter. Silver Lake, named for the man-made Silver Lake Reservoir at its center, is a bohemian community of artists and ethnic families that's popular for nightclubbing and barhopping. Los Feliz is northwest of Silver Lake, centered on Vermont and Hillhurst avenues between Sunset and Los Feliz boulevards; it's slightly tamer and filled with 1920s and 1930s buildings. You'll find tons of unique businesses of all sorts, including artsy boutiques, music stores, and furniture dealers.

Because so many alternative bands call Silver Lake home, it's not surprising to find cutting-edge music stores around every corner. A neighborhood mainstay with lots of

---

  Lingerie Insider

Panty Raid, a very charming boutique, carries brands for the serious lingerie collector such as Cosabella, Mary Green, and Felina, as well as Hanky Panky (cute lace tank tops and boy-short sets), Betsey Johnson, T & C California, Eberjey, and Only Hearts. A selection of hosiery, socks, yoga outfits, loungewear, and gift items—including bath and body products and candles—is also available. 1953 Hillhurst Ave., Los Angeles. *©* 323/668-1888; www.pantyraidshop.com.

abbot kinney BOULEVARD: L.A.'S ANTITHESIS TO RODEO DRIVE

When you're finally fed up with the Rodeo Drive attitude and megamall conformity, it's time to drive to Venice and stroll the eclectic shops along **Abbot Kinney Boulevard.** This refreshingly anti-establishment stretch of street has the most diverse array of shops, galleries, and restaurants in Los Angeles. (Locals still cheer that there are no franchises in the neighborhood.) You can easily spend the entire afternoon here poring over vintage clothing, antique furniture, vintage Vespas, local art, and amusing gifts. Or if you're looking for a unique gift, you'll want to try **Strange Invisible Perfumes,** 1138 Abbot Kinney Blvd. (⟨℗⟩ **310/314-1505;** www.siperfumes.com), where they can custom-make a scent to match your musk. Then there's **Firefly,** 1409 Abbot Kinney Blvd. (⟨℗⟩ **310/450-6288;** www.shopfirefly.com), a local favorite. It's that one store

you can go into and find everything from great baby gifts, stationery, and books to quirky handbags and cool clothing. **DNA Clothing Co.,** 411 Rose Ave. (⟨℗⟩ **310/399-0341;** www.dna clothing.com), is the mother lode for those in search of the coolest, most current styles for men and women at great prices (stylists and costumers often use DNA as their resource for sitcoms and feature films). You'll find all your major brands as well as their own private-label wear, and fresh stock arrives weekly. Take a break to eat at one of the boulevard's many restaurants, including **Joe's** (the best California cuisine in L.A.; p. 92), **Primitivo, Axe, Lilly's, Jin's Patisserie, French Market Café, Tasting Kitchen Gjelina,** and, of course, **Hal's Bar & Grill,** with its live jazz music. Heck, there are even 2 hours of free street parking.

used CDs, collectible disks, and new releases is **Rockaway Records,** 2395 Glendale Blvd. (south of Silver Lake Blvd.; ⟨℗⟩ **323/664-3232;** www.rockaway.com).

Vintage clothing is another big draw in these parts. The most reliable yet eclectic selections to browse through are at **Ozzie Dots,** 4637 Hollywood Blvd. (west of Hillhurst Ave.; ⟨℗⟩ **323/663-2867;** www.ozziedots.com); **Pull My Daisy,** 3908 Sunset Blvd. (at Griffith Park Blvd.; ⟨℗⟩ **323/663-0608**); and **Squaresville,** 1800 N. Vermont Ave. (south of Franklin Ave.; ⟨℗⟩ **323/669-8464**).

Rubbish, 1627 Silver Lake Blvd. (north of Sunset Blvd.; ⟨℗⟩ **323/661-5575;** www.rubbishinteriors.com), specializes in vintage furnishings. One not-to-be-missed highlight is the wacky and eclectic **Soap Plant/Wacko/La Luz de Jesus Art Gallery,** 4633 Hollywood Blvd. (west of Hillhurst Ave.; ⟨℗⟩ **323/663-0122;** www.soapplant.com), a three-in-one business with candles, art books, erotic toys, soap and bathing items, and a large selection of lava lamps. Local fixture **Y-Que,** 1770 N. Vermont Ave. (⟨℗⟩ **323/664-0021;** www.yque.com), almost defies description, selling a variety of stuff ranging from a knockoff *Austin Powers* penis pump to psychedelic lava lamps to L.A. neighborhood T-shirts.

With a focus on small-production, high-quality, affordable wine from around the world, and a large selection of microbrew beer and sake, **Silverlake Wine,** 2395 Glendale Blvd. (⟨℗⟩ **323/662-9024;** www.silverlakewine.com), is a great place to visit. Get your friends together and check out any one of their weekly tastings: Sunday at 3pm, Blue Monday from 5 to 9pm, and Thursday Night Flights from 5 to 9pm (call ahead to confirm times). Located in Sunset Junction (at the southeast corner of

Sanborn Ave. and Sunset Blvd.), the **Cheese Store of Silverlake,** 3926–28 W. Sunset Blvd. (*(C)* **323/644-7511;** www.cheesestoresl.com), sells fine cheeses, wines, and gourmet products such as Revival confections, Latini pastas, Agrumato flavored oils, and McQuade's chutneys. Next door is the West Coast's first **Intelligentsia Coffee & Tea,** 3922 W. Sunset Blvd. (*(C)* **323/663-6173;** www.intelligentsiacoffee. com), where Mac-using hipsters convene for artfully poured lattes and Chemex-brewed, single-origin coffee.

Downtown

Since the late lamented Bullock's department store closed in 1993 (its Art Deco masterpiece salons were rescued to house the Southwestern Law School's library), Downtown has become less of a shopping destination than ever. Although many of the once-splendid streets are lined with cut-rate luggage and electronics stores, shopping here can be a rewarding—albeit gritty—experience for the adventuresome.

Savvy Angelenos still go for bargains in the garment and fabric districts (see "Discount" under "Fashions," later in this chapter); florists and bargain hunters arrive before dawn at the vast **Los Angeles Flower District,** 766 Wall St. (btw. E. 8th and E. 7th sts.; *(C)* **213/622-1966;** www.laflowerdistrict.com), for the city's best selection of fresh blooms; and families of all ethnicities stroll the **Grand Central Market ★★**, 317 S. Broadway (btw. 3rd and 4th sts.; *(C)* **213/624-2378;** www.grandcentral square.com). Opened in 1917, this bustling market has watched the face of Downtown L.A. change while changing little. Today its sawdust-covered aisles serve Latino families, enterprising restaurateurs, and cooks in search of unusual ingredients—stuffed goat heads, mole, plantains, deep-fried smelt, Mexican cane alcohol—and bargain-priced produce. On weekends you'll be greeted by a mariachi band at the Hill Street entrance, near my favorite market feature, the fruit-juice counter, which dispenses 20 fresh varieties from wall spigots and blends the tastiest, healthiest "shakes" in town. Farther into the market, you'll find produce and prepared foods, spice vendors who seem straight out of a Turkish bazaar, and a grain-and-bean seller who'll scoop out dozens of exotic rices and dried legumes. It's open 9am to 6pm daily.

Another of my favorite Downtown shopping zones is **Olvera Street ★★★** (*(C)* **213/680-2525;** www.olvera-street.com), a lively brick pedestrian lane near Union Station that's been lined with stalls selling Mexican wares since the 1930s. Everything that's sold south of the border is available here, including custom leather accessories, huarache sandals, maracas, and—but of course—freshly baked churros. On weekends you're bound to see strolling bolero musicians, mariachis, folk dancers, and performances by Aztec Indians. It's open daily from 10am to about 8pm.

If you're looking to find *the* best shopping deals in handbags, luggage, shoes, costume jewelry, and trendy fashions, then find a parking meter or park in one of the

---

 Downtown Deals

At the base of the Fashion Institute of Design & Merchandising's Downtown campus, you'll find the **FIDM Scholarship Store,** where donated new merchandise is sold at bargain prices. All sales go toward scholarships for FIDM students, so you can shop with the karmic awareness that you're helping the fashion industry's next generation of designers with their tuition. It's located at 919 S. Grand Ave., at W. 9th Street (*(C)* **213/624-1200;** www.fidm.edu).

parking structures from Olympic Boulevard to 12th Street and explore **Santee Alley,** located in the alley between Santee Street and Maple Avenue. Often referred to as the heart of the fashion district, this is where you'll find everything you've ever wanted at bargain prices. Go early on Saturday mornings if you want to blend in with the locals.

Okay, so you have to wake up a little early to experience the **Southern California Flower Market,** 755 Wall St., between 7th and 8th streets (📞 213/627-2482; www.laflowerdistrict.com), but if you do it right—wear comfortable shoes, bring cash, and pick up a cup o' joe—you'll find walking through the myriad of flower stalls a very tranquil experience. Besides the usual buds and stems that you see in *Sunset Magazine,* you'll be surprised to find tropicals such as torch ginger, protea, and bird of paradise. You can purchase flowers by the bundles at amazingly low prices.

The San Fernando Valley

Studio City (Ventura Blvd. btw. Laurel Canyon Blvd. and Fulton Ave.)   Long beloved by Valley residents, Studio City is where you'll find small boutiques and antiques stores, quirky little businesses (many dating from the 1940s and 1950s), and less congested branches of popular chains like Gap, Pier 1 Imports, and Blockbuster. Melanie Shatner, daughter of William, stocks Marc Jacobs and Joie at her chic boutique **Dari,** 12184 Ventura Blvd. (📞 818/762-3274). Fashionistas flock to TV personality Lisa Rinna's **Belle Gray,** 13812 Ventura Blvd. (📞 818/789-4021; www. bellegray.com). Actress Kirsten Dunst's mother has a day spa, **Belle Visage,** 13207 Ventura Blvd. (📞 818/907-0502; www.bellevisage.com), that caters to the young and the beautiful—or at least those in search of youth and beauty. Parking is a cinch on the street except during holiday season, when stores team up to decorate these blocks and often observe extended evening hours. The 4 blocks of Ventura Boulevard between Laurel Canyon Boulevard and Whitsett Avenue are the most concentrated.

Pasadena & Environs

Compared to L.A.'s behemoth shopping malls, the streets of pretty, compact Pasadena are a breeze to stroll. As a general rule, stores are open daily from about 10am, and while some close at the standard 5 or 6pm, many stay open until 8 or 9pm to accommodate the before- and after-dinner/movie crowd.

Old Pasadena ★★   Dating back to the 1880s, the 22-block-long Old Pasadena district (centered on the intersection of Colorado Blvd. and Fair Oaks Ave.; www. oldpasadena.com) offers some of the best shopping in L.A.—*if* it retains the mom-and-pop businesses currently being pushed out by the likes of Banana Republic and Crate & Barrel. Going through its own sort of renaissance, more upscale shopping has been added to the strip, including a **Tiffany & Co.,** 68 W. Colorado Blvd. (📞 626/793-7424; www.tiffany.com), which has become somewhat of an attraction more than a store, and the new (and hugely popular) **H&M** fashion store, 60 W. Colorado Blvd. (📞 626/793-8974; www.hm.com), which now is an anchor to the neighborhood. As you move eastward, the mix of businesses begins to include more eclectic shops and galleries commingling with dusty, pre-yuppie relics, but it's a good segue between Old Pasadena and the Paseo Colorado mall.

Travelers also seem to find something they need at **Distant Lands Bookstore and Outfitters,** 20 S. Raymond Ave. (📞 800/310-3220 or 626/449-3220; www. distantlands.com), a pair of related stores. The bookstore has a terrific selection of maps, guides, and travel-related literature, while the outfitter two doors away offers everything from luggage and pith helmets to space-saving travel accessories.

OTHER PASADENA SHOPPING

In addition to Old Pasadena, there are numerous good hunting grounds in the surrounding area. Antiques hounds might want to head to the **Green Street Antique Row,** 985–1005 E. Green St. (east of Lake Ave.), or the **Pasadena Antique Center,** on South Fair Oaks Boulevard (south of Del Mar Blvd.). Each has a rich concentration of collectibles that can captivate for hours.

You never know what you might find at the **Rose Bowl Flea Market ★,** at the Rose Bowl, 1001 Rose Bowl Dr., Pasadena (✆ **323/560-SHOW** [560-7469]; www. rgcshows.com). The horseshoe-shaped Rose Bowl, built in 1922, is one of the world's most famous stadiums, home to UCLA's Bruins, the annual Rose Bowl Game, and an occasional Super Bowl. **California's largest monthly swap meet,** held here on the second Sunday of every month from 9am to 3pm rain or shine, is a favorite of Los Angeles antiques hounds (who know to arrive as early as 7am for the best finds). Antique furnishings, clothing, jewelry, and other collectibles are assembled in the parking area to the left of the entrance, while the rest of the flea market surrounds the exterior of the Bowl. Expect everything from used surfboards and car stereos to one-of-a-kind lawn statuary and bargain athletic shoes. Admission is $8 after 9am. (Early-bird admission is $10 at 8am, $15 at 7am and $20 from 5–7am.) Free admission for kids 11 and under.

Anglophiles will enjoy **Rose Tree Cottage,** 801 S. Pasadena Ave. (✆ **626/793-3337;** www.rosetreecottage.com), and its charming array of all things British. This cluster of historic Tudor cottages surrounded by traditional English gardens holds three gift shops and a tearoom, where a superb $33 high tea is served thrice daily among the knickknacks (and supervised by the resident cat, Miss Moffett). In addition to imported teas, linens, and silver trinkets, Rose Tree Cottage sells English delicacies like steak-and-kidney pies, hot cross buns, and shortbread. It's also the local representative of the British Tourist Authority and offers a comprehensive array of travel publications.

SHOPPING MALLS
L.A.'s Westside & Beverly Hills

The Beverly Center When the eight-story Beverly Center opened on L.A.'s Westside, there was more than a bit of concern about the impending "mallification" of Los Angeles. Loved for its convenience and disdained for its penitentiary-style architecture (and the "no validations" parking fee), Beverly Center contains about 160 standard mall shops, including the wildly popular **H&M,** and even a few boutiques that are open by advance reservation only (*so* L.A.). It's anchored on opposite sides by Macy's and Bloomingdale's department stores. You can see it from blocks away, looking like a gigantic climbing wall. *Tip:* For a nice bite after a long day of shopping, try the adjacent **Capital Grille,** 8614 Beverly Blvd. (✆ **310/338-0650;** www.thecapitalgrille.com/Locations/LosAngeles/Main.asp), much more civilized than the food court. 8500 Beverly Blvd. (at La Cienega Blvd.), Los Angeles. ✆ 310/854-0071. www.beverlycenter.com.

The Grove ★ Located at the eastern end of the Farmers Market, this massive 575,000-square-foot Vegas-style retail complex is one of L.A.'s most popular megamalls. See "L.A.'s Top Attractions" in chapter 6 for more information. 189 The Grove Dr. (W. 3rd St. at Fairfax Ave.), Hollywood. ✆ 888/315-8883 or 323/900-8000. www. thegrovela.com.

> ### All American Girls
>
> Filled to the brim with all the things young girls love, the **American Girl Place** at the Grove shopping mall at 189 The Grove Dr. (℗ **877/AG-PLACE** [247-5223]; www.americangirlplace.com) features the flagship line of historical dolls and books. Find the contemporary Just Like You dolls, accessories, and girl-size clothing. For a real treat, girls can take in a performance at the American Girl Theater, dine with their dollies at the American Girl Café, and treat their doll to a new coif at the Doll Hair Salon.

Pacific Design Center   Something of an architectural and cultural landmark, the Pacific Design Center is the West Coast's largest facility for interior design goods and fine furnishings. It houses more than 200 showrooms filled with furniture, fabrics, flooring, wallcoverings, kitchen and bath fixtures, lighting, art, and accessories. Locals refer to the PDC as the Blue Whale in reference to its exterior, composed entirely of brilliant blue glass. Technically, businesses here sell to the trade only, and their wholesale prices reflect that. *Tip:* For a small fee, the center will provide a decorator-for-the-day to serve as official broker for your purchases. 8687 Melrose Ave., West Hollywood. ℗ 310/657-0800. www.pacificdesigncenter.com.

Westfield Century City   Since Westfield acquired this open-air shopping center in 2002, it's undergone a massive $150-million renovation in an attempt to transform this lackluster location into the area's premier shopping, dining, and entertainment destination. Along with a sorely needed face-lift, Westfield added 30 new shops, many restaurants, a new flagship 15-screen AMC movie theater, and 260 luxury condominiums. Anchored by **Macy's** and **Bloomingdale's** department stores, it's located on what was once a 20th Century Fox back lot, just west of Beverly Hills. Among the nearly 200 offerings are **Banana Republic, J. Crew, bebe,** and **Sephora.** 10250 Santa Monica Blvd. (at Ave. of the Stars), Century City. ℗ 310/277-3898. www.westfield.com/centurycity.

Westside Pavilion   Located at the intersection of Overland and Pico boulevards on the Westside of Los Angeles, this shopping center has the only **Nordstrom** in the area and attracts a very style-conscious crowd with a taste for the finest in women's fashions, handbags, and shoes. It's within easy access of I-405 and I-10, major arterials to the L.A. area. It boasts a roster of more than 160 specialty shops, such as **BCBG, Aeropostale, Aldo, Banana Republic,** and **Nine West,** as well as the anchor restaurant **Westside Tavern,** a food court, and the two-story **Landmark Theatres.** This mall is big on community and kids' events. 10800 W. Pico Blvd., Los Angeles. ℗ 310/470-8752. www.westsidepavilion.com.

Hollywood

Hollywood & Highland   A sure sign that this formerly seedy section of the city is on the fast track to recovery is the massive $615-million "entertainment complex" at the corner of Hollywood Boulevard and Highland Street (hence the name). Surrounded by souvenir shops and tattoo parlors, the gleaming 8¾-acre center contains all the top-end merchants—Guess, Louis Vuitton, bebe—as well as studio broadcast facilities and the gorgeous **Kodak Theatre,** home of the Academy Awards (really, you'll want to take a peek at this theater). The mall's other centerpiece is Babylon Court; designed after a set from the 1916 film *Intolerance,* the open-air space attempts to re-create an over-the-top golden-age movie set, complete with giant pillars topped with 13,500-pound elephants and a colossal arch that frames the HOLLYWOOD sign in the distance. Parking isn't a problem, as the six-level underground lot can cram in 3,000 cars. 6801 Hollywood Blvd., Hollywood. ✆ 323/817-0200. www. hollywoodandhighland.com.

Pasadena

Paseo Colorado   This open-air mall in the heart of Pasadena is ground zero for local shopaholics. Anchored by Macy's, the two-level, 3-block monolith houses about 140 retailers and restaurants (but few men's fashions), a Gelson's market, a fitness center, a full-service day spa, and a 14-screen multiplex theater. What's unique about the Paseo is the dozens of offices, apartments, and studios built atop the mall, which allows residents easy access to all the daily necessities a city dweller needs to survive. 280 E. Colorado Blvd. (at Marengo Ave.), Pasadena. ✆ 626/795-9100. www.paseo-coloradopasadena.com.

The San Fernando Valley

Americana at Brand ★★   The people behind the Grove opened this outdoor mall in 2008, bringing some top-notch retailers—and a touch of Vegas—to the Valley. There's a Barneys New York Co-Op, H&M, Kitson, Calvin Klein, Sur La Table, and Kate Spade for shopping; an 18-screen movie theater; and restaurants like Katsuya and Frida Mexican Cuisine. During the summer, Good Humor men sell ice-cream treats from old-fashioned trucks; during the winter holidays, there's a nightly fake snowfall to get people in the spirit. It looks pretty much like soapy suds, but for those Angelenos who've never seen snow, it does the trick. 889 Americana Way (at Colorado Blvd. and Brand Ave.), Glendale. ✆ 818/637-8982. www.americanaatbrand.com.

Universal CityWalk ☺   Designed to resemble an almost-cartoonish depiction of an urban street, Universal CityWalk gets a mention because it's unique. Next door to Universal Studios—you must walk through it if you use Universal City's main parking structure—CityWalk is dominated by brightly colored, oversize storefronts. The heavily touristed faux street is home to a number of restaurants, including **Hard Rock Cafe** and **Saddle Ranch Chop House.** In terms of shopping, CityWalk is not worth a special visit—it's got the ubiquitous Abercrombie & Fitch, Guess, and the like. Still, kids will love the carnival atmosphere and the **Universal Studios Store.** Universal Center Dr., Universal City. ✆ 818/622-4455. www.citywalkhollywood.com.

   A Hollywood Production Worth Checking Out

Every Sunday from 8am to 1pm, the **Hollywood Farmers Market** takes place on Ivar Avenue between Hollywood and Sunset boulevards. Along with fresh California-grown produce and flowers, there's plenty of live entertainment, an artisan and crafts fair, and prepared foods from local restaurants. There's even free parking off Vine Street. See "L.A.'s Top Attractions," in chapter 6, for more information.

SHOPPING A TO Z

Adult Toys

WEST HOLLYWOOD

Hustler Hollywood Here's a bit of shopping trivia for you: Teresa Flynt, daughter of *Hustler Magazine* maven Larry Flynt, is the owner of Hustler Hollywood, the largest erotica store in the country. Although the magazine is pretty raunchy, this boutique-style store is surprisingly chic and not the least bit intimidating. Whereas most sex shops are small, cramped, and poorly lit (from what I hear, of course), Hustler Hollywood's entire facade is floor-to-ceiling windows, and merchandise is artfully arranged on well-lit displays throughout the store. Sure, a spot-lit vibrator is still a vibrator, but it's the packaging that makes all the difference. 8920 Sunset Blvd., West Hollywood. © 310/860-9009. www.hustlerhollywood.com.

Antiques

L.A.'S WESTSIDE & BEVERLY HILLS

Del Mano It's worth a visit to this contemporary crafts gallery to see the cool creations—some whimsical, some exquisite—of American artists working with glass, wood, ceramics, and jewelry. 2001 Westwood Blvd., Westwood. © 310/441-2001. www.delmano.com.

HOLLYWOOD

Off The Wall This collection of oversize antiques includes kitschy statues, Art Deco furnishings, carved wall reliefs, Wurlitzer jukeboxes, giant restaurant and gas-station signs, pinball machines, and lots and lots of neon. 7325 Melrose Ave., West Hollywood. © 323/930-1185. www.offthewallantiques.com.

THE SAN FERNANDO VALLEY

Arte International Furnishings Seven warehouses full of carved furniture and wrought iron once sold only to moviemakers and restaurants are now open to the public. This is one of the most fascinating places in North Hollywood. 5356 Riverton Ave., North Hollywood. © 818/769-5090. www.arteshowrooms.com.

Art

SANTA MONICA & THE BEACHES

Bergamot Station ★★★ Once a station for the Red Car trolley line, this industrial space is now home to the Santa Monica Museum of Art, plus two dozen art galleries, a cafe, a bookstore, and offices. Most of the galleries are closed Monday. The train yard is located at the terminus of Michigan Avenue, west of Cloverfield Boulevard.

The wide variety of exhibits changes often: Julius Shulman's black-and-white photo retrospective of L.A.'s Case Study Houses, a provocative exhibit of Vietnam War propaganda posters from the United States and Vietnam, or whimsical furniture constructed entirely of corrugated cardboard. A sampling of offerings includes

---

Stellar Shopping

If you want to mix in some celebrity sightings along with your shopping spree, head to the Beverly Center. A handful of high-end shops here cater to the famous and wealthy, particularly **Hugo Boss** and **D&G**. Other shops like Ed Hardy cater strictly to hopeless fashion victims.

GETTING artsy

the **Gallery of Functional Art** (☏ **310/829-6990**), which features one-of-a-kind and limited-edition furniture, lighting, bathroom fixtures, and other functional art pieces, as well as smaller items like jewelry, flatware, ceramics, and glass. The **Rosamund Felsen Gallery** (☏ **310/828-8488**) is well known for showcasing L.A.-based contemporary artists; this is a good place to get a taste of current trends. **Track 16 Gallery** (☏ **310/264-4678**) has exhibitions that range from pop art to avant-garde inventiveness. 2525 Michigan Ave. (east of Cloverfield Blvd.), Santa Monica. www.bergamotstation.com.

Every Picture Tells A Story ★★★ ☺ This gallery, devoted to the art of children's literature, is frequented by young-at-heart art aficionados as well as parents introducing their kids to the concept of an art gallery. Works by Maurice Sendak (*Where the Wild Things Are*), Tim Burton (*The Nightmare Before Christmas*), and original lithos of *Curious George* and *Charlotte's Web* are featured. Call for events; the store usually combines exhibitions of illustrators with story readings and interactive workshops. 1311-C Montana Ave., Santa Monica. ☏ 310/451-2700. www.everypicture.com.

Books

SANTA MONICA & THE BEACHES

Hennessey + Ingalls This bookstore is devoted to art and architecture, from magnificent coffee-table photography books to graphic arts titles and obscure biographies of artists and histories of art movements. 214 Wilshire Blvd., Santa Monica. ☏ 310/458-9074. www.hennesseyingalls.com.

Small World Books ★ This sunny little shop is located right on the Venice boardwalk, with a friendly and dedicated staff whose mission is helping customers locate that hard-to-find book. Along with a wide selection of titles published by major presses, Small World carries titles published by smaller presses. 1407 Ocean Front Walk, Venice. ☏ 310/399-2360. www.smallworldbooks.com.

L.A.'S WESTSIDE & BEVERLY HILLS

Barnes & Noble This national chain is represented throughout the city. B&N offers discounts on bestsellers and also comfy chairs to shoppers who like to read a bit before they buy. The Westwood branch is one of its largest stores and is conveniently attached to the vast Westside Pavilion shopping mall; there's plenty of free parking downstairs. 10850 W. Pico Blvd. (Westside Pavilion), Los Angeles. ℭ 310/475-3138. www.bn.com. Other branches: Santa Monica (1201 Third Street Promenade; ℭ 310/260-9110) and Pasadena (111 W. Colorado Blvd.; ℭ 626/585-0362).

Book Soup ★★ This is one of L.A.'s most celebrated bookshops, selling mainstream and small-press books and hosting regular book signings and author nights. Book Soup is a great browsing shop; it has a large selection of showbiz books and an extensive outdoor news and magazine stand. 8818 Sunset Blvd., West Hollywood. ℭ 310/659-3110. www.booksoup.com.

C. G. Jung Bookstore & Library This bookshop specializes in analytical psychology, folklore, fairy tales, alchemy, dream studies, myths, symbolism, and other related topics. CDs and DVDs are also sold. 10349 W. Pico Blvd. (east of Beverly Glen Blvd.), Los Angeles. ℭ 310/556-1196. www.junginla.org.

Los Angeles Audubon Society Bookstore A terrific selection of books on nature, adventure travel, and ecology is augmented by bird-watching equipment and accessories. Phone for information on L.A. nature walks. Closed Monday. 7377 Santa Monica Blvd., West Hollywood. ℭ 323/876-0202. www.losangelesaudubon.org.

Traveler's Bookcase ★ This store, one of the best travel bookshops in the West, stocks a huge selection of guidebooks and travel literature, as well as maps and travel accessories. A quarterly newsletter chronicles the travel adventures of the genial owners, who know firsthand the most helpful items to carry. Look for regular readings by well-known travel writers. 8375 W. 3rd St., Los Angeles. ℭ 323/655-0575. www.travelbooks.com.

HOLLYWOOD

Samuel French Book Store This is L.A.'s biggest theater and movie bookstore. Plays, screenplays, and film books are all sold here, as well as scripts for Broadway and Hollywood blockbusters. 7623 Sunset Blvd. (btw. Fairfax and La Brea aves.), Hollywood. ℭ 323/876-0570. www.samuelfrench.com.

PASADENA

Vroman's Bookstore Open for more than 110 years, this is Southern California's oldest and largest independent bookstore. Don't expect dusty shelves and musty smells; it's clean, up to date, and chock-full of everything a book lover would want or need. The visiting-author series is one of the best in the area. Vroman's Fine Writing, Gifts, and Stationery store is right next door. 695 E. Colorado Blvd. (btw. Oak Knoll and El Molino aves.), Pasadena. ℭ 626/449-5320. www.vromansbookstore.com.

CDs & Music

HOLLYWOOD

Amoeba Music ★ Just as movie fans must walk the Hollywood Walk of Fame, fans of music must walk the aisles of Amoeba. With nearly 1 million new and used CDs, LPs, 45s, and 78s, as well as DVDs and other video formats, Amoeba prides itself on its breadth and depth with music of every genre: hip-hop, pop, rock, jazz, country, R&B, folk, classical, blues, reggae, dance, and so on. With the largest collection of vinyl albums in one location anywhere on the planet, Amoeba also stocks a huge assortment of new and vintage music and film-oriented posters. 6400 Sunset Blvd., Los Angeles. ℭ 323/245-6400. www.amoebamusic.com.

Fashions

FOR MEN & WOMEN
Santa Monica & the Beaches

Fred Segal ★★ They've become an L.A. institution, these breezy collections of ultrahip boutiques linked like departments of a single-story fashion maze. Shops include the latest apparel for men, women, and toddlers, plus lingerie, shoes, hats, luggage, cosmetics, workout/loungewear, and a cafe. Fred Segal also has major star-spotting potential (Matt Damon, Cameron Diaz, Sandra Bullock, and Kate Hudson are regulars; David Duchovny reportedly met his wife here when he asked her to help him pick out a suit). The original Fred Segal complex (opened in 1960) is at 8118 Melrose Ave. in West Hollywood (✆ **323/655-3734**), but either is a rewarding shopping foray. 500 Broadway, Santa Monica. ✆ 310/651-4129. www.fredsegal.com.

L.A.'s Westside & Beverly Hills

American Rag First to draw shoppers back to industrial La Brea in the early '80s, American Rag has grown from a small vintage clothing store to include trendy new fashions on its own label, as well as adjacent boutiques selling shoes and children's clothes; there's even a kitchen and housewares shop with a small cafe. Once a best-kept secret of hip teenagers, the American Rag dynasty today draws more tourists than trendsetters. 150 S. La Brea Ave., Los Angeles. ✆ 323/935-3154. www.amrag.com.

L.A. Souvenirs on the Cheap

Ocean Front Walk in Venice Beach is one of the best places in L.A. to shop for inexpensive souvenirs.

H&M ★★ If you haven't heard of H&M, then you obviously don't know a thing about affordably priced fashion. So popular among the city's shopping elite, it created a frenzy when Southern California's first Swedish-brand H&M store opened in Old Pasadena. (People were lined up around the block and even camping out.) The Pasadena location carries only women's fashions, while the larger Beverly Center location has a men's section and a better selection of accessories. Pasadena, 60 W. Colorado Blvd. ✆ 626/793-8974. www.hm.com. Other branch: Beverly Center, 8500 Beverly Blvd. (at La Cienega Blvd.), Los Angeles. ✆ 310/855-1009.

Maxfield ★ Here you'll find some of L.A.'s best-quality avant-garde designs, including men's and women's fashions by Yamamoto, Comme des Garçons, Dolce & Gabbana, Jil Sander, and the like. Furniture and home accessories are also sold. The store's provocative window displays have ranged from sharp political statements to a Jerry Garcia tribute. 8825 Melrose Ave., West Hollywood. ✆ 310/274-8800.

FOR WOMEN & CHILDREN
Santa Monica & the Beaches

CP Shades CP Shades is a San Francisco ladies' clothier whose line is carried by many department stores and boutiques. Fans will love this store, devoted solely to loose, casual cotton and linen separates. CP Shades's trademark monochromatic neutrals are meticulously arranged within an airy, well-lit interior. 2937 Main St., Santa Monica. ✆ 310/392-0949. www.cpshades.com.

L.A.'s Westside & Beverly Hills

Oilily ☺   This colorful line of kids' play clothes came from the Netherlands like a storm, and now kids around town are all sporting candy-bright colors and retro-bold florals. Moms get into the action, too, with a coordinating line of sun wear. 9520 Brighton Way, Beverly Hills. ✆ 310/859-9145. www.oilily-world.com.

Polkadots & Moonbeams   This is actually two stores several doors apart, one carrying (slightly overpriced) hip young fashions for women, and the other a vintage store with clothing, accessories, and fabrics from the 1920s to the 1960s, all in remarkable condition. 8367 W. 3rd St. (vintage store) and 8381 W. 3rd St. (modern store), Los Angeles. ✆ 323/651-1746. www.polkadotsandmoonbeams.com.

Hollywood

Betsey Johnson Boutique   The New York–based designer has brought to L.A. her brand of fashion—trendy, cutesy, body-conscious women's wear in colorful prints and faddish fabrics. 8050 Melrose Ave., Los Angeles. ✆ 323/852-1534. www.betsey johnson.com.

DISCOUNT

Loehmann's   Loehmann's is huge and packed to the rafters with clothes, shoes, and accessories. Most of its stock is name-brand and designer labels, though nothing ultratrendy is represented. The store is popular for business attire, conservative leisure wear, and bargains on fancy dress wear. Known for years as a women's enclave, Loehmann's also has a men's department offering the same great deals. Serious shoppers should check out the Back Room, where heavyweight designers like Donna Karan and Calvin Klein are represented alongside beaded and formal evening gowns. 333 S. La Cienega Blvd. (south of 3rd St.), Los Angeles. ✆ 310/659-0674. www. loehmanns.com.

Los Angeles Fashion District   Reminiscent of the New York garment district but not quite as frenetic, L.A.'s 90-block Fashion District, bordered by 7th, Spring, and San Pedro streets and the Santa Monica Freeway, has dozens of small shops selling designer and name-brand apparel at heavily discounted prices. A concentration of retail women's wear bargains—many by name-brand designers—can be found at the Cooper Design Space, 860 S. Los Angeles St. (at 9th St.). Men should have some luck along the upper blocks of Los Angeles Street, where mostly business attire is displayed, with deep discounts on Hugo Boss, Armani, and other current suits (mainly Italian), plus similar savings on sport coats and shirts. Ties and vests are usually less stylish. Los Angeles Street btw. 7th St. and Washington Blvd. www.fashiondistrict.org.

 Celebrity Cloned Clothing

If your dream is to dress like your favorite celebrity who may have stepped right off the red carpet at one of Hollywood's numerous award shows, then a visit to **A.B.S. by Allen Schwartz** should be on your to-do list. As soon as one of these high-profile events is over (think Golden Globes, SAG Awards, Oscars), A.B.S. has already produced a knockoff version that is every bit as lovely, but much more affordable. 1533 Montana Ave. (at 15th St.), Santa Monica. ✆ **310/393-8770.** www.absstyle.com.

WHERE TO FIND HOLLYWOOD'S
hand-me-downs

Admit it: You've dreamed of being a glamorous movie or TV star—everyone has. Well, don't expect to be "discovered" during your L.A. vacation, but you can live out your fantasy by dressing the part. Costumes from famous movies, TV show wardrobes, cast-offs from celebrity closets—they're easier to find (and more affordable to own) than you might think.

For sheer volume, you can't beat **It's A Wrap,** 3315 W. Magnolia Blvd., Burbank (© **818/567-7366;** www.itsawraphollywood.com). Every item here is marked with its place of origin, and the list is staggering: *Beverly Hills, 90210; House; Eat, Pray, Love; General Hospital; True Blood; As the World Turns; Dexter; Hannah Montana;* and so on. Many of these wardrobes (which include shoes and accessories) aren't outstanding except for their Hollywood origins: Jerry Seinfeld's trademark Polo shirts, for instance, are standard mall-issue. Some collectible pieces, like Sylvester Stallone's *Rocky* stars-and-stripes boxers, are framed and on display. Open Monday through Friday from 10am to 8pm, Saturday and Sunday from 11am to 6pm.

When you're done at It's A Wrap, stop in across the street at **Junk For Joy,** 3314 W. Magnolia Blvd., Burbank (© **818/569-4903;** www.junkforjoy.com). A Hollywood wardrobe coordinator or two will probably be hunting through the racks right beside you at this wacky little store. The emphasis here is on funky items more suitable as costumes than everyday wear (the store is mobbed every year around Halloween). When I visited, the shop was loaded with 1970s polyester shirts and tacky slacks, but you never know what you'll find. Open Tuesday through Saturday from noon to "5-ish" pm.

The grande dame of all wardrobe and costume outlets is **Western Costume,** 11041 Vanowen St., North Hollywood (© **818/760-0900;** www.westerncostume.com). In business since 1912, Western Costume still designs and executes wardrobes for major motion pictures; when filming is finished, the garments are added to the staggering rental inventory. This place is perhaps best known for outfitting Vivien Leigh in *Gone With the Wind.* Several of Scarlett O'Hara's memorable gowns were available for rent until they were auctioned off at a charity event. Western also maintains an outlet store, where damaged garments are sold at rock-bottom (nothing over $15) prices. If you're willing to do some rescue work, there are definitely hidden treasures here. Open for rentals Monday through Friday from 8am to 6pm, and for sales Monday through Friday from 8:30am to 6pm.

Finally, don't miss **Golyester** (below). This shop is almost a museum of finely preserved (but reasonably priced) vintage clothing and fabrics. The staff will gladly flip through stacks of *Vogue* magazines from the 1930s, 1940s, and 1950s with you, pointing out the lavish, star-studded original advertisements for various outfits in their stock. Open every day 11am to 6pm.

VINTAGE
L.A.'s Westside & Beverly Hills

Golyester Before this ladies' boutique opened, the owner's friends would take one look at her collection of vintage fabrics and clothes and gasp, "Golly, Esther!" Hence the whimsical name. You pay a little extra for the pristine condition of hard-to-find

A MECCA FOR HIGH-END vintage

If your style is more Hepburn than Hilton, you won't want to miss the treasure-trove of high-end vintage shopping L.A. has to offer. Doris Raymond's the **Way We Wore,** 334 S. La Brea Ave. (✆ **323/937-0878;** www.thewaywe wore.com), is a favorite among celebs and stylists for vintage Chanel, Balenciaga, and Fortuny. Cameron Silver's **Decades,** 8214½ Melrose Ave. (✆ **323/655-0223;** www.decadesinc.com), is an L.A. institution, where you'll find frocks from Halston, Gucci, Lilly Pulitzer, and Missoni. **Lily et Cie,** 9044 Burton Way (✆ **310/724-5757**), supplies many of the glamour gowns you see on the red carpet. Owner and vintage maven Rita Watnick has an impeccable collection of pieces from important designers like Yves Saint Laurent, Givenchy, and Trigere.

garments like unusual embroidered sweaters from the 1940s and 1950s, Joan Crawford–style suits from the 1940s, and vintage lingerie, but it's worth every penny. 136 S. La Brea Ave., Los Angeles. ✆ 323/931-1339.

Hollywood

Wasteland An enormous steel-sculpted facade fronts this L.A. branch of the Berkeley/Haight-Ashbury hipster hangout, which sells vintage and contemporary clothes for men and women. You'll find leathers and denim as well as some classic vintage, but mostly funky 1970s garb. This trendy store is packed with colorful polyester halters and bell-bottoms from the decade I'd rather forget. 7248 Melrose Ave., Los Angeles. ✆ 323/653-3028. www.wastelandclothing.com.

The San Fernando Valley

Playclothes Men and women alike will marvel at the pristine selection of vintage clothes housed in this boutique, tucked into a burgeoning antiques row west of Coldwater Canyon Avenue. Playclothes approaches its stock with a sense of humor and knows exactly how each item was worn and accessorized in its heyday. 3100 W. Magnolia Blvd., Burbank. ✆ 818/557-8447. www.vintageplayclothes.com.

Hubba Hubba This vintage shop for "guys and dolls" is one of the oldest and longest-standing in all of Los Angeles. Owner Pat Taylor, something of a "character," has been at it since the early '80s. She specializes in mostly '40s through '60s clothing and accessories, so don't come in looking for parachute pants or platform shoes. If you're a fan of *Mad Men*, you'll love this nifty little shop—the costume buyers for the show certainly do. 3220 W. Magnolia Blvd., ✆ 818/845-0636. 3100 W. Magnolia Blvd., Burbank. ✆ 818/557-8447. www.vintageplayclothes.com.

L.A.'S TOP DAY SPAS

L.A.'s Westside & Beverly Hills

Bliss Los Angeles ★ Located at the W Hotel, this outpost of a popular New York spa is part of a new breed of day spas that are more about sass than Zen. You won't find classical or wave-simulated music here; instead, it's rhythm and blues. Forget the lemon water in the women's lounge, and look for the brownie bar. The men get sports magazines, heated shaving cream, and a flatscreen TV in their lounge. There's a retail boutique, three movie-while-you-manicure nail stations, and 10 treatment rooms in the second-floor, 7,000-square-foot space. And just like the vibe, the menu offers up something a little bit different, like the hot milk and almond pedicure ($65 for 60 min.); carrot and sesame-seed body buff ($165 for 90 min.); the "hangover herbie" detoxifying package ($215 for 90 min.); and the ultra-relaxing Blissage 75 massage ($150), what they call a "virtual countdown to 'butter.'" 930 Hilgard Ave. (at the W Hotel), Westwood. © 323/930-0330. www.blissworld.com.

Kinara Spa ★ Whether you're a Hollywood starlet primping for a big night or just pretending to be, Kinara is a one-stop location for everything you'll need. The space is subtle but not bare; calm but not Zen; natural but not serious. Spa services range in price from about $30 to $200, with multitreatment packages starting at $235. Not bad for a place that attracts the toned and the beautiful Halle Berry, Naomi Watts, and Jennifer Garner. But you don't even need to be a star to get star treatment: The Red Carpet facial, one of the most popular treatments, is a custom-blended procedure that exfoliates, brightens, and smoothes the face. **Note:** The onsite cafe has closed. 656 N. Robertson Blvd. (btw. Melrose Ave. and Santa Monica Blvd.), West Hollywood. © 310/657-9188. www.kinaraspa.com.

Ona Spa & Privé Salon ★ Ona means "all things good" in the French Basque dialect, and that's certainly the treatment you'll receive in the hands—or feet of Ona's Daniel Krasofski (one of his signature treatments, the $175 Ona Pada, utilizes the therapist's feet for maximum, stress-relieving pressure), one of the top massage therapists around. This small, full-service day spa specializes in custom treatments using both ancient and traditional techniques, particularly Ayurveda. The massages here run the gamut, from $50 to $95 for a tension-relieving Ona Quick Fix (30- to 50-min. in length) to the $220 Onaaah, a choreographed four-handed tandem Balinese massage. Body and facial enhancements such as laser hair removal, Botox, filler, and chemical peels are also available, as is acupuncture therapy. One of the newest services is the signature Babar Platinum Facial (75 min. for $175), an anti-aging service incorporating cleaning, peeling, masks, facial massage, collagen boosts, rich creams and a dash of pure platinum powder. On the bottom floor of the same building is the **Privé Salon,** one of the city's trendiest salons, where celebrity-sighting is common. 7373 Beverly Blvd. (at N. Fuller Ave.), Los Angeles. Ona: © 323/931-4442 or 931-5559 (Privé). www.onaspa.com.

Peninsula Spa ★★★ *Condé Nast Traveler* recently rated the 4,600-square-foot Peninsula Spa number one in service and number two in treatments for urban spas, and indeed, this is one of the top spots in the U.S. for pampering. Sure, it's pricey, but what would you expect from the only hotel in Southern California to earn both the AAA Five Diamond and Mobil Five Star awards for many years running? **Bonus:** The spa underwent a $7-million revamp, adding an extra 1,000 square feet of space, with mosaic tile work in serene shades of blue and pure white Calacatta marble. The spa is the first in North America to offer Shiffa precious-gem oil treatments, which contain rubies, emeralds, sapphires, and diamonds, and are said to bring healing powers. In addition to the seven treatment rooms, you can opt to have some services in one of the Peninsula's famed cabanas overlooking the 60-foot lap pool. They even offer a good selection of services geared toward the guys, such as the 50-minute Men's Foot Recovery and 60-minute Gentlemen's Facial Rejuvenation. The Roof

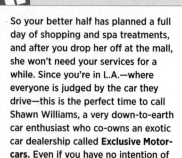

For Bored Non-Shoppers: A Lamborghini Test-Drive

So your better half has planned a full day of shopping and spa treatments, and after you drop her off at the mall, she won't need your services for a while. Since you're in L.A.—where everyone is judged by the car they drive—this is the perfect time to call Shawn Williams, a very down-to-earth car enthusiast who co-owns an exotic car dealership called **Exclusive Motorcars.** Even if you have no intention of buying or leasing a Ferrari or Lamborghini, he'll be happy to talk cars, take you on a tour of his showroom, and perhaps test-drive a new or slightly used Bentley Continental GT, Mercedes SL600, or Porsche Carrera GT. If you're the type that has to have it *now,* you can drive your new baby while vacationing in L.A. (Shawn can arrange financing and insurance while you wait), then either take the car home or have it shipped. He'll be happy to arrange a short-term rental as well (me, I'd go with the black Ferrari F430 Spider F-1). If you want to make an appointment, call Shawn at ✆ **310/558-3300,** or just drop by the showroom at 10534 W. Pico Blvd. near Overland Avenue. It's open Monday through Friday 9am to 6pm, and Saturday 10am to 5pm. Log onto www.emcars.com.

Garden restaurant is the perfect spot for a pre- or post-treatment lunch or tonic. And don't be surprised if you spot an A-lister, as the Peninsula is a perennial celeb favorite. 9882 S. Santa Monica Blvd. (near Wilshire Blvd.), Beverly Hills. ✆ 310/551-2888. www.peninsula.com.

Spa at the Four Seasons Hotel ★★   There's already something so indulgent about the Four Seasons in Beverly Hills, that a caviar facial in the spa seems positively pedestrian. The 4,000-square-foot spa has eight treatment rooms, men's and women's locker rooms, and a menu full of rejuvenating services. The wildly popular Punta Mita Massage uses tequila and sage oil; combined with the Margarita Salt Scrub, it's like a happy hour for your skin. One of the signature treatments—a California Cabana Massage at a private, candlelit poolside cabana—is oh-so-very L.A. Along with the full-service spa, the view-endowed fourth-floor deck features a lap pool, poolside cafe, and glass-walled fitness center, all of which guests are welcome to use before or after a spa treatment. 300 S. Doheny Dr. (at W. 3rd St.), Beverly Hills. ✆ 310/273-2222. www.fourseasons.com/losangeles.

Spa Montage ★★★   This two-floor facility in the new Montage Beverly Hills hotel is as luxurious as you'd expect it to be for the Golden Triangle. It's 20,000 square feet of pure bliss that's inspired by the ancient Andalusia region of Spain, which means lots of water everywhere—a coed mineral pool where couples can relax after their massage, trickling fountains in the whirlpool areas—and lovely mosaic tile work throughout. Treatments focus on well-being, like Fruits of the Orchard, a series of detoxifying baths and wraps filled with fruit extracts and herbs ($270); or get slathered in mud from three different parts of the world in the Three Bowls Ritual ($270). Customized facials are the ultimate in relaxation (starting at $125). Kim Vo, "colorist to the stars," relocated his Beverly Hills salon here. 225 N. Canon Dr., Beverly Hills. ✆ 310/860-7800. www.montagebeverlyhills.com.

Santa Monica

Chocolate Sun ★   A mere 2 blocks away from the beach in Santa Monica, this charming bungalow has attracted accolades from top beauty magazines such as *InStyle, Allure,* and *Shape* for its natural-looking, sunless spray tan using all organically grown and wild-crafted botanicals. Should you want to go to the beach during your visit, not to worry—the treatment is SPF 30. 147 Bay St., Santa Monica. ✆ 310/450-3075. www.chocolatesun.net.

Exhale ★★   Escape the crowds at the Third Street Promenade at this luxury retreat that hails from New York but is so fittingly SoCal, with a yoga studio, well-being workshops, "healing waters" room, eucalyptus saunas, and Core Fusion Pilates classes. You'll find 15,000 square feet of Ohm here, all with a tranquil design and natural aesthetic. The signature Fusion Massage uses therapeutic massage practices from around the world, like rhythmic movements and potent herbal and aromatherapy oils. Before any treatment, you're encouraged to arrive early to sit in the "quiet room" where teas are ceremoniously blended for each individual guest. Remember . . . just breathe. 101 Wilshire Blvd., Santa Monica. ✆ 310/319-3193. www.exhalespa.com.

Ocean Spa & Fitness ★   In the Loews Santa Monica Beach Hotel, Ocean Spa & Fitness is an eco-conscious spa that embraces nurture *and* nature and offers Moor mud wraps, buff body treatments, beauty flash facials, and the signature "Beachcomber" massage with heated tiger clam shells infused with mineral-rich kelp and seawater. 1700 Ocean Ave., Santa Monica. ✆ 866/563-9792. www.santamonica loewshotel.com.

ONE, The Spa ★★   This beach-themed spa—it's designed to resemble a ship—is owned by the tony Shutters on the Beach Hotel but located in a separate building, giving it a little more privacy than the typical hotel spa. Featuring Ole Henriksen's (the "facialist to the stars") all-natural products and services, ONE has a great selection of treatments and day packages with cheeky seaside names like the Clear as Day, a deep detoxifying treatment ($160 for 60 min.), or the Surf's Up pedicure ($130 for 90 min.). I recommend the 90-minute, hot-stone massage that's designed to restore balance to the body ($220). 1 Pico Blvd., Santa Monica. ✆ 310/587-1712. www. shuttersonthebeach.com.

Spa at Le Merigot ★   Le Merigot is a low-key luxury hotel that doesn't try to be anything other than a comfortable place to spend your seaside vacation, and its spa is the perfect place to unwind after a busy day of shopping and sightseeing. The 5,500-square-foot space offers a full range of services, everything from waxing to couples massage. The aestheticians have such a wonderful touch that a 60-minute facial seems to heal more than just your skin: You walk out feeling beautified *and* blissed-out. Non–hotel guests can go in for any treatment (including eyebrow waxes) and still use all the state-of-the-art fitness equipment, pool, saunas, and other hotel amenities before or afterward. 1740 Ocean Ave., Santa Monica. ✆ 310/395-9700. www.lemerigothotel.com.

Downtown

Pho-Siam Thai Spa ★★ 📖   I used to live in Thailand, and there's nothing I miss more than a traditional Thai massage, an ancient healing art that combines yogalike stretching, deep-tissue massage, and therapeutic balms. You walk in tense and stiff and walk out a happy noodle. The family-run Pho-Siam Thai Spa is near Downtown

L.A. at the south end of Echo Park and staffed by a group of Thai women who are well-trained in the art of their homeland's massage. For a mere $50 your body will undergo 60 minutes of such indulgence that you'll be planning a vacation to Thailand by the time you're done. Foot massages, waxes, facials, and couples massages are offered as well, but for the ultimate indulgence, request the 2-hour healing massage, a bargain at $100. Walk-ins are welcome, but it's better to call and make an appointment. Free parking. 1525 Pizarro St. (at Glendale Blvd., 1 block west of Temple St.), Los Angeles. ✆ 213/484-8484. www.phosiam.com.

LOS ANGELES AFTER DARK

Los Angeles didn't invent the word hip, but it certainly holds the patent on it. L.A. has some of the most cutting-edge clubs and bars in the world and is the polestar for the best and brightest in the music scene. Entertainment of all types—from Hollywood Bowl picnic performances to cool jazz venues, retro chic bars, and rock-'n'-roll clubs—can be found in the following pages.

First you need to find out who's performing while you're in town. Check **L.A. Weekly** (www.laweekly.com), a free weekly paper available at sidewalk stands, shops, and restaurants. It has all the most up-to-date news on what's happening in Los Angeles's playhouses, cinemas, museums, and live-music venues. The Sunday **"Calendar"** and Thursday **"Weekend"** sections of the **Los Angeles Times** (www.latimes.com/theguide) are also a good source of information for what's going on throughout the city. For more online info on L.A.'s entertainment scene, see "Website-Seeing: The Best of L.A. Online," in chapter 11.

To purchase tickets in advance, first try buying them directly from the venue to avoid paying a surcharge. If that doesn't work, log on to **Prestige Tickets'** website at www.prestigetickets.com or call ✆ **888/595-6260.** Based in Hollywood for more than 20 years (now relocated to Encino and merged with an East Coast company), it specializes in selling tickets to sporting, theater, concerts, and other entertainment events throughout Los Angeles—at a markup, of course. If all else fails, call **Ticketmaster** (✆ **800/745-3000;** www.ticketmaster.com), but beware of their absurdly high processing fees.

THE LIVE MUSIC SCENE

Los Angeles's music scene is extremely diverse, to say the least, a daunting and dizzying beast. But on any given night, finding something to satisfy any musical taste is easy because this city is at the center of the entertainment industry. Every day countless national and international acts are drawn here. From acoustic rock to jazz-fusion, heavy metal to Latin funk, and up-and-coming to put-to-pasture, L.A. has got it all.

But there's a rub. The big events are easy to find, but by the time you get to town, odds are the good tickets will be gone. The best advice is to plan ahead. On the Internet, both **Ticketmaster** (see above) and concert business trade publication **Pollstar** (www.pollstar.com) have websites that include tour itineraries of acts that are on—or will be going on—the road. Just start your search in advance. For a listing of smaller shows closer to the date of your arrival, both *L.A. Weekly* and the *Los Angeles Times* "Calendar" section have websites (see above). Sometimes tickets may become available at the box office before shows, or when all else fails, try "negotiating" with some of the locals in front of the venue.

Large Concert Venues

Mostly gone are the days of the behemoth stadium shows, excepting, of course, the occasional U2 or Rolling Stones tour. Still, major national and international acts tend to be attracted to some of the city's larger venues.

The crown of Downtown and home to the Lakers and Clippers pro basketball teams is the **Staples Center,** 1111 S. Figueroa St. (📞 213/742-7340; www.staplescenter.com). Along with the new 7,200-seat **Nokia Theatre** (www.nokiatheatre.com), this combination sports/event stadium is the city's primary concert venue. Part of the $4.5-billion, 4-million-square-foot **L.A. LIVE** complex (www.lalive.com)—which opened late 2008 and early 2009 adjacent to Staples and the Los Angeles Convention Center—the Nokia Theatre hosts star-studded award ceremonies and more than 150 live annual performances a year.

Amphitheaters are the staple of national rock and pop concert tours. Los Angeles's two main warriors are the outdoor **Greek Theatre** in Griffith Park, 2700 N. Vermont Ave., Los Angeles (📞 323/665-5857; www.greektheatrela.com), and the indoor **Gibson Amphitheatre** (formerly Universal Amphitheatre), Universal City Drive, Universal City (📞 818/622-4440), each seating about 6,000. Both are among the most accommodating and comfortable facilities for big-name acts. Nearly as beautiful as the Hollywood Bowl, the Greek books a full season of national acts ranging from the White Stripes and Robert Plant to Al Green and Melissa Etheridge. After a recent multimillion-dollar renovation project, the Greek is nicer than ever. Be advised that getting out afterward can still be a problem, as cars are stacked in packed lots, making exiting a painfully slow process.

Gibson Amphitheatre has one advantage over the Greek: It has a roof, so it can book year-round. It's not as aesthetically pleasing, but it is quite comfortable and none of its seats are too far from the stage. For some events, the "Party in the Pit" offers a general admission section next to the stage. In addition to pop stars from the Strokes to Kid Rock, the Universal hot spot has booked such theater events as *The Who's Tommy.* While the neon jungle of Universal's CityWalk doesn't appeal to everyone, it does offer plenty of pregig dining and drinking options.

Orange County's **Verizon Wireless Amphitheatre** (formerly Irvine Meadows), 8800 Irvine Center Dr., Irvine (📞 949/855-8096), which holds 15,000 (including a general-admission lawn *way* in the back), has hosted KROQ's often-spectacular summertime "Weenie Roast" and KIIS FM's "Wango Tango," as well as a plethora of touring rock acts, including recent shows from Dave Matthews Band and Coldplay. If you're going from L.A. on a weekday, get an early start, because Irvine is located at one of the most heavily traveled freeway junctions in the country.

Another popular venue is the **Honda Center** (formerly Arrowhead Pond of Anaheim), 2695 E. Katella Ave. (1 mile east of I-5), Anaheim (© **714/704-2500;** www. hondacenter.com), a combination sports/event stadium that's gaining momentum as a primary concert venue. It's about an hour from Los Angeles via the always-crowded I-5 freeway, but it's convenient to Disneyland-goers (about 8 min. away).

Midsize Concert Venues

The Avalon Hollywood   Formerly known as the Palace, this 1,100-capacity theater and nightclub—just across Vine from the famed Capitol Records tower—has been the site of numerous significant classical to alternative rock shows throughout for more than 60 years; everyone from Frank Sinatra to Nirvana has performed inside this Art Deco gem. After a much-needed makeover when it became the Avalon, club nights feature famous DJs such as Felix da Housecat and Sebastian Ingrosso. 1735 N. Vine St., Hollywood. © **323/462-8900.** www.avalonhollywood.com.

Club Nokia   This is the smaller of the two Nokia venues at L.A. LIVE, holding about 2,300 concertgoers in one open room. For pre- or post-show entertainment, there are touch screens in the lobby to scroll through the history and preview future events. Since it opened in 2008, acts like India.Arie, Joss Stone, and Staind have played here; Prince closed out a trifecta of back-to-back L.A. LIVE shows here in 2009. 800 W. Olympic Blvd., Downtown. © **213/765-7000.** www.clubnokia.com.

El Rey Theatre   Another restored relic of L.A.'s old Art Deco movie theaters, this small venue holds about 1,500 for such performers as Lucinda Williams and Manchester Orchestra. It offers upstairs and downstairs views of the stage, but plan on standing all night as there are usually no seats available. 5515 Wilshire Blvd. © **323/936-6400.** www.theelrey.com.

Hollywood Palladium ★   For such a storied venue—Frank Sinatra and Tommy Dorsey Orchestra performed at the opening show in 1940, and it's hosted everyone from the Grateful Dead and Led Zeppelin to Madonna over the years—there was a threat that it would be torn down to make way for condos. Luckily, Live Nation took over the 4,000-person venue in 2007 and, after a multimillion-dollar renovation, reopened it in 2008 with a concert by Jay-Z. 6215 W. Sunset Blvd., Hollywood. © **323/962-7600.** www.livenation.com.

House of Blues ★   With three great bars, funky Southern art, and a key Sunset Strip location, there are plenty of reasons music fans and industry types keep coming back to House of Blues. Night after night, audiences are dazzled by performances from nationally and internationally acclaimed acts as diverse as Jeff Beck, the Black Eyed Peas, and Motorhead. The food in the upstairs restaurant can be great (reservations are a must), and the Sunday Gospel Brunch, though a bit pricey, puts a mean raise on the roof. 8430 Sunset Blvd., West Hollywood. © **323/848-5100.** www.hob.com.

The Mayan Theatre   Perhaps the strangest yet coolest concert venue in town, with an elaborate decor in the mode of a Mayan temple (or something), this former movie house is a fine relic of L.A.'s glorious past. It seats about 1,000 for such performers as PJ Harvey, house DJs on Friday nights, salsa artists on Saturdays, Mogwai and masked Mexican wresting (Lucha Va Voom). The place is in a part of Downtown that most people don't usually visit, but parking is relatively easy and the interior makes it seem like another dimension. 1038 S. Hill St., Downtown. ✆ **213/746-4674.** www.clubmayan.com.

The Wiltern ★★ Saved from the wrecking ball in the mid-1980s, this 1930s-era Art Deco showcase is perhaps the most beautiful theater in town. Countless national and international acts such as Beck and Audioslave have played here. In addition, plenty of non-pop-music events such as Penn & Teller and Cedric the Entertainer complement the schedule. 3790 Wilshire Blvd., Los Angeles. ✆ **213/388-1400.** www.livenation.com.

The Club Scene

With more small clubs than you can swing a Stratocaster at, Los Angeles is *the* place for live music. Check **L.A. Weekly** (www.laweekly.com) to see who's in town during your visit. Unless otherwise noted, listed clubs admit only patrons 21 and over.

MOSTLY ROCK

The Dragonfly The Dragonfly offers a little bit of everything—the highlight being the long-running weekly hit show *Point Break Live,* with classic scenes from the movie starring a hilarious cast and an audience member chosen totally at random to play Keanu Reeves' starring role (cue cards are provided). Other nights are mostly dance-oriented, and run the gamut from Goth, industrial, jungle and drum & bass. Smokers and the overheated enjoy the cool outdoor patio. 6510 Santa Monica Blvd., Hollywood. ✆ **323/466-6111.** www.thedragonfly.com. Cover $5–$25.

King King ★ I'm not normally keen on Hollywood clubs (too much überhip dig-me crap), but King King is a refreshing change in attitude. The warehouse-size venue feels more SoHo than L.A.: exposed brick walls and ceilings, dark lighting, black velvet curtains, and a square bar on wheels that's moved to accommodate whatever's going on. The last time I was there, I watched a rather disturbing play followed by a sensational rockabilly band. 6555 Hollywood Blvd. (btw. Hudson and Whitley aves.), Hollywood. ✆ **323/960-5765.** www.kingkinghollywood.com. Cover $5–$10.

Largo at the Coronet ★ In 2008, this longstanding music venue moved from its Fairfax Village home to the aging Coronet Theatre near the Beverly Center. After some major refurbishment, the main stage is a comfortable 280-seater, and there's an intimate 60-seat room aptly named The Little Room. There's an eclectic array of performances, ranging from the plugged-in folk set to vibrant trip hoppers, and, pop-music archaeologist Jon Brion continues his amazing Friday-night shows (which are now monthly versus weekly), and it's (thankfully) no longer a dinner theater. Everyone from Fiona Apple to Randy Newman to comedians Sarah Silverman and Will Ferrell has performed here. This is an all-ages club. 366 N. La Cienega Blvd., Los Angeles. ✆ **310/855-0350.** www.largo-la.com.

McCabe's Guitar Shop ★ 🎁 Since 1958 this funky, cluttered music shop has opened its backroom for some memorable acoustic sets from the likes of Doc Watson, Jackson Browne, John Hammond, Aimee Mann, John Lee Hooker, Bill Frisell, Dan Bern, and Ann Wilson. With just 150 seats, McCabe's is intimate in the extreme; the gig would have to be in your living room to get any cozier. A guitar shop first and music venue second, McCabe's doesn't serve alcohol, and tickets are always reasonably

JON BRION live

When it comes to real musical talent, few L.A. music lovers will argue that there's a better all-around musician than **Jon Brion**. At a Los Angeles club called Largo at the Coronet (see above), Brion performs an amazing one-man show that always leaves his audience in awe. Producer, songwriter, and multi-instrumentalist, he has an amazing ability to play multiple instruments simultaneously. (He *is* the house band at Largo.) Brion is famous for making up songs on the spot, usually from titles shouted from the audience. He's also well known for his on-stage antics and idiosyncratic takes on famous classics such as the Beatles and Cheap Trick. Brion on Brion: "It's like spraying musical Raid on the classics, until each dying song flips on its back and wiggles its little musical legs in surrender." His shows tend to start pretty late (for Californians, that is), but it's worth the wait; check the schedule at Largo's website to see when he's playing. And don't be surprised if Elvis Costello or Beck makes a guest appearance. (Kanye West made a cameo rap the last time I was here.)

priced (if hard to get). All ages are admitted. 3101 Pico Blvd., Santa Monica. ✆ **310/828-4497.** www.mccabes.com. Cover $13–$35.

The Roxy Theatre   Veteran record producer/executive Lou Adler opened this Sunset Strip club in the mid-1970s with concerts by Neil Young and a lengthy run of the pre-movie *Rocky Horror Show*. Since then it has remained among the top showcase venues in Hollywood. Although the revitalized Troubadour and such new entries as the House of Blues challenge its preeminence among cozy clubs, you can still find international acts like the soulful Adele and great local bands. 9009 W. Sunset Blvd. ✆ **310/278-9457.** www.theroxyonsunset.com.

The Satellite ★   The wall-to-wall mirrors and shiny brass posts decorating the interior create the feeling that, in a past life, The Satellite must have been the legendary Spaceland. Oh yeah, it was. After almost 20 years, the venue officially changed names in late 2010/early 2011, depending on who you ask. But it's basically the same place that has hosted countless performances by artists such as Pavement, Mary Lou Lord, and Beck, and is still one of the most important clubs on the L.A. circuit. 1717 Silver Lake Blvd., Silver Lake. ✆ **323/661-4380.** www.thesatellitela.com. Cover free–$20.

The Troubadour   This West Hollywood mainstay radiates rock history—from the 1960s to the 1990s, the Troub really has seen 'em all. Audiences are consistently treated to memorable shows from the already-established or young-and-promising acts that take the Troubadour's stage. But bring your earplugs—this beer- and sweat-soaked club likes it loud. All ages are accepted. 9081 Santa Monica Blvd., West Hollywood. ✆ **310/276-6168.** www.troubadour.com. Cover $12–$35.

Villains Tavern ★   Downtown has certainly come up so far as cool nightlife venues opening in its Bunker Hill and South Park neighborhoods, but this L.A. River-adjacent property is truly boundary-pushing. Done up in Steampunk style, all of the pieces fit together nicely here: from a small but satisfying pub grub menu (juicy burger, addictive fried chickpeas) and artisanal, original cocktails to a jarringly friendly crowd and a roster of talented old timey Americana bands. 1356 Palmetto St. ✆ **213/613-0766.** www.villainstavern.com.

Art, jazz, beer, and free—baby, that's for me. That's why I always mark my calendar for the free jazz concerts hosted Friday evenings at the **Los Angeles County Museum of Art,** 5905 Wilshire Blvd., Los Angeles (ℂ **323/857-6000;** www.lacma.org). The museum hosts free concerts in its open central courtyard every Friday night April through Thanksgiving from 6 to 8pm. It's a great way to listen to good music with a glass of wine on a warm Los Angeles evening.

Viper Room   This world-famous club made a splash when it was first opened by actor Johnny Depp and co-owner Sal Jenco back in 1993; Depp is no longer involved, but after a small renovation in 2008, it's still rocking the Strip. With an intensely electric and often star-filled scene, the intimate rock club is also known for unforgettable late-night surprise performances from such powerhouses as the late Johnny Cash, Iggy Pop, Tom Petty, Slash, and Trapt (to name but a few) after headline gigs elsewhere in town. 8852 Sunset Blvd., West Hollywood. ℂ **310/358-1880.** www.viperroom.com. Cover $5–$15.

Whisky A Go-Go ★   This legendary bi-level venue personifies L.A. rock 'n' roll, from Jim Morrison and X to Guns N' Roses and Beck. Every trend has passed through this club, and it continues to be the most vital venue of its kind. With the hiring of an in-house booker a few years ago, the Whisky began showcasing more local talent. All ages are welcome. 8901 Sunset Blvd., West Hollywood. ℂ **310/652-4202,** ext. 15. www.whiskyagogo.com. Cover $10–$25.

BLUES & JAZZ

The Baked Potato   This restaurant/nightspot offers missile-size spuds while hosting a steady roster of jazz performances by local and visiting acts. Guitarist Andy Summers (of Police fame) has been known to pop in now and again. The valley location is a few blocks from Universal City. All ages welcome. 3787 Cahuenga Blvd., Studio City. ℂ **818/980-1615.** www.thebakedpotato.com. 2-drink minimum.

Catalina Bar & Grill   Situated in a rather staid building (I miss the character of the old Cahunega location), this premier supper club manages to book some of the biggest names in contemporary jazz for multinight stints. The acoustics are great and there really are no bad seats. All ages are welcome. Tip: If you don't eat dinner, there's a two-drink minimum required. 6725 W. Sunset Blvd., Hollywood. ℂ **323/466-2210.** www.catalinajazzclub.com. Cover $15–$35.

Fais Do-Do ★   Most nights, this architecturally unique New Orleans–style nightspot hosts jazz, blues, and the occasional rock combo. It's located in a once-upscale suburb west of Downtown, but the surrounding neighborhood has become somewhat sketchy. Originally built as a bank, the building has gone through several jazz-club incarnations. It's even rumored that Miles Davis once graced the stage. The club offers great music in a memorable atmosphere, as well as good Cajun and soul food from the busy kitchen. 5257 W. Adams Blvd., Los Angeles. ℂ **323/931-4636.** www.faisdodo.com. Cover $10–$20.

Harvelle's Blues Club ★   Open since 1931, this Santa Monica bastion of blues claims to be the oldest blues club in Los Angeles. Dark and sexy like a blues club should be, you can always rely on a good local band playing here; many famous musicians have passed through as well, including Albert King and Bonnie Raitt. **_Tip:_** If you get the chance to catch local favorites Café R&B or the Toledo Show, go for it! The mostly 30-and-up crowd usually needs a few cocktails before hitting the dance floor. 1432 4th St., Santa Monica. ☏ **310/395-1676.** www.harvelles.com. Cover $5–$12.

Jazz Bakery 👫   Ruth Price's nonprofit venue was renowned for attracting some of the most important names in jazz to its location in the Helms bakery complex, but due to rising rents, she was forced to move in 2009. At the time of this printing, the club was still looking for a new home, but Price continued to sponsor the same acts in different venues around town. For the most up-to-date information, check the website. ☏ **310/271-9039.** www.jazzbakery.org.

DANCE CLUBS

The once momentous popularity of Latin dance and swing has faded, with the former still enjoying a built-in audience of Latino Angelenos and other lovers of salsa, while the latter is now just a small subculture (RIP The Derby). Though the styles subtly change, DJ culture is forever on the rise locally, featuring noteworthy shows at some cool clubs; such dance clubs, however, can come and go as quickly as you can say "jungle rave." Mere whispers of a happening thing elsewhere can practically relegate a club to been-there-done-that status. Check the *L.A. Weekly* for updates on specific club information.

Bardot   Above the Avalon theater—entrance is up a flight of stairs alongside the side of the building—this club has reinvented itself numerous times since it first opened in 1927. Today the club hosts burlesque nights, live jazz, and DJs spinning everything from classic rock to dance music. There's a bar and lounge, an outdoor courtyard, and a "tent room" filled with plush fabrics and low-lit sconces. You' might need a dinner reservation to get in—the food is nothing special—but it's still better than a bottle-service minimum. 1737 N. Vine St., Hollywood. ☏ **323/462-1307.** www.bardot hollywood.com.

El Floridita 👫   This tiny Cuban restaurant and salsa club is hot, hot, hot. Despite its modest strip-lot locale, it draws the likes of Jennifer Lopez, Sandra Bullock, Jimmy

Dinner & a Show & DJs & Dancing

For a truly surreal spin on the old dinner-and-a movie date night, or for a fun group outing, check out **Hollywood's Supperclub**, 6675 Hollywood Blvd., Hollywood (☏ **323/466-1900**; www.supperclub.com). Based on an all-in-one restaurant, DJ, performance art, and after-party dancing concept that began in Amsterdam, Hollywood's old Vogue theater has been transformed into an avant-garde party space. The evening typically begins in the lobby with an amuse bouche and a shot, then moves to the middle staging room (in neither place are you more than a few feet from a bar), before the curtains are drawn and guests are escorted to their "beds" (more like flat couches). A multi-course meal ensues while DJs spin everything from George Michael to Afrika Bambaataa. Interactivity is key; be it with costumed performers or flirtatious neighbors. From $75 all-inclusive.

Smits, and Jack Nicholson, in addition to a festive crowd of Latin-dance devotees who groove well into the night. The hippest nights continue to be Mondays, when Johnny Polanco and his swinging New York–flavored salsa band get the dance floor jumpin'. 1253 N. Vine St., Hollywood. ✆ **323/871-8612.** www.elfloridita.com. Cover $10.

Roxbury ★   This is *not* the second coming of the storied nightspot that inspired the movie *A Night at the Roxbury*—that was up on the Sunset Strip. This behemoth was born out of one half of the old Ivar club space, and the remodel is one of the more impressive I've seen. What was once done up like the set of *Tron* has morphed into an oasis-like venue built around a throbbing dance floor (while the lotus flower-inspired bar grooves right along with it—no really, parts of it move!). Here you'll find gorgeous 20-somethings and well-heeled gentleman who gladly fork over four figures for bottle service. This is easily L.A.'s hottest mega-club of the moment. 1661 Ivar Ave., Hollywood. ✆ **323/469-0040.** www.roxburyhw.com.

Voyeur ★   As the name suggests, this is a venue built around sex appeal, one that is known primarily for the scantily clad dancers in raised booths and in netting hanging above the main lounge area. Subtle but appreciated design touches include windows brought in from the 1920s era at the original *New York Times* Building and vintage-style naughty photo shoot film strips used as wallpaper. *Tip:* If you're going to bite the bottle service bullet, do it adjacent to the dance floor and DJ booth. Not only do you get proximity to the all the action, those couches are by far some of most comfortable I've tried in a club. 7969 Santa Monica Blvd., West Hollywood ✆ **310/255-1111.** www.voyeur7969.com.

Zanzibar   A DJ'd musical extravaganza in Santa Monica, this club hosts an eclectic mix of hip-hop, Afro funk, boogie, nu jazz, trance, techno, dubstep, and future soul in a Moroccan-style environment with leather ottomans, low upholstered benches, and curtains that you can pull when you want a little privacy. Tip: Food trucks often pull up outside to feed hungry clubbers. 1301 5th St., Santa Monica. ✆ **310/451-2221.** www.zanzibarlive.com. Cover $5–$10.

BARS & COCKTAIL LOUNGES

Akbar ★🍸   On the outside, Akbar isn't much to look at with its brown stucco facade and simple (almost imperceptible) sign. Step inside, though, and you'll find one of the city's more moody rooms. Friendly barkeeps ply the patrons with cocktails from behind the arabesque mirrored bar, and an astonishingly diverse CD jukebox is filled to capacity with tunes old and new. This is a mixed bar that's predominantly gay, but always comfortable for straights. 4356 W. Sunset Blvd. (at Fountain Ave.), Silver Lake. ✆ 323/665-6810. www.akbarsilverlake.com.

Barney's Beanery ★ the original Barney's may not be a high-tech and lounge-y (that would be the Burbank location) or have the sprawling patio (Santa Monica wins that one) of its offshoots, but it is seeped in rock and roll history. Not only was it once part of Route 66, Jim Morrison was a regular (his barstool bears a placard that was dedicated on what would have been his 65th birthday. Janis Joplin had a favorite spot here, too (table no. 20), and you can still see it and the "JJ" initials she carved into it—it's nailed to the ceiling above the new table no. 20. If you stick to pub grub, the food is actually pretty good (I highly recommend the chili). 8447 Santa Monica Blvd. (at Holloway Ave.), West Hollywood. ✆ 323/654-2287. www.barneysbeanery.com.

Basement Tavern The Victorian has long been an area favorite for meetings, weddings, and special events, but has recently debuted a lovely little cocktail bar that is completely open to the public. As the name suggests, the venue is mainly subterranean, though they can accommodate spillover upstairs in the relatively much quieter parlor area (unless there's a special event). Cocktails are creative, as is the use of a relatively small space. The menu is standard fare for a bar, though I was impressed with the tacos. 2640 Main St., Santa Monica. ✆ 310/392-4956. www.libraryalehouse.com.

Beauty Bar It's a proven concept in New York, Las Vegas, and San Francisco: a cocktail lounge/beauty salon. Decorated with vintage salon gear and sporting a hip-retro vibe, the Beauty Bar is both campy and trendy. Where else can you actually get a manicure while sipping cocktails with such names as the Shampoo (a combination of vodka, ginger, bitters and muddled lemons) or the Platinum Blonde (Malibu rum and pineapple)? Known as the martinis & manicures happy hour, the special runs Thursday to Saturday from 7 to 11pm. 1638 N Cahuenga Blvd., Hollywood. ✆ 323/464-7676. www.thebeautybar.com/los_angeles

The Bowery ★ 🍴 This friendly, neighborhood hang is centrally located at the Sunset and Vine intersection, walking distance to the Palladium, the ArcLight movie theaters, and the Pantages Theatre. A sliver of a bar, it features stylish decor with subway tiles and black leather booths; no velvet rope, and no cover charge; a good spirits list, plus eclectic beers and wines; and a great-looking, low-key crowd that might include the occasional celebs trying to prove they are normal people just like us (we saw Jessica Biel one night, Jake Gyllenhaal another). The best part, however, is the thick, juicy burger (get it with the works) and sweet-potato fries, plus other American bistro dishes like fish and chips, charcuterie and cheese plates, and salads. 6268 Sunset Blvd., Hollywood. ✆ 323/465-3400. www.theboweryhollywood.com.

The Brig This ultrahip bar, at the end of the Abbot Kinney strip in Venice, attracts an eclectic crowd of young clubgoers from all over L.A. The spacious main room pumps house beats, creating an atmosphere in which the scantily clad women and well-dressed men vie for attention from the opposite sex. If you're just rolling off the beach, however, don't be worried about being underdressed because at the Brig, less is more (at least early in the evening). If you're lucky enough to get on the lone pool table, you can show off your skills and perhaps attract some of that sought-after attention to yourself. 1515 Abbot Kinney Blvd., Venice. ✆ 310/399-7537. www.thebrig.com.

out & about: L.A.'S GAY & LESBIAN NIGHTLIFE SC

Like San Francisco to the north, Los Angeles has a vibrant and politically powerful gay and lesbian community. Every year in June, this active community comes out (pun intended) in full force for one of the city's most popular events: the **Gay Pride parade,** which all but takes over West Hollywood in the spirit of activism and audacity. If you're in town, this is one party you don't want to miss (see "Los Angeles Calendar of Events," in chapter 2).

Although **West Hollywood (WeHo),** often referred to as Boys Town, is the best-known gay neighborhood in Los Angeles, there are several other noteworthy enclaves. **Silver Lake** has a long-standing gay community that's worked hard to preserve the area's beautiful homes once occupied by the likes of Charlie Chaplin and Cecil B. DeMille. To the west of WeHo, **Venice** also has a strong gay and lesbian presence.

If you're looking for specific info on gay culture in L.A., check out *Frontiers* (✆ **323/930-3220**), one of the most prominent free biweekly gay mags, available in coffeehouses and at newsstands citywide. *L.A. Weekly* and *New Times Los Angeles* also have lesbian and gay articles and listings.

The Abbey ★★★ This is *the* social spot for WeHo's gay scene. It's part coffeehouse, bar, and restaurant, so you can start with lattes in the morning and switch to cocktails in the afternoon. In fact, most of West Hollywood seems to end up here on Saturday nights and/or Sunday mornings for Bloody Marys. The drinks are big—as in 10 ounces big—so sop them up with tasty American comfort food like sliders and pastrami sandwiches. *Tip:* Be sure to try the specialty house-made pickles (double entendre fully intended). Bottom line: The Abbey is not only one of the coolest gay bars in L.A., MTV's Logo Network named it the best in the world—two year's running! But it's open to all. I routinely recommend it as a fun but comfortable place for straight locals to take their visiting gay friends. 692 N. Robertson Blvd., West Hollywood. ✆ **310/289-8410.** www. abbeyfoodandbar.com.

Akbar See "Bars & Cocktail Lounges," below.

Café Was ★★ 🎒 Nightlife impresario turned restaurateur Ivan Kane refers to this happening nightspot as a "bohemian, bistro and cabaret." Part of the large, generic-looking Sunset + Vine complex, you'd never know that such an elegant parlor-style room was secreted inside. Weekly entertainment includes Forty Deuce Fridays, with dancers from Kane's Vegas nightclubs of the same name, plus jazz from big-name producer J.R. Rotem, and occasional sets by Hollywood oddball Jeff Goldblum. *Tip:* The food is nosh-worthy, particularly the dates stuffed with blue cheese and wrapped in bacon. 1521 N. Vine St., Hollywood. ✆ **323/466-5400.** www.cafewas.com.

Circle Bar This hip spot is particularly popular with the post-college crowd. A place to see and be seen, the Circle Bar packs them in nightly. Although it's located in Santa Monica, the scene is often more reminiscent of Hollywood. Its namesake, a large circular bar, gets very crowded on the weekends, but the bartenders pour a stiff drink that normally makes the wait worthwhile. The DJ spins everything from '80s to more progressive beats as the crowd dictates. Students, locals, and struggling actors all dance the night away and get their groove on while looking for that special someone. 2926 Main St., Santa Monica. ✆ **310/450-0508.** www.thecirclebar.com.

Eleven Hormones and hot bods abound throughout this WeHo club's lower bar/lounge and upstairs dining area. Jeffrey Sanker's Fresh, held every Friday, is a popular dance party. 8811 Santa Monica Blvd. (at Larrabee St.), West Hollywood. (*) **310/855-0800.** www.eleven. la. Cover free–$10.

Jewel's Catch One The Catch's claim to fame is that it was the very first out-and-proud African-American "disco." The crowd is somewhat more diverse these days, with both men and women representing. The venue stays open until 3am on popular club nights.4067 W. Pico Blvd., Los Angeles. (*) **323/734-8849.** www.jewelscatchone.com. Cover free–$10.

Micky's ★★ After a 2007 fire, Micky's came back bigger—larger dance floors and an exclusive second-story VIP bar—and more contemporary when it reopened in 2009. A sexy new look might be too much for the older crowd that used to frequent it, but the younger set is happy to have a new club for carousing. In fact, Micky's has now replaced Rage as *the* dance club of choice in West Hollywood on any given night. 8857 Santa Monica Blvd., West Hollywood. (*) **310/657-1176.** www.mickys.com. Cover free–$5.

The Other Side This amiable place reputedly serves the best martini in Silver Lake. It's a handsome and intimate piano bar with plenty of friendly patrons, and the ideal place to meet people if you're new in town—and over 50. Still, it's fun for any age or persuasion. 2538 Hyperion Ave., Silver Lake. (*) **323/661-0618.** www.flyingleapcafe.com.

Rage For almost 20 years, this high-energy, high-attitude disco was the preferred mainstay on WeHo's gay dance-club circuit. In the old days, between turns around the dance floor, shirtless muscle boys self-consciously strutted about—like peacocks flashing their plumes—looking to exchange vital statistics. Now they go to Micky's instead. Sadly, most nights, Rage is no longer ragin'. 8911 Santa Monica Blvd., West Hollywood. (*) **310/652-7055.**

Copa d'Oro ★ The bartenders here know how to make some serious cocktails, from classics like an old-fashioned sidecar to something a little more ambitious like the Sour Kraut, made with mustard and orange marmalade (seriously . . . but it's surprisingly delicious). Tell them what you like from the farmers' market bounty that day, and they'll concoct a fresh and tasty drink. The room is simply designed, just a long bar with banquettes and a few sofas strewn about. It's a great spot to hit right after the beach because it's usually empty at that time—with a good happy hour to boot (only $5 for a proper Manhattan!)—but when it's crowded on the weekends, expect to see lines of the young and fashionable waiting to get in. *Tip:* There's a small but respectable menu of sandwiches and dips. 217 Broadway, Santa Monica. (*) **310/576-3030.** www.copadoro.com.

The Dresden Room ★★ Hugely popular with L.A. hipsters because of its longevity, location, and elegant ambience, "the Den" was pushed into the mainstream of L.A. nightlife thanks to its inclusion in the movie *Swingers*. But it's the timeless lounge act of Marty and Elayne (the couple has been performing there up to 5 nights a week since 1982) that has proven that, fad or no fad, this place is always cool. Not that anything could make disco cool again, but their rendition of "Stayin' Alive" is a kitschy treat. Sidle up to the bar for a glass of the sweet house classic, Blood and Sand cocktail. 1760 N. Vermont Ave., Hollywood.© **323/665-4294.** www.thedresden.com.

El Carmen Opened by L.A. restaurant-and-bar impresario Sean MacPherson, the man with the mescal touch, El Carmen conjures the feel of a back-alley Mexican cantina of a bygone era. Vintage Mexican movie posters, vibrant Latin-American colors, and oil paintings of masked Mexican wrestlers decorate the Quonset-hut interior, while an eclectic jukebox offers an array of tunes from Tito Puente to the Foo Fighters. The busy bar boasts a gargantuan list of more than 100 tequilas and a small menu of tacos, nachos, and guacamole. 8138 W. 3rd St., Los Angeles.© **323/852-1552.**

Father's Office ★★ This offshoot of the tiny original Santa Monica bar that has one of the best burgers in town opened to much fanfare in 2008, but this is definitely a 2.0 version. The space is much bigger, with a fantastic patio filled with communal picnic tables; and the bar has double the microbrews and Belgian beers on tap, plus a state-of-the-art wine tap system and cocktails made with artisanal spirits and mixers (don't even bother asking for a Cosmopolitan). What is similar to the original: the no-reservation policy, which means you might just have to share your table with strangers; no ketchup on premises (people have been known to bring their own); and no substitutions. The meaty burger, topped with blue cheese, arugula, and caramelized onions, remains, as does the tiny shopping cart of sweet-potato fries, but don't miss the seasonal and daily specials written on the blackboards. 3229 Helms Ave., Los Angeles.© **310/736-2224.** www.fathersoffice.com.

The Federal Bar Valley nightlife has never been much of a draw for anyone outside of the neighborhood. Who am I kidding—it's barely been a draw for those that do live there (I'm a native, I should know). Everyone got really excited when Bank Heist opened in this location a few years back, but then a fire shut it down. Now, the Federal is doing it justice, with craft beers, conscientious bartenders and an impressive menu of gastropub fare (I don't know that I've had better chicken wings in this town), along with some serious entrees like a Moroccan-inspired meatloaf and an excellent flat-iron steak with molé sauce. The venue is owned by Knitting Factory Entertainment, which has shuttered its Hollywood location, so expect to see a nice roster of live entertainment upstairs in this old bank building space soon. 5303 Lankershim Blvd., North Hollywood.© **818/980-2555.** www.thefederalbar.com.

Firefly ★ Opened in 2002 by Jeffery Best, a veteran of the Hollywood club scene, this dream of a bar and restaurant is the meeting place of choice for Valley dwellers to drag their Eastside and Hollywood hipster friends. Flavored by '40s noir (think Bogie in *The Big Sleep*), this is a sexy and simple nightspot where visitors can recline on comfy cushions, warm up by the fire pit in the middle of the restaurant, or relax at the patio with its cabana-like tables enclosed by drapes. DJs offer up a pumping mix of soul and ambient sounds, and who knows what could happen in those coed bathrooms? The kitchen has hit or miss over the years, so there's no predicting what the food will be like when you visit. Plan on eating beforehand, though if you need to do dinner just to get in (it's still that happening), go for it—there's nothing else this vibe-y in the Valley. 11720 Ventura Blvd., Studio City.© **818/762-1833.** www.fireflystudiocity.com.

Frolic Room ★ This classic L.A. dive bar is located next door to the Pantages Theatre on Hollywood and Vine. Pumping too-loud music from one of the best CD jukeboxes in Los Angeles, Hollywood vampires hang out with rough-around-the-edges hipsters and old coots getting their fill of stiff, cheap drinks amid the Art Deco decor. **Tip:** The crowd gets really interesting right before and right after shows next door. Then you suddenly get way-overdressed Valley and Beverly Hills types who would never normally hang out in a place like this. It's a bit surreal. Look for Hedy Lamarr's star out front on the Hollywood Walk of Fame ("That's HEDLEY!"). 6245 Hollywood Blvd., Hollywood. (© **323/462-5890.**

Golden Gopher ★ This is the bar that started it all for Cedd Moses, the visionary who can be credited with almost single-handedly reimagining and redefining downtown nightlife. The cocktails are good, the crowd diverse (hipsters to office workers during happy hour to generally well-behaved USC students), and the setting stylish without being pretentious. **Tip:** Though the bar doesn't serve food, they are generally very tolerant about letting you order-in, provided you don't make a mess. Better yet, you can pick up booze for your after-party *inside* the venue. Due to a very old and unusual license, this is one of the few establishments in Los Angeles with a liquor store inside a bar (it conveniently sells breath mints and cigarettes as well). 417 W. 8th St., Downtown L.A. (© **213/614-8001.** www.goldengopher.la.

Good Luck Bar Until they installed a flashing neon sign outside, only locals and hipsters knew about this kung-fu-themed room in the Los Feliz. The dark-red, windowless interior boasts Asian ceiling tiles, fringed Chinese paper lanterns, sweet-but-deadly drinks like the Yee Mee Loo (translated as "blue drink"), and a jukebox with selections ranging from Thelonius Monk to Cher's "Half Breed." The spacious sitting room, furnished with mismatched sofas, armchairs, and banquettes, provides a great atmosphere for conversation or romance. Arrive early to avoid the throngs of L.A. scenesters. 1514 Hillhurst Ave. (btw. Hollywood and Sunset boulevards), Los Feliz. (© **323/666-3524.**

Hemingway's ★ Named after the writer, this library-like bar pays tribute to "Papa" with a wall of typewriters, endless stacks of notebooks piled above the bar and shelves of various tomes throughout. It has a certain stylish cache without going overboard on theme. It also has something else Hemingway loved: cocktails. The menu changes seasonally to reflect fresh produce and the weather (so you'll see heartier drinks in winter and stuff like a Spring Negroni after the equinox). **Tip:** If you get here before it gets packed, the bartenders are usually game to improvise, too. 6356 Hollywood Blvd., Hollywood. (© **323/469-0040.** www.hemingwayslounge.com.

Library Alehouse ★ On Main Street in Santa Monica, this eco-friendly neighborhood bar has 13 international beers on draft, another 25 or so in bottles, and a wine list that includes exclusive California vintages. Its back patio is a serene place to enjoy a warm evening. 2911 Main St., Santa Monica. (© **310/314-4855.** www.libraryalehouse.com.

Lola's The swimming-pool-size martinis are enough reason to trek over to Lola's. From the classic gin or vodka martini for the purist to the chocolate- or apple-flavored concoctions for the adventurous, Lola's has a little something for everyone. Two bars, a billiards table, and plush couches hidden in dark, romantic corners make for an enjoyable setting and plenty of celeb spotting. **Tip:** While it's not known for food, the mac and cheese is delish! 945 N. Fairfax Ave. (south of Santa Monica Blvd.), West Hollywood. (© **323/654-5652.** www.lolasla.com.

Nic's Beverly Hills ★★ Unlike the surrounding Beverly Hills establishments, there's no attitude here, just lots of retro-groovy slippery white leather; bold, colorful stripes; and laid-back locals noshing on cocktail cuisine while listening to good jazz bands and big-band trios. Owner Larry Nicola—a really fun guy to hang out with, by the way—takes pride in his self-anointed title as Vodkateur™, which means he's an expert regarding all things vodka. In fact, he built a walk-in freezer called a Vodbox just so he could have a proper tasting room so his guests can sample the best vodkas from around the world. Give Larry a call and ask him to give you the Vodbox experience when you arrive. I only wish that for a place with a Dean Martin shrine, the cocktails were less girly (a Peachy Keen Cosmo—really?), though they do make a mean Moscow Mule, copper mug and all. *Tip:* Go for the happy hour, stay for the dinner menu, especially for small plates and appetizers that incorporate vodka, such as the steamed artichoke with miso and vodka, and the vodka-cured salmon served with pumpernickel crostini and caper-dill aioli (I dream about this dish). 453 N. Canon Dr., Beverly Hills. ✆ **310/550-5707.** www.nicsbeverlyhills.com.

O'Brien's Pub   O'Brien's offers everything it takes to make a great pub, including more beers on tap than you could possibly attempt to drink in one sitting. The food is far better than pub grub, so come hungry. Three levels and a patio allow you to either post up inside and listen to live bands 6 or 7 nights a week, or grab some sun outside during the day. The clientele is mostly on the young side, but everyone seems to be treated like family. 2941 Main St., Santa Monica. ✆ **310/396-4725.** www.obriensonmain.com.

Red Lion Tavern   A hidden veteran of the Silver Lake circuit, this kitschy, over-the-top German tavern—complete with dirndl-clad waitresses—is where neighborhood hipsters mingle with cranky, working-class German expats. The place serves hearty half-liters of Warsteiner, Becks, and Bitburger, but braver souls—with bottomless bladders—can take on a 1.5-liter boot. The surprisingly good food offerings include schnitzel, bratwurst, and potato pancakes. 2366 Glendale Blvd., Silver Lake. ✆ **323/662-5337.** www.redliontavern.net.

Seven Grand ★★   As mentioned in the Golden Gopher review (p. 225), Cedd Moses made a name for himself by taking downtrodden, historic locations and turning them into cool bars with great design and fantastic cocktails. The neon sign lights up what was once a relatively dark block Downtown (before this bar brought people here), and after walking up a few flights of stairs, passing windows filled with mannequins as hunters and Maker's Mark bottles, you enter a low-lit whiskey mecca. Everything about Seven Grand is masculine—animal heads on the walls, pool tables, a great jukebox—save for the bartendresses in plaid miniskirts. This is one of the best and largest whiskey selections in L.A.—more than 200 kinds of rye, Irish, bourbon, and Scotch, all served neat or on the rocks with special slow-melting cubes. Libations made with fresh-squeezed juices and homemade syrups are worthy, but note that this is not a new-style mixology bar; the emphasis is on classic cocktails. Things get a little more raucous when there's live music in the corner of the room. **Tip:** A small but comfortable patio offers a few booths for smokers. 515 W. 7th St., Downtown. ✆ **213/614-0737.** www.sevengrand.la.

Skybar ✋   Since its opening in hotelier Ian Schrager's refurbished Sunset Strip hotel, the Mondrian, Skybar has been a favorite among L.A.'s most fashionable of the fashionable set. This place was at one time so hot that even the agents to the stars needed agents to get in—rumor has it that one agent was so desperate to gain entrance that he promised one of the servers a contract—but this is a fickle town, and the young and hot have moved on to greener pastures. Nevertheless, the view is still spectacular and you may still get to rub elbows with some of the faces that regularly appear on the cover of *People* (but please don't stare). **Tip:** If you really want to get in, make a dinner reservation at neighboring Asia de Cuba. Unless there's a private event, that usually works (but is at the discretion of the doorman, so dress nicely and tip your waiter well). Be advised that drinks are overpriced, under-poured, and the bartenders are limited in their repertoires. 8440 W. Sunset Blvd., West Hollywood. ✆ **323/848-6025.** www.mondrianhotel.com.

The Standard Downtown ★★   This rooftop bar, located atop the Standard Hotel in Downtown L.A. (formerly Superior Oil headquarters), is surrounded by high office towers and helipads, and the view is magnificent. The skyscrapers act like strangely glowing lava lamps in the night sky as exotic ladies sip exotic cocktails amid water beds and bent-plastic loungers. 550 S. Flower St., Downtown. ✆ **213/892-8080.** www.standardhotels.com.

Thirsty Crow   Named after Aesop's fable about a whiskey-loving bird, this diminutive but ever-friendly Silver Lake bar is all about brown spirits like bourbon and scotch, though they do carry a respectable selection of clear spirits and cocktails (vodka and gin) because, well, this is frou-frou L.A. after all. There are all sorts of vintage trinkets and various antiques, a testament to owner Bobby Green's love for swap-meet steals. **Tip:** An alley-like space makes for a popular, if not comfortably lounge-y smokers' patio. 2939 W. Sunset Blvd., Los Angeles. ✆ **323/661-6007.** www.thirstycrowbar.com.

Three Clubs 👬   In the tradition of Hollywood hipster hangouts trying to maintain a low profile, Three Clubs, sometimes known as the "Three of Clubs" (like the playing card) is absent of any signage indicating where you are. Inside this dark and cavernous lounge, you'll find a youthful, hoping-to-become-a-star-soon set mingling into the night. Even with two rooms, plenty of cushiony sofas, two long bars, and lots of spacious tables, this place is always loud and packed. Entertainment may include burlesque, comedy or live bands. 1123 N. Vine St., Hollywood. ✆ **323/462-6441.** www.threeclubs.com.

Whiskey Blue   When ascending the dramatic backlit staircase and entering the dimly lit, seductive interior, it's hard to believe Whiskey Blue in the W Hotel is on UCLA's Sorority Row. The atmosphere is as chic as the decor, which features high screen partitions, low cushioned couches, sleek private rooms, and a row of carved stumps of wood where manicured martinis may be set. Patrons are encouraged to dress their best, especially on the weekends when the Westside's glitterati come out to this scene to be seen. Hotel guests are given priority entrance. 930 Hilgard Ave., Westwood. ✆ **310/443-8232.**

The Woods   For a concrete jungle like Los Angeles, this strip-mall lounge is a welcome respite in much the same spirit as the Lava Lounge, which once occupied this space. Just as the name implies, teak tables, cedar paneling, and antler chandeliers make you feel like you're drinking in a forest—albeit one with a little Hollywood polish. Get the mint julep. 1533 La Brea Ave., Hollywood. ✆ **323/876-6612.** www.vintagebargroup.com.

Yamashiro ★   Enjoy the view of the city from this pagoda-and-garden perch in the Hollywood Hills. Though the place has long been considered a "special-occasion" Japanese restaurant (more for the view than the food), I prefer to sit in the lounge—Mai Tai in hand—and watch Hollywood's dancing searchlights dot the night sky. There's no cover, but there's also no way around the $7.50 valet parking fee. 1999 N. Sycamore Ave., Hollywood. ✆ **323/466-5125.** www.yamashirorestaurant.com.

The Yard   This Santa Monica gastropub is helmed by Chris "CJ" Jacobson, known to foodies as a contestant on season 3 of *Top Chef*. In addition to fish tacos, fried chicken and lighter salad options, there's also an extensive drink menu featuring artisan beers on tap, boutique wines by the glass, and a market-fresh seasonal cocktail list by mixologist Blake Landis. The venue features local live music, DJs, film screenings, and art. 119 Broadway, Santa Monica. ✆ **310/395-6037.** www.theyardsm.com.

Ye Old Kings Head Although it's in downtown Santa Monica with an oceanview patio, this pub is as authentically British as it gets, serving a host of premium British ales and hard cider on tap, fish and chips, and a variety of other British pub fare. 116 Santa Monica Blvd., Santa Monica. ✆ **310/451-1402.** www.yeoldekingshead.com.

PERFORMING ARTS
Classical Music & Opera

While L.A. is best known for its pop realms (see "The Live Music Scene," earlier in this chapter), other types of music here consist of top-flight orchestras and companies—both local and visiting—to fulfill the most demanding classical music appetites; scan the papers to find out who's performing while you're in the city.

The world-class **Los Angeles Philharmonic** (✆ 323/850-2000; www.laphil. org) is the only major classical music company in Los Angeles, and it got a whole lot more popular in 2003 with the completion of its incredible home: the **Walt Disney Concert Hall** (p. 145), located at the intersection of 1st Street and Grand Avenue in the historic Bunker Hill area. Designed by world-renowned architect Frank Gehry, this exciting addition to the Music Center of L.A. includes a breathtaking 2,265-seat concert hall, outdoor park, restaurant, cafe, bookstore, and gift shop.

Gustavo Dudamel, hailed as one of the most exciting and compelling conductors of our time, has begun his tenure as the new music director of the Los Angeles Philharmonic. Tickets can be hard to come by when celebrity players like Itzhak Perlman, Emanuel Ax, and Yo-Yo Ma are in town. In addition to performances at the Walt Disney Concert Hall, the Philharmonic plays a summer season at the **Hollywood Bowl** (see "Concerts Under the Stars," below).

Slowly but surely, the **Los Angeles Opera** (✆ 213/972-8001; www.losangelesopera.com), which performs at the **Dorothy Chandler Pavilion,** is gaining respect and popularity with inventive stagings of classic pieces, modern operas, visiting divas, and the contributions of high-profile general director Plácido Domingo. The 120-voice **Los Angeles Master Chorale** sings a varied repertoire that includes classical and pop compositions. Concerts are held at the **Walt Disney Concert Hall** (✆ 323/850-2000) September through May.

The **UCLA Center for the Performing Arts** (✆ 310/825-2101; www.uclalive. org) has presented music, dance, and theatrical performances of unparalleled quality for more than 60 years and continues to be a major presence in the local and national cultural landscape. Presentations occur at several different theaters around Los Angeles, both on and off campus. UCLA's **Royce Hall** is the Center's pride; it has even been compared to New York's Carnegie Hall. Standouts from the Center's busy

Fun with Festivals

The L.A. Philharmonic's summer concert series at the Hollywood Bowl is one of the world's largest outdoor music festivals. And the venue itself is the largest natural outdoor amphitheater in the country!

Free Morning Music at Hollywood Bowl

It's not widely known, but the L.A. Philharmonic's summer morning rehearsals are generally open to the public and absolutely free. On Tuesdays and Thursdays, from 9:30am to 12:30pm, you can see the program scheduled for that evening. Non-L.A. Phil rehearsals are only open subject to the artists' discretion. So bring some coffee and doughnuts (the concession stands aren't open) and enjoy the best seats in the house (© **323/850-2000; www. hollywoodbowl.org**).

calendar included the famous Gyuto Monks Tibetan Tantric Choir and the Cinderella story *Cendrillon,* with an original score by Sergei Prokofiev.

Concerts Under the Stars

Also see "The Live Music Scene," earlier in this chapter.

The Greek Theatre ★★   Located inside Griffith Park, this scenic outdoor amphitheater holds 5,800 guests, and has received the accolade of being North America's Best Small Outdoor Venue by trade publication *Pollstar Magazine.* It's been the site of everything from Neil Diamond's infamous *Hot August Night* live concert album to the destination of Russell Brand's maniacal main character Aldous Snow in *Get Him to the Greek.* 2700 N. Vermont Ave. Los Angeles. © 323/665-3125. www.greek theatrela.com.

Hollywood Bowl ★★★ 📷   Built in the early 1920s, the elegant Greek-style natural outdoor amphitheater, cradled in a small mountain canyon, is the summer home of the Los Angeles Philharmonic and Hollywood Bowl orchestras, and often hosts internationally known conductors and soloists on Tuesday and Thursday nights. Friday and Saturday concerts typically feature orchestral swing or pops concerts. The summer season also includes a jazz series; past performers have included Natalie Cole, Dionne Warwick, and Chick Corea. Other events, from standard rock-'n'-roll acts like Radiohead to Garrison Keillor programs, summer fireworks galas, and the annual Mariachi Festival, are often on the season's schedule.

To round out an evening at the Bowl, many concertgoers use the occasion to enjoy a picnic dinner and a bottle of wine—it's one of L.A.'s grandest traditions. You can prepare your own or order a picnic basket with a choice of hot and cold dishes and a selection of wines and desserts from Patina's on-site catering department, which also provides delivery to box seats; call © **323/850-1885** by 4pm the day before you go to place your food order. Arrive a couple of hours before the show starts to dine while listening to the orchestra or band tune up. *Tip:* Lease events, often mainstream pop and rock concerts, have their own rules about what you can and cannot bring in, especially in regards to alcohol, so check if your event is a regular part of the L.A. Phil season, or not, before you head out. 2301 N. Highland Ave. (at Pat Moore Way), Hollywood. © **323/850-2000.** www.hollywoodbowl.org.

Theater

MAJOR THEATERS & COMPANIES

Tickets for most plays cost $10 to $35, although big-name shows at the major theaters can fetch more than $100 for the best seats. **LA Stage Alliance**

Santa Monica's Twilight Dance Series (www.santamonicapier.org/twilight) brings top names to the world-famous Santa Monica Pier for free open-air concerts Thursday nights from early July through mid-August. Join locals, families, singles, and tourists who picnic on the beach while enjoying the sunset and live music.

(📞 213/614-0556), a nonprofit association of live theaters and producers in Los Angeles, offers half-price tickets to more than 100 venues via their Internet-only service at **www.lastagetix.com**. This handy site features a frequently updated list of shows and availability. Tickets can be purchased online with a credit card and they'll be waiting for you at the box office; a service fee is applied depending on the cost of the ticket. *Note:* One caveat of the half-price bargain is that the seating assignments are solely at the discretion of the theater—there's no guarantee you'll be sitting next to your partner (though this is rare)—and you must bring a printed or faxed copy of your e-mail confirmation to the box office.

The all-purpose **Music Center of Los Angeles County,** 135 N. Grand Ave., Downtown, houses the city's top two playhouses: the **Ahmanson Theatre** and **Mark Taper Forum** (📞 213/628-2772; www.centertheatregroup.org). They're both home to the Center Theater Group (www.centertheatregroup.org), as well as traveling productions (often Broadway- or London-bred). Every season, the Ahmanson Theatre (📞 213/628-2772) hosts a handful of high-profile shows, such as the Tony Award–winning *Jersey Boys,* and Oprah Winfrey's musical *The Color Purple.* **Tip:** The best seats in the theater are in the mezzanine section.

The **Mark Taper Forum** is a more intimate theater with a thrust stage—where the audience is seated on three sides of the acting area—that hosts contemporary works by international and local playwrights. Neil Simon's humorous and poignant *The Dinner Party* and Tom Stoppard's witty and eclectic *Arcadia,* which has won three Pulitzer Prizes and 18 Tony Awards, are among the more popular productions performed on this internationally recognized stage.

One of L.A.'s most venerable landmarks, the **Orpheum Theatre,** 842 S. Broadway, at 9th Street (📞 213/749-5171; www.laorpheum.com), reopened after a 75-year hiatus. Built in 1926, this renowned venue has hosted an array of theatrical productions, concerts, film festivals, and television and movie shoots—from Judy Garland's 1933 vaudeville performance to a taping of *American Idol.* The 2,000-seat theater is home to the Mighty Wurlitzer, one of three original theater organs still existing in Southern California theaters.

Across town, the moderate-size **Geffen Playhouse,** 10886 Le Conte Ave., Westwood (📞 310/208-5454; www.geffenplayhouse.com), presents dramatic and comedic works by prominent and emerging writers. UCLA purchased the theater—which was originally built as a Masonic temple in 1929 and later served as the Westwood Playhouse—back in 1995 with a little help from philanthropic entertainment mogul David Geffen. This striking venue is often the West Coast choice of many acclaimed off-Broadway shows, and also attracts locally based TV and movie actors eager for the immediacy of stage work. One popular production featured the world premiere of *Wishful Drinking,* a poignant comedy written and performed by Carrie Fisher. Always audience-friendly, the Playhouse prices tickets in the $35 to $75 range.

You've probably already heard of the **Kodak Theatre,** 6834 Hollywood Blvd. (℃ **323/308-6300;** www.kodaktheatre.com), home of the Academy Awards. The crown jewel of the Hollywood & Highland entertainment complex, this modern beauty hosts a wide range of international performances, musicals, and concerts ranging from Alicia Keys and David Gilmour to the Moscow Stanislavsky Ballet and Sesame Street Live. Guided tours are given 7 days a week from 10:30am to 4pm.

The restored **Pantages Theatre,** 6233 Hollywood Blvd., between Vine Street and Argyle Avenue (℃ **323/468-1770;** www.pantages-theater.com), reflects the full Art Deco glory of L.A.'s theater scene. Opened in 1930, this historical and cultural landmark was the first Art Deco movie palace in the U.S. and site of the Academy Awards from 1949 to 1959. The theater recently presented *Hair, Spring Awakening,* and *West Side Story.*

At the foot of the Hollywood Hills, the 1,245-seat outdoor **John Anson Ford Amphitheatre** (℃ **323/461-3673;** www.fordamphitheater.org) is located in a county regional park and is set against a backdrop of cypress trees and chaparral. It's an intimate setting, with no patron more than 96 feet away from the stage. Music, dance, film, theater, and family events run May through September. An indoor theater, a cozy 87-seat space that was extensively renovated in 1998 and renamed **[Inside] The Ford,** features live music and theater year-round.

Supported by Dustin Hoffman in association with Santa Monica College, the $45-million **Broad Stage** theater (℃ **310/434-3200;** www.thebroadstage.com) has drawn rave reviews for its intimate atmosphere. Its compact design allows patrons to feel as if they're in eye-to-eye contact with the performers from any of the 499 seats in the house. The state-of-the-art theater presents renowned artists and world-class operas, symphonies, musicals, dance companies, film, and theater, under the leadership of artistic director Dale Franzen.

For a schedule at any of the above theaters, check the listings in *Los Angeles* magazine (www.lamag.com), available at most area newsstands, or the "Calendar" section of the Sunday *Los Angeles Times* (www.latimes.com/theguide/); or call the box offices at the numbers listed above.

SMALLER PLAYHOUSES & COMPANIES

On any given night, there's more live theater to choose from in Los Angeles than in New York City, due in part to the surfeit of ready actors and writers chomping at the bit to make it in Tinseltown. Many of today's familiar faces from film and TV spent plenty of time cutting their teeth on L.A.'s busy theater circuit, which is home to nearly 200 small and medium-size theaters and theater companies, ranging from the 'round-the-corner, neighborhood variety to high-profile, polished troupes of veteran

Great Theater, Cheap Tickets

The **Ahmanson Theatre and Mark Taper Forum** offer specially priced $20 "hot" tickets that can be purchased in person at the box office or over the phone. It used to be that you would have to stand in line two hours before a show to get them (if you were lucky); now you can purchase them at any time. Exact seat locations are not discussed; however, all are described as "limited view." Still, it's a great way to experience theater if you are on a budget. All performances are subject to availability, with restrictions.

actors. With so many options, navigating the scene to find the best work can be a monumental task. A good bet is to choose one of the theaters listed below, which have established excellent reputations for their consistently high-quality productions; otherwise, consult *L.A. Weekly* (www.laweekly.com), which advertises most current productions, or call LA Stage Alliance (℗ **213/614-0556;** http://lastagealliance.com) for up-to-date performance listings.

In the same complex as Walt Disney Concert Hall, **REDCAT** (an acronym for the Roy and Edna Disney/CalArts Theater) is a relatively new multiuse forum for cutting-edge performance and media arts. Befitting its ultramodern location, the REDCAT is one of the most versatile and technologically advanced presentation spaces in the world. *Tip:* Be sure to arrive a bit early so you can visit the REDCAT lounge and bookstore for a pre-performance espresso or cocktail—wrapped in signature Frank Gehry plywood, it's one of the best-kept-secret bars in the city. The REDCAT is located at 631 W. 2nd St. at the southwest corner of the Walt Disney Concert Hall (℗ **213/237-2800;** www.redcat.org).

The **Colony Studio Theatre,** 555 N. 3rd St., Burbank (℗ **818/558-7000;** www.colonytheatre.org), was formed in 1975 and has developed from a part-time ensemble of TV actors longing for their theatrical roots into a nationally recognized company. The company produces plays in all genres at the 276-seat Burbank Center Stage, which is shared with other performing arts groups.

Actors Circle Theater, 7313 Santa Monica Blvd., West Hollywood (℗ **323/882-6805;** www.actorscircle.net), is a 47-seater that's as acclaimed as it is tiny. Look for original contemporary works throughout the year.

Founded in 1965, **East West Players,** 120 N. Judge John Aiso St., Downtown (℗ **213/625-7000;** www.eastwestplayers.org), is the oldest Asian-American theater company in the United States. It's been so successful that the company moved from a 99-seat venue to the 200-seat David Henry Hwang Theater in Downtown L.A.'s Little Tokyo (p. 161).

The **L.A. Theatre Works** (℗ **310/827-0808**) is renowned for its marriage of media and theater and has performed more than 500 plays and logged more than 1,000 hours of on-air programming. Performances are held at the Skirball Cultural Center (see "Museums & Galleries," in chapter 6), nestled in the Sepulveda Pass near the Getty Center. In the past, personalities such as Richard Dreyfuss, Julia Louis-Dreyfus, Jason Robards, Annette Bening, and John Lithgow have given award-winning performances of plays by Arthur Miller, Neil Simon, Joyce Carol Oates, and more. For nearly a decade, the group has performed simultaneously for viewing and listening audiences in its radio theater series. Tickets are usually around $49; a full performance schedule can be found online at www.latw.org.

COMEDY

L.A.'s comedy clubs have launched the careers of many comics who are now household names. In addition to the clubs below, check out the alternative comedy featured comedy and stand-up nights at **Largo at the Coronet** with Patton Oswalt and Sarah Silverman, among others (see "Mostly Rock," p. 246), 366 N. La Cienega Blvd. (℗ **310.855.0350;** www.largo-la.com).

Acme Comedy Theater The Acme players provide a barrage of laughs with their improv and sketch comedy acts—a veritable grab bag of funnies. 135 N. La Brea Ave., Hollywood. ℗ **323/525-0202.** www.acmecomedy.com. Cover $8–$17.

The Comedy & Magic Club ★ A Hermosa Beach mainstay since 1978, this popular venue pulls in some of the biggest names in the business—including regular Sunday night gigs by Jay Leno. But it's not unusual to see names like Jerry Seinfeld, Jon Lovitz, Bill Maher or Ray Romano on the marquee either. The room is basically a series of basic tables that jut out from the stage, all surrounded by memorabilia from popular movies and TV shows—such as the infamous "puffy shirt" from *Seinfeld*, and *Austin Powers'* psychedelic suit. The club is 18 and over, and there's a two-item minimum per person, which can be a mix of food and beverage. The food is about what I expected, and though the drinks aren't expensive by Hollywood standards, they are small and weak. 1018 Hermosa Ave, Hermosa Beach. ✆ 310/372-1193; www.comedyandmagicclub.com. Tickets $15–$30.

Comedy Store ★ You can't go wrong here: New comics develop their material, and established ones work out their kinks at this landmark owned by Mitzi Shore (Pauly's mom). The Main Room, which seats 350, features professional stand-ups continuously on Friday and Saturday nights. Several comedians are always featured, each doing about a 15-minute stint. The talent is always first-rate and includes comics who regularly appear on *The Tonight Show* and other shows. The **Original Room,** which seats 150, features a dozen or so comedians back-to-back nightly, whereas the smaller Belly Room is for development. As Mitzi likes to say "Life begins in the Belly," so you never know what you might get there. Sunday and Mondays Potluck night is amateur night: Anyone with enough guts can take the stage for 3 minutes—Lord only knows what you'll see, though celebs have been known to "pop in.". 8433 Sunset Blvd., West Hollywood. ✆ **323/650-6268.** www.comedystore.com. Cover free–$20 plus 2-drink minimum. Always 21+.

Groundling Theater ★ L.A.'s answer to Chicago's Second City has been around for more than 25 years, yet it remains the most innovative and funny group in town. The skits change every year or so, but they take new improvisational twists every night and the satire is often savage. The Groundlings were the springboard to fame for Pee-Wee Herman, Elvira, and former *Saturday Night Live* stars Jon Lovitz, Phil Hartman, and Julia "It's Pat" Sweeney. Phone for showtimes and reservations. 7307 Melrose Ave., Los Angeles. ✆ **323/934-4747.** www.groundlings.com. Tickets $10–$17.

The Improv A showcase for top stand-ups since 1975, the Improv offers something different every night. Although it used to have a fairly active music schedule, the place is now mostly doing what it does best—showcasing comedy. Owner Budd Freedman's buddies—like Jay Leno, Billy Crystal, and Robin Williams—hone their skills here more often than you would expect. But even if the comedians on the bill are all unknowns, they won't be for long. Shows are at 8pm Sunday and Thursday, and at 8:30 and 10:30pm Friday and Saturday. 8162 Melrose Ave., West Hollywood. ✆ **323/651-2583.** www.improvclubs.com. Tickets average $14, plus 2-drink minimum.

Laugh Factory ★ Yes, this is where Michael Richards made his infamous racist comments toward two black men who were heckling him (and where Mr. Richards is no longer welcome). In fact, just about every comedian you've seen on TV—living or dead—has been a regular at the Laugh Factory: Rodney Dangerfield, Dave Chappelle, Robin Williams, Richard Pryor, Jim Carrey, Jerry Seinfeld, and others. The best night to attend is the Friday All Star Comedy show, because you never know when a celebrity guest is going to sneak onstage and try out a new routine. 8001 Sunset Blvd., Hollywood. ✆ **323/656-1336.** www.laughfactory.com. Tickets $20–$35, plus 2-drink minimum).

MOVIES: PLAY IT AGAIN, SAM

This being L.A., the city is saturated with megaplexes catering to high-budget, high-profile flicks featuring the usual big-ticket lures such as Hanks, Jolie, and DiCaprio. But there are times when those polished Hollywood-studio stories just won't do. Below are some nonmainstream options that play movies from bygone eras or those with an indie bent. Consult *L.A. Weekly* (www.laweekly.com) to see what's playing when you're in town.

Film festivals are another great way to explore the other side of contemporary movies. In addition to the American Film Institute's yearly November fete (see "Los Angeles Calendar of Events," in chapter 2), the **Film Independent's Los Angeles Film Festival** (📞 866/345-6337 or 310/432-1240; www.lafilmfest.com) looks at what's new in American indies, short films, and music videos during a weeklong event in late June. Every July since 1982, the **Gay and Lesbian Film Festival** (📞 213/480-7088; www.outfest.org), also known as Outfest, has aimed to bring high-quality gay, lesbian, bi, and transgender films to a wider public awareness. In 1998 the festival became Los Angeles's largest, with more than 32,000 audience members.

Promoting moving pictures as this country's great art form, the **American Cinematheque** in Hollywood (📞 323/466-3456; www.egyptiantheatre.com) presents not-readily-seen videos and films, ranging from the wildly arty to old classics. Since relocating to the historic and beautifully refurbished 1923 **Egyptian Theatre,** 6712 Hollywood Blvd. in Hollywood, American Cinematheque has hosted several film events, including a celebration of contemporary flicks from Spain, a tribute to the *femmes fatales* of film noir, and a retrospective of the films of William Friedkin. Events highlighting a specific individual are usually accompanied by at least one in-theater audience Q-and-A session with the honoree. Note: Sister property, the **Aero Theatre,** 1328 Montana Ave. (📞 310/260-1528), in Santa Monica presents similar programming.

The **Leo S. Bing Theater** at the **L.A. County Museum of Art,** 5905 Wilshire Blvd., Los Angeles (📞 323/857-6010; www.lacma.org), presents a variety of themed film series. Past subjects have ranged from 1930s blonde bombshell films to Cold War propaganda flicks to contemporary British satire (complete with a 3-day *Monty Python's Flying Circus* marathon).

Despite being a multiplex in a bright outdoor mall, **Laemmle's Sunset 5,** 8000 Sunset Blvd., West Hollywood (📞 323/848-3500; www.laemmle.com), features

---

 ## Cinema at the Cemetery

If you prefer your movie settings to be slightly macabre, boy, are you in luck. Every other Saturday in the summer, the **Hollywood Forever Cemetery** hosts civilized screenings of movie classics, which are projected against the cemetery's massive mausoleum wall. Guests are encouraged to arrive early for a BYOB picnic on the lush lawn while listening to DJs spin records. Admission is $10 per person, and parking is $5 per car within the cemetery. Bring a sweater, a flashlight, and—if you're having a picnic— bring a trash bag as well. Hollywood Forever Cemetery is located at 6000 Santa Monica Blvd., between Gower Street and Van Ness Avenue. For more information, log on to www.cinespia.org.

THE WORLD'S MOST PRIVATE public theater

Part of the culture of L.A. is to always avoid standing in line because you're far too important and busy. So it was only a matter of time before someone came up with the idea of treating everyone like a VIP at the movie theater. **ArcLight Cinemas** (🕻 **323/464-4226;** www.arclight cinemas.com) is specifically designed for anyone who abhors rude patrons (ushers keep it quiet), late arrivals (forbidden), searching for seats (reserved in advance by customer preference), uncomfortable chairs (think La-Z-Boy), neck strain (the first rows start 25 ft. from the screen), pimply teenage employees (most of the staff are struggling actors or film students), crappy popcorn (real butter and freshly made caramel popcorn), and paying for parking (4 free hr. are included in the ticket price). And it only gets better: There's a full bar and a groovy lounge where themed cocktails such as the Mordor are served with appetizers.

The ArcLight shows a mix of indie and Hollywood films, and ticket prices—as you would expect—are higher than the industry average: typically $14 for regular shows and up to $16 for weekend nights and holidays, with a $3.50 supplement for 3D films. But the rewards are worth the occasional splurge. The sound and picture quality are so good that filmmakers come here to host Q-and-A sessions, and celebrities such as Brad Pitt and Leonardo DiCaprio prefer the ArcLight's reserved seating system. Be sure to review the "Now Playing" and "Coming Soon" sections at the ArcLight's website to see what movies and Q-and-A sessions are scheduled. It's located at 6360 W. Sunset Blvd., between Vine and Ivar streets. **Note:** There are now 3 additional locations, including Sherman Oaks, 15301 Ventura Blvd. (🕻 **818/501-7033**); Pasadena, 336 E. Colorado Blvd. (🕻 **626/568-8888**); and El Segundo, 831 S. Nash St. (🕻 **310/607-9630**).

films that most theaters of its ilk won't even touch. This is the place to come to see interesting independent art films. There's often a selection of gay-themed movies as well.

The **Nuart Theatre,** 11272 Santa Monica Blvd., Los Angeles (🕻 **310/281-8223;** www.landmarktheatres.com/market/losangeles/nuarttheatre.htm), digs deep into its archives for real classics, ranging from campy to cool. It also features frequent in-person appearances and Q-and-A sessions with stars and filmmakers, and screens *The Rocky Horror Picture Show* (yes, still!) every Saturday at midnight.

Now operated by film enthusiast organization the Cinefamily, fans of silent-movie classics will enjoy the **Silent Movie Theatre,** 611 N. Fairfax Ave. (½ block south of Melrose Ave.), near the Miracle Mile (🕻 **323/655-2520** for recorded program information, or 655-2510 for the main office; www.cinefamily.org).

The **Paley Center for Media,** 465 N. Beverly Dr., Beverly Hills (🕻 **310/786-1025;** www.paleycenter.org), celebrates this country's long relationship with the tube. The museum often features a movie of the month, and it also shows free selections from past television programs (p. 148).

LATE-NIGHT BITES

Finding places to dine in the wee hours is getting easier in L.A., as every year sees more 24-hour and after-midnight eateries staking a place in the culinary landscape.

The Apple Pan ★★ This classic American burger shack, an L.A. landmark, hasn't changed much since 1947—and its burgers and pies continue to hit the spot. *Tip:* There's no formal line here while waiting for a seat. You're on the honor system. Open until 1am Friday and Saturday, and until midnight other nights; closed Monday. See p. 108 for a full review. 10801 W. Pico Blvd., West L.A. ✆ **310/475-3585.**

Canter's Fairfax Restaurant, Delicatessen & Bakery This 24-hour Jewish deli has been a winner with late-nighters since it opened more than 66 years ago. If you show up after the clubs close, you're sure to spot a bleary-eyed celebrity or two alongside the rest of the after-hours crowd, chowing down on a giant pastrami sandwich, matzo-ball soup, potato pancakes, or other deli favorites. Try a potato knish with a side of brown gravy—trust me, you'll love it. 419 N. Fairfax Ave., West Hollywood. ✆ **323/651-2030.**

Dolores's One of L.A.'s oldest surviving coffee shops, Dolores's offers just what you might expect: Naugahyde, laminated counters, lots of linoleum, and comforting predictability. Expect the usual coffee-shop fare of pancakes, burgers, and eggs at this 24-hour joint. 11407 Santa Monica Blvd., Los Angeles. ✆ **310/477-1061.**

Du-par's Restaurant & Bakery ★ Open 24 hours, this popular Valley coffee shop serves early morning "beat the clock" specials from 4 to 6am, and blue-plate specials from 6 to 11am.12036 Ventura Blvd. (1 block east of Laurel Canyon), Studio City. ✆ **818/766-4437.**

Fred 62 Silver Lake/Los Feliz hipsters hankering for a slightly demented take on classic American comfort grub skulk into Fred round-the-clock. See p. 117 for a full review. 1850 N. Vermont Ave., Los Feliz. ✆ **323/667-0062.**

Jerry's Famous Deli ★ Valley hipsters head to 24-hour Jerry's to satiate the late-night munchies. See p. 127 for a full review. 12655 Ventura Blvd. (east of Coldwater Canyon Ave.), Studio City. ✆ **818/980-4245.**

Kate Mantilini ★ Kate's serves stylish nouveau comfort food in a striking setting. It's open until midnight Sunday and Monday, Tuesday through Thursday until 1am, and Friday and Saturday until 2am. See p. 108 for a full review. 9101 Wilshire Blvd. (at Doheny Dr.), Beverly Hills. ✆ **310/278-3699.**

Kitchen 24 The key to this hipster diner's success is location, location, location. Situated in the middle of Hollywood club-land, the design in trendy but still welcoming, and the food is much better than average for a coffee shop. Hearty egg dishes are served all day and night, but there are also burgers, meatloaf and cupcakes. 1608 N. Cahuenga Blvd. (at Selma Ave.), Hollywood. ✆ **310/278-3699.** www.kitchen24.info.

Mel's Drive-In Straight from an episode of *Happy Days*, this 24-hour 1950s diner on the Sunset Strip attracts customers ranging from chic shoppers during the day to rock 'n' rollers at night. The fries and shakes here are among the more popular dishes. 8585 Sunset Blvd. (west of La Cienega Blvd.), West Hollywood. ✆ **310/854-7200.**

101 Coffee Shop A retro coffee shop right out of the early '60s with rock walls, funky colored tiles, comfy booths, and cool light fixtures, all pulled together nicely in a hip yet subdued fashion. Count on tasty grinds until 2:45am (try the breakfast burritos or the creamy mac and cheese). 6145 Franklin Ave., Hollywood. ✆ **323/467-1175.**

The Original Pantry Owned by former Los Angeles mayor Richard Riordan, this Downtown diner has been serving huge portions of comfort food round-the-clock for

Late-Night Bites

LOS ANGELES AFTER DARK

more than 60 years; in fact, they don't even have a key to the front door (there's no lock!). See p. 126 for a full review. 877 S. Figueroa St. (at 9th St.), Downtown. © **213/972-9279.**

Pink's Hot Dogs   Many a woozy hipster has awakened with the telltale signs of a post-cocktailing trip to this greasy street-side hot-dog stand—the oniony morning-after breath and chili stains on your shirt are dead giveaways. Open Friday and Saturday until 3am, and all other nights until 2am. See p. 118 for a full review. 709 N. La Brea Ave., West Hollywood. © **323/931-4223.**

Swingers ★   This hip coffee shop keeps L.A. scene-stealers happy with its retro comfort food. Open daily until 4am. See p. 118 for a full review. There's a second location at 802 Broadway (at Lincoln Ave.; © **310/393-9793**) in Santa Monica. 8020 Beverly Blvd. (west of Fairfax Ave.), Hollywood. © **323/653-5858.**

Toi on Sunset ★   Those requiring a little more *oomph* from their late-night snack should come here. At this colorful and *loud* hangout, garbled pop-culture metaphors mingle with the tastes and aromas of "rockin' Thai" cuisine in delicious ways until 4am nightly. See p. 119 for a full review. 7505½ Sunset Blvd. (at Gardner St.), Hollywood. © **323/874-8062.**

9

LOS ANGELES AFTER DARK | Late-Night Bites

SIDE TRIPS FROM LOS ANGELES

L os Angeles may be one of the world's most stimulating cities, but don't let it monopolize you to the point of ignoring its diverse, scenic side trips—from sun-filled South Coast beach towns (Newport Beach, Huntington Beach, Laguna Beach) to the island oasis of Catalina to the smog-free mountain communities of Big Bear and Lake Arrowhead.

LONG BEACH & THE QUEEN MARY ★

10

21 miles S of Downtown L.A.

The fifth-largest city in California, Long Beach is best known as the permanent home of the former cruise liner Queen Mary and the Long Beach Grand Prix, whose star-studded warm-up race has included hipster Jason Priestley and formerly perennial racer Paul Newman burning rubber through the streets of the city in mid-April.

Essentials

GETTING THERE   See chapter 11 for airport and airline information. Driving from Los Angeles, take either I-5 or I-405 to I-710 south, which leads to both downtown Long Beach and the Queen Mary Seaport.

ORIENTATION   Downtown Long Beach is at the eastern end of the vast Port of Los Angeles; Pine Avenue is the central restaurant and shopping street, which extends south to Shoreline Park and the Aquarium. The Queen Mary is docked just across the waterway, gazing south toward tiny Long Beach marina and Naples Island.

VISITOR INFORMATION   Contact the **Long Beach Area Convention & Visitors Bureau,** 301 E. Ocean Blvd, Ste 1900 (© **800/452-7829** or 562/436-3645; www.visitlongbeach.com). For information on the **Long Beach Grand Prix,** call © **562/981-2600** or check out **www.gplb.com**.

The Major Attractions

Aquarium of the Pacific ★ ☺   This enormous aquarium—one of the largest in the U.S.—is the cornerstone of Long Beach's ever-changing waterfront. Figuring that what stimulated flagging economies in Monterey and Baltimore would work in Long Beach, planners gave their all to this project, creating a crowd-pleasing attraction just across the harbor from Long Beach's other mainstay, the *Queen Mary*. The vast facility—it has enough exhibit space to fill three football fields—re-creates three areas of the Pacific: the warm Baja and Southern California regions, the Bering Sea and chilly northern Pacific, and faraway tropical climes, including impressive re-creations of a lagoon and barrier reef. The aquarium houses more than 11,000 creatures in all, from 150 sharks (some you can touch) prowling a 90,000-gallon habitat to delicate sea horses, moon jellies, and gaggles of tropical birds within the Lorikeet Forest. Learn little-known aquatic facts at the many educational exhibits, or come nose-to-nose with sea lions, moray eels, and other inhabitants of giant tanks, up to nearly three stories high.

100 Aquarium Way, off Shoreline Dr., Long Beach. © 562/590-3100. www.aquariumofpacific.org. Admission $25 adults, $22 seniors 62 and over, $13 children 3–11, free for kids 2 and under. Daily 9am–6pm. Closed Christmas and Toyota Grand Prix weekend (mid-Apr). Parking $8.

The Queen Mary ★   It's easy to dismiss this old cruise ship/museum as a barnacle-laden tourist trap, but it's the only surviving example of this particular kind of 20th-century elegance and excess. From the staterooms paneled lavishly in now-extinct tropical hardwoods to the perfectly preserved crew quarters and the miles of hallway handrails made of once-pedestrian Bakelite, wonders never cease aboard this 81,237-ton Art Deco luxury liner. Stroll the teakwood decks with just a bit of imagination and you're back in 1936 on the maiden voyage from Southampton, England. Don't miss the streamlined modern observation lounge, featured often in period motion pictures; have drinks and listen to some live jazz. Kiosk displays of photographs and memorabilia are everywhere—following the success of the movie *Titanic,* the *Queen Mary* even hosted an exhibit of artifacts from its less fortunate cousin. The Cold War–era Soviet submarine *Scorpion* resides alongside; separate admission is required to tour the sub. *Tip:* Buy a First Class Passage ticket to both the sub and the ship and you'll also get a behind-the-scenes guided tour, peppered with worthwhile anecdotes and details—plus all the bells and whistles (and dramatic lighting effects) of the Ghosts and Legends Tour——well worth the extra $8.

Save Some Cash

If you plan on visiting the *Queen Mary* and the Aquarium on the same day, you can purchase a combined ticket package at either venue for $36 ($20 for kids 5–11). You'll save about $10 (hey, that's a free lunch).

1126 Queen's Hwy. (end of I-710), Long Beach. © 877/342-0738. www.queenmary.com. Admission $25 adults, $22 seniors 55 and over and military, $13 children 5–11, free for kids 4 and under; First Class Passage $33 adults, $29 seniors 55 and over and military, $20 children 5–11, free for kids 4 and under. Daily 10am–6pm. Parking $12.

Where to Stay

Hotel Queen Mary ★ 🛏   The Queen Mary isn't only a piece of maritime history; it's also a hotel. Although the historic ocean liner is considered the most luxurious vessel ever to sail the Atlantic, with some of the largest rooms built aboard a ship, the quarters aren't exceptional when compared to those on terra firma today, nor are the amenities. The idea is to enjoy the novelty and charm of its features, such as the original bathtub water faucets ("cold salt," "cold fresh," "hot salt," "hot fresh")—along with the more modern duplicate features (everything comes in pairs of two). The beautifully carved interior is a feast for the eye and fun to explore, and the weekday rates are hard to beat. Three onboard restaurants are overpriced but convenient (though the new Chelsea Chowder House is showing promise), and the shopping arcade has a decidedly British feel (one shop sells great Queen Mary souvenirs). An expansive Sunday champagne brunch—complete with ice sculpture and harpist—is served in the ship's Grand Salon, and it's always worthwhile to have a cocktail in the Art Deco Observation Bar. If you're too young to have traveled on the old luxury liners, this is the perfect opportunity to experience the romance of an Atlantic crossing—with no seasickness or cabin fever.

1126 Queen's Hwy. (end of I-710), Long Beach, CA 90802. www.queenmary.com.📞 **877/342-0742.** 365 units. From $110 inside cabin; from $164 deluxe cabin; from $360 suite. Many packages available. AE, DC, MC, V. Valet parking $19; self-parking $15. **Amenities:** 3 restaurants; spa. In room: A/C, TV, Wi-Fi ($9.95 per day).

Where to Eat

The Sky Room ★★ CALIFORNIAN/FRENCH   It takes a 40-minute drive from Los Angeles to Long Beach to get a sense of what fine dining must have been like during Hollywood's Golden Age. Built in 1926 and meticulously restored by proprietor Bernard Rosenson, the restaurant's Art Deco–period design inspires oohs and aahs among first-time guests. Awash in brilliant white, the interior's massive pillars, curvaceous ramps, glimmering brass, elevated maple-and-ebony dance floor, and classic jazz band playing enticing dance tunes all combine to create the illusion of dining on a luxury ocean liner (the view of the stately *Queen Mary* certainly enhances the effect). Opulence continues with white Frette linens, custom black-rimmed china, Villeroy & Boch tableware, and a *Wine Spectator*–award-winning wine list. The Californian/French menu offers a pleasing presentation of the classics: scallops with sweet potato puree, Prime rib eye with pommes frites, and osso bucco. I highly recommend that you take the advice of the experienced waitstaff and sommelier; our duo handled the task flawlessly. A night of dinner, drinking, dancing, and romance—what's not to like?

40 S. Locust Ave. (at Ocean Blvd.), Long Beach.📞 562/983-2703. www.theskyroom.com. Reservations recommended. Main courses $27–$45. AE, DC, DISC, MC, V. Mon–Thurs 5:30–9pm; Fri–Sat 5:30pm–midnight; Sun 4:30–9:30pm. Valet parking $7.

Yard House ★ AMERICAN ECLECTIC   Not only does it have one of the best outdoor dining venues in Long Beach, the Yard House also features one of the world's largest selection of draft beers. The keg room houses more than 1,000 gallons of beer, all visible through a glass door where you can see the golden liquids transported to a signature oval bar via miles of nylon tubing to the dozens of taps. The restaurant takes its name from the early colonial tradition of serving beer in 36-inch-tall glasses—or yards—to weary stagecoach drivers. Customers are encouraged to partake in this tradition and can drink from the glass yards, as well as half-yards and traditional pint glasses. Signature dishes range from the tortelike California roll to the crab cake hoagie and an impressive selection of steaks and chops. There's also an extensive list of appetizers—perfect for a tapas-style meal—salads, pasta, and rice dishes, as well as sandwiches and individual pizzas. On sunny days, be sure to request a table on the deck overlooking the picturesque harbor.

401 Shoreline Village Dr., Long Beach. 📞 **562/628-0455.** www.yardhouse.com. Reservations only accepted weekdays until 5pm. Main courses $12–$30. AE, DC, MC, V. Mon–Thurs 11am–midnight; Fri–Sat 11am–2am.

THE SOUTH COAST ★★★

Seal Beach, 36 miles S of Los Angeles; Newport Beach, 49 miles; Dana Point, 65 miles

Whatever you do, don't say "Orange County" here. The mere name evokes images of smoggy industrial parks, cookie-cutter housing developments, and the staunch Republicanism that prevails behind the so-called "orange curtain." We're talking instead about the Orange Coast, one of Southern California's best-kept secrets—a string of seaside jewels that have been compared with the French Riviera or the Costa del Sol. Forty-two miles of beaches offer pristine stretches of sand, tide pools teeming with marine life, ecological preserves, secluded coves, picturesque pleasure-boat harbors, and legendary surf breaks. One option is to do it as a day trip from L.A.—hit the road early for a scenic cruise down Pacific Coast Highway starting at Seal Beach, stop for lunch at Laguna Beach (the prettiest of all the SoCal beach towns), continue south to Dana Point (where the really expensive resorts reside), and then take the freeway back to L.A. (I-5 to I-405). My advice, if you have the time, is to take a full day or two to really relax and enjoy the distinct culture of this area. Who wants to spend a pleasant day at the beach only to spend two hours in traffic on the way back?

Essentials

GETTING THERE   See "Getting There," in chapter 11, for airport and airline information. By car from Los Angeles, take I-5 or I-405 south. The scenic, shore-hugging Pacific Coast Highway (Calif. 1, or just PCH to the locals) links the Orange Coast communities from Seal Beach in the north to Capistrano Beach just south of Dana Point, where it merges with I-5. To reach the beach communities directly, take the following freeway exits: **Seal Beach,** Seal Beach Boulevard from I-405; **Huntington Beach,** Beach Boulevard/California 39 from either I-405 or I-5; **Newport Beach,** California 55 from either I-405 or I-5; **Laguna Beach,** California 133 from I-5; **San Juan Capistrano,** Ortega Highway/California 74 from I-5; and **Dana Point,** Pacific Coast Highway/California 1 from I-5.

Driving the Orange Coast

You'll most likely be exploring the coast by car, so the beach communities are covered in order from north to south. Keep in mind, however, that if you're traveling between Los Angeles and San Diego, Pacific Coast Highway (Calif. 1) is a breezy, scenic detour that adds less than an hour to the commute—so pick out a couple of seaside destinations and take your time.

Seal Beach, on the border between Los Angeles and Orange counties, and a neighbor to Long Beach's Naples Harbor, is geographically isolated by both the adjacent U.S. Naval Weapons Station and the self-contained Leisure World retirement community. As a result, the beach town appears untouched by modern development—it's Orange County's version of small-town America. Take a stroll down Main Street, culminating in the Seal Beach Pier. Although the clusters of sunbathing, squawking seals that gave the town its name aren't around any more, old-timers still fish, lovers still stroll, and families still cavort by the seaside, enjoying great food and retail shops or having a cold drink at Hennessey's tavern.

Huntington Beach—or Surf City, as it's known—is the largest Orange Coast city; it stretches quite a way inland and has seen the most urbanization. To some extent, this has changed the old boardwalk and pier to a modern outdoor mall where cliques of teens coexist with families and the surfers who continue to flock here, drawn by Huntington's legendary place in surf lore. Hawaiian-born George Freeth is credited with bringing the sport here in 1907, and some say the breaks around the pier and Bolsa Chica are the best in California. The world's top wave riders flock to Huntington every August for the rowdy but professional **U.S. Open of Surfing.** If you're around at Christmastime, try to see the gaily decorated marina homes and boats in Huntington Harbor by taking the **Cruise of Lights,** a 45-minute narrated sail through and around the harbor islands. The festivities generally last from mid-December until Christmas; call ✆ 714/840-7542 or visit www.cruiseoflights.org for schedules and ticket information.

 A Special Arts Festival

A tradition for 70 years in arts-friendly Laguna, the Festival of Arts & Pageant of the Masters is held every summer throughout July and August. It's pretty large now, and it includes the formerly "alternative" Sawdust Festival across the street. See "Los Angeles–Area Calendar of Events," in chapter 2, for details, or log on to www.foapom.com.

The name **Newport Beach** conjures comparisons to Rhode Island's Newport, where the well-to-do enjoy seaside living with all the creature comforts. That's the way it is here, too, but on a less grandiose scale. From the million-dollar Cape Cod–style cottages on sunny Balboa Island to elegant shopping complexes such as Fashion Island and South Coast Plaza (an übermall with valet parking, car detailing, limo service, and concierge), this is where fashionable socialites, right-wing celebrities, and business mavens shop. Alternatively, you could explore **Balboa Peninsula**'s historic Pavilion and old-fashioned pier, or board a passenger ferry to Catalina Island.

Laguna Beach, whose breathtaking geography is marked by bold elevated headlands, coastal bluffs, pocket coves, and a very inviting beach, is known as an artists' enclave, but the truth is that Laguna has became so "in" (read: expensive) that it has driven most of the true bohemians out. Their legacy remains, with the annual **Festival of Arts & Pageant of the Masters** (see "A Special Arts Festival," above), as well as a proliferation of art galleries mingling with high-priced boutiques along the town's cozy streets. In warm weather, Laguna Beach has an overwhelming Mediterranean island ambience, which makes *everyone* feel beautifully, idly rich.

San Juan Capistrano, in the verdant headlands inland from Dana Point, is defined by Spanish missions and its loyal swallows. The mission architecture is authentic, and history abounds. Think of San Juan Capistrano as a compact, life-size diorama illustrating the evolution of a small Western town—from Spanish-mission era to secular rancho period, statehood, and into the 21st century. Surprisingly, Mission San Juan Capistrano (see "Seeing the Sights," below) is once again the center of the community, just as the founding friars intended 200 years ago.

Dana Point, the last town south, has been called a "marina development in search of a soul." Overlooking the harbor stands a monument to 19th-century author Richard Henry Dana, who gave his name to the area and described it in *Two Years Before the Mast.* Activities generally center on yachting and Dana Point's beautiful harbor. Nautical themes are everywhere, particularly the streets named for old-fashioned shipboard lights—a hodgepodge that includes Street of the Amber Lantern, Street of the Violet Lantern, Street of the Golden Lantern, and so on. Bordering the harbor is Doheny State Beach (see "Beaches & Nature Preserves," below), one of the very best for its seaside park and camping facilities.

The South Coast

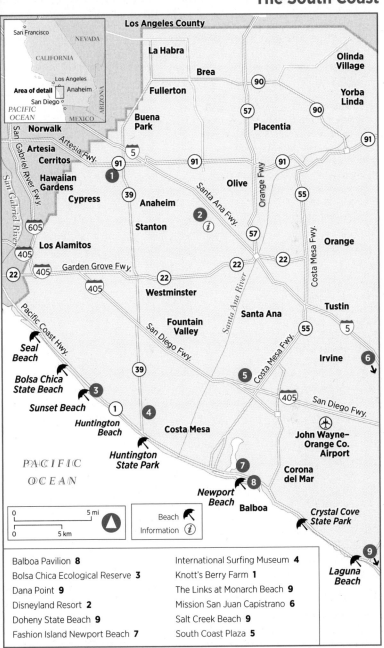

Los Angeles County

La Habra

Brea

Olinda Village

Fullerton

Yorba Linda

Buena Park

Placentia

Norwalk

Artesia
Cerritos

Hawaiian Gardens

Cypress

Anaheim

Olive

Stanton

Los Alamitos

Orange

Garden Grove Fwy.

Westminster

Tustin

Fountain Valley

Santa Ana

Seal Beach

Bolsa Chica State Beach

Sunset Beach

Irvine

Huntington Beach

Costa Mesa

Huntington State Park

John Wayne–Orange Co. Airport

PACIFIC OCEAN

Corona del Mar

Newport Beach

Balboa

Crystal Cove State Park

Laguna Beach

0 — 5 mi	Beach ☂
0 — 5 km	Information ⓘ

Balboa Pavilion **8**

International Surfing Museum **4**

Bolsa Chica Ecological Reserve **3**

Knott's Berry Farm **1**

Dana Point **9**

The Links at Monarch Beach **9**

Disneyland Resort **2**

Mission San Juan Capistrano **6**

Doheny State Beach **9**

Salt Creek Beach **9**

Fashion Island Newport Beach **7**

South Coast Plaza **5**

Enjoying the Outdoors

BEACHES & NATURE PRESERVES The **Bolsa Chica Ecological Reserve,** in Huntington Beach (© **714/846-1114;** www.bolsachica.org), is a 900-acre restored urban salt marsh that's a haven to more than 200 bird species, as well as a wide variety of protected plants and animals. Naturalists come to spot herons and egrets as well as California horn snails, jackknife clams, sea sponges, common jellyfish, and shore crabs. An easy 1.5-mile loop trail begins from a parking lot on Pacific Coast Highway (Calif. 1) a mile south of Warner Boulevard; docents lead a narrated walk the first Saturday of every month. The trail heads inland, over Inner Bolsa Bay and up Bolsa Chica bluffs. It then loops back toward the ocean over a dike that separates the Inner and Outer Bolsa bays and traverses a coastal sand-dune system. This beautiful hike is a terrific afternoon adventure. The Bolsa Chica Conservancy has been working since 1978 on reclaiming the wetlands from oil companies that began drilling here more than 70 years ago. It's an ongoing process, and you can still see those "seesaw" drills dotting the outer areas of the reserve.

Huntington City Beach, adjacent to Huntington Pier, is a haven for volleyball players and surfers; dense crowds abound, but so do amenities such as outdoor showers, beach rentals, and restrooms. Just south of the city beach is 3-mile-long **Huntington State Beach.** Both popular beaches have lifeguards and concession stands seasonally. The state beach also has restrooms, showers, barbecue pits, and a waterfront bike path. The main entrance is on Beach Boulevard, and there are access points all along Pacific Coast Highway (Calif. 1).

Newport Beach runs for about 5 miles and includes both Newport and Balboa piers. It has outdoor showers, restrooms, volleyball nets, and a vintage boardwalk that just may make you feel as though you've stepped 50 years back in time. **Balboa Bikes N Beach Stuff** (© **949/723-1516**), at the corner of Balboa and Palm near the pier, rents a variety of items, from pier-fishing poles to bikes, beach umbrellas, and body boards. The **Southwind Kayak Center,** 17855 Sky Park Circle, Irvine (© **800/768-8494** or 949/261-0200; www.southwindkayaks.com), rents sea kayaks for use in the bay or open ocean at rates starting at $60 per day; instructional classes are available on weekends, with some midweek classes in summer. The center also conducts several easygoing guided outings, including a $55 Back to Nature trip that highlights the marine life around Dana Point.

Crystal Cove State Park (© **949/494-3539;** www.crystalcovestatepark.com), which covers 3 miles of coastline between Corona del Mar and Laguna Beach and extends into the hills around El Moro Canyon, is a good alternative to the more popular beaches for seekers of solitude. (There are, however, lifeguards and restrooms.) The beach is a winding, sandy strip, backed with grassy terraces; high tide sometimes sections it into coves. The entire area offshore is an underwater nature preserve. There are four entrances, including Pelican Point and El Moro Canyon.

Salt Creek Beach Park lies below the palatial Ritz-Carlton Laguna Niguel; guests who tire of the pristine swimming pool can venture down the staircase on Ritz-Carlton Drive to wiggle their toes in the sand. The setting is spectacular, with wide white-sand beaches looking out toward Catalina Island. The park has lifeguards, restrooms, a snack bar, and convenient parking near the hotel.

Doheny State Beach in Dana Point, just south of Dana Point Marina (enter off Del Abispo St.), has long been known as a premier surfing spot and camping site. Doheny has the friendly vibe of beach parties in days gone by: Tree-shaded lawns give way to wide beaches, and picnicking and beach camping are encouraged. There are 121 sites that can be used for either tents or RVs, plus a state-run visitor center featuring several small aquariums of sea and tide-pool life. For more information and camping availability, call ✆ **949/496-6172.**

BICYCLING Biking is the most popular beach activity. A slower-paced alternative to driving, it allows you to enjoy the clean, fresh air and notice smaller details of these laid-back beach towns and harbors. The Newport Beach visitor center (see "Visitor Information," above) offers a free map of trails throughout the city and harbor. Bikes and equipment can be rented at **Balboa Bikes N Beach Stuff,** 601 Balboa Blvd., Newport Beach (✆ **949/723-1516**), and at **Laguna Beach Cyclery,** 240 Thalia St. (✆ **949/494-1522;** www.lagunabeachcyclery.net).

GOLF Many golf-course architects have used the geography of the Orange Coast to its full advantage, molding challenging and scenic courses from the rolling bluffs. Most courses are private, but a few outstanding ones are open to the public. **Monarch Beach Golf Links,** 50 Monarch Beach Resort Dr. N., Dana Point (✆ **949/240-8247;** www.monarchbeachgolf.com), is particularly impressive. This hilly, challenging course, designed by Robert Trent Jones, Jr., offers great ocean views. Afternoon winds can sneak up, so accuracy is essential. Weekend morning greens fees are $165 to $195 ($145 to $175 weekdays). The rates after 1pm drop to $135 weekends and $115 weekdays.

GONDOLA RIDES Newport Harbor's six-mile long stretch of luxury homes and boats provides a picturesque backdrop for mood-setting romance aboard the Venetian-style boats of **Gondola Adventures★★**, 3101 West Coast Hwy., (✆ **949/646-2067**; www.gondola.com). Cozy couples can bundle up beneath blankets as they cruise the canals—tradition dictates that you kiss under every bridge. If you're lucky, your gondolier will amplify the experience—literally—with song. *Tip:* Many a proposal has been accepted via the "message in a bottle" notes that your gondolier can plant for an additional fee. www.gondola.com

Seeing the Sights

Beyond the sights listed below, one of the most popular Orange Coast attractions is **Balboa Island** (www.balboaisland.com). The charm of this pretty little neighborhood isn't diminished by knowing that the island was man-made—and it certainly hasn't affected the price of real estate (it's hard to believe that the original property lots sold for $250). Tiny clapboard cottages in the island's center and modern houses with two-story windows and private docks along the perimeter make a colorful and romantic picture. You can drive onto the island on Jamboree Road to the north or take the three-car ferry from Balboa Peninsula (www.balboaislandferry.com). It's generally more fun to park and take the 30-minute ferry ride as a pedestrian, since the island is crowded and lacks parking, and the tiny alleys they call streets are more suitable for strolling. **Marine Avenue,** the main commercial street, is lined with small shops and cafes that evoke a New England fishing village. Shaved ices sold by sidewalk vendors will relieve the heat of summer.

Balboa Pavilion & Fun Zone ★ ☺ This historic cupola-topped structure, a California Historical Landmark, was built in 1906 as a bathhouse for swimmers in their ankle-length bathing costumes. Later, during the Big Band era, dancers rocked the Pavilion doing the Balboa Hop. Now it serves as the terminal for Catalina Island passenger service, harbor and whale-watching cruises, and fishing charters. The surrounding boardwalk is the Balboa Fun Zone (© **949/673-0408;** www.thebalboa-funzone.com), a collection of carnival rides, game arcades, and vendors of hot dogs and cotton candy. For Newport Harbor or Catalina cruise information, call © **949/673-5245;** for sport fishing and whale-watching, call © **949/673-1434.**

400 Main St., Newport Beach. © **800/830-7744.** www.balboapavilion.com. From Calif. 1, turn south onto Newport Blvd. (which becomes Balboa Blvd. on the peninsula); turn left at Main St.

International Surfing Museum   Nostalgic Gidgets and Moondoggies shouldn't miss this monument to the laid-back sport that has become synonymous with California beaches. You'll find gargantuan longboards from the sport's early days, memorabilia of Duke Kahanamoku and the other surfing greats represented on the Walk of Fame near Huntington Pier, and a gift shop where a copy of the *Surfin'ary* can help you bone up on your surfer slang even if you don't know which foot is goofy.

411 Olive Ave., Huntington Beach. © **714/960-3483.** www.surfingmuseum.org. Free admission. Mon, Wed–Fri noon–5pm; Tues noon–9pm; Sat-Sun 11am–6pm (hours tend to vary, so call ahead).

Laguna Art Museum   This beloved local institution is working hard to position itself as the artistic cornerstone of the community. In addition to a small but interesting permanent collection, the museum presents installations of regional works definitely worth a detour. Past examples include a display of surf photography from the coast's 1930s and 1940s golden era, and dozens of plein-air Impressionist paintings (ca. 1900–30) by the founding artists of the original colony. The museum is also open for extended hours (until 9pm) during Laguna Beach Artwalk, the first Thursday each month, when all are admitted free from 5 to 9pm.

307 Cliff Dr., Laguna Beach. © **949/494-8971.** www.lagunaartmuseum.org. Admission $12 adults, $10 students and seniors, free for children 11 and under. Daily 11am–5pm.

Mission San Juan Capistrano   The seventh of the 21 California coastal missions, Mission San Juan Capistrano is continually being restored. The mix of old ruins and working buildings is home to small museum collections and various adobe rooms that are as quaint as they are interesting. The intimate mission chapel with its ornate baroque altar is still used for religious services, and the mission complex is the center of the community, hosting performing arts, children's programs, and other cultural events year-round.

This mission is best known for its **swallows,** which are said to return to nest every year at their favorite sanctuary. According to legend, the birds wing their way back to the mission annually on March 19, St. Joseph's Day, arriving at dawn; they are said to take flight again on October 23, after bidding the mission farewell. In reality, you'll probably see the well-fed birds here any day of the week, winter or summer. *Tip:* Admission for adults and seniors includes a complimentary audio tour.

26801 Ortega Hwy. (Calif. 74), San Juan Capistrano. © **949/234-1300.** www.missionsjc.com. Admission $9 adults, $8 seniors, $5 children 4–11, free for kids 3 and under. Daily 8:30am–5pm. Closed Thanksgiving, Christmas Eve, Christmas Day and Good Friday (weather conditions can close the Mission unexpectedly).

Where to Stay
VERY EXPENSIVE
Montage Resort & Spa ★★ ☺   The investors behind this 30-acre Arts and Crafts beauty have created yet another reason for big spenders to unwind along the Orange Coast. You can barely see it from the PCH, and the front entrance is rather understated, but as you walk through the lobby and onto the balcony overlooking

the . . . oh my. The change of scenery is so breathtakingly abrupt that it takes composure not to sprint down to the gorgeous mosaic-tiled pool or run barefoot along the sun-kissed beach. It's the same view from the balcony of every room, and you never tire of it.

The Montage Resort is all about style. As soon as you arrive, you're warmly greeted and given a well-rehearsed tour of the resort by attractive khaki-clad employees wearing tailored jackets. The tour ends at the neo-Craftsman-style guest rooms, which are spacious, immaculate, and tastefully decorated with museum-quality plein-air artwork, huge marble bathrooms with oversize tubs and plush robes, 27-inch flatscreen TVs with DVD players, quality dark-wood furnishings, feather-top beds with goose-down pillows, and very inviting balconies. You'll spend very little time here, though, since you'll be lounging by the infinity pool sipping a lemonade, exploring the tide pools, strolling through the hotel's impeccably manicured park and pristine beaches, spoiling yourself rotten with skin treatments and massages at the oceanfront Spa Montage, and sampling chef Craig Strong's imaginative cuisine at the resort's signature restaurant, **Studio.** There's plenty for kids to do as well: They have their own pool and several fun-filled programs to keep them entertained (and, of course, there's the beach).

30801 S. Coast Hwy., Laguna Beach, CA 92651. **www.montagelagunabeach.com.** © **866/271-6953** or 949/715-6000. Fax 949/715-6100. 250 units. $575–$795 double; from $1,295 suite. AE, DISC, MC, V. Valet parking $30. **Amenities:** 3 restaurants; lobby lounge w/live entertainment; children's programs and entertainment; concierge; oceanfront fitness facilities and spa; pool and kiddie pool; room service. *In room:* A/C, flatscreen TV and DVD/CD player, hair dryer, minibar, Wi-Fi ($16 per day).

Pelican Hill Resort ★★ Past grand Romanesque columns on PCH, everything about this luxury resort was inspired by the 16th century architecture of Andrea Palladio. Not just ordinary guest rooms or suites, there are only two main room categories here: bungalow or villa. Bungalows are geared more toward the casual traveler, while villas are intended to accommodate larger groups for longer-term stays. Each bungalow features its own patio (I only wish each had an umbrella to protect against sun or inclement weather—request one that does), a gas fireplace and a gorgeous marble bathroom. The concierge gallery is its own dedicated space of first-rate, multimedia assistance and interactivity.

The two championship golf courses were designed by the celebrated Tom Fazio, and the 23,000 sq. ft. spa provides 22 treatment rooms for blissful escape. One-of-a-kind, the awe-inspiring Coliseum pool features more than a million hand-laid glass tiles. The lovely Northern Italian Andrea restaurant is one of the best on the entire South Coast, making it truly unnecessary to ever leave the property. (The truffled risotto, which is finished in a giant wheel of aged Parmesan, is a must-try.) For kids, Camp Pelican provides activities for recreation and education; teens can enjoy similar amenities.

22701 Pelican Hill Rd., Newport Coast, CA 92657. www.pelicanhill.com. © **800/315-8214** or 949/467-6800. Fax 949/467-6888. 204 bungalows; 128 villas. $795–$995 double; from $1,150 suite. AE, DISC, MC, V. Valet parking complimentary. **Amenities:** 5 restaurants; children's programs; concierge; fitness facilities and spa; 2 championship golf courses; 3 pools; room service; *In room:* A/C, flatscreen TV/DVD, hair dryer, minibar, free Wi-Fi.

Ritz-Carlton Laguna Niguel ★★ After a sorely needed $40-million renovation to keep up with neighboring resorts such as the Montage and St. Regis, this Dana Point grande dame has recaptured its status as one of the top resorts on the Orange Coast. From its vantage on the edge of a 150-foot-high bluff overlooking an idyllic

2-mile-long beach, the scenery from most every window is spectacular (you can spend hours on your balcony admiring the ocean view). The most welcome change is that every guest room and public space has been completely remodeled with a much more chic and contemporary look. The spacious rooms are now outfitted with 42-inch plasma TVs with DVD players, sumptuous furnishings and fabrics, an Italian-marble bathroom with a double vanity, and the very comfortable feather beds. The resort's main restaurant, the surprisingly casual, hallway-adjacent Raya, offers chef Richard Sandoval's flavorful pan-Latin fare, along with gorgeous ocean views. For an impressive selection of cheese, chocolate and fine wines, the small but elegant Eno bar conjures impressive pairings. Other improvements include a new luxury spa and oceanfront fitness center. As always, lush terraces and colorful flower gardens abound throughout the well-tended property, and service—in typical Ritz-Carlton style—is unassuming and impeccable. Garden tours, beach shuttles, surf lessons, and excellent kids' programs are available.

1 Ritz-Carlton Dr., Dana Point, CA 92629. www.ritzcarlton.com. © **800/542-8680** or 949/240-2000. Fax 949/240-0829. 393 units. From $495 garden-view/pool-view double; $645 oceanview double; from $1050 suite. Children 17 and under stay free in parent's room. Midweek and special packages available. AE, DC, DISC, MC, V. Parking $35. **Amenities:** 2 restaurants; lounge; children's programs; concierge; health club; room service; spa; 2 outdoor tennis courts. *In room:* A/C, TV w/pay movies, hair dryer, minibar, Wi-Fi included in the resort fee.

St. Regis Monarch Beach Resort & Spa ★★★

Let's cut to the chase: The St. Regis Monarch Beach Resort is one of the finest luxury hotels I have ever had the pleasure of reviewing. They nailed it with this one, setting a standard for all other resort hotels. Everything oozes with indulgence, from the stellar service to the striking artwork, high-tech electronics, absurdly comfortable beds, stellar restaurants, and a 30,000-square-foot spa that will blow your mind. The $240-million, 172-acre resort opened on July 30, 2001, with a massive star-studded gala, and has since been wooing the wealthy with its gorgeous Tuscan-inspired architecture and soothing ocean views.

Perfection is all in the details, and the St. Regis is full of them: a three-lane lap pool with an underwater sound system; a yoga, spinning, and "movement" studio; a full-service Vogue salon; private poolside cabanas; fantastic cuisine at Michael Mina's popular **Stonehill Tavern** restaurant ★★★; couples' spa treatment rooms with whirlpool baths and fireplaces; an 18-hole Robert Trent Jones, Jr., golf course; and even a private beach club. The guest rooms are loaded with beautiful custom-designed furniture, 32-inch Sony Vega flatscreen TVs with CD/DVD audio systems and a 300-DVD library, huge marble-laden bathrooms with glass shower doors that must weigh 100 pounds, and 24-hour butler service.

The resort's only drawback is that although it's near the beach, unlike the Ritz-Carlton Laguna Niguel and Montage (see above), it's not on it. The view of the terraced pool area, golf course, and shimmering ocean beyond is fantastic, however, and the hotel offers complimentary shuttle service to the 2-mile-long beach, plus exclusive access to the **St. Regis Beach Club,** where attendants set up chairs, towels, and umbrellas, and take food and drink orders. You can even hire a "Surf Butler" to take your measurements for a wet suit, bring out a board, and give you lessons.

1 Monarch Beach Resort Rd., Dana Point, CA 92629. www.stregismb.com. © **800/722-1543** or 949/234-3200. Fax 949/234-3201. 400 units. From $512 resort-view double; from $620 oceanview double; from $775 suite. Golf and spa packages available. AE, DC, DISC, MC, V. Valet parking $30. **Amenities:** 6 restaurants; lounge; wine cellar tasting room; kids' club; concierge; fitness center; 18-hole golf course; 2 Jacuzzis; 3 pools; room service; spa. *In room:* A/C, TV w/DVD library, DVD/CD player, hair dryer, minibar, Wi-Fi ($13 per day).

Surf and Sand Resort ★   The nine-story Surf and Sand Resort has come a long way since it started in 1948 as a beachside motor lodge with 13 units. Still occupying the same fantastic ocean-side location, it now features 152 guest rooms that, despite their simplicity and standard size, feel enormously decadent. They're all very bright and beachy; each has a private balcony with a dreamy ocean view, a marble bathroom accented handsomely with granite, and plush cotton terry robes. *Tip:* Try getting one of the deluxe corner rooms, with an expanded 90-degree view of the California coastline—it's well worth the additional dollars. Also, be sure to check the website for special deals. The hotel's Mediterranean-style **Aquaterra Spa** offers a tantalizing array of personalized massage, skin-care, and body treatments. You'll find the requisite ocean-inspired treatments, but the menu also features eight different specialty massages, each with your choice of four aromatherapy oils. The spa's four Couples Rituals offer themed body treatments followed by a bubble bath for two (the tub has an ocean view) and a massage to finish. The outdoor fire pit areas are also very romantic. **Splashes** restaurant serves breakfast, lunch, and dinner daily in a beautiful oceanfront setting, though the food doesn't live up to the stunning backdrop.

1555 S. Coast Hwy. (south of Laguna Canyon Rd.), Laguna Beach, CA 92651. www.surfandsandresort. com. ✆ **888/869-7569** or 949/497-4477. Fax 949/494-2897. 165 units. $535–$700 double; from $700 suite. AE, DC, DISC, MC, V. **Amenities:** Restaurant; bar; summer children's programs; concierge; fitness room; Jacuzzi; outdoor heated pool; room service; full-service spa. *In room:* TV/DVD, hair dryer, minibar, free Wi-Fi, iPod docking station.

EXPENSIVE

The Balboa Bay Club & Resort ★   Spread out over 15 acres, this bay-front resort retains late '40s charm but with many modern day amenities; it's been a perennially popular destination for the duration. The staff is immensely helpful and takes great pride in its knowledge of the property. Ask a question that someone can't answer off the top of his head, and you just might get an unexpected call from the concierge with the information. Rooms are tastefully appointed with mostly muted tones, though the occasional too-vibrant pattern—floral curtains adjacent to striped chairs could use a retouch. The 1,200 sq. ft. Bay View suites are worth the splurge for their unobstructed waterside sightlines, two separate patios—and privacy between bedroom and living area. There's even a 1/2-bath in the living room. The aptly named **First Cabin** restaurant is reminiscent of a cruise ship, both in terms of offerings—everything from tableside Caesar and dry-aged filet mignon—to the sharply dressed longtime servers.

1221 Coast Hwy., Newport Beach, CA 92663. www.balboabayclub.com. ✆ **888/445-7153** or 949/645-5000. Fax 949/630-4215 160 units. $325–$495 double; from $565 suite. Themed packages are available. Valet parking $28. AE, DISC, MC, V. **Amenities**: 1 restaurant, 1 lounge with live entertainment; concierge; heated pool with hydro spa; room service; spa, salon and fitness center. *In room:* TV/DVD; fridge; Wi-Fi ($13 per day).

Moderate

Blue Lantern Inn ★★   A three-story New England–style gray clapboard inn, the Blue Lantern is a pleasant cross between romantic B&B and modern, sophisticated small hotel. Almost all the rooms, which are decorated with reproduction traditional furniture and plush bedding, have a balcony or deck overlooking the harbor. Each has a fireplace and whirlpool tub. You can have your breakfast here in private (clad in the fluffy robe provided) for an extra $5 per person (totally worth it), or go downstairs to the sunny dining room that also serves complimentary afternoon tea. There's also an exercise room and a cozy lounge with menus for many area restaurants plus loaner items like movies, books, and board games. The friendly staff welcomes you with home-baked cookies at the front desk.

34343 St. of the Blue Lantern, Dana Point, CA 92629. www.bluelanterninn.com. ℰ **800/950-1236** or 949/661-1304. Fax 949/496-1483. 29 units. $175–$600 double. Rates include full breakfast and afternoon tea. AE, DC, MC, V. Free parking. **Amenities:** Complimentary bikes; concierge; exercise room; Jacuzzi. *In room:* A/C, TV/DVD, fridge with complimentary soft drinks, free Wi-Fi.

Casa Laguna Inn & Spa ★   Once you see this romantic terraced complex of Spanish-style cottages amid lush gardens and secluded patios—which offers all the amenities of a B&B *and* affordable prices—you might wonder, what's the catch? Well, the noise of busy PCH wafts easily into Casa Laguna, so light sleepers may be disturbed. Still, the Casa has been a favorite hideaway since Laguna's early days and now glows under the watchful eye of a terrific owner, who has upped the ante by adding a spa. Some rooms—especially the suites—are downright luxurious, with a fireplace, kitchen, bathrobes, CD player, VCR, and other in-room goodies. Throughout the property, Catalina tile adorns fountains, and bougainvillea spills into paths; each room has an individual charm. Breakfast, which is a big focus here (popular recipes are even published on the website) is served in the sunny morning room of the Craftsman-style Mission House, where a cozy living room invites relaxation.

2510 S. Coast Hwy., Laguna Beach, CA 92651. www.casalaguna.com. ℰ **800/233-0449** or 949/494-2996. Fax 949/494-5009. 21 units. $159–$349 double; from $279 suite. Rates include breakfast, afternoon wine, and hors d'oeuvres. Off-season and midweek discounts available. AE, DISC, MC, V. **Amenities:** Jacuzzi; heated outdoor pool; spa. *In room:* TV, free Wi-Fi.

Where to Eat

Options in Seal Beach are limited, but a good choice for seafood is **Walt's Wharf,** 201 Main St. (ℰ **562/598-4433;** www.waltswharf.com), a bustling, polished restaurant featuring market-fresh selections either plain or with Pacific Rim accents.

MODERATE

Crab Cooker SEAFOOD   Since 1951 folks in search of fresh, well-prepared seafood have headed to this bright-red former bank building. Also a fish market, the Crab Cooker has a casual atmosphere of humble wooden tables, uncomplicated smoked and grilled preparations, and meticulously selected fresh fare. The place is especially proud of its Maryland crab cakes, but clams and oysters are also part of the repertoire.

2200 Newport Blvd., Newport Beach. ℰ **949/673-0100.** www.crabcooker.com. Main courses dinner $14–$30, lunch $11–$30. AE, MC, V. Sun–Thurs 11am–9pm; Fri–Sat 11am–10pm.

Harbor Grill SEAFOOD/STEAK   Located in a business/commercial mall right in the center of the Dana Point Marina, the Harbor Grill is enthusiastically recommended by locals for mesquite-broiled ocean-fresh seafood. Hawaiian mahimahi with a mango-chutney baste is on the menu, along with Pacific swordfish, crab cakes, and beefsteaks. I was particularly impressed by the scratch-made sauces and homemade marinades.

34499 St. of the Golden Lantern, Dana Point. ℰ **949/240-1416.** www.harborgrill.com. Reservations recommended. Main courses $19–$29. AE, DC, DISC, MC, V. Mon–Sat 11:30am–10pm; Sun 9am–9pm.

Las Brisas 🔟 MEXICAN SEAFOOD   Las Brisas's breathtaking view of the Pacific (particularly at sunset) and potent margaritas are a surefire combination for a

UPSCALE mall DINING

Leave it to designer-conscious Orange County to plop some of its best restaurants in super-upscale shopping malls. It turns out al fresco **Fashion Island**, 401 Newport Center Dr. (© 949/721-2000; www.shopfashionisland.com), is more than a playground for the *Real Housewives of Orange County*—it's a foodie oasis. Highlights include **Brasserie Pascal** (© 949/263-9400), the more casual but still stylish bistro from acclaimed area chef Pascal Olhats; **Rustica** (© 949/706-8282), a fresh modern Italian temple of gastronomy; and **True Food Kitchen** (© 949/644-2400), a global fusion of healthy goodies. You'll find equally good food at luxury behemoth **South Coast Plaza** (actually in Costa Mesa), 3333 Bristol St. (© 800/782-8888; www.southcoastplaza.com). Both The An Family's Crustacean-offshoot **Anqi** (© 714/557-5679)—a Vietnamese fusion eatery and gourmet noodle bar—and **Charlie Palmer** (© 714/352-2525)—a modern American fine-dining restaurant with an emphasis on wine—are based in Bloomingdale's alone. Nearby there's also **Hamamori** (© 714/850-0880) for refined Japanese cuisine, and **Seasons 52** (© 714/437-5252), for festival but casual American fare and nightly piano music.

muy romantico evening. In fact, it's so popular that it can get pretty crowded during the summer months, so be sure to make a reservation. Affordable during lunch but pricey at dinner, the menu consists mostly of seafood recipes from the Mexican Riviera. Even the standard enchiladas and tacos get a zesty update with crab or lobster meat and fresh herbs. Calamari steak is sautéed with bell peppers, capers, and herbs in a garlic-butter sauce, and king salmon is mesquite-broiled and served with a creamy lime sauce. Although a bit on the touristy side, Las Brisas can be a fun part of the Laguna Beach experience. *Tip:* The patio is considered prime territory at both lunch and dinner, but the birds can detract from the experience. I much prefer an inside window table. You still get the view, without the fuss.

361 Cliff Dr. (off PCH north of Laguna Canyon), Laguna Beach. © **949/497-5434.** www.lasbrisaslagunabeach.com. Reservations recommended. Main courses $10–$27. AE, DC, DISC, MC, V. Mon–Thurs 8am–10pm; Fri–Sat 8am–11pm; Sun 9am–10pm. Valet parking $6.

Summer House CONTEMPORARY AMERICAN   Fashioned after a seaside holiday beach retreat, with lots of cream-colored walls, subtle stripes, and an overall airy vibe, the casual but fresh menu is quite affordable. An ever-popular appetizer, the Kung Pao calamari strikes the right balance of spicy-sweet; for entrees, whole-grain mustard gives a new spin on the Macadamia-crusted mahi-mahi.

2744 East Coast Hwy., Corona Del Mar. © **949/612-7700**. www.summerhousecdm.com. Main courses $10–$18. AE, DISC, MC, V. Daily 11am–9:30pm

Watermarc NEW AMERICAN/SMALL PLATES   The newest sister restaurant to more established area favorites 230 Forest and Opah, this sleek but welcoming bistro pulls off solid small plates during both lunch and dinner service. A large front window provides fun people-watching opps, particularly in the summer during festival season. Skilled servers are as well versed with the food-portion of the menu as they are enthusiastic about the wine list—heed their advice unless you feel strongly about a particular label or varietal. Some standout dishes include the sweet and savory fried

If you're anywhere near San Juan Capistrano, you *have* to stop for breakfast or lunch at the **Ramos House Café**, a petite restaurant in an adorable little old house in San Juan Capistrano's historic Los Rios district. Chef John Humphreys's swoon-inducing menu changes daily, and everything—from his roast turkey hash scramble with apple cider gravy to his corn and buttermilk crab cakes and Southern fried chicken salad—is made from scratch (even the ice cream is turned by hand). And if that's not the best soju bloody mary you've ever had, send me a better recipe. The cafe is at 31752 Los Rios St.—the oldest remaining residential street in California—near the train depot and is open for breakfast and lunch Tuesday through Sunday from 8:30am to 3pm (© **949/443-1342;** www.ramoshouse.com).

Laura Chenel goat cheese with apples and honey, and refreshing ahi watermelon skewers. A handful of regular-sized entrees are available as well.

448 South Coast Hwy,, Laguna Beach. © **949/376-6272.** www.watermarcrestaurant.com. Reservations recommended at dinner. Main courses $21–$34. AE, MC, V. Sun–Thurs 11am–10pm; Fri–Sat 11am–11pm.

10 SANTA CATALINA ISLAND ★★

After an unhealthy dose of the mainland's soupy smog and freeway gridlock, you'll appreciate an excursion to Santa Catalina Island, with its clean air, crystal-clear water, and the blissful absence of traffic. In fact, there isn't a single traffic light on "the Island of Romance." Conditions like these can fool you into thinking that you're miles away from the hustle and bustle of the city, but the reality is that you're only 22 miles off the Southern California coast and *still* in L.A. County.

Because of its relative isolation, out-of-state tourists tend to ignore Santa Catalina—which everyone calls simply Catalina—but those who do make the crossing have plenty of elbowroom to boat, fish, swim, scuba, and snorkel. There are also miles of hiking and biking trails, plus golf and tennis, but the main sport here seems to be barhopping.

Catalina is so different from the mainland that it almost seems like a different country, remote and unspoiled. In 1919 the island was purchased by William Wrigley, Jr., the chewing-gum magnate, who had plans to develop it into a fashionable pleasure resort. To publicize the new vacationland, Wrigley brought big-name bands to the Avalon Ballroom and moved the Chicago Cubs, which he owned, to the island for spring training. His marketing efforts succeeded, and Catalina soon became a world-renowned playground, luring such celebrities as Laurel and Hardy, Cecil B. DeMille, John Wayne, and even Winston Churchill.

In 1975 the Santa Catalina Island Conservancy—a nonprofit operating foundation organized to preserve and protect the island's nature habitat—acquired about 88% of Catalina Island, protecting virtually all of the hilly acreage and rugged coastline that make up what is known as the interior. In fact, some of the most spectacular areas can be reached only by arranged tour (see "Exploring the Island," p. 285).

Santa Catalina Island

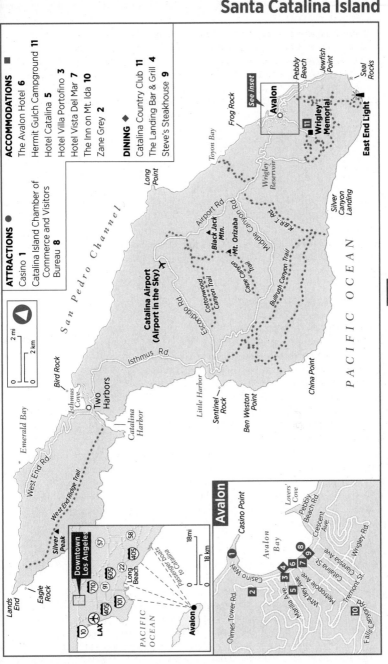

See Inset

ACCOMMODATIONS ■
The Avalon Hotel **6**
Hermit Gulch Campground **11**
Hotel Catalina **5**
Hotel Villa Portofino **3**
Hotel Vista Del Mar **7**
The Inn on Mt. Ida **10**
Zane Grey **2**

DINING ◆
Catalina Country Club **11**
The Landing Bar & Grill **4**
Steve's Steakhouse **9**

ATTRACTIONS ●
Casino **1**
Catalina Island Chamber of Commerce and Visitors Bureau **8**

SIDE TRIPS FROM LOS ANGELES | Santa Catalina Island

10

Essentials

GETTING THERE   The most common way to get to and from the island is on the **Catalina Express** ferryboat (© **800/481-3470;** www.catalinaexpress.com), which operates up to 30 daily departures year-round from Long Beach, San Pedro, and Dana Point. High-speed catamarans make the trip in about an hour. Captain's and Commodore Lounge upgrades are available. Round-trip fares are $67 for adults, $60 for seniors 55 and over, $51 for children ages 2 to 11, and $4 for infants. Fares for Dana Point are $2 more, except for infants. In San Pedro, the Catalina Express departs from the **Sea/Air Terminal,** Berth 95; take the Harbor Freeway (I-110) south to the Harbor Boulevard exit, and then follow signs to the terminal. In Long Beach, boats leave from the **Catalina Landing;** take I-710 south into Long Beach. Stay to the left, follow signs to downtown, and exit at Golden Shore. Turn right at the stop sign and follow around to the terminal on the right; parking is in the structure on the left. In Dana Point, boats depart from Dana Wharf Sportfishing. From San Diego, take I-5 north and exit at Beach Cities Hwy. 1; turn left at Dana Point Harbor Drive, then left at Golden Lantern. Call ahead for reservations. *Note:* Check-in at the ticket window is required and begins 1 hour prior to each departure. Passengers must be checked in, holding tickets, and ready to board at least 15 minutes prior to departure (I suggest 30 minutes ahead to be on the safe side), otherwise the reservation will be canceled and the credit card will be charged for the full amount of the round-trip fare. Luggage is limited to 70 pounds per person; reservations are necessary for bicycles, surfboards, and dive tanks; and there are restrictions on transporting pets. You can leave your car at designated lots at each departure terminal; the parking fee is around $10 per 24-hour period.

The **Catalina Flyer,** 400 Main St., Balboa (© **949/673-5245;** www.catalina info.com), the largest passenger-carrying catamaran on the West Coast, departs daily from Newport Beach's historic Balboa Pavilion. The boat leaves once a day at 9am and returns to Newport at 4:30pm daily. Travel time is about 75 minutes each way. Round-trip fares are $68 for adults, $63 for seniors, $51 for children 3 to 12, and $4 for infants. Pets are not allowed.

Island Express Helicopter Service, 1175 Queens Way Dr., Long Beach (© **800/2-AVALON** [228-2566] or 310/510-2525; www.islandexpress.com), flies from Long Beach (regularly) or San Pedro (seasonally) to Avalon in about 15 minutes. The expense is definitely worth the thrill and convenience, particularly if you're prone to seasickness. It flies on demand between 8am and sunset year-round, charging $104 plus tax each way, or $200 round-trip. The weight limit for luggage, however, is a mere 25 pounds. It also offers brief air tours over the island; prices vary. In Long Beach, the heliport is located a few hundred yards southwest of the *Queen Mary.*

Cart Culture

One of the first things you'll notice when you arrive in Avalon, the only city on the island, is the abundance of golf carts in a comical array of styles and colors. Since Avalon is the only city in California authorized by the state legislature to regulate the number of vehicles allowed to drive on city streets, there are no rental cars and only a handful of privately owned vehicles. For information on renting a golf cart, see "Getting Around," below.

The 149-passenger catamaran **Catalina–Marina del Rey Flyer,** 13737 Fiji Way, Marina del Rey (📞 **310/305-7250;** www.catalinaferries.com), departs from Fisherman's Village at Marina del Rey. Schedule varies. Travel time to Avalon is 1¾ hours. Round-trip fare is $90 for adults, $82 for seniors, $69 for children 2 to 11, and $5 for infants.

VISITOR INFORMATION The **Catalina Island Chamber of Commerce and Visitors Bureau,** P.O. Box 217, Avalon, CA 90704 (📞 **310/510-1520;** fax 310/510-7606; www.catalinachamber.com), located on the Green Pleasure Pier, distributes brochures and information on island activities, hotels, and transportation.

ORIENTATION The picturesque town of **Avalon** is both the port of entry for the island and the island's only city. From the ferry dock, you can wander along Crescent Avenue, the main road along the beachfront, and easily explore adjacent side streets.

Northwest of Avalon is the village of **Two Harbors,** accessible by boat or shuttle bus. Its twin bays are favored by pleasure yachts from L.A.'s various marinas, so there's more camaraderie and a less touristy ambience overall.

GETTING AROUND Once in Avalon, take **Catalina Taxi Service** (📞 **310/510-0025**) from the heliport or dock to your hotel, and enjoy the quick and colorful trip through town (don't blink or you'll miss it). Only a limited number of cars are permitted on the island; visitors are not allowed to drive cars on the island, and most residents motor around in golf carts (many of the homes only have golf-cart-size driveways). Don't worry, though—you'll be able to get everywhere you want to go by renting a cart yourself or just hoofing it, which is what most visitors do.

If you want to explore the area around Avalon beyond where your feet can comfortably carry you, rent a mountain bike or tandem from **Brown's Bikes,** 107 Pebbly Beach Rd. (📞 **310/510-0986;** www.catalinabiking.com). If you'll be exploring, you'll want to rent a gas-powered golf cart from **Cartopia Golf Cart Rentals** on Crescent Avenue at Pebbly Beach Road (📞 **310/510-2493**), or **Island Rentals** (📞 **310/510-1456**), across from the boat terminal. Both companies offer a map of town for a self-guided tour. Rates are about $50 per hour plus a deposit. You must be 25 or older to drive.

Exploring the Island

ORGANIZED TOURS The Santa Catalina Island Company's **Discovery Tours** (📞 **800/322-3434** or 310/510-TOUR [510-8687]; www.visitcatalinaisland.com) has a ticket and information office at the Green Pier and the Tour Plaza, in the center of town. It offers the greatest variety of excursions from Avalon; many last just a couple of hours and don't monopolize your whole day. Tours are available in money-saving combo packs; inquire when you call.

Noteworthy excursions include the **Cape Canyon,** which takes you into the heart of Catalina's "outback" in an open-air four-wheel-drive Mercedes Benz Unimog Vehicle. The tour's rugged route includes the American bald eagle and Catalina Island fox habitats at Middle Ranch, lunch at Airport-in-the-Sky, and plenty of photo stops ($107 adults, $96 seniors and children). You can also try the **Undersea Tour,** a leisurely 45-minute cruise of Lover's Cove Marine Preserve in a semi-submersible vessel that allows you to sit 5 feet under the water in a climate-controlled cabin where you comfortably observe Catalina's kelp forests by day or night ($32 adults, $23 kids, $28 seniors; discount on night rates). The **Casino Tour** is a fascinating 50-minute look at the style and inventive engineering of this elegant ballroom (see "Catalina's

CATALINA'S GRAND casino

No trip to Catalina is complete without taking the **Casino Tour** (see "Organized Tours," above). The Casino Building, Avalon's world-famous Art Deco landmark, is not—and never was—a place to gamble your vacation money away (*casino* is an Italian word for a place of entertainment or gathering). Rather, the incredibly ornate structure (the craftsmanship inside and out is spectacular) is home to the island's only movie theater and the world's largest circular ballroom.

Virtually every big band of the '30s and '40s played in the 158-foot-diameter ballroom, carried over CBS radio beginning with its grand opening in May 1929. Today it's a coveted venue for elaborate weddings, dances, gala dinners, and the Catalina Jazz Festival. The 3-week **Jazz-Trax Festival** (© **866/872-9849;** www.jazztrax.com) takes place every October. To experience the festival, be sure to book your tickets and accommodations as far in advance as possible.

Grand Casino," below; $19 adults, $17 seniors, $14 kids). The Casino also offers a Behind the Scenes Tour ($31 adults, $23 kids, $27 seniors) where you visit the "green rooms" used by Errol Flynn, Cary Grant, and all the Big Bands. Walk across the stage where Benny Goodman played; visit the projection room with the original 1929 equipment on display; and gain unprecedented access to other backstage areas. Both tours include admission to the Catalina Island Museum. The nighttime **Flying Fish Boat Trips** (seasonal) are a 50-minute Catalina tradition in searchlight-equipped open boats ($24 adults, $21 seniors, $18 kids).

Newer tours include the Catalina Zip Line Eco Tour and the Sea Trek Undersea Adventure as well as Snuba and the GPS Ranger Walking Tour. Beginning almost 600 feet above Avalon, the **Zip Line Eco Tour** ($99 per person) is a way to see Catalina like never before. The nearly 4,000-foot zip line comprises five separate zips across Descanso Canyon and ends by the seashore at Descanso Beach, with speeds reaching 45 mph and heights of more than 300 feet. Each zip ends at a specially designed platform with spectacular views of the surrounding island interior and ocean, and interpretative signage highlighting the flora and fauna.

Where the zip-line tour provides a view of Catalina from above, the **Sea Trek Undersea Adventure** ($103 per person) and **Snuba** ($69 per person) gives a glimpse from below (no prior diving experience is necessary). Beneath the waves, participants may find themselves surrounded by teeming schools of mackerel or anchovies, observing sea lions or a solitary bat ray gliding through the blue water, or even catching a glimpse of an octopus or California lobster hiding among the rocks.

The **GPS Walking Tour,** which meanders through the streets of Avalon, offers visitors their own personal high-tech guide to experience the sights at their own pace. The GPS-enabled multimedia units ($15 per device) lead the way, pointing out landmarks and historical points of interest using audio, video, and photos. The tour accommodates up to six people per unit, and guests have ample time to complete the tour.

VISITING TWO HARBORS If you want to get a better look at the rugged natural beauty of Catalina and escape the throngs of beachgoers, head over to Two Harbors, the quarter-mile "neck" at the island's northwest end that gets its name from the "twin harbors" on each side, known as the Isthmus and Catalina Harbor. An excellent

Santa Catalina Island

SIDE TRIPS FROM LOS ANGELES

starting point for campers and hikers, Two Harbors also offers just enough civilization for the less-intrepid traveler.

The **Banning House Lodge** (✆ **800/626-1496;** www.visitcatalinaisland.com/twoharbors) is a 12-room bed-and-breakfast overlooking the Isthmus. The clapboard house was built in 1910 for Catalina's pre-Wrigley owners and has seen duty as on-location lodging for movie stars like Errol Flynn and Dorothy Lamour. Peaceful and isolated, the simply furnished but comfortable lodge has spectacular views of both harbors. Peak season rates range from $160 to $280, including deluxe continental breakfast,, and they'll even give you a lift from the pier.

Everyone eats at the **Harbor Reef Restaurant** (✆ **310/510-4215**) on the beach. This nautical, tropical-themed saloon/restaurant serves breakfast, lunch, and dinner, the latter consisting of hearty steaks, ribs, swordfish, and buffalo burgers in summer. The house drink is sweet "buffalo milk," a potent concoction of vodka, crème de cacao, banana liqueur, milk, whipped cream, and nutmeg.

WHAT TO SEE & DO IN AVALON Walk along horseshoe-shaped Crescent Avenue, past private yachting and fishing clubs, toward the landmark Casino building. You can see the Art Deco theater for the price of a movie ticket any night. Also on the ground floor is the newly renovated Catalina Island Museum (✆ 310/510-2414; www.catalinamuseum.org), which explores 7,000 years of island history, including fascinating exhibits of archaeology, steamships, big bands, and natural history. The museum has also been updated with more advanced technology, like flatscreen TVs, and more interactive exhibits. Admission is $5 for adults, $4 for seniors, $2 for children 5 and over, and free for kids 4 and under; it's included in the price of Discovery's Casino Tours (see "Catalina's Grand Casino," above). The museum is open daily from 10am to 5pm.

Around the point from the Casino is the **Descanso Beach Club** (✆ **310/510-7410**), a mini–Club Med nestled in a private cove just past the famous Casino Building. While you can get on the beach year-round, the club's facilities—an open-air restaurant and two bars, live music, beach area, volleyball lawns, dance area, fire rings on the beach, private cabana and chaise longue rentals, and thatched beach umbrellas (bring your own towels or be prepared to purchase them)—are only open from spring to October. The Descanso Beach Club also serves as an activity headquarters, where guests can rent kayaks, stand-up paddle boards, snorkeling and scuba gear, as well as book massage and golf tee times, plus tours. Admission is $2.

Instant Massaging

After a full day of island activity, why not pamper yourself with a relaxing professional massage in the privacy and comfort of your hotel room? Make a reservation with **Catalina Sea Spa** (✆ 310/510-8920; www.catalinamassagebymichelle.com) and Michelle will tote her table and oils to you. She specializes in sports, deep tissue, Swedish, Thai, Swede-Thai combo, and pregnancy massage. Other treatments include sugar glow, foot scrubs, peppermint scalp massage, couples massages, and lavender or honey facial massages. Michelle works in 50- to 80-minute increments, offers packages, and caters to groups. If you're just visiting for the day, Michelle offers her own pampering facility for you to visit. Prices range from $85 to $135.

About 1½ miles from downtown Avalon is **Wrigley Memorial and Botanical Garden** (© **310/510-2595**). The specialized gardens, a project of Ada Wrigley, showcase plants endemic to California's coastal islands. It's open daily from 8am to 5pm; admission is $5 for adults, free for children 11 and under.

Diving, Snorkeling & Sea Kayaking ★

Snorkeling, scuba diving, and sea kayaking are among the main reasons mainlanders head to Catalina. Catalina Island's naturally clean water and giant kelp forests teeming with marine life have made it a renowned diving destination that attracts experts and beginning divers alike. **Casino Point Marine Park,** Southern California's first city-designated underwater park, was established in 1965 and is located behind the Casino. Due to its convenient location, it can get outrageously crowded in the summer (just like everything else at that time of year).

Catalina Divers Supply (© **800/353-0330**; www.catalinadiverssupply.com) runs two full-service dive shops: one from a large trailer behind the Casino at the edge of Avalon's underwater park, where it offers guided snorkeling tours and introductory scuba dives; and another at the Green Pier, where it launches boat dives aboard the *Scuba Cat*. The three best locations for snorkeling are **Lover's Cove Marine Preserve, Casino Point Marine Park,** and **Descanso Beach Club. Catalina Snorkeling Adventures,** at Lover's Cove (© **877/SNORKEL** [766-7535]), offers snorkel-gear rental. Snorkeling trips that take you outside of Avalon depart from **Joe's Rent-a-Boat** (© **310/510-0455**), on the Green Pier.

At Two Harbors, stop by **West End Dive Center** (© **310/510-4272**). Excursions range from half-day introductory dives to complete certification courses—but note that all are off-shore, not boat-based. It also rents snorkel gear and offers kayak rental, instruction, and tours.

Hiking & Biking

When the summer crowds become overwhelming, it's time to head on foot for the peacefulness of the interior, where secluded coves and barren, rolling hills soothe frayed nerves. Visitors can obtain a free **hiking permit** at the Conservancy Office (125 Clarissa Ave.; © **310/510-2595**; www.catalinaconservancy.org), where you'll find maps, wildlife information, and friendly assistance from Conservancy staffers who love to share their knowledge of the interior. It's open daily from 8:30am to 4:30pm, and closed for lunch on weekends. Among the sights you may see are the many giant buffalo roaming the hills, scions of movie extras that were left behind in 1929 and have since flourished.

More than 200 miles of trails beckon both the "tennis shoe" hiker and the experienced trekker. The granddaddy of them all is the Trans-Catalina Trail, a 37.2-mile trail that transverses the entire island.

Mountain biking is allowed on the island's designated dirt roads but requires a $35 permit that must be purchased in person at the Conservancy Office (see above; dial ext. 100).

Beaches

Unfortunately, Avalon's beaches leave much to be desired. The town's central beach, off Crescent Avenue, is small and completely congested in peak season. Be sure to claim your spot early in the morning before it's full. **Descanso Beach Club** (see "What to See & Do in Avalon," above) offers the best beach in town but also gets crowded very quickly. Your best bet is to kayak out to a secluded cove that you'll have virtually to yourself.

Where to Stay

If you plan to stay overnight, be sure to reserve a room in advance because most places fill up quickly during the summer and holiday seasons. There are only a handful of hotels whose accommodations and amenities actually justify the rates that they charge. Some are downright scary, so book as far in advance as possible to get a room that makes the trip worthwhile. Don't stress too much over your accommodations, as you'll probably spend most of your time outdoors. Keep in mind that the best time to visit is in September or October when the water is warm, the crowds have somewhat subsided, and hotel occupancy is easier to come by. If you're having trouble finding a vacancy, try calling the Catalina Chamber of Commerce & Visitors Bureau (© **310/510-1520**); they keep daily tabs on last-minute cancellations.

For Travelers Who Use Wheelchairs

Visitors who use wheelchairs should request a room at **Hotel Metropole** (© **800/300-8528** or 310/510-1884; www.hotel-metropole.com). One of the most modern properties in Avalon, it has an elevator, a large sun deck that overlooks Avalon Bay, a shopping complex, and a very convenient location in the heart of Avalon.

VERY EXPENSIVE

The Inn on Mt. Ada ★★   When William Wrigley, Jr., purchased Catalina Island in 1921, he built this ornate hilltop Georgian Colonial mansion as his summer vacation home. It's now one of the finest small hotels in California. The opulent inn—considered to be the best in town for its luxury accommodations and views—has several ground-floor salons, a clubroom with a fireplace, a formal library, and a sunroom where tea, cookies, and fruit are always available. The best guest room is the Grand Suite, fitted with a fireplace and a large private patio. Amenities include a golf cart during your stay. An early-morning continental breakfast, a hearty full breakfast, a light deli-style lunch, appetizers, fresh fruit, freshly baked cookies, soft drinks, beers, wines, and champagne are included in the rate. *Tip:* Even if you find that it's sold out or too pricey to fit your budget, make a breakfast or lunch reservation and enjoy amazing views from the Inn's spectacular balcony. Reservations are taken 1 month in advance; space is limited for non-overnight guests. *Note:* The entire property shuts down every January for annual maintenance.

398 Wrigley Rd. (P.O. Box 2560), Avalon, CA 90704. www.innonmtada.com. © **800/608-7669** or 310/510-2030. Fax 310/510-2237. 6 units. Nov–Apr $375–$550 double and $640 suite, May–Oct $415–$550 double and $765 suite. Rates include 2 meals daily. AE, MC, V. **Amenities:** Restaurant; free harbor/heliport transfer. *In room:* TV, hair dryer, no phone, free Wi-Fi.

EXPENSIVE

The Avalon Hotel   The Avalon Hotel was originally developed at the turn of the 20th century as the Pilgrim Club, a gentleman's club that vanished in the great fire of 1915. After many incarnations, the dilapidated property was finally renovated to become one of the island's most luxurious hideaways. The cozy Craftsman-style hotel is decked out in rich, hand-carved mahogany and imported slate tastefully accented with handmade tile and local artwork. Catalina's silhouette is artfully etched into the slate, stained glass, and light fixtures, while shadow boxes showcase island memorabilia throughout the hotel's homey public space. Guest rooms, which come in a variety of sizes, feature garden or ocean views (some with balconies) and an incredibly comfy queen- or king-size Supple-Pedic memory foam bed.

124 Whittley Ave. (P.O. Box 706), Avalon, CA 90704. www.theavalonhotel.com. ✆ **310/510-7070.** Fax 310/510-7210. 15 units. Mid-Nov to mid-June $195–$435 double; mid-June to mid-Sept $295–$545 double. Rates include continental breakfast. AE, MC, V. **Amenities:** Free harbor/heliport transfer. *In room:* TV/DVD, fridge, hair dryer, Ethernet chords available for complimentary rental.

MODERATE

Hotel Villa Portofino ★   Enjoy European elegance on the oceanfront from your courtyard room or deluxe suite after a warm welcome from the hotel's efficient and friendly staff. The hotel boasts renovated rooms and a spacious rooftop deck overlooking the bay that is perfect for people-watching, sunbathing, cocktail sipping, or just enjoying the fantastic view. Some rooms have luxurious touches like fireplaces, balconies, deep soaking tubs, and separate showers. The hotel is just steps away from the beach, shops, and sights.

111 Crescent Ave. (P.O. Box 127), Avalon, CA 90704. www.hotelvillaportofino.com. ✆ **888/510-0555** or 310/510-0555. Fax 310/510-0839. 35 units. May–Oct $150–$375 double, from $285 suite; winter $115–$315 double, from $225 suite. Rates include continental breakfast, beach towels, and chairs. AE, DC, MC, V. **Amenities:** Award-winning restaurant. *In room:* A/C, TV, fridge, hair dryer, free Wi-Fi.

Hotel Vista Del Mar   The hotel's location smack-dab in the middle of town, lush garden atrium courtyard, lovely balcony with views of the harbor, and friendly staff make it an island favorite for families and couples alike. The oceanview suites with double Jacuzzi tubs are fantastic but hard to secure, as the only two are booked by regulars almost year-round.

417 Crescent Ave. (P.O. Box 1979), Avalon, CA 90704. www.hotel-vistadelmar.com. ✆ **800/601-6836** or 310/510-1452. 15 units. Apr–Nov $175–$265 double, $325–$495 suite; Dec–Mar $145–$185 double, $250–$400 suite. Rates include continental breakfast and freshly baked cookies and milk in the evening. AE, DISC, MC, V. *In room:* A/C, TV/VCR, fridge, minibar, free Wi-Fi.

INEXPENSIVE

Our recommended choices for inexpensive lodgings are **Hotel Catalina** (✆ **800/540-0184** or 310/510-0027; www.hotelcatalina.com), a well-maintained Victorian-style hotel just a half-block from the beach, with tons of charm, family cottages, a courtyard with beautiful stained glass, and large verandas with bay views; **Zane Grey** (✆ **310/510-0966;** www.zanegreypueblohotel.com), a Hopi-style pueblo built in 1926 and former home of American author Zane Grey, situated above town and equipped with a cozy living room with fireplace and piano, free shuttle service, and a swimming pool; and **Hermit Gulch Campground** (✆ **310/510-8368;** www.visitcatalinaisland.com), one of Avalon's three campgrounds, which can be crowded and noisy in peak season. Campsites can be tough to secure, especially when hotels are booked, so it's a good idea to make reservations in advance. The walk to town and back can be draining, so hop on the red trolley that runs you back and forth to town for a couple dollars each way.

Where to Eat

Along with the choices below, recommended Avalon options include the **Avalon Grille,** a new American restaurant with patio seating and a full bar. It's on the waterfront in the center of town, across from the Green Pleasure Pier (✆ 310/510-7494). On the Two Harbors side of the island, the **Harbor Reef Restaurant** is the place to eat; see "Exploring the Island," earlier.

EXPENSIVE

Catalina Country Club ★ CALIFORNIAN   You'll find some of Avalon's most elegant meals at the landmark Catalina Country Club, whose stylish Spanish-Mediterranean clubhouse was built by William Wrigley, Jr., during the 1920s. The club exudes a chic and historical atmosphere; the menu is peppered with archival photos and vintage celebrity anecdotes. Sit outdoors in an elegant tiled Fountain Terrace courtyard, or inside the intimate, exquisite dining room. The executive chef infuses new American cuisine with creative influences from around the world, using free-range, organic meats; fresh produce; and seafood from environmentally sensitive fisheries. *Note:* The club is only a few minutes from the waterfront but uphill.

1 Country Club Dr. (above Sumner Ave.). ✆ **310/510-7404.** Reservations recommended. Main courses $12–$30 dinner. AE, DISC, MC, V June–Oct Thurs–Sun 4pm to closing including live music on the patio on Thursdays.

MODERATE

The Landing Bar and Grill AMERICAN   With a secluded heated deck overlooking the harbor, the Landing is one of the most romantic dining spots in Avalon. It boasts beautiful Spanish-style architecture and is located in the historic El Encanto Center that manages to attract as many jeans-clad vacationers as dressed-up islanders. The menu is enticing, with local seafood offerings, pasta, Mexican cuisine, and gourmet pizzas that can be delivered to your hotel room if you wish.

Intersection of Crescent and Marilla aves. ✆ **310/510-1474.** Reservations recommended. Main courses $11–$22. AE, DISC, MC, V. Tues–Sun 11am–3pm and 4–10pm (subject to change in winter).

Steve's Steakhouse AMERICAN   Step up above the busy bayside promenade into a fantastic collage of museum-quality photos capturing the Avalon of old. This setting overlooking Avalon Bay feels just right for the hearty menu of steaks, seafood, and pasta—all of which can be ordered at the full bar as well as in the dining room. Catalina swordfish is their specialty, along with excellent cuts of meat. You can also make a respectable repast of appetizers such as oysters and sashimi.

417 Crescent Ave. (directly across from the Green Pier, upstairs). ✆ **310/510-0333.** Reservations recommended on weekends. Main courses $20–$32 dinner, $9–$18 lunch. AE, DISC, MC, V. Daily 11am–3pm and 5–10pm.

INEXPENSIVE

My favorite for a low-bucks meal is the **Casino Dock Café** (✆ **310/510-2755**), with live summertime entertainment, marina views from the sun-drenched deck, breakfast burritos loaded with homemade salsa, and kicking bloody marys.

Barhopping

Note: Avalon doesn't have listed street addresses, but all these bars are within stumbling distance of each other on the main drag. The **Chi Chi Club** (✆ **310/510-9211**), the "noisy bar in Avalon" referred to in Crosby, Stills, and Nash's song "Southern Cross," is the island's only dance club and quite a scene on summer weekend evenings—the DJ spins an eclectic mix of dance tunes. **Luau Larry's** (✆ **310/510-1919**) is Avalon's signature bar that everyone must visit; its tacky tiki theme and signature Wicky Wack drink kicks you into island mode as soon as you step inside. Go where the locals go and swill beers at the **Marlin Club** (✆ **310/510-0044**), Avalon's oldest drinking hole, or catch the Dodgers game at **J. L.'s Locker Room** (✆ **310/510-0258**).

Shopping

You won't have any trouble finding that must-have Catalina key chain or refrigerator magnet, as Crescent Avenue is lined with a myriad of schlocky souvenir shops. There are, however, a few stores that do offer unique and tasteful items. **C. C. Gallagher** (☎ **310/510-1278**) carries high-end gifts and also is a coffee shop; it's best for finding beautiful art, music, and jewelry created by local artists. **Buoys and Gulls** (☎ **310/510-0416**) offers men's and women's wear such as Reyn Spooner islander shirts, Nautica, Hurley, and Billabong. The **Steamer Trunk** (☎ **310/510-2600**) is loaded with unique gifts to take home to the dog sitter or neighbor who collected your mail. **Leo's Drugstore** (☎ **310/510-0189**) is the obvious spot to pick up the sunscreen that you forgot to pack. **Von's,** located on Metropole Avenue in the center of town, and **Von's Express** on Catalina Avenue, are Avalon's main grocery stores where you'll find all your staples.

SANTA BARBARA ★★★

92 miles NW of L.A.; 45 miles S of Solvang; 105 miles S of San Luis Obispo

by Kristin Luna

Between palm-lined Pacific beaches and the sloping foothills of the Santa Ynez Mountains, this prosperous resort community presents a mosaic of whitewashed stucco and red-tile roofs, and a gracious, relaxed attitude that has earned it the sobriquet American Riviera. It's ideal for kicking back on gold-sand beaches, prowling the shops and galleries that line the village's historic streets, and relaxing over a meal in one of many top-notch cafes and restaurants.

Downtown Santa Barbara is distinctive for its Spanish-Mediterranean architecture. But it wasn't always this way. Santa Barbara had a thriving Native American Chumash population for hundreds, if not thousands, of years. The European era began in the late 18th century around a Spanish *presidio* (fort) that's been reconstructed in its original spot. The earliest architectural hodgepodge was destroyed in 1925 by a powerful earthquake that leveled the business district. Out of the rubble rose the Spanish-Mediterranean town of today, a stylish planned community that continues to enforce strict building codes.

Visit Santa Barbara's waterfront on a Sunday, and you're sure to see the weekly **Arts and Crafts Show,** one of the city's best-loved traditions. Since 1965, artists, craftspeople, and street performers have been lining grassy Chase Palm Park, along Cabrillo Boulevard.

Essentials

GETTING THERE By car, U.S. 101 runs right through Santa Barbara; it's the fastest and most direct route from north or south (1½ hr. from Los Angeles, 6 hr. from San Francisco).

By train, **Amtrak** (☎ **800/USA-RAIL** [872-7245]; www.amtrak.com) offers daily service to Santa Barbara. Trains arrive and depart from the **Santa Barbara Rail Station,** 209 State St. (☎ **805/963-1015**). Fares can be as low as $32 (round-trip) from Los Angeles's Union Station.

ORIENTATION State Street, the city's primary commercial thoroughfare, is the geographic center of town. It ends at Stearns Wharf and Cabrillo Boulevard; the latter runs along the ocean and separates the city's beaches from touristy hotels and

Santa Barbara

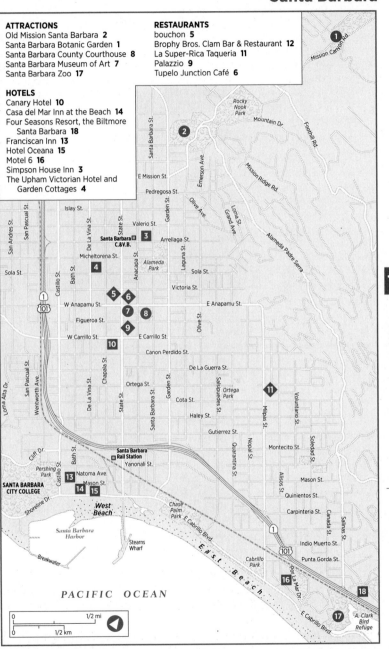

ATTRACTIONS
Old Mission Santa Barbara **2**
Santa Barbara Botanic Garden **1**
Santa Barbara County Courthouse **8**
Santa Barbara Museum of Art **7**
Santa Barbara Zoo **17**

HOTELS
Canary Hotel **10**
Casa del Mar Inn at the Beach **14**
Four Seasons Resort, the Biltmore
  Santa Barbara **18**
Franciscan Inn **13**
Hotel Oceana **15**
Motel 6 **16**
Simpson House Inn **3**
The Upham Victorian Hotel and
  Garden Cottages **4**

RESTAURANTS
bouchon **5**
Brophy Bros. Clam Bar & Restaurant **12**
La Super-Rica Taqueria **11**
Palazzio **9**
Tupelo Junction Café **6**

10

SIDE TRIPS FROM LOS ANGELES | Santa Barbara

restaurants. Electric shuttles provide frequent service along these two routes, if you'd rather leave the car behind.

VISITOR INFORMATION   The **Santa Barbara Conference and Visitors Bureau,** 1601 Anacapa St. (☏ **805/966-9222;** www.santabarbaraca.com), distributes maps, brochures, an events calendar, and information. It's open Monday through Saturday from 9am to 5pm, and Sunday from 10am to 5pm.

Be sure you pick up a copy of the *Independent,* Santa Barbara's free weekly, with articles and events listings; and *Explore Santa Barbara,* a compact visitor's guide published by the local paper, the *Santa Barbara News-Press.* Both are also available at shops and sidewalk racks throughout town.

Seeing the Sights
HISTORIC DOWNTOWN
Following a devastating 1925 earthquake, city planners decreed that all new construction would follow codes of Spanish- and Mission-style architecture. In time, the adobe-textured walls, rounded archways, glazed tile work, and terra-cotta rooftops came to symbolize the Mediterranean ambience that still characterizes Santa Barbara. The architecture also gave a name to the **Red Tile Tour,** a self-guided walking tour of historic downtown. The visitor center (see "Visitor Information," above) has a map/guide of the tour, which can take anywhere from 1 to 3 hours, including time to visit some of the buildings, and covers about 12 blocks in total. Some of the highlights are destinations in their own right.

Santa Barbara County Courthouse ★   Built in 1929, this grand "palace" is considered the local flagship of Spanish colonial revival architecture (you undoubtedly saw its facade on TV during the Michael Jackson trial). It's certainly the most flamboyant example, with impressive facades, beamed ceilings, striking murals, an 85-foot-high observation clock tower, and formal sunken gardens. Free guided tours are offered on Monday, Tuesday, and Friday at 10:30am.

1100 Anacapa St. www.santabarbaracourthouse.org. ☏ **805/962-6464.** Free admission. Mon–Fri 8am–5pm; Sat–Sun and holidays 10am–4:30pm.

Santa Barbara Museum of Art ★   This little jewel of a museum feels more like the private gallery of a wealthy collector. Its leaning is toward early-20th-century Western American paintings and 19th- and 20th-century Asian art, but the best displays might be the antiquities and Chinese ceramics. In addition, there are often visiting exhibits featuring small but excellent collections from other establishments.

1130 State St. www.sbmuseart.org. ☏ **805/963-4364.** Admission $9 adults; $6 seniors 65 and over, students, and children 6–17; free for children 5 and under; free for everyone every Sun. Tues–Sun 11am–5pm.

ELSEWHERE IN THE CITY
Stearns Wharf ★, at the end of State Street (www.stearnswharf.org), is California's oldest working wharf. It attracts visitors for strolling, shopping, dining, and exploring its exhibits, which include a Sea Center with aquariums and an outdoor touch-tank. Although the wharf no longer functions for passenger and freight shipping as it did when built in 1872 by local lumberman John C. Stearns, local fishing boats still dock to unload their daily catch. Consider taking a narrated sunset harbor cruise aboard the *Harbour Queen* at **Captain Don's** (☏ **805/969-5217;** www.stearnswharf.org). Public parking on the wharf is free with merchant validation.

Ganna Walska Lotusland 🏛 This secluded, lavishly landscaped 37-acre estate is renowned for exotic plants and mysterious garden paths. Named for the estate's vivacious European-born mistress and the romantic, lotus-filled ponds in her gardens, the estate reflects the late Madame Walska's eccentricity and the skill of her prestigious gardeners. She was especially fond of succulents and cactuses, interspersing them artistically among native plants and decorative objects. Assembled when money was no object and import regulations were lenient (mostly in the 1940s), the garden contains priceless rare specimens—even prehistoric plants that are extinct in the wild. Advance reservations are required. Montecito is a 5-minute freeway drive south of downtown Santa Barbara. *Note:* Advance reservations are required and are available up to 6 months in advance.

695 Ashley Rd., Montecito. www.lotusland.org. ✆ **805/969-9990.** Admission $35 adults, $10 children 5-18, free for children 4 and under. 2-hr. guided tours mid-Feb to mid-Nov Wed–Sat 10am and 1:30pm.

Old Mission Santa Barbara ★ Established in 1786 by Father Junípero Serra and built by the Chumash Indians, this is a rare example in physical form of the blending of Indian and Hispanic spirituality. This hilltop structure is called the Queen of the Missions for its twin bell towers and beauty. It overlooks the town and the Channel Islands beyond. Self-guided tour booklets are available in six languages.

2201 Laguna St. (at Los Olivos St.). www.santabarbaramission.org. ✆ **805/682-4713.** Admission $5 adults, $4 seniors, $1 children 11 and under. Mon–Fri 9am–4:30pm.

Santa Barbara Botanic Garden 🏛 The Botanic Garden is devoted to indigenous California plants. More than 5.5 miles of meandering trails on 65 acres offer glimpses of cactuses, redwoods, wildflowers, and much more, many arranged in representational habitats or landscapes. The gardens were established in 1926. You'll catch the very best color and aroma just after spring showers.

1212 Mission Canyon Rd. (a short drive uphill from the mission). www.sbbg.org. ✆ **805/682-4726.** Admission $8 adults, $6 seniors 60 and over and children 13-17, $4 children 2-12, free for children 1 and under. Daily 9am–5pm (till 6pm Mar–Oct).

Santa Barbara Zoo ★ ☺ When you're driving around the bend on Cabrillo Boulevard, look up—you might spot the head of a giraffe poking through the palms. This zoo is an appealing, pint-size place, where all 700 animals can be seen in about 30 minutes. Most live in natural, open settings. For more stimulation, try the Discovery Area, miniature train ride, and small carousel. The picnic areas (with barbecue pits) are underused and especially recommended.

500 Niños Dr. (off Cabrillo Blvd.). www.santabarbarazoo.org. ✆ **805/962-5339,** or 962-6310 for recorded information. Admission $12 adults, $10 seniors and children 2-12, free for children 1 and under. Daily 10am–5pm; last admission 1 hr. before closing. Parking $5. Open Thanksgiving 10am–3pm. Closed Christmas.

Beaches

East Beach is Santa Barbara's favorite beach, stretching from the Santa Barbara Zoological Gardens to Chase Palm Park and the wharf. Nearer the pier you can enjoy manicured lawns, tall palms, and abundant facilities; to the east are many volleyball courts, plus the Cabrillo Pavilion, a recreational center, bathhouse, and architectural landmark dating from 1925. Picnic areas with barbecue grills, showers, and clean, well-patrolled sands make this beach a good choice for everyone.

On the other side of Santa Barbara Harbor is **Leadbetter Beach,** less sheltered than those to the south and popular with surfers. It's reached by following Cabrillo Boulevard after it turns into Shoreline Drive. This beach is also a great place to watch pleasure boats entering or leaving the harbor. Leadbetter has basic facilities, including restrooms, picnic areas, and a metered parking lot.

Two miles west of Leadbetter is secluded but popular **Arroyo Burro Beach County Park,** also known as Hendry's Beach. This gem has a grassy park beneath the cliffs and a white crescent beach with great waves for surfing and bodysurfing. There are volleyball nets, picnic areas, and restrooms.

Outdoor Activities

BIKING & SURREY CYCLING   A relatively flat, palm-lined 2-mile coastal pathway, perfect for biking, runs along the beach. More adventurous riders can pedal through town (where painted bike lanes line many major routes, including one up to the mission). These routes and many more are outlined in the *Santa Barbara County Bike Map,* a free and comprehensive resource available at the visitor center or by calling **Traffic Solutions** at ✆ **805/963-7283.**

Wheel Fun Rentals, 23 E. Cabrillo St. (✆ **805/966-2282;** www.wheelfun rentals.com), rents well-maintained beach cruisers, mountain bikes, tandem bikes, and an Italian four-wheel surrey that seats three adults; rates vary. It's open daily from 8am to 8pm.

BOATING   The **Santa Barbara Sailing Center,** 133 Harbor Way at the Santa Barbara Harbor (✆ **800/350-9090** or 805/962-2826; www.sbsail.com), rents sailboats from 21 to 50 feet in length, as well as paddle boats, kayaks, and motorboats. Both skippered and bareboat charters are available by the day or the hour. Sailing instruction for all levels of experience is also available. Coastal, island, whale-watching, dinner-cruise, and adventure tours are offered on the 50-foot sailing catamaran *Double Dolphin.* Open 9am to 6pm spring and summer; 9am to 5pm fall and winter.

GOLF   At the **Santa Barbara Golf Club,** 3500 McCaw Ave., at Las Positas Road (✆ **805/687-7087;** www.sbgolf.com), there's a great 6,009-yard, 18-hole course and a driving range. Unlike many municipal courses, the Santa Barbara Golf Course is well maintained and presents a moderate challenge for the average golfer. Greens fees are $30 to $40 Monday through Friday for 18 holes and $40 to $50 on weekends. Optional carts rent for $28.

The 18-hole, 7,000-yard **Sandpiper,** at 7925 Hollister Ave. (✆ **805/968-1541;** www.sandpipergolf.com), is a scenic oceanside course that's rated as one of the top public courses in the U.S. It also has a driving range. Weekend greens fees are $159, and the cart fee is $16.

HIKING   The foothill trails in the Santa Ynez Mountains above Santa Barbara are perfect for day hikes. In general, they aren't overly strenuous. Trail maps are available at **The Travel Store,** 12 W. Anapamu St. (at State St.; ✆ **800/546-8060**); at the visitor center (see "Visitor Information," above); and from **Traffic Solutions** (✆ **805/963-7283**).

One of the most popular hikes is the **Seven Falls/Inspiration Point Trail,** an easy trek that begins on Tunnel Road, past the mission, and skirts the edge of Santa Barbara's Botanic Garden (which contains some pleasant hiking trails itself).

SKATING   The paved beach path that runs along Santa Barbara's waterfront is perfect for in-line skating. **Wheel Fun Rentals,** 23 E. Cabrillo St. (© **805/966-2282;** www.wheelfunrentals.com), rents skates and all the requisite protective gear. It's open daily from 8am to 8pm.

WHALE-WATCHING   Whale-watching cruises are offered between late December and late March, when Pacific gray whales pass by on migratory journeys from their breeding lagoons in Baja California, Mexico, to their Alaskan feeding grounds. **Shoreline Park,** west of the harbor, has high bluffs ideal for land-based whale-spotting. Sea excursions are offered by both **Captain Don's Harbor Tours** (© **805/969-5217;** www.stearnswharf.org), on Stearns Wharf, and the **Condor** (© **888/77-WHALE** [779-4253] or 805/882-0088; www.condorcruises.com), located at 301 W. Cabrillo Blvd. in the Santa Barbara Harbor.

Shopping

State Street from the beach to Victoria Street is the city's main thoroughfare and has the largest concentration of shops. Many specialize in T-shirts and postcards, but there are a number of boutiques as well. If you get tired of strolling, hop on one of the electric shuttle buses (25¢) that run up and down State Street.

Also check out **Brinkerhoff Avenue** (off Cota St., btw. Chapala and De La Vina sts.), Santa Barbara's "antiques alley." Most shops here are open Tuesday through Sunday from 11am to 5pm. **El Paseo** (814 State St.) is a picturesque shopping arcade reminiscent of an old Spanish street. It's built around an 1827 adobe home and is lined with charming shops and art galleries. **Paseo Nuevo,** on the other side of State Street, is a modern outdoor mall, featuring familiar chain stores and cafes, and anchored by a Nordstrom department store.

Where to Stay

Before you even begin calling around for reservations, keep in mind that Santa Barbara's accommodations are expensive—especially in summer. Then decide whether you'd like to stay beachside (even more expensive) or downtown. Santa Barbara is small, but not small enough to happily stroll between the two areas.

The free one-stop reservations service **Hot Spots** (© **800/793-7666** or 805/564-1637; www.hotspotsusa.com) keeps an updated list of availability for about 90% of the area's hotels, motels, inns, and B&Bs. Reservationists are available Monday through Saturday from 9am to 9pm, and Sunday from 9am to 4pm.

VERY EXPENSIVE

Four Seasons Resort, The Biltmore Santa Barbara ★★★   This gem of the American Riviera manages to adhere to the most elegant standards of hospitality without making anyone feel unwelcome. It's easy to sense the ghosts of golden-age Hollywood celebs such as Greta Garbo, Errol Flynn, and Bing Crosby, who used to play croquet on the hotel's perfectly manicured lawns and then head over to the private Coral Casino Beach & Cabana Club—because that's exactly what privileged guests are *still* doing. Rooms have white plantation shutters, light-wood furnishings, and full marble bathrooms. Guests can amuse themselves on the 20-acre property with a putting green or shuffleboard courts. In addition to two dining rooms, the Biltmore offers a Sunday brunch that draws folks from all over. The Spa, a multimillion-dollar, Spanish-style facility, boasts numerous treatment rooms, a swimming pool and two huge whirlpool baths, a fitness center, and 10 oceanview suites with fireplaces, in-room bars, changing rooms, and twin massage tables.

1260 Channel Dr. (at the end of Olive Mill Rd.), Santa Barbara, CA 93108. www.fourseasons.com/santa barbara. ℂ **800/819-5053** or 805/969-2261. Fax 805/565-8323. 207 units. $470–$8,000 double; from $1,250 suite. Extra person $55. Children 18 and under stay free in parent's room. Special midweek and package rates available. AE, DC, MC, V. Valet parking $20; free self-parking. **Amenities:** 4 restaurants; 2 lounges; complimentary bikes; health club; 2 outdoor heated pools; room service; spa services; 3 lit tennis courts; whirlpool. *In room:* A/C, TV/VCR w/pay movies, hair dryer, high-speed Internet, minibar.

EXPENSIVE

Canary Hotel ★★★   Formerly the Andalucia, the Canary Hotel's combination of Moroccan flair and Spanish culture fits in perfectly with downtown Santa Barbara's casual elegance. In fact, one night's visit at the centrally located establishment will make any subsequent stay in a boutique hotel pale in comparison. Every last detail has been carefully thought out and each piece of furniture finely crafted. All bedrooms boast four-poster beds, Matelasse linens, flatscreen TVs, and yoga DVDs and mats. The hotel has no spa but offers a menu of massages, facials, and other nurturing treatments performed in-room. The rooftop's heated pool and Jacuzzi offer stunning views of the surrounding Santa Ynez mountains, nearby Channel Islands, and downtown. The hotel even caters to canines with Club Canario, a pooch program that includes a cushy bed with hotel linens, dog tags, grooming kit, treats, and a Frisbee.

31 W. Carrillo, Santa Barbara, CA 93101. www.canarysantabarbara.com. ℂ **877/468-3515** or 805/884-0300. Fax 805/884-8153. 97 units. $405–$765 double. Packages available. AE, MC, V. Dogs accepted. **Amenities:** Restaurant; bar; concierge; fitness center; room service. *In room:* TV/DVD, minibar, MP3 docking station, Wi-Fi.

Simpson House Inn ★★★   The Simpson House is genuinely something special. Rooms within the 1874 Historic Landmark main house are decorated to Victorian perfection, with extras ranging from a claw-foot tub and antique brass shower to skylight and French doors opening to the manicured gardens; romantic cottages are nestled throughout the grounds. The rooms have everything you could possibly need, but most impressive are the extras: the gourmet Mediterranean hors d'oeuvres and Santa Barbara wines served each afternoon, the enormous video library, and the full gourmet breakfast (delivered on delicate china). Fact is, the Simpson House goes the distance—and then some—to create the perfect stay. Although this property is packed into a relatively small space, it still manages an ambience of country elegance and exclusivity—especially if you book one of the cottages.

121 E. Arrellaga St. (btw. Santa Barbara and Anacapa sts.), Santa Barbara, CA 93101. www.simpsonhouseinn.com. ℂ **800/676-1280** or 805/963-7067. Fax 805/564-4811. 15 units. $255–$615 double; $595–$605 suite and cottage. 2-night minimum on weekends. Rates include full gourmet breakfast, evening hors d'oeuvres, and wine. AE, DISC, MC, V. **Amenities:** Complimentary bikes; concierge. *In room:* A/C, TV/VCR, hair dryer, minibar.

MODERATE

Casa del Mar Inn at the Beach ✦   A half-block from the beach (sorry, no views), Casa del Mar is an excellent-value Spanish-architecture inn with one- and two-room suites in addition to standard-size rooms. All the rooms were recently remodeled with fresh modern touches while still maintaining the Mediterranean feel. The flower-sprinkled grounds are well maintained, with an attractive sun deck and Jacuzzi (but no swimming pool), and the staff is eager to please. Many rooms have kitchenettes, and a variety of different room configurations guarantee something to suit your needs (especially families). Guests may order in-room spa treatments, and golf packages can be arranged. *Tip:* Despite the hotel's multitude of rates, rooms can often be an unexpected bargain. Also check the website for Internet-only specials.

18 Bath St., Santa Barbara, CA 93101. www.casadelmar.com. © **800/433-3097** or 805/963-4418. 21 units. $144–$269 double. Extra person $10. AE, DC, DISC, MC, V. Free parking. From northbound U.S. 101, exit at Cabrillo, turn left onto Cabrillo, and head toward the beach; Bath is the 2nd street on the right after the wharf. From southbound U.S. 101, take the Castillo exit and turn right on Castillo, left on Cabrillo, and left on Bath. Pets accepted for $15. **Amenities:** Jacuzzi. *In room:* TV, hair dryer, kitchen or kitchenette and fridge in some units.

Hotel Oceana ★ If you're going to vacation in Santa Barbara, you might as well stay in style and on the beach—ergo, at the Hotel Oceana, a "beach chic" hotel with an oceanfront setting and an L.A. makeover. The 2½-acre Spanish Mission–style property consists of four adjacent motels built in the 1940s that have been merged and renovated into one sprawling hotel. The result is a wide range of charmingly old-school accommodations—everything from apartments with real day beds (great for families) to courtyard rooms and deluxe oceanview suites—with bright modern furnishings. The beach and jogging path are right across the street, and the huge lawn is perfect for picnic lunches. *Note:* Yes, you will probably be paying over $250 per night for a gussied-up motel room with no air-conditioning, but that's the going rate for oceanfront accommodations in Santa Barbara.

202 W. Cabrillo Blvd., Santa Barbara, CA 93101. www.hoteloceanasantabarbara.com. © **800/965-9776** or 805/965-4577. Fax 805/965-9937. 122 units. $250–$360 double. 2-night minimum for weekend reservations. AE, DC, DISC, MC, V. **Amenities:** Denny's restaurant adjacent; fitness room; 2 swimming pools; spa; whirlpool; sun deck. *In room:* TV, CD player, fridge, hair dryer, Wi-Fi.

The Upham Victorian Hotel and Garden Cottages This conveniently located inn combines the intimacy of a B&B with the service of a small hotel. Built in 1871, the Upham is the oldest continuously operating hostelry in Southern California. Somewhere the management made time for upgrades, though, because guest accommodations are complete with all the modern comforts. The hotel is constructed of redwood, with sweeping verandas and a Victorian cupola on top. It also has a warm lobby and a cozy restaurant.

1404 De La Vina St. (at Sola St.), Santa Barbara, CA 93101. www.uphamhotel.com. © **800/727-0876** or 805/962-0058. Fax 805/963-2825. 50 units. $195–$290 double; from $340 suite and cottage. Rates include continental breakfast and afternoon wine and cheese. AE, DC, MC, V. **Amenities:** Restaurant. *In room:* TV.

INEXPENSIVE

All the best buys fill up fast in the summer months, so be sure to reserve your room—even if you're just planning to stay at the reliable **Motel 6,** 443 Corona del Mar Dr. (www.motel6.com; © **800/466-8356** or 805/564-1392), near the beach.

Franciscan Inn The Franciscan is situated in a quiet neighborhood just a block from the beach, near Stearns Wharf. This privately owned and meticulously maintained hotel is an affordable retreat with enough frills that you'll still feel pampered. The small but comfy rooms feature a country-tinged decor and finely tiled bathrooms. Services include free local calls and afternoon cookies with spiced cider, hot cocoa, and tea or coffee in the lobby. Most second-floor rooms have unobstructed mountain views, and some suites feature fully equipped kitchenettes. The inn stacks up as a great family choice that's classy enough for a romantic weekend too.

109 Bath St. (at Mason St.), Santa Barbara, CA 93101. www.franciscaninn.com. ✆ **800/663-5288** or 805/963-8845. Fax 805/564-3295. 53 units. Summer (mid-May to mid-Sept) $165–$180 double, $195–$230 suite; winter $125–$160 double, $145–$180 suite. Extra person $10. Rates include continental breakfast and afternoon refreshments. AE, DC, MC, V. Free parking. **Amenities:** Heated outdoor pool; whirlpool. *In room:* A/C, TV/VCR, hair dryer, Wi-Fi.

Where to Eat

EXPENSIVE

bouchon ★★ CALIFORNIAN   You can tell that this warm and inviting restaurant is passionate about wine just from its name—*bouchon* is French for "wine cork." And not just any wines—those of the surrounding Santa Barbara County. Have fun by enhancing each course with a glass (or half-glass); knowledgeable servers help make the perfect match from among 50 different Central Coast vintages available by the glass. The seasonally composed and regionally inspired menu has included dishes such as smoked Santa Barbara albacore "carpaccio," arranged with a tangy vinaigrette and shaved imported Parmesan; luscious sweetbread and chanterelle ragout cradled in a potato-leek basket; local venison sliced and laid atop cumin spaetzle in a shallow pond of green pep-percorn–Madeira demiglacé; and monkfish saddle fragrant with fresh herbs and accom-panied by a creamy fennel-Gruyère gratin. Request a table on the heated front patio, and don't miss the signature chocolate "molten lava" cake for dessert.

9 W. Victoria St. (off State St.). ✆ **805/730-1160.** www.bouchonsantabarbara.com. Reservations rec-ommended. Main courses $25–$35. AE, DC, MC, V. Daily 5:30–10pm.

MODERATE

Brophy Bros. Clam Bar & Restaurant ★★ SEAFOOD   This place is most known for its unbeatable view of the marina, but the dependable fresh seafood keeps tourists and locals coming back. Dress is casual, portions are huge, and favorites include New England clam chowder, cioppino, and any one of an assortment of seafood salads. The scampi and garlic-baked clams are consistently good, as is all the fresh fish, which comes with soup or salad, coleslaw, and pilaf or french fries. A great deal is the hot-and-cold shellfish combo platter for $15. Ask for a table on the narrow deck overlooking the harbor. ***Be forewarned:*** The wait at this small place can be up to 2 hours on a weekend night.

119 Harbor Way (off Cabrillo Blvd. in the Waterfront Center). ✆ **805/966-4418.** www.brophybros.com. Reservations not accepted. Main courses $9–$19. AE, MC, V. Sun–Thurs 11am–10pm; Fri–Sat 10am–11pm.

Palazzio ★ ITALIAN   I should tell you up front: This family-style restaurant is not a good place for a first date. The fresh garlic bread, which is this State Street staple's raison d'être—and the reason so many UCSB students have no problem putting on the legendary Freshman Fifteen—is potent. Offered in half-order, "normal," or fam-ily-style sizes, the main courses aren't half bad, either, though normal dishes, such as their capellini with chicken meatballs and penne alla puttanesca, could easily feed two. (I didn't manage to plow my way through even half of my Papa Ruby's rigatoni.)

1026 State St. ✆ **805/564-1985.** www.palazzio.com. Main courses $16–$18. AE, MC, V. Mon–Thurs 11:30am–3pm and 5:30–11pm; Fri 11:30am–3pm and 5:30pm–midnight; Sat 11:30am–midnight; Sun 11:30am–11pm (kitchen closes 1 hr. before the restaurant daily).

Pane e Vino ★ ITALIAN   This popular Italian trattoria offers food as authentic as you'd find in Rome. The simplest spaghetti topped with basil-tomato sauce is so good, it's hard to understand why diners would want to occupy their taste buds with more complicated concoctions. But this kitchen is capable of almost anything. Pasta puttanesca, with tomatoes, anchovies, black olives, and capers, is always tops. Pane e Vino also gets high marks for its reasonable prices, service, and casual atmosphere. Although many diners prefer to eat outside on the patio, some of the best tables are in the charming, cluttered dining room.

1482 E. Valley Rd., Montecito (a 5-min. drive south of downtown Santa Barbara). ✆ **805/969-9274.** www.panevinosb.com. Reservations required. Main courses $10–$35. AE, MC, V. Mon-Sat 11:30am-9pm.

Tupelo Junction Café ★★ SOUTHERN   Most trendy restaurants have expiration dates, but the countrified Tupelo Junction has proven immune to such patterns. The unpretentious cafe, which produces Southern cuisine with a healthy California touch, is juxtaposed among the European labels and designer boutiques of State Street. Lemonade and mimosas are served in mason jars, and Jolly Ranchers are generously doled out with the bill. If you're in Santa Barbara long enough to dine at Tupelo only once, plan your pit stop for brunch: The pumpkin oatmeal waffle with candied walnuts and caramelized bananas is divine, and the apple beignets with crème anglaise aren't to be taken lightly. On Thursday nights, the venue hosts live music, with an array of alcohol and appetizer specials on tap.

1218 State St. ✆ **805/899-3100.** www.tupelojunction.com. Breakfast and lunch $5–$16; dinner $13–$29. AE, MC, V. Daily 8am-2pm and 5-9pm.

INEXPENSIVE

La Super-Rica Taqueria ★ MEXICAN   Looking at this humble street-corner shack, you'd never guess it was blessed with an endorsement by the late Julia Child. The tacos here are authentic and no-nonsense, with generous portions of filling piled onto fresh, grainy corn tortillas. My favorites are the *adobado* (marinated pork), *gorditas* (thick corn *masa* pockets filled with spicy beans), and flank steak. A dollop of house-made salsa and green or red hot sauce is the only adornment required. Sunday's special is *pozole,* a stew of pork and hominy in red-chile sauce. On Friday and Saturday, the specialty is freshly made tamales (if the Dover sole tamales are one of the specials, order them—they're incredible). **Tip:** Always check the daily specials first, and be sure to ask for extra tortillas, no matter what you order.

622 N. Milpas St. (btw. Cota and Ortega sts.). ✆ **805/963-4940.** Most menu items $4–$10. No credit cards. Daily 11am-9pm.

Stacky's Seaside SANDWICHES   This ivy-covered shack filled with fishnets, surfboards, and local memorabilia has been a local favorite for years. A classic seafood dive, its menu of sandwiches is enormous, as are most of their pita pockets, hoagies, and club sandwiches. A sign proudly proclaims HALF OF ANY SANDWICH, HALF PRICE—NO PROBLEM, and Stacky's has made a lot of friends because of it. Choices include the Santa Barbaran (roasted tri-tip and melted jack cheese on sourdough), the Rincon pita (jack and cheddar cheeses, green Ortega chilies, onions, and ranch dressing), and a hot pastrami hoagie with Swiss cheese, mustard, and onions. Heck, they even serve a PB&J for $4. And if you like fish and chips, they nail it here. Stacky's also serves breakfast, featuring scrambled-egg sandwiches and south-of-the-border egg dishes. An order of crispy fries is enough for two.

2315 Lillie Ave., Summerland. ✆ **805/969-9908.** Most menu items under $10. AE, DISC, MC, V. Mon-Fri 6:30am-7:30pm; Sat-Sun 7am-7:30pm. 5 min. on the freeway from Santa Barbara—take the Summerland exit, turn left under the freeway, and then take the 1st right.

BIG BEAR LAKE & LAKE ARROWHEAD ★★

100 miles NE of downtown L.A.

These two deep-blue lakes, close to one another in the San Bernardino mountains, have long been favorite year-round alpine playgrounds for city-weary Angelenos.

Big Bear Lake is popular with skiers as well as boaters (it's much larger than Arrowhead, and equipment rentals abound), and in the past decade the area has received a much-needed face-lift. Big Bear Boulevard was widened to handle high-season traffic, and downtown Big Bear Lake (the "Village") was spiffed up but retains its woodsy charm. In addition to two excellent ski slopes less than 5 minutes from town, you can enjoy the comforts of a real supermarket and several video-rental shops, all especially convenient if you're staying in a cabin. Most people choose Big Bear over Arrowhead because there's so much more to do, from boating, fishing, and hiking to snow sports, mountain biking, and horseback riding. The weather is nearly always perfect at this 7,000-foot-plus elevation: If you want proof, ask CalTech, which operates a solar observatory here to take advantage of nearly 300 days of sunshine per year.

Lake Arrowhead has always been privately owned, as is apparent from the affluence of the surrounding homes, many of which are gated estates rather than rustic mountain cabins. The lake and the private docks lining its shores are reserved for the exclusive use of homeowners, but visitors can enjoy Lake Arrowhead by boat tour or use of the summer-season beach clubs, a privilege included in nearly all private-home rentals. Reasons to choose a vacation at Lake Arrowhead? The roads up are less grueling than the winding ascent to Big Bear Lake and, because of its lower elevation, Arrowhead gets little snow (you can forget those pesky tire chains). It's very easy and cost-effective to rent a luxurious house from which to enjoy the spectacular scenery, crisp mountain air, and relaxed resort atmosphere—and if you do ski, the slopes are only a half-hour away.

Essentials

GETTING THERE   Lake Arrowhead is reached by taking Hwy. 18 from San Bernardino. The last segment of this route takes you along the aptly named **Rim of the World Highway,** with its breathtaking view over the valley on clear days. Hwy. 18 then continues east to Big Bear Lake, but to get to Big Bear Lake, it's quicker to bypass Arrowhead by taking Hwy. 330 from Redlands, which meets Hwy. 18 in Running Springs. During heavy-traffic periods, it can be worthwhile to take scenic Hwy. 38, which winds up from Redlands through mountain passes and valleys to approach Big Bear from the other side.

Note: Nostalgia lovers can revisit legendary **Route 66** on the way from Los Angeles to the mountain resorts, substituting scenic motor courts and other relics of the "Mother Road" in place of impersonal I-10.

VISITOR INFORMATION   National ski tours, mountain-bike races, and one of Southern California's largest Oktoberfest gatherings are just some of the events held year-round. Contact the **Big Bear Lake Resort Association,** 630 Bartlett Rd., Big Bear Lake Village (© **800/4-BIG-BEAR** [424-2327] or 909/866-7000; www.bigbearinfo.com), for schedules and information. They also provide information on sightseeing and lodging and will send you a free visitors guide.

Big Bear Lake & Lake Arrowhead

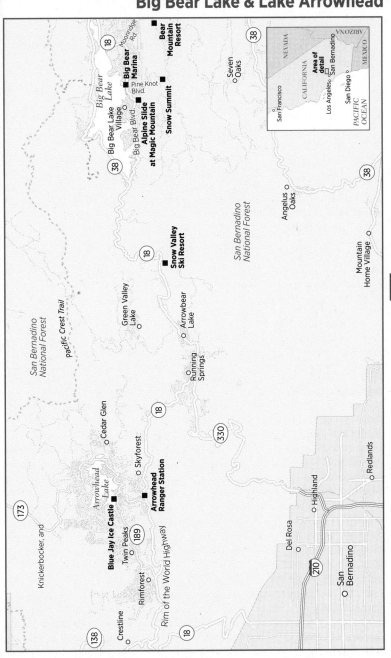

In Lake Arrowhead, contact the **Lake Arrowhead Communities Chamber of Commerce** (℅ **909/337-3715;** www.lakearrowhead.net). The visitor center is in the Lake Arrowhead Village lower shopping center.

ORIENTATION   The south shore of Big Bear Lake was the first resort area to be developed here and remains the most densely populated. Hwy. 18 passes first through the city of Big Bear Lake and its downtown village; then, as Big Bear Boulevard, it continues east to Big Bear City, which is more residential and suburban. Hwy. 38 traverses the north shore, home to pristine national forest and great hiking trails, as well as a couple of small marinas and a lakefront bed-and-breakfast inn (see the Windy Point Inn on p. 308).

Arrowhead's main town is Lake Arrowhead Village, on the south shore at the end of Hwy. 173. The village's commercial center is home to factory-outlet stores, about 40 chain and specialty shops, and the Lake Arrowhead Resort (p. 309). Minutes away is the town of Blue Jay (along Hwy. 189), where the Blue Jay Ice Castle skating rink is located (see "Winter Fun," below).

Enjoying the Outdoors

For up-to-date info on what outdoor activities are available in the region, call the **Big Bear Mountain Resorts Activities** hot line at ℅ **909/866-5766,** or log on to their website at www.bigbearmountainresorts.com.

In addition to the activities described below, there's a great recreation spot for families near the heart of Big Bear Lake: **Alpine Slide at Magic Mountain,** 800 Wildrose Lane (℅ **909/866-4626;** www.alpineslidebigbear.com), has a year-round bobsled-style Alpine Slide, a splashy double water slide open from mid-June to mid-September, and bunny slopes for snow tubing from November to Easter. The dry Alpine Slide is $4 a ride, the water slide is $12 for an unlimited pass, and snow play costs $25 per day, including tube and rope tow.

WATERSPORTS

BOATING   You can rent all kinds of boats—including speedboats, rowboats, paddleboats, pontoons, sailboats, and canoes—at a number of Big Bear Lake marinas. Rates vary only slightly from place to place: A 14-foot dinghy with an outboard runs around $30 per hour; pontoon (patio) boats that can hold large groups range in size and price from $65 to $90 per hour or $180 to $250 for a half-day. **Pine Knot Landing** (℅ **909/866-2628;** www.pineknotlanding.com) is the most centrally located marina, behind the post office at the foot of Pine Knot Boulevard in Big Bear Lake. **Big Bear Marina,** 500 Paine Rd. at Lakeview (℅ **909/866-3218;** www.bigbear marina.com), is close to Big Bear Lake Village and also rents a variety of watercraft.

FISHING   Big Bear Lake brims with rainbow trout, bass, and catfish in spring and summer, the best fishing seasons. Pine Knot Landing, Gray's Landing, and Big Bear Marina (see "Boating," above) all rent fishing boats and have bait-and-tackle shops that sell licenses.

JET-SKIING, WATER-SKIING & WAKE BOARDING   Personal water craft (PWCs) are available for rent at **Big Bear Marina** (see "Boating," above). **North Shore Landing,** on Hwy. 38, 2 miles west of Fawnskin (℅ **909/878-4-FUN** [4386]; www.800bigbear.com), rents jet skis and two- and three-person WaveRunners at rates ranging from $90 to $115 per hour plus gas. Call ahead to reserve your craft and check age and deposit requirements.

OTHER WARM-WEATHER ACTIVITIES

GOLF The **Bear Mountain Golf Course,** Goldmine Drive, Big Bear Lake (© 909/585-8002; www.bigbearmountainresorts.com), is a 9-hole, par-35, links-style course that winds through a gently sloping meadow at the base of the Bear Mountain Ski Resort. The course is open daily April through November. Weekend greens fees are $30 and $47 for 9 and 18 holes, respectively. Both riding carts and pull carts are available. Call ahead for tee times.

HIKING Hikers love the **San Bernardino National Forest.** The gray squirrel is a popular native, so you may see them scurrying around gathering acorns or material for their nests. You can sometimes spot deer, coyotes, and American bald eagles, which come here with their young in winter. The black-crowned Steller's jay and the talkative red, white, and black acorn woodpecker are the most common of the great variety of birds in this pine forest.

The best choice for a short mountain hike is the **Woodland Trail,** which begins near the ranger station. The best long hike is a section of the **Pacific Crest Trail,** which travels 39 miles through the mountains above Big Bear and Arrowhead lakes. The most convenient trail head is at Cougar Crest, half a mile west of the Big Bear Ranger Station.

The best place to begin a hike in Lake Arrowhead is at the **Arrowhead Ranger Station** (© 909/382-2782), in the town of Skyforest on Hwy. 18, a quarter-mile east of the Lake Arrowhead turnoff (Hwy. 173). The staff will provide you with maps and information on the best area trails, which range from easy to difficult. The **Enchanted Loop Trail,** near the town of Blue Jay, is an easy half-hour hike. The **Heaps Peak Arboretum Trail** winds through a grove of redwoods; the trail head is on the north side of Hwy. 18, at an auxiliary ranger kiosk west of Running Springs.

The area is home to a **National Children's Forest,** a 20-acre area developed so that children, people in wheelchairs, and the visually impaired can enjoy nature. To get to the Children's Forest from Lake Arrowhead, take Hwy. 330 to Hwy. 18 east, past Deer Lick Station; when you reach a road marked 1N96 (open only in summer), turn right and go 3 miles.

HORSEBACK RIDING **Baldwin Lake Stables,** southeast of Big Bear City (© 909/585-6482; www.baldwinlakestables.com), conducts hourly, lunch break, and sunset rides along a wide variety of terrains and trails—all with spectacular vistas—including the Pacific Crest Trail, which includes expansive views of the Mojave Desert. It's open year-round.

MOUNTAIN BIKING Big Bear Lake has become a mountain-biking center, with most of the action around the Snow Summit ski area (see "Winter Fun," below), where a $15 lift ticket will take you and your bike to a web of trails, fire roads, and meadows at about 8,000 feet. The lake's north shore is also a popular destination; the forest-service ranger stations (see "Hiking," above) have maps to the historic Gold Rush–era Holcomb Valley and the 2-mile Alpine Pedal Path (an easy lakeside ride).

Bear Valley Bikes, 40298 Big Bear Blvd. (© 909/866-8000), rents quality mountain bikes for about $10 an hour or $40 a day. At Lake Arrowhead, bikes are permitted on all hiking trails and back roads except the Pacific Crest Trail. See the local ranger station for an area map. Visitors can rent gear from the **Lake Arrowhead Resort** (© 909/336-1511) or **Above & Beyond Sports** (© 909/867-5517), 32877 Hwy. 18, Running Springs.

WINTER FUN

ICE-SKATING The **Blue Jay Ice Castle,** at North Bay Road and Hwy. 189 (© **909/337-0802;** www.icecastle.us), near Lake Arrowhead Village, was a training site for world champion Michelle Kwan and boasts former "Olympic Coach of the Year" Frank Carrollon on its staff. Several public sessions each day—as well as hockey, broomball, group lessons, and private parties—give nonpros a chance to enjoy this impeccably groomed "outdoor" rink, open on three sides to the scenery and fresh air.

SKIING & SNOWBOARDING When the L.A. basin gets wintertime rain, skiers rejoice, for they know snow is falling up in the mountains. The last few seasons have seen abundant natural snowfall at Big Bear, augmented by snowmaking equipment. While the slopes can't compare with those in Utah or Colorado, they do offer diversity, difficulty, and convenience.

Snow Summit, at Big Bear Lake (© **909/866-5766;** www.bigbearmountainresorts.com), is the skiers' choice, especially because it installed its second high-speed quad express from the 7,000-foot base to the 8,200-foot summit. There are also green (easy) runs, even from the summit, so beginners can enjoy the Summit Haus lodge and breathtaking lake views from the top. Advanced risk-takers will appreciate three double-black-diamond runs. The resort offers midweek, beginner, half-day, night, and family specials, as well as ski and snowboard instruction. Other helpful Snow Summit phone numbers include advance lift-ticket sales (© **909/866-5841**) and a snow report (© **800/BEAR-MTN** [232-7686]).

The **Bear Mountain Resort,** at Big Bear Lake (© **909/866-5766;** www.big bearmountainresorts.com), has the largest beginner area, but experts flock to the double-black-diamond Geronimo run from the 8,805-foot Bear Peak. Natural-terrain skiers and snowboarders will enjoy legal access to off-trail canyons, but the limited beginner slopes and kids' areas get pretty crowded in season. One of two high-speed quad expresses rises from the 7,140-foot base to 8,440-foot Goldmine Mountain; most runs from here are intermediate. Bear Mountain has a ski-and-snowboard school, abundant dining facilities, and a well-stocked ski shop.

The **Snow Valley Ski Resort,** in Arrowbear, midway between Arrowhead and Big Bear (© **909/867-2751;** www.snow-valley.com), has improved its snowmaking and facilities to compete with the other two major ski areas, and it's the primary choice of skiers staying at Arrowhead. From a base elevation of 6,800 feet, Snow Valley's 13 chairlifts (including 5 triples) can take you from the beginner runs all the way up to black-diamond challenges at the 7,898-foot peak. Children's programs, night skiing, and lesson packages are also available.

ORGANIZED TOURS

LAKE TOURS The ***Big Bear Queen*** (© **909/866-3218;** www.bigbearmarina. com), a small version of a Mississippi-style paddle-wheeler, cruises Big Bear Lake on 90-minute tours daily from late April to the end of November. The boat departs from Big Bear Marina (at the end of Paine Ave.). Tours are $18 for adults, $16 for seniors 65 and older, $12 for children ages 3 to 12, and free for kids under 3. Call for reservations and information on the special Sunday brunch, champagne sunset, and dinner cruises.

Fifty-minute tours of Lake Arrowhead are available year-round on the ***Arrowhead Queen*** (© **909/336-6992**), a sister ship that departs hourly each day between 10am and 6pm from Lake Arrowhead Village. Tours are $16 for adults, $14 for seniors, $10 for children 3 to 12, and free for kids under 3. It's about the only way to really see this alpine jewel, unless you know a resident with a boat. Highlights include celebrity homes—past and present—famous film locations, and the occasional bald eagle or two.

Where to Stay

BIG BEAR LAKE

Vacation rentals are plentiful in the area, from cabins to condos to private homes. Some can accommodate up to 20 people and can be rented on a weekly or monthly basis. For a wide range of rental properties, all pictured in detail online, contact the **Village Reservation Service** (📞 **800/693-0018** or 909/866-9689; www.village reservations.net), which can arrange for everything from condos to lakefront homes, or call the **Big Bear Lake Resort Association** (📞 **800/4-BIG-BEAR** [442-4232]; www.bigbear.com) for referrals on all types of lodgings.

Besides the places below, I also recommend **Apples Bed & Breakfast Inn,** 42430 Moonridge Rd. (📞 **909/866-0903;** www.applesbigbear.com), a crabapple-red New England–style clapboard that blends hotel-like professionalism with B&B amenities (and lots of frilly touches); and **Gold Mountain Manor,** 1117 Anita Ave. (📞 **800/509-2604** or 909/585-6997; www.goldmountainmanor.com), a woodsy 1920s lodge that's now an ultracozy, affordable B&B.

Best Western Big Bear Chateau ☺ This European-flavored property is one of only two traditional full-service hotels in Big Bear. Its location—just off Big Bear Boulevard at the base of the road to Bear Mountain—makes the Chateau a popular choice for skiers and families (kids 17 and under stay free in their parent's room, and there are also children's activities). The rooms are modern but more charming than your average Best Western, with tapestries, brass beds, antique furniture, gas fireplaces, and marble bathrooms with heated towel racks and many with whirlpool tubs. The compound is surrounded by tall forest. The casual Le Bistro restaurant serves a free continental breakfast each morning for guests.

42200 Moonridge Rd. (P.O. Box 1814), Big Bear Lake, CA 92315. www.bestwestern.com. 📞 **800/232-7466** or 909/866-6666. Fax 909/866-8988. 80 units. Winter $120–$259 double; summer $100–$150 double. Children 17 and under stay free in parent's room. Winter-ski, romance, and summer-fun packages available. AE, DISC, MC, V. **Amenities:** Restaurant; lounge; game room; Jacuzzi; heated outdoor pool. *In room:* A/C, TV, hair dryer, free Wi-Fi.

Grey Squirrel Resort ☺ This is the most attractive of the many cabin-cluster-type motels near the city of Big Bear Lake, offering a wide range of rustic cabins, most with fireplace and kitchen. They're adequately, if not attractively, furnished—the appeal is the flexibility and privacy afforded large or long-term parties. Facilities include a heated pool that's enclosed in winter, a fire pit and barbecues, volleyball and basketball courts, and completely equipped kitchens.

39372 Big Bear Blvd., Big Bear Lake, CA 92315. www.greysquirrel.com. 📞 **800/381-5569** or 909/866-4335. Fax 909/866-6271. 18 cabins. $79–$176 1-bedroom cabin; $138–$160 2-bedroom cabin; $218–$239 3-bedroom cabin. Value rates available; higher rates on holidays. AE, DISC, MC, V. Pets accepted for $10 per day. **Amenities:** Jacuzzi; heated indoor/outdoor pool. *In room:* TV/DVD, kitchen (some units), free Wi-Fi.

Knickerbocker Mansion Country Inn ★ Innkeepers Thomas Bicanic and Stan Miller faced quite a task reviving this landmark log house; when they moved in, it was empty of all furnishings and suffered from years of neglect. But Knickerbocker

Mansion has risen to become the most charming and sophisticated inn on the lake's south side; chef Bicanic, who honed his craft in L.A.'s culinary temple Patina restaurant, is now serving intimate gourmet dinners at the Bistro at the Mansion on Friday and Saturday evenings. The pair scoured antiques stores in Big Bear and Los Angeles for vintage furnishings, creating a warm and relaxing ambience in the grand-yet-quirky house of legendary local character Bill Knickerbocker, who assembled it by hand almost 90 years ago. Today's guest rooms are a cedar-paneled dream, with luxury bed linens, cozy bathrobes, modern marble bathrooms with deluxe Australian shower heads, and refreshing mountain views. After Bicanic's memorable breakfast, you can spend the day relaxing on veranda rockers or garden hammocks; Big Bear's village is also an easy walk away.

869 Knickerbocker Rd. (P.O. Box 1907), Big Bear Lake, CA 92315. www.knickerbockermansion.com. ℂ 877/423-1180 or 909/878-9190. Fax 909/878-4248. 8 units. $125–$170 double; $225 suite. Rates include full breakfast, refreshments, and snacks. AE, DISC, MC, V. *In room:* TV/VCR/DVD, hair dryer, free Wi-Fi.

Windy Point Inn ★   A contemporary architectural showpiece on the scenic north shore, the Windy Point is the only shorefront B&B in Big Bear; ergo, all guest rooms have a view of the lake. Hosts Val and Kent Kessler's attention to detail is impeccable: If you're tired of knotty pine and Victorian frills, here's a grown-up place for you, with plenty of romance and all the pampering you can stand. Every room has a wood-burning fireplace, feather bed, private deck, and DVD player (guests may borrow DVDs from the inn's plentiful collection); some also feature whirlpool tubs and luxurious state-of-the-art bathrooms. The welcoming great room features a casual sunken fireplace nook with floor-to-ceiling windows overlooking the lake, a telescope for stargazing, a baby grand, and up-to-date menus for every local restaurant. You might not want to leave the cocoon of your room after Kent's custom gourmet breakfast (only an option in the Coves and the Shores rooms), but if you do, you'll be pleasantly surprised to find that you are dining with only your party—meal times are staggered for privacy. There's a wintertime bald eagle habitat just up the road, and the city of Big Bear Lake is only a 10-minute drive around the lake.

39015 N. Shore Dr., Fawnskin, CA 92333. www.windypointinn.com. ℂ 909/866-2746. Fax 909/866-1593. 5 units. $145–$265 double. Rates include welcome cookies, full breakfast. Midweek discounts available. AE, DISC, MC, V. *In room:* TV/DVD (for movies only; no TV channel reception) CD player (some units), fridge, hair dryer, no phone.

LAKE ARROWHEAD

Arrowhead has far more private homes than tourist accommodations, but rental properties abound, from cozy cottages to mansions; many can be economical for families or other groups. Two of the largest agencies are **Arrowhead Cabin Rentals** (ℂ 800/244-5138 or 909/337-2403; www.arrowheadrent.com) and **AAA Resorts Rentals** (ℂ 800/743-0865 or 909/337-4413; www.lakearrowheadrentals.com). Overnight guests in rentals enjoy some resident lake privileges—ask when you reserve.

Two other options are **Chateau du Lac,** 911 Hospital Rd. (ℂ 909/337-6488; www.chateau-du-lac.com), an elegant and contemporary four-room B&B with stunning views of the lake; and the **Saddleback Inn,** 300 S. Hwy. 173 (ℂ 800/858-3334 or 909/336-3571; www.saddlebackinn.com), an inn and restaurant that still boasts historic charm while offering some up-to-date amenities, all at a prime location in the center of the village.

Lake Arrowhead Resort & Spa ★★ ☺ A $20-million resort-wide transformation greatly improved every part of this sprawling resort—including a new full-service, luxurious **Spa of the Pines** and **Bin 189** restaurant—but its location is still its most outstanding feature. On the lakeshore adjacent to Lake Arrowhead Village, the hotel has its own beach, plus docks that are ideal for fishing. The newly renovated rooms are decked out with 32-inch swiveling flat-panel TVs, Essential Elements body and hair care products, and Anichini linens; most have balconies, king-size beds, and fireplaces as well. The suites, are equipped with kitchen amenities and whirlpool tubs and floor heaters in the bathrooms. The hotel caters primarily to groups and sports a businesslike ambience during the week, but you'll spend most of your time on the beach anyway. A full program of supervised children's activities, ranging from nature hikes to T-shirt painting, is offered on weekends year-round.

27984 Hwy. 189, Lake Arrowhead, CA 92352. www.laresort.com. ℂ **800/800-6792** or 909/336-1511. Fax 909/744-3088. 173 units. $179–$349 double; $309–$785 suite. AE, DC, DISC, MC, V. **Amenities:** 1 restaurant; babysitting; children's programs; fitness center; Jacuzzi; outdoor pool (summer only). *In room:* A/C, flat-panel TV w/pay movies, hair dryer, minibar, free Wi-Fi.

Pine Rose Cabins ★ ☺ Pine Rose Cabins is a good choice for families. On 5 forested acres about 3 miles from the lake, the wonderful free-standing cabins offer lots of privacy. Owners David and Tricia DuFour have 15 cabins, from romantic studios to a five-bedroom lodge, each decorated in a different theme: The Indian cabin has a tepee-like bed; the bed in Wild Bill's cabin is covered like a wagon. Multibedroom units have stocked kitchens and separate living areas; for all cottages, daily maid service is available at an extra charge. There are lots of diversions on hand, including swing sets, croquet, tetherball, and Ping-Pong.

25994 Hwy. 189 (P.O. Box 31), Twin Peaks, CA 92391. www.pinerose.com. ℂ **800/429-PINE** (7463) or 909/337-2341. Fax 909/337-0258. 17 units. $109–$189 studio for 2; $149–$229 1-, 2-, and 3-bedroom cabins for up to 10 people; $325–$550 large-group lodges. Ski packages available. AE, DISC, MC, V. Pets accepted for $10 per night and $100 refundable deposit. **Amenities:** Jacuzzi; outdoor heated pool. *In room:* TV/VCR, kitchen, high-speed Internet access ($5 per day).

Where to Eat
BIG BEAR LAKE
A reliable option for all-day dining is **Stillwell's,** 40650 Village Dr. (ℂ **909/866-3121,** ext. 3). You might otherwise bypass it, because Stillwell's is the dining room for convention-friendly Northwoods Resort at the edge of the village. Despite the unmistakable hotel feel, its American/Continental menu is respectable, with something for everyone, noted attention to detail, and fair prices (rare in this mountain resort town). Another in-hotel dining option is the restaurant **Bin 189** at the Lake Arrowhead Resort & Spa (see above).

Note: Hours of operation often change depending on the season and weather conditions, so be sure to call ahead to see if these restaurants are open.

The Captain's Anchorage STEAK/SEAFOOD   Historic and rustic, this knotty-pine restaurant has been serving fine steaks, prime rib, seafood, and lobster since 1947. Inside, the dark, nautical decor and fire-warmed bar are just right on blustery winter nights. It's got one of those mile-long soup-and-salad bars, plus some great early bird and weeknight specials.

Moonridge Way at Big Bear Blvd., Big Bear Lake. ℂ **909/866-3997.** www.captainsanchorage.com. Reservations recommended. Full dinners $18–$40. AE, MC, V. Sun–Thurs 4:30–9pm; Fri–Sat 4:30–10pm.

Himalayan Restaurant ★ INDIAN/NEPALESE To say that the Himalayan is the best Indian eatery in the Big Bear area is a self-fulfilling prophesy—in fact, it's the only one. But when an Indian expat shares this sentiment, you take notice. The simple dining room is run by casual waiters more likely to be in baseball hats than turbans, but the menu reflects the soul of the subcontinent. And they aren't afraid of spice, so think twice before ordering anything hot. Particularly good is the clay-roasted tandoori lamb sekuwa with mint sauce. There are more familiar dishes like chicken tikka masala and spinach paneer as well.

672 Pine Knot, Big Bear Lake. © **909/878-3068**. www.himalayanbigbear.com. Main courses $7.95–$16. MC, V. Mon, Tues, Thurs, Sun 11am–9pm; Fri–Sat 11am–10pm. Closed Wednesday.

LAKE ARROWHEAD

For a mountain community, Lake Arrowhead has a few surprisingly good dining options. It's worth venturing beyond your hotel to some of the local haunts. These include the **Lake Arrowhead Sports Grille**, 27200 State Hwy. 189, Blue Jay (©)**909/744-8785**), a local's favorite pub; the **Royal Oak,** 27187 Hwy. 189, Blue Jay Village (© **909/337-6018**), an expensive American/Continental steakhouse; and **Belgian Waffle Works,** dockside at Lake Arrowhead Village (© **909/337-5222**), a bargain coffee shop with Victorian decor, known for flavorful waffles with tasty toppings.

Moderate

Casual Elegance 🎁 MODERN AMERICAN If you can make it past the unfortunate moniker (truly, what were they thinking?), you'll be glad you did, as the food here could hold its own in a much more competitive market. The bi-level space is small, and the seating can seem downright French at times, but it's worth it for exquisitely cooked cuts of lamb, among other typical entrée choices of Atlantic salmon and chicken breast. *Note:* All entrees are served as part of a 4-course set menu.

26848 Hwy. 189, Blue Jay © **909/337-8932**. www.casualelegancerestaurant.com. Main courses $22–$34. AE, DISC, MC, V. Weds–Sun 5–9pm.

The Grill at Antlers Inn ECLECTIC AMERICAN A rustic retreat sought out by special occasion-celebrating locals, as well as curious tourists, both come for the friendly atmosphere and whimsical fare. It's a fun spot for folks that don't take food too seriously, meaning you can be happy with something as wild as tempura avocado with raspberry remoulade appetizer, or a simple rib-eye steak--with purple whipped potatoes. *Tip:* In winter, the mulled wine here is exceptional.

26125 State Hwy. 189. Twin Peaks © **909/336-2600**. www.thegrillatantlersinn.com. Main courses $16–$34. DISC, MC, V. Tues–Sat 4:30pm–close; Sun 10am–2am and 4:30pm–close.

PLANNING YOUR TRIP TO LOS ANGELES

11

Although the best vacations are the ones that allow for spontaneity, there's no substitute for a little pre-trip research when it comes to planning a great vacation. Ergo, this entire chapter contains practical information to help you prepare the perfect trip to L.A., including topical websites, recommended pre-trip arrangements, ideal times to visit, and local resources for those with specialized needs.

GETTING THERE

By Plane

Five airports serve the Los Angeles area. Most visitors fly into **Los Angeles International Airport** (© **310/646-5252;** www.lawa.org/lax), better known as LAX. This behemoth—ranked sixth in the world for number of passengers handled—is oceanside, between Marina del Rey and Manhattan Beach. LAX is a convenient place to land; it's within minutes of Santa Monica and the beaches, and not more than a half-hour from Downtown, Hollywood, and the Westside (depending on traffic, of course). Despite its huge size, the nine-terminal airport has a straightforward, easy-to-understand design. Free **shuttle buses** connect the terminals and stop in front of each ticket building. Special minibuses accessible to travelers with disabilities are also available. Call **310/646-6402** for more information. **Travelers Aid of Los Angeles** (© **310/646-2270;** www.travelersaid.org) operates booths in every terminal.

There are eight short-stay (and expensive) parking lots within the main concourse building and a long-stay park on 96th Street and Sepulveda Boulevard. A free bus service runs between this car park and the terminals. A free 24-hour **Cell Phone Waiting Lot** is at 9011 Airport Blvd. for drivers picking up passengers. It can be very easy to miss, so keep an eye out for the big post office—it's right next door. You can find extensive information about LAX—including maps, parking, shuttle-van information, and links to weather forecasts—online at **www.lawa.org.** All car-rental agencies are in the neighborhood surrounding LAX, within a few minutes' drive; each provides a complimentary shuttle to and from the airport.

For some travelers, one of the area's smaller airports might be more convenient than LAX. **Bob Hope Airport** (BUR; 2627 N. Hollywood Way, Burbank; ✆ 818/840-8840; www.bobhopeairport.com) is the best place to land if you're headed for Hollywood or the valleys—and it's even closer to Downtown L.A. than LAX. The small airport has especially good links to Las Vegas and other southwestern cities. **Long Beach Municipal Airport** (LGB; 4100 Donald Douglas Dr., Long Beach; ✆ 562/570-2600; www.lgb.org), south of LAX, is the best place to land if you're visiting Long Beach or northern Orange County and want to avoid L.A. **John Wayne Airport** (SNA; 18601 Airport Way, Santa Ana; ✆ 949/252-5200; www.ocair.com) is closest to Disneyland, Knott's Berry Farm, and other Orange County attractions. **Ontario International Airport** (ONT; 1923 E. Avion St., Ontario; ✆ 909/937-2700; www.lawa.org/ont) is not a popular airport for tourists; businesspeople use it to head to San Bernardino, Riverside, and other inland communities. However, it's convenient if you're heading to Palm Springs, and also a viable choice if you're staying in Pasadena.

By Car

Los Angeles is well connected to the rest of the United States by several major highways. Among them are I-5, which enters the state from the north; I-10, which originates in Jacksonville, Florida, and terminates in Los Angeles; and U.S. 101, a scenic route that follows the western seaboard from Los Angeles north to the Oregon state line.

If you're driving **from the north,** you have two choices: the quick route, along I-5 through the middle of the state; or the scenic route along the coast. Heading south along I-5, you'll pass a small town called Grapevine. This marks the start of the mountain pass with the same name. Once you've reached the southern end of it, you'll be in Canyon Country, just north of the San Fernando Valley, which is the start of Los Angeles County. To reach the beach communities and L.A.'s Westside, take I-405 south (hello, traffic!); to get to Hollywood, take California 170 south to U.S. 101 south (this route is called the Hollywood Freeway the entire way); I-5 will take you along the eastern edge of Downtown and into Orange County.

If you're taking the **scenic coastal route** from the north, take U.S. 101 to I-405 or I-5, or stay on U.S. 101, following the instructions above.

If you're approaching **from the east,** you'll be coming in on I-10. For Orange County, take California 57 south. I-10 continues through Downtown and terminates at the beach. If you're heading to the Westside, take I-405 north. To get to the beaches, take California 1 (Pacific Coast Hwy., or PCH) north or south, depending on your destination.

From the south, head north on I-5 at the southern end of Orange County. I-405 splits off to the west; take this road to the Westside and beach communities. Stay on I-5 to reach Downtown and Hollywood.

Here are some **driving times** if you're on one of those see-the-USA car trips: From Phoenix, it's about 350 miles, or 6 hours (okay, 7 if you drive the speed limit) to Los Angeles via I-10. Las Vegas is 265 miles northeast of Los Angeles (about a 4- or 5-hr. drive). San Francisco is 390 miles north of Los Angeles primarily on I-5 for the fastest route (6–7 hr.), and San Diego is 115 miles south (about 2 hr.).

If you're visiting from abroad and plan to rent a car in the United States, you probably won't need the services of an additional automobile organization. If you plan to buy or borrow a car, automobile-association membership is recommended. **AAA,** the

American Automobile Association (*©* **800/222-4357;** www.aaa.com), is the country's largest motor club and supplies its members with maps, insurance, and, most importantly, emergency road service. **Note:** Foreign driver's licenses are usually recognized in the U.S., but you should get an international one if your home license is not in English.

International visitors should note that insurance and taxes are almost never included in quoted rental car rates in the U.S. Be sure to ask your rental agency about additional fees for these. They can add a significant cost to your car rental.

By Train

Amtrak (*©* **800/USA-RAIL** [872-7245]; www.amtrak.com) connects Los Angeles with about 500 American cities. As with plane travel along popular routes, fares fluctuate depending on the season and special promotions. As a general rule, heavily restricted advance tickets are competitive with similar airfares. Remember, however, that those low fares are for coach travel in reclining seats; private sleeping accommodations cost substantially more.

The *Sunset Limited* was Amtrak's regularly scheduled transcontinental service, originating in Florida and making 52 stops along the way as it passed through Alabama, Mississippi, Louisiana, Texas, New Mexico, and Arizona before arriving in Los Angeles. Unfortunately, Hurricane Katrina wiped out the Jacksonville to New Orleans section. Though it is being rebuilt, a reopening date has not been scheduled. Cross-country travel typically means a change of trains in either Chicago or New Orleans. Amtrak's *Coast Starlight* travels along the Pacific Coast between Seattle and Los Angeles. This stylish train (with its wonderfully scenic route) has been steadily growing in popularity.

Amtrak also runs trains along the California coast, connecting San Diego, Los Angeles, San Francisco (with bus connections in the case of the latter), and all points in between. Multiple trains run every day. One-way fares for popular segments can range from $25 (Los Angeles–Santa Barbara) to $31 (Los Angeles–San Diego) to $67 (San Francisco–Los Angeles); but, again, fares fluctuate.

Ask about special family plans, tours, and other money-saving promotions. You can call for a brochure outlining routes and prices for the entire system; up-to-date schedules and fares are also available on Amtrak's comprehensive—but often unwieldy—website (www.amtrak.com). Better yet, log on to Amtrak's California website: **www.amtrakcalifornia.com**. It's far more user-friendly and lists only California schedules and special fares.

The L.A. train terminus is **Union Station,** 800 N. Alameda St., on Downtown's northern edge. Completed in 1939, this was the last of America's great train depots—a unique blend of Spanish Revival and Streamline Moderne architecture (see "Architectural Highlights," in chapter 6). From the station, you can take one of the taxis that line up outside; board the Metro Red Line to Hollywood or Universal City; or take the Metro Gold Line to Pasadena. If you're headed to the San Fernando Valley or Anaheim, Metrolink commuter trains leave from Union Station; call *©* **800/371-LINK** (371-5465), or visit www.metrolinktrains.com.

International visitors can buy a USA Rail Pass, good for 15, 30, or 45 days of segmented travel on Amtrak (*©* **800/USA-RAIL** [872-7245]; www.amtrak.com). The pass is available through many overseas travel agents. See Amtrak's website for the cost of travel within the western, eastern, or northwestern United States. With a foreign passport, you can also buy passes directly from some Amtrak locations, including San Francisco, Los Angeles, Chicago, New York, Miami, Boston, and Washington, D.C., though prices are usually higher in person. Reservations are generally required and should be made as early as possible. California rail passes are also available.

GETTING INTO TOWN FROM THE AIRPORT (LAX)
By Car

To reach **Santa Monica** and other northern beach communities, exit the airport, take Sepulveda Boulevard north, and follow the signs to California 1 (PCH) north. You *can* take I-405 north, but you'll be sorry you did—that stretch of freeway is always heavily congested.

To reach **Redondo, Hermosa, Manhattan,** and the other southern beach communities, take Sepulveda Boulevard south and then follow the signs to California 1 south.

To reach **Beverly Hills** or **Hollywood,** exit the airport via Century Boulevard and then take I-405 north to Santa Monica Boulevard east.

To reach **Downtown** or **Pasadena,** exit the airport, take Sepulveda Boulevard south, then take I-105 east to I-110 north.

Tip: If you're going to rent a car at LAX, avoid arriving during midweek mornings or evening rush hour, particularly if you have to get on dreaded I-405. You'll save yourself several hours of stop-and-go misery if you time it right.

By Car Service

For about the same price you would pay for a taxi to and from LAX, you can hire a personal car service, which is far more convenient and luxurious. **M and M Car Service** (✆ **310/738-9898** or 285-0193; www.mandmcarservice.com) provides friendly and reliable car service both to and from LAX, with rates starting at $50 (gratuity not included) for car service to LAX from Santa Monica, and slightly more for LAX pickup. M and M also provides car, limousine, and SUV service throughout the greater L.A. region for shows, restaurants, scenic cruises, and special occasions.

By Shuttle

Many city hotels provide free shuttles for their guests; ask when you make reservations. **SuperShuttle** (✆ **800/BLUE-VAN**258-3826 or 310/782-6600; www. supershuttle.com) offers regularly scheduled minivans from LAX to any location in the city, as does **Prime Time Shuttle** (✆ **800/RED-VANS** [733-8267] or 310/536-7922; www.primetimeshuttle.com). Fares can range from about $15 to $35 per person, depending on your destination. If you're a group of three or more, it probably will

---

 A Shortcut to LAX

One of the city's busiest interchanges is from the Santa Monica Freeway (I-10) to the San Diego Freeway (I-405) on the way to LAX—many a tourist has missed a flight because of this beastly bottleneck. Therefore, if you're heading to LAX for your flight home, the scenic route may prove to be the fastest. From the Santa Monica Freeway (I-10) westbound, exit south to La Brea Avenue. Go right on Stocker Street and then left on La Cienega Boulevard. Veer right on La Tijera Boulevard and left on Airport Boulevard, then follow the signs. You can use this trick from West Hollywood and Beverly Hills as well—simply take La Cienega south, continuing as above.

Instead of renting a boring ol' car to cruise the Sunset Strip, why not rent a motorcycle? Even better, why not rent a Harley? **EagleRider** (11860 S. La Cienega Blvd., Hawthorne; ☏ 800/501-8687 or 310/536-6777; www.eaglerider. com), the world's largest motorcycle rental and tour company, will rent you a mild-mannered Sportster 883cc for about $101 per day. Leather chaps are optional, but a motorcycle license is required. Other quality L.A.-based Harley motorcycle-rental companies include **Route 66 Riders** (4161 Lincoln Blvd., Marina del Rey; ☏ 888/434-4473 or 310/578-0112; www.route66 riders.com) and **Ride Free Motorcycle Tours** (4848 W. 136th St., Hawthorne; ☏ 310/978-9558; www.ridefree.com). Keep the rubber side down.

be cheaper and far more convenient to take a cab. Reservations aren't needed for your arrival, but are required for a return to the airport.

By Metro Rail
Budget-minded travelers heading to Downtown, Universal City, or Long Beach can take L.A.'s Metro Rail service from LAX. An airport shuttle can take you to the Green Line light-rail station; from there, connections on the Blue, Gold, and Red lines can get you where you're headed. It's a good idea to contact your hotel for advice on the closest station. The service operates from 5am to midnight, and the combined fare is less than $3—but you should be prepared to spend 1 to 2 hours in transit. Call the **Los Angeles County Metropolitan Transit Authority (MTA)** at ☏ 323/GO-METRO (466-3876), or see **www.metro.net** for information.

By Public Bus
The city's MTA buses also go between LAX and many parts of the city. Phone **MTA Airport Information** (☏ 323/GO-METRO [466-3876]; www.metro.net) for the schedules and fares. If you arrive at LAX and your hotel is in Santa Monica, you can hop aboard the city's **Big Blue Bus** (☏ 310/451-5444; www.bigbluebus.com). It's a slow ride, but the $1 fare is hard to beat. Bus information is available in the baggage claim area of every LAX terminal.

By Taxi
Taxis are at the arrivals level under the yellow sign outside each terminal. Be sure to ask for a list of prices to various major destinations before setting off. There's a flat price of $47 between LAX and Downtown Los Angeles; expect to pay at least $45 to Hollywood, $35 to Beverly Hills, $30 to Santa Monica, and $75 to the Valley and Pasadena. But wait—there's more. You'll also have to pay an airport surcharge of $2.50 for trips originating from LAX.

Car Rentals
Los Angeles is one of the cheapest places in America to rent a car. The major national car-rental companies usually rent economy- and compact-class cars for about $40 per day (hybrids $80–$90) and $200-plus per week, with unlimited mileage. All the major car-rental agencies have offices at the airports and in the larger hotels; I highly recommend booking a car online before you arrive, such as **Simply Hybrid Rental Cars** (☏ 888/359-0055; www.simplyhybrid.com) or **Enterprise Rent-A-Car** (☏ 800/261-7331 or 310/649-5400; www.enterprise.com).

If you're thinking of splurging on a dig-me road machine such as a Maserati, Ferrari, Rolls-Royce, Lamborghini, or Hummer, the place to call is **Beverly Hills Rent-A-Car,** 9732 Little Santa Monica Blvd., Beverly Hills (ⓒ **800/479-5996** or 310/337-1400; www.bhrentacar.com). There are additional locations in Hollywood, Santa Monica, LAX, and Newport Beach, with complimentary delivery to local hotels or pickup service at LAX.

GETTING AROUND

By Car

Need I tell you that Los Angeles is a car-crazed city? L.A. is a sprawling metropolis, so you're really going to need some wheels to get around easily (there *is* public transportation in L.A., but you probably don't want to rely on it). An elaborate network of well-maintained freeways connects this urban sprawl, but you have to learn how to make sense of the system and cultivate some patience for dealing with the traffic—purchasing one of those plastic-covered fold-out maps is a smart investment; purchasing a GPS navigation system is a better one (don't count on your smartphone if you are without a co-pilot—the hands-free driving law is strictly enforced). For a detailed view of L.A.'s freeway system, see the tear-out map tucked inside the back cover.

L.A.'S MAIN FREEWAYS

L.A.'s extensive system of toll-free, high-speed (in theory, anyway) freeways connects the city's patchwork of communities, though most visitors spend the bulk of their time either along the coastline or on the city's ever-trendy Westside (see "Neighborhoods in Brief," in chapter 3, for complete details on all of the city's sectors). The system works well to get you where you need to be, although rush-hour (roughly 7–9am and 3–7pm) traffic is often bumper-to-bumper, particularly on the dreaded I-405. Here's an overview of the city's main freeways (best read with an L.A. map in hand):

U.S. 101, called the Ventura Freeway in the San Fernando Valley and the Hollywood Freeway in the city, runs across L.A. in a roughly northwest-southeast direction, from the San Fernando Valley to the center of Downtown. You'll encounter heavy rush-hour traffic.

California 134 continues as the Ventura Freeway after U.S. 101 reaches the city and becomes the Hollywood Freeway. This branch of the Ventura Freeway continues directly east, through the valley towns of Burbank and Glendale, to I-210 (the Foothill Fwy.), which takes you through Pasadena and out toward the eastern edge of Los Angeles County.

I-5, otherwise known as the Golden State Freeway north of I-10, and the Santa Ana Freeway south of I-10, bisects Downtown on its way from Sacramento to San Diego.

I-10, labeled the Santa Monica Freeway west of I-5, and the San Bernardino Freeway east of I-5, is the city's major east-west freeway, connecting the San Gabriel Valley with Downtown and Santa Monica.

I-405, known as the San Diego Freeway, runs north-south through L.A.'s Westside, connecting the San Fernando Valley with LAX and southern beach areas. *Tip:* This is one of the area's busiest freeways; avoid it as much as possible (and like the plague during rush hour).

If you're driving to or from Santa Monica and the Westside communities—Beverly Hills, West Hollywood, Century City—try to avoid Santa Monica Boulevard during rush hour. Both Olympic and Pico boulevards parallel Santa Monica Boulevard and are usually far less congested. (Pico Blvd. is my savior.)

I-105, Los Angeles's newest freeway—called the Century Freeway—extends from LAX east to I-605.

I-110, commonly known as the Harbor Freeway, starts in Pasadena as California 110 (the Pasadena Fwy.); it becomes an interstate in Downtown Los Angeles and runs directly south, where it dead-ends in San Pedro. The section that is now the Pasadena Freeway was Los Angeles's first freeway, known as the Arroyo Seco when it opened in 1940.

I-710, also known as the Long Beach Freeway, runs in a north-south direction through East Los Angeles and dead-ends at Long Beach. Crammed with big rigs leaving the port in San Pedro in a rush, this is the ugliest and most dangerous freeway in California.

I-605, the San Gabriel River Freeway, runs from I-405 near Seal Beach to the I-210 interchange at Duarte. It follows the San Gabriel River (hence the moniker), roughly paralleling I-710 to the east. Most importantly, it gets you through the San Gabriel Valley up to the edge of the San Gabriel Mountains.

California 1—called Hwy. 1, the Pacific Coast Highway, or simply PCH—is more of a scenic parkway than a freeway. It skirts the ocean, linking all of L.A.'s beach communities, from Malibu to the Orange Coast. It's often slow going due to all the stoplights, but is far more scenic than the freeways.

A complex web of surface streets complements the freeways. From north to south, the major east-west thoroughfares connecting Downtown to the beaches are **Sunset, Santa Monica, Wilshire, Olympic, Pico,** and **Venice boulevards.**

L.A. DRIVING TIPS

Many Southern California freeways have designated **carpool lanes,** also known as High Occupancy Vehicle (HOV) lanes or "diamond" lanes (after the large, white diamonds painted on the blacktop along the lane). Most require two passengers (others three), and they have rigidly enforced zones where you can't leave the HOV lane for several miles at a time (I've missed many an exit because of this rule). Most on-ramps are metered during even light congestion to regulate the flow of traffic onto the freeway; cars in HOV lanes can usually pass the signal without stopping. Although there are tales of drivers sitting life-size mannequins next to them to beat the system, don't use the HOV lane unless you have the right numbers—fines begin around $350.

Keep in mind that California has a seat-belt law for both drivers *and* passengers, so buckle up before you venture out.

Here are a few more tips for driving around:

o **Allow more time than you think it will actually take to get where you're going.** You need to make time for traffic and parking. Double your margin in weekday rush hours, from 7 to 9am and again from 3 to 7pm. Also, the freeways tend to be much more crowded than you'd expect all day on Saturdays, especially heading toward the ocean on a sunny day.

o **You may turn right at a red light after stopping unless a sign says otherwise.** Likewise, you may turn left on a red light from a one-way street onto another one-way street after coming to a full stop.

o **Plan your exact route before you set out.** Know where you need to exit the freeway and/or make turns—especially lefts—and merge well in advance. Otherwise, you're likely to find yourself waving at your freeway exit from an inside lane or your turnoff from an outside one. Pulling over and whipping out your map if you screw up is never easy, and it's near impossible on the freeways. Better yet, bring your smartphone and use its map app (as long as you can do it hands-free), or rent a car that has a GPS unit.

o **Pedestrians in Los Angeles have the right of way at all times,** so stop for people who have stepped off the curb.

o **Get detailed driving directions to your hotel.** Save yourself the frustration of trying to find your hotel—plot it on a map and call the hotel for the best route.

PARKING

Explaining the parking situation in Los Angeles is like explaining the English language—there are more exceptions than rules. In some areas, every establishment has a convenient free lot or ample street parking; other areas are pretty manageable as long as you have a quick eye and are willing to take a few turns around the block, but there are some frustrating parts of town (particularly around restaurants after 7pm) where you might have to give in and use valet parking. Whether there's valet parking depends more on the congestion of the area than on the elegance of the establishment; the size of an establishment's lot often simply won't allow for self-parking. These days, restaurants and nightclubs rarely provide a complimentary valet service; more often than not they charge between $5 and $15. Some areas, like Santa Monica and Beverly Hills, offer self-park lots and garages near the neighborhood action; costs range from $2 to $10. In the heart of Hollywood and on the Sunset Strip, self-park lots can run up to $20. Most of the hotels that are listed in this book offer both self-parking and/or valet parking, which ranges from $10 to $40 per day.

 Freeway Names & Numbers

Locals refer to L.A. freeways by both their numbers and their names. For example, I-10 is both "the 10" and "the Santa Monica Freeway."

Here are a few more parking tips to remember:

o **Beware of parking in residential neighborhoods.** Many areas allow only permit parking, so you will be ticketed and possibly towed (especially in the West Hollywood and Beverly Hills neighborhoods).

o **Have plenty of quarters on hand.** Angelenos scrounge for parking-meter quarters like New Yorkers do for laundry coinage: They are the equivalent of pure gold. Save yourself some hassle and just buy a roll or two at your bank before you leave home. Note: More and more cities are now accepting credit cards and/or converting to centralized parking machines, but in areas with the old-style meters, many businesses maintain a no-change policy, unless you make a purchase.

- **Be creative.** Case the immediate area by taking a turn around the block. In many parts of the city, you can find an unrestricted street space less than a block away from eager valets.
- **Read posted restrictions carefully.** You can avoid a ticket if you pay attention to the signs, which warn of street-cleaning schedules and those sneaky rush-hour "no parking" zones.
- **Don't lose your car in a parking garage.** This seems like obvious advice, but you'd be surprised how easily you can lose your car at an L.A. megamall. Most garage levels and subsections are letter-, number-, and color-coded, so make a mental note after you lock your car.

By Public Transportation

There are visitors who successfully tour Los Angeles entirely by public transportation (I've met them both), but we can't honestly recommend that plan for most readers. L.A. is a metropolis that's grown up around—and is best traversed by—the automobile, and many areas are inaccessible without one. As a result, an overwhelming number of visitors rent a car for their stay. Still, if you're in the city for only a short time, are on a very tight budget, or don't expect to be moving around a lot, public transport might be for you.

The city's trains and buses are operated by the **Los Angeles County Metropolitan Transit Authority (MTA;** ✆ **213/922-2000;** www.mta.net), and MTA brochures and schedules are available at every area visitor center.

By Bus

Spread-out stops, sluggish service, and frequent transfers make extensive touring by bus impractical. For straight shots, short hops and occasional jaunts, however, buses are economical and environmentally correct. However, I don't recommend riding buses late at night.

The basic bus fare is $1.50 for all local lines, with transfers costing 35¢. A Metro Day Pass is $6 and gives you unlimited bus and rail rides all day long; these can be purchased while boarding any Metro Bus (exact change is needed) or at the self-service vending machines at the Metro Rail stations. *Note:* Up to two kids age 4 and under may travel free with each fare-paying adult.

The **Downtown Area Short Hop (DASH)** shuttle system operates buses throughout Downtown and Hollywood. Service runs every 5 to 30 minutes, depending on the time of day, and costs just 35¢. Contact the Department of Transportation (✆ **213/808-2273;** www.ladottransit.com) for schedules and route information (it's pretty confusing—you'll definitely need a weekday *and* weekend map).

The **Cityline** shuttle is a great way to get around West Hollywood on weekdays and Saturdays (9am–6pm). For 50¢, it'll take you from La Brea Ave. and Fountain Ave. all the way to Beverly Blvd and San Vicente Blvd area near Cedars-Sinai Hospital. For more information, call ✆ **800/447-2189.**

Public-Transport Tip

The L.A. County Metropolitan Transit Authority (MTA) website, www.metro. net, provides all the practical information you need—hours, routes, fares—for using L.A.'s nearly invisible network of public transportation (buses, subways, light rail).

THE BEST OF L.A. online

Keep in mind that this is a press-time snapshot of leading websites—some may have crashed, evolved, changed, or moved by the time you read this. My favorite? The Los Angeles Yelp website **(http://www.yelp.com/la)**—it's an extremely popular site for "Yelpers" (faithful site users) to share their candid opinions of just about every hotel, restaurant, and club in the city.

- **Yelp.com**: The beauty of Yelp is that anyone can write a review, which is certainly democratic, but it also means credibility runs the gamut. If you pay close attention to the language employed, the examples given and look for patterns, it's easy to read between the lines. Yelp offers not only reviews of individual venues, but also themed lists, discussion forums, and a section dedicated to the most bookmarked pages each month—a good indication of what's currently hot and trendy.

- **LA.COM**: The content has been scaled way back here, but there's still a decent selection of blog-like content and event info.

- **www.latimes.com/theguide/**: Hosted by the *L.A. Times,* the **Find Local section** is loaded with entertainment and nightlife reviews and listings in greater Los Angeles. Use the pull-down menu for categories ranging from "Theater & Dance" to "Family & Festivals." Other topics include restaurants, art and museums, and Southern California side trips. Use the search box to zoom in on whatever you're seeking. Online ticket

purchasing via Ticketmaster is available as well.

- **www.at-la.com**: This is the home page of **@LA,** whose exceptional search engine provides links to close to 60,000 sites in thousands of categories relating to all of Southern California.

- **www.lamag.com**: This online edition of *Los Angeles* magazine offers "The Guide," an oft-updated listing of L.A.'s theater, music scene, museums, and more, as well as an excellent "Dining Out" guide listing hundreds of restaurants organized geographically.

- **www.discoverlosangeles.com**: The **L.A. Convention & Visitors Bureau** (also known as LA INC.) lets you browse its site by region or category; view sample itineraries keyed to selected neighborhoods, activities, ethnic themes, or type of visitor; and use the "Plan Your Vacation" section to assemble a hotel/rental car/activity itinerary based on your interests.

- **www.santamonica.com**: Everything you could possibly want to know about travel and tourist information in Santa Monica is covered in this vibrant website hosted by the Convention & Visitors Bureau. Also available is an online reservation system with comprehensive information on hotels and motels.

- **www.beverlyhillscvb.com**: This official site of the Beverly Hills Visitors Bureau is as perfectly manicured as Beverly Hills itself, offering tons of practical information (including an indispensable map of parking lots, complete with rates), plus extras like a short historical walking tour and a list of spas and salons as long as Cher's wigs.

- **www.lastagealliance.com**: LA Stage Alliance is an association of live theaters and producers in Los Angeles (and the organization that puts on the yearly Ovation Awards, L.A.'s answer to Broadway's Tonys). The website is a great place to look for small and midsize productions, plus information on which shows are currently on sale at the half-price.

- **www.visitwesthollywood.com**: The West Hollywood Convention & Visitors Bureau hosts this frequently updated guide to everything to see/do/eat/buy in WeHo, as it's come to be known. Learn about the Avenues of Art & Design (a district of L.A.'s best galleries and showrooms), plus browse extensive activity and service guides for WeHo's prominent gay and lesbian community.

- **www.tvtickets.com**: This is your online source for free tickets to dozens of sitcoms and talk shows. The site, hosted by Audiences Unlimited, Inc., includes a taping schedule, studio information, news about shows, updates on specials, and just about everything else you need to help you figure out what show you'd like to catch.

- **www.disneyland.com**: Check out the resorts, dining facilities,

travel-package options, and activities and rides in the Magic Kingdom at Disneyland's official website. Get specific hours and ride closures in advance by selecting the day of your visit; this site is guaranteed to rev up your enthusiasm level. Also visit **Disneyland: Inside & Out** (**www. intercotwest.com**), an independent guide to Disneyland with updates on activities, rides, entertainment, and the ever-expanding Disneyland resort; consult tips on what to bring, best times of year to visit, and more.

- **www.universalstudioshollywood. com**: Take a virtual tour of the Universal Studios Hollywood attractions, view current show schedules, check out special ticket offers (and purchase tickets online), or play games based on Universal's most popular rides.

- **www.laweekly.com**: Straight from the pages of the alternative *L.A. Weekly* paper, this site combines listings with social commentary. It has an events calendar, arts listings and critiques, and restaurant reviews.

- **www.losangeles.com**: This is the L.A. feature of Boulevards New Media, whose national alternative websites emphasize travel, arts, entertainment, contemporary culture, and politics.

- **www.festivalfinder.com** or **www. festivalusa.com**: These sites can locate music and other festivals in and around Los Angeles.

By Rail & Subway

The **MetroRail** system is a sore subject around town. For years, the MTA has been digging up the city's streets, sucking in huge amounts of tax money, and pushing exhaust vents up through peaceful parkland—and for what? Let's face it, L.A. will never have New York's subway or San Francisco's BART. Today the system is still in its infancy, mainly popular with commuters from outlying suburbs. Here's an overview of what's currently in place:

The **Metro Blue Line,** a mostly aboveground rail line, connects Downtown Los Angeles with Long Beach. As with all other metro rail lines, it operates daily from 5am to midnight.

The **Metro Red Line,** L.A.'s first subway, opened a highly publicized Hollywood–Universal City extension in 2000. The line begins at Union Station, the city's main train depot, and travels west underneath Wilshire Boulevard, looping north into Hollywood and the San Fernando Valley.

The **Metro Purple Line** subway starts at Union Station, shares six stations with the Red Line Downtown, and continues to the Mid-Wilshire area.

The **Metro Green Line** runs for 20 miles along the center of I-105; the Glenn Anderson (Century) Freeway, and connects Norwalk in eastern Los Angeles County to LAX and Redondo Beach. A connection with the Blue Line offers visitors access from LAX to Downtown L.A. or Long Beach.

The **Metro Gold Line** is a 14-mile link between Pasadena and Union Station in Downtown L.A. Stops include Old Pasadena, the Southwest Museum, and Chinatown.

The base Metro fare is $1.50 for all lines. A Metro Day Pass is $6 and weekly passes are $20. Passes are available at Metro Customer Centers and local convenience and grocery stores. For more information on public transportation—including construction updates, timetables, and details on purchasing tokens or passes—call **MTA** at ℂ **213/922-2000** or, better yet, log on to their handy website at **www.metro.net**.

By Taxi

Distances are long in Los Angeles, and cab fares are high; even a short trip can cost $20 or more. Taxis currently charge $2.85 at the flag drop, plus $2.70 per mile. A service charge of $2.50 is added to fares originating from LAX. Beware, there's also an additional charge of 30¢ for each 37 seconds on delay, and if you know anything about L.A. traffic, that can really add up fast.

Except in the heart of Downtown, cabs will usually not pull over when hailed. Cabstands are at airports, at Downtown's Union Station, and at major hotels. To ensure a ride, order a taxi in advance from **Checker Cab** (ℂ **323/654-8400**), **L.A. Taxi** (ℂ **213/627-7000**), or **United Taxi** (ℂ **800/822-8294**).

[FastFACTS] LOS ANGELES

Area Codes Within the past 30 years, L.A. has gone from having a single area code (213) to a whopping seven. Even residents can't keep up. As of press time, here's the basic layout: Those areas west of La Cienega Boulevard, including Beverly Hills and the city's beach communities, use either the **310 or 424** area codes. Portions of Los Angeles County east and south of the city, including Long Beach, are in the **562** area. The San

Fernando Valley has the **818** area code, while points east—including parts of Burbank, Glendale, and Pasadena—use the **626** code. What happened to 213, you ask? The Downtown business area still uses **213.** All other numbers, including Griffith Park, Hollywood, and parts of West Hollywood (east of La Cienega Blvd.) now use the area code **323.** If it's all too much to remember, just call directory assistance at ✆ **411.**

Automobile Organizations   Motor clubs will supply maps, suggested routes, guidebooks, accident and bail-bond insurance, and emergency road service. The **American Automobile Association (AAA)** is the major auto club in the United States. If you belong to a motor club in your home country, inquire about AAA reciprocity before you leave. You may be able to join AAA even if you're not a member of a reciprocal club; to inquire, call AAA (✆ **877/428-2277;** www.aaa.com). AAA has a nationwide emergency road service telephone number (✆ 800/AAA-HELP [222-4357]).

Business Hours   Offices are usually open weekdays from 9am to 5pm. Banks are open weekdays from 9am to 5pm or later and sometimes Saturday mornings. Stores typically open between 9 and 10am and close between 5 and 6pm from Monday through Saturday. Stores in shopping complexes or malls tend to stay open late: until about 9pm on weekdays and weekends, and many malls and larger department stores are open on Sundays.

Customs   Every visitor 21 years of age or older may bring in, free of duty, the following: (1) 1 U.S. quart of alcohol; (2) 200 cigarettes, 50 cigars (but not from Cuba), or 3 pounds of smoking tobacco; and (3) $100 worth of gifts. These exemptions are offered to travelers who spend at least 72 hours in the United States and who have not claimed them within the preceding 6 months. It is forbidden to bring into the country almost any meat products (including canned, fresh, and dried meat products such as bouillon, soup mixes, and so on). Generally, condiments including vinegars, oils, pickled goods, spices, coffee, tea, and some cheeses and baked goods are permitted. Avoid rice products, as rice can often harbor insects. Bringing fruit and vegetables is prohibited since they may harbor pests or disease. International visitors may carry in or out up to $10,000 in U.S. or foreign currency with no formalities; larger sums must be declared to U.S. Customs on entering or leaving, which includes filing form CM 4790. For details regarding U.S. Customs and Border Protection, consult your nearest U.S. embassy or consulate, or **U.S. Customs** (www.customs.gov).

For information on what you're allowed to bring home, contact one of the following agencies:

U.S. Citizens: U.S. Customs & Border Protection (CBP), 1300 Pennsylvania Ave., NW, Washington, DC 20229 (✆ **877/287-8667;** www.cbp.gov).

Canadian Citizens: Canada Border Services Agency, Ottawa, Ontario, K1A 0L8 (✆ **800/461-9999** in Canada, or 204/983-3500; www.cbsa-asfc.gc.ca).

U.K. Citizens: HM Revenue & Customs, Crownhill Court, Tailyour Road, Plymouth, PL6 5BZ (✆ **0845/010-9000;** from outside the U.K., 020/8929-0152; www.hmce.gov.uk).

Australian Citizens: Australian Customs Service, Customs House, 5 Constitution Ave., Canberra City, ACT 2601 (✆ **1300/363-263;** from outside Australia, 612/6275-6666; www.customs.gov.au).

New Zealand Citizens: New Zealand Customs, The Customhouse, 17–21 Whitmore St., Box 2218, Wellington, 6140 (✆ **04/473-6099** or 0800/428-786; www.customs.govt.nz).

Disabled Travelers   Los Angeles's spirit of tolerance and diversity has made it a welcoming place for travelers with disabilities. Strict building codes make most public facilities and attractions extremely accessible (though some historic sites and older buildings simply can't accommodate drastic remodeling), and the city provides many services for those with disabilities.

The **Los Angeles County Commission on Disabilities** (📞 **213/974-1053**) provides telephone referrals and information about L.A. for those with physical disabilities.

Organizations that offer a vast range of resources and assistance to travelers with limited mobility include **MossRehab** (📞 **800/CALL-MOSS** [225-5667]; www.mossresource net.org), the **American Foundation for the Blind** (AFB; 📞 **800/232-5463**; www.afb.org), and **SATH** (Society for Accessible Travel & Hospitality; 📞 **212/447-7284**; www.sath.org). **Air Ambulance Card** (www.airambulancecard.com) allows you to select top-notch hospitals in case of an emergency, either domestically or internationally.

Drinking Laws   The legal age for purchase and consumption of alcoholic beverages is 21; proof of age is required and often requested at bars, nightclubs, and restaurants, so it's always a good idea to bring ID when you go out.

Do not carry open containers of alcohol in your car or any public area that isn't zoned for alcohol consumption. The police can fine you on the spot. Don't even think about driving while intoxicated.

Driving Rules   See "Getting There" and "Getting Around" sections earlier in this chapter.

Electricity   Like Canada, the United States uses 110–120 volts AC (60 cycles), compared to 220–240 volts AC (50 cycles) in most of Europe, Australia, and New Zealand. Downward converters that change 220–240 volts to 110–120 volts are difficult to find in the United States, so bring one with you.

Embassies & Consulates   All embassies are located in the nation's capital, Washington, D.C. Some consulates are located in major U.S. cities, and most nations have a mission to the United Nations in New York City. If your country isn't listed below, call for directory information in Washington, D.C. (📞 **202/555-1212**) or check **www.embassy. org/embassies**.

The embassy of **Australia** is at 1601 Massachusetts Ave. NW, Washington, DC 20036 (📞 **202/797-3000**; www.usa.embassy.gov.au).

The embassy of **Canada** is at 501 Pennsylvania Ave. NW, Washington, DC 20001 (📞 **202/682-1740**; www.canadainternational.gc.ca/washington). Other Canadian consulates are in Buffalo (New York), Detroit, Los Angeles, New York, and Seattle.

The embassy of **Ireland** is at 2234 Massachusetts Ave. NW, Washington, DC 20008 (📞 **202/462-3939**; www.irelandemb.org). Irish consulates are in Boston, Chicago, New York, San Francisco, and other cities. See website for complete listing.

The embassy of **New Zealand** is at 37 Observatory Circle NW, Washington, DC 20008 (📞 **202/328-4800**; www.nzembassy.com). New Zealand consulates are in Los Angeles, Salt Lake City, San Francisco, and Seattle.

The embassy of the **United Kingdom** is at 3100 Massachusetts Ave. NW, Washington, DC 20008 (📞 **202/588-6500**; http://ukinusa.fco.gov.uk). Other British consulates are in Atlanta, Boston, Chicago, Cleveland, Houston, Los Angeles, New York, San Francisco, and Seattle.

Emergencies   Call 📞 **911** to report a fire, call the police, or get an ambulance anywhere in the United States. This is a toll-free call (no coins are required at public telephones).

If you encounter traveler's problems, call the Los Angeles chapter of the **Traveler's Aid Society** (📞 **310/646-2270**; www.travelersaid.org), a nationwide, nonprofit, social service organization that helps travelers in difficult straits. Its services might include reuniting families separated while traveling, providing food and/or shelter to people stranded without cash, and even emotional counseling.

Family Travel   If you have enough trouble getting your kids out of the house in the morning, dragging them thousands of miles away may seem like an insurmountable challenge. But family travel can be immensely rewarding, giving you new ways of seeing the world through smaller pairs of eyes.

Baby Gear & Babysitters

Babyland rents strollers, cribs, car seats, and the like from its store located at 7134 Topanga Canyon Blvd. (📞 **818/704-7849**). Rates vary; expect to spend around $45 per week for strollers and $55 per week for a crib. If you need a babysitter in L.A., contact the **Baby-Sitters Guild** (📞 **818/552-2229** or 310/837-1800), named the city's best by *Los Angeles* magazine. The concierge at larger hotels can also often recommend a reliable sitter.

To make things easier for families vacationing in L.A., I've included three family-friendly sidebars that highlight the best hotels (p. 77), restaurants (p. 123), and attractions (p. 159) for parents and kids. Also watch for the "Kids" icon throughout this guide.

Gasoline (Petrol) At press time, in the U.S., the cost of gasoline (also known as gas, but never petrol), is at an all-time high (about $4 per gallon). Taxes are already included in the printed price. One U.S. gallon equals 3.8 liters or .85 imperial gallons.

Health Overall, L.A. is a healthy place to visit, although people with respiratory problems should keep in mind that L.A.'s air quality can often be poor, particularly in the valleys in the mid- to late summer (too many cars, too little wind). When the air quality is really bad, warnings are aired on local TV and radio stations encouraging people to avoid outdoor activities. If you're concerned about smog levels affecting your vacation, you can contact the **South Coast Air Quality Management District** at 📞 **800/CUT-SMOG** (288-7664) or www.aqmd.gov, which also publishes "Air Quality Forecast/Advisories" for the greater L.A. region. ***Tip:*** If you want to avoid the summer smog, stay and play along the coast. The light offshore breezes usually keep the beach communities relatively smog free.

Also, for people not used to so much sun—L.A. averages 320 sunny days a year—be sure to protect yourself from the sun's rays by wearing appropriate clothing (long-sleeve shirts, wide-brim hats) and/or using sunscreen with an SPF rating of at least 30 and broad-spectrum UVA/UVB protection.

Holidays Banks, government offices, post offices, and many stores, restaurants, and museums are closed on the following legal national holidays: January 1 (New Year's Day), the third Monday in January (Martin Luther King, Jr., Day), the third Monday in February (Presidents' Day), the last Monday in May (Memorial Day), July 4 (Independence Day), the first Monday in September (Labor Day), the second Monday in October (Columbus Day), November 11 (Veterans Day/Armistice Day), the fourth Thursday in November (Thanksgiving Day), and December 25 (Christmas). The Tuesday after the first Monday in November is Election Day, a federal government holiday in presidential election years (held every 4 years, and next in 2012).

For more information on holidays see "Los Angeles Calendar of Events," in chapter 2.

Hospitals The centrally located (and world-famous) **Cedars-Sinai Medical Center,** 8700 Beverly Blvd., Los Angeles (📞 **310/423-3277**), has a 24-hour emergency room staffed by some of the country's finest doctors.

Insurance For information on traveler's insurance, trip cancellation insurance, and medical insurance while traveling, please visit www.frommers.com/tips.

Internet Access Los Angeles is totally wired. You'll find that many cafes have wireless access, as do most hotels, coffee shops, and even fast-food joints.

Legal Aid If you are "pulled over" for a minor infraction (such as speeding), never attempt to pay the fine directly to a police officer; this could be construed as attempted bribery, a much more serious crime. Pay fines by mail, or directly into the hands of the clerk of the court. If accused of a more serious offense, say and do nothing before consulting a lawyer. Here the burden is on the state to prove a person's guilt beyond a reasonable doubt, and everyone has the right to remain silent, whether he or she is suspected of a crime or actually arrested. Once arrested, a person can make one telephone call to a party of his or her choice. International visitors should call your embassy or consulate.

LGBT Travelers   When the city of **West Hollywood** was incorporated in 1984, it elected a lesbian mayor and a predominantly gay city council. West Hollywood, also known as WeHo, has been waving the rainbow flag ever since. While L.A.'s large gay community is too vast to be contained in this 2-square-mile city, West Hollywood has the largest concentration of gay- and lesbian-oriented businesses and services. Santa Monica, Venice, Silver Lake, and Studio City are other lesbian and gay enclaves.

There are many gay-oriented publications with information and up-to-date listings, including *Frontiers,* a Southern California–based biweekly; Metro Source magazine, a New York and L.A.-based monthly. The periodicals above are available at most newsstands citywide.

The **International Gay and Lesbian Travel Association** (IGLTA; ✆ 954/630-1637; www.iglta.org) is the trade association for the gay and lesbian travel industry, and offers an online directory of gay- and lesbian-friendly travel businesses and tour operators.

Gay.com Travel (http://daily.gay.com/travel or www.outtraveler.com) is an excellent online successor to the popular *Out & About* print magazine. It provides regularly updated information about gay-owned, gay-oriented, and gay-friendly lodging, dining, sightseeing, nightlife, and shopping establishments in every important destination worldwide.

The following travel guides are available at many bookstores, or you can order them from any online bookseller: *Spartacus International Gay Guide, 40th Edition* (www.spartacusworld.com/gayguide); *Odysseus: The International Gay Travel Planner, 17th Edition;* and the *Damron* guides (www.damron.com), with separate, annual books for gay men and lesbians.

Mail   At press time, domestic postage rates were 28¢ for a postcard and 44¢ for a letter. For international mail, a first-class letter of up to 1 ounce costs 98¢ (75¢ to Canada and 79¢ to Mexico); a first-class postcard costs the same as a letter. For more information go to **www.usps.com**.

If you aren't sure what your address will be in the United States, mail can be sent to you, in your name, c/o General Delivery at the main post office of the city or region where you expect to be. (Call ✆ **800/275-8777** for information on the nearest post office.) The addressee must pick up mail in person and must produce proof of identity (driver's license, passport, and so on). Most post offices will hold your mail for up to 1 month, and are open Monday to Friday from 8am to 6pm, and Saturday from 9am to 3pm.

Always include zip codes when mailing items in the U.S. If you don't know your zip code, visit http://zip4.usps.com.

Medical Requirements   Unless you're arriving from an area known to be suffering from an epidemic (particularly cholera or yellow fever), inoculations or vaccinations are not required for entry into the United States.

Money & Costs   Frommer's lists exact prices in the local currency. The currency conversions quoted below were correct at press time. However, rates fluctuate, so before departing consult a currency exchange website such as http://www.xe.com/ to check up-to-the-minute rates.

THE VALUE OF THE U.S. DOLLAR VS. OTHER POPULAR CURRENCIES

US$	Can$	UK£	Euro (€)	Aus$	NZ$
1.00	0.97	0.62	0.71	0.97	1.31

It's always advisable to bring money in a variety of forms on a vacation: a mix of cash, credit cards, and ATM cards. You should also have enough petty cash upon arrival to cover airport incidentals, tipping, and transportation to your hotel. You can always withdraw money upon arrival at an airport ATM, but you'll still need to make smaller change for tipping. **Note:** Many banks impose a fee every time you use a card at another bank's ATM, and that fee is often higher for international transactions (up to $5 or more) than for domestic ones (where they're rarely more than $2). In addition, the bank from which you withdraw cash may charge its own fee. To compare banks' ATM fees within the U.S., use **www.bankrate.com**. Visitors from outside the U.S. should also find out whether their bank assesses a 1% to 3% fee on charges incurred abroad. One way around these fees is to ask for cash back at grocery, drug, and convenience stores that accept ATM cards and don't charge usage fees (be sure to ask). Of course, you'll have to purchase something first.

The most common bills in the U.S. are the $1 (a "buck"), $5, $10, and $20 denominations. There are also $2 bills (seldom encountered), $50 bills, and $100 bills. (The last two are usually not welcome as payment for small purchases.)

Coins come in seven denominations: 1¢ (1 cent, or a penny); 5¢ (5 cents, or a nickel); 10¢ (10 cents, or a dime); 25¢ (25 cents, or a quarter); 50¢ (50 cents, or a half dollar); the gold-colored Sacagawea coin, worth $1; and the rare silver dollar.

WHAT THINGS COST IN LOS ANGELES	US$
Taxi from the airport to Downtown	46.50
SuperShuttle from LAX to West Hollywood area	26.00
Fine for expired parking meter	35.00–60.00
Double room at the Beverly Hills Hotel (absurdly expensive)	530.00
Double room at the Beach House at Hermosa Beach (expensive)	229.00
Double room at the Venice Beach House (moderate)	150.00
Double room at the Sea Shore Motel (inexpensive)	110.00
Lunch for one at Cafe Pinot (moderate)	22.00
Bacon Chili Cheese Dog at Pink's	4.90
Dinner for one, without wine, at Koi (expensive)	50.00
Dinner for one, without wine, at Border Grill (moderate)	25.00
Dinner for one, without wine, at Good Stuff (inexpensive)	12.00
Cup of coffee at Philippe the Original	0.09
Cup of coffee at the Peninsula Hotel	5.75
2-hour StarLine Movie Star's Home Tour	39.00
Admission to the Hollywood Wax Museum	12.95
Admission to the Getty Museum	Free
Full-price movie ticket	15.00

Newspapers & Magazines   The *Los Angeles Times* (www.latimes.com) is a high-quality daily with strong local and national coverage. Its "Find Local" section (http://findlocal.latimes.com) is an excellent guide to entertainment in and around L.A., and includes listings of what's doing and where to do it. The *L.A. Weekly* (www.laweekly.com), a free weekly listings magazine, is packed with information on current events around town. *Los Angeles* magazine (www.lamag.com) is a city-based monthly full of news, information, and previews of L.A.'s art, music, and food scenes. **World Book & News Co.,** at 1652 N. Cahuenga Blvd. (℃ **323/465-4352**), near Hollywood and Vine and Grauman's Chinese Theatre, stocks lots of out-of-town and foreign papers and magazines. No one minds if you browse through the magazines, but you'll be reprimanded for thumbing through the newspapers. It's open 24 hours.

Passports   Virtually every air traveler entering the U.S. is required to show a passport. All persons, including U.S. citizens, traveling by air between the United States and Canada, Mexico, Central and South America, the Caribbean, and Bermuda are required to present a valid passport. *Note:* U.S. and Canadian citizens entering the U.S. at land and sea ports of entry from within the Western Hemisphere must now also present a passport or other documents compliant with the Western Hemisphere Travel Initiative (WHTI; see www.getyouhome.gov for details). Children 15 and under may continue entering with only a U.S. birth certificate, or other proof of U.S. citizenship.

See http://www.frommers.com/tips/ for information on how to obtain a passport. See "Embassies & Consulates," above, for whom to contact if you lose yours while traveling in the U.S.

Passport Offices

○ **For Residents of Australia**   Contact the **Australian Passport Information Service** at ℃ **131-232,** or visit the government website at www.passports.gov.au.

○ **For Residents of Canada**   Contact the central **Passport Office,** Department of Foreign Affairs and International Trade, Gatineau, QC K1A 0G3 (℃ **800/567-6868;** www.ppt.gc.ca).

○ **For Residents of Ireland**   Contact the **Passport Office,** Setanta Centre, Molesworth Street, Dublin 2 (℃ **01/671-1633;** www.foreignaffairs.gov.ie).

○ **For Residents of New Zealand**   Contact the **Passports Office** at ℃ **0800/225-050** in New Zealand or 04/474-8100, or log on to www.dia.govt.nz.

○ **For Residents of the United Kingdom**   Visit your nearest passport office, major post office, or travel agency or contact the **United Kingdom Passport Service** at ℃ **0870/521-0410.**

○ **For Residents of the United States**   To find your regional passport office, either check the U.S. State Department website (www.state.gov) or call the **National Passport Information Center** toll-free number (℃ **877/487-2778**) for automated information.

Pets   If you're thinking of taking your pet along with you to romp on a California beach, make sure you do a little research. For one thing, dogs are restricted from most public beaches in the L.A. area. To find out where you can bring man's best friend, check out the online **Pets Welcome** service (www.petswelcome.com). The site also lists pet-related publications, medical travel tips, and resources.

A good book to carry along is *The California Dog Lover's Companion: The Insider's Scoop on Where to Take Your Dog,* a 900-page source for complete statewide listings of fenced dog parks, dog-friendly beaches, and other indispensable information.

Los Angeles has strict leash laws (including stiff penalties for failing to pick up waste), prompting the formation of a dog owner/supporter group called **Freeplay** (℃ **310/379-1207;** www.freeplay.org). Contact them for the latest developments on dog-related issues, including information on off-leash parks around town.

In the event that your pet requires medical care while you're visiting, call or visit the **California Animal Hospital,** 1736 S. Sepulveda Blvd., stes. A–B (south of Santa Monica Blvd.), Los Angeles (📞 **310/479-3336**). The **Animal Surgical & Emergency Center** (📞 **310/473-1561**), 1535 S. Sepulveda Blvd., is open 24 hours a day. The website **www.thepetplace.org** is another good source for emergency animal clinics.

Police   In an emergency, dial 📞 **911.** For nonemergency police matters, call 📞 **213/485-2121;** in Beverly Hills, dial 📞 **310/550-4951.**

Safety   For a big city, Los Angeles is relatively safe, and requires only that you use common sense (for example, don't leave your new video camera on the seat of your parked car). However, in neighborhoods such as East L.A. and parts of Downtown (at night especially), it's a good idea to pay attention to your surroundings.

Avoid carrying valuables with you on the street, and don't display expensive cameras or electronic equipment. Hold on to your handbag, and place your wallet in an inside pocket. In theaters, restaurants, and other public places, keep your possessions in sight.

Remember also that hotels are open to the public, and in a large hotel, security may not be able to screen everyone entering. Always lock your room door—don't assume that inside your hotel you are automatically safe.

Driving safety is important, too. If you drive off a highway into a questionable neighborhood, leave the area as quickly as possible. If you have an accident, even on the highway, stay in your car with the doors locked until you assess the situation or until the police arrive. If you're bumped from behind on the street or are involved in a minor accident with no injuries, and the situation appears to be suspicious, motion to the other driver to follow you. Never get out of your car in such situations. Go directly to the nearest police precinct, well-lit service station, or 24-hour store (again, having that GPS handy is key). Report the incident to the police department immediately by calling 📞 **911.** This is a free call, even from pay phones.

Senior Travel   Nearly every attraction in Los Angeles offers a senior discount; age requirements vary, and specific prices are listed in chapter 6. Public transportation and movie theaters also have reduced rates. Don't be shy about asking for discounts, but always carry some kind of identification, such as a driver's license, that shows your date of birth.

Members of **AARP,** 601 E St. NW, Washington, DC 20049 (📞 **888/687-2277;** www.aarp.org), get discounts on hotels, airfares, and car rentals. AARP offers members a wide range of benefits, and anyone 50 and over can join.

Smoking   Heavy smokers are in for a tough time in Los Angeles. Smoking is banned in public buildings, sports arenas, elevators, theaters, banks, lobbies, restaurants, offices, stores, bed-and-breakfasts, most small hotels, and bars. That's right—as of January 1, 1998, you can't even smoke in a bar in California. The only exception is a bar where drinks are served solely by the owner. Implemented in March 2011, there are now further restrictions on smoking in outdoor-dining areas. Bar patios are being targeted next. Entire hotel properties are increasingly 100-percent smoke-free. Once upon a time, people would turn a blind eye, but now that fines are so heavy, this is no longer true.

Taxes   The United States has no value-added tax (VAT) or other indirect tax at the national level. Every state, county, and city may levy its own local tax on all purchases, including hotel and restaurant checks and airline tickets. These taxes will not appear on price tags. Sales tax in Los Angeles is 9.75%. Hotel tax is charged on the room tariff only (which is not subject to sales tax) and is set by the city, ranging from 12% to 17% around Southern California.

Telephones   Many convenience groceries and packaging services sell **prepaid calling cards** in denominations up to $50; for international visitors, these can be the least expensive way to call home. Many public pay phones at airports now accept American Express,

MasterCard, and Visa credit cards. **Local calls** made from pay phones in most locales typically cost 35¢. Most long-distance and international calls can be dialed directly from any phone. **For calls within the United States and to Canada,** dial 1 followed by the area code and the seven-digit number. **For other international calls,** dial 011 followed by the country code, city code, and the number you are calling.

Calls to area codes **800, 888, 877,** and **866** are toll-free. However, calls to area codes **700** and **900** (chat lines, bulletin boards, "dating" services, and so on) can be very expensive—usually a charge of 95¢ to $3 or more per minute, and they sometimes have minimum charges that can run as high as $15 or more.

For **reversed-charge or collect calls,** and for person-to-person calls, dial the number 0 then the area code and number; an operator will come on the line, and you should specify whether you are calling collect, person-to-person, or both. If your operator-assisted call is international, ask for the overseas operator.

For **local directory assistance** ("information"), dial **411;** for long-distance information, dial 1, then the appropriate area code and **555-1212.**

Time   Los Angeles is in the Pacific Standard Time zone, which is 8 hours behind Greenwich Mean Time and 3 hours behind Eastern Standard Time.

The continental United States is divided into **four time zones:** Eastern Standard Time (EST), Central Standard Time (CST), Mountain Standard Time (MST), and Pacific Standard Time (PST). Alaska and Hawaii have their own zones. For example, when it's 9am in Los Angeles (PST), it's 7am in Honolulu (HST), 10am in Denver (MST), 11am in Chicago (CST), noon in New York City (EST), 5pm in London (GMT), and 2am the next day in Sydney.

Daylight saving time is in effect from 1am on the second Sunday in March to 1am on the first Sunday in November, except in Arizona, Hawaii, the U.S. Virgin Islands, and Puerto Rico. Daylight saving time moves the clock 1 hour ahead of standard time.

Tipping   In hotels, tip **bellhops** at least $1 per bag ($2–$3 if you have a lot of luggage) and tip the **chamber staff** $1 to $2 per day (more if you've left a disaster area for him or her to clean up). Tip the **doorman** or **concierge** only if he or she has provided you with some specific service (for example, calling a cab for you or obtaining difficult-to-get theater tickets). Tip the **valet-parking attendant** $1 to $2 every time you get your car.

In restaurants, bars, and nightclubs, tip **service staff** and **bartenders** 15% to 20% of the check, tip **checkroom attendants** $1 per garment, and tip **valet-parking attendants** $1 to $2 per vehicle.

As for other service personnel, tip **cabdrivers** 15% of the fare; tip **skycaps** at airports at least $1 per bag ($2–$3 if you have a lot of luggage); and tip **hairdressers** and **barbers** 15% to 20%.

Toilets   You won't find public toilets or "restrooms" on the streets in most U.S. cities, but they can be found in hotel lobbies, bars, restaurants, museums, department stores, railway and bus stations, and service stations. Large hotels and fast-food restaurants are often the best bet for clean facilities. Restaurants and bars in resorts or heavily visited areas may reserve their restrooms for patrons.

Visas   For information about U.S. visas, go to **http://travel.state.gov** and click on "Visas." Or go to one of the following websites:

Australian citizens can obtain up-to-date visa information from the **U.S. Embassy Canberra,** Moonah Place, Yarralumla, ACT 2600 (✆ **02/6214-5600**) or by checking the U.S. Diplomatic Mission's website at **http://canberra.usembassy.gov.**

British subjects can obtain up-to-date visa information by calling the **U.S. Embassy Visa Information Line** (✆ **09042/450-100**) or by visiting the "Visas to the U.S." section of the American Embassy London's website at **www.usembassy.org.uk.**

Irish citizens can obtain up-to-date visa information through the **Embassy of the USA Dublin,** 42 Elgin Rd., Ballsbridge Dublin 4, Ireland (**℃ 353/1-668-8777;** http://dublin. usembassy.gov).

Citizens of **New Zealand** can obtain up-to-date visa information by contacting the **U.S. Embassy New Zealand,** 29 Fitzherbert Terrace, Thorndon, Wellington(**℃ 644/462-6000**), or get the information directly from the website at **http://newzealand.usembassy.gov**.

Visitor Information

The **Los Angeles Convention and Visitors Bureau (LA INC.; ℃ 800/228-2452** or 213/624-7300; www.discoverlosangeles.com) is the city's main source for information. In addition to maintaining an informative website, answering telephone inquiries, and sending free visitors kits, the bureau provides two **walk-in visitor centers:** Downtown at 685 S. Figueroa St. at West 7th Street (Mon–Fri 9am–5pm), and in Hollywood at the Hollywood & Highland Center, 6801 Hollywood Blvd. at Highland Avenue (Mon–Fri 10am–10 pm and Sat–Sun 10am–7pm).

Many Los Angeles–area communities also have their own information centers and often maintain detailed and colorful websites that are loaded with timely information. These include the following:

- The **Beverly Hills Visitors Bureau,** 239 S. Beverly Dr. (**℃ 800/345-2210** or 310/248-1015; (http://www.beverlyhillsbehere.com), is open Monday through Friday from 8:30am to 5pm.

- The **Hollywood Arts Council,** P.O. Box 931056, Hollywood, CA 90093 (**℃ 323/462-2355;** www.discoverhollywood.com), publishes the magazine *Discover Hollywood,* a seasonal publication that contains listings and schedules for the area's many theaters, galleries, music venues, and comedy clubs; the current issue is always available online. You can also load up on info at the **Hollywood Visitor Center,** 6801 Hollywood Blvd., (**℃ 323/467-6412**), on the first level of the Hollywood & Highland mall (near the Kodak Theatre's entrance).

- The **West Hollywood Convention and Visitors Bureau,** 8687 Melrose Ave., M-38, West Hollywood, CA 90069 (**℃ 800/368-6020** or 310/289-2525; www.visitwesthollywood.com), is located in the Pacific Design Center and is open Monday through Friday from 8:30am to 6pm.

- The **Santa Monica Convention and Visitors Bureau** (**℃ 800/544-5319** or 310/393-7593; www.santamonica.com) is the best source for information about Santa Monica. The Palisades Park walk-up center is located near the Santa Monica Pier, at1920 Main St., Ste. B, Santa Monica, CA 90405.), and is open daily from 10am to 4pm. Also check out **www.malibu.org** for information about Malibu, to the northwest.

- The **Pasadena Convention and Visitors Bureau** 300 E. Green St.(**℃ 626/795-9311;** www.pasadenacal.com), is open Monday through Friday from 8am to 5pm.

Local tourist boards also are great for information regarding attractions and special events, but they often fail to keep a finger on the pulse of what's "in" in L.A., especially with regard to dining, culture, and nightlife. Several city-oriented newspapers and magazines offer more up-to-date info. *L.A. Weekly* (www.laweekly.com), a free listings magazine, is packed with information on current events around town. It's available from sidewalk news racks and in many stores and restaurants around the city.

The *Los Angeles Times* "Calendar" section of the Sunday paper, a good guide to the world of entertainment in and around L.A., includes listings of what's doing and where to do it. The *Times* also maintains a comprehensive website at www.latimes.com/theguide/. Information is culled from the newspaper's many departments and is always up to date. If you want to check out L.A.'s most immediate news, the *Times*'s main website is **www.latimes.com**.

Los Angeles magazine (**www.lamag.com**) is a glossy city-based monthly full of real news and pure gossip, plus guides to L.A.'s art, music, and food scenes. Its calendar of events gives an excellent overview of goings-on at museums, art galleries, musical venues, and other places. The magazine is available at newsstands around town and in other major U.S. cities; you can also access stories and listings from the current issue on the Internet. Cybersurfers can visit @ **L.A.**'s website, **www.at-la.com**; its search engine, though somewhat tedious, provides links to more than 23,000 sites relating to the L.A. area, including many destinations covered in chapter 10.

To read numerous blogs about the Los Angeles scene, log onto **LA.COM**'s blog page at www.la.com/pluck/blogs. For a more esoteric array of L.A.-based blogs, try **Metroblogging Los Angeles** at http://blogging.la.

Index

See also Accommodations and Restaurant indexes, below.

General Index

Accommodations

Restaurants